THE LIGHT SHINES ON IN THE DARKNESS

Robert J. Spitzer, S.J., Ph.D.

THE LIGHT SHINES ON IN THE DARKNESS

Transforming Suffering through Faith

Volume Four of the Quartet:
Happiness, Suffering, and Transcendence

IGNATIUS PRESS   SAN FRANCISCO

Nihil obstat: Pia de Solenni, S.Th.D.

Imprimatur: +The Most Reverend Kevin J. Vann, J.C.D., D.D.
Bishop, Diocese of Orange
March 22, 2017

Cover design by John Herreid

ISBN 978-1-58617-957-1
Library of Congress Control Number 2015948645
Printed in the United States of America ⊗

*In loving memory of my mother and father, whose faith
in times of suffering inspired and edified me.*

*And to Joan Jacoby, Camille Pauley, and Jacinta Connall—
who transformed every scholarly and administrative idea into books,
articles, and organizational realities.*

In the beginning was the Word,
and the Word was with God, and the Word was God.
He was in the beginning with God;
all things were made through him, and without him was
not anything made that was made.
In him was life, and the life was the light of men.
The light shines in the darkness, and the darkness has not overcome it.

—John 1:1–5

CONTENTS

Phase One:
Theological Preparation for Suffering
Foundations 1–3

Chapter One: In the Twinkling of an Eye

First Foundation: Conviction about the Resurrection
(Eternal Life and Love)

Chapter Two: *Who* God Is—and Is Not

Second Foundation: Affirming the Unconditional Love of God

Chapter Three: I Am with You Always

Third Foundation: Recognizing God's Presence in Our Suffering

**Phase Two:
Contending with Suffering in the Short-Term
Foundations 4–5**

Chapter Four: "Take This Cup Away from Me"

Fourth Foundation: Spontaneous Prayers in Times of Suffering

Chapter Five: Fear Is Useless

Fifth Foundation: Mitigating Fear and Choosing Consolation

Phase Three:
Benefitting from Suffering in the Long-Term
Foundations 6–9

Chapter Six: Love One Another as I Have Loved You

Sixth Foundation: The Unity of Suffering and Love
in Self-Sacrifice

Chapter Seven: Finding Light in the Darkness

Seventh Foundation: Interior and Exterior Opportunities of Suffering

Chapter Eight: Mystical Self-Offering

Eighth Foundation: Offering Suffering as a
Loving Self-Sacrifice

Chapter Nine: The Spirit of Truth Will Guide You

Ninth Foundation: Following the Inspiration and
Guidance of the Holy Spirit

A Vexing Question and a Synopsis of the Relationship among Suffering, Freedom, Love, and God

Chapter Ten: Why the All-Loving God Allows Suffering

ACKNOWLEDGMENTS

I am most grateful to Joan Jacoby—whose invaluable work transformed my thoughts once again into a full manuscript—for typing multiple copies of each chapter, making helpful editing suggestions, and helping with research. I am particularly grateful for her appreciation of the subject, and her undying patience.

I am also grateful to Karlo Broussard and Juliana Gerace for their important input and assistance on preparing the manuscript, and to Joseph Miller for his editorial suggestions and encouragement.

I would also like to express my appreciation to the Board and friends of the Magis Institute who gave me the time and resources to complete this Quartet.

INTRODUCTION

We have taken a rather lengthy path through three volumes to get to this challenging issue within our consideration of transcendent happiness. In the first volume of the Quartet we queried into what the most meaningful kind of happiness and fulfillment might be, and resolved that three inner powers or capacities point the way to true, perfect, and lasting dignity and destiny—empathy, conscience, and transcendent awareness. With respect to the third capacity, we discovered five distinct manifestations of transcendent awareness—perfect truth, perfect love, perfect justice/goodness, perfect beauty, and perfect home. When we viewed the implications of these powers in their relationship to one another, we concluded that the only way we could find eternal happiness is through a supreme interpersonal Being—who is present in our five transcendental desires, and in the depths of our conscious and unconscious psyche. This led us to Saint Augustine's declaration: "For Thou hast made us for Thyself—and our hearts are restless until they rest in Thee!"[1]

We arrived at this conclusion by exploring four levels of happiness, proceeding from material-external happiness (Level One) to ego-comparative happiness (Level Two). We paused at Level Two because so many within our culture believe it to be "true happiness", only to find themselves experiencing profound emptiness, jealousy, fear of loss of esteem, inferiority, superiority, ego-sensitivity, self-pity, resentment, and loneliness. We showed that the way out of these negative feelings of the comparison game is to move toward Levels Three and Four, which lead to a more pervasive, enduring, and deep purpose in life—contribution, love, noble endeavor, transcendence, and communion with the Divine.

This led to another discovery: that Level Three happiness alone is not able to satisfy and fulfill us at the highest levels of our being. Though Level Three purpose in life can bring relief to the negative

---

[1] Saint Augustine, *Confessions*, trans. F.J. Sheed, ed. Michael P. Foley (Indianapolis: Hackett Publishing, 2006), Book I, Chapter 1, p. 1.

emotions of the comparison game, it cannot overcome other negative emotions connected with our desire for communion with a personal transcendent Being. We discovered that *worldly* purpose, love, and home could not overcome four negative states on the cosmic or transcendent level: *cosmic* emptiness, loneliness, alienation, and guilt. The meaning and love of this world—no matter how powerful and full—cannot satisfy our yearning for and calling to transcendent purpose and home. This was confirmed by a study of the American Psychiatric Association indicating that nonreligiously affiliated individuals have significantly greater anxiety, meaninglessness, familial tensions, past substance abuse, and suicide attempts than the religiously affiliated.[2]

We then asked how cosmic emptiness, loneliness, alienation, and guilt can be alleviated. This led to a fivefold path taken by religiously affiliated people throughout the world, through association with a church, participation in sacred rites, the pursuit of transcendent wisdom, and engagement with the personal transcendent Being through prayer. This led to an examination of contemplative prayer and prayers of interior transformation along with special consideration of how to recognize and follow the inspiration and guidance of divine providence in our lives. We concluded that if the personal transcendent Being were unconditionally loving, we could be perfectly and eternally happy, which led to three questions:

1. Can we be sure that there is *really* a personal transcendent Being?
2. If so, is the personal transcendent Being unconditionally loving?
3. If so, then why does He allow suffering and evil within the world?

This led us to three additional explorations in three subsequent volumes.

[2] See Kanita Dervic et al., "Religious Affiliation and Suicide Attempt", *American Journal of Psychiatry* 161, no. 12 (December 2004): 2303–8, http://ajp.psychiatryonline.org/article.aspx ?articleid=177228. See also Thomas D. Williams, "Religious People Much Happier Than Others, New Study Shows", Breitbart News Network, December 24, 2014, http://www .breitbart.com/national-security/2014/12/24/religious-people-much-happier-than-others -new-study-shows.

In response to the first question, we examined several kinds of evidence for our transcendent nature and the existence of a personal transcendent Being in *The Soul's Upward Yearning: Clues to Our Transcendent Nature from Experience and Reason* (Volume II). We began with our universal, fundamental, irreducible experience of the numen (a mysterious, fascinating, overwhelming, inviting "wholly Other") manifest to both our conscious and unconscious psyche. We used Rudolf Otto's seminal study of this phenomenon, *The Idea of the Holy*,[3] to study the *interior* manifestation of the Divine, and complemented this with the extensive studies of Mircea Eliade on the intuition of the sacred and its centrality to religion throughout the world.[4] We deepened this study by exploring John Henry Newman's phenomenal investigation of conscience,[5] as well as Jung's and Tolkien's examination of unconscious archetypal myth and symbolism.[6]

Yet the question still lingered: How do we know that these fundamental experiences originate in a *real* personal transcendent Being? This led us to an exploration of three kinds of *external* evidence: Bernard Lonergan's proof of God,[7] an examination of the veridical evidence for survival of human consciousness after bodily death (from major medical studies of near-death experiences),[8] and

[3] Rudolf Otto, *The Idea of the Holy: An Inquiry into the Non-Rational Factor in the Idea of the Divine and Its Relation to the Rational* (New York: Oxford University Press, 1958).

[4] Mircea Eliade, *The Sacred and the Profane: The Nature of Religion* (New York: Harcourt Brace Jovanovich, 1987).

[5] John Henry Newman, unpublished manuscript entitled "Proof of Theism", in *The Argument from Conscience to the Existence of God*, ed. Adrian Boekraad and Henry Tristram (London: Mill Hill, 1961).

[6] See Carl Jung, *The Archetypes and the Collective Unconscious*, in *Collected Works of C. G. Jung*, vol. 9, pt. 1, trans. R. F. C. Hull (Princeton, N.J.: Princeton University Press, 1981). See also Joseph Pearce, "J. R. R. Tolkien: Truth and Myth", *Lay Witness*, September 2001, http://www.catholiceducation.org/en/culture/literature/j-r-r-tolkien-truth-and-myth.html.

[7] See Bernard Lonergan, *Insight: A Study of Human Understanding*, in *Collected Works of Bernard Lonergan* 3, ed. Frederick E. Crowe and Robert M. Doran (Toronto: University of Toronto Press, 1992), Chapter 19. This proof was systematically summarized in Volume II, Chapter 3.

[8] This evidence was systematically summarized in Volume II, Chapter 5. The five principle studies are as follows: Sam Parnia et al., "AWARE—AWAreness during REsuscitation—A Prospective Study", *Resuscitation*, October 6, 2014, http://www.resuscitationjournal.com/article/S0300-9572%2814%2900739-4/fulltext; Pim van Lommel et al., "Near-Death Experience in Survivors of Cardiac Arrest: A Prospective Study in the Netherlands", *The Lancet* 358, no. 9298 (2001): 2039–45; Kenneth Ring, Sharon Cooper, and Charles Tart, *Mindsight:*

contemporary scientific evidence for a transcendent creation[9] from the Borde-Vilenkin-Guth proof,[10] the second law of thermodynamics (entropy),[11] and anthropic coincidences at the Big Bang.[12] We found each kind of evidence to be probative in its own right, and in combination, to be mutually corroborative and complementary, validating the existence of God and a transcendent soul as reasonable and responsible.

We investigated other evidence for a transcendent soul from Gödel's proof of human nonalgorithmic mathematical awareness,[13] David Chalmers' "Hard Problem of Consciousness",[14] and contemporary studies of the five transcendental desires for perfect truth, love, goodness, beauty, and home.[15] We concluded from the combined evidence the high likelihood that human beings have a transphysical consciousness (soul) capable of self-awareness, genuine creativity, transcendental reflection, and survival after bodily death. We showed how such a transphysical soul could interact with the

---

Near-Death and Out-of-Body Experiences in the Blind (Palo Alto, Calif.: William James Center for Consciousness Studies at the Institute of Transpersonal Psychology, 1999); Janice Holden, *Handbook of Near Death Experiences: Thirty Years of Investigation* (Westport, Conn.: Praeger Press, 2009); Mario Beauregard, *Brain Wars: The Scientific Battle over the Existence of the Mind and the Proof That Will Change the Way We Live* (New York: HarperOne, 2012).

[9] This evidence is summarized in Appendix I of Volume II. It is also explained in Robert J. Spitzer, *New Proofs for the Existence of God: Contributions of Contemporary Physics and Philosophy* (Grand Rapids, Mich.: Eerdmans, 2010).

[10] Arvind Borde, Alan Guth, and Alexander Vilenkin, "Inflationary Spacetimes Are Not Past-Complete", *Physical Review Letters* 90, no.15 (2003): 151301-1–151301-4.

[11] Thomas Banks, "Entropy and Initial Conditions in Cosmology", January 16, 2007, http://arxiv.org/abs/hep-th/0701146.

[12] See Paul Davies, *The Accidental Universe* (New York: Cambridge University Press, 1982). See also Roger Penrose, *The Emperor's New Mind* (Oxford: Oxford University Press, 1989).

[13] Kurt Gödel, "Über formal unentscheidbare Sätze der Principia Mathematica undverwandter Systeme I", *Monatshefte für Mathematik und Physik* 38 (1931): 173–98. See also John Lucas, "Minds, Machines, and Gödel", *Philosophy* 36 (1961): 120; Roger Penrose, *Shadows of the Mind* (Oxford: Oxford University Press, 1994).

[14] David Chalmers, "Facing Up to the Problem of Consciousness", *Journal of Consciousness Studies* 2, no. 3 (1995): 200–19. See also David Chalmers, *The Conscious Mind: In Search of a Fundamental Theory* (London: Oxford University Press, 1997).

[15] See Lonergan, *Insight*; Bernard Lonergan, *Method in Theology* (New York: Herder and Herder, 1972); Karl Rahner, *Spirit in the World* (New York: Herder and Herder, 1968); Hans Urs von Balthasar, *The Glory of the Lord: A Theological Aesthetics*, trans. Erasmo Leiva-Merikakis, vol. I (Edinburgh: T&T Clark, 1982); Roger Fry, "Retrospect", in *Vision and Design*, ed. J.B. Bullen (Mineola, N.Y.: Dover Publications, 1998).

physical brain through a model proposed by Sir Karl Popper and Sir John Eccles, as well as Michael Polanyi and Bernard Lonergan.[16] We also concluded to the high likelihood of a unique, unrestricted act of thinking that is the Creator of everything else (God)—who is present to our consciousness and invites us to Himself and eternal life, love, and goodness.

The above evidence justified an affirmative answer to our first question: Can we be sure that there is a personal transcendent Being? This led naturally to the second question: Is this personal transcendent Being unconditionally loving? We explored this question in the third volume of the Quartet—*God So Loved the World: Clues to Our Transcendent Destiny from the Revelation of Jesus*. This investigation took us first to the nature of love—*agapē*[17] (Chapter 1), and then to Jesus' revelation of His Father's unconditional love (Chapter 2), and Jesus' own unconditional love (Chapter 3). We reflected on how Jesus' revelation of God's unconditional love correlated with our transcendental desire for perfect love, and noted how this was verified by the overwhelming love of "the bright white light" reported by many patients who had near-death experiences. Yet, this correlation begged for independent corroboration of Jesus' divine authority. We found this corroboration in His Resurrection and glory,[18] gift of the Holy Spirit,[19] and miracles by His own

---

[16] This is explained in Chapter 5 of Volume II.

[17] This is a distinctly Christian concept, which signifies the kind of love arising out of concern for *the other* as intrinsically good and lovable. It seeks no reward other than to help and serve *the other*, which is why it is the ground of forgiveness, compassion for the marginalized, and love of enemies. See Volume III (Chapter 1) of this Quartet.

[18] In Chapter 4 of Volume III, we explored the historicity of Jesus' Resurrection in the arguments of Saint Paul, the arguments of N. T. Wright, and the evidence from the Shroud of Turin. The evidence from the Shroud of Turin is scientifically compelling and is explained in detail in Volume III, Appendix I. Recent dating tests (2012) show that the Shroud very probably originated at the time of Jesus, and recent imaging technology reveals that the Shroud's image probably originated with a burst of vacuum ultraviolet radiation shorter than one forty-billionth of a second at an intensity of several billion watts—exceeding all known ultraviolet light sources today—from the corpse inside the Shroud. This is interpreted as a remnant of Jesus' Resurrection. See N. T. Wright, *The Resurrection of the Son of God* (Minneapolis: Fortress Press, 2003). See also Frank Viviano, "Why Shroud of Turin's Secrets Continue to Elude Science", *National Geographic*, April 17, 2015, http://news.nationalgeographic .com/2015/04/150417-shroud-turin-relics-jesus-catholic-church-religion-science/.

[19] This was explored in Chapter 5 of Volume III. We examined evidence of the power of the Spirit manifest through the name of Jesus in the apostolic Church (James Dunn and

authority.[20] We concluded from this that it is reasonable and responsible to believe in Jesus' divine authority to reveal God's unconditional love as well as His intention to bestow eternal resurrection upon those who are open to His message and call to love (*agapē*).

We now confront the third question: If God is unconditional love, then why does He allow suffering and evil in the world? At first glance, suffering seems to contradict God's unconditional love and the possibility of transcendent happiness, undermining the evidence and analysis given in the previous three volumes of the Quartet. As we shall see, this prima facie judgment does not correspond either to the nature of love or the conditions for personal freedom. Suffering is not opposed to love—it *leads* to it, to its authenticity and purification; to empathy, humility, forgiveness, compassion, good for the world, and good for the Kingdom. Suffering is not opposed to transcendent happiness; it is an indispensable pathway to it.

This may seem paradoxical, but in light of Jesus' promise of an unconditionally loving resurrection and our need to embrace empathetic, forgiving, and compassionate love *freely*, the paradox loosens its grip, allowing divine light to emerge from sufferings' seeming darkness. Is this merely Christian imagination—or is it the *really real*? Is it a fiction invented to make God more appealing, and suffering more tolerable, or is it the necessary outcome of the interface of love, freedom, personal identity, and eternal love? Readers will have to decide for themselves, but Jesus' answer is clear: suffering is the essential path to the optimization of freedom, the purification of love, and an eternal life of love and joy with the Trinity and the Blessed. Hopefully, this volume will shed light on this difficult, yet life-giving divine mystery—light that will help readers to transform their suffering into freedom, love, and eternal salvation.

John P. Meier) and in the contemporary Church (e.g., Craig Keener). See James Dunn, *Jesus and the Spirit: A Study of the Religious and Charismatic Experience of Jesus and the First Christians as Reflected in the New Testament* (Philadelphia: Westminster Press, 1975). See also John P. Meier, *A Marginal Jew: Rethinking the Historical Jesus*, vol. 2, *Mentor, Message, and Miracles* (New York: Doubleday, 1994); Craig Keener, *Miracles: The Credibility of the New Testament*, 2 vols. (Grand Rapids, Mich.: Baker Academic Publishing, 2011).

[20] This was explained in Chapter 5 of Volume III, using the analysis of John P. Meier and Raymond Brown. See Meier, *Marginal Jew*. See also Raymond Brown, *An Introduction to New Testament Christology* (New York: Paulist Press, 1994).

I. A Personal Lesson from the
"Book of Life's Challenges"

Suffering can be a remarkably positive inspiration and power—when we view it within the context of love and eternal life. I did not appreciate this in my earlier years, but have come to realize that it is the high point of wisdom, if we have faith in a loving God. I have struggled with my eyesight since I was thirty years old and can now understand the incredible value and opportunity of that struggle in my journey to come closer to God in love. For many years, when my eyes took another turn for the worse, I would go through yet another bout of frustration and anxiety—frustration, because I made the fatal error of comparing my diminished abilities with what I was once able to do, and anxiety, because I was not certain whether the new level of disability would end my productivity or people's respect for my capacity to "deliver". Looking back on it, I can honestly say that those frustrations were nothing more than an exercise in futility and that the anxieties—in every case—were completely unwarranted.

Let me say for the moment that this initial negative reaction to suffering was really about *perspective*—how I viewed suffering and challenge, not so much the suffering or the challenge itself. I was not able to help myself. When the next level of disability came, I looked at it from a self-centric point of view. It seemed that the shocking development of "one more dreaded decrease in eyesight" caused me, despite my faith, to turn into myself. I suppose that this was just human nature, but I have learned one thing—the sooner I get over it, by putting myself into the hands of God and looking for the opportunity that will come through His guidance, the better off I am.

If I did not have faith in a loving God, and hope in eternal life with Him, I don't think I would have a positive outlook on suffering, and I certainly would not be able to view it as an opportunity. I am not a stoic, so I wouldn't have been able to see suffering as a way of cultivating strength, courage, self-discipline, self-sufficiency, invulnerability, and autonomy. Some of these stoic "benefits" of suffering, such as self-sufficiency, invulnerability, and autonomy, run contrary to empathy, compassion, and humility, and so I do *not* view them as real benefits, but rather as negatives. The other characteristics—strength, self-discipline, and courage—can be positive, but they are not ends in themselves; they are only *means* to greater ends, such as contribution to others and the common good, to the objectives of love.

So, if stoic benefits of suffering are either elusory or partial, what are its *real* enduring benefits? I have come to believe that these can only be seen through the lens of *love* that may be initially defined as a "recognition of the unique goodness of individuals that induces a sense of empathy and unity with them, making it just as easy, if not easier, to do the good for them as to do the good for myself". Inasmuch as suffering can lead to greater humility, empathy for the needy, and compassion, it can free us to contribute to others and the common good without counting the cost, which advances the cause of love. I believe this to be a much higher purpose in life than the stoic characteristics mentioned above.

In my life, love alone is not sufficient to make *complete* sense out of suffering. If suffering is to make *complete* sense, it would have to lead not only to transitory love, but to enduring and even eternal love; it would have to lead not only to a contribution to others and the common good, but also to the Kingdom of God. If suffering could lead to a *permanent* freedom from egocentricity, domination, self-absorption, and self-idolatry, and through this, to a *permanent* appreciation and communion with other people and a supreme Being, then suffering would be far more intelligible, but still not completely intelligible.

In order for suffering to make *perfect* sense, it would have to be combined with grace to help us use the suffering to achieve the objective of perfect love. Suffering provides a remarkably powerful inducement to move toward greater empathy, humility, compassion, and purpose in life, but I have always found that I need even more help—more inspiration and guidance to peel back the layers of inauthenticity, egocentricity, and autonomy that impede my freedom to move toward authentic love. This is what I mean by "grace". Thus, if suffering is to make perfect sense, it would have to be situated within the context of perfect love, eternal life, and a perfectly loving supreme Being to provide the grace and mercy to help us use suffering to ultimately achieve perfect freedom to love.

When I looked upon these three conditions for "perfectly intelligible suffering" as a young man, I came face-to-face with the revelation of Jesus Christ. I realized that this is precisely what Jesus promised—it was the core of His message for all of us:

1. God (His *Abba*) is unconditional love—the Father of the Prodigal Son.
2. The Father's and Jesus' objective is to bring all of us to eternal life in an unconditionally loving communion with them.
3. Jesus' revelation and gift of the Holy Spirit is intended to provide the grace, inspiration, and guidance to attain greater freedom to love.

If Jesus' revelation is true, then suffering can be (and is) perfectly intelligible.

This implication of Jesus' teaching led me on a search to confirm the existence of God, the soul, and the historical Jesus. I was able to discover enough evidence of these things when I was younger to incite my desire for transcendent happiness and to make recourse to Jesus' revelation and the inspiration of the Spirit to find the opportunities in suffering. The rest, as they say, is history.

The reader may have noticed that there is a strong correlation between the three components of my search and the previous two volumes of this Quartet. As noted above, I wrote these two volumes to set out the contemporary evidence for the truth of these three transcendent realities, so that the "leap of faith" would not have to be "across the Grand Canyon". If readers are in anyway skeptical about the unconditionally loving God, His intention to bring us to His Resurrection, and the efficacy of the Spirit in guiding us to it, I would ask them to read these two volumes and also the sources referenced in them. The more we know the reality of God, Jesus, and our transcendence, the better will be our pursuit of transcendent happiness and our conversion of suffering into eternal love.

It should not be thought that evidence alone can lead to faith. There is an indispensable component of intention, decision, and choice involving the heart that must accompany whatever evidence we might use. God gives us room to decide freely to come to Him. In the words of Dostoyevsky, "He will not enslave us to a miracle."[21] Thus, we can never be completely compelled by the evidence, even overwhelming probative evidence, to believe in, seek, and

[21] Fyodor Dostoyevsky, "The Grand Inquisitor", in *The Brothers Karamazov*, trans. David McDuff (New York: Penguin, 2003), p. 320.

attach ourselves to God. There will always be room to decide—to choose God as the objective of our *heart's* desire. If we are to attach ourselves to God, we will have to *want* this; indeed, we will have to want *Him*, and the life of unconditional love He promises. This means we will have to detach ourselves from attitudes and ways of life contrary to love—egocentricity, domination, pride, envy, greed, and other vices. Detaching ourselves from these vices does not mean *perfect* detachment—that would be virtually impossible—but rather *intending* to detach ourselves from them with the help of God over the course of time. In sum, if the desire to be with God *is* present, then the above evidence will likely be sufficient to allow reasonable and responsible assent to faith; however, if the desire to be with God is *not* present, then even the most perfectly probative evidence will not be sufficient to support our faith—we will always find a way to avoid its conclusion.

Let us return to the contention with which we started—if I did not have faith in a loving God, and hope in eternal life with Him, I would not have a positive outlook on suffering, and I certainly would not be able to view it as integral to ultimate meaning, dignity, and destiny. Christian faith can make the difference between an essentially embittered and negative life or a positive life—a life in decline or a life toward transcendence, a nihilistic outlook or an absolutely positive outlook. In light of this overwhelmingly positive transformative power of Christian faith, I will use it as the overarching lens to interpret suffering in this book.

Even if we bring a deep and strong Christian faith to our lives, suffering can still surprise us and, in its initial phases, hit us hard. So we must be patient with our human nature even as we are focusing on bringing our faith to bear on our suffering. It is difficult to fight our human nature. Sometimes, when suffering comes out of the blue, I experience many of the same reactions as someone who just received news about having a terminal illness—undergoing most of the five stages of death and dying (denial, anger, bargaining, depression, and acceptance).[22] I think all of us have natural negative and defensive reactions to suffering that depend in part on our personalities and the kind of suffering we are undergoing. If you have a personality

---

[22] See Elizabeth Kübler-Ross, *On Death and Dying: What the Dying Have to Teach Doctors, Nurses, Clergy and Their Own Families* (New York: Scribner, 2014).

like mine, you probably would not go through a stage of denial, but move immediately to a stage of frustration (anger and resentment) and anxiety about the future.

You would then experience a bargaining stage—where you make promises to God to be a much better person if He would simply minimize your suffering. You might even get creative and promise major increases in productivity in God's service, if He would give you a "little" miracle. And when that doesn't work, you might feel a temporary impasse. If God does not redress the suffering, you will probably reach a decision point where you will face two options: either give into depression, frustration, apathy, and despair, or turn in faith to God and pray not so much for an alleviation of your suffering, but that this new challenge bring humility, empathy, compassion, faith, and new opportunities to serve others and to serve the Kingdom.

Other personalities will have different "natural reactions" to suffering. A melancholic personality may be more inclined to phases of depression; a choleric personality might have an extended phase of anger; and a phlegmatic personality might have an earlier sense of resignation. Whatever the case, if we have dealt with suffering on several occasions, we will notice certain natural proclivities that characterize our initial reaction before we turn to the Lord in faith.

The intensity with which we go through our "natural negative reaction" to suffering also depends on the kind of suffering we are enduring. Grief over the passing of a loved one—parent, child, or close friend—generally produces the most intense reaction. Since we are not able to bring our relative or friend back to life, we might skip the bargaining process—and find ourselves in a state of intense loneliness and emptiness. Though these feelings are almost inevitable at first, we cannot afford to prolong them, because they can set us on a self-destructive path. At this juncture we will want to use some of the spontaneous prayers discussed in Chapter 4 to connect us with the loving God and the Holy Spirit. This will help us gain perspective through faith, prayer, and the Lord's grace.

There are two things to be learned from the above initial reactions to suffering. First, reacting to suffering in a negative (and even self-centered) way is psychologically and physiologically human. It is not a lack or crisis of faith, but only a *natural* reaction. The Lord understands this reaction, because He created us and knows us through and through. Even when we feel bitter resentment He is not "turned off"

to us, but rather tries to break through to us, help us, and guide us to
the eternal opportunities in our suffering.

Secondly, the more quickly we turn to the Lord for help—putting
on the perspective of faith to see the divine opportunity within
suffering—the better off we will be. When we turn to the Lord in
our suffering—through prayer, openness to the Holy Spirit, seeking
the Lord's perspective on the opportunities within our suffering—we
will likely feel a sense of deep peace, beyond *our* capacity to produce.
This peace is frequently the beginning of a new journey or adventure
with the Lord, who uses our suffering to guide and lead us to new
perspectives on happiness and success, to deeper forms of courage
and love, and to new opportunities to serve others and the Kingdom.
The initial feeling of "supernatural peace" introduces consolation and
light into our initial desolation and darkness—interrupting the process of dwelling on frustration, anxiety, loneliness, emptiness, and the
pain intrinsic to it all. This light not only interrupts the darkness; it
illuminates the way out of it. When we feel this peace and sense this
light, our job is to put our trust in the Lord, to remember that He
is leading us ultimately to our *transcendent and eternal destiny* with Him,
and to follow the light as best we can.[23]

Following the light is not as easy as it might seem. Sometimes
when we are trying to follow the light, we can be drawn back into
the darkness because we dwell too much upon it or the events that
led up to it. This has the peculiar effect of taking our focus off the
supernatural sense of peace, the light, and the Holy Spirit, who is
guiding us. Like Peter leaving the boat to come to Jesus, we take our
eyes off of Him because we are concerned about the power of the
waves beneath us, and we begin to sink. Yet this too is very typical.
When I do it, I react very much like Peter, saying, "Lord, save me!"
and Jesus reaches out, restores my sense of peace, and reintroduces
me to His light—until I lapse again.

Unfortunately, my reaction is not as quick as Peter's. When I falter, I generally go through another bout of frustration or resentment,
followed by another bout of anxiety about the future, followed by
another bout of darkness. Sometimes I talk myself out of asking the

---

[23] Sometimes we can unconsciously block God's peace and consolation during our times
of suffering. See Chapter 5, Section IV, for an explanation of how to move beyond these
unconscious blocks by "choosing consolation".

Lord for help by thinking to myself, "I must be making all of this up—this peace and light is not God's light, but only the Spitzerian light of ultimate rationalization." Some cynical strand within me fastens onto this negative thought and gives itself over to Murphy's Law—"Whatever can go wrong, will go wrong"; and so if I am sensing God's light in the darkness, it must be me—and not God—because that is the dictate of Murphy's Law. I can laugh at this logic when I am not overcome by it, but when I am overcome by it, it really puts a damper on my ability to see and follow God's light—which is *really there*.

What I'm trying to say here is that "seeing God's light in the darkness" is not a *simple*, one-off event—"Oh, now I see God's light in the darkness—I'll just follow it, and I will soon be out of the darkness." Would that it were that simple! Unfortunately the complexity of our psychological mindset, emotions, histories, and capacities forces us to do a "retake" of "finding and following the light" several times—at least if you are anything like me. However, there is one important note of consolation in all these "retakes"—every time we do a retake, we do it a little better, because *the Lord* is really leading us out of the darkness, and when we refocus on His light, He inspires us to see it more clearly and brightly, making it harder to repeat our fall into Murphy's Law to the same degree and extent. We don't fall nearly as hard or as long the second, third, and fourth times along the path. Thus, "seeing God's light in the darkness" is a bumpy journey—with some pretty good pitfalls along the way—but it is filled with God's inspiration, guidance, and providential care, coming through our little acts of trust, courage, resoluteness, and hope, amid all the bumps. Make no mistake about it—the light is always pointing toward our eternal salvation with the Lord as well as to our ability to help others move to that salvation as well. If we follow that light—no matter how many bumps we encounter and times we "retake"—it will lead us to His Kingdom and help us to lead others to it as well.

II. The Purpose of This Book— Seeing Light in the Darkness

Suffering is darkness, leading to light—if we let it. The darkness of suffering requires no explanation. We have all felt it in times of grief, pain, deprivation, physical weakness, psychological anxiety, setbacks, loss, and failure. Most nonmasochists do not rejoice in the darkness of suffering. In its initial moments, it hurts, distresses, enervates, isolates, threatens, and discourages—obscuring and even eclipsing the light of love, joy, and peace that calls us to our true home.

There is no need to remain in the darkness, because we have been told by Jesus that there is light—love, joy, peace, and home—in every kind and instance of suffering, light that can transform us into a perfect reflection of God's unconditionally loving nature. If we want to overcome the darkness—to transform it into even greater light than we experienced before the darkness—we will have to be able to see the light in the darkness, and then follow it. But this can be a challenge, because the darkness of suffering can be quite overwhelming—and when suffering is particularly acute, the darkness can seem all-encompassing.

Fortunately we are not left alone in our suffering—most of us have friends and family to help and support us, and *all* of us have Jesus as well as His Father and Holy Spirit. As we shall see throughout this volume, Jesus has made multiple promises to us—and every one of them is true, certainly in my life, and in the lives of those with faith. What are some of these promises?

- "Blessed are the sorrowing, for they shall be consoled" (Mt 5:4; my translation).
- "Come to me, all who labor and are heavy laden, and I will give you rest" (Mt 11:28).
- "Truly, truly, I say to you, he who hears my word and believes him who sent me, has eternal life" (Jn 5:24).
- "I am the light of the world; he who follows me will not walk in darkness, but will have the light of life" (Jn 8:12).
- "Truly, truly, I say to you, you will weep and lament, but the world will rejoice; you will be sorrowful, but your sorrow will turn into joy" (Jn 16:20).

If we take Jesus' promises to heart—if we believe that He will fulfill them now and in His Kingdom—then we will begin to see His light in the darkness: His Spirit guiding us to the fullness of our eternal dignity, identity, and destiny.

The objective of this book is to point to the light in the darkness—the light of Jesus, His Father, and the Holy Spirit—so that we might more easily see and follow it. Jesus' light uses and transforms the darkness into *eternal and perfect* love, peace, and joy. Ironically, the path from imperfect to perfect light, as well as imperfect to perfect love, joy, and peace, almost inevitably goes through the darkness, but if we have faith in the promises of Jesus, the light will intensify through the darkness, and it will lead to the love and joy of Jesus Himself. As He assured His disciples before His Crucifixion and death: "These things I have spoken to you, that my joy may be in you, and that your joy may be full. This is my commandment: love one another as I have loved you" (Jn 15:11–12). Yet if we are to experience His perfect and eternal love and joy, we must have faith—trusting in Him, and His Father.

It is one thing to trust in God when life is going well, and quite another to do so when we are suffering. The problem is, at the very moment when we need faith the most, it can seem the most elusive. Though faith can reveal Jesus' light in the darkness, the darkness can also obscure our faith. The ways in which darkness does this are quite well-known, and we will want to be alert to its influence. If we fall prey to the allies of darkness—resentment, frustration, fear, anxiety, callousness, skepticism, and cynicism—our faith will be weakened and even undermined, leaving us powerless within the darkness. Hence, we will want to note the causes of the allies of darkness so that we can avoid and overcome them. This book addresses these causes at some length—false notions of God, false notions of God's will in times of suffering, inability to pray, unawareness of the opportunities in suffering, false expectations about happiness and life, superficial definitions of love, being ungrateful for life's gifts, unawareness of how the Holy Spirit inspires and guides us in times of suffering, and false notions about God's expectations and desires for us. Notice that these causes of darkness arise out of either a false impression of the truth or unawareness of the truth about God, His love, and His desire to bring us to Himself.

If we are alert to the allies of darkness and their causes—and we strive to avoid and overcome them—then suffering will not undermine faith; our efforts will have precisely the opposite effect, allowing faith to overcome and transform suffering. We will have to be strong in our conviction about God, the soul, and Jesus if suffering is to have this enormously positive effect in our lives. Given the importance of this life-transforming and salvific effect, we need to take time to study the evidence for God, the soul, and Jesus so that our conviction will be like that of the saints who underwent such remarkable transformations in spirit and love that they brought the culture, Church, and world to a whole new level of light and love in Christ.[24]

The more we are convinced about the truth of God, the soul, and Jesus, the more we will trust in the unconditional love of God, the promise of resurrection, and the goodness, beauty, efficacy, and fulfillment of love—and the more we trust in these truths, the more our suffering will be transformed into love. Suffering will become an indispensable instrument of our freedom to love, detaching us from egocentric attitudes contrary to love. It will become an inspiration and a power to serve others and the Kingdom, an impetus for gratitude, prayer, and trust in the Lord—an invitation to enter into an ever-deeper, more trusting relationship with the Lord, a call to imitate Jesus in His suffering, and the entryway to a life of loving self-sacrifice for others and the Kingdom. Thus, it is imperative to appropriate as much evidence and knowledge as we need to make the truth of Jesus—about the Resurrection, love, and His Father's unconditional love—come alive in our hearts. If we do this, suffering will no longer be vexing; it will be the indispensable vehicle for transforming us into the reflection of God's unconditional love—and therefore, the pathway to our eternal salvation, and the eternal salvation of others whom we have been inspired to serve.

One major truth lies at the foundation of every chapter of this book—suffering is not incompatible with love; suffering plus Christian faith leads to ever-greater love. As we shall see, suffering in the context of Christian faith is a primary impetus for courage, empathy, generosity, humility, and compassion—all of which are integral to Jesus' view of love (*agapē*). Suffering also detaches us from egocentricity, power, the need to dominate, and self-idolatry—and so it can free us to love as Jesus did, with gentleness, humble-heartedness, understanding, forgiveness, and self-sacrifice. In the context of faith, suffering is powerfully positive—so much so that it can cause people

---

[24] As noted above, this evidence is explained in detail in Volumes II and III of this Quartet.

to sacrifice themselves completely to serve others and the Kingdom, like Saint Francis of Assisi, Saint Ignatius Loyola, Saint Peter Claver, and Saint Teresa of Calcutta. In the context of faith, there is almost no limit to the good that suffering can produce—and no limit to the suffering that can be alleviated by those who love.

The greater our faith, the more useful this book will be. Therefore, it may be helpful for readers who have doubts about the unconditional love of God—or even doubts about the existence of God—to review the chapters dedicated to these topics in the previous two volumes. This review will make this book particularly useful for recognizing Christ's light in the darkness—and following it toward eternal salvation. It will also help us to lead others to their salvation.

III. Nine Christian Foundations for Suffering Well

There are nine major Christian foundations for interpreting suffering and growing through it. If we internalize these nine foundations, they will condition the way we encounter suffering. Instead of suffering hitting us, knocking us down, and enervating our spirit, these nine foundations can help us engage the negativity of suffering within a realistic positive Christian context. This can give us insight, inspiration, and strength while forming a conduit for God's grace to transform suffering from something negative to something profoundly positive within the framework of eternal, unconditional love.

These nine foundations enable suffering to work miracles—opening the way to humility where once there was pride; to compassion where once there was hardness of heart; to gentleness and acceptance where once there was domination and control; to courage where once there was faintness of heart; to transcendent meaning in life where once there was a reduction of self to materialism; to community and common cause where once there was autonomy and self-sufficiency; to an awareness of grace, providence, and the power of the Holy Spirit where once there was mere self-reliance; and to the anticipation of perfect truth, love, goodness, and home where once there was cosmic emptiness, loneliness, and alienation. Yes, suffering is negative—it causes pain, dejection, anxiety, and self-alienation, but it also has incredibly great potential to transform our meaning in life from base superficiality to wise profundity, to move us from the first two levels of happiness to the third and fourth levels of happiness, and to move us out of the profound darkness and falsity of self-idolatry, to surrender to God's transforming power and guidance. All these transformations will be vital to our life in the Kingdom of Heaven, for Heaven awaits the transformation of our hearts, so that we become more like the One who has loved us first. If suffering can help us to move along that path, then we will be much closer to our goal before we pass into the arms of the loving God.

The nine Christian foundations for "suffering well" will be presented as follows:

1. Conviction about eternal life and the resurrection (Chapter 1)
2. Who God is and is not—according to Jesus (Chapter 2)
3. God's presence in our suffering (Chapter 3)
4. Spontaneous prayers in times of suffering (Chapter 4)
5. Mitigating fear and choosing consolation (Chapter 5)
6. The unity of suffering and love in self-sacrifice (Chapter 6)
7. Awareness of the opportunities of suffering (Chapter 7)
8. Offering up our suffering as self-sacrifice in imitation of Jesus (Chapter 8)
9. Following the inspiration and guidance of the Holy Spirit (Chapter 9)

The nine Christian foundations for suffering well can be divided into three phases:

1. Theological preparation for suffering (foundations 1–3)
2. Contending with suffering in the short-term (foundations 4–5)
3. Benefitting from suffering in the long-term (foundations 6–9)

The preparatory phase is meant to help readers strengthen and solidify their faith and hope in the resurrection, and to refine belief in God and His presence in times of suffering. This phase is essential in our increasingly materialistic and agnostic culture. We need empirical, scientific, intuitive, logical, and historical evidence to counteract skepticism about transcendence and resurrection—evidence for both the heart and mind. We need to recapture the unconditionally loving God to avoid the false notions of God that conflict with Jesus' revelation of His Father as Abba—the Father of the Prodigal Son. We also need to examine carefully Jesus' teaching about God's presence in our suffering, so that we do not fall prey to the belief that He uses suffering to punish us or is indifferent to our pain and grief. God can cause suffering to help someone turn from a self-destructive life but this is not punishment—it is Divine Assistance.

If we do not take this preparation seriously, we can lose faith and hope in God when suffering strikes, which could blind us to the reality of His presence, grace, consolation, and redemption. This blindness makes suffering not only a waste, but also an impetus toward darkness and lower levels of meaning. Therefore, the sooner and more seriously we prepare ourselves by engaging in the first three Christians foundations (Chapters 1–3), the more likely we are to benefit from our suffering—in the present and in the eternal future.

The second phase (contending with suffering in the short-term) is meant to give three essential tools to mitigate emotional debilitation as well as loss of meaning, direction, and interpersonal connection during times of suffering:

1. Spontaneous prayers, which can be immediate conduits of grace
2. Practical techniques for mitigating fear and anxiety
3. Practices to help us choose and accept consolation

These tools are indispensable for contending *positively* with suffering. Without them, we can become overwhelmed by the fear, emptiness, loneliness, darkness, frustration, anger, meaninglessness, anxiety, dissociation, and despondency that can often flood into our consciousness when suffering occurs. The prayers, tools, and techniques (given in the fourth and fifth foundations) not only help to mitigate these negative conditions, but begin the process of positive transformation. Spontaneous prayers can focus us on the opportunities of suffering; natural virtues can help us form backup plans and lifetime associations and friendships that can give our lives new direction; and choosing consolation can deepen our relationship with God—not just during times of suffering, but throughout the rest of our lives.

The third phase (benefitting from suffering in the long-term) focuses us on the opportunities that suffering provides for our and others' salvation. It does this by calling us out of superficial meaning in life, deepening our faith, and helping us develop in freedom, virtue, love, and personal actualization. Suffering goes far beyond helping us to *our* salvation—it prepares us to help *others*, sometimes thousands of others, toward their salvation. It does so by purifying our freedom and love so that it becomes more like that of Jesus, making us more authentic witnesses to His truth and salvation. Yet suffering brings with it another more mystical blessing. As we shall see, it can—when offered to God as loving self-sacrifice in imitation of Jesus—produce incredible grace to strengthen the Mystical Body and help those in most need of mercy.

Suffering is filled with opportunities for us, both individually and interpersonally. It helps us contribute to community, culture, society, church, and the whole order of salvation. If we know what to look for in faith, then darkness can accentuate the light of salvation, refining our freedom and love to ever-greater degrees of authenticity and holiness. The combination of faith and suffering is so powerful, it can transform our whole being into a living and loving self-sacrifice for goodness and salvation. Hence, when we have contended with the debilitating effects of suffering in the short-term, we will want to focus on the opportunities of suffering promised by Jesus in the long-term—opportunities leading to our salvation that make us into "grace" for others' salvation.

Hopefully the explanation of these nine foundations of Christian suffering will enable you to discover the inspiration, grace, and power of love in your suffering—and through this, to travel far along the path to your salvation, while leading others to their salvation. This is the light that Christ brought into the darkness—the light of ultimate, eternal, redemptive, salvific love.

PHASE ONE

Theological Preparation for Suffering

Foundations 1–3

Chapter One

In the Twinkling of an Eye

First Foundation: Conviction about the Resurrection (Eternal Life and Love)

Introduction

In the First Letter to the Corinthians, Saint Paul sums up the Christian vision of suffering by proclaiming the definitive victory of Christ's Resurrection over death and decay:

> Behold! I tell you a mystery. We shall not all sleep, but we shall all be changed, in a moment, in the twinkling of an eye, at the last trumpet. For the trumpet will sound, and the dead will be raised imperishable, and we shall be changed. For this perishable nature must put on the imperishable, and this mortal nature must put on immortality. When the perishable puts on the imperishable, and the mortal puts on immortality, then shall come to pass the saying that is written: "Death is swallowed up in victory. O death, where is your victory? O death, where is your sting?" (15:51–55)

At the end of this verse, Saint Paul cites a text from Isaiah 25:8: "[God] will swallow up death for ever", which refers to a prophecy about the coming of the Kingdom of God. Isaiah compares God's Kingdom to a messianic banquet,[1] which points not only to the overcoming of

---

[1] Jesus alludes to the image of the messianic banquet in Isaiah 25:5–11, by saying: "I tell you, many will come from east and west and sit at table with Abraham, Isaac, and Jacob in the kingdom of heaven" (Mt 8:11). In so doing, He reveals that the messianic banquet of Isaiah will be both universal and timeless. See the explanation of this in Volume III, Chapter 7, Section II.A.

39

death, but to the redemption of all suffering—physical, psychological, and spiritual:

> [God] will swallow up death for ever, and the Lord GOD will wipe away tears from all faces, and the reproach of his people he will take away from all the earth, for the LORD has spoken. It will be said on that day, "Behold, this is our God; we have waited for him, that he might save us. This is the LORD; we have waited for him; let us be glad and rejoice in his salvation." (25:8–9)

For Saint Paul, Jesus' Resurrection is the fulfillment of Isaiah's prophecy, and therefore, the redemption of all suffering where every tear will be wiped away and transformed into joy.

For this reason, Paul and all the disciples situate the Resurrection at the center of Christian doctrine because virtually every dimension of Christian life draws its strength and fulfillment from it. Saint Paul is so adamant about the foundational status of the Resurrection that he declares:

> But if there is no resurrection of the dead, then Christ has not been raised; if Christ has not been raised, then our preaching is in vain and your faith is in vain. We are even found to be misrepresenting God, because we testified of God that he raised Christ, whom he did not raise if it is true that the dead are not raised. For if the dead are not raised, then Christ has not been raised. If Christ has not been raised, your faith is futile and you are still in your sins. Then those also who have fallen asleep in Christ have perished. If for this life only we have hoped in Christ, we are of all men most to be pitied. (1 Cor 15:13–19)

Inasmuch as the Resurrection provides the context for the *whole* of Christian life, it also provides the context through which Christians suffer. This connection between suffering (the Cross) and the Resurrection is particularly important, because the Resurrection provides meaning and redemption to the seeming negativity of suffering, transforming it into a pathway toward unconditional love and eternal joy.

For Jesus, the Cross is inseparable from the Resurrection. In every instance that Jesus predicts His Passion, He also predicts His Resurrection.[2] Furthermore, in His polemic with the Pharisees,

---

[2] Mark recounts three Passion-Resurrection predictions (see 8:31; 9:31; 10:34). Matthew follows Mark in this regard (see 16:21; 17:23; 20:19).

He symbolically connects the two events: "Destroy this temple, and in three days I will raise it up" (Jn 2:19).[3] Perhaps the most telling connection occurs with respect to the Transfiguration. In Mark's account (which is paralleled by both Matthew and Luke), Jesus makes His first prediction of the Passion (including a prediction of His Resurrection). This is closely followed by Jesus' teaching about the cost of discipleship—to take up our *cross* and follow in His steps—which is then followed by another prediction of Jesus' Resurrection: "Truly, I say to you, there are some standing here who will not taste death before they see the kingdom of God come in power" (Mk 9:1).[4] These predictions of the Cross and Resurrection come to a completion in the recounting of the Transfiguration, which is a prefigurement of Jesus' Resurrection. Apparently, Jesus wanted to assure Peter, James, and John (who were leaders among the disciples) *before* the occurrence of the Passion that Jesus would in fact rise in glory, and that this would be the ultimate context in which Jesus' Cross would be interpreted. At the end of the Gospels, Jesus' Passion and death is followed by the discovery of the empty tomb, after which He appears in glory to His disciples.

Inasmuch as Jesus' Passion and Resurrection anticipate our own suffering, death, and resurrection (see 1 Cor 15:49), we should view our suffering in the same way that Jesus viewed His—namely, through its inseparable connection to *our* resurrection in glory with Him.

I. Faith in Our Resurrection

Since the Resurrection is the context through which Christians should view suffering, we will want to be as convinced as possible about its veracity. As we shall see, the more confident we are in our resurrection, the more positive our suffering will become. Though there is a tremendous amount of corroborative evidence for our

---

[3] This same prediction is recounted in Jesus' trial in the Gospel of Matthew: "This fellow said, 'I am able to destroy the temple of God, and to rebuild it in three days'" (26:61).

[4] This passage refers to Jesus' Resurrection, not to the Second Coming. In it, Jesus predicts that His Resurrection will be in *glory*—the glory of God Himself. This prediction is followed by the Transfiguration, which is a prefigurement of Jesus' Resurrection in *glory*, transformed in light, and whiteness. This is borne out in the Resurrection of Jesus Himself (see Volume III, Chapter 4).

resurrection (see below), it will never lead to faith unless we are open to God and His will for us. Without this openness, no amount of corroborating evidence will ever convince us, for we will look for every possible way of extricating ourselves from it. The truly great part about God's gift of freedom is that we can never be forced to believe in something we don't *want* (choose) to believe in. If people want to believe in a flat earth, they can still find "convincing" reasons to do so, even if they are rejected by the entire scientific community.

How can we achieve reasonable and responsible belief in the Resurrection? After all, it happened about two thousand years ago. The basic answer is belief in the apostolic testimony, because the apostles were eyewitnesses to it and are worthy of our trust. Yet for those who cannot "cross the threshold of belief" on this basis alone, there are four other kinds of evidence *directly* accessible to us *today*:

1. The application of criteria of historicity
2. Scientific evidence from the Shroud of Turin
3. Corroboration by medical studies of near-death experiences
4. Contemporary miracles done in the name of Jesus, or through the intercession of His Mother

Before discussing these four contemporary kinds of evidence, we will want to consider the most basic one: trust in the apostolic testimony.

Those who have read the New Testament with care will probably have discovered the worthiness of its authors. I recall my first careful reading of the New Testament in college when it struck me that the authors of the Gospels could have embellished the accounts of miracles and the Resurrection beyond their rather prosaic form. Indeed, they seemed to underplay these "deeds of power" so much that the actual event appeared somewhat anticlimactic. What really amazed me was that all three major accounts of Jesus' risen appearances to the apostles in Matthew, Luke, and John reported *doubts*! Though these doubts were not absolute (for the apostles clearly witnessed the appearance of a powerful divine reality that they later discovered to be the risen Jesus), it made no sense to me that the authors would be honest enough to plant the seed of "doubt" in a text attempting to elicit belief. Why would they have done this if they had not intended to tell the whole truth and nothing but the truth?

Furthermore, when I compared the exorcism stories (which were dramatic) to the miracle stories (which were quite subdued), I got the feeling that an editor went through the miracle stories to take out the exciting parts. Why would an author conclude these stories with "Go now and don't tell anybody about this"? When I later studied the Gnostic Gospels,[5] I was struck not only by the hyperbole in them, but also by their departure from the canonical teaching of Jesus. In stark contrast to this, the four canonical evangelists were unbelievably sober, respectful of the oral tradition they received, and faithful to Jesus' teaching about truth, goodness, and love. The writing of the texts corresponded splendidly with their content, which made them, at least on the surface, believable.

I also marveled at the *humility* of the authors and the people about whom they wrote. The inclusion of insults leveled at Jesus by the religious authorities (e.g., "He casts out demons by the prince of demons" [Mt 9:34]), the failings and weaknesses of the apostles (e.g., Peter, Thomas, and Matthew), and the accusation that the apostles stole Jesus' body from the tomb, and so forth, showed the interest the evangelists had in putting the truth before the reputation of Christianity's foundational leaders. If those leaders had not had the humility to tell the whole truth, I wondered, wouldn't they have asked the evangelists to use their editorial pens a little more assiduously? Humility speaks convincingly about the reliability of witnesses and authors.

Most importantly for me, the *tone* of the Gospel texts seemed "just right". The Gospels manifested an interest in *my salvation, my soul, and my virtue*. The texts were not written in a soft and flattering way to gain my approval, but rather in a challenging, almost "off-putting", way to help me toward salvation, to call me out of

---

[5] The Gnostic Gospels are a set of apocryphal works attributed falsely to Jesus' disciples and friends. They were written several decades after the four canonical Gospels (Matthew, Mark, Luke, and John) during the second half of the second century to the fourth century. Their authors are not accepted authorities within the apostolic Church (as the four canonical Gospels), but rather considered to be spiritual writers who were heavily influenced by Gnostic philosophy (which attempts to achieve spiritual freedom through special knowledge or enlightenment). The so-called Christian Gnostics who wrote these texts departed from apostolic Christianity by advocating salvation not only through Jesus Christ, but through enlightenment proposed by its spiritual leaders. As can be seen from their miracle stories, their view of salvation and miracles was considerably different from that of Jesus' and, in some cases, is ridiculous and fantastic.

self-delusion and darkness into the light of Christ's love. "Tough love" can dissuade more converts than it persuades. If the evangelists had been more interested in "winning converts" instead of "helping souls", the Gospels would have been written quite differently—avoiding the "tough love".

There was something about the collective ethos of the New Testament writers that attracted me, despite its challenging tone, and I wanted to be part of it. Though I knew I was far from the ideal they set, I wanted to be like them, on the same mission as they were, with the same trust and love of the One about whom they were writing. The more I read the New Testament, the more I was confirmed in this truth of the heart—the foundation of my faith.

Though the truth of the *heart* is the foundation of faith, there may be some who need extra confirmation of the *mind* to become convinced of the reality of the risen glory to which they are called by Jesus. If you, the reader, are one of these individuals, I would ask that you review the chapters of Volumes II and III mentioned below in the four areas of contemporary evidence for the Resurrection.

The first area of evidence concerns criteria of historicity that can be evaluated just as well today as two thousand years ago. In Volume III, Chapter 4, we explained four kinds of evidence for the historicity of Jesus' Resurrection:

1. Saint Paul's list of witnesses to the Resurrection who were still alive at the time of Paul's writing—and could be asked for verification. Paul makes clear that they had everything to lose and nothing to gain by testifying to Jesus' Resurrection (Sections III.A and III.B).
2. N. T. Wright's exploration of the failure of first-century messianic movements, and Christianity's starkly contrasting success. Can this be explained without the Resurrection and gift of the Holy Spirit? (Section IV.A).
3. N. T. Wright's examination of the Christian mutations to Second Temple Judaism's doctrine of Resurrection. How can these be explained without the disciples witnessing the risen Christ in the way reported by the Gospel narratives? (Section IV.B).
4. The likelihood that Jesus' tomb was empty and that the religious authorities knew this to be true. Given the unlikelihood

that Jesus' disciples would have stolen His body or that anyone else would have done so, then the question arises: How did His body disappear? (Section V).

The second area of evidence concerns the Shroud of Turin, the purported burial cloth of Jesus. This evidence is assessed in detail in Volume III, Appendix I of the Quartet. Some readers may think that the cloth was debunked by the 1988 carbon testing, but the subsequent work of Dr. Raymond Rogers and others shows that the sample used for the tests was clearly not from the original Shroud, and that the procedure to obtain the sample was seriously flawed.[6] Moreover, recent dating procedures by Dr. Raymond Rogers and Dr. Giulio Fanti (and his teams) indicate a dating very close to the time of Jesus' Crucifixion and Resurrection. In four separate dating procedures, these scientists and engineers show that the cloth very probably originated around the time of Jesus' Crucifixion. Fanti averaged his three tests (Fourier transformed infrared spectroscopy, Raman laser spectroscopy, and mechanical tension compressibility tests) and obtained a mean of 33 B.C. (plus or minus 250 years), with 95 percent confidence (see Section II.B).

There are three other circumstantial dating methods that show almost conclusively that the Shroud could not have originated in thirteenth- or fourteenth-century France (as the 1988 carbon testing supposedly showed):

- Max Frei's pollen samples (see Section II.C.1),
- Alan Whanger's digital photography of Roman coins on the eyes of the man in the Shroud (see Section II.C.2), and
- remarkable similarities (120 blood imprints) between the Shroud of Turin and the facecloth of Jesus—the Sudarium of Oviedo (see Section II.C.3).

---

[6]See Volume III, Appendix I, Section II.A, for a list of the inexplicable flaws in the procedure to gather the sample for the 1988 carbon testing. The problems are so flagrant that Dr. Rogers published in the peer-reviewed journal *Thermochimica Acta* the following: "The combined evidence from chemical kinetics, analytical chemistry, cotton content, and pyrolysis-mass-spectrometry *proves* that the material from the radiocarbon area of the shroud is significantly different from that of the main cloth. The radiocarbon sample was thus not part of the original cloth and is invalid for determining the age of the shroud." Raymond N. Rogers, "Studies on the Radiocarbon Sample from the Shroud of Turin", *Thermochimica Acta* 425, nos. 1–2 (January 20, 2005): 189–94; emphasis mine.

These three kinds of evidence show an origin of the cloth in *Judea* (near Jerusalem) *before* A.D. 600—and very probably near the time of Jesus (the Roman coins on the man's eyes were minted by Pontius Pilate in Judea in A.D. 29). The combined evidence plus the unique features of Jesus' Crucifixion on the Shroud indicate that it is very probably His burial cloth.

In addition to the above, there is considerable evidence of a transphysical light phenomenon (suggestive of Jesus' transphysical Resurrection) on the cloth. This is explained in detail in Volume III, Appendix I, Section III. The cloth has five enigmas that are very difficult to explain by any known physical process:

1. The fact that the image is limited to the uppermost surface of the fibrils and does not penetrate to the medulla of the fibers. This implies that the image was not produced by chemicals or vapors of any kind.

2. The fact that the image is not a scorch (but rather discoloration coming from dehydration). This implies that the image could not have been produced by slowly dissipating radiation (which would have scorched it).

3. The image is a perfect photographic negative in which the image intensity is related to the distance of the cloth from the body. Thus, the image was present regardless of whether the cloth touched the body. This implies that radiation, not chemicals or vapors, was the source of image formation.

4. There is a double image on the frontal part of the cloth (a more intense image on the front surface, nearest the body, and a less intense image on the back surface, furthest from the body, without any effects between the two surfaces). This implies that the radiation was surrounding both surfaces of the cloth, implying that the cloth collapsed into a mechanically transparent body.

5. Parts of the frontal image, particularly the hands, show an image that is resolvable into three dimensions, in which the inside skeletal parts of the hand are proportionately related to the surrounding exterior flesh on the hand. This again implies that the cloth collapsed into *and through* a mechanically transparent body.

How can these enigmas be explained by a single event? In 2010, six physicists from three research centers (Frascati Research Center, the University of Padua, and Casaccia Research Center) were able to do so under experimental conditions by creating a burst of ultraviolet radiation through an excimer laser. According to Paolo DiLazzaro, director of the six-member team:

> We have irradiated a linen fabric having the same absolute spectral reflectance of the Turin Shroud ... with pulsed deep-UV radiation emitted by an ArF excimer laser. We have shown that 12 ns, 193 nm laser pulses are able to color a very thin layer on the linen yarn.... The colorless inner part of a few fibers ... suggests that we have locally achieved a coloration of the outermost part of the fibers. To the best of our knowledge, this is the *first* coloration of a linen material resembling the very shallow depth of coloration ... observed in the Turin Shroud fibers.[7]

The only way to produce the particular shallow coloration on the Shroud—without chemicals, vapors, or scorching—is by means of an incredibly short burst of vacuum ultraviolet radiation, which requires an excimer laser. It would take fourteen thousand excimer lasers across the length and width of the body to do this. According to DiLazzaro:

> [The ultraviolet light necessary to form the image] exceeds the maximum power released by all ultraviolet light sources available today. It would require pulses having durations shorter than one forty-billionth of a second, and intensities on the order of several billion watts.[8]

Furthermore, this incredibly special light would have to have been emitted by every three-dimensional point of the body simultaneously in a fashion that would surround both sides of the cloth. This is the only known way to explain the fourth and fifth enigmas given above. In view of the fact that no known physical process can explain how a decaying corpse could produce such an intense, short burst, and all-encompassing light form, we must, as Dr. John Jackson notes, make recourse to a transphysical cause:

[7] Paolo Di Lazzaro et al., "Deep Ultraviolet Radiation Simulates the Turin Shroud Image", *Journal of Imaging Science and Technology*, July–August 2010, p. 6; emphasis mine.

[8] Quoted in Frank Viviano, "Why Shroud of Turin's Secrets Continue to Elude Science", *National Geographic*, April 17, 2015, http://news.nationalgeographic.com/2015/04/150417-shroud-turin-relics-jesus-catholic-church-religion-science/.

In the case of the Shroud image, the cloth did collapse *into* and *through* the underlying body structure. As a physicist, I admit to having my own difficulties with this concept, but I also know that scientists must be ready to overturn even their most hallowed principles if observation warrants.[9]

In conclusion, the Shroud of Turin is very probably the burial cloth of Jesus, and it has imprinted on it what appears to be a relic of His Resurrection—a relic of one forty-billionth of a second of intense light emitted from every three-dimensional point within a mechanically transparent body. It corroborates the Gospel and Pauline accounts of Jesus' changed body, prefigured by the Transfiguration.

The third area of evidence concerns recent medical studies of near-death experiences (NDEs). It is explained in Volume II, Chapter 5, of the Quartet. There are several important longitudinal studies of near-death experiences worthy of consideration. Principal among these are the studies of Dr. Samuel Parnia at Southampton University (2014),[10] Dr. Pim van Lommel (reported in the prestigious British medical journal *The Lancet*),[11] Dr. Kenneth Ring's study of near-death experiences of the blind,[12] and Dr. Janice Holden's analysis of veridical evidence in NDEs from thirty-nine independent studies.[13] There are additional careful longitudinal studies[14] as well as many

[9]John P. Jackson, "An Unconventional Hypothesis to Explain All Image Characteristics Found on the Shroud Image" in *History, Science, Theology and the Shroud*, ed. A. Berard (St. Louis: Symposium Proceedings, 1991), http://theshroudofturin.blogspot.com/2012/01/john-p-jackson-unconventional.html.

[10]Sam Parnia et al., "AWARE—AWAreness during REsuscitation—A Prospective Study", *Resuscitation*, October 6, 2014, http://www.resuscitationjournal.com/article/S0300-9572(14)00739-4/abstract.

[11]Pim van Lommel et al., "Near-Death Experience in Survivors of Cardiac Arrest: A Prospective Study in the Netherlands", *The Lancet* 358, no. 9298 (2001): 2039–45.

[12]Kenneth Ring, Sharon Cooper, and Charles Tart, *Mindsight: Near-Death and Out-of-Body Experiences in the Blind* (Palo Alto, Calif.: William James Center for Consciousness Studies at the Institute of Transpersonal Psychology, 1999); Kenneth Ring and Madelaine Lawrence, "Further Evidence for Veridical Perception during Near-Death Experiences", *Journal of Near-Death Studies* 11, no. 4 (Summer 1993): 223–29.

[13]See Janice Holden, *Handbook of Near Death Experiences: Thirty Years of Investigation* (Westport, Conn.: Praeger Press, 2009).

[14]There are ten major studies worth examining: T. K. Basford, *Near-Death Experiences: An Annotated Bibliography* (New York: Garland, 1990); P. Fenwick and E. Fenwick, *The Truth in the Light: An Investigation of Over 300 Near-Death Experiences* (New York: Berkley Books,

studies reported in the *Journal of Near-Death Studies* published by the International Association for Near-Death Studies (peer-reviewed).[15]

The above studies detail three major ways of verifying the survival of human consciousness after bodily death:

1. Reported veridical data (all major longitudinal studies)[16]
2. Visual perception of the blind (primarily Ring and van Lommel)
3. Personal information about deceased individuals[17]

Each of these kinds of evidence can be verified by independent researchers after the fact, and all of them are exceedingly difficult (if not impossible) to explain by merely physical or physiological theories (such as hallucinations, anoxia, narcotics, stimulation of the

1995); Bruce Greyson and C.P. Flynn, eds., *The Near-Death Experience: Problems, Prospects, Perspectives* (Springfield, Ill.: Charles C. Thomas, 1984); G. Roberts and J. Owen, "The Near-Death Experience", *British Journal of Psychiatry* 153 (1988): 607–17; M.B. Sabom, *Recollections of Death: A Medical Investigation* (New York: Harper and Row, 1982); C. Zaleski, *Otherworld Journeys: Accounts of Near-Death Experience in Medieval and Modern Times* (Oxford: Oxford University Press, 1987); Raymond Moody, *The Light Beyond* (New York: Bantam Books, 1988); Bruce Greyson, "Seeing Dead People Not Known to Have Died: 'Peak in Darien' Experiences", American Anthropological Association, November 21, 2010, http://onlinelibrary .wiley.com/doi/10.1111/j.1548-1409.2010.01064.x/abstract; E.W. Cook, B. Greyson, and I. Stevenson, "Do Any Near-Death Experiences Provide Evidence for the Survival of Human Personality After Death? Relevant Features and Illustrative Case Reports", *Journal of Scientific Exploration* 12 (1998): 377–406; Emily Kelly, B. Greyson, and I. Stevenson, "Can Experiences Near Death Furnish Evidence of Life After Death?" *Omega: Journal of Death and Dying* 40 (2000): 39–45.

[15] See the website of the International Association for Near-Death Studies at https://iands .org/research/index-to-nde-periodical-literature/topics-outline.html for a complete index of 135 topics concerned with research and longitudinal studies of NDEs (website was last updated April 23, 2013).

[16] Explored in the following fourteen studies (most mentioned above): Parnia et al., "AWAreness during REsuscitation"; van Lommel et al., "Near-Death Experience"; Kenneth Ring and Evelyn Elsaesser Valarino, *Lessons from the Light: What We Can Learn from the Near-Death Experience* (New York: Insight Books, 2006); Janice Holden, *Handbook of Near Death Experiences*; Basford, *Near-Death Experiences*; Fenwick and Fenwick, *Truth in the Light*; Greyson and Flynn, *Near-Death Experience*; Roberts and Owen, "Near-Death Experience"; Sabom, *Recollections of Death*; Zaleski, *Otherworld Journeys*; Moody, *Light Beyond*; Greyson, "Seeing Dead People"; Cook, Greyson, and Stevenson, "Do Any Near-Death Experiences Provide Evidence?"; Kelly, Greyson, and Stevenson, "Can Experiences Near Death Furnish Evidence?"

[17] Primarily the following: Greyson, "Seeing Dead People"; Pim van Lommel, *Consciousness beyond Life* (New York: HarperOne, 2010); Raymond A. Moody, *Reunions: Visionary Encounters with Departed Loved Ones* (New York: Random House, 1993); Cook, Greyson, Stevenson, "Do Any Near-Death Experiences Provide Evidence?"; Kelly, Greyson, and Stevenson, "Can Experiences Near Death Furnish Evidence?"

temporal lobe, etc.—see Volume II, Chapter 5, Section IV). A brief explanation of each kind of evidence will help to clarify this. For a more detailed explanation, see Volume II, Chapter 5, Section III.

Reported Veridical Data. Frequently, during near-death experiences, the transphysical component leaves the body, but does not go immediately to an otherworldly domain. Instead, it remains in the resuscitation room or in close or remote proximity to the body. This transphysical component is self-conscious and can see, hear, and remember. Its memories can be recalled after patients return to their bodies. Some of these reports have highly unusual or unique characteristics that are not part of ordinary resuscitation or hospital procedures. Many of these reports can be verified by independent researchers after patients return to their bodies. When all of these conditions have been met and the unusual accounts have been verified to be 100 percent accurate, they are termed "veridical". Virtually every peer-reviewed study reports multiple instances of such veridical data. For some remarkable examples of this data, see Volume II, Chapter 5, Section III.A.

Visual Perception of the Blind during Clinical Death. Ring, Cooper, and Tart,[18] and van Lommel,[19] did focused studies on the near-death experiences of the blind. These patients (most whom were blind from birth) were able to see (most for the first time) during their near-death experience. These accounts show that patients who do not have the capacity to see through their *physical* bodies, report visual data accurately about their experiences during clinical death. Some of this data is veridical (highly unusual and therefore difficult, if not impossible, to guess).[20] Ring found that 80 percent of blind people had visual perception during clinical death, and that these perceptions were clear and accurate. For examples of these, see Volume II, Chapter 5, Section III.B. This data is virtually impossible to explain through any current *physical* hypothesis such as hallucination, anoxia, temporal lobe stimulation, or narcotics (see Volume II, Chapter 5, Section IV).

---

[18] Ring, Cooper, and Tart, *Mindsight.*
[19] Van Lommel et al., "Near-Death Experience".
[20] See Ring, Cooper, and Tart, *Mindsight*, and Ring and Valarino, *Lessons from the Light*, pp. 80–82.

Meeting Deceased Persons in a Transphysical Domain. Many patients undergoing clinical death are moved from the physical world to an otherworldly or heavenly domain. Some of them see themselves crossing a border into a beautiful paradise in which many are greeted by deceased relatives or friends, Jesus, or a loving white light. Some patients may experience two or more of these phenomena. Some patients who are greeted by deceased relatives do not recognize them, because they died before the patient was born. These individuals often introduce themselves and reveal hitherto unknown facts about themselves that the patients' relatives or friends are subsequently able to verify. For specific examples of this, see Volume II, Chapter 5, Section III.C.

Given the large number of verified cases of consciousness surviving bodily death (thousands) and the above three kinds of evidence that cannot be explained by current physicalist hypotheses, it is highly probable that human consciousness can and does survive physical death. This evidence corroborates the reality of postphysical existence, but it goes even further—it corroborates some of Jesus' claims about life after physical death. Three points are relevant here:

1. The transphysical state of patients is not conditioned by physical laws (they can pass through walls, they are unaffected by gravity, etc.). The risen Jesus manifested these same qualities (e.g., see Jn 20:19).

2. The bodies of patients are transformed and spiritlike, resembling some of the features attributed to Jesus' risen body in the Gospel Resurrection narratives (e.g., see Lk 24:37). Furthermore, when patients pass over to the other side and see deceased friends and relatives, they report that these individuals are transformed, spiritlike, and beautiful. There is one important difference between these reports and Jesus' risen appearance. Jesus' body is transformed in *power* and *glory*, having the appearance of divinity. This is not reported of patients having a near-death experience.

3. About 99 percent of patients who have and recall a near-death experience unreservedly indicate that it is filled with love. Those who see the white light report that it is overwhelmingly loving, and they also report that their friends and relatives are

filled with love. Children frequently report that they encounter Jesus, who is loving and caring. This correlates with Jesus' teaching about the unconditional love of God and the unconditional love and joy of eternal life (a major theme in the Gospel of John).

These similarities corroborate both the Gospel accounts of Jesus' risen appearance and Jesus' preaching about the nature of eternal life. Jesus' teaching goes beyond the evidence of near-death experiences, indicating that transphysical life is *eternal* (which NDEs intimate, but do not directly corroborate) and that love in His Kingdom will be unconditional and perfect joy (which again NDEs intimate, but cannot directly corroborate).

The evidence of NDEs alone is sufficient to reasonably affirm the high probability of life after physical death. When it is seen in the context of the Christian witness to Jesus' Resurrection (and His teaching about the Resurrection), it also corroborates and complements Christian revelation.

The fourth area of evidence concerns the miracles done in the name of the risen Jesus and through the intercession of the Mother of Jesus. This evidence is examined in Volume III, Chapter 5, of the Quartet. Recall from that chapter that the meteoric rise of Christianity, in the face of the public humiliation and execution of its Messiah, required a sufficient historical cause, because it was so radically different from every other messianic movement whose messiah was killed. N. T. Wright, Raymond Brown, and John P. Meier show that this sufficient cause is both the Resurrection of Jesus and the apostles' power to perform healings and miracles in a similar fashion to Jesus (with the important exception that Jesus performed miracles by His own authority while the apostles performed them in *His name*). John P. Meier notes in this regard:

> There was a notable difference between the long-term impact of the Baptist and that of Jesus. After the Baptist's death, his followers did not continue to grow into a religious movement that in due time swept the Greco-Roman world. Followers remained, revering the Baptist's memory and practices. But by the early 2d century A.D. any cohesive

group that could have claimed an organic connection with the historical Baptist seems to have passed from the scene. In contrast, the movement that had begun to sprout up around the historical Jesus continued to grow—amid many sea changes—throughout the 1ˢᵗ century and beyond. Not entirely by coincidence, the post-Easter "Jesus movement" claimed the same sort of ability to work miracles that Jesus had claimed for himself during his lifetime. This continued claim to work miracles may help to explain the continued growth, instead of a tapering off, of the group that emerged from Jesus' ministry.[21]

The name of Jesus was extraordinarily powerful, galvanizing the Holy Spirit within the apostles and disciples of the early Church, and enabling them to perform the same miraculous cures as Jesus. If Jesus had not risen from the dead, and if He had not preached the truth about His Father and the Resurrection, then how could His name have such remarkable power in the apostolic Church *until this very day*? Why would this name bestow transphysical power on the disciples if God did not intend to validate the Resurrection and teaching of Jesus? These same miraculous powers in the name of Jesus persist to this day. One does not have to look far to see the millions of testimonies to the power of Jesus' name used to evoke the charismatic manifestation of the Holy Spirit. A simple Internet search shows millions of results devoted to the Holy Spirit, healings, miracles, prophesy, and tongues that resemble those recounted by Luke and Paul almost two thousand years ago.[22] Scholars such as Craig Keener have chronicled hundreds of modern, medically documented miracles occurring through the power of the Holy Spirit in Jesus' name.[23] There is certainly no shortage of evidence for the risen power of Jesus in the current age.

Additionally, there is excellent medical assessment of miracles done through the intercession of Mary, the Mother of Jesus. A truly

[21] John P. Meier, *A Marginal Jew: Rethinking the Historical Jesus*, vol. 2, *Mentor, Message, and Miracles* (New York: Doubleday, 1994), p. 623.

[22] A simple Google search on the Internet for "Holy Spirit healing" currently yields 11,200,000 results; for "Holy Spirit miracles" there are 7,220,000 results; for "Holy Spirit prophecy" there are 5,480,000 results; and for "Holy Spirit tongues" there are 3,490,000 results.

[23] See Craig Keener, *Miracles: The Credibility of the New Testament*, 2 vols. (Grand Rapids, Mich.: Baker Academic Publishing, 2011).

excellent source of these documented miracles is the International Medical Committee of Lourdes. Its selection criteria are so rigorous that of the thousands of miracles that have occurred at Lourdes, it has only definitively approved of sixty-nine (as of 2015). However, those sixty-nine miracles are incredibly well-documented and deserve the readers' scrutiny.[24]

In conclusion, the veracity of the apostolic testimony to the Resurrection of Jesus can be corroborated with a high degree of probability by the historical analysis of the Resurrection narratives, the evidence of the Resurrection from the Shroud of Turin, the high probability of human consciousness surviving bodily death—which correlates with Christian accounts of the Resurrection—and the miracles done in the name of Jesus from the time of the apostolic Church until today.

As previously noted, the apostolic testimony and the above four areas of evidence will not be convincing to those who are not open to the salvation and message of Jesus. However, if we are open to the salvation and message of Jesus, the combined evidence for life after bodily death and Jesus' Resurrection will likely form a reasonable and responsible basis for belief in our resurrection. This is precisely what is required to enter into the Christian view of suffering. If you, the reader, continue to be in doubt about the resurrection (eternal life in unconditional love), I would strongly advise reviewing the chapters and sections mentioned above—and if doubts continue, then review the scientific and medical sources referenced in those chapters.

II. Hope in Our Resurrection

Before discussing the nature of our risen life, it is important to note that if we seek God with a sincere heart, and try in our actions to do His will according to the dictates of our conscience, we will be led into His risen life.[25] None of us will be able to follow the teachings

---

[24] See their website at http://en.lourdes-france.org/deepen/cures-and-miracles/the-international-medical-committee.

[25] The Dogmatic Constitution on the Church (*Lumen Gentium*) indicates that "those who, through no fault of their own, do not know the Gospel of Christ or his Church, but who nevertheless seek God with a sincere heart, and, moved by grace, try in their actions to do his will as they know it through the dictates of their conscience—those too may achieve

IN THE TWINKLING OF AN EYE

of Jesus *perfectly* during our lifetime, and so the word "try" in the previous sentence is important. Jesus makes clear that if we fail multiple times—even as egregiously as the prodigal son—His Father will accept us into His heavenly Kingdom if we contritely ask for forgiveness, just as the father of the prodigal son was moved to accept his son into the household unconditionally when he expressed his contrition. Thus, we should not fall prey to doubts that undermine our hope. If we try in our actions to do God's will as Jesus has taught, and if we turn back to God for forgiveness when we have failed, we should have confidence that the unconditional love of Jesus and His Father will bring us to the promised resurrection.

We should not doubt that the Lord will forgive us as many times as we have failed, for if He asks Peter to forgive his brother seventy times seven times—a virtually endless number of times—we can be sure that the Lord will do precisely the same for us, so long as we ask sincerely. Jesus makes this point powerfully in the Parable of the Tax Collector and the Pharisee who go up to the Temple to pray. The tax collector—considered to be a very serious egregious sinner in first-century Israel—simply stands at a distance and prays contritely, "God, have mercy on me, a sinner." Jesus declares emphatically, "I tell you that this man, rather than the other, went home justified [ready for salvation] before God" (Lk 18:13–14; my translation).

Saint Paul understood how important this confidence in the unconditional love of God is—not only for the sake of warding off discouragement and despair, but also for interpreting the cross (suffering) in our lives. In his Letter to the Romans, Paul presents an argument for Christian hope grounded in the teaching and self-sacrifice of Jesus on the Cross:

> If God is for us, who is against us? He who did not spare his own Son but gave him up for us all, will he not also give us all things with him? Who shall bring any charge against God's elect? It is God who justifies; who is to condemn? Is it Christ Jesus, who died, yes,

---

eternal salvation" (no. 16), in *Vatican Council II, Vol. 1: The Conciliar and Postconciliar Documents*, trans. Austin Flannery (Northport, N.Y.: Costello Publishing, 1975), p. 376. We can infer a doctrine of salvation *for Christians* from this. For Christians, "the will of God" is defined by the teachings of Jesus. Hence, Christians will attain eternal salvation if they seek God and *try* to do His will by following the teachings of Jesus. If we fail at times to do God's will, we can confidently rely on the unconditional forgiving love of His Father.

who was raised from the dead, who is at the right hand of God, who indeed intercedes for us? (8:31–34)

Paul's argument is probative, for if God allowed His Son to sacrifice Himself completely for us, then there is *nothing* that He would not do to save us and bring us to eternal life—that is, He would do anything and everything to bring us into His eternal Kingdom.

This news is already beyond belief, but Paul goes further: if God would do anything and everything to bring us to eternal life, then no person or group of persons—no spirit or group of spirits—can successfully block us from God's salvific intention. Therefore, if we try to do God's will as Jesus taught us, and ask sincerely for forgiveness when we have failed to do so, then God's salvific intention will lead us to His Kingdom. We should have confidence in this—particularly during times of suffering.

In the Letter to the Ephesians, we are given a prayer and declaration about how to have this powerful confidence in the salvific will of God; Saint Paul prays

> that Christ may dwell in your hearts through faith; that you, being rooted and grounded in love, may have power to comprehend with all the saints what is the breadth and length and height and depth, and to know the love of Christ which surpasses knowledge, that you may be filled with all the fullness of God. Now to him who by the power at work within us is able to do *far more* abundantly than all that we ask or think, to him be glory in the Church and in Christ Jesus to all generations, for ever and ever. Amen. (3:17–21; emphasis mine)

Saint Paul prays that we will know the breadth and length and height and depth of Christ's love, which is the fullness of God; for if we gain a mere glimmer of this love—which is beyond all knowledge—we will know with confidence that God will do *far more* to bring us to His eternal salvation than we can possibly "ask or think". Therefore, if we ask God for eternal salvation, believing in His unconditional love, He will grant us far more than anything we could have hoped for.

When we are suffering acutely, we will want to make recourse to this radical hope in the salvific intention of the unconditionally loving God. Anything less could cause us to falter at the very moment we must believe in our risen glory with Him.

III. The Nature of Our Resurrection—
Spirit, Glory, Love, and Beauty

How might we best understand the connection between the Cross and the Resurrection? By *returning* to the viewpoint of the disciples, evangelists, and other witnesses—many of whom heard His preaching and saw His glorious transformation after His Resurrection. These early witnesses had a good idea about the risen life awaiting them with Jesus. If we get a good sense of this risen life, we can superimpose it on the crosses we experience. This will enable us to use these crosses as a pathway to the glorious life to come.

We have already discussed the heavenly Kingdom in Volume III (Chapter 7, Section II) of this Quartet, so we will only need to summarize three points characterizing the viewpoint of the disciples and earliest witnesses to Jesus' Resurrection:

1. The glorious spiritual transformation of our bodies
2. The love of God and the heavenly community
3. The glorification of the whole of creation

Seen in the light of the risen life (our true dignity and destiny), no cross—no suffering of any kind—can be ultimately tragic. For God will bring perfect, absolute, and eternal consolation out of every desolation—especially death. As we shall see, the Holy Spirit uses these crosses to deepen us in love and guide us to this heavenly destiny. Though crosses are painful, debilitating, undermining, and enervating, they are also liberating, refocusing, guiding, and transforming—when seen in the light of the resurrection.

Let us turn to the first dimension of resurrection in Christ: the spiritual and glorious transformation of our bodies. As noted in Volume III (Chapter 4), Saint Paul and the Gospel writers indicate that Christ's risen body was transformed in glory, power, and spirit.[26] Saint Paul states that we will be raised like Jesus (1 Cor 15:49). So what does Paul mean by our being raised in glory, power, and spirit?

---

[26]See 1 Cor 15:42–44. See also the analysis of the Resurrection narratives in Volume III, Chapter 4, Section II.

We may obtain some clues from Jesus' Transfiguration, which is a prefigurement of His risen glory[27]: "[H]is garments became glistening, intensely white, as no fuller on earth could bleach them" (Mk 9:3). Some exegetes see this as a transformation in bright light, where Jesus' body is still noticeable, but luminescent. The Gospel accounts of Jesus' risen appearance also indicate that His body was no longer subject to physical laws, for He was able to appear seemingly from nowhere (and disappear just as easily) and able to appear in closed rooms without going through doors. There is also the implication that Jesus transcended the pain of His Crucifixion—for though His wounds are present, they are apparently no longer painful. The implication is that after our deaths, we will undergo the same kind of transformation—from perishable to imperishable, from dishonor to glory, from weakness to power, and from natural body to spiritual body (1 Cor 15:42–44). We will be free from pain, physical laws and constraints, and the decay of the flesh. We will be transformed in spirit—dazzlingly bright and luminescent, like Jesus in His glory.

This corresponds to a comment Jesus made to the Sadducees about our status in eternal life: "[I]n the resurrection [people] neither marry nor are given in marriage, but are like *angels* in heaven" (Mt 22:30; emphasis mine). The reference to "angels" is consistent with Old and New Testament usage, signifying the personification of divine power, divine wisdom, and divine action.[28] Jesus does not mean that our embodiment will be "cancelled", but that it will be enhanced by the qualities Paul refers to in 1 Corinthians 15: glory, power, and spirit.

The second dimension of the resurrection is most important, for it is not limited to the transformation of our bodies, but of our soul or spirit. Saint Paul implies that we will be taken into a condition of *perfect love*, which is eternal by its very nature (1 Cor 13:7–8, 13). He describes what perfect love would consist in—namely, perfect patience and kindness; the complete absence of envy, boasting, pride,

---

[27] According to McKenzie "[in the Transfiguration], the change described in the appearance of Jesus suggests the change which is implied in the resurrection narratives.... The transformation of the body into glory in the resurrection is also mentioned by Paul (1 Co 15:40–44)." John L. McKenzie, *Dictionary of the Bible* (New York: Macmillan Publishing, 1965), p. 898.

[28] See ibid., pp. 31–32.

dishonoring of others, self-seeking, anger, and resentment of wrongs. It is perfect protection, trust, hope, and perseverance (see I Cor 13:4–8). He further implies that no pain, suffering, or evil can separate us from this love of God (Rom 8:35–39).

Jesus provides concrete images to fill in Paul's association of the resurrection with perfect love. As noted in Volume III, Chapter 7, Section II.A, Jesus uses the image of the messianic banquet to convey the love and joy of the Kingdom of Heaven. It will resemble a perfect banquet with all the foods we like, with all the people we would want to be with, and they will all be like "family" to us. For Jesus, table fellowship with "friends who are like family" provides a good image of the intimacy, affection, friendship, empathy, consideration, patience, kindness, respect, conviviality, co-responsibility, and joy that the Kingdom of Heaven represents.

The Gospel of John uses other "family" images to convey the closeness and "friendship-family" of the Kingdom of Heaven: "In my Father's house are many rooms; if it were not so, would I have told you that I go to prepare a place for you? And when I go and prepare a place for you, I will come again and will take you to myself, that where I am you may also be" (14:2–3). This image of *home* is meant to convey our intimate participation in Jesus' (and the Father's) family, and that we have our own special place in it. There are other images of family closeness and the "love and joy of good friends" conveyed through Jesus' relationship with His Mother, the Twelve, Martha, Mary, Lazarus, and Mary Magdalene—as well as the table fellowship He enjoys with friends, religious officials, and sinners.

The Gospel of John might be called the "Gospel of *love*". Love is so foundational that John uses it fifty-six times—at the center of both his narratives and discourses. John refers to himself as the disciple whom Jesus *loved*, which indicates that he derived his very heart and essence from that love (see Jn 13:23; 19:26; 20:2; 21:7; 21:20). The central commandment of the Gospel is to "love one another as I have loved you", calling us to a love that Jesus demonstrated in action (Jn 15:12; see Jn 13:34). Jesus links this primacy of love to the Kingdom of Heaven when He says:

> If you keep my commandments, you will abide in my love, just as I have kept my Father's commandments and abide in his love. These

things I have spoken to you, that my joy may be in you, and that your joy may be full. (Jn 15:10–11)

Only in the Kingdom of Heaven will Jesus' joy be ours, and our joy complete. Hence, perfect love (loving one another as Jesus has loved us) characterizes the Kingdom of Heaven.

Those who have "crossed over to the other side" in near-death experiences report almost universally that "overwhelming love" is the primary characteristic of their experience. Frequently, these individuals are taken up into a loving white light in which they not only experience overwhelming love, but learn to love themselves and others in the same way. Others have experienced the love of family and friends, and still others, the love of Jesus.[29] One person describes this universal experience as follows:

> I became very weak, and I fell down. I began to feel a sort of drifting, a movement of my real being in and out of my body, and to hear beautiful music. I floated on down the hall and out the door onto the screened-in porch. There, it almost seemed that clouds, a pink mist really, began to gather around me, and then I floated right straight on through the screen, just as though it weren't there, and up into this pure crystal clear light, an illuminating white light. It was beautiful and so bright, so radiant, but it didn't hurt my eyes. It's not any kind of light you can describe on earth. I didn't actually see a person in this light, and yet it has a special identity, it definitely does. It is a light of perfect understanding and perfect love.... And all during this time, I felt as though I was surrounded by an overwhelming love and compassion.[30]

The third dimension of the Kingdom of Heaven is the redemption of all creation. Though the joy that comes from the redemption of human relationships and love is primary in the Christian view of Heaven, Saint Paul makes clear that our joy will be brought to completion when the whole of creation is redeemed:

---

[29] The experience of overwhelming love is so central to near-death experiences that a simple Internet search for "Love, near-death experiences" yields 9,310,000 results. Many of these experiences are also published in books and journals.

[30] Raymond A. Moody, *Life after Life* (New York: HarperCollins, 1975), pp. 53–54. There are many other testimonies to the intense love of the white light and Jesus that are accessible through an Internet search of "love in near death experiences".

I consider that the sufferings of this present time are not worth comparing with the glory that is to be revealed to us. For the creation waits with eager longing for the revealing of the sons of God; for the creation was subjected to futility, not of its own will but by the will of him who subjected it in hope; because the creation itself will be set free from its bondage to decay and obtain the glorious liberty of the children of God. We know that the whole creation has been groaning with labor pains together until now; and not only the creation, but we ourselves, who have the first fruits of the Spirit, groan inwardly as we wait for adoption as sons, the redemption of our bodies. For in this hope we were saved. (Rom 8:18–20)

Paul's vision inspired a conception of Heaven as an intensely beautiful place where nature—plants, animals, bodies of water, and so on—take on a spiritual magnificence that inspires awe and wonder. Though these images are reconstructions of Paul's vision for creation, they are borne out by a multitude of reports about a "heavenly domain" encountered during near-death experiences.[31] Though overwhelming love is the primary and central dimension of "crossing to the other side", many have conjointly experienced an intense beauty in a heavenly domain.

The above three dimensions of the heavenly Kingdom contextualize the suffering we endure on this earth. They show that we will be brought to fulfillment in our souls and bodies, in our consciousness and love, with family and friends, and in the splendor of God and the redemption of nature.

Thus we do not want to forget the promise of Jesus: "Blessed are the sorrowing, for they shall be comforted" (Mt 5:4; my translation), and, "Come to me, all who labor and are heavy laden, and I will give you rest" (Mt 11:28). As noted in the Introduction, these promises are absolute, indicating Jesus' intention to remove and redeem

---

[31] There are several good descriptions available on the Internet. For the experience of Dr. Mary Neal, see the following: Billy Hallowell, " 'Beyond Science': Doctor Says She Visited Heaven during a Near-Death Experience—and What She Learned Haunted Her for Years", Blaze.com, February 9, 2015, http://www.theblaze.com/stories/2015/02/09/doctor-who-claims-she-visited-heaven-during-near-death-experience-says-she-learned-something-there-that-haunted-her-for-years/. For dozens of other experiences, search the following online: "Heaven, near death experiences".

all suffering in the Kingdom of Heaven. A passage in the Book of Revelation sums up the belief of the disciples and the early Christian Church about the redemption of suffering:

> [God] will wipe away every tear from their eyes, and death shall be no more, neither shall there be mourning nor crying nor pain any more, for the former things have passed away. (21:4)

The removal and redemption of pain and suffering in the afterlife is explicitly mentioned in the accounts of many near-death experiences. The clinical death of Linda Stewart gives a detailed account of this phenomenon. She was wracked not only with great physical pain from a debilitating disease, but also with severe depression, and the spiritual pain of being taught that God was angry, wrathful, and punishing. As her disease progressed, and her pain grew worse, Linda let go of her physical body and described the following experience:

> When I finally gave up my will to live, relinquishing my life unto death was sublimely easy after my long illness and loss of everything that had made life worthwhile for me. The decision to leave this world hung suspended in an extended moment of absolute quiet. Passionless, I watched my spirit leave my body as a feeling of "otherness" engulfed me. I felt a strange detachment from my physical body and the life I had created. I was no longer connected to a pitiful, suffering mass of flesh. I was not that body and yet, I still existed but in a new state of being. Gone was the wrenching pain that had accompanied my every waking moment. The strain of expanding my lungs to gasp for air had disappeared. Fatigue, which had weighted my life for years, had lifted. Depression no longer drained my mind of hope. Sight and sounds did not sear my head with pain, leaving me emotionally bereft. And yet, I still existed. I felt weightless and calm.... Although I knew I was not in the lifeless body lying on my bed, and that the eyes and brain I had previously identified as mine, were in that inanimate object with which I no longer identified, I was still aware of sight and thoughts and sensations. I observed my new reality with tranquility.... I became aware of a deep sense of peace and warmth that permeated my senses.... I was suddenly buffeted by a powerful, energetic force that swooped beneath and lifted me, carrying me upward.... Barely conscious, my only awareness was a sensation of rising. I seemed to be traveling upward at an unimaginable speed. A clean sensation of wind

rushed over my face and body with tremendous force and yet there was no discomfort. Vast distances seemed to fly by me and the higher I rose, the more my head cleared. I became aware of a deep sense of peace and warmth that permeated my senses.... Confused, because the energy that had enveloped me had a definite presence, I tried to see what was happening and who was carrying me; who or what cared so deeply for me? I felt peaceful and loved immeasurably. I knew I was in the arms of a being who cherished me with perfect love and carried me from the dark void into a new reality.... With the eyes of my soul body, I looked to see what held me in such love and I beheld a radiant, Spirit being, so magnificent and full of love that I knew I would never again feel the sense of loss. I have no way of explaining how, but I knew the Spirit was Christ. It was not a belief, perception or understanding, but my recognition of Christ came from my new perspective of spirit.... I did not see the Spirit as I had seen Jesus of Nazareth depicted in paintings, but the innate knowing of my heart remembered and acknowledged Christ. The radiant Spirit was Christ, the manifestation and expression of pure love.[32]

Linda experienced precisely what is promised by Jesus and expressed in the Book of Revelation. Her physical pain and debilitation was transformed into peace and warmth, which permeated her senses; her depression and malaise was transformed by a sense of being unconditionally loved; and her spiritual pain that came from a misconception about God was replaced by the overwhelming awareness that God is perfect love and that He is one with Jesus Christ. Linda's experience typifies that of thousands of others who have crossed over from this world to the next—an experience where every tear is wiped away and replaced by the consolation of the loving God promised by Jesus.

Belief in Jesus' promise to remove and redeem all suffering—and bring us into a domain of perfect love and joy is essential to the Christian experience of "suffering well". When we affirm this truth, suffering can no longer be ultimately tragic. Yes, it can produce terrible pain, grief, loneliness, emptiness, fear, and frustration, but these

---

[32] Kevin Williams, *Nothing Better Than Death* (Bloomington, Ind.: Xlibris Corp., 2002). The testimony of Linda Stewart can also be found on the Internet: Kevin Williams, "Linda Stewart's Near-Death Experience", Near-Death Experiences and the Afterlife, 2014, http://www.near-death.com/experiences/notable/linda-stewart.html.

negative states are only *temporary* if we believe in the resurrection and put the redemption of our suffering into the hands of the loving God.

If the evidence for our resurrection detailed in Section I above (historical criteria, near-death experiences, the Shroud of Turin, and miracles in the name of Jesus) has *any* validity, then we can be reasonably certain that God *will* wipe away all of our pain and replace it with unconditional warmth, peace, love and joy. He will make use of every bit of our suffering to lead us and others into the Kingdom of His unconditional love. Bearing this in mind, we can proceed to several other points in the Christian interpretation of suffering.

IV. The Resurrection Transforms All Suffering and Death

The most fundamental Christian foundation of suffering is conviction about eternal life with the unconditionally loving God. If this really is our destiny (as Jesus said), then no suffering, not even the most intense grief of losing a child, is *ultimately* tragic. Yes, the pain of such loss and grief can be unbelievably intense, but it need not be overwhelming to the point of despair, because it is not the end of the story—of the child, the parents, and everyone else affected. Death and loss are intensely negative *moments* within an ultimately loving eternity. The same holds true for every other kind of suffering— physical pain and deprivation, psychological pain and deprivation, weakness, loss of socioeconomic means, humiliation, rejection, and callous hatred; all these things are mere redeemable passing states within an ultimately loving eternity.

Jesus views our passing lives in this world as a time for choosing who we are and who we will become. This idea of "self-definition" is central to the Christian view of suffering. For Jesus, this life is not an end in itself, but only a brief moment—though a very significant moment—for choices and preparation for the life to come. Saint Paul summarizes this in the Second Letter to the Corinthians as follows:

So we do not lose heart. Though our outer nature is wasting away, our inner nature is being renewed every day. For this slight momentary affliction is *preparing* for us an eternal weight of glory beyond all comparison, because we look not to the things that are seen but to the things that are unseen; for the things that are seen are transient, but the things that are unseen are eternal. (4:16–18; translation mine)

Later, in the Letter to the Romans, he expresses it this way:

[W]e are children of God, and if children, then heirs, heirs of God and fellow heirs with Christ, provided we suffer with him in order that we may also be glorified with him. I consider that the sufferings of this present time are not worth comparing with the glory that is to be revealed to us. (8:16–18)

Then why is there death? Why do we have to bring this life to a close before we can proceed to eternal life? Death is significant for only one major reason—to compel us to make the fundamental decisions that will define our eternal character. Death makes us realize that we will not be able to continue this life indefinitely, which means we will have to start leaving a legacy sooner rather than later—defining who we are with respect to others and defining what matters most to us in life (Level One, or Two, or Three, or Four). In short, we must declare in intention, word, and action who we are and who we are likely to become. Will we orient our lives toward good or evil, virtue or vice, actions that build up others or tear them down, and actions that are loving or hateful? Death means that the path we choose—though it can be changed in midcourse or even at the end of life—will ultimately define who we are. We will *not* be able to reverse course *forever*—there will be a point at which our intentions, words, and actions will be definitive.

What about children who die unexpectedly before engaging in truly self-defining choices and actions? We have to leave these matters in God's hands. Does God give them a chance to make such decisions after they die? Perhaps He does, but we must bear in mind that God is absolutely predisposed to the salvation of any innocent child. As Jesus teaches, "I tell you that in heaven [children's] angels always behold the face of my Father who is in heaven" (Mt 18:10), and again, "Truly, I say to you, unless you turn and become like children, you will never enter the kingdom of heaven" (Mt 18:3). It is worth noting here that according to the International Association for

Near-Death Studies, 85 percent of children undergoing clinical death have a "heavenly" near-death experience.[33] It is also significant that this large percentage of children (who had an NDE) have virtually no death anxiety for the rest of their lives—which is quite different from the normal population[34] (see Volume II, Chapter 5).

Though Saint Paul sees the importance of death in calling us to faith,[35] he states confidently that with resistance to sin and faith in the redemptive power and Resurrection of Jesus, death has no power over us:

> For this perishable nature must put on the imperishable, and this mortal nature must put on immortality. When the perishable puts on the imperishable, and the mortal puts on immortality, then shall come to pass the saying that is written: "Death is swallowed up in victory. O death, where is your victory? O death, where is your sting?" (1 Cor 15:53–55)

For Jesus, eternal life with Him and His Father is the consolation of unconditional love with everyone in the heavenly Kingdom. As we saw above, He likens this to a perfect and perpetual messianic banquet, and being like angels in Heaven (Mt 22:30). This eternal consolation in love, spirit, and glory puts an end to suffering and transforms the whole of suffering and death into complete fulfillment and joy. This is the essence of Jesus' preaching at the Sermon on the Plain in the Gospel of Luke:

> Blessed are you poor, for yours is the kingdom of God. Blessed are you that hunger now, for you shall be satisfied. Blessed are you that weep now, for you shall laugh. Blessed are you when men hate you, and when they exclude you and revile you, and cast out your name as

---

[33] International Association for Near-Death Studies, "Children's Near-Death Experiences", last updated July 14, 2014, http://iands.org/childrens-near-death-experiences.html.

[34] See Cherie Sutherland, "Near Death Experiences of Children", in *Making Sense of Near-Death Experiences: A Handbook for Clinicians*, ed. Karuppiah Jagadheesan, Anthony Peake, and Mahendra Perera (London: Jessica Kingsley Publishers, 2012), pp. 63–79.

[35] "Why, we felt that we had received the sentence of death; but that was to make us rely not on ourselves but on God who raises the dead; he delivered us from so deadly a peril, and he will deliver us; on him we have set our hope that he will deliver us again" (2 Cor 1:9–10). See also Rom 6:5; 2 Cor 4:11–12.

evil, on account of the Son of man! Rejoice in that day, and leap for joy, for behold, your reward is great in heaven. (6:20–22)

So if Jesus' intent is to lead us into eternal love and joy and to redeem our suffering through this love and joy, why is there a Hell? In Volume III (Chapter 7, Section III), we looked at the reason why an unconditionally loving God would allow for even the possibility of Hell—a place that Jesus acknowledges to be dark, lonely, and sad (see Mt 25:30; 13:42; Lk 16:23–24). We indicated, in conformity with the *Catechism of the Catholic Church*, that Hell is a state of definitive *self*-exclusion from God and the blessed in His Kingdom (no. 1033). Why would anyone exclude himself from God and the blessed? Apparently some people might *choose* (over the course of their lives) to reject God and love. Some people might *prefer* autonomy, domination, ego-centricity, and self-idolatry to love—appreciation of others, equality with others, giving oneself to others, and surrendering in love to God. Since God has made us free to define who we are and where we will find our "happiness", He will accommodate those who prefer egocentricity and dominion instead of love and loving self-surrender.

God does not want anyone to choose this life of ego-centricity, domination, and self-idolatry, because He knows it will involve loneliness, pain, emptiness, and darkness, but He allows us to choose it because He has given us the ultimate dignity of defining ourselves and choosing our "eternal happiness". Though He is incredibly saddened by anyone who chooses self-exclusion from love—from Him and the blessed—He will not force us to take His gift of loving salvation. If some choose "antilove", God cannot bring them into the Kingdom of Love, for they would undermine the dynamic of love in Heaven. Thus God must keep the domain of antilove separate from the domain of love.

Ironically, when God created us in His own image with the freedom to define ourselves and to choose our happiness, He had to allow us to definitively reject Him, others, love, and His Kingdom. He does not send anyone to Hell, but accommodates a state that can be chosen by an individual in which He, love, and the blessed are *absent*. In order to give us ultimate dignity, He has to accommodate ultimate separation from Himself and love. Thus, God does not cause eternal suffering to anyone—He allows us to enter into a state of separation in order to accommodate our choice to reject Him and the joy of love.

One final question must be addressed: Is the risen life of Jesus available to *everyone*? In Section II above, we examined the Church's declaration on this matter in its Dogmatic Constitution on the Church (*Lumen Gentium*):

> Those who, through no fault of their own, do not know the Gospel of Christ or his Church, but who nevertheless seek God with a sincere heart, and, moved by grace, try in their actions to do his will as they know it through the dictates of their conscience—those too may achieve eternal salvation. (no. 16)

This is complemented by a declaration from *Gaudium et Spes* (the Pastoral Constitution on the Church), which explains that the redemptive act of Jesus and the actions of the Holy Spirit are actively involved in saving *all* people of good will:

> The Christian is certainly bound both by need and by duty to struggle with evil through many afflictions and to suffer death; but, as one who has been made a partner in the paschal mystery, and as one who has been configured to the death of Christ, he will go forward, strengthened by hope, to the resurrection. All this holds true not for the Christian only but also for all men of good will in whose hearts grace is active invisibly. For since *Christ died for all*, and since all men are in fact called to one and the same destiny, which is divine, we must hold that the Holy Spirit offers to all the possibility of being made partners, in a way known to God, in the paschal mystery.[36] (no. 22)

What can we conclude from this? We may confidently believe that God so loved the world that He created us with the ultimate dignity to define ourselves for all eternity—and with the ultimate destiny of eternal life with Him and the blessed in the community of unconditional love and joy. This dignity and destiny is the ultimate context through which suffering and death are to be interpreted. Suffering and death are not ends in themselves—they are not definitive, and not even long-term conditions. For Jesus and the loving God, suffering

---

[36] In *Vatican Council II: Conciliar and Postconciliar Documents*, pp. 923–24; emphasis mine.

and death are punctuated realities that incite us to *choose* who we are and who we will become—necessary moments in the process of self-definition, our ultimate dignity. Since they are temporary, there can be tragedy, but no *ultimate* tragedy; grief, but no *ultimate* grief; weakness, anxiety, and pain, but no *ultimate* weakness, anxiety, and pain; and sadness, but no *ultimate* sadness—no despair. Therefore, suffering and death are transcended by love, joy, and life—the only real absolutes—in the Kingdom of God. As Jesus affirms in the Gospel of John:

> These things I have spoken to you, that my joy may be in you, and that your joy may be full. This is my commandment, that you love one another as I have loved you. (15:11–12)

In the context of the resurrection, life is *ultimately* and *eternally* meaningful, joyful, loving, good, and beautiful. In this context, suffering and death find their place in a *temporary* process of self-definition and simply disappear without trace of negativity or tragedy in the eternity of the resurrection. Saint Paul teaches us how to live according to this belief and hope in the Letter to the Philippians:

> Indeed I count everything as loss because of the surpassing worth of knowing Christ Jesus my Lord. For his sake I have suffered the loss of all things, and count them as refuse, in order that I may gain Christ and be found in him, not having a righteousness of my own, based on law, but that which is through faith in Christ, the righteousness from God that depends on faith; that I may know him and the power of his resurrection, and may share his sufferings, becoming like him in his death, should I by any means attain[37] the resurrection from the dead. Not that I have already obtained this or am already perfect; but I press on to make it my own, because Christ Jesus has made me his own. Brethren, I do not consider that I have made it my own; but one thing I do, forgetting what lies behind and straining forward to what lies ahead, I press on toward the goal for the prize of the upward call of God in Christ Jesus. (3:8–14; my translation)

[37] The Greek phrase *ei pōs katant* is best translated as "if (*ei*) by any means (*pōs*) I should attain (*katant*)". It is better rendered in English as "if I should by any means attain". Paul uses the indefinite adverb *pōs* to avoid being presumptuous about declaring his salvation. It does not mean he lacks confidence in the saving power of Christ, which is the precise point of this whole passage in the Letter to the Philippians.

V. An Overview of the Christian Interpretation of Suffering

The purpose of this section is to give a brief overview of what will be explained throughout the rest of this book. It is meant to give you, the reader, a *general* idea about the Christian interpretation of suffering—a big picture that will allow you to see how the major pieces of this puzzle fit together. If you are tempted to ask why the points in the following summary are true, just wait—the answer will hopefully be provided in the next nine chapters. For the moment it will be sufficient to understand the foundational insights of Jesus and the early Church on one of the most challenging questions of human existence. The Christian view of suffering may be described through six major insights.

A. First Christian Insight: Suffering Is Completely Redeemed in the Resurrection

By now it will be evident that the first and most foundational Christian insight concerns the redemption of suffering in the eternal life of unconditional love. It may be characterized as follows: our life is eternal, and intended by Jesus to be unconditional love and joy. Therefore our life in the physical universe is but a mere blip on the landscape of eternity. Though this life has definitive significance (see the second, third, and fifth insights below), it will be changed at the moment of death—and so its temporal and physical features should not be absolutized.

As noted in the previous section, the Christian Church teaches that all people "who nevertheless seek God with a sincere heart, and, moved by grace, *try* in their actions to do his will as they know it through the dictates of their conscience", may achieve the resurrection of unconditional love.[38] For Christians, the "dictates of their conscience" are based on the teachings of Jesus. Recall that the requirement for salvation is not the achievement of perfection in doing God's will, but *trying* in our actions to do God's will. God knows that precious few of us will be able to achieve perfection in

---

[38] See the full citation from *Lumen Gentium*, no. 16, in Section IV above; emphasis mine.

doing His will before we die, and so He accepts sincere repentance for shortcomings and our good faith *efforts*.

According to Jesus, this choice to seek God with a sincere heart and to try to do His will can be made even at the last moment.[39] When the choice is made, and when Christians put their faith in Jesus, this life can no longer be ultimately tragic. Jesus promised that all suffering would be transformed into perfect love and joy in His Kingdom, meaning that even the worst of disasters will be perfectly redeemed for all eternity. Hence Saint Paul can say with great confidence:

> We are afflicted in every way, but not crushed; perplexed, but not driven to despair; persecuted, but not forsaken; struck down, but not destroyed; always carrying in the body the death of Jesus, so that the life of Jesus may also be manifested in our bodies. (2 Cor 4:8–10)

B. Second Christian Insight: The Purpose of Suffering

For Christians, the redemption of suffering in an eternal life of unconditional love is not *the whole* story. Suffering has a significant purpose *in this life*—it *helps* us move toward that eternal salvation. In the perspective of Christian faith, suffering purifies love—it does not undermine it. Without faith, this perspective is difficult to see, but *with* faith in the unconditionally loving God, this central insight becomes quite powerful—not only leading us to our salvation, but enabling us to lead others to their salvation.

As will be discussed in Chapters 7 and 10, suffering provides the impetus for six major opportunities:

1. It can shock us out of a superficial Level One–Two purpose and identity, and point the way to a Level Three–Four purpose and identity.
2. It provides the impetus to grow in our faith and deepen our trust in God, which leads to our salvation, and frequently to the salvation of others.

---

[39] See, for example, Mt 20:1–16 (Parable of the Late Laborers), and Lk 15:11–32 (Parable of the Prodigal Son). Jesus reflects this attitude in His ministry with sinners, eating with and calling even the worst of sinners (e.g., tax collectors and prostitutes) to the Kingdom of Heaven through their choice and faith in Him.

3. It provides the conditions for need and interdependence, which in turn incites the call to serve and contribute to others and to make the world a better place.
4. It provides the impetus to grow in natural virtues—endurance, courage, fortitude, prudence, rationality, and temperance.
5. It provides the impetus to purify and deepen our love (*agapē*), particularly in the areas of empathy, humility, forgiveness, compassion, and the "acceptance of compassion".
6. It provides the conditions for serving, strengthening, and building the Kingdom of God on Earth—and to bring hope and the good news of salvation to the world.

Each of these six opportunities has a "self-definitional" quality. The more we follow the opportunities of suffering, the more deeply we define our hearts and ourselves as "living for the kingdom, others, and the human and divine community". Were it not for suffering, we would not have the same impetus to move beyond a self-centric nature—beyond self-sufficiency, autonomy, domination, and self-worship; we would not have the same opportunity to leave a legacy of contribution, compassion, and good for the Kingdom and the community; we would be left without the challenges that call us to courage, effort, commitment, and love—left to a kind of infancy of "being taken care of" instead of taking care of others; and we would be deprived of the opportunity to make sacrifices for others, the Kingdom, and other noble causes—left to a nonsublime innocence.[40]

Though suffering causes pain, loss, grief, and other negative emotional states, Jesus did not view it as *essentially* negative, because in the context of faith it can lead toward our and others' salvation. Saint Paul develops this theology of "positive suffering" in two major passages. The first passage, from the Letter to the Romans, concerns the role of suffering in developing natural virtue:

> [W]e rejoice in our sufferings, knowing that suffering produces endurance, and endurance produces character, and character produces hope, and hope does not disappoint us, because God's love has been poured into our hearts through the Holy Spirit who has been given to us. (5:3–5)

[40] These points will be taken up extensively in Chapter 7.

Saint Paul's perspective is that suffering plus faith will lead to virtue and love. He spells out some of these virtues in the above passage— endurance, character, and hope, all of which open us to the love of God poured into our hearts by the Holy Spirit. This love of God leads to an increase in trust and a deepening of our capacity for love.

Another passage from the Second Letter to the Corinthians is central to the Christian interpretation of suffering:

> And to keep me from being too proud [*hyperōmai*—self-exalted, proud, conceited] by the abundance of revelations, a thorn was given me in the flesh, an angel of Satan, to torment me. Three times I besought the Lord about this, that it should leave me; but he said to me, "My grace is sufficient for you, for my power is made perfect in weakness." I will all the more gladly boast of my weaknesses, that the power of Christ may rest upon me. For the sake of Christ, then, I am content with weaknesses, insults, hardships, persecutions, and calamities; for when I am weak, then I am strong. (12:7–10; my translation)

Paul's thorn in the flesh is very probably a *physical* infirmity, and many exegetes believe that he had significant problems with his vision,[41] but he remained intentionally vague about this to allow others with different kinds of suffering the greatest latitude to identify with him and his interpretation of redemptive suffering. So what is Paul's interpretation of the "opportunity of suffering"? He names two specific benefits:

- It prevents him from becoming conceited (proud).
- His weaknesses are the means through which Jesus' power is perfected within him.

---

[41] There are several indications of Paul's difficulties with vision. He seems to have dictated most of his letters to scribes (e.g., Tertius, who transcribed the Letter to the Romans). What he does write for himself, he pens with large print (Gal 6:11), indicating possible difficulties with seeing. Furthermore, in Galatians 4:15, Paul tells the Galatians, "For I bear you witness that, if possible, you would have plucked out your eyes and given them to me." What would have been the purpose of that, if Paul did not need their eyes? In Acts 23:3–5, Paul, who was a former Pharisee, claims that he did not recognize the high priest standing in full regalia in front of him—referring to him as a "whitewashed wall" (23:3). This passage makes little sense if Paul had clear vision.

For Saint Paul, there are far worse things than suffering—namely, the darkness of pride and conceit. Pride and conceit gave him the false impression that he was more important than others and his life more valuable than others. This bloated sense of self-importance could have led him away from the Lord into a self-idolatrous darkness—which he feared. So, he felt incredibly blessed by the Lord to be given his thorn in the flesh—which caused him to stumble, be embarrassed, and be dependent on others. He probably found this very difficult to accept at first—as manifest by his pleading with God to take it away three times (over and over and over again many times). His reticence to accept the thorn is probably attributable to the dignity and pride he felt due to his education, intelligence, his ability to speak and write, and his obvious charisma and leadership ability.

If Paul really did have problems with his vision, and took pride in his independence and leadership, he may have felt dependent and weak when he required assistance to travel and write. Furthermore, embarrassing incidents, such as not recognizing a high priest in full regalia (Acts 23:3–5), would have been humiliating. Yet when it became apparent that the Lord would not take away his thorn in the flesh, he saw the light—he had been rescued from real darkness, the darkness of egocentricity and self-idolatry. Moreover, his thorn opened him to the strength and grace of Christ, helping him toward his salvation while making him a light to others' salvation. When this light became apparent, and he saw his thorn as one of the greatest gifts ever given to him—more precious than his charisma and his ability to speak, write, and lead—he proclaimed that he would boast first in his weakness instead of his strength, for when he was weak, it was then that he was truly strong.

C. Third Christian Insight: Suffering as Loving Self-Offering

Suffering is not beneath God—He *enters into it* in order to dignify it, give us an example, and turn it into a perfect gift of love. Jesus proclaims Himself to be the exclusive Son of the Father (see Volume III, Chapter 6), who comes into the world to be with us, heal our infirmities, forgive our sinfulness, rescue us from evil, and to bring us to the fullness of His perfectly loving salvation through an unconditional act of love. In so doing, He shows us the intrinsic dignity and positivity of suffering as loving self-sacrifice.

Jesus endured suffering—willingly entering into complete self-sacrifice in order to show us that suffering is *not* the undermining of our dignity and destiny, but rather their fulfillment. Self-offering for the sake of humanity is central to Jesus' view of love (*agapē*). In Volume III (Chapter 3) of the Quartet, we showed that Jesus interpreted His impending Passion and death as an act of complete self-sacrifice—a complete gift of self, which is His definition of love. Inspired by the Fourth Suffering Servant Song (Is 52:13—53:12) and Psalm 22 (His dying words), Jesus proceeds toward Jerusalem and His impending death confident that His self-offering to the Father on behalf of all humanity would be the unconditional act of love that would dispel the darkness of Satan and human hearts. Trusting in His unconditionally loving Father, He turned Himself into a loving sacrificial offering for the forgiveness of sins and freedom from death—for everyone. His Eucharistic words, echoing Isaiah 53:12, reveal this universal loving self-sacrificial intention. He decided to take the place of both a sin offering and the Paschal lamb, intending to create an act of unconditional love that would lead to freedom from darkness and evil, and usher us into His Father's eternal light and love.

The early Church understood that the self-sacrificial meaning of suffering was not limited to Jesus' suffering and death alone. It proclaimed that all of us have the same opportunity to imitate Jesus by offering our suffering to the Father as an act of self-sacrifice (love) for the life of the world. Saint Paul was keenly aware of this when he declared:

> Now I rejoice in my sufferings for your sake, and in my flesh I complete what is lacking in Christ's afflictions for the sake of his body, that is, the Church. (Col 1:24)

Paul is not saying here that he *has* to make up for an intrinsic deficiency in Jesus' suffering, but rather that Jesus has given us the opportunity to join Him in His self-sacrificial act for the sake of His body, the Church—and for all who are in need.

For Jesus, Saint Paul, and the early Church, every life can have inestimable value for universal salvation. Everyone—no matter what one's state, station, or health—can have the most profound effect on the salvation of humanity by imitating Jesus in His act of self-sacrifice on the Cross, including those who are profoundly sick, depressed, immobile, and in all other ways lacking in autonomy and bodily power. The more profound the suffering, the more profound the act of self-sacrificial love can be. The ultimate irony of life is that we can have the most redemptive and salvific impact on the world when we are most profoundly debilitated and suffering—even to the point of dying and death.

The greater our suffering, the greater our self-offering to the Father, and the greater our act of self-offering, the greater our act of love for the life of the world. Indeed we could make a ministry— our life's ministry—out of offering our suffering to the Father for the life of the world, joining ourselves to the redemptive love initiated by Jesus.

D. Fourth Christian Insight: God's Presence and Guidance

Jesus entered into the depths of human need, healing the sick, redeeming sinners, and even enduring the highest levels of physical and emotional pain. In so doing, He showed us His willingness to be present to us and suffer with us. Jesus showed definitively that God is not aloof (as philosophers such as Aristotle believed), but is completely and intimately involved in everything we are experiencing and doing—particularly our suffering.

As implied above, suffering is an inevitable part of human existence for several reasons. First, free will entails the possibility of causing suffering to others; therefore, God cannot prevent us from causing such suffering without simultaneously depriving us of free will. Secondly, a world without suffering would have no challenge, no opportunity to sacrifice ourselves for a noble cause, no possibility to make the world a better place, no possibility to be purified in love through weakness and vulnerability, no possibility to grow in natural virtue such as courage and prudence, and no possibility to build the Kingdom of God. If God had made a painless, perfect world, with perfectly self-sufficient individuals, we would miss out on life's most important challenges, choices, contributions, virtues, and opportunities for self-definition. Life would no doubt be easier, but incredibly less significant, for we would have nothing to say about who we are and who we will become—nothing to prove our mettle; nothing to establish our principles, virtues, and ideas.

God wanted us to have freedom throughout eternity, self-definition throughout eternity, purified love throughout eternity, and the privilege of loving others and building the Kingdom throughout eternity, and so God created a short span in an imperfect world filled with human evil to give us the opportunity to choose and define ourselves according to love or egocentricity, faith or self-idolatry, and contribution to others or domination of others, with the intention that we would choose the path to our eternal salvation with Him. In order for God to allow us these choices, He had to create us in a world of freedom and challenges, open to the inevitability of suffering, for a short time. But He had no intention of leaving us alone in this inevitable suffering.

So God willed from all eternity not only to reveal Himself to us, but to make Himself intimately present to us—particularly in our times of suffering—through the Incarnation of His Son. More than this, He planned to give us His Holy Spirit to inspire us, protect us, guide us, and open new doors. He also planned to give us consolation and support from the Church community, the sacraments, and His Word—and through His Spirit, to orchestrate a "conspiracy of providence" to help us use our suffering for our and others' salvation.

How can we know when the Spirit is inspiring and guiding us? How can we detect the "conspiracy of divine providence" around us? How do we control fear and anxiety, and maintain peace? How can we best follow God's grace to achieve the greatest opportunity and benefit from our suffering? These questions are answered in detail in Chapters 5 and 9. For the moment, suffice it to say that the consolation, inspiration, and guidance of the Holy Spirit *can be* known and followed, if we seek God's will, pray for His assistance, and make the best use of our pain, weakness, and sacrifices. Saint Paul speaks of this as "living in the Holy Spirit" and instructs his disciples in Rome as follows:

> For all who are led by the Spirit of God are sons of God. For you did not receive the spirit of slavery to fall back into fear, but you have

received the spirit of sonship. When we cry, "Abba! Father!" it is the Spirit himself bearing witness with our spirit that we are children of God, and if children, then heirs, heirs of God and fellow heirs with Christ, provided we suffer with him in order that we may also be glorified with him.... Likewise the Spirit helps us in our weakness; we do not know how to pray as we ought, but the Spirit himself intercedes for us with sighs too deep for words. And he who searches the hearts of men knows what is the mind of the Spirit, because the Spirit intercedes for the saints according to the will of God. We know that in everything God works for good with those who love him, who are called according to his purpose. (Rom 8:14–17, 26–28)

E. Fifth Christian Insight: Radical Transformation in Holiness and Love

We are invited to a level of holiness and love that is truly heroic. Though it is not necessary for salvation, it helps us to help others toward salvation in extraordinary ways. It characterizes the lives of Christianity's greatest saints. Though God will lead to salvation all who seek Him with a sincere heart and *try* to do His will according to the dictates of their conscience, He also desires that we deepen our holiness (freedom to love) so that we will be completely swept up in the service of others and the Kingdom—swept up in the alleviation of suffering and the salvation of souls. Suffering is integral to this high level of freedom to love.

In Chapter 6, we will discuss this remarkable freedom in the lives of Saint Francis of Assisi, Saint Ignatius Loyola, Saint Peter Claver, Saint Teresa of Calcutta (Mother Teresa), and Saint Thérèse of Lisieux, along with some uncanonized saints. What all of them have in common is a tremendous love of Jesus arising out of appreciation and gratitude for His Passion and Crucifixion, which causes them to give everything and suffer everything for the sake of the one they love. Their hearts were set free (set afire) by the love that Christ had for them, and so they naturally serve the most destitute, impoverished, diseased, and enslaved, as well as those in *spiritual* darkness—the misled, angry, faithless, despairing, cynical, and skeptical.

They brought the light and hope of Christ not only through their service and contribution, but also by their genuine love, which fed the hearts of those in most need of help and consolation. Suffering was integral to their extraordinary freedom to love—though they sought to alleviate it in others, they embraced it in themselves, offered it to Jesus, and recognized it as a manifestation of their love as it had been a manifestation of Jesus' love for them. They found in its darkness an irrepressible light—a proof of love, and a gift of self to the One who had loved them in exactly the same way. Jesus is the primary inspiration of this love in the history of the world. Though it had been anticipated, even foretold, by the two passages of Scripture to which Jesus makes recourse (the Fourth Suffering Servant Song of Isaiah in Is 52:13—53:12 and Psalm 22), it was Jesus who concretized it in His own life, bringing it to its fulfillment in His Passion and death. At that moment, suffering and love became complementary, inseparable, and synergistic—a power to redeem the world.

F. Sixth Christian Insight: The Impetus of Suffering in the Progress of Culture and Social Organization

In Chapter 10 we discuss not only the individual spirit, but the collective human spirit, which forms culture and historical momentum. As we look at the history of human suffering and culture, we may notice that suffering has provided an impetus for us to build a social and cultural reality with historically ascending levels of efficacy and goodness in the areas of justice, rights, legal systems, governance systems, medicine, biology, chemistry, physics, psychology, sociology, and every other discipline that has as its noble end the advancement of the common good. Without suffering in the world, it seems highly unlikely that any of this would have arisen out of the collective human spirit in the course of history. Though these ascending levels of efficacy and goodness have been punctuated by negative and even tragic declines, the collective human spirit seems to reemerge on an ever greater level. It does not seem that the collective human spirit is *solely* responsible for this ascending momentum, because it has also given birth to tremendous darkness and evil. If this is correct, it points to a higher Spirit (God's Spirit)—who is not only Lord of individuals, but the Lord of culture and history.

The progression of culture and history depends on leaders, people, and communities who seek to move toward *cultural* and *societal* ideals in Levels Three and Four. When the challenges of suffering are met by such leaders and individuals, the Holy Spirit can galvanize the collective human spirit to bring forth new levels of civility, justice, and love. Without these leaders and individuals, history may find itself in a downward and destructive cycle. However, if faith remains, particularly the faith inspired by Jesus that animates justice and love, then suffering will continue to move the collective human spirit ever closer to the ideal of God's Spirit. This is the challenge that Christianity makes not only to its own leaders, but to the secular cultures in which it operates. We are all called to make that challenge—to inspire our fellow citizens and to fight those who would drag culture and society to a lower plane (mere Level One and Two purpose).

VI. Conclusion

The six Christian insights into suffering are built upon the foundation of the resurrection—an eternal resurrection into unconditional love and joy; a resurrection of the body transformed in spirit, power, light and glory; a resurrection into a community: that is, a family, a banquet, a home (a *perfect* home). This foundational belief in resurrection gives purpose to suffering in the *here and now*. For Christians, suffering calls us out of superficiality, deepens our faith, and purifies and deepens our love (*agapē*). In other words, suffering interpreted through faith helps us to move toward the resurrection of unconditional love—and prepares us to help others toward that same fulfillment. Thus, suffering has inestimable positive value—in the context of faith.

Jesus taught us that suffering has even greater value—it can be offered to the Father as a loving self-sacrifice for the salvation of souls and the strength of the Mystical Body of Christ. This purpose of suffering also derives its remarkably positive power from the Resurrection and the risen Christ, who is the body through which all Christians, in this world and the next, are unified and nourished (see 1 Cor 12:27 and Rom 12:5). When we offer our sufferings to God in loving self-sacrifice, we strengthen every part of the risen body of Christ (see Col 1:24), which has exceedingly positive value. The greater our suffering—offered as loving self-sacrifice in imitation of Jesus—the more positive the effects upon the Mystical Body of Christ.

Jesus did not leave us alone in our suffering "to figure it out for ourselves". He is lovingly and peacefully present to us—and sends His Spirit to help us see His light in the darkness, the way to salvation, and the way to help others to their salvation through the purification of our faith and love.

We conclude with a passage from Karl Rahner, who describes our dignity and destiny in the light of infinite eternal love:

> God wishes to communicate himself, to pour forth the love which he himself is. This is the first and the last of his real plans and hence of his real world too. Everything else exists so that this one thing might be: the eternal miracle of infinite Love. And so God makes a creature whom he can love: he creates man. He creates him in such a way that he *can* receive this Love which is God himself, and that he can and must at the same time accept it for what it is: the ever astounding wonder, the unexpected, unexacted gift.[42]

With this vision of our dignity and destiny in mind, we may now proceed to the other eight Christian foundations of suffering.

---

[42] Karl Rahner, *Foundations of Christian Faith: An Introduction to the Idea of Christianity*, trans. William Dych (New York: Crossroad Publishing, 1982), pp. 123–24; emphasis mine.

Chapter Two

Who God Is—and Is Not

Second Foundation: Affirming the Unconditional Love of God

Introduction

A false notion of God can easily undermine our prayer, peace of mind, and capacity to grow in times of suffering. Even worse, such false notions can lead us *away* from God—and to the brink of despair. In view of this, we must first review Jesus' revelation of who God is (Section I) and then examine six common false notions of God that impede our capacity to suffer well (Section II). This should provide a foundational view of God through which to see His presence in times of suffering (Chapter 3). This view will also help us understand *to whom* we are praying when suffering comes (Chapter 4).

I. Who God Is—according to Jesus

Before examining *Jesus'* definitive revelation of God, we will want to make a fundamental clarification: God is not merely a *"what"*; He is a *"who"*, a personal and interpersonal Being. In responding to contemporary cultural challenges about God, the soul, and transcendence, we can become too narrowly focused on the *attributes of God* that can be proven or objectively validated. This takes our focus off of God's personal, emotional, and relational dimensions. For example, in Lonergan's proof for the existence of God, we arrive at a God which is a unique, uncaused, unrestricted act of thinking that creates everything else. Each attribute in the definition is demonstrated in the proof. Though such proofs are important and valid,

82

they leave us more with a "what" than a "who". The same holds true for approaching God from the evidence of science. We arrive at a "God" who is the probable Creator of physical reality, who transcends physical space and time, and is superintelligent. Once again, this view of God says little about God's personhood, compassion, and interpersonal relationship with us.

Little wonder that so many of history's philosophers and scientists have viewed God in an unemotional, impersonal, and distant way. Aristotle viewed Him as the unique, efficient, and final cause of everything else, but did not see Him *relating*—and certainly not personally relating—to anything or anyone in the sublunar sphere (the domain of human beings).[1] Einstein viewed God in a similar distant way:

> Certain it is that a conviction, akin to religious feeling, of the rationality and intelligibility of the world lies behind all scientific work of a higher order.... This firm belief, a belief bound up with a deep feeling, *in a superior mind* that reveals itself in the world of experience, represents my conception of God.[2]

Classical and modern deism affirm the existence of an intelligent Creator from logical proof and the evidence of science, but generally reject any relational encounter between the one uncaused God and us.[3]

We may infer from this that the *mind* alone cannot grasp the personal and loving dimensions of God; but this should not surprise us, because intellection alone cannot grasp these characteristics in human

---

[1] "Aristotle speaks of God, the immovable prime mover, in quasi-mystical terms. God is pure actuality and as such, perfect; he is alive, but he is impassible, since it is the desire that the highest heaven feels for him that makes heaven move while God himself loves nothing and no one; it would be detrimental to his perfection to act on something other than himself, or to think of something other than himself: God is 'thought thinking itself'." Jacques Brunschwig and Pierre Pellegrin, *Greek Thought: A Guide to Classical Knowledge* (Cambridge, Mass.: Harvard University Press, 2000), p. 569.

[2] Albert Einstein, *Ideas and Opinions*, trans. Sonja Bargmann (New York: Crown Publishers, 1954), p. 262; emphasis mine.

[3] There is an exception to this called "warm modern deism", which allows for certain limited encounters between God and man. See the following modern deism website: http://en.wikipedia.org/wiki/Deism.

beings either.[4] If we are to experience these characteristics in both God and ourselves, we will have to move beyond the domain of isolated intellection, and turn to our other four powers—empathy, conscience, aesthetic awareness, and transcendent-spiritual awareness (of perfect love, goodness, beauty, and home). We have described these powers in Volumes I and II of this Quartet.[5]

Some readers may object that turning to these other nonrational or quasi-rational powers is less certain than intellection, making our affirmation of an interpersonal God "less reasonable and responsible". This is erroneous because allowing our other four powers to enter into our conception of God does *not* lessen what the mind alone can affirm about a unique uncaused unrestricted act of thinking (Lonergan) or a superintelligent, trans-spatio-temporal Creator of the universe (science). Our nonrational powers only *add to* the rational foundations of logic and science.

Even if we do not ascribe the same kind of *objective* verifiability to the contents of our nonrational powers, we should not reject them as false or unreal simply because they are subjective and intersubjective. Do people deny the reality of their love for their children, or their children's love for them, because that love is not grasped through cognitive understanding, logical assessment, and rational judgment? Does anyone deny the intrinsic beauty of a mountain, seascape, or sunset because it is not grasped through rational intellection? Though some people may deny the reality of the contents of conscience, most still believe that the feelings of guilt and shame on the one hand and nobility and honor on the other represent intrinsic moral qualities of the actions we are about to perform or have performed.

If we believe that these powers make us aware of important dimensions of *reality* in *this world*—love, intrinsic beauty, and intrinsic moral qualities of actions—why would we not believe the same for a transcendent Being that we rationally affirm to be the uncaused Creator of all else that is? Why would we unnecessarily limit our awareness and experience of the source of everything, including ourselves? Why would we think that our four nonintellective powers

[4]For a detailed description of the powers of intellection, see Volume II, Chapter 3, Sections I, II, V, and VI.

[5]For a description of empathy and conscience, see Volume I, Chapter 1, Section IV. For a description of aesthetic awareness and transcendent awareness, see Volume II, Chapters 1, 2, and 4.

decrease our intellective power? By doing this, we unnecessarily limit our view of reality to the merely intellective, and unnecessarily limit God to a "what", excluding loving, personal, and relational dimensions from Him. If we can reasonably and responsibly affirm the existence of God, why would we not be open to the possibility of personal qualities in this unrestricted act of understanding, this conscious Being?

If such openness is reasonable and responsible, then we will want to look for other evidence of the transcendent Being's personal and interpersonal qualities. If He is the source of all creation—which resulted in *our* having personal and interpersonal qualities—why wouldn't we think that He would have these same qualities, and be using them to be in relationship with us?[6] Why would we assume the opposite? Uncovering this "other evidence" was the purpose of Volume II of this Quartet. A brief review of some of this evidence may prove helpful.

Those who are suspicious of nonrational approaches to God may want to start with the veridical data of near-death experiences and then examine the common experiences of those who have gone "to the other side—to the overwhelmingly *loving* white light". This group may also want to take the route of Plato, to examine three transcendentals that are manifestations of perfect inclusivity and unification: perfect love, perfect goodness, and perfect beauty. Recall from Volume II (Chapter 4) that these transcendentals would have to be intrinsic to the One unrestricted act of thinking because there can only be one perfectly inclusive reality.[7] If Plato's insight is correct, then the unique unrestricted act of thinking would also be perfect

---

[6] God does not have these qualities in the same way we do. He possesses them through an unrestricted act of existence and thinking. Since we cannot understand this, we can only apprehend it analogously.

[7] An outline of the five steps for proving the other three transcendental qualities in the unique unrestricted act of thinking is as follows: (1) The proof that there must be *at least* one reality that exists through itself (uncaused), and that such a reality would have to be unrestricted in intelligibility—an unrestricted act of thinking (see Volume II, Chapter 3, Sections III.A and B). (2) The proof that there can be *only* one reality that is unrestricted in intelligibility (see Volume II, Chapter 3, Section III.C). (3) The proof that this one unrestricted reality must be purely inclusive, because any exclusion from itself would indicate a restriction to its intelligibility (see Volume II, Chapter 4, Section I.B). (4) The proof that a purely inclusive reality is also a perfect unifying reality (see Volume II, Chapter 4, Section I.B). (5) The proof that there are four kinds of perfect unification—a perfect act of thinking, a perfect act of love, a perfect act of goodness, and perfect beauty (see Volume II, Chapter 4, Sections I–III).

love, perfect goodness, and perfect beauty—all the dimensions of perfect inclusivity. This introduces at least the possibility of personal, moral, and loving qualities within the Deity.

For those open to nonrational approaches to God, there is considerable evidence of God's interpersonal and loving qualities. We might begin with the numinous experience (elucidated by Rudolf Otto)—the conscious and unconscious sense of the mysterious, fascinating, overwhelming, inviting "wholly Other", which grounds our innate desire for the spiritual, sacred, and religious (see Volume II, Chapter 1). We might also examine the transcendent dimension of the contents and feelings of conscience (so important for Kant and Newman; see Volume II, Chapter 2, Section II), as well as our awareness of the struggle between cosmic good and evil manifest in the archetypal myths and symbols coursing through our dreams (see Volume II, Chapter 2, Section III). If it is reasonable to believe that these experiences have an origin in a transcendent Being who is purely inclusive—and therefore perfectly empathetic and loving—a Being who manifests Himself as overwhelming love in near-death experiences, then we will want to move beyond merely rational conceptions of God to pursue a relationship with a personal transcendent Being who is already present to us as goodness and love.

If we believe that such an interpersonal and loving Being is present to us, we will want to carefully examine the revelation of Jesus Christ, for this is precisely the view of God that He reveals through His words and actions, the view of God corroborated by His miracles, Resurrection, and gift of the Spirit—the view of God made perfectly manifest in His loving self-sacrificial death. If we believe that God cannot be reduced to a "what"—that He is a "who", a personal and loving "who"—then we will want to affirm Jesus' view of His Father, whom He proclaimed to be not only love, but *unconditional* love.

Recall Jesus' most fundamental revelation about His Father, given through the name "*Abba*": affectionate, caring, compassionate, understanding Father. Recall also that names in Semitic culture reflect the heart and nature of a person, and so this name that carries with it the depth of childlike trust, affection, and security expresses the heart and essence of God Himself.

Recall also Jesus' consummate revelation of the heart of His Father in the Parable of the Prodigal Son (Lk 15:11–32). As noted in Volume III, Chapter 2, this parable is not so much about the prodigal son as it is about the son's father who represents Jesus' Divine *Father*. This father is the central character in both parts of the parable—concerned first with the younger prodigal son and then with the obedient older son.

With respect to the first part of the story, recall that after the younger son has shamed and betrayed his father, family, election, country, law, and God, he makes himself completely impure by living with pigs, which were regarded as extremely unclean animals. After all this, the father, representing God, runs out to meet him with joy, throws his arms around him, and kisses him, then forgives his transgressions, takes care of his temporal needs (with sandals), treats him like royalty (with a tunic), accepts him back into the family 100 percent (with the signet ring), and celebrates his homecoming (by killing the fatted calf). Jesus' implication is clear: if God loves a completely egregious sinner (by first-century Jewish standards) so much, then He must love us in the same way—unconditionally.

In the second part of the story, the older son, though obedient to his father, refuses to show mercy or forgiveness to his brother, preferring to leave him cast out without hope of redemption in a hostile world. He resents his father's mercy and goodness so much that he berates his father and refuses to come back into the family home. Recall the father's reaction to him: he shows no indignation or anger at his son's resentment, rejection, and scolding. He understands his son's reaction, and so offers him all his remaining property, begging him to come into the house.

Now try to get a sense of the father's interior disposition and love from these two parts of the story. Hold on to that notion of God, because it is precisely what Jesus came to reveal about Himself and His Father! Now, make this notion of God the standard or criterion by which to judge all other explicit and implicit notions of God.

For those preferring a more straightforward description of God's personal and relational qualities from Christian teaching, I would recommend turning to the Hymn to Love in 1 Corinthians 13:4–7, and substituting "God" for "love" throughout the hymn. Since God is unconditionally loving, I would add "unconditionally" before each adjective. The original form of the hymn is as follows:

> Love is patient and kind; love is not jealous or boastful; it is not arro-gant or rude. Love does not insist on its own way; it is not irritable or resentful; it does not rejoice at wrong, but rejoices in the right. Love bears all things, believes all things, hopes all things, endures all things.

When we make the above two substitutions, we get a good description of God's personal loving and relational qualities:

> God is unconditionally patient and unconditionally kind; God is not jealous or boastful; he is not arrogant or rude. God does not insist on his own way; he is not irritable or resentful; he does not rejoice at wrong, but rejoices in the right. God bears all things, believes all things, hopes all things, endures all things.

This adapted hymn and the image of the father of the prodigal son can keep us on track in our thinking about God, which should help us be attentive to the common false notions of God that can exacer-bate our suffering and undermine our spiritual lives.

One final point: we can infer from Jesus' revelation that our rela-tionship with God really matters to Him; it really affects His sub-jective, personal, and relational state of consciousness. Though God does not need to be in relationship with us to be "what" He *is* in His nature and power—the unique, uncaused, unconditionally lov-ing, perfectly good, unrestricted act of self-consciousness and thought capable of creating everything that exists—He *chooses* to enter into a relationship with us that can affect His subjective state of conscious-ness. God continuously and unconditionally loves *every* one of us, even those who reject Him. Our rejections affect His subjective con-scious state. Yet the acceptance of this is part of His love, His desire to create freely loving creatures, for when we accept His love and try to grow close to Him, His joy is overwhelming, like the father whose son returned from a life of rejection and self-destruction. Though God does not need us to be *what* He is, He *chooses* to be in relationship with us because our acts of love bring Him overwhelm-ing joy. This is *who* God is—according to Jesus.

II. Who God Is Not—according to Jesus

When we acknowledge God's interpersonal, loving, and caring qualities and dispositions, we have to be quite certain about what those dispositions are truly like; for if we are mistaken, even slightly mistaken, in our conceptions of these qualities, we can frustrate our relationship with Him, undermine our prayer, and grow distant from Him. We might then exclude His grace and love from our suffering, and even from our entire lives. Thus, we will want to examine the most common misconceptions of God's personal and interpersonal states, so that we can turn to the revelation of Jesus in our times of suffering—and throughout our lives.

In Volume III (Chapter 7), we briefly discussed several common false notions of God. Since these notions of God can be so destructive, and even induce despair, during times of suffering, we must examine each one in detail to be certain that readers will be able to identify them in their many guises and manifestations, and to see their falsity in light of Jesus' revelation of Abba and the Father of the Prodigal Son. The six most common and destructive false notions of God are

1. "the angry god",
2. "the payback god",
3. "the domineering god",
4. "the terrifying god",
5. "the stoic god", and
6. "the disgusted god".

We will discuss each in turn.

A. "The Angry God"

We will give a more extensive treatment of this false notion of God than the other five for two reasons. First, it lies at the root of the other false notions of God, and second, there appears to be more evidence for it than the other five in the New Testament. Once we have properly explained "the angry god", the falsity of the other five notions will become more evident.

The idea of an angry God does not correspond to Jesus' teaching about the father of the prodigal son or His teaching about anger. Furthermore, when the supposed indications of God's anger in the New Testament are interpreted properly, they have the *opposite* meaning—not indicating God's anger, but God's compassion and mercy. Contrary to popular belief, Jesus did not indicate or imply that God is angry, in the sense of having antagonistic, resentful, and retributive feelings toward us—but we are getting ahead of ourselves here, so let us begin with the view of God present in Israel *before* Jesus arrived on the scene. We can then proceed to examine how Jesus superseded that tradition and emphasized instead the revelation of God as unconditional love, manifest in both His words and actions.

The idea of God as passionately angry, resentful, and retributive comes from the Old Testament. As McKenzie notes:

> [The anger of God] is an essential part of the biblical conception of God as endowed with a vigorous personality. He is a "living God," active, with a moral will to whose execution He is not indifferent; furthermore, His anger is only one feature of his personality as described in the Bible and must be understood in the context of its motivation and of other personal traits.[8]

In the Old Testament, God is portrayed as capable of retributive anger that sometimes necessitates punishment, even down to the fourth generation (see Ex 34:6–7; Deut 5:8–10; Lev 26:39). God often expresses this negative and retributive passion toward the people of Israel for a variety of transgressions, such as infidelity, idolatry, unbelief, breaking the law, and inhumanity.[9]

Though God has other more positive moods and emotions in the Old Testament (e.g., concern and care for His chosen people), the frequency of expressions of anger led many Christians to a view of God similar to that of eighteenth-century puritanical preaching.[10] Is

---

[8]John L. McKenzie, *Dictionary of the Bible* (New York: Macmillan Publishing, 1965), p. 32.

[9]See Ex 32; Num 11:1; 12:9; 13:25–14:35; 18:5; 32:10–14; Deut 1:34; 9:8, 19; Jas 2:14; 3:8; 10:7; 1 Kings 14:15; 2 Kings 22:17; Jer 4:4; 8:18; 14:19; 16:38; 20:8; Hos 5:10; 8:5; 13:11; Is 9:11; 9:16; 9:18, 20; Ezek 5:13; 7:3, 8. See also McKenzie, *Dictionary of the Bible*, p. 32.

[10]For example, the sermon of Jonathan Edwards views God as follows: "The God that holds you over the pit of hell, much as one holds a spider, or some loathsome insect over the

this view of God justified? Did Jesus accept this Old Testament view? Did He supersede it? As we shall see, there is considerable reason to believe that Jesus did supersede the Old Testament view of God, because He *never* directly attributes anger to God in the Gospels. Indeed, antagonistic and retributive anger stands in tension with His teaching about the Father. This requires considerable explanation.

Let us begin with the contention that Jesus *never* speaks of the anger of God or His Father in any of the Gospels. Some exegetes[11] have pointed to one possible exception to Jesus' universal silence about God's anger: Luke 21:23, a discourse about the end times in which Jesus says, "Alas for those who are with child and for those who are nursing in those days! For great distress shall be upon the earth and wrath [*orgē*] upon [*en*] this people." This is a very weak reference to *God's* anger. First, the supposed reference to *God's* anger is only *implied*, but not stated. The text says that there will be wrath upon this people", but is this wrath necessarily due to God's anger, or the anger intrinsic to the tumult of nations? We cannot be sure. Secondly, Luke's reference to *orgē* in his apocalyptic discourse is unique and is not referenced in either the Marcan (Mk 13) or the Matthean (Mt 24) apocalyptic discourses. Thus, the reference to *orgē* may be a *Lucan* redaction. In any case, its absence in the other two apocalyptic discourses—as well as the rest of the Gospels—indicates that it is *not* an essential part of Jesus' view of His Father.

Jesus felt free to modify and enhance teachings of the Old Testament. When interpreting the Law of Moses, He supersedes to well-known parts of the Torah in the six antitheses of the Sermon on the Mount (Mt 5:21–48). Recall that each antithesis begins with the phrase "You have heard it said ...", after which He gives a prescription or proscription of the Mosaic Law. He then follows with a modification or enhancement of that prescription or proscription with the phrase "*But I* say to you ...", in which He contrasts

___

fire, abhors you, and is dreadfully provoked: his wrath towards you burns like fire; he looks upon you as worthy of nothing else, but to be cast into the fire." Jonathan Edwards, "Sinners in the Hands of an Angry God", sermon delivered in Enfield, Connecticut, July 8, 1741, Christian Classics Ethereal Library, accessed January 31, 2016, http://www.ccel.org/ccel /edwards/sermons.sinners.html.

[11] See McKenzie, *Dictionary of the Bible*, p. 33.

His teaching with that of the Mosaic Law.[12] Though Jesus accepts the general validity of the Torah (see Mt 5:19–20), He also sees Himself as having sovereign authority over it.[13] He used this sovereign authority to modify and enhance the law, subjecting it to the primacy of love (*agapē*). By doing this, He also modifies the image of God, whom He reveals to be perfect love.[14] This is particularly true with respect to anger. When Jesus subjects the interpretation of the law to the primacy of love, He prohibits anger (an interior disposition opposed to love), which the Mosaic code permits. The implication is clear: if God is unconditional love, and anger is opposed to love, then God's heart and nature are opposed to anger.

Jesus' prohibition of anger supersedes its acceptance in the Mosaic code: "I say to you that every one who is angry with his brother shall be liable to judgment" (Mt 5:22).[15] Jesus goes even further by prohibiting *expressions of anger*, such as "*Raca*" and "you fool" (Mt 5:22). In doing this, Jesus shifts the focus from external behavior to the interior attitude that can incite it. He does this not only to prevent the cause of violent actions, but to help believers embrace the fundamental attitude that reflects the heart and perfection of God: love. For Jesus, anger, in the sense of having antagonistic, resentful, and retributive feelings, is opposed to love. In this sense, anger will not only incite us to unloving behaviors, but undermine our interior disposition.

There are other feelings and behaviors associated with anger that do not fall under the above definition, such as dismay at someone's victimizing behavior or giving a *stern* warning to a child not to play in the street. These actions *are* consistent with love, and even promote

---

[12] See John L. McKenzie, "The Gospel according to Matthew", in *Jerome Biblical Commentary*, ed. Raymond E. Brown, Joseph A. Fitzmyer, and Roland E. Murphy (Englewood Cliffs, N.J.: Prentice Hall, 1968), p. 71.

[13] See also Benedict Viviano, "The Gospel according to Matthew", in *The New Jerome Biblical Commentary*, ed. Raymond E. Brown, Joseph A. Fitzmyer, and Roland E. Murphy (Englewood Cliffs, N.J.: Prentice Hall, 1990), p. 641.

[14] The Father's perfect love is best manifest in His love of enemies. This is the perfection of love to which all of us are called: "But I say to you, Love your enemies and pray for those who persecute you, so that you may be sons of your Father who is in heaven.... You, therefore, must be perfect, as your heavenly Father is perfect" (Mt 5:44–45, 48).

[15] See Viviano, "Gospel according to Matthew", p. 642.

it, though they may look aggressive. Hence, they do not come under Jesus' prohibition of anger. Jesus' prohibition of anger extends only to those manifestations of it that are fundamentally opposed to the beatitudes: humble-heartedness, gentle-heartedness, forgiveness, compassion, and peacemaking.[16]

Jesus connects His reinterpretation of the law (fulfilled by love) with the heart and nature of the Father (unconditional love) in the sixth and final antithesis, which is meant to give meaning to the previous five. Here He reveals that the Father's perfection is best characterized by His love of enemies, which is followed by His call to all of us to imitate the Father in this radical form of love. The Father's perfect love includes not only His external love of enemies, but also His interior dispositions that give rise to this love. One of these interior dispositions, expressed in the first antithesis, is "not growing angry".

We might look at it the opposite way around—if we suppose that the Father is angry, then that would imply that anger is not inconsistent with His love; and if we are called to imitate Him in love, then we would be permitted to be angry, which contradicts Jesus' prohibition of it. Besides, it is unthinkable that Jesus would brand a particular attitude as unethical ("subject to judgment") while proclaiming that the Father (who is perfectly good) possesses that attitude.

This conclusion (concerning the Father not being angry) is corroborated by Jesus' other revelations about the Father. As noted above, Jesus' address of God as "Abba" (which He encourages His disciples to use) is virtually unique. It appears nowhere in the Old Testament, and only in a few passages of rabbinical literature. This address is meant to convey "an affectionate and caring father for his child", not "an angry and retributive father". Furthermore, Jesus' use of the prodigal son parable shows a very different view of God than that expressed in the Old Testament. Instead of God (the father in the story) reacting to the sinful son with anger, in the sense of "antagonism, resentment, and retribution", he responds with joy and love at the son's return, complete forgiveness, and complete restoration to the family.

When we combine the above considerations, it is difficult to believe that Jesus viewed His Father as angry in the sense of having

---

[16] See Volume III, Chapter 1, for an explanation for "poor in spirit" as humble-heartedness, meek as "gentle-heartedness", and "mercy" as "forgiveness and compassion".

antagonistic, resentful, and retributive feelings toward "sinful peo-ple". If this is correct, then how can New Testament passages that imply God's anger be understood? Though Jesus does not speak explicitly of divine anger, some readers have *inferred it* from the fol-lowing New Testament passages:

1. Saint Paul's use of "wrath of God", particularly in three pas-sages in the Letter to the Romans (1:18; 5:9; 12:19)
2. Jesus' references to Gehenna[17] and "wailing and grinding of teeth" (Mt 8:12; 13:42, 50; 22:13; 24:51; 25:30; Lk 13:28, NAB)
3. Jesus' cleansing of the Temple (knocking over the tables of the money changers, etc.)
4. Jesus' seemingly angry and harsh rhetoric toward the Pharisees

At first glance, it may seem hard to believe that all these indications of supposed divine anger have a virtually opposite meaning from that suggested by their harsh tone, but if we distinguish among the many conditions that could be interpreted as anger, we can see a way in which the above four passages can have positive outcomes instead of negative, hostile, and retributive ones. What are some of these con-ditions that could be interpreted as anger?

- A hostile emotion or mood
- An attitude of antagonism, resentment, and retribution
- A negative judgment toward us or others
- An expression of frustration, disappointment, or regret
- An expression of warning or passionate conviction
- A provocative statement intended to challenge or induce change

As can be seen, some of these conditions have negative outcomes, while others have positive outcomes—or are intended to have posi-tive outcomes. As we shall see, the latter applies to the four passages we will now examine. The four passages under consideration fall

---

[17] "Gehenna" can refer to a specific valley that was accursed and unholy because of a cult of human sacrifice. It became a trash dump, and known for the filth and fire associated with it. It took on the meaning of a place of eternal fire and eternal misery in the New Testament, and probably has this meaning when used by Jesus.

under the second category, those that are intended to have positive outcomes.

1. The "Wrath of God" in the Pauline Letters

Let's begin with the first implication of God's anger: Paul's use of "wrath of God". Does "wrath of God" really mean an angry disposition, emotion, or attitude of God? There are no indications of this in Saint Paul; rather, "wrath of God" is an expression he borrows from the Old Testament to refer to the negative *judgment* that unjust people justly deserve. According to McKenzie, a common meaning of "God's anger or wrath" in the Old Testament is "an outpouring of his moral will and his justice".[18] This meaning is closely connected with judgment, particularly, "the negative *judgment* that unjust people justly deserve". About half of the mentions of "wrath of God" in the Pauline Letters concern the "just deserts" of unjust or sinful people (Rom 1:18; 3:5–7; 12:19–20), and about half are concerned with Jesus saving us from the wrath of God (1 Thess 1:10; 5:9; Rom 5:9).

It should be mentioned at the outset that if by "wrath of God" Paul meant "an antagonistic, resentful, retributive disposition, emotion, or attitude of God", then Paul's second use of this phrase (Christ saving us from the wrath of God) would be unintelligible. Why? The Father would not have sent his Son into the world in a complete act of self-sacrificial love to save us from His antagonistic or resentful mood, feeling, or attitude. If the Father really has such feelings (which Jesus did not attribute to Him), then He should have been able to control them on His own without subjecting His Son to complete self-sacrifice. Thus, the only way that these passages make any sense is if the Father sends His Son into the world to save us from "the negative judgment that we deserve for our unjust and disobedient deeds".

If this is Paul's meaning of "wrath of God" in the contexts of Christ saving us from wrath, why would we not assume that it is his meaning in the other contexts as well? When we interpret "wrath of God" as "the negative judgment we deserve for our sinfulness" instead of "a hostile, antagonistic, or retributive mood or outburst",

---

[18] McKenzie, *Dictionary of the Bible*, p. 32.

all of the above uses of "wrath of God" in the Pauline corpus make much more sense. If this is true, then Saint Paul is not saying that *God* is angry in the sense of having antagonistic and retributive feelings toward us, but rather that *we* through our deeds have built up a negative judgment against *ourselves*, which God chose to overcome by sending His Son into the world to give us an unconditional act of self-sacrificial love.

Thus, the focus of "wrath of God" is not *God's* mood, but rather *our* "just deserts" from which the *love* of God manifest in Jesus must save us. Therefore, Saint Paul is not encouraging us to *fear* God's antagonistic mood, but rather to call upon the *love* of God (manifest in Jesus) to save us from the negative judgment we deserve. He is not implying that God is hateful, but rather that He is unconditionally loving—the only Being capable of saving us from *our* prideful and hard-hearted propensities.

2. Jesus' Use of "Gehenna" and "Wailing and Grinding of Teeth"

If Jesus' Father is not angry, then how are we to understand "Gehenna" and "wailing and grinding of teeth?" In the previous chapter (Section IV), we explained that Hell is a state of *self*-exclusion from God. God does not want to send anyone to Hell—and He certainly would not do this out of a sense of retribution or anger. He allows those who prefer Hell (a state of hatred opposed to love, of domination opposed to care, of pride and arrogance as opposed to humility and gratitude, and of self-idolatry as opposed to worship of the true God) to choose it. Since this state is completely incompatible with Heaven (in which love, care, humility, gratitude, and worship of the true God are opposed to hatred, envy, domination, pride, arrogance, egocentricity, and self-idolatry), He has to keep the two states separated from one another.[19]

If the motives of Jesus and His Father are fundamentally compassionate and forgiving, then we must conclude that Jesus speaks about the pain intrinsic to the state of Hell, not out of anger or retribution, but as a *warning* borne out of *love* to those who may be inclined to reject Heaven and choose Hell. He and His Father do not consign

---

[19] An extensive explanation of this is given in Volume III, Chapter 7, Section III.

people to Hell because they are angry with them, but rather are incredibly saddened when people choose to reject Heaven in favor of Hell. As with fallen angels, Jesus and His Father allow these individuals to choose according to their heart's treasure. Thus, these passages should *not* be interpreted as Jesus *threatening* us in a state of outrage and revulsion, but precisely the opposite. Jesus loves all of us in the same way the father loved the prodigal son, and He (Jesus) loved the repentant thief on the cross. Jesus and His Father are never revolted by us and never stop loving us, even if we are deeply immersed in sin and darkness. So why does Jesus use the images of "Gehenna" and "wailing and grinding of teeth" if He really loves sinners?

The simple answer is, He wants to *warn* us about the enticement of vice and evil. The problem is that evil always looks beautiful for a *short* time. It brings with it the apparent promise of happiness— the pleasure of sensorial and sexual indulgence, the pleasure of control and even domination, the pleasure of pride and self-idolatry. Yet Jesus knows that these "pleasures" are short-lived, very addictive, and a wide road into darkness, emptiness, loneliness, destruction of others, and destruction of self: in other words, a road into pain and misery—"Gehenna"—where there will be "wailing and grinding of teeth".

Jesus' awareness of our capacity to *choose* a path antithetical to love causes Him to give us a *blunt warning* to refocus our purpose in life toward *love* (*agapē*) before we become caught up in the deception and darkness of evil (self-indulgence, domination, and self-idolatry). Though his words *sound* like a threat, they are not meant to be one, for they are not said out of anger, disgust, or hatred, but out of *love*. His warnings are definitely meant to *shock* and *disturb* us so that we will call the elusive happiness of evil into question, so that we will see this false happiness as it really is—destruction of others and destruction of self.

Yes, Jesus expresses these warnings *passionately*, not because He is filled with indignation, anger, hatred, and threats, but because He is passionately *concerned* about how we use our freedom to love (and stay in the light) *or* not to love (and go into the darkness). When a parent warns a child passionately—"Don't touch the stove! Don't cross the street! Don't play with matches! If you do, you are really going to be sorry!"—they do not do so out of a state of anger, disgust, and threat, but rather out of a sense of concern and love for their children and the people around them. The same holds true for the Lord of love.

Some people are particularly disturbed by Jesus' story about the king's division of the sheep from the goats, and his attitude toward the goats: "Depart from me, you cursed, into the eternal fire prepared for the devil and his angels" (Mt 25:41). If there is any passage in the New Testament that indicates Jesus' anger, it's this one. Yet this passage, despite the harshness of the rhetoric, should be read in the same way as all other passages about "Gehenna" and "wailing and grinding of teeth"—namely, as rhetoric that is meant to *shock* and *disturb* us into reflecting on certain kinds of conduct. It is a warning against letting ourselves go too far into the darkness. The harshness of the rhetoric does not indicate the anger of God, but rather the seriousness of the warning. The harsher the rhetoric, the more shocking and disturbing the warning.

When the king says, "Depart from me, you cursed, into the eternal fire prepared for the devil and his angels", he is telling us not about *God's* anger but the state of *our* souls. He is holding a mirror up to our spiritual condition—accursed and like that of the devil. Some might respond, "Even if this is not about the anger of God but about our spiritual condition, it's still very insulting!" Jesus does not intend to insult us—He is trying to point to a *reality*, a *truth* about ourselves that is meant to shock and disturb us into *changing* our conduct and the disposition of our hearts.

So why does Jesus reserve such harsh rhetoric for this particular offense regarding the hardness of heart? For Jesus, hardness of heart is the key indicator of a dark spiritual condition. In addition to the fact that hardness of heart adversely affects the people around us, it also adversely affects *us*—pulling us more and more into the darkness. So Jesus *lovingly* calls us to the *truth* about our darkness that is shocking, disturbing, and difficult to hear. His intention is not to hurt us, but to use the shock to call us into the light—the joy of humble, gentle, forgiving, compassionate *love*.

3. Jesus' Cleansing of the Temple

We may now consider the third seeming indication of God's anger: Jesus' apparent anger toward the money changers and merchants in the Temple. Some may believe that since Jesus ostensibly grew angry and even violent toward the money changers and merchants in the Temple, and since He is divine, then His anger and violence in the Temple reveal God's anger and violence toward us. This interpretation is overly simplistic and fails to recognize that Jesus is performing a prophetic action. In movies about the life of Jesus, He is portrayed as going into the Temple precincts and suddenly becoming enraged by the money changers and merchants, getting so out of control that he turns violent, knocking over tables and chairs. Is that what truly happened? There is a very good reason to believe that it is not. Jesus had been in the Temple precincts witnessing the actions of the money changers and merchants many times; yet on none of those occasions did He even look askance at the day-to-day activities of these individuals. Why on this one occasion does He seem to fly into rage and resentment? Were the merchants doing something especially egregious? No, they were conducting business as usual.

So what was so special about this occasion? Did it provoke Jesus' rage and violence, *or* was it the occasion for something quite different that was *not* an act of spontaneous rage? As might be suspected from Jesus' completely different attitude toward the merchants on that particular day, His action was not an act of spontaneous rage—but something else.

N. T. Wright provides the incisive clue to Jesus' unusual action. It is not borne out of anger or violence, but rather is a prophetic action (quite similar to that of Nehemiah five centuries earlier) that initiates the imminent destruction of the Temple and its replacement by *Jesus Himself* and His eschatological movement. For Wright[20] and his student Nicholas Perrin,[21] Jesus believed that part of His mission was to supersede the Temple—to replace the static brick-and-mortar Temple in Jerusalem with His living word and living presence throughout the world. Many groups within Israel (e.g., the Essenes) believed that the Temple was already defunct and that it was being run by wicked priests. Jesus goes beyond these groups by saying that even if the Temple were not run by a corrupt administration, it would still

---

[20] See N. T. Wright, *Jesus and the Victory of God* (Minneapolis, Minn.: Fortress Press, 1996), pp. 490–501.

[21] See Nicholas Perrin, *Jesus the Temple* (Ada, Mich.: Baker Academic, 2010).

have to be replaced by a dynamic, redemptive eschatological power transcending space and time—namely, *Himself*.

When Jesus entered the Temple precincts, He was very *well prepared* to initiate the time of His Passion and Resurrection leading to the new Jerusalem that would be worldwide ("for all nations"). This process was to begin with a series of prophetic actions in the Temple precincts carefully designed to show

1. His authority over the Temple,
2. His judgment of the Temple administration,
3. the impending destruction of the Temple, and
4. its replacement with Himself (the New Temple).

When He drove out the merchants and buyers and disallowed people from carrying anything in the Temple area, He established His authority over the old Temple and its administration. When He overturned the tables and seats of the money changers and sellers, He prophetically initiated the impending destruction of the old Temple. His action is more than a prediction; as a prophetic gesture, it sets history on an inevitable course that is brought to completion only when the Temple is destroyed (in A.D. 70). When He subsequently declares, "Is it not written, 'My house shall be called a house of prayer for all the nations'? But you have made it a den of robbers" (Mk 11:17), He renders judgment against the Temple and its administration. Instead of making the Temple a house of prayer for all nations, the Temple administration had corrupted it and mired it in "the things of this world". When Jesus' judgment against the Temple administration is combined with His prophetic action of overturning the money changers' tables and chairs, it signified and anticipated not only the destruction of the Temple, but something new that would become a "house of prayer for *all* the nations".

Later, Jesus interprets His prophetic actions in the Temple cleansing. He tells the Parable of the Wicked Vintners (Mk 12:1–12), which allegorically describes the persecution of Israel's prophets, culminating with the murder of the vineyard owner's (God's) beloved son. The owner then comes back, destroys the tenants, and gives the vineyard to others. Though Jesus does not directly say that He is the beloved Son of the vineyard owner (God), He implies it when He declares, "Have you not read this Scripture: 'The very stone which the builders rejected has become the cornerstone; this was the Lord's doing, and it is marvelous in our eyes'?" (Mk 12:10). Notice what Jesus has done: if He really is the beloved Son in the parable, and the beloved Son is the "very stone which the builders rejected [that] has become the cornerstone", then Jesus is the cornerstone of the New Temple; indeed, He is the New Temple—He is the something new that will become a "house of prayer for *all* the nations".

If Wright and Perrin are correct, then Jesus' actions in the Temple area are not a spontaneous outburst of anger and violence, but rather a very carefully thought-out series of *prophetic* actions signifying, anticipating, and initiating the destruction of the old order (centered on the Jerusalem Temple) and replacing it with a new worldwide order (the New Temple in Himself). These actions will find their completion first in the rejection of Jesus, His subsequent torture and death, His Resurrection, the gift of the Holy Spirit, the establishment of the Christian Church, and the destruction of the Temple and its administration. Thus, Jesus did not display spontaneous rage and violence, but rather prophetically initiated the judgment and destruction of the corrupt old order, which would lead to a universal new order culminating in the resurrection of unconditional love.

4. Jesus' Harsh Rhetoric toward the Pharisees

We are now prepared to consider the fourth and final seeming indication of God's anger: Jesus' harsh rhetoric toward the Pharisees. No doubt Jesus bluntly criticized and insulted the Pharisees—"Woe to you,... Pharisees, hypocrites!" (Mt 23:13, 15, 23, 25, 27, 29); "Woe to you, blind guides" (Mt 23:16); "You blind fools!" (Mt 23:17); "[Y]ou are like whitewashed tombs, which outwardly appear beautiful, but within they are full of dead men's bones and all uncleanness" (Mt 23:27). After pronouncing seven woes against them, Jesus says:

> Thus you witness against yourselves, that you are sons of those who murdered the prophets. Fill up, then, the measure of your fathers. You serpents, you brood of vipers, how are you to escape being sentenced to Gehenna? (Mt 23:31–33; my translation)

Were these accusations and reprimands borne out of anger?

It is essential at the outset to be clear about what we interpret as anger. For a twenty-first-century American, accusing a group of being "full of dead men's bones and all uncleanness", not to mention "serpents [and] brood of vipers being sentenced to Gehenna", would be viewed as so insulting that it must be borne out of anger or rage. But is this a proper interpretation of Jesus' words and actions? There are several initial clues that it is not. First these insults contradict what Jesus proscribes in the Sermon on the Mount:

> But I tell you that anyone who is angry with a brother or sister will be subject to judgment. Again, anyone who says to a brother or sister, "Raca," [a pronouncement of contempt] is answerable to the court. And anyone who says, 'You fool!' will be in danger of the fire of hell. (Mt 5:22; my translation)

When Jesus calls the Pharisees *fools*, does He really mean to say that they *are* fools? If so, would this not contradict His admonition against this very pronouncement? Do His accusations really indicate anger and contemptuousness toward the Pharisees (contradicting the above admonitions)? If Jesus is not to be inconsistent, and even hypocritical, then there must be another explanation.

The explanation lies in the fact that Jesus wants to *provoke* a *debate* with the Pharisees about who has legitimate religious *authority*—that is, who properly represents the word, intention, and will of God. In order to show that his authority is superior to that of the Pharisees, Jesus uses two criteria:

1. authenticity versus hypocrisy, and
2. faithful adherence to the teachings of Moses and the prophets (their self-professed teachers).

For Jesus, winning this debate is essential because the Pharisees have distorted the words of their teachers, implied God's disinterest in and disdain of sinners, and replaced "being made righteous by God" with their own self-righteousness. All three of these distortions are leading people away from God, causing sinners and "ordinary people" to lose hope. Moreover, the Pharisees endanger *themselves* because they are under the illusion that they can make themselves righteous. Inasmuch as they cannot, they jeopardize their salvation.

For Jesus, the misrepresentation of Moses and the prophets undermines the will of God for the people of Israel. The exclusion of sinners from the Kingdom completely misrepresents the intention and heart of His Father, leading sinners to conclude falsely that God does not love them and there is no hope for their salvation. Finally, the Pharisee's self-righteousness will lead to their self-destruction, which saddens Jesus and His Father and prompts Him to provoke and challenge the Pharisees to turn from their self-righteousness and surrender humbly to the loving God.

Though Jesus wanted to stop the Pharisees from undermining the hope of sinners, misinterpreting the law, and pursuing self-destructive self-righteousness, He did not feel malice toward them. Indeed He formulates the second part of the Parable of the Prodigal Son *for them.* According to Jeremias, the loyal and beloved older son represents the Pharisees.[22] Notice that the Father (God) loves His older son (the Pharisees), and so He comes out to meet His son, pleads with him (humbling Himself before him), accepts His son's insults ("you never gave me even a young goat to feast on with my friends" [Lk 15:29, NAB]), gives him all his property, and begs him to come into the house with these words:

> Son, you are always with me, and all that is mine is yours. It was fitting to make merry and be glad, for this your brother was dead, and is alive; he was lost, and is found. (Lk 15:31–32)

If Jeremias is correct, then Jesus (and His Father) *loves* the Pharisees and wants them to be saved ("to come into the house"). Yes, He is *distressed* that the Pharisees are falsely discouraging sinners and misleading the people, but this distress at the Pharisees' words and actions should not be confused with antagonistic, resentful, and retributive anger, leading to hatred, rejection, or contempt for them. Such an interpretation not only contradicts the father's love for the older son, but also Jesus' teaching about anger and contempt. It is one thing to be distressed and desperate to change the Pharisees' hearts and actions, and quite another to be antagonistic, resentful, retributive,

---

[22] For this interpretation of the "older son" as the Pharisees, see Joachim Jeremias, *The Parables of Jesus* (London: SCM Press, 1972), p. 130. See also Volume III (Chapter 2, Section III.C) of this Quartet.

hateful, and contemptuous. The former interpretation of Jesus' harsh rhetoric to the Pharisees is quite consistent with the rest of Jesus' words and actions, but the latter is not.

Is Jesus' harsh rhetoric *solely* a manifestation of His distress and desperation to change the Pharisees' hearts and actions—or is there something more? In His prophetic role, Jesus uses techniques similar to that of Israel's classical prophets who used harsh rhetoric— sometimes very harsh rhetoric—to call Israel's leaders and "false prophets" back to the truth and way of Yahweh. The objective of the harsh rhetoric was first to *shock* Israel's leaders and false prophets into listening to the true prophet; they were probably wondering, "What's this? How dare he say that to us? Who does he think he is?" The second objective was to *challenge* the teaching and actions of Israel's leaders and false prophets, and thereby to challenge the legitimacy of their authority, particularly before Yahweh. The third objective was to *provoke* them into a debate where they will have to account for their teachings and actions, exposing the falsity of their ways—and therefore the illegitimacy of their authority.[23]

When Jesus uses harsh rhetoric against the Pharisees, He imitates the way the classical prophets treated the false prophets of Israel; He confronts their false teaching, and through this, the legitimacy of their authority. John the Baptist also uses this prophetic technique to challenge the Pharisees:

> [W]hen he saw many of the Pharisees and Sadducees coming for baptism, he said to them, "You brood of vipers! Who warned you to flee from the wrath to come? Bear fruit that befits repentance, and do not presume to say to yourselves, "We have Abraham as our father"; for I tell you, God is able from these stones to raise up children to Abraham. (Mt 3:7–9)

When Jesus uses this technique against the Pharisees, He does not make reference (as John does) to the wrath of God. Instead, He challenges their self-righteousness, reveals their inauthenticity, and points the way to a compassionate and forgiving heart. However, He does

---

[23] See Bruce Vawter, "Introduction to Prophetic Literature", in *The New Jerome Biblical Commentary* (Englewood Cliffs, N.J.: Prentice Hall, 1968), pp. 186–97, particularly p. 189. See also McKenzie, *Dictionary of the Bible*, pp. 694–98, particularly p. 695.

share one thing in common with John: He uses harsh rhetoric to provoke and challenge the Pharisees. This rhetoric is not a manifestation of antagonistic and retributive anger against them personally. Indeed, Jesus never attacks an individual Pharisee, scribe, or lawyer, but only the group. Like the classical prophets, He shocks the Pharisees, challenges their teaching, and provokes them into a debate to expose their falsity and illegitimacy.

Was it necessary for Him to be so harsh by using "brood of vipers" "dead men's bones", etc.? In Jesus' view, it was, because anything less would not have had enough shock value to provoke the Pharisees to defend the legitimacy of their authority. His rhetoric was so provocative that they could not allow Jesus to get away with such overt challenges, and so they had only two choices: to respond to Him or get rid of Him.

No doubt the words "hypocrites", "fools", "blind guides", "serpents", and "brood of vipers" are all insults, but these insults are not meant as a contemptuous and hateful degradation but rather as a *provocation*. They are meant to elicit the response, "Those are fightin' words." So, is Jesus looking for an argument? Absolutely! He is trying to goad the Pharisees into a debate, to make them defend themselves, with the hope that they will reach one of two inevitable results: either they will not be able to make a cogent defense for themselves, or they will have to resort to some transparently self-contradictory rationale for their actions. When the Pharisees accuse Jesus of casting out demons by the power (authority) of Beelzebul, He is able to expose the contradiction easily: "[I]f Satan casts out Satan, he is divided against himself; how then will his kingdom stand?" (Mt 12:26). It really does not matter how the Pharisees respond—whether they refuse to answer or they make recourse to some transparent self-contradiction, Jesus has won the day. Their teaching is inadequate to resolve His challenge, which throws the legitimacy of their authority into question.

Jesus has a third motive for using harsh rhetoric with the Pharisees, beyond expressing His distress and desperation, and exposing the illegitimacy of their teaching and authority. He wants the Pharisees to recognize the *precarious* spiritual condition in which they, as Israel's religious leaders, are living. Their self-righteousness is not only a danger to God's people; it is a danger to *themselves*. When Jesus tells the story of the tax collector and the Pharisee in the Temple, He says that the Pharisee was "standing toward himself and praying" (Lk 18:11; my translation), implying he was praying to himself (instead of to God). After recounting the Pharisee's self-righteous prayer, Jesus says, "I tell you he [tax collector] went home justified before God, but the [Pharisee] did not, for all those who exalt them-selves will be humbled, and those who humble themselves will be exalted" (Lk 18:14; my translation).

The Pharisees are so confident that their adherence to the law will save them that they do not see the consequences of their arrogance, lack of compassion, domination of others, and self-idolatry. Jesus' rhetoric, though harsh, is focused on *lovingly* helping them to move beyond their significant blind spots. Evidently He was successful in helping Nicodemus, Joseph of Arimathea, and many of the Jewish scribes who became early Christian converts. The end of the Parable of the Prodigal Son does not indicate whether the older son (rep-resenting the Pharisees) goes back into the house; it concludes only with the father's humble and loving plea to do so.

5. Conclusion

What might we now conclude about the anger of God? Though God is portrayed as passionately, antagonistically, and retributively angry in many parts of the Old Testament, Jesus never uses the term "anger" (*orgē*) of God and never directly indicates that God is angry in any sense or on any level. This supersedes the theology of the Old Testament. Though Jesus gives no *direct* indications of God's anger, some people have seen implications of it in four areas: (1) Paul's use of "wrath of God", (2) Jesus' use of "Gehenna" and "wailing and grinding of teeth", (3) Jesus' cleansing of the Temple, and (4) Jesus' harsh rhetoric toward the Pharisees. Closer inspection of these four implications of God's anger, however, indicate something quite dif-ferent from antagonistic, resentful, retributive moods or feelings on the part of God.

Paul's use of "wrath of God" does not indicate the above antago-nistic, resentful, retributive *feelings* on the part of *God*, but rather the negative *judgment* that human *beings* deserve for their hard-heartedness, arrogance, domination, self-idolatry, and destruction of others. For

Paul, Christ *saves* us from that negative judgment we deserve; He is not saving us from God's antagonistic feelings toward us.

Jesus' use of "Gehenna" and "wailing and grinding of teeth" are meant *not* as an indication of God's antagonistic retributive feelings toward us, but rather as a *warning* about the defining power of personal freedom to choose hard-heartedness, pride, domination, self-idolatry, and destruction of others over compassion, humility, contribution, and worship of the true God. These warnings are meant to *shock* us into a reconsideration of the way we are living—not to make ourselves perfect overnight "or else!" but rather to call upon the mercy and grace of God to help us reorient our path from darkness into the light of eternal love. Without this conversion—this "reorientation of ourselves" away from "antilove" toward love—we could find ourselves *choosing* a life of darkness, emptiness, alienation, loneliness, and self-destruction: "Gehenna" and "wailing and grinding of teeth".

Jesus' cleansing of the Temple was not a spontaneous violent outburst toward a group of money changers doing their regular business, but rather a prophetic action directed at the religious authorities to initiate the process of replacing the old Temple, which had become corrupt and was restricted to Jerusalem, with a worldwide "house of prayer": the temple of Himself. It was the first prophetic step in a process that would include His Passion, death, Resurrection, gift of the Spirit, and the destruction of the Jerusalem Temple. This prophetic action was intended not as an indication of God's violent temper, but as a *loving* action that would replace a corrupt and ineffective Temple administration with a universal efficacious vehicle for the salvation of the world.

Finally, Jesus' harsh rhetoric toward the Pharisees is not an indication of Jesus' (and God's) antagonistic, resentful, retributive anger toward mankind. Rather, it was an expression of Jesus' distress and desperation to change the attitude of the religious authorities—intentionally used to shock, challenge, and provoke the religious authorities to defend and expose their illegitimate teachings and authority. Furthermore, it was meant to provoke the Pharisees to see the dangerous spiritual path of self-righteousness upon which they had embarked, not out of a sense of resentment and retribution, but out of profound love for them, like the father's plea to his older son.

If the above analysis is correct, then Jesus very probably did not intend to indicate or imply that God (His Abba) had antagonistic, resentful, and retributive anger toward us—even in our most sinful and evil state. Rather, He extends unconditional mercy toward us, patiently awaits our repentance, joyfully rushes out to meet us, lovingly gives us the family ring, and kills the fatted calf. Jesus makes a clean break with the anger and retribution of God in the Old Testament and replaces it with his Abba, reflected in the heart of the prodigal son's father.

In view of this, we will want to embrace the father of the prodigal son as our image of God when we enter into prayer—particularly prayer during times of suffering. As such, we can be confident in God's mercy, patience, kindness, and affection—without having to take steps to avoid or assuage a potential outburst of God's antagonistic and retributive anger. Though confident in God's forgiving love, we must be genuinely contrite for our sins, while trying to grow in humility, gentleness, forgiveness, and compassion. If we do these things, we can be sure that the Father, Jesus, and the Holy Spirit will help us along the path of life to the eternal salvation prepared for us. We don't have to make ourselves righteous—indeed, as Jesus told the Pharisees, we can't make ourselves righteous—but thanks be to God for our Lord and Savior Jesus Christ.

As we enter into prayer reverently, humbly, and contritely, we can be filled with confidence, affection, hope, and joy. God is not the "sword of Damocles waiting to lop off our heads"; He is Jesus' Abba—the Father of the Prodigal Son—who welcomes us into the adventure of grace and salvation.

B. "The Payback God"

The "payback god" is a subspecies of the angry god, except the emphasis is placed more on retribution than on angry feelings. The Old Testament makes reference to God's desire for retribution, even down to the fourth generation (Ex 34:6–7; Deut 5:8–10; Lev 26:39; Job 4:3–6). We normally make recourse to this false notion when we are surprised by some form of suffering—sickness, debilitation, or a negative change in our life (such as a loss of a job). Instead of viewing

God as Abba, the Father of the Prodigal Son, our minds turn to guilt for past offenses: "I did something wrong ten years ago, and now I have to pay; God has been waiting around for a time when I am particularly vulnerable—I deserve it." The truth of the matter is, we may in *justice* deserve some kind of retribution for our past offenses, but that is *not* the way God (Jesus' Father) works. As Jesus taught us, the Father of the Prodigal Son is interested in forgiveness, *mercy*, and restoration, not in the punishment that justice demands.

Furthermore, the Sermon on the Mount is dedicated to an over-arching theme—that mercy triumphs over justice. If God were interested primarily in justice, Jesus would not have said, "Turn the other cheek," but rather, "Slap his cheek too!" He would not have said, "Love your enemies and do good to those who hate you," but rather he would have cited Psalm 139:21–22: "Do I not hate them that hate you, O LORD? And do I not loathe them that rise up against you? I hate them with perfect hatred; I count them my enemies." If Jesus were interested in retribution, he would not have repudiated the Old Testament dictum "eye for eye, tooth for tooth" (Ex 21:24; Lev 24:20; Deut 19:21; cf. Mt 5:38), but would have reinforced it. Instead of holding up the Good Samaritan as a paradigm of virtue, he could have followed the thinking of Eliphaz who told Job that he deserved all his suffering because of his sin (Job 4:1—5:1). Further-more, Jesus asks His disciples to forgive one another "seventy times seven" (Mt 18:22)—a prime number (seven) times ten times a prime number, signifying an unending number of times. Since forgiveness entails a release from the strict prescriptions of justice, it again signi-fies the triumph of mercy over justice.

Inasmuch as Jesus asks us to make mercy triumph over justice (in the above passages) and that this kind of love imitates the perfection of His Father (Mt 5:48), then we may infer that the Father is the essence of how "mercy triumphs over judgment" (Jas 2:13). He is not the "pay-back god", but rather an unrestrictedly merciful Father—not interested in retribution any more than the father of the prodigal son.

This notion of the payback god is typical among those who have encountered suffering and are uncertain about the meaning of Jesus' revelation. These individuals are likely to believe that God needs or wants to punish them for past sins or injustices. This strong sense of God kicking sinners to the side of the road and repudiating them—giving them their "just deserts"—can exacerbate fear and guilt, blind us to the opportunity and salvation in suffering, and cause us to run from God instead of trusting Him. It is not consistent with the Father of the Prodigal Son, and it violates Jesus' view that suffering is not punishment for sin.[24] As such, we should try to banish it from both our conscious and unconscious minds.

C. "The Domineering God"

Those who have been raised with and continue to subscribe to the "angry god" (Section II.A above) can easily move to the idea that God is domineering. Old Testament passages about God's anger (see above II.A); jealousy (e.g., Ex 20:5; 34:14); power, as in "Lord of hosts", another way of saying, "Lord of heaven's armies" (which appears more than two hundred times in the Old Testament, appearing first in 1 Sam 1:3);[25] and punishment of sinners and enemies (see above II.B) can give the impression that God not only is the highest of all beings, but also wants us to know and recognize His superiority. This implies that God wants to put us in our proper place and wants us to be wholly subservient and surrender to His superior and dominant will. It is a short leap from here to the "domineering god" to whom we can attribute the attitudes of dominating personalities we have known. When we do this, "god" can become "a domineering boss, an uncontrollable ego, an authoritarian parent, or a great dictator".

This view of God is disempowering and eviscerating and will likely impede and even undermine our relationship with Him. During times of suffering, it is disastrous because we are led to believe that we are suffering either because we are "nothing" in His eyes or because

---

[24] "[F]or he makes his sun rise on the evil and on the good, and sends rain on the just and on the unjust" (Mt 5:45).

[25] Though the Old Testament attributes jealousy to God, its primary intention is to signify Yahweh's prohibition of other competitor cults to the people of Israel. For modern audiences, the focus on the prohibition of competitor cults is lost, and so we tend to focus on the emotion of jealousy. Jesus does not attribute this emotion or attitude to God. The same holds true for the "power of god", in the sense of being the leader or authority of heaven's armies. This designation comes from a "warrior culture". Jesus does not view His Father in this way.

we are mere pawns on a cosmic chessboard; God is so far above us that we are mere cannon fodder or "playthings". If we really believe in such a god, suffering could lead to abject despair, and if we revolt against such a god, it could lead to unbelief. In either case, it will leave our spiritual and psychic lives in ruins. Though we can easily slip into this view in times of suffering, it is completely incompatible with the teaching of Jesus (see below) and, as such, should be resisted—and replaced with trust in Jesus' perfectly loving Father.

Let us return to the idea that the domineering god wants us to be subservient and surrender to Him. Notice that this notion of "surrender" is quite different from the Christian view of "surrender", which comes from being forgiven and loved, giving rise to trust. The former kind of surrender resembles that of a defeated army accepting the terms of a dominant victor—which crushes our freedom and spirit. This is opposed to Christian surrender, which liberates us through the purification of our will from egoism toward empathetic and compassionate love.

Jesus' Father is the complete antithesis to the "domineering god". Jesus does not portray His Father as superior, overbearing, authoritarian, and disdainful—nor does He portray Him as jealous, leader of an army, or intent on punishment. As repeatedly noted above, Jesus portrays His Father as the father of the prodigal son who has every right (according to the Old Covenant) to disown his son for all of the harm he has done to his family, people, and religion. He certainly did not have to divide his property and give it to his younger son before his death and before his older brother. He could have simply said, "How dare you—get out of my presence you ungrateful wretch!" Yet he does nothing like this, choosing instead to give his son half of the estate before it is due to him, and taking him back fully after he has squandered it on dissolute living in the land of the Gentiles. When the younger son returns from squandering his father's property and humiliating him, the father doesn't give him a lecture—he doesn't even ask the following question: "Why did you do this to us?" He simply turns to the servants to tell them to take care of his son's needs—restoring him back to the family 100 percent and then throwing a party to celebrate it. Thus, Jesus portrays His Father as not only perfectly compassionate and forgiving, but also perfectly *humble*.

The idea of a perfectly humble God may seem counterintuitive to us because God as Creator would imply perfect power and being— *unrestrictedly* powerful. Though this is true (see Volume II, Appendixes I and II), we cannot counterpose "power" and "love". There are several passages in the Old Testament that portray God as both powerful and gentle—treating His *people* with just punishments as well as the love of a mother:

> But Zion said,
> "The LORD has forsaken me,
> my Lord has forgotten me."
> "Can a woman forget her sucking child,
> that she should have no compassion on the son of
>   her womb?
> Even these may forget,
> yet I will not forget you.
> Behold, I have engraved you on the palms of my hands;
>   your walls are continually before me." (Is 49:14–16;
>   my translation)

Jesus advances this idea of God's gentle love by first superseding God's supposed anger and retributive punishment (see above II.A), and secondly, by focusing not just on the "*people* Israel" (a term used throughout the Old Testament), but also on each individual person, particularly the most lowly and needy. These emphases blend perfectly not only with the attributes of the prodigal son's father, but also with the first and third Beatitudes—"Blessed are the poor in spirit [the humble-hearted]" (Mt 5:3); "Blessed are the meek [the gentle-hearted]" (Mt 5:5).[26]

Recall from Volume I (Chapter 9) and Volume III (Chapter 2) that the Beatitudes reflect the heart of the Father. Jesus attributes the same qualities to Himself in Matthew 11:29: "[F]or I am gentle and lowly in heart."

---

[26] For the translation of "poor in spirit" as "humble-hearted" and "meek" as "gentle-hearted" see Volume I (Chapter 9, Section II.A) and Volume III (Chapter 2, Section III.A).

The complementarity between God's unrestricted power and His perfect humility and gentleness is also manifest in the names that Moses and Jesus give to God. Moses says that God's name is Yahweh—which is Aramaic for the verb "to be". W. F. Albright believes it is the causative tense of "to be"—and its full expression is Yahweh ser-yiweh ("He brings into being whatever comes into being").[27] Recall that for the Hebrew people, a name is more than a linguistic token to reference an object or idea. It represents the nature, essence, or heart of someone or something. Thus, in the name Yahweh we sense the *power* of God—the Creator of all being out of the abyss (nothing). He is the Master of the universe, the source of all things, and absolute power.

Jesus knew well what the name Yahweh signified, yet He had no difficulty revealing another name (i.e., address) that seemed to stand in stark contrast to it—namely, Abba. As noted earlier, "Abba" signifies not only "Father", but also how a child might view his father—as affectionate, gentle, trustworthy, and protective (see Volume III, Chapter 2, Section III.B). It might be roughly translated as "Daddy". At first glance we might sense the same tension as that felt by the scribes and Pharisees, who were more than likely wondering, "Are you really saying that the Master of the universe, the Creator, the Absolute power is 'daddy'?" This is precisely what Jesus is saying—absolute power is absolute love, which is absolute humility, gentleness, affection, trustworthiness, and protection. The revelation of Jesus is that there is no contrast between power and love—God is, as it were, loving power and empowering love.

When Jesus becomes incarnate in *little* Bethlehem in *little* Israel, in a *humble* stable of *humble* parents, we should not be surprised, because this is precisely the way absolute power would manifest itself if Jesus' name for God is correct. Again, we should not be surprised that Jesus chose to give Himself to us completely in an act of self-sacrifice, suffering, and death—for this is precisely how absolute power would manifest itself as absolute love. Thus, it is the same thing to say that "God *created* the universe" as to say "God *loved* the universe into existence." The "logic" of Jesus is the logic of love that says that power *is* humility, gentleness, affection, and "littleness". This equation of

[27] McKenzie, *Dictionary of the Bible*, p. 317.

power and love is well recognized by Christian mystics such as Saint
John of the Cross:

> Since He is the virtue of supreme *humility*, He *loves you* with supreme
> humility and esteem and *makes you His equal*, gladly revealing Him-
> self to you in these ways of knowledge, in this His countenance is
> filled with graces, and telling you in this His union, not without great
> rejoicing: "*I am yours and for you* and *delighted* to be what I am so as to
> be yours *and give myself to you.*"[28]

So what is the significance of this revelation? If Yahweh really is
Abba, if Jesus and His Father really are perfect humility and gentleness, and if Jesus' Father is properly manifest by the father of the
prodigal son, then God is anything but domineering; He is the antithesis of it: He is perfect humility, gentleness, affection—perfect Abba.

In view of this, we can go before the Lord in prayer with confidence that we will not be dominated, "put down", vitiated, insulted,
rendered powerless, disdained, or trivialized. We don't have to be
concerned that our act of surrender will lead to complete subser-
vience, self-immolation, and loss of our self-identity and freedom.
Rather, when we go to prayer we can feel confident that God will
enhance us, dignify us, treat us with utmost dignity and respect, and
empower us in love—and we can hear Him saying: "*I am yours and
for you* and *delighted* to be what I am so as to be yours *and give myself
to you.*"[29]

D. "The Terrifying God"

The "terrifying god" arises out of a combination of the angry god
and the domineering god. In this misconception, God is seen as
angry with us because of our sinfulness and compelled to "punish
and humiliate us" because He has the power and right to do so. He is
completely indifferent about sending us to Hell for eternity, so if we

---

[28] Saint John of the Cross, "The Living Flame of Love", in *The Collected Works of St. John
of the Cross*, trans. Kieran Kavanaugh and Otilio Rodriguez (Washington, D.C.: ICS Publications, 1979), p. 613; emphasis mine.

[29] Ibid; emphasis mine.

step out of line, we can be reasonably sure that we will be cast into the netherworld without a care or even a thought. In order to give us fair warning of what is to befall us if we step out of line, He asks us to remember his anger, superiority, and right to punish us—the specter of abject terror. The mere sight of His overwhelming and terrifying presence so threatens us that we immediately understand, "We had better stay in line, or we're really going to get it!" As noted above, this view was promoted by Jonathan Edwards and other like-minded preachers who portrayed God as "the god that holds you over the pit of hell, much as one holds a spider, or some loathsome insect over the fire, abhors you, and is dreadfully provoked".

Many religious individuals today follow Jonathan Edwards in promoting the terrifying god, believing that it will "scare people into faith" and hold them in moral rectitude. They go beyond the "angry and domineering god" by adding a critical feature—God's complete indifference to our well-being and redemption. The more they remove care, compassion, sympathy, and love from God, the more they make Him into a character straight out of Hollywood's *Psycho, Friday the 13th, Halloween,* and *Silence of the Lambs.* Now He is really scary, so you better not mess with Him!

This view of God is completely contrary to the revelation of Jesus, and its proponents' strategy to "win converts and hold them in moral rectitude" is remarkably unsuccessful. Though it may persuade a few people to be religious and moral (by inducing neurotic fear and defensiveness), it generally leads to a rejection of God and a revolt against religion, because it is hard to believe that God would be indifferent to everyone's well-being and salvation.

As we shall show, Jesus taught that God is *not* indifferent to our well-being and salvation; He is infinitely concerned to bring it about. This means that preaching the *false* terrifying, angry, domineering, uncaring god is not helping the divine cause. By giving a completely false view of God, it undermines growth in the spiritual life, religious community, and the Kingdom of God. If we are to redress this unnecessary disaster, we must expose its falsity and renounce it altogether.

The terrifying god also undermines the process of healing and redemption of suffering. Suffering is already filled with fear and other anxieties—particularly fear of the future. The last thing we need to do is add to those fears by praying to the terrifying god. Suffering also leads to feelings of isolation and loneliness, but praying to an angry, uncaring, indifferent, antagonistic, resentful, retributive, and domineering god will cause us to run even faster and harder away from the very source of our help and redemption.

The "terrifying god" appears occasionally in the Old Testament,[30] but it is infrequent. Jesus makes no recourse to it because He has superseded it in His teaching about the Father—as Abba, the Father of the Prodigal Son. Moreover, the terrifying god is in tension with Jesus' mission as the beloved Son sent by God—not to scare the world, but to save it in an act of self-sacrificial love. Jesus' name ($Y\bar{e}\check{s}\bar{u}\check{a}$'), which points to His essence, means "Yahweh is salvation." This means that Jesus' very essence is the salvation of Yahweh. Everything Jesus does in His mission manifests His *care* for the sick, the poor, the downtrodden, and sinners. He cares for people not only in their temporal needs, but more importantly, in their spiritual needs—teaching them how to stay on the path to salvation, the path He created Himself through His Incarnation, self-sacrificial love, Resurrection, gift of the Spirit, and Church. Jesus put care and compassion at the center of His moral teaching as well as His teaching about God. The Beatitudes, the Parable of the Good Samaritan, and the Parable of the Prodigal Son, as well as His life of compassion and service, show unequivocally that He and His Father are caring, compassionate, redeeming, saving, empathizing, self-sacrificing *love*. Saint Paul states this clearly:

> If God is for us, who is against us? He who did not spare his own Son but gave him up for us all, will he *not also* give us all things with him? Who shall bring any charge against God's elect? It is God who justifies; who is to condemn? (Rom 8:31–33; emphasis mine)

The idea that God could be in any way uncaring is completely alien to Jesus, His Father, and Christianity. In view of this, the idea of a terrifying god should be rejected and renounced.

---

[30]Job describes his reaction to God during his suffering as terror: "[God] is unchangeable and who can turn him? What he desires, that he does. For he will complete what he appoints for me; and many such things are in his mind. Therefore I am terrified at his presence; when I consider, I am in dread of him. God has made my heart faint; the Almighty has terrified me" (Job 23:13–16). Jeremiah hears the Lord saying, "Do you not fear me?" declares the Lord. "Do you not tremble before me?" (Jer 5:22).

In sum, Jesus' teaching is completely opposed to the three pillars of the terrifying god—His supposed anger, domineering ego, and indifference to salvation. As such, we do not have to fear God (in the negative sense described above). That is why Saint John tells us that in Jesus, all fear is driven out by love:

> There is no fear in love, but perfect love casts out fear. For fear has to do with punishment, and he who fears is not perfected in love. (1 Jn 4:18)

In Chapter 5, we will show that Jesus and the New Testament writers do not advocate fear of God and do not give a single positive assessment of fear in any context. Indeed, Jesus encourages His followers in all cases to *avoid* fear, and in their relationship with God, to replace fear with trust (see Mk 5:36 and Lk 8:50).

If Jesus so completely rejects fear and the terrifying god, why does the Old Testament sometimes treat the fear of God so positively? For example, in Proverbs 9:10 fear of God is said to be "the beginning of wisdom", and in Ecclesiastes 12:13 fearing God and keeping His commandments is said to be "the whole duty of everyone". The answer may be found in two distinct dimensions of the concept of "fear of God": a negative one (as described above) and a positive one that associates fear with awe, the recognition of God's power, splendor, glory, majesty, and mystery.

The English term "fear" and the Greek term *phobos* are used to translate no less than eleven Hebrew terms[31]—some of them (like those mentioned above) are negative and superseded by Jesus' teaching about the unconditional compassion of God, but some of them are positive, emphasizing reverence, respect, awe, worship, and adoration. The positive meaning of "fear" is related to a passage from Psalm 2:11, which says, "Serve the LORD with fear, with trembling rejoice." Contemporary readers may be asking, "How do fear and trembling go together with rejoicing?" They don't go together if your view of fear is negative—terror, horror, and dread before the terrible anger, punishment, indifference, and destructiveness of God. However, they do go together when fear is positive, evoking a sense

---

[31] Eugene Merrill, "Fear," in *Baker's Evangelical Dictionary of Biblical Theology*, ed. Walter Elwell (Grand Rapids, Mich.: Baker Books, 1996), http://www.biblestudytools.com /dictionaries/bakers-evangelical-dictionary/fear.html.

of humility, creatureliness, and worship before the overwhelming yet benevolent Creator God.

Recall that this positive fear is intrinsic to the numinous experience[32] and is the foundation for the essential attitudes of creatureliness—reverence, worship, awe, veneration, and adoration. This positive kind of fear is not only compatible with rejoicing, but also with love, goodness, and beauty—with what is transcendentally holy or sacred, with majesty, glory, and splendor. It is completely compatible with the teaching of Jesus and was integral to His own spiritual life with the Father. So long as we do not confuse this notion of fear with the negative one (evoking terror), we will be able to enjoy the Psalms, Proverbs, and other Wisdom literature in the light of Jesus' unconditionally loving Father.

E. "The Stoic God"

The "stoic god" embraces stoic virtues and expects us to do so as well. In this view, God is exceedingly rational, nonemotional, imperturbable, self-disciplined, unsympathetic, "tough-minded", dissatisfied with mediocrity, and detached. He is like Mr. Spock on *Star Trek*, but with much greater power, less care for friends (like Captain Kirk), and more serious. The stoic god expects us to pursue qualities like His own—and to move the fulcrum of our lives from being dependent to being independent, from being emotional to being logical, from being vulnerable to being impervious, and above all, from being weak to being strong. When suffering comes, He expects us to suppress emotion, "take the hit", be self-sufficient, and use the experience to gain greater rationality, discipline, and courage (the three stoic virtues). This will enable us to have more control over ourselves and our lives—and to rise above mediocrity. Needless to say, the stoic god is quite distinct from the Father of Jesus, portrayed by the father in the prodigal son parable.

Though Christians consider rationality, self-discipline, and courage to be important natural virtues (see Chapter 7, Section I.B),

---

[32] See Rudolf Otto, *The Idea of the Holy: An Inquiry into the Non-Rational Factor in the Idea of the Divine and Its Relation to the Rational* (New York: Oxford University Press, 1958). See also Volume II (Chapter 1) of this Quartet.

they acknowledge other higher virtues such as *agapē*, which includes compassion, contribution to the good of others, self-sacrifice, empathy, and humility. They recognize that the above stoic virtues are essential for the practice of *agapē*; however, they cannot be ends in themselves—this is reserved for *agapē* alone. For Christians, exaggerating the three stoic virtues can lead to undesirable and even immoral conduct. For example, if we consider *self-discipline* to be an end in itself, it could lead to pride and narcissism. If we view *rationality* as an end in itself, it could undermine affection, care, and compassion—and promote an elitist intelligentsia. If we consider physical and mental strength as an end in itself, it could lead to cruelty and disdain for the weak. If *agapē* does not guide the stoic virtues to their proper ends, then they can lead to the opposite of *agapē*—hard-heartedness, coldness, elitism, and disdain.

The stoic god resembles the god of Aristotle and the deists, who emphasized God's unrestricted power and intellect, while deemphasizing emotion, empathy, care, and other seemingly "soft" feelings.[33] Strange as it may seem, many Christians mistake the stoic god for the Christian God, and so they believe that God wants them to be disciplined, strong, and rational without having to be empathizing, caring, merciful, and humble. As such, they believe that "God" *wants* them to suffer so that they will become stronger, more self-sufficient, more impervious to pain, and more disciplined. They also tend to believe that God thinks that "harder and tougher is better—and that the more pain we can endure without complaint, the more virtuous we are."

If God were a stoic, this contention would be true. But if God is like the father of the prodigal son, then He has a very different viewpoint—He does not want us to develop stoic virtues as ends in themselves, but rather as *means* to the end of *agapē*. He wants us to develop courage, strength, fortitude, and temperance *for the sake* of love. Furthermore, Jesus' Father is not indifferent to us—even when we have been callous and indifferent to him. He continually calls us to the love that He unceasingly manifests toward us—profoundly loving us by respecting, caring for, and delighting in us.

If Christians falsely believe that the God of Jesus is the stoic god, then they will have difficulty relating to Him, which will diminish their capacity for love instead of enhancing it. Their suffering will not

---

[33] See the explanation in Section I above.

lead to greater faith, hope, and love, but rather to greater toughness, self-sufficiency, and cool indifference. In times of suffering, they will believe that God is saying, "Stop the whimpering and simpering— toughen up and get over it! 'What does not kill you will make you stronger.'" This view of God might have been appropriate for the Roman Legion, but it was certainly not part of Jesus' revelation.

The "stoic god" is not only incompatible with Christianity, but also with the Old Testament, which portrays God as intensely inter- ested in His people—not indifferent to them; He has high and low feelings, which are not considered to be weaknesses but strengths; He is "our keeper" and wants us to be "our brother's and sister's keeper". If stoicism does not come from the Judeo-Christian tradition, where does it come from?

Stoicism had its origins in Athens, but found its flourishing in Rome—particularly in the philosophy of Seneca, Epictetus, and the emperor Marcus Aurelius. The stoics held that perfect calm could be attained through three virtues—self-discipline, fortitude, and clear rational thought. Self-discipline includes restraint (temperance) toward passions and stimuli that may interfere with rational thought, deliberation, and judgment. Fortitude is the courage and commit- ment required to put our best rational thoughts into action. Thus, rational thought and judgment lie at the base of stoic life, and self- control and fortitude support them. When we are perfectly rational, we feel calm—enabling us to maintain a sense of equilibrium no matter how difficult and adverse our external circumstances may be.

Stoic values are noble, and they are highly prized by modern cul- ture. They are also valued by Christians—though Christians view them *only* as means to the end of *agapē*, but not as ends in them- selves. If Christians forget this distinction, they can be easily pulled into the perspective of modern culture, causing them to lose sight of the true end of life (*agapē*) and the true nature of God (uncon- ditional *agapē*). "God" then becomes progressively more stoic— emphasizing "stronger, harder, better, faster, and more", instead of "humble-heartedness, gentle-heartedness, patience, kindness, for- giveness, compassion, and genuine care and concern for the weak as well as the strong".

The nobility of stoic values makes them quite seductive for Chris- tians, particularly Christian leaders. Who doesn't want to be rational, self-disciplined, courageous, calm, and composed in times of danger and turbulence? Aren't these the virtues of a leader? Are they not admirable and noble? Of course they are, but when they are not accompanied by justice and love (*agapē*), they can become callous, cold, hard-hearted, and uncaring.[34] They can lead to societal dictums like "survival of the fittest", "the strongest and most capable are more deserving of life and political protection", "carry your own weight and I will carry mine"—dictums that characterize Rome, with its justification of slavery, gladiatorial combat, aggressive war, empire building, and strict social stratification. Stoic values by themselves, without justice and love (*agapē*), can lead to abject heartlessness, cruelty, social injustice, dehumanization, and a culture of death.

There is further difficulty with stoicism; it tends to undermine *agapē*—humility, empathy, compassion, mercy, forgiveness, and self-sacrifice—by suggesting that they breed weakness and dependence in individuals, which leads to weakness within society and culture. Christians do not want weak individuals, societies, and cultures any more than stoics do. However, they don't want unmitigated strength, "strength at any price", either. Christians want strength, independence, rationality, and courage *directed toward* justice and love— toward the common good and the Golden Rule; toward our true transcendent dignity and destiny; toward this world and the next. We must remember that a strong society without just, humane, and respectful values is completely uncivilized; it quickly turns into a totalitarian state, which suppresses every value except the strength of the state, similar to Rome, Nazi Germany, Stalinist Russia, and other vicious societies. In view of this, stoic virtues cannot stand alone; they need to be complemented by justice and *agapē* (contribution,

[34] Recall the words of Seneca, who disdained feelings of compassion and pity: "The wise man uses foresight, and keeps in readiness a plan of action.... He, consequently, will not suffer pity, because there cannot be pity without mental suffering.... He will bring relief to another's tears, but will not add his own; to the shipwrecked man he will give a hand, to the exile shelter, to the needy alms.... He will do these things with unruffled mind, and a countenance under control. The wise man, therefore, will not pity, but will succor.... Pity is akin to wretchedness; for it is partly composed of it and partly derived from it.... Pity is a weakness of the mind that is over-much perturbed by suffering, and if anyone requires it from a wise man, that is very much like requiring him to wail and moan at the funerals of strangers." Lucius Seneca, *De Clementia*, in *World Essays*, Loeb Classical Library, trans. John W. Basore, vol. 1 (London: W. Heinemann, 1928), 2.6–7.

service, humility, empathy, care, compassion, mercy, forgiveness, and self-sacrifice).

Given the above, Christians can ill afford to turn the Father of Jesus into the stoic god. If they do, they will take the heart of Jesus' revelation right out of Him—reconfiguring Him from an approachable God of love to a distant god of strength, from the God who invites us to Himself, saying, "Come to me, all who labor and are heavy laden, and I will give you rest" (Mt 11:28), to the god who stands aloof—uncaring and indifferent, like Seneca's wise man:

> The wise man, therefore, will not pity, but will succor.... Pity is akin to wretchedness; for it is partly composed of it and partly derived from it.... Pity is a weakness of the mind that is over-much perturbed by suffering.[35]

If stoic values must be complemented by justice and *agapē* to prevent them from becoming heartless, cruel, unjust, inhumane, and deadly, then modern societies will need spokesmen to communicate and defend these "higher values". Who better than Christians to take on this responsibility? Christians have the teaching of Jesus to guide them, the Father of Jesus to grace them, and the Spirit of Jesus to inspire them. Yet if Christians are to assume this responsibility, they will have to resist the cultural allure of mere stoic values, and the implication that God loves strength more than compassion. They will have to be strong in a nonstoic way—strong in faith, humility, gentleness, compassion, and forgiveness. This will take courage, an altogether different kind of courage than that advocated by the stoics.

F. "The Disgusted God"

The disgusted god is a subspecies of both the domineering god and the stoic god. He has very high standards for our conduct, and the ideals for which we are to strive, and high expectations for our progress toward those ideals. Like a parent or boss with high expectations, He disdains low achievers, is impatient with slow progress, and

---

[35] Ibid.

intolerant of regression and failure. When expectations are not met, He unhesitatingly expresses disappointment and disdain, punishing us with "the silent treatment and rejection".

Slow progress over the long-term or multiple failures in the short-term elicit a response of disgust—"Joe/Mary, I have done everything imaginable for you, given you an excellent family, provided excellent education and catechesis, given you talents with which to progress, and here you are limping along. You haven't met a single moderate expectation since the day you were born. I have reduced my standards and criteria for success, and still you limp. You are a colossal disappointment, and if there is no improvement, I'll just have to cut my losses with you. Let's get cracking; I'm waiting." Humorous as this example might be, there are many people who not only implicitly feel but explicitly believe that God looks at them in this way. He is the *Judge*, the superior Judge devoid of understanding, patience, kindness, and toleration of weakness. Though the Old Testament hints at some of the above characteristics, it does not present God in this way; God's judgment is concerned ultimately with justice and fidelity, not with high standards, stretch goals, progress markers, and disdain for low achievers. Instead of the Old Testament, the reader will recognize the roots of this god in the "stoic god".

This view of God is typical among those who have a strong sense of personal responsibility. They hold themselves to a high standard of accountability in their productivity and quality of work, and believe that God operates according to similar criteria. Though the Lord certainly wants us to be responsible for our lives, and to move to higher levels of happiness/purpose in life, He is not a demanding boss who expresses disappointment, and even disdain, when quality and productivity do not meet "stretch expectations". God does not want to be our "boss"; He wants to be our *Father* (our *Abba*), who is caring, understanding, affectionate, and protective. When our performance slips, He does not want to put us on probation or fire us; He wants to lead us back to Himself. His relationship with us is personal, not "task oriented".

Furthermore, God is not a demanding parent expecting better grades, athletic performance, and social adeptness with each passing day, and who expresses disappointment and disgust when expectations are not met. Rather, God is the infinitely patient and compassionate

Father of the Prodigal Son who accepts us back into the family—100 percent, with exuberance and joy, even after we have failed at just about everything. His intention is not to show us who's boss and who's better, and to lay a control trip on us to do things His way; He is not on a "control trip", but the very opposite: a "freedom trip". He is not concerned with our doing things *His* way and meeting *His* productivity standards, but rather with leading us to our salvation without violating our freedom. Obviously, He would *like* us to do things His way, because it would be easier for *us* and more conducive to our salvation. However, He will not compromise our freedom in order to do this; hence, He will not try to control us overtly or covertly manipulate us to do what He wants. His objective is to help us to get to the finish line: His heavenly Kingdom, through our free decisions and choices.

Since the "disgusted god" does not conform to Jesus' revelation of Abba as the Father of the Prodigal Son or to God's respect for our free will, we need to reject it by replacing it with the revelation of Jesus.

III. Conclusion

Each of the above false notions of God can appear to be reasonable, appropriate, and credible. Once they gain credibility in our minds and hearts, they are hard to change—at which point they do incalculable harm to our spiritual lives, and those of the people we touch. They are particularly deleterious during times of suffering, because they close us off to God, making prayer impossible and grace unreachable.

If you the reader find yourself susceptible to one or more of these false notions of God, I would suggest reviewing the rebuttals provided above. We may briefly summarize them as follows.

The "angry god" is present in the Old Testament, but Jesus never mentions it in the Gospels. Nevertheless, this idea seems to be implied by four New Testament expressions or actions of Jesus. Closer scrutiny reveals that these expressions and actions supersede an angry god. Saint Paul was not implying that God is angry but that Jesus came to *save* us from the "wrath of God", the negative judgment we justly deserve for our deeds. Jesus' use of "Gehenna" and "wailing and grinding of teeth" does not indicate that God is cavalierly condemning people to Hell, but that He is warning us not to pursue the path of self-absorption, hard-heartedness, domination, and self-idolatry that could induce us to *choose* Hell. Jesus' cleansing of the Temple was not a manifestation of spontaneous rage, but a carefully planned prophetic action designed to replace the old Temple in Jerusalem with the new universal Temple in Himself, which had as its ultimate objective the salvation of the world. Jesus' harsh tone toward the Pharisees was not a manifestation of antagonistic, resentful, or retributive anger, but the use of a well-known prophetic method (practiced by John the Baptist and Old Testament prophets) to engage the Pharisees in a debate about their doctrine and authority and to warn them about the spiritual peril of their self-righteousness. All of these actions and expressions point to the love of Jesus and His Father—not to an angry god.

Since the "payback god" is a subspecies of the "angry god", its justification proves false for the same reasons. God is no more interested in paying us back for mistakes made and sins committed than the father of the prodigal son. He is not interested in vengeance at all, but in forgiveness seventy times seven times.

Though the "domineering god", who wants to show us His superiority and make His authority felt, has roots in the Old Testament, it is absent in the New Testament. Jesus' teaching supersedes this view, particularly the name "Abba" and its connection to the Father of the Prodigal Son, His advocacy of humility and gentle-heartedness, and His admonition to His disciples not to make their authority felt. The character of His ministry also supersedes the domineering god. The Christian mystical tradition has long embraced this, as expressed by Saint John of the Cross: "I am yours and for you and delighted to be what I am so as to be yours and give myself to you."

The "terrifying god" also has roots in the Old Testament, but not in the way that Jonathan Edwards (the eighteenth-century Puritan preacher) would suggest: "The God that holds you over the pit of hell, much as one holds a spider, or some loathsome insect over the fire, abhors you, and is dreadfully provoked." The Old Testament is filled with references to Yahweh's love of His people, and the New Testament is centered on proclaiming the God who unconditionally loves us. There is no indication in the New Testament of God being uncaring or indifferent to our salvation. Indeed, everything in the preaching and actions of Jesus *militates against* these ideas and shows God's intense and unconditional love for us and desire for our salvation.

Though the "stoic god" does not have roots in either the Old Testament or the New Testament, it seems to make sense in light of contemporary cultures' admiration for the stoic virtues—rationality, strength, self-discipline, and courage/fortitude. Though Christianity has held to the importance of these virtues, it has never made them primary, because they are subordinate to *agapē*—care, compassion, empathy, humility, and self-sacrifice for the good of others. Christians have long recognized that stoic values without *agapē* as their end and perfection lead almost inevitably to every kind of indignity, callous marginalization, and persecution. If we attribute only stoic virtues to God, we risk creating the belief that God is rational but devoid of emotion; helpful but without compassion; tough-minded but without gentle-heartedness; and superior without being humble-hearted. If we believe that of God, then we will also believe He expects this of us, which is spiritually disastrous because He expects precisely the opposite according to Jesus.

Since the "disgusted god" is a subspecies of both the "domineering god" and the "stoic god, its justification proves false for the same reasons. In view of this, we should not think that God is more concerned with "harder, faster, better, and best" than with *agapē*—compassion, care, empathy, humility, and self-sacrifice. God has but two principal concerns: leading us and others to His eternal salvation. He helps us toward this salvation with a humble, gentle, compassionate, and understanding heart, which has no trace of disrespect, disdain, or disgust, but only a perfect parent's undying love.

In conclusion, if you the reader find yourself believing in one of the above false notions of God, review the rebuttals of them and find a good spiritual director who can help you affirm the spiritual goal given to all Christians in the Letter to the Ephesians, where Saint Paul prayed that

Christ may dwell in your hearts through faith; that you, being rooted and grounded in love, may have power to comprehend with all the saints what is the breadth and length and height and depth, and to know the love of Christ which surpasses knowledge, that you may be filled with all the fulness of God. Now to *him* who by the power at work within *us* is able to do *far more abundantly* than all that we ask or think, to him be glory in the Church and in Christ Jesus to all generations, for ever and ever. Amen. (3:17–21; emphasis mine)

Chapter Three

I Am with You Always

Third Foundation: Recognizing God's Presence in Our Suffering

Introduction

If we are to turn to God for help in times of suffering, then we must be confident of how He views our suffering, helps to alleviate it, and enables us to grow through it. If we interiorly appropriate this theology *before* encountering suffering, it can save us considerable distress, particularly from misinterpreting God's motives and actions. It can also provide guidance to see God's providential hand leading us to optimal goodness, growth, and love through our suffering. As will be clear, this theology borrows points from the Old Testament, but it is fundamentally Christian. In order to understand the Christian perspective, it may be helpful to examine first the Old Testament view of suffering, which is thoroughly presented in the Book of Job. We can then separate what Jesus keeps of the Old Testament tradition from what He leaves behind. This will be particularly important to avoid misinterpretations of God's motives coming from an Old Testament theology modified by Jesus.

I. The Old Testament View of Suffering— The Book of Job

Much of Middle Eastern culture from the fifteenth century B.C. through the third century B.C. was polytheistic and almost completely unaware of the monotheism, covenants, and commandments of the Hebrew people. The dominant view of suffering and evil was that suffering is caused by capricious gods using human beings as pawns in their games, disputes, and wars. As a result, there was no question about why a just or good God would cause suffering to just or good people—the gods were neither just nor good, so no problem.

The teaching of Moses (twelfth century B.C.) changes this because he insists that the one God is a just lawgiver who is concerned, and even loves, the people of Israel. This shift in the religious and legal climate causes a problem: Why would a good God cause suffering and evil to good people? (the problem of theodicy).

In the ancient Hebrew view, nature is under the direct causal influence of God. Thus, God causes all natural events; there is nothing that escapes His divine intention and action. For the Hebrews, then, God does not *allow* suffering or evil to happen by *allowing* nature to follow its course; He *causes* suffering to occur.

This presents a major problem in Old Testament theology because the Torah and the Psalms teach that God rewards righteous people, protects them from suffering, and helps them to prosper.[1] Conversely, the same God is displeased with unjust and impious people, punishing them down to the fourth generation.[2] The combination of God's strict justice (prospering the righteous and punishing the unjust) and God's direct causation of all natural events presents a problem: Why would the just and good God cause nature to bring suffering to righteous people?

This problem becomes a major theme in Old Testament Wisdom literature, and the central theme of the Book of Job. The Book of

---

[1] This is a recurrent theme in the Psalms and Wisdom literature. Some examples are the following:

"The righteous flourish like the palm tree, and grow like a cedar in Lebanon" (Ps 92:12).
"In his days may righteous flourish, and peace abound, till the moon be no more!" (Ps 72:7).
"For you bless the righteous, O LORD; you cover him with favor as with a shield" (Ps 5:12).
"Many are the afflictions of the righteous; but the LORD delivers him out of them all" (Ps 34:19).

[2] God punishes sinners and their children to the third and fourth generations (see Ex 20:5). See also Ex 20:6; 34:7; Num 14:18; Deut 5:9–10. This is also a recurrent theme in the Psalm and Wisdom literature (see Prov 12:21). Psalm 58 is a prayer for God to punish the wicked. In Psalm 139, the Psalmist professes that he hates sinners: "O that you would slay the wicked, O God.... Do I not hate them that hate you, O LORD? And do I not loathe them that rise up against you? I hate them with perfect hatred; I count them my enemies" (139:19, 21–22).

Job (written perhaps in the seventh century B.C., though the date is still an open question)[3] represents the major strands of theodicy (theology of suffering and evil) that influenced the Old Testament. There are four discernible strands of thought presented in the text:

1. Suffering is caused by the devil, to test a good person as a challenge to God.
2. Suffering is a punishment for offenses committed by individuals or their parents, grandparents, or great-grandparents.
3. Suffering is a challenging condition produced by God to help people learn wisdom and abandon folly.
4. Suffering is a great mystery known to God alone, and we should not question Him in this regard, but remain faithful to Him no matter how miserable life is or might become.

The third and fourth strands come from the Elihu discourses, which were probably written by a different author than the first part of the Book of Job (containing the first two strands of theodicy). They were probably composed at a later date to correct and add to the original version.[4]

The first strand (Satan accuses Job [Job 1:1—2:13]) tries to resolve the problem of God causing evil to a righteous man (Job) by shifting the agency of evil to Satan, who in this period is not viewed as an evil spirit or demon but as a heavenly prosecutor or accuser given the charge to test the genuineness of people's faith. God is no longer the direct cause of the suffering and evil endured by Job, but rather Satan, the prosecutor who acts independently of God and tries to prove the disingenuousness of Job's supposed faith. God seems somewhat blameless for allowing the accuser to test Job, because if Job's faith is genuine, God will restore the blessings He had formerly given him.

The second strand (Job is blamed for sin by his friends [Job 3:1— 25:1]) is common to the most ancient parts of the Old Testament tradition—namely, that suffering and evil are punishment by God for

---

[3] R. A. F. McKenzie and Roland E. Murphy, "Job", in *The New Jerome Biblical Commentary*, ed. Raymond E. Brown, Joseph A. Fitzmyer, and Roland E. Murphy (Englewood Cliffs, N.J.: Prentice Hall, 1990), p. 467.

[4] Ibid.

sin. If a person *seems* blameless for such suffering, then either he does not know how sinful he really is (as Job's friend suggests[5]) or the suffering came from the sin of previous generations. In the latter view, God can punish the sinfulness of people down to the fourth generation (Ex 34:6–7; Deut 5:8–10; Lev 26:39), and so suffering could be the fault of the father, grandfather, or great-grandfather. In this sense, God is not to blame for the suffering of the innocent; He is only the administrator of strict justice. The blame for the suffering of the innocent is placed squarely on the shoulders of the guilty party (or his parents, grandparents, or great-grandparents) who committed the sin.

The third strand (affliction as medicinal or pedagogical) is found in Elihu's first discourse, second thesis (Job 33:19–24). Elihu suggests that affliction itself is medicinal and a teacher. It can help us to be humble, to open our hearts to God, and through this can lead us to deeper wisdom. Furthermore, suffering can be an impetus or stimulus to repent—and to learn our proper place before God (Job 36:ff.). This interpretation of suffering is retained by the Christian Church, particularly by Saints Peter and Paul (see below Section II.D).

The fourth strand (the conclusion of the Elihu speeches [Job 36–37]) emphasizes the impenetrable mystery of suffering. According to Elihu, there are two ideas of which we can be certain: (1) that God is just (more just than we can fathom), and (2) that God is so wise and powerful, He cannot be fully understood by us. In this view, the suffering of the innocent does not contradict the justice of God, because God is perfectly just. Therefore, suffering of the seemingly innocent person must be just in the infinite wisdom and power of God.

II. Jesus' Revised View of Suffering

Jesus revises the Old Testament view of suffering in several important ways. We will discuss His revision of each of the four strands of the Old Testament interpretation of suffering in turn.

---

[5] Job's friends ostensibly come to console him, but are convinced that God is retributive, and so they believe that Job must have sinned in some way that either he is not admitting to them or to himself. They come with Psalms of penance, but Job responds with Psalms of innocence. Thus, he is forced to defend both his righteousness and God's love for him, which his friends will not accept. This leads Job to consider them enemies. See ibid.

A. Jesus' Supersedes the First Two Strands of the
Old Testament Interpretation of Suffering

With respect to the first strand, Jesus' view of Satan has evolved since the time of Job. For Him, Satan is not so much a prosecutor in a "heavenly courtroom" whose task is to test and challenge the genuineness of people's faith; rather, Satan is an evil fallen angel, a demonic spirit who is a tempter, liar, and destroyer of human beings and their capacity for love. One of Jesus' primary missions is to defeat the rule of Satan, and to orient us back toward God. For Jesus, God did not and does not use Satan as a means to test the genuineness of people's faith; rather, He has sent His only Son into the world to defeat Satan and to exorcise him from individuals and the world through the name of Jesus. Though the Book of Revelation retains the notion of Satan as accuser (Rev 12:10), this meaning is otherwise absent from the New Testament.

Jesus also abandons the second strand of the Old Testament interpretation of suffering, that suffering is a punishment for sin. He does so because it stands in tension with three more fundamental theological viewpoints: (1) His view of God (the Father) as unconditional love, (2) His view that the highest interior virtue is compassion (care for sinners as well as the needy), and (3) His view of the perfection of love (*agapē*) as "love of enemies". In Matthew 5:43–48, Jesus encourages His disciples to love their enemies (instead of seeking retribution and punishment). He says that this is precisely what His heavenly Father does, and for this reason, "[H]e makes his sun rise on the evil and on the good, and sends rain on the just and on the unjust" (Mt 5:45).

Jesus' view of God and virtue requires that He abandon the second strand of suffering as punishment for sin. As we saw in the previous chapter (and Volume III, Chapter 2), Jesus identifies God with the father of the prodigal son, who loves the worst of sinners, is overjoyed by their return, and restores them to the fullness of life when they turn back to him (Lk 15:11–32). This is completely consistent with Matthew's Sermon on the Mount, in which Jesus identifies the Father's perfection with love of enemies (Mt 5:48). This love of enemies and evildoers stands in tension with a God who punishes sinners down to the fourth generation and reserves His love for the righteous alone. How can the same God forgive His enemies (relinquishing punishment and penalty) while punishing them down to the fourth generation? In order for Jesus to be consistent with His insistence that we imitate the Father's compassion for enemies by forgiving them seventy times seven times (a virtually endless number of times; see Mt 18:22), He supersedes the idea of suffering as primarily punishment for sin and says that God causes rain (something negative) to fall on *both* the righteous and sinners, and that God causes His sun to shine (something positive) on *both* sinners and the righteous. In the Gospel of Luke, Jesus states outright, "[L]ove your enemies ... and you will be sons of the Most High; for he is kind to the ungrateful and selfish" (Lk 6:35). If Jesus had not abandoned the idea of God's retribution for suffering, it would have undermined His view of God, love, and virtue. At this juncture, Jesus superseded the Old Testament view of suffering.

B. Jesus' Modification of the Third Strand of the Old Testament Interpretation of Suffering

Jesus, Saint Paul, and Saint Peter retain much of the third strand of the Old Testament view of suffering—the medicinal and pedagogical value of suffering. God was seen by the early Church to use suffering to prevent a person from taking a path leading to self-destruction and destruction of others. Saint Paul is struck blind, which causes him to abandon his persecution of the Church (see Acts 9:8; 13:11; 22:11); Jesus rebukes Peter to prevent Him from resisting the Cross as an essential part of His mission (see Mt 16:23 and Mk 8:33); and Jesus insults and publicly repudiates the Pharisees to show them the way out of self-righteousness, which He believes misguides their followers and places their salvation in jeopardy (see multiple passages in Matthew 23).

Saint Paul also appeals to the third strand of the Old Testament view of suffering in the famous passage from 2 Corinthians 12:7:

[T]o keep me from being too elated by the abundance of revelations, a thorn was given me in the flesh, a messenger of Satan, to harass me, to keep me from being too elated.

We discussed this passage in Chapter 1; it is repeated here only to show that Paul views suffering as both medicinal and pedagogical—a grace from God, to help him on his journey toward salvation (eternal life with the loving God).

This view of suffering is central to the lives of virtually every saint, and figures prominently in the biographies or autobiographies of Saint Augustine, Saint Francis of Assisi, and Saint Ignatius Loyola (see Chapter 6, Section IV). Though central, it can be misinterpreted, and so we will want to give a proper explanation of God's motives in using it. Even slight misinterpretations can lead to needless anguish, ruptures in our relationship with God, and abandonment of God and the Church. Standing behind every misinterpretation of suffering is an erroneous view of God. Before examining these misinterpretations of God's motives in suffering, we will want to establish His true motives as revealed by Jesus. So how does God use suffering for medicinal or pedagogical purposes according to Jesus and the Church? He does so in two ways:

1. To lead us to our salvation
2. To help us help others to their salvation

We will explain this in detail throughout the rest of this book, but for the moment suffice to say that God uses suffering caused by others and nature to lead us away from lifestyles and beliefs that are self-destructive and destructive of others. He also uses it to shock us out of superficial meaning in life (which seeks nothing more than ego-comparative advantage), to help us pursue contributive, empathetic, conscientious, and transcendent meaning in life. In so doing, He helps us purify our authenticity, natural virtue, and love, helping us to grow in empathy, humility, forgiveness, and compassion. He even uses suffering to help develop leaders of culture, society, and the Church, who will help to advance the common good and build His Kingdom. If we are open to these "opportunities of suffering" (Chapter 7) and follow the inspiration of the Holy Spirit toward them (Chapter 9), we will assuredly be lead toward our salvation and be prepared to help others toward their salvation.

Notice that the above objectives of God are commensurate with Jesus' revelation of Abba, the Father of the Prodigal Son. However, there are other so-called objectives or motives of God that are not compatible with Jesus' view of the Father, and must be rejected before they cause us or others psychological and spiritual damage. We might formulate a general rule based on the content of the previous chapter: any interpretation of suffering that implies the angry god, the payback god, the domineering god, the terrifying god, the stoic god, or the disgusted god is incompatible with the revelation of Jesus, and should be rejected. Three common misinterpretations of suffering that imply the above false notions of God are that

1. God uses suffering to punish us,
2. God uses suffering to toughen us up, and
3. God is indifferent to our pain and challenges.

We have already discussed Jesus' explicit rejection of the first misinterpretation of God's motives in suffering—punishing us for our sins or the sins of our parents or grandparents. In addition to this explicit rejection, we can apply the above rule and recognize that this view of God's motives would imply both the angry god and the payback god.

The second erroneous view of God's motives—"suffering is good for us and will toughen us up"—implies the domineering god, the stoic god, and the disgusted god. If God were so motivated, His primary objective would not be humility, empathy, forgiveness, and compassion, but rather strength, indifference, and self-sufficiency. Instead of trying to give us "hearts of flesh", He would be creating "hearts of stone", precisely the opposite of Ezekiel's prophecy (Ezek 36:26).

The third erroneous view of God's motives—His supposed indifference to our suffering—implies the stoic god who stands aloof and detached in the midst of our pain and challenges. We have already shown the contradiction between this and Jesus' view of God in the previous chapter, but it requires additional attention because it is so easily "conjured up" in times of suffering.

In modern culture, we expect quick solutions to problems—medications that will alleviate pain and disease, information and advice from the Internet, instant communication with family and friends, and so forth. Though none of us would want to give up these benefits, we have lost something in the process—the patience to wait for the opportunities of suffering. When those opportunities do not quickly materialize, we begin to think that God is doing nothing for us or through us in our suffering, and therefore, He does not care about us. Nothing could be further from the truth.

As we shall see, the benefits of suffering are "benefits of the *heart* and *spirit*", which take far more time to solidify and mature than benefits of the body and intellect. We can start an exercise program or a diet and see progress in relatively short order, or study a text in mathematics or business and learn useful procedures and techniques in a few hours. As we continue in our diet, exercise program, and learning programs, we *notice* progress and feel a great sense of satisfaction. Unfortunately, in the domain of the heart and spirit, progress comes more slowly—and is harder won. Learning a lesson in virtue, such as courage or temperance, or a lesson in the spiritual life, such as contemplative or examined prayer, or a lesson in love, such as humility, gentleness, or compassion, all require greater nuance, focus, *and time.* It frequently entails *detaching* ourselves from former beliefs and habits that are gratifying and fulfilling, and instead focusing ourselves on what Saint Paul calls the higher things of faith, hope, and love (see 1 Cor 13:13). Thus, if we are to benefit from suffering in our culture, we will have to become, in some sense, countercultural; we will have to be patient, focused, and determined, when every indication in the culture tells us, "You should not have to wait, endure hardship, and look intently for 'a silver lining'!" Unfortunately, if we follow the culture too closely, we will never benefit from our suffering, and worse, we will think that God is doing nothing—and does not care.

The temptation to believe that God is indifferent or uncaring in our times of suffering must be vigorously resisted, for if we fall prey to it, we will not be committed to prayer, be open to His inspiration and grace, or focused on the meaning, virtue, contribution, love, transcendence, and salvation to which He is leading us. By submitting to this temptation, in a state of cool resignation and insipient despair, we cut off the Holy Spirit, divine grace, and the lasting benefits of suffering.

An important clarification: most of the time, God does not directly *cause* suffering. He works through the suffering caused by ourselves, others, social structures, and nature (all of which will be discussed in detail later). When suffering happens, the Holy Spirit enters into our interior life and social surroundings and begins His work of guidance and inspiration. If we keep our eyes of faith open, we can receive the same kinds of grace as Saint Paul, Saint Augustine, Saint Francis, Saint Ignatius, and Saint Thérèse.

In conclusion, we must hold fast to the teaching of Jesus, who not only preached the love of His Father, but entered into suffering in every imaginable way to be with us in our times of pain, and to show us the way from darkness into light. Jesus suffered and died to solidify our trust in His and the Father's compassion, particularly during times of suffering and sin. Therefore, we will want to cultivate our patience, our focus on "the higher things", and our trust in God. We will have to reinforce our belief that God is filled with great compassion and love for us in our grief, pain, and challenges while He is working through our suffering to guide us toward higher meaning, deeper love, and greater wisdom—on our way to salvation.

How do we reconcile God's compassion with His "medicinal and pedagogical purpose" in times of suffering? As will be explained below, He has six objectives, four of which are primary and equally important. The other two are secondary and equally important on that plane. God's primary objectives are our salvation, others' salvation, the maintenance of our freedom, and the maintenance of others' freedom. His secondary objectives are the alleviation of our suffering and the alleviation of others' suffering. We might frame these six objectives, and two priorities, in a general concept—God will alleviate our and others' suffering in a way that will optimize salvation for all of us, without undermining our and others' freedom. The reverse is also compatible with Christian revelation—God will *not* alleviate our or others' suffering if it leads away from our or others' salvation or undermines our or others' freedom. So, for example, God will not perform a miracle if it undermines our or others' freedom or leads away from our or others' salvation.

Notice that God will not direct His compassion solely toward *our* personal salvation—He must be equally concerned with the salvation of others whose lives are affected by us. Similarly, God will not restrict His concern to maintaining *our* freedom; He must also maintain the freedom of those whom we touch—or will touch in the future. Thus when God alleviates our suffering, He finds a way to optimize salvation for all of us while maintaining our and other's freedom in doing so. He must also be conscious of how the alleviation of our personal suffering will affect the alleviation of others' suffering, and then He must optimize this sixfold objective not only in the present, but into the future, even the distant future. Orchestrating these six objectives (and two priorities) for the entire interconnected and interdependent human community is only within the capacity of a Being with unrestricted intelligence, power, and compassion. Thus, God's plan to alleviate suffering is completely beyond *our* capacity to understand. This leads us to Jesus' revision of the fourth strand of the Old Testament interpretation of suffering.

C. Jesus' Modification of the Fourth Strand of the Old Testament Interpretation of Suffering

The fourth strand of the Old Testament interpretation of suffering holds that suffering (and its alleviation by God) is an impenetrable mystery—and that we must simply trust in the justice and wisdom of God without, as Elihu says, arrogantly asserting the superiority of *our* view of justice and wisdom. Elihu's position is grounded in the unknowability of God's will to bring justice out of sin, innocence, reward, suffering, and punishment. Jesus makes this "calculus" even more unknowable by reinterpreting God's will for us and the world. He declares that God is interested in justice only insofar as it advances the cause of perfect forgiveness, compassion, and love. Though God seeks justice for all, He goes far beyond this by unendingly forgiving us for our sins, unceasingly loving us in our weakness, and unqualifiably helping us when we least deserve it—like the father of the prodigal son. How can we possibly understand God's will and plan for us without having a perfectly compassionate heart? Obviously, we cannot.

In view of this, we are even more challenged in our ability to comprehend God's plan. We would not only have to understand God's perfect justice and wisdom (as Elihu says); we would also have to comprehend perfect compassion and love. Additionally, we would have to understand how God is using His "conspiracy of providence" to achieve His sixfold objective in the alleviation of suffering for all people into the distant future. The unknowability of God's will and plan requires, as Elihu teaches, a fundamental act of humility before God. More than this, it requires, as Jesus says, a radical act of trust in God's perfectly compassionate and loving providential care.

Without these radical acts of humility and trust, we are likely to put our judgment about suffering above that of God—and given the limitations of our judgment, we are likely to be wrong, wrong about how God should bring about our and others' salvation, preserve our and others' freedom, and alleviate our and others' suffering. This will not only lead to multiple errors in judgment and choices along life's way, but will also likely cause a deep mistrust of God, a rupture in our relationship with Him, and a foreclosing of His grace in moving us and helping us on our path to salvation.

It may seem heartless for Elihu to have called Job arrogant for believing that he had been treated unjustly and abandoned by God, because Job was inflicted with pain and deprived of everything—yet he was innocent. Surely Elihu could have been a bit more compassionate toward Job in those circumstances. Perhaps so, but for Elihu, Job had crossed a line. It is one thing to *feel* abandoned by God, and quite another to accuse God of being unjust. When Job did this, he set his judgment and understanding above that of God's. For Elihu, this is not just a lack of humility; it is an unbelievably arrogant affront to God.

Though Jesus would agree with Elihu's concern that we be humble and respectful before God, He does so because the contrary will cause *us* great difficulty—and perhaps great harm. Accusing God of injustice is dangerous because, as noted above, it will likely lead to an abandonment of trust in God, anger toward Him, a rupture in our relationship with Him, and a foreclosure of His capacity to guide us and others to salvation through our suffering. Given Jesus' new perspective, we might conclude that His advocacy of radical humility and respect before God is essential for *our* peace, sanity, development, and salvation.

Can we glean anything form Elihu's judgment of Job in light of Christ's teaching? Yes, but it is a challenging truth. Though we may be justified in feeling abandoned, hurt, bewildered, angry, and depressed when confronted with seemingly undeserved suffering (by comparison with others), we cross a *self-destructive* line when we fail to remain humble before God's compassionate, wise, and salvific will for us. If we abandon a stance of humble trust and surrender to God, and succumb to outrage at seeming injustice, we move into a dark domain in which we no longer believe in His capacity or desire to help us—a domain of resentment and even hatred toward the One who loves us. This means we have no one to rely on besides ourselves and the human community. We begin to lose our sense of salvation and eternal life; we foreclose ourselves to His guidance, grace, and inspiration; and ultimately give ourselves over to this darkness—which can envelop us and take us into its emptiness and despair.

So how do we know when we are crossing the line from legitimate feelings of abandonment, anger, hurt, bewilderment, and depression into the dark domain that leads to despair? How do we know when our legitimate feelings of abandonment, anger, and bewilderment are becoming tainted with the arrogance that crosses the line into the domain of resentment, hatred, and nihilism? This occurs when we accuse God of being something that He is not—something contrary to the revelation of Jesus. Sometimes our feelings of abandonment, anger, and bewilderment generate accusatory thoughts against God— "*You* are not a just God; *you* are not compassionate. I don't care what anyone says!" or "*You* don't care about me or anyone else—if you did you would do something about this." Sometimes we explicitly express these accusations—but sometimes we hold them in, turning them over again and again in the back of our minds like a dark prayer of resentment. In either case, we turn our anger at a difficult *situation* into resentment and hatred *toward God*, our feelings of abandonment and hurt into rejection *of God*, and our feelings of sadness and depression into a rejection of the hope offered *by God*—moving us into despair. If we are to escape the clutches of radical despair, we will want to reverse course the moment we reflectively grasp its presence. This will entail turning back to God, asking for forgiveness, and opening ourselves to the salvation to which He will lead us—if we allow Him to do this *His* way.

Even if we enter into the dark zone of resentment and despair— and even if this causes us to abandon or reject God—we can always return to Him. As noted many times above, God continues to love us even in our most sinful and arrogant moments—even when we counterpoise our will to His, and even if we set ourselves up as His enemy.

Thus, if we find ourselves accusing God of injustice, and reflectively grasp our error—and our vulnerability in it—we can always return to Him like the prodigal son, assured of His acceptance, joy, and love.

D. Suffering and the Sin of Adam

There is one last lesson we can learn from Jesus and the Book of Job. When we or others ask why God has allowed suffering to happen in our lives, the *whole* answer is not contained in the simple response "It was the sin of Adam" (see Gen 2:17; 3:16, 19). Indeed, the Gospels and the Book of Job never make an appeal to the sin of Adam or the Fall to explain suffering. Instead, as noted above, the Book of Job appeals to the testing of people by Satan, the punishment of sinful people by God, the medicinal and pedagogical benefits of suffering, and the mystery and incomprehensibility of suffering. Jesus supersedes the first two reasons and comprehensively enhances the other two. As implied above, Jesus and the Christian Church teach three major benefits of suffering:

1. Suffering helps us to reach for higher meaning, deeper love, and eternal salvation (see Chapter 7).
2. Our choices in the midst of suffering and death help us to define our eternal identity (see Chapter 7).
3. Suffering can be turned into self-sacrificial love for the redemption of the world in imitation of Jesus (see Chapter 8).

Though Saint Paul appeals to the sin of Adam to explain both death and our concupiscence (see Rom 5:12, 19), he does not specifically connect suffering (beyond that of death and concupiscence) to it. His purpose for doing this is to show that death and concupiscence come through one man (Adam) and are redeemed through the love and grace of one man (Jesus Christ).

Yet, the question remains: Why didn't Jesus and the Book of Job appeal to the sin of Adam to explain suffering? Why did they give so many other alternative explanations? Apparently, the sin of Adam is not the *whole* reason for human suffering. The sin of Adam causes the fall of human nature—which in its original state was in harmony with God, other humans (i.e., Eve), and nature. Once the sin of Adam

occurred, all three of these harmonies were disrupted and undermined, leading to a state of *hardship* in our relationships with God,
others, and nature. This state of hardship is not definitive—in the
sense of our being condemned to experience *only* hardship in our
relationship with God, others, and nature. God provides a way to
mitigate these hardships, and to make our lives better—the discipline
of the law (which mitigates the adversity in our relationship with
Him and others) and the discipline of hard work and prudence which
enables us to cultivate and "civilize" nature. In this way, we can
be reasonably happy—experiencing moments of peace amid conflict
and war, and moments of surplus amid times of drought and severe
weather.

This is precisely the condition in which Job finds himself before
Satan convinced God to test the genuineness of his faith. Job was a
just man—a practitioner of virtue, the law, and hard work—and as
a result, he had a good family, many lands and possessions, and many
friends. Thus, the central question of the Book of Job is not, why is
there hardship in the world—friction between us, God, nature, and
one another? That question could have been answered by appealing to the sin of Adam in the Book of Genesis. Again, the question
is not, how did Job mitigate the hardships that came through the
sin of Adam so that he could have a reasonably happy life? This
question could have been answered by appealing to the promises of
Moses concerning the efficacy of the law and hard work in mitigating suffering and receiving God's promise of favor and prosperity.
The above two questions and their answers are *assumed* by the Book
of Job. So what is the central question of the Book of Job? Why
did the just man Job—who was prosperous and happy because he
followed the law, worked hard, and therefore enjoyed the favor of
God and the fruits of his labors—find himself in terrible suffering
and destitution? This is precisely the question that the vast majority
of us who are trying to be good and faithful people ask when deep
suffering afflicts us. To answer this question with the perfunctory
comment "You're suffering because of the sin of Adam" doesn't
answer the question. It only serves to frustrate people who are trying
to reconcile their attempts to follow virtue, the law, and the Lord
with seemingly undeserved and unexpected suffering. If we want to
answer *this third* question, then we will have to consider the third
and fourth strands of the Old Testament interpretation of suffering

in the Book of Job as well as Jesus' comprehensive enhancement of them. The elucidation of Jesus' answer is the purpose of this book.

III. God's Presence in Our Suffering—Seven Points

Bearing the above in mind, we may now craft a lens through which to view God's participation in our suffering and our response to Him. If we look through this lens when suffering comes, we will be predisposed to avoid the traps leading to resentment and rejection of God and, consequently, to apathy, malaise, and despair. We will also be disposed to follow the inspiration and guidance of the Lord to reach higher meaning in life, deeper love, and ultimately eternal salvation. This lens has seven filters that describe God's viewpoint during our suffering (according to Jesus) and how we can appropriately and beneficially respond to it. Commit these seven filters to mind and heart because they will help you through your pain into the salvation prepared for you from the beginning of time.

A. God's Six Objectives in Alleviating Suffering

By now it will probably be apparent that God's highest objective is not the immediate alleviation of our suffering. He has four higher objectives to consider while doing this: your salvation, others' salvation, the maintenance of your freedom, and the maintenance of others' freedom. Furthermore, while alleviating our personal suffering, He must also consider another objective: the alleviation of others' suffering. If we do not bear these six objectives in mind, we can fall into several traps from which we will find it difficult to extricate ourselves.

For example, we might ask the Lord, "Please just give me a miracle to alleviate my suffering", and then feel bewildered when He does not comply. We might think, "I'm not asking for the world, just a slight reversal of the genetic mutation leading to my eye disease; that shouldn't be too hard." Before concluding to God's absence or indifference, we may want to consider that such a miracle might not be good for us, that the challenges we or others face might actually help us to grow in empathy, compassion, higher purpose, humility, and courage—all of which might help us and others on the path to salvation. We may also want to consider that if God gives *us* a miracle, He might have to give others similar miracles for the sake of consistency, to avoid favoritism.

In order to give everybody a miracle, He would likely have to mitigate the whole domain of natural laws and forces. As a result, we would have no idea about what to expect from one moment to the next—after all, somebody next door could pray for a miracle and "poof!" the laws of nature are suspended again—and again—and again! Consider that if we live in such a world, we would never be able to predict the future, in which case we could not anticipate the consequences of our actions. As a result, we would not be able to make free rational choices. This would render meaningless our *plans* to do good, to avoid evil, and to be compassionate and contributive. Why even bother to get together with others for the sake of making the community or world a better place? All we would need to do is pray for a miracle—and "poof!"—all done! Evidently, this could undermine our freedom, creativity, collective efforts, and, yes, our path to salvation.

In sum, God would never alleviate our suffering in a way that could even slightly undermine our or others' path to salvation or our or others' freedom. Once the above four higher objectives are in the process of being met, He will then proceed to the alleviation of suffering for all of us. God's power and creativity to alleviate suffering amid these other four higher objectives cannot be underestimated—and so we must keep ourselves focused on the *unexpected* opportunities that arise in the midst of our suffering. The main point to remember is, if we trust in God, and His six objectives for the alleviation of suffering, then He will help us to grow through our suffering, help us to help others through their suffering, and bring us to His eternal fullness of joy and love.

B. God Loves Us Passionately and Compassionately in Our Suffering

The Lord views our suffering, even suffering caused by our sinfulness, with unmitigated compassion, like a perfectly loving parent—like the father of the prodigal son. Though God wants us to bear with our sufferings courageously by trusting in Him, He does not want us to become hardened stoics, devoid of feelings and insensitive to the feelings of others. God intimately understands our pain acutely like Jesus, who felt the pain of those He healed and forgave, and like the father of the prodigal son, who rushed out to meet his son with great joy, knowing the pain he must have suffered.

In the Gospel of John, Jesus proclaims that He and the Father are one (Jn 10:30) and that the Father is in Him, and He in the Father (Jn 10:38). He further declares that to see Him *is* to see the Father (Jn 14:9). We might infer from this that the Father and Jesus are not only united in being, but also united in their compassion—they experience one another and us through a similar affective lens. Thus, when we read in that same Gospel that "Jesus wept" at the death of His friend Lazarus—empathizing with the pain of Martha, Mary, and their friends (Jn 11:34–35)—we can legitimately attribute similar compassion to His Father, who shares His affective disposition. Furthermore when Jesus weeps over Jerusalem (Lk 14:41–44), we may infer that the Father also has similar compassion for the fate of His people. We may also infer that the Father empathizes with the pain of Jesus in the Garden of Gethsemane and every dimension of His Crucifixion. Thus, Jesus reveals that not only He, but His Father, intimately understands our pain. Thus, the Father draws close to us in sympathy and compassion during our times of suffering as Jesus did to Martha, Mary, and her friends.

Saint John of the Cross, Carmelite companion of St. Teresa of Avila describes God's compassionate and empathetic love as follows:

> ... [S]ince He is the virtue of supreme *humility*, He *loves you* with supreme humility and esteem and *makes you His equal*, gladly revealing Himself to you in these ways of knowledge, in this His countenance filled with graces, and telling you in this His union, not without great rejoicing: '*I am yours and for you* and *delighted* to be what I am so as to be yours *and give myself to you*.'[6]

As may by now be evident, God is not a loveless being, but quite the contrary—He is oriented in every way toward a single objective: unconditional love.

---

[6] Saint John of the Cross, 1979, "The Living Flame of Love" in *The Collected Works of Saint John of the Cross*, trans. Kieran Kavanaugh and Otilio Rodriguez (Washington, D.C.: ICS Publications), p. 613.

So how does God look upon us in our suffering? He draws close to us and enters into it. He cannot help Himself; this empathy and sympathy is intrinsic to His unconditionally loving nature. If we open ourselves to this fundamental disposition of God toward us, we will become more and more like Him—growing in empathy and sympathy for others in their suffering, and compassionately responding to it. As we become transformed in this love, we will share in His risen glory; as Saint Peter notes:

> In this you rejoice, though now for a little while you may have to suffer various trials, so that the genuineness of your faith, more precious than gold which though perishable is tested by fire, may redound to praise and glory and honor at the revelation of Jesus Christ. (1 Pet 1:6–7)

C. God Creates Us in an Imperfect World Filled with Challenges

The Lord created us in a condition that will *inevitably* present us with suffering and challenges. He gave us freedom and was well aware of our capacity to misuse it for the sake of selfishness and evil, which will cause suffering. He created us in an imperfect world that He knew would cause us hardship, challenges, and suffering. As noted above, His reason for doing this is not explained completely by the sin of Adam—which only explains how we came to be at odds with both nature and other people. The question in the Book of Job goes beyond this, because Job believes in the promises that God made to Moses—that if he is a just person, God would reward him with a life that is essentially happy and secure. Thus, Job's problem reflects the problem of most people today: If we have been essentially just and righteous people, then why are we being made to suffer? This question will be answered in this and the next three subsections. For the moment we will take the first part of the explanation: Why would God create an imperfect world that can cause challenges and suffering?

As we have said above, this imperfect world (with its inevitability of death) compels us to make choices sooner rather than later—choices that respond to our vulnerability and need, and to the vulnerability and need of others; choices to move to higher or lower levels of happiness and purpose in response to our fears, jealousies, ego-sensitivities, emptiness, and loneliness.

Thus, we should not be surprised when suffering comes, suffering caused by our personal choices, others' choices, and the natural world. When these sufferings come, we must be prepared to turn to the Lord in trust and to make the choices that suffering elicits from us—choices to move higher in our view of happiness and purpose; choices to develop humility, empathy, and compassion through our vulnerability and weakness; choices to help others in their suffering and need; and choices to build up the Kingdom of God and bring hope to the world. If we find ourselves doing the opposite—going to a lower view of happiness and purpose, growing in anger, resentment, and bitterness; undermining others in their weakness and vulnerability; and tearing down the Kingdom of God (as repayment for our "unjustified misery")—we should *stop* and consider the unconditional love of God, the eternal salvation He has prepared for us, and His six objectives in alleviating suffering. We should stop being shocked at our unexpected challenges and get about the creative and loving business of choosing to make the world a better place. If we do not, we will lose the deeper significance of our lives and relegate ourselves to a superficial world of bitterness, self-pity, and isolation. It need not be so, if we remember that suffering is inevitable and that it has a very loving divine purpose.

D. God Does Not Cause Suffering as a Punishment for Sin

As explained above (Section II.A), the unconditionally loving God revealed by Jesus does not cause suffering as a punishment for sin—not even egregious sin. Jesus declared that "God causes his sun to shine on *both* the good and the evil and causes his rain to fall on *both* the just and the unjust" (Mt 5:45; my translation), a declaration that reversed one thousand years of Jewish thought and doctrine. Furthermore, He forgives us more than seventy times seven times (a virtually limitless number), and the perfection of His love consists principally in His love (forgiveness) of enemies.

In view of this, we should resist the thought that suffering is punish-ment or retribution for our sins because it has been superseded by Jesus' solemn teaching. Hence when suffering comes, we should not say, "I deserve it—God is paying me back for what I did two years ago." When we say this, we ignore the teaching of Jesus and turn God into "the payback god". We then begin to believe that God is not inter-ested in alleviating our pain and helping us benefit from our suffering, but only in meting out justice. As a result, we exclude Him (and His grace) from our suffering, developing a callous or stoic resignation to deal with it. This will likely deafen us to the inspiration and guidance of the Holy Spirit, causing us to miss the major benefits that could have come from our suffering—a change of life, a new opportunity, a chance to grow in humility, empathy, compassion, and faith, and a chance to make a positive difference to the world and God's Kingdom.

Though we might believe that accepting our suffering as "just deserts for our sins" is an act of humble faith (and perhaps it is), it is nevertheless wrong about the mind and heart of God. It implies that God is more interested in doling out punishment than being compassionate—more interested in ensuring we receive our just des-erts than growing in love toward His Kingdom. Nothing could be further from the truth—and the more we persist in "believing" in this false God, the more our suffering will be wasted, our growth impeded, and our faith weakened. Thus when we find ourselves say-ing, "Well, I deserve it—I'm getting repaid for my sins," we must stop and consider the revelation of Jesus, who put compassion above punishment and love above justice.

E. God Does Not Directly Cause All Suffering

Most of the time God does not directly cause suffering. At first glance this may be confusing, because as noted above, the ancient Hebrew worldview assumed that God *directly causes* everything to happen in the natural world. If there's a thunderstorm, God caused it; if there is an earthquake, God caused it; and so forth. Jesus also seems to adhere to this worldview as seen in Matthew 5:45, for "he makes[7] his

---

[7] Literally, makes to arise His sun (*anatellei*—"*ana*" = "to make" and *tellei* = "to arise").

sun rise on the evil and on the good, and sends rain[8] on the just and the unjust."

So if Jesus believes that God causes the sun to shine and sends rain, who are *we* to say that He doesn't? We are not saying that God does not *ultimately* cause the sun to rise and the rain to fall—He certainly does since He is the cause of the *existence* of both the sun and the rain. However, according to the contemporary scientific worldview, God does not *directly* cause the sun to rise and the rain to fall. He could do these things, but prefers instead that they be generated by a series of *secondary causes* that operate through the natural laws and constants He designed and infused in the universe at its creation.

The idea of "secondary causation" is commensurate with Christian thought, and originated from it. Saint Thomas Aquinas discovered this idea by reconciling Aristotle's four causes with the requirements for personal freedom and the existence of chance events. Aquinas argued that God could not be the direct cause of every action in the world; otherwise, chance and personal freedom would be impossible.[9] Furthermore, Aristotle's teleological view of causation allowed natural objects to be responsible for their proper effects. Even though the first cause is necessary to ground the existence and motion of all subsequent causes, those subsequent causes—after being brought into existence and action—can actualize their own proper ends.[10] After synthesizing these concepts, Aquinas concluded that God (the First Cause) created the natural world so that various objects are responsible for causing their own proper effects and so they have *intrinsic* activity and qualities capable of achieving these ends. This central idea provided the intellectual framework for the emergence of natural science.[11]

---

[8] "Sends rain"—*brechei*. *Brechei* can mean either to rain or to send rain, but the latter is preferred because of the subject "He" ("God"). The former translation makes no sense with this subject—"He (God) rains on the just."

[9] Saint Thomas Aquinas, *Summa Theologica* I, q. 22, art. 2.

[10] See Saint Thomas Aquinas, *Commentary on Aristotle's Physics*, trans. Richard J. Blackwell, Richard J. Spath, and W. Edmund Thirlkel, Books I–II (New Haven, Conn.: Yale University Press, 1963), http://www.dhspriory.org/thomas/Physics.htm.

[11] See Stanley L. Jaki, *The Origin of Science and the Science of Its Origin* (Edinburgh: Scottish Academic Press, 1978). Jaki makes the case that secondary causation led to the methodology of natural science.

Aquinas' idea of secondary causation is intrinsic to contemporary physics and is an integral part of Big Bang cosmology.[12] According to this view, the parameters of all causation and natural objects were infused in the universe at the Big Bang 13.8 billion years ago. As the universe unfolded in its first second of existence, all four universal forces with their intrinsic qualities, magnitudes, and parameters expressed themselves independently—the gravitational force, then the strong nuclear force, then the weak force, and then the electromagnetic force. These forces interacted in universal space-time as the universe expanded, which eventually gave rise to the natural objects and forces we know today. Though the whole universe must be brought into being and maintained in being by God (the First Cause), the forces in the universe *can* act toward their proper ends as true causes. God did not have to create the universe in this way, but we surmise that He did—given the remarkable consistency of our physical laws throughout the history of the whole universe.

Of course God could interrupt, interfere with, or supersede these natural laws, by causing a miracle; however, we must assume that He does this only sparingly, for the reasons mentioned above. Recall that if He performed miracles regularly, we would not know what to expect, and if we did not know what to expect, we would not be able to be rational about future plans—in which case we would not be truly *free*. Recall also that God is always concerned to protect our freedom— for this is the only way that our love can be our own, allowing us to remain creatures made in the image and likeness of Him.

Is this distinction really important? I believe it is, because if we do not expect that God is going to allow natural laws and natural events to take their natural courses—and we believe that He is going to perform a miracle every few minutes (interrupting the laws of nature)— then we will have a *false* expectation of both God and nature, and this false expectation will lead to a belief that God *directly* causes pain, deprivation, and calamities, which *in fact*, He does not. Rather, God allows nature to follow its natural course so that we will know what to expect and thereby be able to deal with the natural world rationally and intelligently—allowing us to be free.

[12] See Volume II, Appendix I, of the Quartet for a detailed explanation of Big Bang cosmology.

Yes—God *does* perform miracles, but He does so within the framework of the six objectives mentioned above—the promotion of our and others' salvation, the preservation of our and others' freedom, and the alleviation of our and others' suffering. Miracles interrupt the possibility of rational expectations, and therefore the process of rational decision making intrinsic to freedom. So, if God performs a miracle knowing that it has the potential to undermine our and others' freedom—we can be sure that He does so because our or others' *salvation* is at stake.

Thus, it would not be wise to ask, "Why did you take my eyesight away?" or "Why didn't you prevent my tire from blowing out so I could have avoided an accident?" or "Why didn't you prevent the earthquake that killed so many people?" These questions ignore the world of natural causes and the six objectives of God in alleviating suffering. Recall that God did not *cause* these sufferings—He *allowed* them to occur through the natural forces and laws He created in our universe, and He did not prevent them, because it would have interfered in some way with the salvation and freedom of the people affected.

As we shall see (in Chapters 7 and 10), there are some things far worse than suffering and an imperfect world—such as a "perfect" world that offers no challenges to superficial definitions of happiness and purpose; no challenges to self-sufficiency, egocentricity, self-indulgence, and narcissism; and no challenges that require us and others to make a positive difference for the common good and the building of God's Kingdom. Such a "perfect world" would be filled with incredibly superficial people and would not elicit humility, compassion for the weak and needy, self-sacrifice for noble endeavors, and legacies left for the betterment of the world and God's Kingdom. As many theologians (beginning with Saint Paul) have reasoned, the world of suffering is a far better place than this "perfect world"—and a much better path to our eternal salvation (see 2 Cor 12:7–10).

So what is a wise way to approach suffering caused by natural forces? First, assume that this suffering occurred not because God directly caused it, but because it came from the natural course of natural forces and laws. Secondly, assume that a miracle is not essential for our or others' salvation—and so God decides instead to maintain the natural order for the sake of our freedom. Thirdly, ask the Lord to alleviate your suffering *within* the framework of *His* other *five objectives*—our and others' salvation, the preservation of our and others' freedom, and the alleviation of others' suffering. This will enable us to keep focused on how the Holy Spirit is working through our suffering, instead of being preoccupied by the false suppositions that God intentionally caused our suffering or intentionally did not give us a deserved or needed miracle.

If we keep ourselves focused on the way the Holy Spirit *really* works, we will begin to see the clues to what might be called the "conspiracy of divine providence", gradually manifesting itself in new opportunities to change our life's path and enhance our effectiveness and ability to serve the Kingdom. We will also discover a deepened awareness about happiness, purpose in life, freedom, love, authenticity, and virtue. At the same time, we will discover that our personal and others' suffering is being alleviated in the most unexpected, broadened, and deepened ways. If we keep ourselves focused on the way the Holy Spirit *really* works, we will be surprised—not by natural forces taking their natural course, but by supernatural grace bringing its immense scope of salvation and freedom into *our* personal life. This will no doubt be an adventure, leading toward the "breadth and length and height and depth" of the love of Christ (Eph 3:18)—an adventure opening upon the fullness of eternal joy with the unconditionally loving God.

At the beginning of this subsection, we noted that *most* of the time God does not *directly* cause suffering. Rather, it comes from our choices, others' choices, and an imperfect natural world. Does God *sometimes directly* cause suffering? He can—particularly when someone is on the path to self-destruction or the destruction of others. However, we must remember that if God does this, it would have to lead to salvation and could not interfere with freedom. Thus, instances of God directly causing suffering are quite rare. In the case of Saint Paul, Jesus caused him to be temporarily blinded. We must assume that this did not interfere with Paul's freedom to come into the Christian Church. Jesus must have been aware that Paul needed a "wake up call", to incite him to think and pray about the One he had been persecuting—which in turn led him, after three years in the desert, to a *free* choice to join and lead the Christian Church.

Examples like that of Saint Paul are difficult to find because the vast majority of suffering that happens to saints and ordinary Christians comes from the usual three nondivine causes—our choices, others' choices, and nature. For example, the emptiness that led Saint Augustine to find God came from *his* choice to stay away from Jesus, the commandments, and the Church; the cannonball that hit the leg of Saint Ignatius Loyola—though remarkably aimed—came from *his* choice to stand on the highest point of the fortress as well as the natural forces of propulsion and gravity working on cannonballs; the physical suffering endured by Saint Thérèse of Lisieux at the end of her life was due to the ordinary progression of tuberculosis; and the cosmic emptiness, loneliness, and alienation that incites many people to search for God is not caused directly by God but rather by their choice to ignore the transcendental part of their nature. In sum, the instances of God directly causing suffering are rare, because doing so generally undermines freedom—and sometimes the path to salvation.

F. God Is Especially Present to Us in Our Suffering

God does not leave us alone and abandoned in our suffering. It is perfectly natural to *feel* abandoned and alone when suffering comes, because suffering makes us turn in on ourselves—initially. At first, we focus on our pain and confusion—our interior states. This interior focus tends to isolate us from the outside world, suggesting that we are alone—and therefore abandoned.

However, there is a vast gulf between *feelings* and *rationality*—and valid as our feelings are, they do not and cannot represent the whole story, because they are *precognitional*—"*prior* to thinking". If we want the *whole* story, we will have to employ our *knowledge* of how God works through our suffering, which would include the above five subsections along with the present one. The New Testament is not alone in urging us to believe in the presence of God throughout our sufferings. Psalm 46 states this explicitly:

> God is our refuge and strength,
>   a *very present* help in trouble.
> Therefore we will not fear though the earth should change,
>   though the mountains shake in the heart of the sea....
>
> "Be still, and know that I am God.
>   I am exalted among the nations,
>   I am exalted in the earth!"
> The LORD of hosts is with us;
>   the God of Jacob is our refuge. (vv. 1–2, 10–11; emphasis
>   mine)

We see this also in Psalm 23:

> The LORD is my Shepherd, I shall not want....
> Even though I walk through the valley of the shadow of
>   death, I fear no evil;
> for you are with me; your rod and your staff, they comfort
>   me. (vv. 1, 4)

This is certainly the perspective of Jesus, in His own suffering. Recall from Volume III (Chapter 3) that Jesus' recitation of "My God, my God, why have you forsaken me?" (Mk 15:34) refers to the *whole* of Psalm 22. As we explained, this Psalm is a Psalm of hope—expressing a belief not only in God's presence during our times of suffering, but also in His bringing goodness and salvation (for the world) from it. It is instructive that the Psalm begins with *feelings* of abandonment and forsakenness, but then recounts the *knowledge* of how God was present and victorious in the sufferings of His people:

> In you our fathers trusted;
> they trusted, and you delivered them.
> To you they cried, and were saved;
> in you they trusted, and were not disappointed. (Ps 22:4–5)

The Psalmist then speaks of his *knowledge* that God is present in his suffering:

For he has not despised or abhorred the affliction of the
    afflicted;
and he has not hidden his face from him, but has heard,
    when he cried to him. (v. 24)

The Psalm concludes with God bringing goodness and salvation for
the world from the suffering of the Innocent One:

All the ends of the earth shall remember and turn to the
    LORD;
and all the families of the nations shall worship before
    him. . . .
To him, indeed, shall all who sleep in the earth bow
    down;
before him shall bow all who go down to the dust,
and he who cannot keep himself alive.
Posterity shall serve him;
men shall tell of the Lord to the coming generation,
and proclaim his deliverance to a people yet unborn,
saying that he has done it. (vv. 27, 29–31; my translation)

It is sometimes quite difficult to interrupt our initial feelings of
abandonment, isolation, dismay, or even frustration and anger to
allow rationality its proper place in our encounter with suffering.
Our initial feelings can be so powerful that they take over our consciousness. Nevertheless for our sake, the truth's sake, and the whole
story, we must cultivate a *discipline* of allowing rationality and knowledge into our otherwise occupied conscious space. No matter how
valid we believe our feelings to be, we cannot allow ourselves to be
persuaded that they contain the *whole* truth about suffering, and so we
must interrupt those feelings through an act of the will and prayer,
so that we can begin the process of remembering and thinking—
remembering the promises of Jesus, the words of the Psalms, and the
works of God throughout our lives.

As we begin this process of remembering and thinking, we will
notice a calming of our feelings, which occurs because our consciousness is now focused on something different—something cerebral,

positive, and reflective. We will notice something similar to the experience of the Psalmist in Psalm 22, who moves from feelings of abandonment to remembrance of the works of God in Israel, to belief in God's presence in his suffering, and to hope in the salvation and good that will come from it. And that makes all the difference!

There is a story entitled "Footprints in the Sand", which reflects the above transition from feelings to remembrance—then to reflection, and then to prayer, inspiration, and redemption:

> One night I had a dream. I dreamed I was walking along the beach with the Lord. Across the sky flashed scenes from my life. For each scene, I noticed two sets of footprints in the sand, one belonging to me and the other to the Lord. When the last scene of my life flashed before me, I looked back at the footprints in the sand. I noticed that many times along the path of my life there was only one set of footprints. I also noticed that it happened at the very lowest and saddest times of my life. This really bothered me and I questioned the Lord about it: "Lord, you said that once I decided to follow you, You'd walk with me all the way. But I have noticed that during the most troublesome times in in my life there is only one set of footprints. I don't understand why when I need you most you would leave me."
>
> The Lord replied: "My precious child, I love you and would never leave you. During your times of trial and suffering, when you see only one set of footprints, it was then that I carried you."[13]

In the future, when we are overwhelmed by feelings of abandonment and anger, we will want to call forth the discipline to interrupt those feelings with rationality and prayer. We will want to remember the promises of Jesus, the six objectives of God, the resurrection that awaits us, and the presence of Jesus in our suffering. These remembrances and thoughts form a doorway for God to enter into our consciousnesses during our suffering with peace, inspiration, and guidance toward an objective that we cannot clearly see. Nevertheless, we can be sure that the Holy Spirit will direct us toward new opportunities for the future, a heightened view of happiness and purpose, depth of virtue and love, and above all our eternal resurrection

[13] Mary Stevenson, "Footprints in the Sand". See Carolyn Carty's version at www.wowzone.com/fprints.htm.

in the love of Christ. If we fail to remember that God is and wants to be present to us in our sufferings—if we allow only the overwhelming feelings of pain to occupy our consciousness—we will screen out the important data of remembrance and thought, as well as the grace of the Holy Spirit coming through it. This will pave the way for us to enter into the eros of death, and nothing good will come from that. So give the Lord of love a chance—interrupt the feelings of grief and pain, remember the revelation of Jesus, and follow the inspiration that proceeds from it, even if you do not see it clearly. You will not be disappointed by the result.

G. Humility and Trust—Give God the Benefit of the Doubt

The preceding six points were concerned with how *God* is present in our suffering. This final point is concerned mostly with *us*, how we can best connect with God in our suffering. To do this, we might return to the advice of Elihu to Job—that the safest and truest stance we can have before God in our suffering is *humility*. As we have noted many times above, we cannot possibly know how God is operating through our and others' suffering, because we do not understand perfectly our and others' past, present, and future, the path to our and others' salvation, the preservation of our and others' freedom, and the alleviation of our and others' suffering. Furthermore, we have cloudy minds and hearts—which give rise to cloudy judgments, making it virtually impossible to understand God's perfect justice and compassion in the light of the perfect eternal love and joy He desires to give us. As Elihu implies, if we are *not* humble, we are likely to be far from the truth about God, ourselves, and our neighbor—we would be living in the context of inauthenticity and falsity, which is likely to undermine everything we are, do, and seek.

Jesus adds another dimension to Elihu's sage advice: trust. When a synagogue leader came to Jesus asking Him to heal his daughter, the report came that she had already died. Jesus responds by telling the synagogue leader, "Fear is useless—what is needed is trust" (Mk 5:36; Lk 8:50; my translation). We will discuss Jesus' repudiation of "fear" in Chapter 5; for the moment, we will look only into "trust". The Greek word translated as "trust" in Mark 5:36 and Luke 8:50 is *pisteue* (from *pisteuo*)—which means "belief" in the special New Testament sense. According to the *New American Standard New Testament Greek Lexicon*, this special sense denotes "the conviction and trust to which a man is impelled by a certain inner and higher prerogative and law of soul".[14]

When Jesus used this term, He did so, not only in the sense of "trusting in the wisdom and power of God," but also "trusting in the loving *heart* and providence of His Father". This trust in both the power and loving intent of God can dispel not only fear, but also the feelings of abandonment, isolation, anger, and resentment. It is a trust grounded in love—an awareness of God's and Jesus' loving intent.

This trust goes further than Elihu's humility. Notice that humility originates from within ourselves. When we recognize the infinite wisdom, intelligence, and power of God, we accept our inability to understand fully who He is, how He thinks, and how He works. It is like praying, "I will defer to your judgment, Lord, because I do *not* understand your unsurpassable mind and power." Though this stance is true and wise, it stops short of recognizing any real qualities or characteristics of God—preferring, as it were, to stand at a distance, acknowledging complete inadequacy.

Jesus' advocacy of trust (in the above sense) complements Elihu's distant stance. Jesus invites us into the *heart* of God by revealing His name (His essence) to be Abba (Daddy)—the Father of the Prodigal Son. Though Jesus would agree with Elihu that no person can possibly understand the mind and power of God, he would say that we have the capacity to partially understand the *heart* of God. He goes even further when he implies that we can know the heart of the Father enough to trust that He would not do anything contrary to perfect love and our salvation. This trust—working with the grace of God—can reduce, and sometimes dispel, fear, grief, abandonment, isolation, anger, and resentment. It is trust not built on *our* thoughts and will alone but rather on a *relationship* with the loving God—a relationship grounded in the revelation, Crucifixion, and Resurrection of Jesus—all of which combine to show not only the truth of

---

[14] *New American Standard New Testament Greek Lexicon*, s.v. "Pisteuo", accessed January 17, 2016, http://www.biblestudytools.com/lexicons/greek/nas/pisteuo.html.

His preaching, but also His divine power and status, and through these, the efficacy of His and the Father's perfect love.

When we open ourselves to Jesus' words and build a relationship with Him and His Father, our trust grows. It can grow so profoundly that we not only believe in God's presence and grace in our suffering— we *know* it; we become aware of His peace, sensing that everything is going to be okay; everything is going to be brought into the love and consolation of God's eternal salvation, brought about in His own way, in His own time, and assuredly brought about if we but trust in Him. This will be taken up extensively in Chapter 9 (Section I. B).

H. Five Habits of the Heart

So how might we summarize the combined advice of Elihu and Jesus in forming our attitude before God in times of suffering? How might we best connect with God so that we might best experience His consolation, grow from our suffering, help the world and the Kingdom of God, and inherit the salvation prepared for us by Him? We might develop five habits of the heart.

First, it is prudent to avoid unjustified accusations against God's justice, love, compassion, and salvific intent in times of our and others' suffering. These accusations are born of a false pretention to know more about God, His plan, and His justice and love than we could possibly know. Such pretentions as Elihu suggests lead us into a fog of inauthenticity, hubris, and unwarranted self-reliance, which is destined to fail. They cannot bring us to our true dignity (made in the image and likeness of God) and our true destiny (eternal salvation with the loving God); they will only give us feelings of anger and resentment that separate us from the God who is trying to help us.

Second, in times of suffering—and indeed at all times—assume a posture of humility before the wisdom, justice, and power of God. We do not do this because God wants us to "grovel" before His superior presence—God has absolutely no interest in our groveling. He is hoping that we will recognize His love and accept His invitation to draw closer to Him in that love. So why should we be humble before His presence? For the reasons suggested by Elihu: it is the truth, and if we don't live according to that truth, we are likely to rely on ourselves more than Him—to do it "our way" instead of "His way".

Yet if His way is the way of infinite wisdom and love, then humility will lead us to our true dignity, happiness, fulfillment, and destiny, in which case humility is not a surrender out of fear to the overwhelming power of God but rather a surrender in love to the compassionate heart of God. Humility is not a crushing defeat, but a liberating victory.

Elihu did not know this last point about humility—he recognized it solely for its truth. However, Jesus builds on this truth by revealing the loving heart of the Father that gives rise to another truth—that surrender to God is not humiliation, but rather liberation into the perfectly loving will of God.

Third, in light of Jesus' revelation of His and the Father's love, we will want to give God the benefit of the doubt in times of suffering. Jesus' revelation is supported by His ministry of healing, exorcisms, and raising of the dead, as well as His Crucifixion, which all manifest His unconditional love. It is also supported by His promise of our resurrection, for which there is considerable evidence (see Chapter 1).[15] In light of this revelation (and the evidence for it), we can make a *rational* judgment to trust in the God of Jesus Christ, even when we *feel* completely alone, abandoned, depressed, and resentful. This process is discussed in Chapter 9 (Section I.B).

During the times when our emotional state might be at the point of boiling over or giving up, rationality can step in to bring God's promises and grace into focus, which can lead to a sense of calm. As noted above, this may require an act of the will to interrupt the flow of negative emotions that can get carried away by a curious masochistic fascination. The strange pleasure that can come from our negative emotions may be described as "the eros of death", the pleasure of considering our ultimate demise to be our ultimate act of freedom. Before we reach such a state, we must stop ourselves in our tracks with an act of *fiat* ("Let it be done") that dictates, "I will not indulge this death-dealing pleasure anymore!"

---

[15] Chapter 1 contains a summary of this evidence from historical criteria, the Shroud of Turin, near-death experiences, and miracles done in the name of Jesus. This evidence is discussed in much greater detail in Volume II, Chapter 5 (near-death experiences) and Volume III, Chapter 4 (historical criteria), Volume III, Chapter 5 (contemporary miracles done in the name of Jesus), and Volume III, Appendix I (Shroud of Turin).

Fourth, when the interruption of our negative feelings has momentarily occurred, we must use another act of the will to introduce *rationality* into our consciousness: we need to think about the unconditional love and promises of Jesus. Depending on our personality, we might do this by considering His promises to redeem our suffering: "Blessed are the sorrowing [grieving], for they *shall* be comforted" (Mt 5:4; translation mine). We might also take a more contemplative approach and consider Jesus entering into our suffering through His Passion and Cross, to sacrifice Himself completely for us in an unconditional act of love (see Chapter 8). We could also take a more analytical approach and consider the evidence for Jesus' Resurrection that is manifest in historical criteria, new scientific evidence on the Shroud of Turin, contemporary medical studies of near-death experiences, and medical studies of miracles done in His name (see Chapter 1). Whatever we choose, we must let our minds do "some of the talking", as well as our hearts, and in light of this, to give God the benefit of the doubt. At this point, our minds will be liberating our hearts, which will allow our hearts to liberate our minds.

Fifth, let God's grace into the process through prayer. I would suggest any combination of the spontaneous prayers given in the next chapter. Repeat these prayers until you sense the peace of the Lord beginning to dawn in your consciousness, and then pledge your trust to Him. Once you have made this pledge of trust, begin the creative and loving discipline of looking for the ways the Holy Spirit is leading you—the new paths He might be opening, the old paths He might be closing, the new heights of happiness and purpose He may be inspiring, the new depth of love He may be encouraging, and the new ways of serving the world and the Kingdom, to which He may be guiding. We will take all of this up in detail in Chapters 6–9.

IV. Conclusion

The above considerations complete Phase I of our approach to suffering—theological preparation. If we maintain a strong rational belief in the resurrection and the unconditional love of God (Chapters 1 and 2), avoid the six false notions of God that destroy our relationship with Him (Chapter 2), and believe in Jesus' revelation about God's presence in our suffering (this chapter), we will not only be able to constructively contend with suffering in the short-term (Phase II, Chapters 4–5), but also optimally benefit from it in the long-term (Phase III, Chapters 6–9). We now turn to the second phase of "suffering well"—spontaneous prayers, mitigating fear, and choosing consolation.

PHASE TWO

Contending with Suffering in the Short-Term

Foundations 4–5

Chapter Four

"Take This Cup Away from Me"

Fourth Foundation: Spontaneous Prayers in Times of Suffering

Introduction

We now proceed to the fourth Christian foundation for suffering well—prayer. In the previous chapter, we tried to paint a general picture of how God is present to us in our suffering, by looking at His six objectives, the compassion He feels for us, and the way He works through our humility and trust. We also looked at some of the erroneous views of God's interaction with our suffering— God causing suffering to punish sin, directly causing all natural occurrences, and being stoically indifferent. We further examined some healthy and unhealthy attitudes toward suffering, and how these positively and negatively affect the ways God can work through suffering. We concluded with some thoughts about going beyond the domain of negative feelings when suffering strikes, paying special attention to the role of rationality as a conduit for grace and consolation. These attitudes and dispositions about God and ourselves can help us avoid useless anxieties and resentments and prepare us to deal with and benefit from our suffering.

Spontaneous prayers are short (one to ten words) and therefore easily remembered and recalled. They can be recited several times, particularly when we are overcome by fear and anxiety. They call us out of ourselves and invite the Lord into our consciousness. Since God immediately responds to our pleas for help, these prayers produce remarkable results, even if we do not recognize them right away. Sometimes the grace of these prayers can be felt and seen quite rapidly. The most common manifestations of this quick grace are

- a sense of peace, indicating "everything is going to be okay", and
- a sense of direction about the future.

The peace coming from prayer and grace can be quite palpable. Much of the time, we know we are not producing this peace by ourselves, but that there is another personal Being connecting with, inspiring, and guiding us. This peace can mitigate our feelings of fear and anxiety, and fill us with a sense of confidence and hope in the future.

The second manifestation of "quick grace" is a general sense of where the future may lead. This is often accompanied by confidence that God is leading us toward that future. It is by no means a clear intuition or thought about the future, but more like a conviction about the *direction* to which God is pointing us. It is very much like God's request of Abraham:

> Now the LORD said to Abram, "Go from your country and your kindred and your father's house to the land that I will show you. And I will make of you a great nation, and I will bless you, and make your name great, so that you will be a blessing. I will bless those who bless you, and him who curses you I will curse; and by you all the families of the earth shall bless themselves." (Gen 12:1–3)

God asks Abram to leave everything he knows—his country, family, and livelihood—and go to an unspecified place that He will show him. At this point, Abram has a direction and a promise, and as he follows it, it becomes clearer and clearer. Through faith, we can make Abram's experience of following the Lord our own.

When we come face-to-face with suffering, repeated short prayers are perhaps the best ones that will provide a conduit to God's grace—not because God can't work through long prayers, but because we are not in a peaceful enough frame of mind to compose them. Remember, as *The Cloud of Unknowing* states, "A short prayer pierces the heavens."[1]

So what are these prayers that become a conduit for God's peace and guidance? There are fifteen of them, which I and others have

---

[1] Anonymous, *The Cloud of Unknowing*, ed. James Walsh (New York: Paulist Press, 1981), p. 193.

found very useful (see the chart at the end of this chapter). However, they should be viewed as only a "starter selection".[2] The reader will want to edit them according to preference, and add to them as well. If the reader can remember no other prayer, then commit to memory the final one in this list, "Thy loving will be done." As will be seen, it is the prayer of Jesus and sums up all other spontaneous prayers in times of fear and anxiety.

I. Prayers for Help

We should not disregard simple prayers, because *God* does not disregard them. Throughout the New Testament Jesus responds to the simplest pleas with an outpouring of compassion and healing power. Bartimaeus, the blind man by the side of the road, is calling after Jesus, "Son of David, have mercy on me!" Although he is rebuked and told to be quiet, he continues to cry out, repeating his plea for mercy. Jesus then tells His disciples to call Bartimaeus. When Bartimaeus meets Jesus, Jesus asks, "What do you want me to do for you?" To which Bartimaeus responds, "Master, let me receive my sight." Jesus says immediately, "Go your way; your faith has made you well" (Mk 10:47–52). In another passage, the father of a demoniac begs Jesus to help his son, pleading, "[I]f you can do anything, have pity on us and help us." Jesus responds, "If you can! All things are possible to him who believes." The father then answers, "I believe; help my unbelief!"—at which point Jesus expels the unclean spirit (Mk 9:22–25). We see the very same pattern again when a man with leprosy kneels before Jesus and says, "If you will, you can make me clean." Jesus responds, "I do will it. Be made clean" (Mk 1:40, NAB).

Notice that these individuals are at the margins of society and have become accustomed to being ignored. They probably did not believe they deserve to be heard—let alone receive a healing. Bartimaeus is told to be quiet, but Jesus alone hears him, acknowledges him, and heals him. The demoniac and his father are probably viewed

---

[2] The spontaneous prayers given in this book are focused on suffering. In the sequel to this Quartet entitled *Called out of Darkness: Contending with Evil through Virtue and Prayer* (San Francisco: Ignatius Press, forthcoming), I consider other spontaneous prayers concerned with temptations, forgiveness, and contending with evil.

as sinners because of the son's possession by an unclean spirit, but Jesus approaches the growing crowd and engages the boy's father: "How long has he had this?" (Mk 9:21). He not only hears the man's plea but cares enough about the boy to inquire about him and exorcise him. The leper is viewed as an "untouchable" who is supposed to keep his distance from everyone, but Jesus touches him and then heals him.

A. God Hears and Answers Our Prayers for Help

In view of these healings and many others in the New Testament, we must assume that Jesus is attentive to us—no matter what our station or condition in life—and that He wants to hear us, and in fact does hear us when we make even the simplest of pleas: "Lord, please help me." When we turn to Him in faith and need, He immediately responds by giving us relief that will not undermine our salvation and freedom.

There is nothing wrong with repeating the request multiple times every day; the Lord does not get tired of it or find fault with us asking. However, by repeating it many times, we will probably not be able to make the Lord go faster, particularly if going faster will undermine our or others' salvation or freedom.

As always, we will want to look for the signs of opportunity to change our life; go on new paths; deepen our humility, compassion, love, and faith; and increase our service to others, the common good, and the Kingdom of God. These signs may not manifest themselves in the way we might expect or according to the timing we prefer, but we must keep our eyes focused on the doors opening before us, even for weeks and sometimes months, for God will not disappoint us. When we see the open doors, we will want to use the rules for discernment given in Chapter 9 (Section II).

B. Does God Want Us to Suffer?

Many faithful people are hesitant to pray for help because of misconceptions and questions about the will of God. The most challenging misconceptions come from the question, does God want us to suffer?

The term "want" here has many levels. On one level, Jesus' revelation indicates that God does *not* want us to suffer. He is not indifferent to our pain, grief, anxiety, and debilitation. Indeed, Jesus entered into suffering to reveal its dignity and efficacy; His Father is present to us in our suffering, empathizing with us in the same way as loving parents. Furthermore, He sends His Holy Spirit to guide us through it to our true dignity and destiny. So we might say that on the level of God's empathy and sympathy, He does *not* want us to suffer any more than loving parents *want* their children to suffer.

Yet just as loving parents *allow* their children to enter into situations that might cause suffering (e.g., going to school, playing sports, taking on a challenging task, etc.), God *allows* us to enter into situations that could cause suffering. Why? Because such challenges can lead to growth, knowledge, emotional maturity, friendships, associations, courage, fortitude, prudence, and a myriad of other skills and virtues needed to move from childhood to fully contributive adults. Yet, God *wants* far more from our suffering than mere maturity toward adulthood; He *wants* our eternal salvation—He *wants* choices that will not only bring us to the fullness of eternal and unconditional love, but those that will help others to that same eternal dignity. And so God allows us to enter into an imperfect world with unjust people to provide the challenging context in which choices must be made, choices that will lead to eternal self-definition—choices that open upon empathy, humility, compassion, contribution, transcendence, faith, and ultimately, salvation.

So, does God *want* us to suffer? On one level, He does not want us to feel pain and discomfort, but on another level, like loving parents, He *allows* us to enter into challenging situations so that we might freely choose the eternal and unconditionally loving destiny for which He has prepared us. A more detailed explanation of why God allows us to experience suffering will be taken up in Chapters 7 and 10, but a brief explanation here may help readers to pray more effectively and efficaciously during times of suffering. There are three dimensions to this question which require different answers:

1. Why does God allow us to cause suffering to *others*?
2. Why does God allow us to cause suffering to *ourselves*?
3. Why does God allow *nature* to cause suffering to us?

We will discuss each in turn.

1. *Why does God allow us to cause suffering to* others? He does this to maintain our *freedom*, so that our love can be our own. If God did not allow us to cause suffering to other people, He would not have allowed us to *choose* loving acts over against the possibility of *choosing* nonloving acts, and if He did not allow us this choice, then our love would not be our own; it would not originate within us. We would be reduced to mere robots *programmed* for love alone by the "Divine Programmer". Mere robots are not enough for God, who intends to create us in *His* own image. Thus, in order for God to create us with this ultimate dignity, He has to allow us the possibility of choosing nonloving activities, so that our love could originate from within us and be our own. When He gave us the possibility of choosing nonloving activities, He allowed us to cause suffering to others. God has no other option—if He does not want to create mere robots, He must allow us the possibility of causing suffering to others.[3]

2. *Why does God allow us to cause suffering to* ourselves? He does this because we must have the possibility of freely choosing actions, attitudes, identity, and purpose that are superficial, egotistical, self-absorbed, unvirtuous, heartless, and self-idolatrous, so that our choice to do the opposite—to be compassionate, humble, contributive, virtuous, and faith-filled—will be *our own*. This follows from the same kind of reasoning used to respond to the first question. Note that superficial, egotistical, self-absorbed, unvirtuous, heartless, and self-idolatrous attitudes and identity produce emptiness and the negative emotions of the comparison game (see Chapter 7, Section II).[4] These negative feelings will persist and grow if people do not choose Levels Three and Four. If God did not allow us to choose superficiality and egocentricity—leading to the pain of emptiness and the comparison game—we would not be able to choose compassion, contribution, transcendence, and faith as our main purpose

[3] See Chapter 10 (Section I) for a detailed explanation.
[4] For an extensive explanation of these negative emotions, see Volume I, Chapter 3.

and self-identity. These positive attitudes and behaviors would therefore not originate from within us, but only from the "Divine Programmer".

3. *Why does God allow* nature *to cause suffering?* God creates us in an *imperfect* natural condition so that there will be vulnerability and need in the world. This vulnerability and need provide the *opportunity* to be compassionate, contributive, courageous, and self-sacrificing. Vulnerability and need also make it difficult for anyone to be self-sufficient, and so they provide the opportunity to care for others and receive care, to be compassionate and receive compassion, to sacrifice ourselves and to receive others' self-sacrifice (see Chapter 10, Section II.B). They also call us into an interdependent community to support common cause for the common good (see Chapter 10, Section II.A). Vulnerability and need also provide the opportunity to turn to *God* not only for our *ultimate* fulfillment, but also for the inspiration and grace to freely move toward that fulfillment (see Chapter 7, Section II.B).

So let's review: Does God want us to suffer? God does not *want* us to experience pain, deprivation, grief, and hardship any more than a good parent. He *allows* suffering so that we can have the freedom to make our love our own, so that it will not be only the instructions of a divine programmer. He also allows suffering so that we can freely choose the attitudes that will give us meaning, purpose, and identity in life, such as choosing which of the four levels of happiness will be the most important. Finally, He allows suffering to create a condition of weakness and vulnerability that requires a response of either egoism or love, hard-heartedness or compassion, exploitation or service of the weak, in order to enter into a common cause for the good or to do nothing, to petition God for help or to play "God" for the vulnerable.

This gives rise to another question: If God doesn't want us to suffer, then why doesn't He alleviate it more *quickly?* As noted in Chapter 3 (Sections II and III), God alleviates suffering within the framework of His six objectives, the first four of which are higher priorities than the alleviation of suffering—the promotion of our own and others' salvation, the protection of our own and others' freedom, and *then* the alleviation of our own and others' suffering.

Within the contours of these six objectives God *will* alleviate our suffering as quickly as possible. Some may conjecture that God could "speed things up" by working a few more *miracles*, but as explained in the previous chapter, God works only as many miracles as His six objectives will allow. For example, if our suffering is helping us to define our purpose in life (toward Levels Three and Four), then alleviating that suffering too quickly with a miracle would interfere with His first objective. Similarly, if God performs too many miracles, then we would not have any sense of what the future would bring—and if we cannot anticipate our future, we cannot make informed free choices. Given that God is much more aware of our needs and futures—relative to our salvation and freedom—it is best not to second-guess why, when, and where He will work a miracle.

We are now led to yet another question: Doesn't God expect us to help ourselves? Yes, God does expect us to use our intelligence, learning, energy, creativity, friendships, and any other procurable resource to protect ourselves from suffering as well as a means to alleviate it. He gave us natural powers and abilities to help ourselves and others—and so we must presume that He means for us to use those abilities. Thus when we are suffering or encounter others' suffering, He does not expect us to "shut up, ignore it, and take it", or to subscribe to the spirituality of "we will just sit here and wait while He takes care of our problems." This would be tantamount to encouraging us to be like children who avoid homework and studying, and then pray before an exam, "Lord, please give me the right answers." Rather, God wants us to develop our natural powers and virtues from repeated *choices*. He would not do anything to undermine the process of developing virtue—for this is essential to our eternal self-definition.

So if God expects us to help ourselves, why ask for help? Even though God expects us to use our capabilities, make free decisions and choices toward the good, and work toward our goals and objectives, He is well aware of the fact that many things are beyond our control. He knows we need His help, and He wants to help us; yet He will not force that help on us, and so He frequently waits for us to ask Him. Sometimes He acts without our asking, particularly when we are headed for imminent trouble, but most of the time He reflects the intention of Jesus, who awaited the freedom and faith of those who asked for healing.

God will not disappoint us. When we ask for His help in faith, He responds according to His six objectives. I have lived my life with this expectation, and as I look back on it now—more aware of what God must do to secure our salvation and freedom—I can see clearly that He has not disappointed me. Of course, I cannot see everything in the past with perfect clarity, because I cannot possibly know all the intersections between my own and others' salvation and freedom, but from what little I can see (literally and figuratively), His providence seems remarkably clear, and so I have become accustomed to expecting it.

We are now in a position to ask one of the favorite questions of my doctoral dissertation director, Paul Weiss: Why does God want us to pray for our needs? If He is omniscient and He loves us, why doesn't He simply anticipate our needs and take care of them *before* we ask Him? The basic answer is, once again, human freedom. God does not want us to pray because *He* is in need of additional supplications, but rather because He wants *us* to want and choose His help *freely*. If we do not expressly ask for His help, then we constrain Him to *impose* His help on us, which He typically will not do.

If a relationship with God matters to us, then it will not be difficult to pray for His help, and if we pray for His help, He will not have to impose Himself on us, for we have freely allowed Him to come into our lives. Alternatively, if a relationship with God really doesn't matter to us, then asking for His help would be difficult, either because we would not think to do it or we might feel uncomfortable about asking a stranger to help us. Thus, our freedom comes into play *before* our prayers of petition, because those prayers presume that we freely want and choose to be in a relationship with God that will make praying natural, rather than unnatural and difficult.

We now come to a question that bothers many faithful Christians: Isn't it presumptuous to ask God to protect us from suffering or to help alleviate it quickly? Shouldn't we just accept the suffering that comes our way and contend with it patiently and quietly? Isn't it wrong to try to escape suffering and avoid the cross? This view is often complemented by the thought that asking God to prevent or alleviate suffering is unworthy—and that we should take life's and God's crosses with humility and appreciation. Though we should accept our crosses with humility and trust, the idea that "asking for God's help is unworthy" is simply *wrong*. We can adduce this from

Jesus' view of God, His prayer in the Garden of Gethsemane, and the Our Father.

Let's begin with Jesus' view of God. The view that it is unworthy to ask God for help in times of suffering does not come from Jesus, but rather from one of the false notions of God discussed in Chapter 2, "the stoic god". As noted there, this view conflicts with Jesus' revelation of God as Abba—the Father of the Prodigal Son and His views of love (empathy, humility, and compassion) as the highest "commandment". God is not asking us to "quit whimpering and take the pain", but to trust Him and follow His Spirit on the path to love and salvation; He is not asking us to develop granite faces and hearts of stone, but hearts of compassion like that of the Good Samaritan. Yes, Jesus and His Father ask us to bear with our sufferings trustingly, patiently, and courageously, but always within the context of our loving relationship with them. Our courage, patience, and trust should not be borne out of stoic strength, but out of reliance on God's love, guidance, protection, and salvific intention.

In sum, Jesus' view of God is antithetical to the stoic one, and when we combine this with God's deep compassion and love, it becomes clear that God *really does* want us to pray that suffering *not* befall us. This prayer is subject to the condition mentioned above: the avoidance of suffering cannot impede our salvation—or our freedom.

C. *"Abba, . . . Take This Cup Away from Me"*
(Mk 14:36, NAB)

Jesus' prayer in the Garden of Gethsemane shows definitively that prayers for the avoidance or lessening of suffering are *not* unworthy of us, or incommensurate with God's will. The Synoptic Gospels have three versions of this prayer, but Mark's version is probably the first to be composed, reflecting Jesus' original prayer.[5] Each version

---

[5] Notice that Mark uses "Abba", Jesus' personal, familiar, and trusting address of His Father. Matthew uses "my Father", which is an "Abba" substitute in the context of a prayer of Jesus. According to Jeremias, "We have every reason to suppose that an *Abba* underlies every instance of *pater* (*mou*) or *ho patēr* in his words of prayer." Joachim Jeremias, *New Testament Theology*, vol. 1 (New York: Charles Scribner and Sons, 1971), p. 65. Mark's retention of the Aramaic "Abba" suggests that his version is the original prayer uttered by Jesus.

is instructive for the Christian view of suffering. My italics below indicate the points of difference.

- Mark 14:36: "Abba, Father, *all things* are possible to you; *remove* this chalice from me; yet not what I will, but what you will."
- Matthew 26:39: "My Father, *if* it be possible, *let* this chalice *pass* from me; nevertheless, not as I will, but as thou will."
- Luke 22:42, NAB: "Father, *if* you are *willing, take* this cup away from me; still, not my will, but yours, be done" (emphasis mine).

These three versions of Jesus' prayer reflect differences in tone and spirituality. Assuming that Mark's version is closest to that of Jesus' (because of the Abba reference—see note 5 above), it is worth noting how direct and confident Jesus' petition to the Father is—so much so, that Matthew and Luke "tone it down". In Mark's version, Jesus uses the familiar name "Abba", after which He says that "all things are possible to you". Why would Jesus tell His Father something He already knew? He is giving a rationale for His request. We might phrase it this way: "Abba, Father, [*since*] all things are possible for you, take this cup away from me."

Matthew softens this petition in two ways. First, he changes Jesus' assertion ("all things are possible to you") into a conditional form— "*if* it be possible". Second, he changes the *direct* request, "take this cup away from me", to "*let* this cup pass from me". In Matthew's Gospel, Jesus does not ask the Father *directly* to *intervene* on His behalf ("take this cup from me"), but *only* to allow it to "pass from Him".

Luke has the same inclination as Matthew, and puts the request in the conditional—"*if* you are *willing*". He specifies Matthew's conditional "if it be possible" as the Father's volition. This reflects the last part of the prayer—"still, not my will, but yours, be done." By emphasizing Jesus' openness to the Father's will, Luke deemphasized Jesus' direct and confident appeal to the Father (in Mark).

When we contrast Mark's version with that of Luke's, we feel the internal tension between the two parts of Jesus' prayer: "take this cup away from me" and "still, not my will, but yours, be done." Though Luke's version puts the emphasis on God's will, we should not lose the directness of Jesus' request reflected in Mark—"all things are possible to you; *remove* this chalice from me". Why is this relevant? If *Jesus* can make an assertive, direct, and confident request of the Father to take away His suffering, then it could not be an offense, a disappointment, a dishonor, or a presumption (transgressing the limits of what is appropriate or permissible) for *us* to do so. The conclusion seems inescapable: there is nothing wrong with asking God to "take our cup of suffering away from us" so long as we add Jesus' caveat: "but not what I will but what you will." We may be confident in following Jesus' example to do so.

This confidence is also manifest in the final petition of the Our Father. The last two lines of the Our Father are rendered in English as "lead us not into temptation, but deliver us from evil." This is a misleading translation, even though it is old and venerable, because the contemporary meaning of temptation would suggest that God is leading us toward a situation of sin. Evidently this is not the will or objective of God, but that of His adversary—the Evil One. So, how should these two lines be translated? The Greek verse may be literally translated as follows: "And do not be bringing us into [*eisenegkEs*] the trial [*peirasmon*] but rescue us [*nusai*] from the evil one [*ponErou*]." Though *peirasmon* (trial) can mean temptation interiorly into sin, it does not fit this context for the reason mentioned above. A better translation is "trial", which means an adversity, affliction, or trouble that can test or prove the faith or holiness of believers.[6] So what is Jesus telling us to pray for? Pray that you not be subject to any affliction, adversity, or trouble that would put your faith to the test. He then adds that we should pray also to be rescued from the Evil One.

Once again we see Jesus encouraging us to ask for relief from trials, suffering, and evil: "Abba, Father, do not subject me to any affliction, adversity, or trial that could put my faith to the test, and rescue me from evil and the Evil One."

We may conclude Section I with the following observation about Jesus' unconditional promise to answer our prayers:

Ask, and it will be given you; seek, and you will find; knock, and it will be opened to you. For every one who asks receives, and he who

---

[6]See Joseph Thayer, *Thayer's Greek-English Lexicon of the New Testament: Coded with Strong's Concordance Numbers* (Peabody, Mass.: Hendrickson Publishers, 1995), no. 27:5, s.v. "*peirasmon*". See also Bible Hub, Online Bible Suite, no. 3986, s.v. "*peirasmon*", Thayer's Greek Lexicon, accessed January 18, 2016, www.biblehub.com/greek/3986.htm.

seeks finds, and to him who knocks it will be opened. (Mt 7:7–8; Lk 11:9–10)[7]

This absolute promise is followed by Jesus' assurance that His Father, who loves us unconditionally, would want to give us more than even the most loving human father:

[W]hat man of you, if his son asks him for bread, will give him a stone? Or if he asks for a fish, will give him a serpent? If you then, who are evil, know how to give good gifts to your children, how much more will your Father who is in heaven give good things to those who ask him! (Mt 7:9–11)

The implication is clear: God loves us without limit, and therefore His will is to optimize love, goodness, and salvation, for us and through us. Given this, then He *will* grant us everything we ask for so long as it does not impede our own or others' salvation, freedom, or the optimal alleviation of our own and others' suffering. If our petitions are commensurate with His unconditionally loving will, then He *will* grant them. As I noted earlier, I believe that this promise has been kept by God in my own life, and I have every reason to believe that it will be kept in the lives of others. Life may not be optimally easy, but it can be optimally salvific and loving, if we try to follow God's will.

II. "Hail Mary, Full of Grace" (Lk 1:28)

Most Catholics have been taught the Hail Mary prayer since childhood. I certainly remember learning the Hail Mary and praying it every evening before my family and I went to bed; then, in the second grade, I began to use it quite frequently on my own, especially when I was not confident during spelling tests and other challenges.

---

[7] The unconditional nature of the promise to answer prayers is also reflected in the Gospel of John: "Whatever you ask in my name, I will do it, that the Father may be glorified in the Son" (14:13). "In that day you will ask nothing of me. Truly, truly, I say to you, if you ask anything of the Father, he will give it to you in my name" (16:23).

For some Catholics, the Hail Mary evokes beliefs and feelings that most other spontaneous prayers do not—the sense of Mary as a caring mother, as well as the belief that she really does want to be near us and help us. As a child, I never really questioned these interior dispositions and beliefs, because they seemed correct, and this quality transformed my prayers of petition. Mary was there and she cared for me like a mother; all I had to do was ask for what I needed.

As an adolescent, I had many questions about my faith. I wanted evidence for the existence of God, the Trinity, the historical Jesus, miracles, and several Church doctrines, but the one belief I can't ever remember questioning was the presence and care of the Blessed Mother. I knew this belief could be questioned, but I had a *feeling* that I did not *have to* do this.

As a child I used to look upon the big crèche scene displayed in our home at Christmas time, and it evoked for me a sense of peace, home, and family. The Holy Family's home, which was essentially a simple barn, *felt* like *my* home, and since Mary was integral to that home, I *felt* that *her* home was *my* home—and *her* family, *my* family. I look back on it now and consider this intuition of peace-home-family to be more than a childhood insight. It was a grace, a conviction supported by the Holy Spirit, a *truth* emblazoned on my *heart*.

When such "graced truths" occur, we have a certitude and confidence going beyond the evidence of the mind; it *feels* so certain that we do not believe we have to question it. This is precisely how I felt about the peace-home-family of both the Holy Family and Mary, which, in its turn, gave me confidence about her presence and care when I was in need. I am not sure why I received this grace, and I know there are many Catholics who have not received it either in childhood or adulthood, but the Lord seems to have thought it fitting, or perhaps necessary, for a well-meaning young man who was about to question virtually everything else.

After examining the evidence for God and Jesus, and opening myself to the Father of the Prodigal Son, it occurred to me that God was not calling us as *autonomous individuals* to Himself alone (a sort of "one on one" relationship) but rather calling us as *interpersonal persons* into a huge family that had its origins in His Holy Family. If this is what God was doing, then He would want to select a human mother for the Incarnation of His Son[8], and this mother would have to resemble Him in humility and compassion, with the exception that she would be a more feminine version of this kind of love. My sense of the Blessed Mother's presence and care (as well as the biblical description of her) communicated this "feminine version of humble and compassionate familial love".

I truly sensed a harmony between mind and heart. I knew that what I *felt* when reading the Parable of the Prodigal Son was quite similar to what I had *felt* while looking at the crèche scene—a sense of *home*, a sense of *belonging*, a sense of *family*, which presented to my heart an awareness of peace and love beyond the merely human.

Many believers, like my mother, do not need empirical or analytical evidence to support their faith; their conviction of the heart is more than sufficient. God has a way of assuring us of His presence and love at Mass, in a church, during familiar prayers, in the celebration of liturgical seasons, in the lives of saints, in living traditions, in religious art and music, religious community, prayer services, Bible studies, and combinations of these icons of His love. If we allow ourselves to accept His presence and love in them, then our conviction in the divine family-home will grow more deeply. Yet if we have a more analytical, empirical, scientific, or questioning temperament, we should pursue the abundance of evidence provided for us *by* God (see Volumes II and III of this Quartet). God provides this evidence precisely because He knows that some of us will need it, even acutely.

Whether or not we need evidence, the experience of divine family-home will be enhanced by prayers to and symbols of our Blessed Mother Mary. As noted above, I believe this sense of divine family-home is a *special* grace given to us through the intercession of Jesus' Mother, who is our mother, and this special grace imparts comfort, peace, and trust, particularly during times of suffering.

My hope in presenting this intercessory prayer early in the chapter is to help you integrate this sense of divine family-home into your relationship with the Lord, and thereby into all the other spontaneous prayers for help during times of suffering. It will enhance the depth of peace, comfort, security, affection, and assurance coming from both

[8] See Volume III (Appendix II) for an explanation of the Trinity and the Incarnation of the Son—the Second Person of the Trinity.

the Father and Mother of Jesus. I have one other hope in presenting this prayer: that you see more deeply the divine family into which you are called, and the unique and irreplaceable role you play in it, whenever you invoke the names of Jesus *and* Mary.

This last point is very important, because as noted above, we are not being called into a "one on one" relationship with God alone, but rather to an interpersonal relationship with the Holy Trinity and the Holy Family. This means that we have to use the "logic" of *family* love to understand the dynamic of the heavenly home to which we are called. This family logic is not exemplified by competition for love and sibling rivalry, but rather by co-responsibility for one another, sharing and compounding of love, and rejoicing in others' belovedness within the family.

Using the terminology of Volume I of the Quartet, the Holy Family transcends Level One and Level Two happiness (external pleasure and ego-comparative happiness) and must be understood in terms of Level Three and Level Four happiness (contributive generative love that recognizes the transcendent mystery of self and others). If a family's dynamic is fundamentally Level One or Level Two, it will be characterized by internal competition for love and sibling rivalry. However, if it is based on Levels Three and Four, it will be characterized by co-responsibility for the good of others, sharing love with others, and rejoicing in the transcendent belovedness of others (see Volume I, Chapters 3 and 4).

This Level Three-Four logic of love leads us back to an insight of Archbishop Fulton J. Sheen recounted in Volume I, Chapter 7. In responding to a listener who asked, "By praying to Mary aren't you taking away something from Jesus?" he responded, "Well, if I love your mother, does that mean I love you any less?" We can extend Sheen's insight further by asking, "If I love your mother, doesn't that enhance my love for you?" If the listener's family was at Level One or Level Two happiness, he might have been perplexed by the question or thought, "Yes, I *would* be loved less!" However, if his family was at Level Three or Level Four, the answer would have been apparent— love of one family member does not take away from another; it only enhances it through the compounding effect of the Level Three and Level Four family dynamic. With this as background, we may now move to the loving power of the prayer itself.

Before I pray the Hail Mary, I frequently say, "I know you are here—and I know you include me in your family of beloved ones." Then I begin with the words of the angel Gabriel, completed by the words of Elizabeth—"Hail Mary, full of grace, the Lord is with thee; blessed are you among women, and blessed is the fruit of your womb, Jesus" (cf. Lk 1:28, 42). This focuses my attention on the grace and favor Mary was given because of her humility, love, and faith. It also focuses my attention on Jesus—"the fruit of [her] womb". For me the addition of Jesus' name to Elizabeth's greeting enhances my awareness of being included in the divine family—Jesus is my brother, Mary is my mother, and Jesus' Father (Abba) is *my* father. I feel like a young boy who is spending the night at his best friend's house—and whose mother and father love me like one of their own. At this juncture, I am confident enough to ask for anything that a full-fledged family member could ask.

The rest of the prayer is pure comfort, because I know that Mary is, as mother, deeply inclined to do what we ask of her so long as it conforms with the will of God—"Holy Mary, Mother of God, pray for us sinners now and at the hour of our death. Amen."

Some readers may misinterpret the expression "Mother of God", which does not in any way mean "mother of the divine nature of Christ". As the famous Church historian Jaroslav Pelikan has noted, the term *Theotókos* (the accent is important) should be translated as "the one who gives birth (*tókos*) to the one who is God" (*Theos*).[9] This literal translation indicates that Mary gave birth to the one who was *already* divine, indicating that Mary is not the human mother of divinity itself.

Now let us return to the prayer. When we ask our Blessed Mother for her help, she intercedes with the Lord on our behalf just like any good mother might do for a needy child. This consideration causes me to flash back to the Wedding Feast at Cana, where Jesus had not volunteered to help the hosts who had embarrassingly run out of wine. When Mary sees the problem, she tells Jesus about it, but He refuses to get involved, saying, "O woman, what have you to do with me? My hour has not yet come" (Jn 2:4). Nevertheless,

[9]See Jaroslav Pelikan, *Mary through the Centuries* (New Haven, Conn.: Yale University Press, 1998), p. 55.

His Mother knows His heart, and that He will not turn her down, and so she confidently tells the servants, "Do whatever he tells you" (Jn 2:5).

The above does not imply that Jesus would not listen to our requests without the intercession of His Mother. Jesus and His Father are unconditionally loving and will respond with *full* efficaciousness to our requests within the contours of their six objectives, with or without the intercession of Mary. However, it is sometimes easier *for us* to ask a mother for help before asking our father or brother, because a mother's empathy and compassion are qualitatively different from a father's or a brother's. Neither Jesus nor His Father will be offended if we find it easier to channel our petitions through the empathy and compassion of the Blessed Mother, because they created us and know well what we need to connect more intimately with *them.* The Lord could not possibly be jealous if we found it easier to connect with Him through Mary; after all, He selected her to be the Mother of the *family* that would become the communion of saints: that is, to become *our* mother, thus giving her the role of any other mother—to provide a connection to our Father, brothers, and sisters. Indeed the Lord is absolutely delighted to have us turn to His incarnate Son's Mother to connect with both Him and His Son, because He wants to give us every possible option and freedom to come to Him. In my own case, I *sometimes* find it easier to connect with the Father and Jesus directly, but sometimes I find it more conducive to connect with them through the intercession of our Blessed Mother. I am absolutely certain that God is delighted by whatever path I take, so long as I am trying to connect with Him.

One last thought about the final part of the prayer, "Pray for us sinners." I was once told by a graduate student in theology that he thought that this petition was yet another manifestation of the Church's obsession with sin. I responded that I had precisely the opposite thought—namely, that the use of the word "sinners" meant that I did not have to be perfect to ask for the Blessed Mother's help. When I ask, "Pray for us sinners," I don't have to worry about whether I am a deserving son or an underserving son, or very probably a combination of both. I can come to my mother as I am, with good and imperfect qualities, as a mixed blessing who feels comfortable asking her for help to connect with her Son and His Divine Father.

When we assemble the different parts of this prayer, the sense of divine family-home with the peace, comfort, assurance, and trust that comes with it, and the ready access given us to the Father, Jesus, and the whole communion of saints through the Blessed Mother, we can see the loving hand of God giving us His *fullness*. This fullness includes a perfectly loving and empathetic Mother, who stands with the Father and Jesus at the center of a huge family—an indescribably deep family-home, which is God's ultimate gift to us. This is the breadth, height, depth, and fullness of God's love evoked by saying the simple words, "Hail Mary, full of grace ..."

III. "Lord, Do Not Let Any of This Suffering Go to Waste"

We might expand the prayer "Lord, do not let any of this suffering go to waste" as follows: "Lord, do *not* let any of this suffering go to waste; make optimal *good* come out of it for *me, others*, and *Your Kingdom*." This prayer does not ask God to alleviate suffering immediately, but rather assumes God's six objectives: the promotion of our own and others' salvation as well as the preservation of our and others' freedom, *then* the alleviation of our own and others' suffering. The highest good God can bring out of our suffering is our own and others' salvation.

This salvation can take many forms:

- To be extricated from a dark and deadly path or area of our lives
- To pursue a higher level of happiness and meaning in life
- To appropriate a deeper capacity for humility, empathy, and compassion
- To be given opportunities to make a positive difference in our families, organizations, communities, and culture
- To be given opportunities to serve better and build the Kingdom of God and the People of God
- To offer up our suffering as self-sacrificial love for the good of the Church and all those in need, in imitation of Jesus

There is a remarkable freedom embedded in this prayer because it takes our focus off of getting immediate relief and places it on asking

God to bring optimal good—optimal salvation—out of our suffering. When we do this, we acknowledge that God is going to work for our best interests, which gives us the freedom to let God work *His* plan of salvation through us, to do it *His* way, according to *His* timetable. This freedom is critical because if we keep imposing *our* methods and timetables on God, we will only grow more frustrated and discouraged when He does not adhere to them. We might even begin to think that He does not care about us, because He is not listening to us. As will by now be clear, He most certainly *is* listening to us, but He has chosen to place His plan above ours, because *our* plan is likely to undermine our salvation and freedom.

Many long-standing religious people can make the mistake of stepping into the above flawed viewpoint by ignoring God's six objectives and making subtle suggestions for how God could best alleviate suffering. I have found myself doing this many times—and praying one of the worst of all possible prayers: "Lord, I know my situation quite well—and I thought You might appreciate my perspective on how best to alleviate my suffering. I took the liberty of making a five-step, easily phased-in plan that could get You through the major contours of this problem in a relatively short time—now hear me out." From this point, it is easy to put an addendum on the prayer by suggesting the following: "Lord, I thought I might also provide You with some recommended timelines to help You see how *we* might best expedite my plan—I hope You don't mind."

Kidding aside, it is all too easy to believe in the wisdom, and even the infallibility, of a desired plan of action, and to become silently resentful toward God for not expediting it. When I find myself feeling this kind of resentment during my suffering, I do not have to look very far—a simple review of the expectations I had for the alleviation of my suffering reveals the above humorous prayer. I had imposed these expectations on God, and when He had not let me undermine my own and others' salvation and freedom, I became frustrated and resentful. I had made *my* expectations and wisdom more important than God's salvific plan. Once revealed, the solution was simple: I had to tell myself, "Spitzer, get out of the Lord's way—and your own best interests!" and follow it up with our familiar prayer, "Lord, would *You* please make optimal good come out of my suffering?"

This incisive intervention restores my freedom to allow God's plan for my own and others' salvation to take precedence over my plan for the quick alleviation of suffering, which will be infinitely better for me and others in the long-term. As I keep myself focused on this priority, I find my frustration, dashed expectations, resentments, and isolation held at bay—while gaining the openness to look for what *God* wants me to see and where He is leading me.

As I continue to struggle with my worsening eyesight, this prayer has become a lifesaver. In recent years the decline in my eyesight has accelerated dramatically. When I notice a new decline—which I can no longer deny because it is forcing me to be more tentative and careful about what I'm doing and where I'm walking—my first reaction is to growl, "One more darn thing to struggle with! Now I'm going to have to ask for help in doing something else, and whatever recognition I had of natural beauty is slipping away. Lord, if it's not too late for a miracle ... " When I'm just about to turn in on myself—partially in lament and self-pity, ignoring all of the advice given above—this spontaneous prayer comes to the rescue. After completing my growl, I take two deep breaths and I say, "Okay, Lord, do not let any of this suffering go to waste. Make optimal good come out of it." The anxiety and frustration begin to subside, and I realize that these new deficits are having a profoundly good effect on my own and others' salvation.

There is still another long-term benefit coming from the above prayer. It leads to a little more detachment from my desire to be autonomous and self-sufficient—from what Saint Ignatius called "inordinate attachments to myself, my power, and my glory". This leads to greater *surrender* to God, which Saint Ignatius recognized to be true spiritual freedom. Each new deficit, when followed by the above spontaneous prayer, opens me to greater trust in God and *His* priorities. My heart and mind conform a little bit more to His heart and mind, and this enables me to *let go* of my desires for self-interest, autonomy, self-aggrandizement, and power. Along with this freedom, I get an extra bonus: greater empathy for those who have similar or different struggles, leading to an increase in compassion.

The above transformative outcome is worth the deficit, frustration, and fear that I might temporarily feel, because the former is incomparably deeper and eternal while the latter is only superficial and temporal. In the end, I realize that my growling prayer was a big mistake, which incites me to a new prayer: "Whoops, I may have been a little hasty and impatient, Lord—I'm thinking straight again. I know You're leading me, guiding me, inspiring me, and saving me." If you're anything like me, I recommend this prayer as an essential means for sanity as well as following God's guidance toward your own and others' salvation.

IV. "Lord, Snatch Victory from the Jaws of Defeat"

The prayer "Lord, snatch victory from the jaws of defeat" is essential when a situation has grown out of control—with so many possibilities for increasingly bad results that we cannot keep track of them. We all experience these situations—where problems seem to be compounded again and again. It begins with one or two things going wrong and then something else—perhaps with the family or friends—and then something at work goes wrong, and then when you're leaving work in a completely dilapidated condition you get a flat tire, and people are screaming at you, "Get out of the way!" These scenes happen to just about everyone—including those living in a monastery.

When such situations occur, my first reaction is to try to deal with this network of problems calmly and rationally; however, as the pressure begins to build, and I am trying to handle it all myself, I can feel myself reaching the limits of my cognitional capabilities, patience, and hope for the future. When such multiple calamities occur, I have a curious tendency to believe that *everything* depends on *me*, and that I am responsible for the solution to every part of every problem. I then create a false sense of urgency, which requires faster solutions to each problem than is really necessary. I then top it off by creating a plan of resolution with impossibly high steps—attainable only by Hercules and a few others. I have now made my *difficult* situation into a virtually *impossible* one. In my sense of self-induced panic, I become overwhelmed with the sense of imminent defeat—that my whole world is crumbling around me, and that "I'm going down!" At the point of seeing nothing but defeat, I say the prayer, "Okay, Lord, snatch victory from the jaws of defeat. It's up to You!"

This little spontaneous prayer has the capacity to move me from *self*-reliance to trust in the Lord's "conspiracy of providence". I sometimes repeat it by saying, "Lord, *You* snatch victory from the jaws of defeat. *You* use your wisdom and power to untangle this web of problems—I'm going to remain in the background for the moment." When I say this, I find that my first fatal error—believing that *I* have to resolve all problems—is mitigated. It seems that the Holy Spirit reaches into my consciousness and gives me enough peace to let go of my obsessive need to solve the entangled web of problems all by myself, right now.

After the peace comes a wisdom—not borne out of my panic but by a rationality and awareness both *within* and *beyond* me. It is almost as if the Holy Spirit has joined forces with my natural, rational consciousness to begin the process of asking reasonable questions: Is there anyone who might be able to help me with one or more of these problems? Which problems are the most urgent and the most serious, and how should I—and others—prioritize them? What kind of a backup plan can we formulate if everything does not go perfectly? What kind of a backup plan can we formulate if everything goes worse than might be expected? As we shall see in the next chapter, rationality has its own remarkable calming effect—not only does it help us untangle the web of problems leading toward confusion and panic; it keeps our consciousness focused on our cognitive side instead of our emotional one.

There is one more gift of the Holy Spirit coming through this prayer (and others like it). It might be described as a sense of inspired hope for the future, a confidence that everything will be all right, or that life will be better than before the suffering. It is an inspiration of the Holy Spirit and may be compared to inspired confidence in a rational truth for which we do not have all the evidence or complete understanding. I recall when I was younger reading C. S. Lewis' *Miracles* and *Mere Christianity*. As I moved through the pages, I kept thinking to myself, "That's right; this is really truth!" When I finished the books, it occurred to me that I really didn't understand his points with perfect clarity, and in many cases, didn't know why I *felt* his theses to be true. I later found through research and rational reflection that his theses were true, causing me to ask, "How could I have been so sure of the truth of these theses before I understood the evidence in support of them?" Once again, I concluded that my sub-conscious was not that smart, and that the Holy Spirit galvanized certitude within my *heart*. I have had similar experiences recognizing the falsity of "purported theological truths" that I read or heard. I would keep thinking, "I don't know why this is wrong, but I am certain *that it is*." Sometimes this feeling of "false doctrine" can be so strong that it practically shouts at me.

The same kind of "certitude of the heart" can occur with respect to the future, particularly in times of suffering. When I pray the above spontaneous prayer (or another similar one), I frequently *feel* confident that everything is going to be okay, even though I cannot discern how or why. Sometimes I don't know where to begin the process of unraveling a multifaceted problem, but I frequently get a sense of which questions to ask, where to put my priorities, and who can help. No doubt some of this comes from my experience and practical intelligence, but the *confidence* that frequently accompanies my thoughts, priorities, and actions is surprising indeed—so mysterious that it almost seems to come from a different voice, reflecting a more confident heart and mind.

V. "I Give Up—You Take Care of It"

The spontaneous prayer "I give up—You take care of it" has the same effect as the prayer given immediately above; it inspires peace, wisdom, and hope in the future that "joins forces" with our natural rational faculties, enabling us to get through particularly complex and seemingly hopeless situations. You may want to use this prayer in place of the previous one, or in addition to it—particularly if you are feeling a sense of complete powerlessness.

I discovered this prayer in Rome back in 1980. I had been sent to the Gregorian University to take all of my theology classes in Italian. I went to Italy two months earlier without background in Italian to attain "fluency". I was reasonably confident that after studying the language in Perugia, I would be able to understand my classes. My first class on the first day was an exegesis class on the Gospel of Matthew taught by a Cuban professor who spoke Italian faster than the Italians (with a Spanish accent). I was not able to understand

25 percent of what he was saying, and began to panic. I kept thinking to myself that I was going to "go down". What would I say to my provincial? To my classmates? "Here I am, back in the United States. I couldn't understand anything and I flunked out."

Realizing that circumstances were out of my control, I muttered, "I give up, Lord. You take care of it!" When I said this it seemed like steam came out of my ears. A pressure was relieved by simply giving it over to the Lord, who could providentially bring some good out of my predicament. As a matter of fact, He did. The moment this prayer enabled me to calm down, I became content with understanding partial sentences and concepts. I could then begin to make sense out of the general line of thought, which in turn built my confidence, and in turn enabled me to understand more. As the semester progressed, I began to understand far more of what the professor was saying and eventually made it to the final exam, where the professor gave two or three choices of questions for various passages of Scripture. I was able to choose questions that pertained to the last parts of the course, thereby hiding my inadequate understanding of the first part. In the end, I did quite well. (Thank You, Lord!)

Evidently, much of that success was attributable to my *natural* gradual appropriation of the Italian language and exegetical method; however, much of it was attributable to the graces mentioned above that joined forces with my natural rational faculties—*peace*, which enabled me to calm down and listen, *wisdom*, which enabled me to focus on what I could understand instead of what I could not understand, and *confident belief* that the unseen solution to my problem was about to come, and when it did, to seize upon it. These graces were galvanized through the above simple prayer "I give up, Lord—You take care of it."

VI. "Lord, Push Back This Darkness and Foreboding"

Foreboding is a complex phenomenon. Some of it can come from feelings of anxiety and depression, which our conscious or unconscious psyche projects into the future—so it is internally, psychologically induced. To those who, like myself, are not materialists, there is another side to foreboding—a genuine premonition about darkness or evil in the future. I am uncertain about the cause of such premonitions—whether they are a warning from God, harassment from an evil spirit, or a kind of psychic protention (intrusion) into an impending future. They could be the result of two or three of these causes. Whatever the cause, I believe that foreboding is not completely psychological—and that it does portend some kind of future darkness. I believe this for the simple reason that most of the time I experience it, something dark does in fact happen a few days later. It contains not only a sense of darkness, but powerlessness toward the darkness, and resembles the descriptions of it by prophets (like Jeremiah, Ezekiel, and Isaiah), mythologists (like Thomas Malory and J. R. R. Tolkien), and litterateurs (like Sophocles and Shakespeare).

When these premonitions are accompanied by the feelings of powerlessness and anxiety, I refuse to entertain them. I give them over to the Lord immediately by saying the simple prayer "Lord, push back this darkness and foreboding." I even use my hands to gesture pushing back against something tangible and palpable, while I repeat the prayer, "Lord, push it back." Since I'm fairly sure that something dark or harmful is about to happen to me, I also use this follow-up prayer: "Lord, take care of the dark situation that is about to befall me—please protect me and minimize the harm that may come to me." I frequently repeat that prayer until the foreboding begins to subside. Most of the time, the foreboding *does* subside. It does so in stages—first, it loses its bite and intensity, then it gradually weakens, and finally after some time, a sense of normalcy or even consolation occurs. I can think of only a few occasions when the sense of normalcy-consolation did not occur, though the sense of foreboding decreased considerably.

In virtually all the above cases, my sense of foreboding did foretell something dark and harmful, but it turned out that it was not nearly as harmful or disruptive as it could have been. Sometimes I can see clearly that I have dodged a bullet—even several bullets, and in a few cases, a cannonball or Howitzer shell, which has caused me to believe that the Lord heard my prayer and did in fact protect me. Of course a naturalist would ascribe all the dodged bullets to natural causes, amazing coincidences, and remarkable luck. However, I do not subscribe to this, because continuous manifestations of luck that last for decades are highly unlikely.

Obviously I cannot guarantee that the Lord will protect me or any of us from the consequences of malicious or erroneous intent through the use of this or other similar prayers. All we can know is that the Lord will act according to the six objectives mentioned above, and that if we ask Him to help us, He will minimize the harm that can come to us within the parameters of those objectives.

Sometimes the Lord will not be able to minimize the harms portended by foreboding, because it would be contrary to our salvation or freedom. The most obvious example of this is His own Son in the Garden of Gethsemane. As Luke describes it, Jesus had such a dark and agonizing premonition of what was to befall Him that His sweat became like drops of blood (see Lk 22:44).[10] This led Jesus to pray the petition discussed in Section I.C above: "Abba, Father, [since] all things are possible for you, take this cup [of suffering] away from me, but not what I will but what you will" (see Mk 14:36). Jesus knew that His Father loved Him unconditionally and that He desired to protect Him and minimize the harm that would come to Him, but also knew of the Father's will to advance the salvation of everyone; and so, even with His agonizing premonition, He submits to the will of the Father, which initiates His act of unconditional love for the salvation of the world.

It may be helpful here to recall some of the points made above about God's will concerning our suffering (Section I.B). Recall that God does *not* want us to suffer any more than He wanted His Son to suffer. However, He *allows* suffering from others, ourselves, and nature for a variety of reasons:[11]

- To help with our own and others' eternal salvation (e.g., inciting us to move from superficiality to deeper meaning in life, toward greater compassion, care, virtue, humility, and self-sacrifice, and providing opportunities for us to do good for the people and world around us as well as the Kingdom of God)

---

[10] Hematidrosis (sweating blood) is a rare condition brought on by extreme stress and anxiety. It is frequently preceded by severe headaches and abdominal pain.

[11] See Chapter 10 on why an all-loving God allows suffering.

- To make possible, protect, and foster our personal freedom and the freedom of others so that our love can be our own, and not merely a loving program from the "Divine Programmer"
- To use imperfections in nature to provide the vulnerability and need that gives us the opportunity to make an optimal positive difference to others, the common good, and the Kingdom of God

If we pray to the Father of Jesus, we can be sure that He will either prevent our suffering or tone down our suffering, or lead us through suffering in the most expeditious way possible to optimize our salvation, while protecting our freedom. When we pray, "Lord, push back the foreboding and prevent or minimize the harm it portends according to Your will," He will begin the process of preventing or minimizing suffering, and if it is not possible to prevent or minimize it because of the requirements of our salvation or freedom, He will find a way to lead us through it expeditiously to achieve his six-fold purpose.

We may now sum up some of the above points. First, prayer is indispensable, because God operates within our freedom, and He will not anticipate our need and impose a solution to it without our free desire, choice, and involvement. He wants us to recognize Him, open ourselves to Him, and make Him a part of our lives. If we do not pray for help because we do not know any better, then God will help us without our asking. However, if we reject God, or refuse His help, we leave Him with only one option: to find a method of helping us that will *not* violate our freedom. This may mean allowing us to slip into cosmic loneliness, emptiness, and alienation, to experience the negative emotions of the comparison game, and to sense our powerlessness to fulfill our desires for perfect truth, love, goodness, beauty, and home.

Second, God does not need our prayers to make Himself feel better; *we* need our prayers so that God can make us be and feel better. God certainly enjoys our prayers when they are oriented toward deepening our relationship with Him, and He is saddened when we reject His love and help. However, God does not need our prayers to be who and what He is: "the unique, unrestricted, unconditionally loving source of everything that exists". Recall from Chapter 2

(Section I) that God is what He is independently of us, but His sub-jective interpersonal state (the state of His consciousness in relation to us) is very much affected by how we relate to Him.

Third, if we ask the Lord to deliver us from trials and evil, which can be felt in foreboding or premonition, then God will try to min-imize this harm or evil, within the parameters of His six objectives. This is not only promised by Jesus, but also borne out in my own and others' experiences.

Fourth, the idea that God does not want us to pray for the avoid-ance of suffering or evil (because it would be cowardly, unworthy, or impious) is not Christian, but only stoicism with a Christian face. As we saw with Jesus' prayer in the Garden of Gethsemane and the final petition of the Our Father, Jesus clearly encourages us to pray for the prevention and minimization of suffering—and if this is not consistent with God's will, to pray that our suffering will optimize our salvation.

Finally, if we do not pray to the Lord to push back our foreboding, and to minimize the harmful effects that it portends, then we need-lessly suffer either out of ignorance or a false sense of pride. If I am going through an airport bumping into pillars and counters (because of my poor eyesight), and someone comes up to me and asks, "May I help you?" and I say to him, "No, thank you; don't trouble yourself. I can get along okay," and then I continue to bump into pillars, I am foolish for turning down someone's help in order to maintain pride-fully what I can no longer do.

With all this in mind then, when foreboding strikes, pray, "Lord, push back the foreboding," and as the foreboding begins to subside, pray, "Lord protect me from the harm portended by that foreboding." God, within the parameters of His six objectives, will take care of the rest.

VII. "Lord, You Are the Just, Wise, and Merciful Judge—You Take Care of It"

Oftentimes, suffering is caused by the thoughtlessness, callousness, ego-centricity, selfishness, greed, envy, and pride of others. The suf-fering that these unjust actions produce have multiple components;

they cause harm to us, our families, our well-being, and our reputation, and also strike a blow to our self-worth, dignity, and trust in others. When trusted colleagues, friends, and family members perpetrate an unnecessary and unjustified harm, it shocks us because it abuses the trust that we placed in them, and it wounds us because it devalues our worth and dignity. When we recover from the shock and initial feelings of degradation, we can't help ourselves; we almost instinctively feel anger, and if we do not quell these feelings, they can grow significantly over the course of time. As we "stew and brew" over them, they can turn into hatred and a desire for cruel vengeance. We can become consumed by this destructive anger, and it can actually undermine our productivity and relationships with others, leading to bitterness about life. It can also lead to a desire for retribution *beyond* the offense done to us—violence begetting violence and vengeance begetting vengeance.

Though this anger may in fact be defensible because of the seriousness of an unjustified offense against us, it will not come to a good end, but will likely undermine or destroy our life, the life of the perpetrator, and the lives of the people we touch. Shakespeare's *Hamlet* illustrates this well. Recall that Hamlet had every right to be angry at his uncle Claudius for killing his father and marrying his mother, but his anger leads him to unwittingly kill Polonius, whom Hamlet mistook for Claudius because he was hiding behind a curtain. This unleashes a whole series of events from the drowning of Ophelia (Polonius' daughter whom Hamlet was courting) to the duel between Laertes (Polonius' son) and Hamlet. The duel leads to the death of both Laertes and Hamlet and indirectly to the death of Gertrude (Hamlet's mother). Though his uncle Claudius probably deserved to die, Hamlet's unrestrained anger ultimately leads to the unwitting deaths of five other individuals who did not deserve to die: Polonius, Ophelia, Laertes, his mother, and Hamlet himself.

Shakespeare's rendition of the destruction of the innocent by supposedly justified anger gives great credibility to the teaching of Jesus, who changed the Old Testament's toleration for anger into a prohibition of it: "But I say to you that every one who is angry with his brother shall be liable to judgment" (Mt 5:22). The power of anger to harm the innocent unwittingly is one of the reasons Jesus advocates for forgiveness. The other reason is He sees goodness and the potential for redemption in *every* individual, even the most egregious sinners whom He actively pursues and forgives. Jesus did not believe that any person should simply be "written out" of the Book of Life, because there is always potential to turn away from sin and to move toward redemption. For Jesus, this meant giving everyone a chance to "turn around", no matter what he might have done. This "chance to turn around" is our act of forgiveness, which means *forgiving others from the heart* (see Mt 6:14; 18:35)—letting go of our justified anger and desire for retribution (arising out of unjustified offenses against us). Jesus felt that this act of forgiveness was so important for Christian life and the possibility of love that it is mentioned more often than any other moral teaching in the New Testament.[12] It also underlies Jesus' teaching to love our enemies, and pray for those who hate us (see Mt 5:44).

So how can we let go of this justified anger and desire for retribution when it is beginning to consume us? How can we avoid the destructive power of anger, which could lead to the unwitting harm of the innocent? How can we release ourselves from bondage to this anger? How can we give our brothers and sisters a chance to redeem themselves in the face of unjustified harm? How can we mitigate and even detach ourselves from "our right" to exact punishment for unjustified harms done to us? If you are anything like me, it is almost impossible to do this *by yourself.* I am not able to simply forget about it. Every time I try "to simply forget about it", I remember the offense *even more*, and this causes me to get angrier and desire greater retribution. I can sometimes remember my father's sage advice: "Put yourself into his shoes, and then judge him." But every time I do that, I think to myself, "But I'm not like that rat; I would not have done to him what he did to me!" It seems that every "trick" I try turns back on itself and leads to even greater feelings of anger, insult, degradation, bitterness, and retribution. I seem to be locked into a spiral where I am suffering more than the perpetrator, and I am powerless to let it go.

When I discover my powerlessness to "let it go", *I hand it all over to God.* I do this by letting God be the judge instead of me. Though I do not have the interior strength to let go of an unjustified offense, I do have the *trust* to let God do what I know He can do—to judge

[12] See Rudolph Schnackenburg, *The Moral Teaching of the New Testament* (New York: Herder and Herder, 1965), p. 100.

wisely, justly, and mercifully—and so I say, "Lord, You are the just, wise, and merciful Judge—You take care of it." "It" here refers to the negative situation that includes both the injustice perpetrated on me and the person who perpetrated the injustice.

Using this prayer to put the whole painful matter into God's hands has worked wonders for me. On one occasion, for example, I felt I was dealt with unfairly by someone who intended to undermine my academic advancement and reputation. My initial anger toward him was so great that my friends did not believe I was capable of writing a balanced response that would be politically effective; apparently, my anger and indignation were obvious. I began to use this prayer again and again, handing the matter over to the just, wise, and merciful Judge; and over the course of several days, I felt that He was taking the matter out of my hands and telling me that He had it under control, and that I would not have to worry about it anymore. Of course I did not hear a voice inside my head saying these words, but I had a strong intuition and feeling that this was precisely what He was doing. Slowly but surely, despite myself, I felt myself letting the matter go, and as I did so, my anger began to dissipate. The more it dissipated, the freer I became to let the just, wise, and merciful Judge have it *all*, take the *whole* matter—"I don't want to hold on to to *any* of it anymore; I don't even want to think about it."

I won't say I became completely indifferent to the situation, but I can say that on a scale of one to ten, my "anger and indignation level" went from about a nine to about a three, enabling me to write a balanced, politically effective response. It also gave me a great deal of peace. I no longer woke up at two o'clock in the morning thinking uncharitable thoughts about the perpetrator. Instead, I woke up at my normal time with hopes that he might be healed of his biases. This prayer was effectively a prayer for my enemies, which allowed forgiveness to transform anger and feelings of retribution into hope for healing.

VIII. "Thank You"

I speak about the prayer "Thank You" with some trepidation in the context of suffering, because it can give rise to misunderstandings and resentments. However, its correct use in the context of suffering is so powerful that it is worth providing some preparatory insights and taking the chance that readers will understand them.

Some readers might be thinking that saying the prayer "Thank You" during a time of suffering is either masochistic or an oxymoron. Why would we thank the Lord for something that appears to be essentially negative? We are not thanking the Lord for *suffering*, but rather for the good things we have had in life, and still have in life, amid the suffering we are experiencing. When we are grateful for the good things we have, it restores our sense of being blessed and loved by God—even if we experience feelings of abandonment by God during times of suffering.

Without a sense of gratitude, the feelings of loss and deprivation experienced in times of suffering can easily turn into feelings of isolation and abandonment, which can in turn become feelings of melancholy and despair. These feelings can grow in intensity until they begin to take over our consciousness. When this happens, every experience we have, every person we meet, every opportunity that comes before us, and even the future itself become tainted with isolation, abandonment, melancholy, and possibly despair. These feelings have a life of their own, producing a downward vortex, which becomes increasingly difficult to escape. The first and most important way to loosen the grip of these negative feelings is the presence of God. One of the simplest and best ways to invite Him into our consciousness is through the spontaneous prayers mentioned above (in Sections I–VI).

These prayers can be greatly complemented by recognizing the way God has blessed us in our past and present life. When we recognize our blessings, we acknowledge His favor and love for us, which opens us to the affectionate, merciful, healing, and redeeming grace that He is bestowing on us. When we suffer, we frequently obsess on the bad news and tune out the good news, but when we think about and feel gratitude for our blessings, we begin tuning in to the good news of God once again.

When Israel was in trouble, the prophets not only explained what went wrong in Israel's past, but also what went *right*. Instead of focusing the people on their bad circumstances, they reminded them of how good God had been to Israel. Virtually every spiritual writer recommends remembering and recounting the blessings of the Lord as a way of breaking the spell of dejection, abandonment, melancholy, and despair that can overtake us—completely.

A good way of doing this is to acknowledge first our supernatural blessings: for example, our transcendent and eternal souls, our redemption by Jesus, and the gift of the Holy Spirit and the Church to guide us, and then our natural blessings: for example, our families, friends, education, talents, and opportunities, and even the beauty of nature, music, architecture, etc. As we review these blessings, we need only say, "Thank You," because this one simple phrase, this one simple prayer, connects us with both God and His love through His blessings.

This practice has been quite beneficial in my own life. As mentioned earlier, I have a degenerative eye problem, which began when I was thirty-one years old. It has been getting progressively worse and will ultimately result in complete blindness in a few years. When I was younger, the effects of the degeneration were less noticeable, but my emotional reaction to them was stronger. At this point, each decrease in vision is very noticeable, but my reaction to it is almost inconsequential. The reason for this is that I have become accustomed to a threefold discipline:

1. Situating this temporary problem in the context of *eternal life* with the Lord
2. *Trusting* that the Lord will give me the capacity and resources to deal with the additional loss of self-sufficiency
3. Being able to *thank* the Lord for all the good He has done for me both supernaturally and naturally throughout my life—and even through the steady decrease of my vision

With respect to the third point, when I reflect on the blessings I have been given, even in the midst of my eye problems, I know that I am living a blessed life. I am grateful for my relationship with the Lord; my call to apostolic mission; my talents for thinking, speaking, and writing; and my family and friends—as well as the incredible opportunities to serve the Kingdom of God and to help people toward salvation. This leads to the realization that my effectiveness has grown tremendously despite my eye problems—or should I say because of them.

In my thirties and forties, it was difficult to thank the Lord for my eye problem, particularly when facing more degeneration. But now after having lived with the problem for many years, I know that it has bestowed many spiritual gifts upon me—increased humility, empathy for others, greater trust in God, and whole new directions in life, including starting the Magis Center, going on worldwide lecture tours, and writing multiple books. I don't think I would have pursued these things nearly as concertedly and actively were it not for the eye problem, which pushed humility and empathy to the forefront of my mind, while making me realize that if I wanted to publish my ideas about faith and reason, I had better do it as soon as possible, while I still had some autonomy (see Chapter 7).

When a new decrease in vision occurs, I now thankfully recall the wonderful supernatural and natural gifts I have been given, as well as the blessings that have come through my eye problem; and this lifts up my trust, hope, and spirit, at the very moment I would have previously felt dejection. Thus, in my life, thanksgiving during times of suffering has been the opposite of masochism and contradiction; it has been a lifesaver, an openness to grace, and an enhancer of trust, hope, and spirit.

Saint Ignatius Loyola formulated his final contemplation in the *Spiritual Exercises*, called the "Contemplation to *Attain Divine Love*", on the basis of giving God thanks for both the supernatural and natural blessings in our lives. When we give God sincere thanks for our blessings, His love becomes apparent, which enables us to *trust* Him, even in times of suffering. This trust, in turn, enables us to hope in our future, look for His guidance, recognize His providential hand, and see the potential for good—to us, others, the Church, and the world—that can come from our suffering.

One final clarification: we should never force ourselves to be thankful to God for something we perceive to be inherently negative. By doing this, we reduce God to an unjust despot who orders us to be grateful for freezing conditions, dirt floors, and a cup of gruel. Moreover, we exhaust ourselves trying to put a happy face on a condition that is tearing us apart interiorly. Nothing good will come from this exercise in futility, because it comes neither from God nor good common sense. Thus, our best strategy is to thank God for the things we can perceive as good, which will allow the light of His love, redemption, and consolation to reemerge in our consciousness. When this begins to happen, we will want to look for the

opportunities in our suffering (see Chapter 7), and as these opportunities appear, to give Him thanks for the hard road that led to
those opportunities.

IX. "God, Be Merciful to Me a Sinner!" (Lk 18:13)

The prayer "God, be merciful to me a sinner!" (Lk 18:13) is particularly important for those with a Level Four purpose in life or who
are moving concertedly toward it, because Level Four (transcen-
dent/spiritual) individuals can suffer when their relationship with
God is disturbed by sin. I will speak about this spontaneous prayer
from the vantage point of the Christian tradition, but it can be used
with slightly different interpretations in other non-Christian spiritual traditions (see Volume II, Chapters 1 and 2). For the moment,
suffice it to say that for Jesus, sin is equivalent to "unlove"—
attitudes and behaviors that undermine love, "the unity with other
human beings whereby doing the good for them is just as easy, if
not easier, than doing the good for ourselves".[13] Jesus describes
these attitudes and behaviors quite thoroughly in Matthew's Sermon on the Mount (see Mt 5–7) and Luke's Sermon on the Plain
(see Lk 6:17–49). When we engage in such behaviors, we not only
cause harm to others, but also to ourselves, for they can pull us into
spiritual darkness, with its concomitant feelings of alienation from
self, God, and the human community. This can be deeply painful
on many levels.

As by now may be clear, this pain does not come from *God* withdrawing from us or punishing us in anger or disgust, but from *us*
entering into a condition or situation that obscures and interferes
with *our* ability to relate to Him. Our desire to be with Him, act
on His behalf, and draw closer to Him gradually diminishes, and
soon we find ourselves feeling quite alone and empty. Though God
has not left us, we cannot sense His loving presence through the

---

[13] The term "good" here is meant in the sense of Levels Three and Four—contributive
and transcendent good. It may also include some Level One and Level Two goods, such as
material goods, sensorial pleasures, status, and self-esteem that are consistent with love and
faith. There are other Level One and Level Two "goods" that may not be consistent with
love and faith; these are not included in the idea of "good" given in the definition of love.

darkness surrounding us. When the feelings of alienation and lone-liness become acute enough, Level Four people are inclined to turn to Him like when Peter was sinking into the water and crying out to Jesus, "Lord, save me" (Mt 14:30). This plea for help is the perfect context for repentance and prayers of forgiveness.

Before moving to these prayers, it may prove helpful to give a shorthand discussion of Jesus' teaching on sin (unlove) in the Sermon on the Mount. This can be accomplished by making recourse to the medieval synthesis of His Sermon—the Seven Deadly Sins. This synthesis is an excellent way to check our spiritual health because it is concerned with both interior attitudes and behaviors. Since I will be writing another book on this matter,[14] I will here only list the sins: gluttony/drunkenness, lust/infidelity, sloth, greed, anger, envy, and pride. Much has been written about these sins and the dark-ness, alienation, emptiness, loneliness, self-destructiveness, and harm to others they cause. For the moment, I will depend on the reader's intuitive grasp of these sins as well as the capacity to undermine love, other people, and our relationship with God.

Let us return to the cry of Peter when he realized he was in trouble ("Lord, save me"). The moment he utters this plea, Jesus *immediately* extends His hand to Peter and catches him. God helps us in just the same way—immediately. When we begin to sense His loving presence breaking through *our* darkness, we will want to move to a prayer of repentance, which is a twofold prayer, a prayer of *regret* for allowing ourselves to move away from the Lord of light and love, and a prayer of *resolve* to try our best to stay on the path to love—that is, to temper our egocentric, domineering, and self-idolatrous desires so that we will not undermine love for others and God.

With respect to the prayer of regret, my favorite is the one expressed by the tax collector at the back of the Temple: "God, be merciful to me a sinner!" (Lk 18:13). It should be remembered that tax collectors were considered egregious sinners in first-century Judaism, and so he had much for which to be sorry. Yet the humil-ity and sincerity of his request, which expressed his need for God

---

[14] That is, *Called out of Darkness: Contending with Evil through Virtue and Prayer.* This section is by no means an exhaustive treatment of that book, but only a method of prayer to help with reconciliation and spiritual healing.

and his desire to be with Him, was sufficient for Jesus to declare, "I tell you, this man went down to his house justified [before God] rather than the other" (Lk 18:14). Recall that justification before God means readiness for salvation. For Jesus, the tax collector's sincere prayer of need and regret opened the door to salvation and Heaven. I take his declaration to be absolutely true; when I find myself wandering off the path of light into the darkness, crying out like Peter, "Lord, save me," I say immediately, "God, have mercy on me, for I am a sinner." My dread of the darkness and emptiness in which I find myself produces a heightened awareness of my need to be saved from drowning by Jesus, and so my prayer of regret is filled with sincerity; I *do* regret moving away from Him, and I *do* want His mercy with all my heart, so that I too may go to my "house justified"—restored to the light and love of Jesus, the light and love of sanity and salvation.

My prayer of resolve follows quite naturally: "Lord, I will *try* with all my heart not to go back to the road to darkness." I cannot promise the Lord that I will succeed in my resolve, because I feel like the disciples in the Garden of Gethsemane: "[T]he spirit indeed is willing, but the flesh is weak" (Mt 26:41). Nevertheless, my resolve is sincere. I trust that my imperfect resolve and my likely imperfect "follow-through" will be acceptable to the Lord, for I am given hope by His acceptance of Peter after three denials. Recall that Peter promised that he would never deny Jesus: "Though they all fall away because of you, I will never fall away.... Even if I must die with you, I will not deny you" (Mt 26:33, 35). No doubt Peter's resolve was completely sincere, but he failed in that resolve—three times. He bitterly regretted his weakness, but trusted that the Lord would accept him again. He demonstrated this by diving into the water to greet Jesus when He appeared after His Resurrection (see Jn 21:7). Jesus not only accepts Peter's regret and contrition; He also commissions him as leader of the Church (see Jn 21:15–17). I cannot help but think that the Lord will treat me in exactly the same way. If my prayer of resolve is sincere, but my follow-through is less than perfect, He will take me back if I sincerely ask Him—again and again.

Saint Paul acknowledges this same weakness of the "flesh", but does not give up, trusting that the Lord's unconditional saving love will bring him to where he cannot bring himself—to his eternal salvation in Christ Jesus, his Lord:

> We know that the law is spiritual; but I am carnal, sold under sin. I do not understand my own actions. For I do not do what I want, but I do the very thing I hate. Now if I do what I do not want, I agree that the law is good. So then it is no longer I that do it, but sin which dwells within me. For I know that nothing good dwells within me, that is, in my flesh. I can will what is right, but I cannot do it. For I do not do the good I want, but the evil I do not want is what I do. Now if I do what I do not want, it is no longer I that do it, but sin which dwells within me.... Wretched man that I am! Who will deliver me from this body of death? Thanks be to God through Jesus Christ our Lord! (Rom 7:14–20, 24–25)[15]

Saint Paul clearly experiences a bifurcation within himself, a spirit that is willing but flesh that is weak (Jesus' perception of the apostles' behavior in the Garden of Gethsemane). Saint Paul believes that his true intention is to follow the law and teaching of Jesus, but he experiences base urges within himself that drag him away from it. His higher self wants to follow the law and Jesus, but the base urges within his flesh block his way. He is clearly frustrated by these base desires, exclaiming, "Wretched man that I am!" Nevertheless, he does not consider these base urges to be his *true* self, and so he does not give up, but rather asks, "Who will deliver me from this body of death?" At this point he turns to Jesus, his Lord, *confidently* aware that Jesus will bring him to where he cannot bring himself: to complete spiritual freedom, the capacity to *do* fully what he *wants* to do in his spirit—to become his true self.

We must have the same confidence of Peter and Paul in the forgiving, redeeming, and healing love of Jesus; otherwise, we will not be able to bridge the gulf between our willing spirits (our true selves) and the weakness of our flesh. Without this confident trust in the love of Jesus, we will not be able to reach true spiritual freedom, the capacity to *do* what we truly *want* to do—to follow Jesus in virtue and love. Let us then say with the confidence of Saints Peter and Paul, "Lord, save me," and know that Jesus *will* pull us out of our

---

[15] I discuss this passage thoroughly in *Called out of Darkness*.

turbulent waters, deliver us from our "body of death", and bring us to our true selves in His heavenly Kingdom.

My prayers for forgiveness do not end here. When I was in the novitiate, I doubted the sincerity of my prayers of regret. I would harbor little thoughts in my mind like, "I can't hide my insincerity and ulterior motives from God; He knows everything, and I know I'm harboring all kinds of insincerity and ulterior motives somewhere down there, and therefore, I'm still in trouble." When my novice master asked me, "What's troubling you?" I told him the whole matter. He looked up at me and said, "I detect a closet Pelagian;[16] *you* don't have to be perfectly sincere. I don't think anybody can be. *God's unconditional* love makes up for whatever insincerity and ulterior motives that lurk in the depths of our hearts." I thought to myself, "Whew, that's a relief!" He went on to explain that if we regret our sin because it has caused separation from the God who loves us, God accepts it unconditionally, even if we cannot be perfectly sincere or devoid of ulterior motives. So he suggested that after saying my tax collector's prayer of regret and my prayer of resolve to stay out of the darkness, I add the following prayer: "Lord, I accept your forgiveness."

I asked him if such a prayer might be presumptuous, to which he responded, "We have to be presumptuous about accepting God's unconditional love—if presumptuous means being overly confident in *God's* love." I thought to myself, "Well that makes sense—if God's love is really *unconditional*, then I *should* be able to be not only confident in it, but '*overly* confident' and even '*absolutely* confident' in it." He went on to explain that we should have the same confidence in Jesus' Father as we had in our own parents when we were *children*; after all, Jesus taught us to address His Father with a childlike name, trust, and appeal: "Abba."

I reflected back upon some experiences of my childhood when I had done some "doozies"—fighting on the playground, disobeying direct instructions, and sneaking off to my grandmother's house for a tuna sandwich when I was supposed to be going to catechism class. When the errors of my ways were detected by my parents, they informed me of their displeasure, and I was sent to my room

---

[16] Pelagianism in the modern interpretation holds that we can save ourselves by our own efforts alone.

for a prolonged period of time. After a while I reemerged tenta-
tively and expressed my sincere apology: "Mom and Dad, I am really
sorry. I knew better than that." My parents would always accept me
back—and more to the point, I *accepted* their forgiveness unhesitatingly, without doubt and with absolute confidence, with the heart of
a child.

This reflection led me to Jesus' declaration: "[W]hoever does not
receive the kingdom of God like a little child shall not enter it" (Lk
18:17). It occurred to me that "I think I understand that passage.
What is it in the heart of a child that will so readily and confidently
receive the Kingdom of God? What is it in the heart of a child that
is lost in adults?" I get it: being childlike—*unquestioning* trust in love,
particularly the unconditional love of good parents and God. Adolescents and adults may get jaded over the course of time, but children
really do have a pure and unquestioning trust in the ones who are
supposed to love them. I resolved from that day forward that I would
use my novice master's additional prayer with the unquestioning trust
of a child: "Lord, I presumptuously, like a child, accept the forgiveness of Your unconditionally loving heart."

I add one more prayer to the above set when it is relevant: "Lord,
make good come out of whatever harm I might have caused."
There are many occasions in which I may say or do something
too quickly, carelessly, or even heartlessly, and it suddenly occurs to
me—invariably at three o'clock in the morning—that my action
or statement could be misinterpreted, giving rise to hurt feelings or
resentment. If I am unsure of whether a harm has been caused or
the situation would be further complicated by my trying to clarify
it, I put it into *God's hands* with the above simple prayer. It amazes
me how often and effectively this prayer works. It seems the Holy
Spirit reaches right into the heart of someone who could have been
offended by a careless or even heartless remark or action for which
I was responsible—and gives that person new perspective about
the statement, my motives, or my personal weaknesses. Frequently
enough they come up to me and say, "Father Spitzer, when you first
said this I was really taken aback, but now I can see what you meant
and why you said it." They then proceed to give an even better interpretation to my statement or actions than the one I had intended! My
one thought is, "Whew, thank You, Holy Spirit!" Some of the most

remarkable manifestations of grace in my life have come through the use of that prayer, and I can guarantee that the Holy Spirit works in all of our hearts in ways that are unseen, powerful, compassionate, sensitive, and beautiful.

When Level Four people, particularly Christians, find themselves straying from the love of Christ—and begin to feel the cosmic emptiness, darkness, loneliness, and alienation, arising out of this movement away from the light—I recommend immediate action. Start with Peter's prayer in his moment of panic, "Lord, save me" (Mt 14:30), and then proceed to the prayer of the tax collector, "God, be merciful to me a sinner!" (Lk 18:13). As you repeat these prayers and the light and peace begin to return, make your prayer of resolve: "Lord, I will try with all my heart to walk in Your light and love." Try to find ways to stay close to Christ on your journey, avoiding proclivities, thoughts, and actions that could cause you to stray again. Then say, "Lord, I accept your forgiveness." Repeat this prayer until you can say it with the trust of a child's heart. Then, if relevant, turn to the Spirit for help in reconciling yourself with others by using the following simple prayer: "Lord, make good come out of whatever harm I might have caused." These prayers will help you to stay in the light of Christ, and through it, to remain in the peace, security, and love of the One who will bring ultimate good out of all individual words, actions, and endeavors.

X. "Thy Loving Will Be Done"

The reader will no doubt recognize the prayer "Thy will be done" (Mt 6:10) as the second petition in the Our Father, taught to us by Jesus (Mt 6:9–13; Lk 11:2–4). Though the petition is quite short, it is immensely powerful when properly understood and prayed. So what is the "will of God" that Jesus asks us to pray for? It is to optimize love, goodness, and salvation for us and through us. This requires explanation.

In Chapter 2, we examined Jesus' name for God (Abba) as revealing His essence or inner core. We then showed that the meaning of "Abba" is exemplified by the father in Jesus' Parable of the Prodigal Son, who is affectionate, unrestrictedly forgiving, compassionate, and filled with joy, graciousness, and generosity. For Jesus, the Father's *will* is the same as His identity or inner core—namely, unconditional love manifest in affection, forgiveness, compassion, generosity, and joy. Another way of saying this is that His will seeks to optimize goodness, love, and salvation for us and through us.

We sometimes think that *God's will* is different from this—that instead of optimizing goodness, love, and salvation for us and through us, it undermines them. This viewpoint does not come from the revelation of Jesus, but from one or more of the six false notions of God considered in Chapter 2. It seems that we give credence to the idea of an "angry god", "payback god", "domineering god", "terrifying god", "stoic god", and "disgusted god", and then combine it with our belief in Murphy's Law ("The most likely turn of events is the one that will be most problematic"). This generates a notion of God's will similar to the sword of Damocles hanging over our heads. If we say to God, "Thy will be done," the sword will fall and lop off our heads. We then say, "If you didn't want your head lopped off, then you should never have opened yourself to God's will; you'd better be careful what you pray for—you just might get it!" This view of the will of God is precisely the opposite of what Jesus intended, and it is so far from the truth that it cannot be connected with the New Testament Scriptures. Nevertheless, we hold on to it because we are still persuaded by one or more of the false notions of God.

When I was a young man in my first year of novitiate (the beginning phase of training for Jesuits), I was still theologically and spiritually unformed, and as a result, I was still influenced by various aspects of the terrifying god, stoic god, and disgusted god. This led to my implicit view that God's will was something unknowable, something unpredictable, which could spring up and bite me—hard!

Before we retired to bed, we had final prayers that concluded with the prayer of Saint Ignatius Loyola called the *Suscipe*. It is an extended form of the prayer "Thy will be done" and goes like this:

Take Lord, receive,
all my liberty, my memory, my understanding, my entire will,
whatsoever I have or hold, You have given to me.
I give it all back to You; dispose of it wholly
according to Your *will*.
Give me only Your love and Your grace,
and that's enough for me, and I ask for nothing more.

I found this prayer to be both difficult and tormenting, because I really didn't trust the Lord enough to give Him "all my liberty, my memory, my understanding, and my entire will". I really had no idea what He would do with them the minute I gave them to Him. He could really teach me a lesson in humility and take away my memory and understanding, which I valued *very* much. As the words came out of my mouth, I was making a complementary mental plea: "But *pleeaaase* don't annihilate my memory and understanding!"

When I revealed my strange prayer to the novice master, he informed me that my view of God was of unknown origin; it certainly wasn't Christian, and it seemed to elude the virtues of virtually every other known world religion. For the first time in my life, I had to confront the terrifying and the stoic god. I then began the slow process of replacing these images with the Father of the Prodigal Son and began to affirm the Lord's genuine personal love for me. As this transition occurred, I could feel a sense of hope taking shape within my consciousness, and then a sense of trust that led me to a remarkable discovery: that God's will was not the sword of Damocles; it didn't conform to the warning "You better watch out when you ask for the will of God; you just might get it!" I began to see with increasing conviction that God wanted nothing more than to optimize love, goodness, and salvation in me and to use my gifts to optimize them in others. When I saw this, I gained a great freedom to pray the *Suscipe*. When I prayed, "Take my memory," I understood this to mean, "Use my memory to optimize love, goodness, and salvation in me and for the people I touch," and when I prayed, "Take my understanding," I was asking Him to use my understanding for the same loving and salvific purpose. I trusted Him to do this, and I have since found that my trust was totally warranted, because my life continues to be bestowed with remarkably good salvific effects. If the prayer of Saint Ignatius can do this, then so also can the briefer prayer "Thy loving will be done."

This prayer may be substituted for any of the spontaneous prayers mentioned above, because God's optimally loving and salvific will is the best way to deal with our sufferings, problems, anger, fear, and temptation. I have grown accustomed to praying it at least twenty times per day, and it seems not only to calm me down, but to infuse me with a sense of trust and hope in God's loving will. This in turn enables me to be open to God's grace manifesting itself in little and great ways during my times of suffering. I become attuned to the "Spirit's voice" in the remarks of others, the books I'm reading, the programs I'm listening to, and the conspiracy of providence around me (see Chapter 3, Section III.E), and slowly but surely I am led to the opportunities of suffering that the Spirit wants me to see (see Chapter 7). Frequently, the Spirit manifests Itself by galvanizing a sense of certitude within my spirit. I might hear a phrase in a conversation or on a radio program and think almost immediately, "Yes, that is right, and that's important; there is a clue here to explain the meaning of my suffering. I need to take this in and think about it." When I take the "hint" from the Holy Spirit and pay attention to this "sense of certitude", I find invaluable clues, such as changes to my life's path, changes of attitude, new opportunities to be pursued, dangers to be avoided, deepening of certain insights, and modifications of my relationships with others—and even modifications of long-standing ways of thinking.

If we pray this prayer in trust, and we keep ourselves focused on the "Spirit's voice", we will not be disappointed. Our suffering *will* lead to the six objectives of God, which will optimize love, goodness, and salvation in us and through us.

XI. Conclusion

The following diagram contains the spontaneous prayers addressed in this chapter. You might want to print a copy for easy reference so that you can begin integrating them into your life, before suffering comes. Many of these prayers can be used to bring God's grace into the ordinary circumstances of life, and so using them early and often will bear fruit.

There are several other spontaneous prayers that are not discussed in this volume, but will be discussed in the sequel to this Quartet, prayers that are concerned with virtue, vice, and temptation. The whole of Chapter 8 will be devoted to the prayer "Lord, I offer my suffering to You as self-sacrificial love for the good of the Kingdom and the world."

Spontaneous Prayers in Times of Suffering

- "Lord, help me."
- "Abba, Father, all things are possible to you; remove this chalice from me; yet not what I will, but what you will" (Mk 14:36).
- "Hail Mary, full of grace ..." (Lk 1:28).
- "Lord, do not let any of this suffering go to waste; make optimal good come out of it for me, others, and Your Kingdom."
- "Lord, snatch victory from the jaws of defeat."
- "I give up—You take care of it."
- "Lord, push back this darkness and foreboding."
- "Lord, You are the just, wise, and merciful Judge—You take care of it."
- "Thank You."
- "God, be merciful to me a sinner!" (Lk 18:13).
- "Lord, save me" (Mt 14:30).
- "Lord, I accept your forgiveness."
- "Lord, I will try with all my heart to walk in Your light and love."
- "Lord, make good come out of whatever harm I might have caused."
- "Thy loving will be done."

We might conclude the above consideration of spontaneous prayers by reiterating how important they are—as short and incisive—for inviting the Lord into our suffering when we really need Him. By doing this, we will be able to manage fear and anxiety *more* quickly and successfully, which is the subject of the next chapter.

Chapter Five

Fear Is Useless

Fifth Foundation: Mitigating Fear and Choosing Consolation

Introduction

Up to this point, we have addressed four foundations for suffering well:

1. Interpreting suffering in the context of eternal life with the unconditionally loving God
2. God is Abba—the Father of the Prodigal Son—as distinct from the six false notions of God
3. God's presence to us in our suffering, and His six objectives for alleviating it
4. Prayer during times of suffering—aiming toward His loving will

These four foundations lay the groundwork for mitigating fear and anxiety through both natural and spiritual means, which leads ultimately to choosing God's consolation.

There are two distinct sources of anxiety that accompany suffering:

1. the fear, grief, loneliness, foreboding, and depression coming from negative *events outside* of our control, and
2. the resentment and anger coming from the unjustifiable or hurtful misdeeds of *others*.

We have already addressed the second kind of anxiety in the previous chapter (Section VII), where we noted that forgiveness is the only way to mitigate the anxieties of others' unjustifiable misdeeds. Even though anger and resentment may be justified—as Hamlet's certainly was—its consequences can destroy us and the lives of innocent people, and so it is critical to follow the teaching of Jesus and to forgive those who trespass against us, even outrageously. I recommended the prayer "Lord, you are the just, wise, and merciful Judge—You take care of it." Praying in this fashion allows the loving grace of God to permeate our hearts, which enables us to let go of our justified anger and resentment over the long-term—a movement from bondage into freedom.[1]

The primary focus of this chapter will be on the first source of anxiety—the fear, grief, loneliness, foreboding, and depression coming from *events* outside of our control, such as the death of a friend or relative, loss of a job, debilitating disease, physical pain, and so forth—and how Christians can mitigate these anxieties through prayer, grace, reason, and natural virtue.

Jesus supersedes the Old Testament view of "fear of God" and teaches His disciples that fear and anxiety are mostly negative and should be replaced by trust in God. Since this view may present confusion, we will begin this chapter with an examination of eight critical passages on fear and anxiety in the New Testament (Section I), then proceed to a spiritual approach to mitigating fear and anxiety based on those passages (Section II), and then consider four tactics from natural reason and virtue that complement Christian spiritual practice (Section III). We will conclude with the important consideration of *choosing* consolation during times of suffering (Section IV).

I. The Negativity of Fear according to Jesus

In Chapter 3, we addressed Jesus' response to a synagogue leader who had just heard the news that his daughter had died. He said, "Do not

---

[1] In his masterful work *Ressentiment*, Max Scheler shows how resentment leads at once to Nietzschean nihilism and the elitist egalitarianism underlying totalitarianism. Both views are utterly destructive to self and others. Scheler shows that the only way out of this darkness is the abandonment of resentment through forgiveness grounded in Jesus' teaching on love of neighbor. See Max Scheler, *Ressentiment*, ed. Lewis B. Coser (Milwaukee, Wis.: Marquette University Studies in Philosophy, 1994).

fear, only trust" (Mk 5:36). We concentrated on the second part of that statement—the need for trust—and now we must turn to the first part, the uselessness or negativity of fear and anxiety.

There may be some confusion surrounding this issue because Jesus has a mostly negative view of fear while the Old Testament seems to be mostly positive about the fear of God. This difference can be explained by linguistic considerations. According to Eugene Merrill, the Greek term *phobos* is used to translate numerous terms in Hebrew, ranging from mild unease to full-blown terror. He notes further that "fear of God" is so central to the spirituality of the Old Testament that it has its own subcurrent of development, distinct from other uses of the term. Fear of God is viewed as virtuous and generally means an awareness of God's superior power, which causes at once terror, awe, respectful worship, and obedient surrender.[2]

In Chapter 2 (Section II.D, "The Terrifying God"), we spoke about two meanings of "the fear of God" in the Old Testament—(1) fearing Yahweh's anger and punishment for infidelities, and (2) being struck with awe and moved to reverence at the majesty, beauty, splendor, and glory of God. As explained in Chapter 2, the first sense is superseded by Jesus' teaching, but the second sense is quite compatible with it. Nevertheless, the New Testament does not use "fear of God" in either sense, revealing Jesus' desire to detach "fear" from God.

Jesus and the other New Testament writers not only tend to avoid mentioning the fear of *God*, but also advocate refraining from fear in most of its forms. There are eight major passages in which Jesus—and the other New Testament writers—teach their disciples about fear. All of them reveal that fear is useless and negative and should be replaced by trust in the unconditionally loving God, whom Jesus taught us to address as "Abba"—the Father of the Prodigal Son. A brief examination of each of these passages will manifest Jesus' and the Christian Church's aversion to fear.

The first and most instructive text comes from Jesus' comment to the synagogue leader at the news of his daughter's death—"Fear is

[2]Eugene Merrill, "Fear", in *Baker's Evangelical Dictionary of Biblical Theology*, ed. Walter Elwell (Grand Rapids, Mich.: Baker Books, 1996), http://www.biblestudytools.com /dictionaries/bakers-evangelical-dictionary/fear.html.

useless, what is needed is trust" (Mk 5:36; Lk 8:50; my translation). According to Meier, the passage about the synagogue leader is filled with Aramaic words, Semitisms, and proper names that indicate a probable origin in Jesus.[3] Thus, the radical break with the Old Testament on the efficacy of fear very likely goes back to Jesus Himself. Indeed it would be hard to imagine that any of the evangelists would have made such a radical break from the Old Testament tradition without relying on the authority of Jesus. What is even more interesting is the strong aversion to fear in the writings of Saints Paul, Peter, and John (as discussed below). This strong aversion is also very likely attributable to the stated preference of Jesus. Therefore, we will have to take His teaching seriously—particularly during times of suffering. The other seven major passages will make this contention clear.

The second major passage from Matthew 6:25–34 is an extensive declaration and plea to refrain from anxiety, seek first the Kingdom, and trust in the Father. In this passage, Jesus goes through the various causes of anxiety and repeats His declaration and plea three times—making it, as it were, a solemn declaration:

> Therefore I tell you, *do not be anxious* about your life, what you shall eat or what you shall drink, nor about your body, what you shall put on. Is not life more than food, and the body more than clothing? Look at the birds of the air: they neither sow nor reap nor gather into barns, and yet your heavenly Father feeds them. Are you not of more value than they? And which of you by being anxious can add one cubit to his span of life? And why are you anxious about clothing? Consider the lilies of the field, how they grow; they neither toil nor spin; yet I tell you, even Solomon in all his glory was not clothed like one of these. But if God so clothes the grass of the field, which today is alive and tomorrow is thrown into the oven, will he not much more clothe you, O you of little faith? Therefore *do not be anxious*, saying, "What shall we eat?" or "What shall we drink?" or "What shall we wear?" For the Gentiles seek all these things; and your heavenly Father knows that you need them all. But seek first his kingdom and his righteousness, and all these things shall be yours as well. Therefore *do not be anxious* about tomorrow, for tomorrow

---

[3] See John P. Meier, *A Marginal Jew: Rethinking the Historical Jesus*, vol. 2, *Mentor, Message, and Miracles* (New York: Doubleday, 1994), pp. 780–81.

will be anxious for itself. Let the day's own trouble be sufficient for the day. (emphasis mine)

The Greek term *merimnate* (from *merimnaō*—"be anxious") indicates "to be worried or negatively preoccupied about something". Though it is distinct from fear (*phobos*), Jesus treats it in the same way—as a mental condition that is useless, debilitating, and best replaced by trust in God. We might wonder why Jesus is so adamant about the negativity of anxiety—indicated by His threefold repetition of the declaration, and the two reassurances of God's assistance during our times of need (God takes care of the birds of the sky and the lilies of the field). One can only speculate, but if the whole Christian spiritual tradition has anything to say about it, the answer probably lies in the fact that anxieties or worries make us turn in on ourselves, giving rise to a sense of isolation and loneliness that undercuts our connection with God. The more we worry, the more isolated we feel, which in turn creates a distance between us and the One who can help us. It is difficult to trust in God when we feel that He is so distant from us—and once this trust is undermined, we become victims of every form of depression and hopelessness. Jesus knew well that the sooner we turn to God for help, the sooner we will be able to resist the negative power of anxiety, which will in turn enable us to get about the business of seeking opportunities in our suffering (see Chapter 7), and offering our worries and concerns to the Lord as a self-gift for the salvation of the world (see Chapter 8).

We may now proceed to the third major passage about fear, which is perhaps the most confusing, for it seems to advocate fearing God instead of refraining from it. In Matthew 10:28–31, we read:

[D]o not fear those who kill the body but cannot kill the soul; rather fear him who can destroy both soul and body in Gehenna. Are not two sparrows sold for a penny? And not one of them will fall to the ground without your Father's will. But even the hairs of your head are all numbered. Fear not, therefore; you are of more value than many sparrows. (my translation)

It may be thought that this passage advocates the fear of God because Jesus says, "[R]ather fear him who can destroy both soul and body in Gehenna." The standard interpretation of this text by Catholic exegetes is represented by Benedict Viviano. He contends that "the one who can destroy both soul and body in Gehenna" is God. However, the *whole* passage does not advocate fearing God, but rather, the alleviation of fear. Viviano views this passage as a rabbinical comparison—if God cares so much about trivial things, then how much more does He care about you—trust in His care.[4] In this passage the rabbinical comparison may be stated as follows: God cares about every sparrow (the cheapest item in the marketplace), and if He cares so much about these least significant things, how much more does He care about *you*—a human being with a soul made in His very image? If God cares so much about you, then you can trust Him above fearing Him—and if you can do this, then you need not fear anything or anyone.This is why Jesus concludes the passage by saying "fear not, therefore"—which can be equivalently translated as "therefore, do not fear anything."[5]

   N. T. Wright offers an alternative interpretation, advocating that "the one who can cast soul and body into Gehenna" is Satan. He notes first that it would be highly unusual for Jesus to refer to His Father in such a negative way (the One "who can destroy both soul and body in Gehenna").[6] He further notes that it is a *warning* given to the disciples in the context of Jesus' commission to them (in both Matthew 10:5–42 and Luke 10:1–42), a warning that stands in *contrast* to the Father's loving care portrayed in the next verse. So who is Jesus warning the disciples to fear? Wright contends it is the one who *desires* to lead us to Gehenna—Satan:

> Some have seen "the one who can cast into Gehenna" as YHWH; but this is unrealistic ... again and again—not least in the very next verse of this paragraph—Israel's god is portrayed as the creator and sustainer, one who can be lovingly trusted in *all circumstance*, not the one who waits with a large stick to beat anyone who steps out of line.... The one who can kill the body is the *imagined* enemy, Rome. Who then

---

[4] See Benedict Viviano, "The Gospel According to Matthew", *The New Jerome Biblical Commentary*, p. 652.
  [5] Ibid.
  [6] See Christopher Evans, *Saint Luke* (London: SCM Press, 1990), p. 515.

is the real enemy? Surely not Israel's own god. The real enemy is the accuser, the satan.[7]

According to Wright, Jesus did not view His Father as "the accuser", but rather as "the one who could be lovingly trusted in *all* circumstances", which is clearly manifest in the following two lines of the passage: "Are not two sparrows sold for a penny? And not one of them will fall to the ground without your Father's will. But even the hairs of your head are all numbered." If God so lovingly cares for and protects us, how can He be viewed as the one who casts into Gehenna?

Whether we hold to the standard interpretation espoused by Viviano or the alternative one espoused by N. T. Wright, God is the one we must trust, the one who can protect us and save us. If we trust in Jesus' Father, the conclusion Jesus draws in the above passage follows: "Fear not, therefore," implying that if we remain close to the God who loves us—and turn to Him for protection against Satan—then we will not have *anything* to fear.

In both interpretations, this passage is consistent with the other major passages on fear in the New Testament. We may now turn to the fourth major passage on fear, which comes from John 14:27:

> Peace I leave with you; my peace I give to you; not as the world gives do I give to you. Let not your hearts be troubled [*tarassestho*], neither let them be afraid [*deiliato*, "timid or afraid"].

The general context of this passage is Jesus' discourse on the Holy Spirit—whom He calls "Paraclete" ("Helper", "Advocate", or "Counselor"). He concludes the passage by saying that peace is His gift to us. This peace goes far beyond any peace the world can bring. It is a prime gift of the Holy Spirit that casts out all fear, because it is not only the assurance but the reality of God's salvific intention. Vawter describes it as follows:

> Jesus concludes his words of consolation. *Peace is my gift to you:* "Peace" (šālôm) was and is the common Jewish formula of greeting and farewell. The word had a much deeper significance, however, as

---

[7] N. T. Wright, *Jesus and the Victory of God* (Minneapolis: Fortress Press, 1996), pp. 454–55; emphasis mine.

an expression of the harmony and communion with God that was the seal of the covenant (cf. Nm 6:26). Hence it came to have an eschatological and messianic meaning (cf. Is 9:6), virtually the same as "salvation." It is this spiritual tranquility that Christ gives, which has no resemblance to what the world gives. Because Christ is this gift that he gives, Eph 2:14 can call him "our peace."[8]

The peace that Jesus gives is His very self—which includes His Spirit, His communion with God, and His salvation. When we have faith in Jesus, He bestows a peace on us, which includes His Spirit and the assurance of our salvation. This peace is so deep, wide, and powerful that it counteracts every imaginable fear. As long as we remain in Him, we sense His salvation, His assurance, and His communion with the Father, which mitigates our fears. This is His foremost intention.

We now move from the Gospels to the Epistles for our fifth major passage on fear. In Paul's Letter to the Philippians, he writes:

> Rejoice in the Lord always; again I will say, Rejoice. Let all men know your forbearance. The Lord is at hand. *Have no anxiety [merimnate] about anything*, but in everything by prayer and supplication with thanksgiving let your requests be made known to God. And the peace of God, which surpasses all understanding, will keep your hearts and your minds in Christ Jesus. (4:4–7; emphasis mine)

Paul here gives an absolute declaration to avoid anxiety (*merimnate*)— "have no anxiety about *anything*". The Greek term here is similar in meaning to that used in Matthew 6:25–34 (discussed above)— worrying or being negatively preoccupied. As in the previous Johannine passage, Paul links the avoidance of anxiety to the peace of Christ that comes from prayers of petition and thanksgiving. When Paul declares that we avoid worrying about *anything*, he is not suggesting that we do this on our own—like a stoïc. Instead he provides a formula to help us mitigate all anxieties—first, with confidence we are to bring our prayers and petitions to the Lord (see the spontaneous prayers of Chapter 4). Along with these prayers, we are to bring our

---

[8] Bruce Vawter, "The Gospel according to John", in *The Jerome Biblical Commentary*, ed. Raymond E. Brown, Joseph A. Fitzmyer, and Roland E. Murphy (Inglewood Cliffs, N.J.: Prentice Hall, 1968), p. 454.

acts of thanksgiving for the blessings we have received this day and throughout our lives (see Volume I, Chapter 9). These prayers of petition and acts of thanksgiving will galvanize the Holy Spirit within us, who will bring us peace beyond all understanding—a peace that is capable of mitigating *every* anxiety. With this peace and freedom from fear—with the assurance of God and His salvation—we will not be able to help ourselves; we will be living in the joy of God Himself, and so Paul proclaims, "Rejoice in the Lord always; again I will say, Rejoice."

We may now proceed to the sixth major passage concerning fear from the First Letter of John:

> There is no fear [*phobos*] in love, but perfect love casts out fear. For fear has to do with punishment, and he who fears is not perfected in love. (4:18)

In this remarkable passage, the Johannine author declares fear to be defunct in light of the perfect love of God. The context for this passage is the forthcoming judgment of the Lord—at death and the Parousia. The Johannine author here is saying that children of Christ need not fear either God or the judgment of God because their salvation is already assured by their good-faith attempt to live according to Jesus' commandment to love. If we live in love, then the love of Christ will protect us from the judgment of justice leading to punishment. Therefore, our good attempt to follow the commandment of Jesus to love drives out *all fear* because the love of Jesus saves us from any punishment we might deserve. If we are still "locked into" fearing God and His judgment, then we do not know the love of Jesus, meaning that we are probably not attempting to live in accordance with that love.

We might reverse this and say that when we try to live in accordance with the love of Jesus, we will become confident in His unconditional love for us, and in so doing, be confident that He does not desire to punish us but rather to save us unreservedly. Thus, there is no need to fear, because fear is linked to punishment. In this sense, then, love drives out all fear—fear is defunct in light of the perfect love of God.

We now proceed to the seventh major passage on fear from the First Letter of Peter:

> Now who is there to harm you if you are zealous for what is right? But even if you do suffer for righteousness' sake, you will be blessed. Have *no fear* [*phobēthēte*] of them, *nor be troubled* [*tarachthēte*], but in your hearts reverence Christ as Lord. (3:13–14; emphasis mine)

The context here is similar to Matthew 10:26–31, which concerns fear of deriders and persecutors, but Peter does not want to limit his declaration to this context alone, and so he includes anxieties (*tarachthēte*) about anything. Peter, like the evangelists, is not advocating that we become good stoics and put on a granite face but rather that we derive our strength from Jesus, who dwells in our hearts. How? By reverencing Jesus as Lord (as divine). When we believe in our minds that Jesus is the Son of God, and reverence Him in our hearts for the message and redemption He brought, then we will know that there is no ultimate tragedy in this world and that He will redeem all our suffering in His eternal Kingdom. This leads to tranquility of heart, and the mitigation of fear and anxiety.

The eighth and final passage concerned with fear also comes from the First Letter of Peter:

> Humble yourselves therefore under the mighty hand of God, that in due time he may exalt you. Cast all your anxieties [*merimnan*] on him, for he cares about you. (5:6–7)

This passage resembles Matthew 10:26–31, which argues that because God cares for us, we do not need to fear Him, and if we do not need to fear Him, then we do not need to fear anything or anybody. For Peter, God's perfect care and love for us is grounded in the gift of His Son to us:

> You know that you were ransomed from the futile ways inherited from your fathers, not with perishable things such as silver or gold, but with the precious blood of Christ, like that of a lamb without blemish or spot.... Through him you have confidence in God, who raised him from the dead and gave him glory, so that your faith and hope are in God. (1 Pet 1:18–19, 21)

With great confidence in the God who loves us so much that He sent His only-begotten Son into the world to redeem us through His blood, we can cast all our anxieties onto the Lord, and if we do that,

He will take our fear and anxieties from us and bring consolation out of the temporary sufferings of this world.

II. A Spiritual Approach to Mitigating Fear and Anxiety

Before considering four *natural* means for mitigating fear and anxiety, we will want to recall the primacy of faith, prayer, and grace in this process. Recall that fear and anxiety are essentially negative and destructive, and they undermine our spirits and relationship with God. As such, they will play into the false views of God, suffering, and ourselves (discussed in Chapters 2 and 3). If we succumb to these false views, they will not only exacerbate our suffering, but also undermine our relationship with God—the very One who is trying to help us. Therefore, fear and anxiety should be mitigated as quickly as possible by turning to the Lord in trust and prayer. I would strongly suggest using some of the spontaneous prayers given in the previous chapter to begin this process, because they are short, easy to repeat, and proven conduits of God's grace.

Even if you feel completely overwhelmed—and are attacked by panic or despondency—force yourself in faith to start saying a familiar prayer like the Hail Mary, so that the Blessed Mother can help you to attain calm through reliance on her Son. You may then want to photocopy the list of spontaneous prayers given at the end of the previous chapter and say them in conjunction with other familiar prayers like the Our Father or decades of the Rosary. If you reach out to God, He will reach back to you and comfort you. If we open ourselves to Him, we "will" feel a change in our psyche. As Saint Paul says:

> Blessed be the God and Father of our Lord Jesus Christ, the Father of mercies and God of all comfort, who comforts us in all our affliction, so that we may be able to comfort those who are in any affliction, with the comfort with which we ourselves are comforted by God. For as we share abundantly in Christ's sufferings, so through Christ we share abundantly in comfort too. (2 Cor 1:3–5)

Prayer not only helps us to achieve a preliminary state of calm; it opens us to the inspiration of the Holy Spirit, which helps us to use the four natural tactics for mitigating fear and anxiety (mentioned below, Section III). When I open myself to God's grace through prayer, I often find that I am intellectually open, creative, serendipitous, synthetic, and comprehensive. For example, when I am forming backup plans (see the first tactic below), my prayers open me to the inspiration and guidance of the Holy Spirit, which frequently leads to serendipitous discoveries of alternative plans, friends who can help, means of mitigating damage, etc. Though we might think that serendipity is pure luck, or a spectacular function of our creative subconscious, I find that serendipitous discoveries occur far more frequently when I pray than when I don't. This has caused me to think, "Perhaps my creative subconscious is less spectacular than the inspiration of the Holy Spirit—imagine that!"

Speaking of imagination, I have also found that my creative and synthetic imagination is far more free and expansive after I have prayed than when I have not. I am not here proposing a full-blown Augustinian theory of divine ideas, but rather a "half-blown" one, for I believe that the Holy Spirit works within our creative subconscious and directs us toward "serendipitous" discoveries in a subtle way—allowing us to come to the main insight ourselves. If this is your experience, I would recommend that you begin the process of mitigating fear through prayer, because you will find that it produces not only a preliminary calm but also a remarkable, creative, serendipitous, and synthetic dimension to your practical imagination and insight. If you are anything like me, you will be marveling at how fortunate and insightful you are—or should I say "you *and the Holy Spirit*".

III. Four Tactics for Mitigating Fear from Natural Reason and Virtue

There is a fundamental principle in the theology of grace—"grace builds on nature". This principle does not mean that grace *needs* to build on nature or that grace is not sufficient without nature, but rather, that grace does not negate or undermine nature—it complements nature and brings it to fulfillment. God made natural powers and virtues so that we could operate within the natural world through our natural powers. Though grace brings our natural powers and virtues to fulfillment, we can still perform natural functions in the natural world without making recourse to God's *supernatural* power. Of course all natural powers—and the natural world itself—are created and maintained in existence by God, but He does this in a way that allows us to have control over what might be called "secondary causes" in the natural order (see Chapter 3, Section III.E).

Since grace complements and fulfills nature, God expects us to develop our natural powers and virtues to enable grace to work optimally through them. For example, people educated in philosophy can be more effective in their understanding and interpretation of revealed truth; people who have developed the natural virtues of prudence, justice, courage, and temperance are better able to practice supernatural love; and people who have cultivated practical wisdom and "know-how" can be more effective leaders in the building of God's Kingdom on earth (e.g., starting churches, schools, hospitals, etc.). Furthermore, people with developed natural powers and virtues can also be more successful in communicating and promoting a dialogue between church and state, faith and reason, the City of God and city of man, etc. In view of this, we might expect that God wants us to develop the natural powers and virtues that will complement His grace during times of suffering.

What *natural* powers and virtues are most important in dealing with suffering? I would maintain that they are our powers of reason and empathy and the virtues of prudence and courage. Of course, other powers such as conscience, or virtues such as justice and temperance, are also important but not as much as reason, empathy, prudence, and courage. Since I have already discussed the power of reason in Volume II (Chapter 3) and the power of empathy in Volume I (Chapter 1) of this Quartet, I will restrict myself to a brief discussion of the virtues of prudence and courage below.

The classical definition of "virtue" is a good habit—that is, a habit that orients our natural powers toward a good end, or away from a bad end. Socrates (as well as other classical philosophers) identified four natural virtues as most important, affecting the whole range of human conduct: prudence, justice, fortitude (courage), and temperance. As noted above, prudence and courage are most relevant in the area of suffering.

"Prudence" refers to the habit of mind that focuses our power of reason toward the ends of wisdom and practical effectiveness. "Wisdom" means "knowing what is most important for an optimally meaningful and fulfilled life"—for example, the four levels of happiness addressed in the first volume of this Quartet. "Practical effectiveness" refers to the "know-how" to get things done, to work well with people, to be organized and effective in our use of time, and the ways of procuring needed resources to achieve our plans.

In order to develop these two aspects of prudence, we must first acquire knowledge of them. For wisdom, we might want to begin with studying the four levels of happiness and why the third and fourth levels lead to an optimally meaningful and fulfilling life—and why the first two levels alone lead to a less meaningful life, as well as emptiness and the negative emotions of the comparison game. This will give us enough wisdom to begin orienting our actions and plans toward the higher levels of meaning and fulfillment. In order to obtain knowledge of practical effectiveness, we might want to consult some good practical guides on how to work well with people, formulate effective goals and plans, and organize our time in an effective and balanced way toward those goals.

Once the knowledge is acquired, we have completed the first part of the process. The second part of the process requires more diligence—we have to *use* the knowledge we have acquired *repeatedly* in our daily actions so that they become reinforced habits in our lives. Once these habits are formed, our actions will be focused on optimal meaning, fulfillment, and practical effectiveness—and after a while, we won't even have to think about it. They will flow naturally from us.

"Courage" is part of the virtue of "fortitude", which refers to the effective use of our *will*power. Our "will" is the power or drive to transform ideas into reality through embodied action. Strong-willed people get things done—while weak-willed people remain on the level of ideas and dreams. In the broadest sense, "fortitude" is that habit of the will to keep moving forward in the midst of obstacles and challenges. It is a habit of resolving to stay the course—to contend courageously with challenges, and not to grow weary amid the many obstacles that might potentially block our goals and plans.

Since fortitude and courage are habits of the will, they need to be complemented by prudence—a habit of the mind. A strong will without prudence can be both foolish and vicious. Conversely, prudence needs to be complemented by fortitude, for what does it benefit a person to have wisdom and practical knowledge without the will to put them into practice? We all know people who are intelligent and gifted who remain solely on the level of ideas and dreams. It is an incredible waste of talent and life.

The following four *natural* tactics for dealing with fear and anxiety synthesize the powers of reason and empathy and the virtues of prudence and courage. They complement the graces that come through prayer (discussed above in Section II), and with those graces, help us manage and grow through the fear and anxiety intrinsic to suffering.

A. First Tactic: Using Reason and Prudence to Confront Fear and Anxiety

Some people have a naturally calm temperament—even in times of great danger. Their composure under pressure incites great admiration, and so they are frequently promoted to leadership positions. Many of us are not so naturally gifted, but that does not mean that we cannot *gain* composure by using our power of reason and the virtue of prudence. When danger approaches or we anticipate problematic or debilitating events, many of us become charged with fear or paralyzed with terror. Whether we are flush with panic or ice cold with terror, our emotions are undermining effective mitigating plans and actions. If we do not have natural composure, how can we avoid succumbing to these emotions? The simple answer is, *think!* Though panic and terror can cloud our minds, we can "turn on" the thinking process by simply asking ourselves *practical* questions. The five most important practical questions are the following:

- Can any part of this problem be averted or mitigated right away?
- If everything goes wrong, what are some backup plans I can live with?
- Who can help me with advice or needed action?
- How can I lessen the impact of all or part of this problem?
- What factors need to be mitigated now and which ones can wait until later?

Surprisingly, when we focus on one or more of these practical questions, the engagement of our reasoning process distracts and even inhibits the emotional onslaught of panic or terror—it is almost as if our rational concentration on answering these questions pushes the flood of emotions to the periphery of our consciousness. It is important to commit the above five questions to memory because *these specific* questions are what "turn on" the rational reflection process in times of fear, panic, terror, and anxiety. If we do not have these questions ready at hand, we will effectively start the thinking process in the midst of panic and terror. However, if we remember them, and latch on to one or more of them, our concentration on them pushes the negative emotions aside, and as we begin to create potential solutions—or even potential scenarios that could lead to solutions— we can actually diminish the fear and anxiety, because we can begin to see a way out of the problem causing them. The more we think and create potential solutions, the more we mitigate fear and anxiety. Eventually, we can mitigate some parts of the problem, recruit some people to help and advise us, and create some backup plans we can live with. Though our backup plans may not be ideal and the advice and help we receive less than perfect, they will generally enable us to manage our situation sufficiently to avert a crisis.

Can rationality and prudence be combined with faith and spirituality? Absolutely! Sometimes spontaneous prayers or common prayers like the Hail Mary can bring grace and consolation before we engage the five practical questions given above. The combination of supernatural peace and rational reflection is usually complementary and synergistic—that is, their combined effect can be greater than the sum of their parts. The peace and consolation of prayer can make the reasoning process more effective. Recall that prayer and grace can enhance our imagination and creativity, enabling us to discover additional potential solutions (see above, Section II). Furthermore, the action and grace of God can give us enhanced confidence in the efficacy of our mitigation efforts, planning efforts, and requests for help.

God's peace and inspiration are not meant to replace reason and prudence—they supplement them. Many children have learned the hard way that their prayers for help to pass an exam must be accompanied by the prudential requirement to study for it. When prayer and prudence are combined, they complement each other in mitigating fear, clarifying ideas, and achieving our best effort.

B. Second Tactic: Seeking the Help of Other People

Along with prayer and natural virtue (reason, prudence, and courage), the help of family members, friends, colleagues, and associates can also significantly mitigate fear and anxiety. Sometimes friends and families are not able to do something constructive or give helpful advice, but their presence to us during challenging times can mitigate anxiety—particularly the anxiety that comes from feeling alone and abandoned. Much has been written about how suffering leads not only to feelings of anxiety, but to feelings of isolation, which can heighten anxiety significantly—even to a breaking point. Evidently prayer—a relationship with the Lord—can also help mitigate these feelings of isolation, but the degree to which prayer is effective in doing this is dependent on our awareness of God's presence in our daily lives. This awareness of God's presence grows as we practice our faith—participate in a church, pray, and follow the guidance and inspiration of the Holy Spirit.[9] If someone is relatively new to the practice of faith, then friends will be a crucial source of support to alleviate feelings of isolation and to mitigate anxiety during times of suffering.

Friends can be helpful in two major ways. First, they can bring comfort and psychological support through their love, which can alleviate feelings of isolation and restore a sense of peace and composure. Second, they can offer significant help to alleviate the problems connected with our suffering. We might call the first kind of friend "a supportive friend" and the second kind "a practical friend". Frequently, different friends have to fulfill these two roles, because a person's closeness to us may be unrelated to his ability to help us in some practical way. It is advisable to seek the help of *both* kinds of friends. We sometimes forget to do this because when we turn to a

---

[9]For a complete explanation of these practices, see the following in Volume I of this Quartet: Chapter 6 (participation in a church), Chapter 7 (contemplative prayer), Chapter 8 (following the inspiration and guidance of the Holy Spirit), and Chapter 9 (the Examen Prayer, prayer of transformation through the consciousness).

loving friend for comfort, we don't ask ourselves whether he has the practical ability to help us—and vice versa. Thus, if we first turn to a *loving* friend, we will want to make sure that he has the practical ability to help us, and if he doesn't, to find another friend or associate who can fill that role. Conversely, if we turn first to a *practical* friend, we will want to make sure that he has the ability to give us the attention, comfort, and psychological support we need to alleviate our feelings of isolation, emptiness, and darkness. If not, then we should find another *loving* friend to fill that role.

What constitutes a good *loving* friend? If we have a choice, it would be a friend with whom we share history, trust, principles, faith, and commitment. We must be able to be vulnerable and open with him, and we must believe that his love for us is genuine. Intimacy is not required, but it can be helpful and synergized with the other previously mentioned characteristics. Spouses are frequently ideal loving friends; so also are our parents and siblings to whom we are tightly bonded. Friends outside of our family can also fill this role—particularly if they have the aforementioned qualities of loving friendship.

What constitutes a *practical* friend? You might want to ask yourself some of the following questions to determine a friend's capacity to offer practical help and advice:

- Is my friend or family member committed to Levels Three and Four happiness and purpose in life—does he have a developed sense of love and faith?
- Does my family member or friend have strengths and skills that I do not possess?
- Does my friend or family member possess the above natural virtues of reason, prudence, and courage?
- Can my family member or friend do something to help me concretely—or connect me with someone who could do so?
- Do I have enough respect for this family member or friend to allow him to help me with practical advice?

An ideal *practical* friend would be able to do something in all of the above areas; however, ideal practical friends can be hard to find, so we are generally constrained to find more than one practical friend who can help us in *some* of the above areas.

Extroverts prefer to talk through problems with a trusted friend, while introverts prefer to think things through on their own and then ask for help in implementation. I would recommend that extroverts take the list of the five rational questions given in the previous subsection, sit down with their practical friend, and try to "talk through the answers" together. As noted previously, once we engage in reason and prudence, anxiety and fear diminish because we are developing a concrete plan to mitigate our problems. It really doesn't matter whether we engage in reason and prudence with a friend or by ourselves, so long as we engage in it.

Once we develop a plan—with or without a friend—we must get to the second dimension of practical friendship: asking for help. Again, diverse personalities will approach this differently. Those who have a very strong sense of autonomy and self-sufficiency will be more reticent to ask for help than people who are more "relational"— who view themselves in a more interpersonal way. Those with a greater sense of autonomy should exercise extreme prudence in this regard, because it is all too easy to run from asking for help when help is truly needed. This reticence frequently leads to disasters that could have been avoided with one or two simple questions. Many people have their self-image wrapped up in an extreme idea of self-possession and self-sufficiency. Though being strong, self-possessed, and self-sufficient is important for many of life's challenges, it is not all-important. Indeed, an extreme view of this can be very unhealthy because it can undermine the prerequisite for all friendship, intimacy, and love—namely, self-communication.

How can we make a quick determination of whether we are grounding our self-image in an *unhealthy* view of self-possession and autonomy? If our need to be self-possessed is hindering or undermining our development in self-communication, then it is unhealthy. Readers who fall into this category may want to reduce the degree to which self-possession controls their self-image—and then work on ways to communicate themselves better to others. If you have difficulty communicating feelings and ideas, then try to put some of your "affective thoughts" into your communication. Failure to develop the capacity for self-communication generally leads to mistakes and missed opportunities—because it presumes that we have all the needed perspectives, knowledge, skills, and access to opportunities within our own limited being. Anyone who subscribes to this is probably suffering, at least slightly, from self-delusion—destructive self-delusion. Having suffered from this self-delusion myself, I would suggest following the advice of Shakespeare: "To thine own self be true, / And it must follow, as the night the day, / Thou canst not then be false to any man."[10]

In sum, during times of suffering we will want to be watchful for both loving and practical friends—and in the selection of practical friends, to keep focused on those who can complement and add to our knowledge, skills, perspective, opportunities, and helpful associates. Extroverts will want to take the list of five practical questions (given in the previous subsection) to practical friends and talk through those questions with them. Those who have shaped their self-image around self-possession and self-sufficiency will want to let go of that extreme view to allow for practical self-communication. This will allow them to ask for help when the need really arises.

C. Third Tactic: Reshaping Our Expectations of Happiness

There is an adage about happiness: "Much of our happiness depends on what we *think* will make us happy." Another way of saying this is that happiness comes from psychology—what we *think* we must have in order to be happy, which is often more influential than the *real* circumstances of our life. Frequently, we cannot change the latter, but we can certainly change the former. When we *think* that we cannot be happy without X, Y, or Z, and we lose X, Y, or Z because of some unforeseen circumstance, we will very likely be unhappy. Many kinds of suffering are connected with *loss*, and if we combine this loss with the thought that we cannot be happy, we can transform the pain of loss into full-blown depression—and even despair. For example, if I explicitly think—or implicitly believe—that I cannot be happy without normal vision, and I begin to experience a loss of vision, then my expectation of unhappiness becomes a self-fulfilling prophecy, and I exacerbate the pain of losing my vision with anticipation of an unhappy life. This thought or belief can become so prevalent

[10] *Hamlet*, Act 1, Scene 3, lines 78–80 (Polonius' last speech to his son, Laertes).

in my psyche that I lose all hope for happiness and fulfillment—and then the joy of life is replaced by a pervasive sadness, and depression begins to take hold.

We have all known friends—or perhaps parents—who lose a spouse and suffer tremendous pain of loss. You may have heard that person say, "I love my spouse so much and he was so central to my life that I simply cannot be happy without him—for me, life is over." Needless to say, allowing this belief to become "our reality" has led many to an early death—prior to which life had become a profound emptiness and darkness. No doubt the pain of losing a beloved produces tremendous loneliness, emptiness, and darkness, but when we add to it the belief that we "cannot be happy without him", the loss can easily move to despair and even to self-destructive thoughts.

Even though we may temporarily believe that we cannot be happy without a particular person, without a particular job, without the full use of our faculties, without a particular home, or without being able to live in a particular region, it is very probably *not true*. Such beliefs are common when the pain of loss first strikes because we have probably had an extensive history of being happy with that particular person or job or use of faculties, etc. Nevertheless, when we ask people who have used their imaginations to reconceive the future after their loss, we see that after a certain period of time, they have learned how to be happy once again. They may still mourn or regret their loss, but they do not say, "I cannot be happy without him or it." Sometimes these new paths lead to whole new kinds of happiness that were previously unimagined. This frequently happens with individuals who were formerly living on Levels One or Two and became motivated to move to Levels Three or Four because of the pain of their loss.

So how can we reinvent our view of happiness? How can we get beyond the entrenched viewpoint formed by years of happiness before loss? How can we get on with our lives after our previous view of happiness is no longer possible? Two tactics are of paramount importance. First, we must stop repeating the refrain in our *conscious mind* that "I cannot be happy without X, Y, or Z." By doing this, we not only make ourselves more unhappy in the present moment; we also program our unconscious mind to generate feelings of despondency and hopelessness in the future. It is not enough to stop repeating the familiar refrain—"I can't be happy without X, Y, or Z"; we must repeat the opposite unfamiliar refrain—"I *can* be happy without X, Y, or Z; I just don't know how that is going to look."

People of faith know that this unfamiliar refrain is not mere wishful thinking—to trick the conscious and unconscious psyche out of hopeless and despondent thoughts or beliefs. The Holy Spirit inspires and guides us through His "providential conspiracy" to a new view of ourselves, our lives, and even our happiness—and while He does this, He opens paths of opportunity that will enable this new self to be happy and fulfilled in hitherto unimagined ways. All we need do is be open to His inspiration and guidance (see Volume I, Chapter 8) and the new levels of happiness to which He is calling us (see Volume I, Chapters 4 and 5).

Once we have disentangled ourselves from our previous view of happiness, we must replace the old view with a new one; and so our second tactic for dealing with false expectations is to use our imagination to reinvent our view of happiness and ourselves. As noted above, extroverts will want to engage in this activity with a practical friend while introverts will probably prefer to do so on their own. People of faith will want to open themselves to the guidance and inspiration of the Holy Spirit by using the guideposts and rules of discernment given in Chapter 9. All three of the previously mentioned aids to alleviating fear and anxiety—God, reason, and friends—can be helpful to our imagination in its process of reinventing our view of happiness. If we do not fail to use our imagination with the help of God, reason, and friends, we will very likely find a new way of life which may well make us even happier than before.

Once we move beyond the false belief that we cannot be happy without X, Y, or Z, we will likely finish the project of reinventing our happiness, because we will probably be unwilling to victimize ourselves through a failure of imagination.

D. Fourth Tactic: Avoid Negative Comparisons

There is one sure way to add anxiety to our moments of suffering—make negative comparisons. As noted above, much of suffering is connected with loss. So if we compare ourselves after the loss to what we were like before the loss, we will not be able to avoid frustration and resentment. I am a veritable expert at this because my vision loss has been gradual, and so there is an opportunity every few months to make another comparison to the past, which reveals yet another frustrating loss. I can't help myself—when I notice a new decrease in vision, the frustration and resentment well up within me. Frustration at new losses is difficult to control, precisely because it is new, and it forces itself upon me—I cannot ignore it. I know I am going to have to get adjusted to these new circumstances because I won't be able to function as quickly as before—I'll have to be more careful and use more techniques to prevent mishaps.

Creative adaptation to new losses is essential. As my vision has declined over the years, I have learned one thing—it will probably continue to decline unless I receive a new medical treatment or God grants me a miracle. Thus I know that if new treatments and miracles have not been a part of my life, I should *expect* another loss in the near future, and when it predictably comes, I should take two deep breaths and *resign* myself to the inevitable. Suffering from expected losses is so much easier to take when I don't get myself worked up into a lather, but instead resign myself to my new condition, put myself in God's hands, and get about the business of creatively adapting to the additional loss.

This is not stoic resignation, but Christian resignation, because the source of my detachment from loss does not come from within me—personal strength and courage—but rather from trusting in the loving God who always seems to take care of me, and to use my suffering as a lever for interior and exterior transformation (see Chapter 7). This kind of Christian resignation enables me to transfer my focus from my loss and myself to the new interior opportunities coming through that loss. Making this "trusting resignation" a discipline leads not only to sanity and peace, but to new opportunities in life. I imagine that everyone who feels the pain of aging goes through something similar.

When we can no longer deny or hide these losses from ourselves, we are left with only three options: (1) persisting in resentment, anxiety, and bitterness (with incidental desires to end it all); (2) stoic resignation (which puts the focus on our strength, courage, and resolve); or (3) Christian resignation, in which we place ourselves in the hands of God's loving providence, and creatively adapt to our new circumstances with the certainty that opportunity and transformation will be close at hand. The first option gradually leads to despair, the second option puts the focus on ourselves instead of the opportunity and transformation in the future, and the third presents a peaceful and creative pathway to eternal salvation in the loving God.

I also have a habit of reliving past long-term losses—for example, when I am being driven down the highway, and everything is blurry, I will think to myself, "I used to be able to see the beauty of the mountains and the sky, and the ocean ...", at which point my frustration, anxiety, and resentment levels begin to rise. It's a form of self-torture that is completely unnecessary, because I can still be happy, productive, faith-filled, and contributive without being able to see the beauty of the mountains and the sky, etc. Moreover, the brain has an interesting way of adapting to its new circumstances; I have become much more sensitive to auditory beauty—the beauty of so many different kinds of bird songs and even the symphony of bird songs at dawn and dusk; the beauty of the wind blowing through the chimes and the feel of the wind as I walk down the outside corridor of the House of Prayer (where I live); the beauty of people's voices and their various tones of affection and trust and goodness; and so much more.

My proclivity to compare myself today with a time prior to my loss comes up in many ways. When I have to ask someone for a ride, I can slip into the following thought: "Boy, I remember the times when I could just get into a car and drive"; or when I have to ask people for help in reading, I think to myself, "I wish I could just pick up a book again and read whatever I want whenever I want." As always, this leads to an increase in anxiety, frustration, and resentment, which is completely unnecessary self-torment. Why? Because I have already adapted to these circumstances without a loss of productivity or contribution. Indeed, the experience of loss has deepened me immeasurably, made me more sensitive to the weaknesses of others, and opened me to the Lord in unexpectedly profound ways. Though I have lost autonomy in driving and reading, I experience new kinds of companionship with those who help me in these areas.

The point I am making is that comparisons of ourselves after a loss to a previous state before the loss is unproductive, anxiety producing, and inhibits our creative imagination to adapt to our new life circumstances. Our power to adapt and the creativity of imagination that we can bring to this process are truly remarkable, but the sure way of undermining them is to compare ourselves with what we once had or what we once were able to do.

So how do we begin the process of Christian resignation? By using three important tools discussed above: "fiat", "spontaneous prayer", and "rationality". The first tool in stopping negative comparisons is to make an authoritative act of the will, which is sometimes called "fiat". My favorite way of doing it is to tell myself, "Stop it!" or "Stop it; this is going to destroy you." Use whatever words you like, but make sure they focus your willpower on bringing an immediate end to the negative comparison. The more you let the negative comparison captivate your imagination, the harder it will be to begin the process of prayer and rationality.

After fiat, I proceed to prayer by using some of the spontaneous prayers similar to the ones given in the previous chapter: "Lord, do not waste one scintilla of this suffering—make some good come out of it for me, others, or Your Mystical Body", or "I give up—You take care of it", or "Father, if it be Your will, let this cup pass from me, but if not, then Thy loving will be done." Sometimes frustration can well up right in the middle of saying these prayers. When it does, I simply tell the Lord what I am thinking and feeling—and then I pray the above prayers.

Once I am able to attain a sense of calm with the Lord, I begin the process of practical thought: How can I adapt to this new loss? Do I need additional assistance? Are there any aids or technology that will help me? When I am relatively calm, I am genuinely surprised by how creative and flexible I can be. As I am thinking, I am careful not to slip back into the comparison: "I recall how much easier it was just a week ago." If this begins to occur, I go right back to fiat: "Stop it!"

Sometimes, particularly during my travels in airports, people will express frustration because I ask a question which is obvious or I am slow in getting through a line, etc., and sometimes I can hear people chuckling at some awkward move I might have made. I feel embarrassed and humiliated when these things first occur, but I don't want to take those humiliations home with me and replay the tapes again and again before I go to bed. So, I use the same threefold technique above. First, I tell myself, "Stop it!" I sometimes have to repeat it several times. I then use my favorite Examen Prayer:[11] "Lord Jesus, help

---

[11] See Volume I (Chapter 9, Section III) for an explanation of the Examen Prayer.

me to be humble-hearted—especially in times of humiliation—with You, who are perfectly humble-hearted."

Jesus endured the greatest of humiliations when people were taunting and laughing at Him. Instead of using His divine authority and power to protect Himself or show Himself to be the true Messiah, he simply endured the humiliation in order to offer it up as self-sacrifice—unconditional love—for the life of the world (see Chapter 8). This helps me immensely, because I know that following the example of Jesus will lead not only to *my* sanctification, but also the sanctification of the people I touch, and even the people I do not know or see. Moreover, I truly love the Lord, and so I truly delight in following Him. This prayer (and my desire to follow the Lord) enables me to turn these little trials into humble-heartedness and gentle-heartedness *with Jesus*, which is a great gift—not only for me but for the many others who have to live with me.

I live in a community that hosts guest priests from all over the United States and Canada. Some of the guests will tell my community members, "It's really edifying to see how happy Bob seems to be despite the vision loss he has experienced in the last few years." My community members tell them that this is not phony, because I don't have any regrets, and I don't make any negative comparisons; I am happy with the pathway toward salvation and service to the Kingdom laid out for me by the Lord, "for when I am weak, then I am strong" (2 Cor 12:10).

Perspective is incredibly important. If we can make the future's opportunities and grace-filled adventure more significant than the lost capabilities of the past, we will not only avoid self-inflicted pain, but be open to the opportunities the Holy Spirit will surely bring. This will enable the Lord to lead us into His eternal Kingdom of Love.

IV. Choosing God's Consolation

When fear and anxiety are mitigated, we experience a sense of calm, but this calm comes from the *absence* of fear and anxiety, which is distinct from a positive feeling of peace and consolation. When fear and anxiety begin to dissipate, we get a sense of relief, but peace, in the sense of consolation, is more than this. Peace in the positive spiritual sense includes an awareness of being in an *empathetic* relationship with God, or in *communion* with the Mystical Body of Christ.

We have all experienced the consolation arising out of friend-ship with another person. This consolation is more than a feeling; it is an *experience* of *real* interpersonal empathy and unity. We might mistakenly think of it as a merely *subjective* state of mind, but it is really an experiential state of mind arising out of an *objective* state of unity with another individual. This experience cannot be produced by taking a mood-altering drug, because these chemical agents cannot produce the empathy and response of another consciousness. Hence they cannot produce a positive experience of companionship and "home"—or an experience of care and love—but only relief from anxiety combined with some sense of well-being or *euphoria*.

Let us return to the theme of *spiritual* peace and consolation. It is analogous to the experience of peace and consolation coming from human friendship—from the *experience* of harmony, complemen-tarity, security, and "home" produced by another's consciousness, except that spiritual peace and consolation do not come from a *human* consciousness, but from a *divine* one.

When God becomes present to our consciousness, He can do so in an overt way in which we feel—and can even be overwhelmed by—an experience of empathy, unity, love, joy, and "home".[12] He does this occasionally to lead us in a particular direction, confirm a decision, or in the final stages of mystical life—to create a portal to Himself.[13] Though we might want God to be overwhelmingly pres-ent to us in this way, all the time, He will not do this, because He wants us *to choose* Him and His way of life, which means being far more subtle than overwhelming us with joy, unity, and "home". He

[12] See Volume I, Chapter 8, for a description of affective consolation in the spiritual life. See also the descriptions of extraordinary consolation in the following works: C. S. Lewis, *Surprised by Joy: The Shape of My Early Life* (New York: Harcourt, Brace, Jovanovich, 1966); Evelyn Underhill, *Mysticism: A Study in the Nature and Development of Man's Spiritual Con-sciousness* (London: Methuen, 1930); Saint Teresa of Avila, "The Book of Her Life", in *The Collected Works of St. Teresa of Avila*, trans. Kieran Kavanaugh and Otilio Rodriguez (Wash-ington, D.C.: ICS Publications, 1976), 1:31–308; Saint John of the Cross, "The Living Flame of Love", in *The Collected Works of St. John of the Cross*, trans. Kieran Kavanaugh and Otilio Rodriguez (Washington, D.C.: ICS Publications, 1979), pp. 569–649.

[13] See Volume I, Chapter 8, for a detailed explanation of spiritual consolation.

wants our love to spring from a resonance with His message about love, virtue, and salvation—before He continuously sustains us with consolation and ecstasy. For this reason, most Christian mystics agree that our spiritual life progresses along three stages:

1. The purgative stage, where we free ourselves from attachments to "the glories of this world" to embrace Christ's ideal of virtue and love
2. The illuminative stage, which is characterized by increasing enlightenment and detachment from the world
3. The unitive stage, in which the soul has attained a state of perfection and is united to God in love and joy[14]

Assuming that most of us are somewhere in the purgative stage, or perhaps in the illuminative stage (which is difficult to attain, and more infrequent), then God's presence to us will not be manifest as overwhelming affective consolation—most of the time. Some of us will have experiences of this kind of consolation—similar to C. S. Lewis' "stabs of joy" (recounted in his early autobiography *Surprised by Joy*),[15] but these will be intermittent and generally used by God to lead us in a new direction, or make us aware of His loving, beautiful, and joy-filled consciousness. Most of the time, God will manifest Himself to us through *ordinary* consolation—a sense that He is present, that His light is stronger than the darkness. When we experience this kind of consolation, we have a sense of peace and a taste of "ultimate home" that keeps alienation, emptiness, and darkness at bay. This is the kind of consolation that Paul speaks about in the Letter to the Philippians:

Have no anxiety about anything, but in everything by prayer and supplication with thanksgiving let your requests be made known to God.

[14]See Chapter 6, Section IV.D, on Saint Teresa of Calcutta. See also the description of these three stages in Benedict Groeschel, *Spiritual Passage: The Psychology of Spiritual Development* (New York: Crossroads, 1984), pp. 1–60. See also Teresa of Avila, "The Book of Her Life".

[15]See Lewis, *Surprised by Joy*. I discussed this kind of "affective consolation" in Volume I, Chapter 8, Section II, giving examples from the life of C. S. Lewis, myself, and well-known Christian saints.

And the peace of God, which passes all understanding, will keep your hearts and your minds in Christ Jesus. (4:6–7)

How can we as ordinary pilgrims open ourselves to the peace of Christ, especially during times of suffering? We need to *choose* it. This can be accomplished through three practices:

1. Choosing to remove our emotional blocks to consolation
2. Entering into the domain of the sacred (through church, an icon, or religious objects like a Bible or a rosary)
3. Acknowledging God's presence, and offering simple prayers

By doing these things, we freely invite God into our consciousness, and most of the time, if it is consistent with our own and other's salvation, He will enter. Sometimes He will enter right away; sometimes He will delay a few hours; and sometimes He will delay even longer—but to ordinary people like ourselves (who are not going through a dark night of the soul[16]), He will come; and when He does, He will manifest Himself as "positive peace", a sense of being at home with Him, or with "the communion of saints". These feelings may not be overwhelmingly joyful, but they will be peaceful— empathetically peaceful, the peace of being in communion with a being of great wisdom, strength, and love, who loves us and wants to be with us.

How do we engage in these three practices which allow God to enter into our hearts? Before discussing each one, it is important to bear one principle in mind: "keep it *simple*", as simple as Saint Thérèse of Lisieux's "little way".[17]

---

[16] This state of the spiritual life occurs during the latter part of the illuminative stage, prior to the unitive stage, and can be a very long period of aridity, often called "the desert experience". It is explained in Chapter 6, Section IV.D, with respect to the life of Saint Teresa of Calcutta.

[17] For a brief incisive summary of Saint Thérèse's "little way", see Paul Marie De La Croix's "St. Therese's Life in the Carmel of Lisieux and the Influence of Her 'Little Way'", taken from *Carmelite Spirituality*, EWTN, accessed June 8, 2016, http://www.ewtn.com /therese/carmel.htm (see Paul Marie De La Croix, *Carmelite Spirituality in the Teresian Tradition* [Washington, D.C.: Institute of Carmelite Studies, 1994]). Her spiritual autobiography is filled with simple practices to stay in communion with the Lord. See the references to it in Chapter 8, Section III.

With respect to the first practice (choosing to remove our emotional blocks to consolation), we might wonder why anyone would want to block God's consolation in times of suffering. Most people don't *want* to block God's consolation; the circumstances surrounding their suffering lead them into erroneous and even dark decisions. Some people "give up" when suffering comes, and so they believe that consolation will *never* come. Some people are angered by their new negative circumstances, so they blame God and distance themselves from Him. They have no intention of seeking consolation from the One with whom they are angry. Others believe they deserve the suffering they have received, and so they mistakenly believe that the "payback god" has justly inflicted punishment on them (see Chapter 2, Section II.B). Still others who deeply resent their suffering refuse to be consoled; they hold on to their suffering as if it were a prized possession, an unpayable debt: "I will never forgive you for this pain I am enduring; my unforgiveness toward you is one of my greatest accomplishments." Still others become entranced by their suffering; they are thrown into bewilderment and a state of abeyance. They become enervated and lose the desire and energy to crawl out of their listless state, allowing themselves to be perpetually paralyzed by it.

Most of us have emotional dispositions, personalities, and histories that "tend toward" one or more of the above attitudes, and when suffering comes, we "naturally" move toward these dispositions without really thinking about them. Hence we find ourselves in a resentful, listless, unforgiving, or dark frame of mind without knowing how we got there. We don't even recognize that we have slipped into the darkness—we are "just there" unreflectively.

What makes matters worse, when we are in this negative frame of mind, we become convinced of its "truth". Most of us will recognize that when we are in a dark mood or frame of mind, we tend to believe the bad news as if it were truth itself—and disbelieve the good news as if it were false prima facie. Dark moods favor dark "truths".

Most of us will also recognize that when we are not in a state of darkness, we do not view darkness to be true a priori. Instead, we look to evidence of the mind and heart to determine truth. Rather than giving credence to Murphy's Law, we look for light where it can be reasonably and responsibly found. This is the habit we will want to foster even when we are immersed in darkness.

If we are going to choose consolation (choose to allow God into our hearts), we will have to recognize how our moods can affect our perception, affirmation, and rejection of the truth, and then we must look to the evidence and confront "dark truths" with that evidence. If we look at the darkness soberly, we will likely see that it conflicts with the unconditionally loving God, the teaching of Jesus Christ, our call to eternal joy, and the way God has worked with us in the past. We can gain this sobriety initially by considering the evidence for our resurrection (Chapter 1), the unconditionally loving heart of God (Chapter 2), and the way that God works through our suffering for our own and other's salvation (Chapter 3). When we see the conflict between our dark frame of mind and the truth of Jesus Christ, we have to *choose* the evidence and respect the light of truth. When I do this, I make an intentional act of the will, saying, "I am going to get over this mood and choose Christ—the hope, the light, and the truth of the unconditionally loving God." Some may say that this is easier said than done. Perhaps so, but if we do not *choose* the truth of God, and as a consequence, do not *choose* God's consolation, then we consign ourselves to the darkness; and if we let the darkness last long enough, we condemn ourselves to it.

Some readers may be thinking that the above advice is the attitude of Pollyanna: "I will just mindlessly wish myself into a happier reality and future." I truly hope that most of you are not thinking this; otherwise, I have wasted a lot of ink on Volumes II and III of this Quartet, not to mention Chapters 1 through 4 of this volume. The difference between Pollyanna and Jesus Christ is that there is reasonable and responsible evidence for believing that He and His promise of resurrection into unconditional love are *true*. Pollyanna prefers happiness to truth; Jesus revealed that truth *is* eternal happiness in unconditional love. Only a cynic would proclaim the hope of Jesus Christ to be "too good to be true" without examining the evidence upon which this hope is founded.

Recall that there are two kinds of evidence in support of Jesus' promise of our resurrection:

1. Evidence of the heart
2. Evidence of the mind

242 CONTENDING WITH SUFFERING IN THE SHORT-TERM

Let us first consider evidence of the heart, which reveals interiorly what Jesus taught exteriorly—that love (*agapē*) is the highest meaning, goodness, and reality, and therefore, the highest truth about life, human dignity, and fulfillment—therefore, about God Himself. This truth cannot be affirmed by empirical evidence or logical proof; it is known intuitively, when our powers of empathy, conscience, and transcendent meaning are focused on our experience of being loved and loving others. This experience and intuition call us to affirm the truth of love, though we can choose to ignore or deny it. If we affirm that love is our highest meaning, dignity, and destiny, and through this affirm Jesus' teaching on the unconditional love of God, then we will also know *in our hearts* that God would not have created us with the desire for eternal and unconditional love and also created our nature to be fulfilled by it, without intending to fulfill it.[18] This conviction of the heart can stand alone without any complementary evidence of the mind.

We may now turn to the second kind of evidence—that of the mind. For those in need of additional evidence for the resurrection— particularly in response to materialistic objections—we presented four major kinds of evidence in Volumes II and III of this Quartet (summarized in Chapter 1, Section I of this volume).[19] They are

1. the historical evidence of Jesus' Resurrection, using criteria of historicity (Volume III, Chapter 4),
2. evidence of the Resurrection from the Shroud of Turin (Volume III, Appendix 1),
3. evidence of survival of human consciousness after bodily death from medical studies of near-death experiences (Volume II, Chapter 5), and
4. evidence of miracles performed in the name of Jesus (i.e., the risen Jesus) in the early Church and in the contemporary Church (Volume III, Chapter 5).

[18] This was discussed extensively in Volume III, Chapter 1, of this Quartet.

[19] In addition to the four kinds of evidence listed here, we also presented two philosophical proofs of God in Volume II (Chapter 3 and Appendix 2), evidence of an intelligent Creator from contemporary physics (Volume II, Appendix 1), the evidence of the numinous experience and the intuition of the sacred (Volume II, Chapters 1 and 2), and evidence from the four transcendental desires (Volume II, Chapter 4).

At this juncture, the reader may want to review the above kinds of evidence in Volumes II and III of this Quartet, as well as Chapter 1 (Section I) of this volume. Though this evidence will never be *perfectly convincing* for the reasons mentioned in Chapter 1, it should be significant enough to ground *reasonable and responsible belief*, which is the difference between Christian faith and unexamined optimism.

After reviewing the evidence of the heart and mind, we will want to confront our emotional blocks to choosing consolation by examining them in light of this evidence. We will want to see the falsity of these negative frames of mind and use our reasonable and responsible belief to get over them—and to reject the negative spell and control of these emotional dispositions. To address these frames of mind, if you are a passionate personality (like yours truly), you might use the following words of Jesus: "Get behind me, Satan!" (Mt 16:23); if you are of a more gentle temperament, you might say, "I am not going to fall for this one again." Once you have made your act of the will, turn to the Lord in prayer and ask Him to help you reinforce it. It will probably take more than one act of the will to gain control over persistent emotional blocks to consolation. So be prepared to confront those negative blocks with the truth again and again. Each time you do this, ask the Lord for help to confirm the truth in your heart, as well as your mind. If the research of Dr. Martin Seligman is correct, we should be able to overcome, at least partially, the most persistent negative and pessimistic frames of mind by learning, will, and habit.[20] Imagine the power of that act of the will backed by the evidence of heart and mind—confirmed by the grace of God through prayer.

This brings us to the second practice for choosing consolation: entering into the domain of the sacred (through church, icons, and religious objects such as a Bible or a rosary). Up to now, we have been talking about our *interior* frame of mind—confronting dark and

---

[20]Dr. Martin Seligman, the father of positive psychology, has written a book distinguishing between "learned helplessness" and "learned optimism", which shows the importance of *choosing*, of making an act of the will, to overcome "collapse into helpless inactivity". If we combine Seligman's *choice* to extricate ourselves from negative states of mind with the evidence for the promise of our resurrection and the teaching of Jesus as well as the confirmation of this evidence by God through prayer, we can overcome the most persistent of negative and pessimistic moods. See Martin Seligman, *Learned Optimism: How to Change Your Mind and Your Life* (New York: Simon and Schuster, 1998), pp. 205–53.

negative mindsets with the evidence and truth of Jesus Christ, and our *choice* to control the former with the latter. But God's grace is not limited to our thinking processes and choices; it can also come to us from *exterior* manifestations of the sacred—through a church community, a church building, the Mass, sacraments, and sacramentals (e.g., blessed religious pictures or statues). Though the conscious mind is attuned to reasons and choices, the unconscious mind is attuned to symbols, ambience, and ethos (collective beliefs, feelings, and spirit). God's grace works through both dimensions of the human psyche. Hence, when suffering occurs, we can simply go into a church and, without thinking anything, become attuned to the presence of God in that place—with its symbols, ethos, and ambience. Being still in a sacred place can open us to God's consolation. Similarly, we can hold an open Bible in our hands (without reading it) and open ourselves to consolation. Simply gazing upon a religious picture or statue, or contemplating an icon, can produce the same effect. "Entering into the domain of the sacred" can bring great peace of mind—and heart.

Some readers may be thinking that this is a nice "feel good" trick to get our unconscious mind focused on something more positive and optimistic. Though this may be partially true, it is not the *whole* truth. Sacred places, symbols, art, and objects are not simply stimulants of positive feelings; they are *icons*, portals to God and conduits of grace.

In Volume II (Chapter 1) of this Quartet, we spoke of the numinous experience and the sense of the sacred. We discussed Rudolf Otto's view that the numinous experience is not a mere psychic stimulation, but an experience of something mysterious, or more properly, *someone* mysterious, fascinating, and inviting. It is an experience of *the numen*—the holy One, the conscious and interpersonal Other. Earlier in this section, we spoke about the difference between a *feeling* induced by a mood-altering drug versus the *experience* of being in relationship with and at home with another consciousness. When we enter into the domain of the sacred with faith—whether it be through a sacred place, sacred symbols, art, or objects—the psychic state is decidedly one of an *experience* of relationship and home with another consciousness, not a human consciousness, but a mysterious, overwhelming, fascinating, inviting consciousness that elicits awe,

worship, wonder, and, above all, *peace*. This experience is not so
much a sense of increased pleasure (a psychic high) as an experience
of being comforted, supported, and reassured (at home), from which
we derive the word "consolation" (from the Latin *consolare*—"to
offer solace, comfort, or encouragement"). Consolation is not merely
a "good feeling"; it is an offer from a *conscious interpersonal Being* of
comfort or encouragement.

In Volume II (Chapter 2), we discussed Mircea Eliade's warning
about "modern nonreligious man", who abandons his sense of transcendence and loses his faith, as well as his sense of *icon*, the ability
to enter into a sacred domain in faith through which he experiences
relationship with and home in the sacred and mysterious Other. Eliade indicates that this will cause nonreligious man to lose his sense of
ultimate meaning, destiny, and home, which will in turn cause alienation from himself—he will not feel at home in the cosmos or in his
own being. Furthermore, he will lose the capacity to "enter a sacred
domain" and to sense the comfort, peace, and home of the sacred interpersonal Other who manifests Himself through sacred places, symbols, and objects.[21] Modern nonreligious man will be deprived of
ultimate meaning, dignity, fulfillment, or home, and he will be at a
loss to find a way out of cosmic alienation, emptiness, and loneliness.
Little wonder the American Psychiatric Association and the Austin
Institute find that nonreligiously affiliated people are more unhappy
and despondent than religiously affiliated ones.[22]

My point here is that we should never abandon our sense of sacred
place, symbol, and object because it seems passé or unsophisticated.
This is tantamount to giving ourselves a lobotomy because the culture says it's cool. The evidence of the mind and heart testify to
the primacy of love, the Resurrection, and the revelation of Jesus
Christ, which not only validates our ultimate meaning, dignity,
and fulfillment, but also the reality of the numen and its presence
within us. Since God wants to give consolation—comfort, peace, and

---

[21] See the extensive analysis in Volume II, Chapter 2, Sections I.B and I.C.

[22] See Kanita Dervic et al., "Religious Affiliation and Suicide Attempt", *American Journal of Psychiatry* 161, no. 12 (December 2004): 2303–8, http://ajp.psychiatryonline.org/article.aspx?articleid=177228. See also Austin Institute, "Are Religious People Happier?", January 23, 2015, http://www.austin-institute.org/research/media/are-religious-people-happier/.

encouragement through sacred places and objects—we should allow ourselves to receive and enjoy His consolation. To do otherwise is to stay in the darkness naïvely, or perhaps better, to choose it.

This brings us to the third practice for choosing consolation: acknowledging God's presence and offering simple prayers. When we have positioned ourselves in a sacred place, like a church, or we are in proximity to a sacred object, such as a Bible, a sacred image, or a sacred object, like a rosary, we will want to acknowledge the presence of God in a very simple way: "Lord, I know You are present here", or "Lord, I know You are beside me." You may add other short phrases that express your relationship with God, such as, "Lord I know You love me, and I know You are here." Or, "Lord, I know You want to be with me; I know You are here with me." These affirmations of the truths taught to us by Jesus are essential because they keep us focused on the disposition of God's heart toward us, and stave off the false notions of God that can sometimes emerge from the unconscious part of our psyche (see Chapter 2). Some may be thinking that this is a presumptuous practice, because we are presuming what God would be saying: "How can we say, 'Lord, I know You love me', when He has not directly told us at that moment that He loves us?" Jesus *has* made it abundantly clear that His Father and He are unconditional love (Volume III, Chapters 2 and 3). He has also made it abundantly clear that He wants to save us and will help us in every way possible, within the parameters of our freedom, to enter the Kingdom of Heaven. We do not have to make sure that this truth applies to each of us in particular, or to any particular time, because God's salvific intention is for everyone and for all times. As the blessing of the Paschal candle at Easter Vigil proclaims, "Christ yesterday and today, the beginning and the end, Alpha and Omega— all time belongs to Him, and all the ages, to Him be glory and power through every age for ever. Amen."

It is perfectly okay to presume the words of Jesus, particularly when they are His words and intentions for all people for all ages. To begin prayer by acknowledging the loving and salvific intention of Jesus for us, even when we have sinned egregiously, is truth and consistent with the will of the One who loves all sinners and welcomes them as the Good Shepherd and the Father of the Prodigal Son. So let us with great confidence begin our path to consolation by

1. confronting our emotional blocks with the evidence of heart and mind given above,
2. positioning ourselves in a sacred place or near a sacred object or objects, and
3. acknowledging God's presence and love by saying something like, "Lord, I know You are here, and I know You love me."

Now all we need do is ask for what we want—peace, consolation, salvation, protection, guidance, inspiration, and the loving will of God. We don't even have to ask specifically for peace; we can ask for other gifts of God, and peace will come through those petitions. For example, after I acknowledge God's presence and love for me, I say the following: "Abba, Father, Thy loving will be done; Lord Jesus, save me and protect me; Holy Spirit, inspire me and guide me." When I ask for these gifts, I frequently experience the peace and consolation of God before anything else. God knows what we need, and He will bestow peace on us when we ask Him, so long as it is consistent with our salvation and freedom. Jesus has promised this unconditionally:

> Come to me, all who labor and are heavy laden, and I will give you rest. Take my yoke upon you, and learn from me; for I am gentle and lowly in heart, and you will find rest for your souls. For my yoke is easy, and my burden is light. (Mt 11:28–30)

I generally say the above prayer many times, and sometimes dozens of times, because asking for these gifts keeps me connected with God, and the longer I am connected to Him both consciously and unconsciously, the more His consolation breaks through the darkness of suffering, freeing me to pursue the opportunities in suffering (Chapters 7 and 8). For the moment, we will want to remember that receiving the Lord's consolation is in many ways dependent on our choice. We must choose to confront the deceptions of darkness with the light of truth, by reflecting on the evidence of heart and mind, positioning ourselves in sacred places or near sacred objects, acknowledging the Lord's love and presence, and asking for what we need. If peace is consistent with our salvation, God will give it, along with a sense of His empathy and care. We are not alone in our suffering; He is all around us, and if we choose it, He will manifest His peace to help us through times of tribulation.

V. Conclusion

There is far too much information in this and the previous chapter to remember, and I do not suggest that you do so. However, you may want to keep either this book or a photocopy of this and the previous chapter in a place where you can remember it when suffering comes. Some spouses and friends have told me that they benefitted by reading to one another some of my older notes on suffering. This is especially true if suffering is impacting both spouses or both friends. There is no better way of learning and appropriating practical information than when you really need it. Once you have used Jesus' teachings, spontaneous prayers, and the above practical advice during times of need, I suspect it will stay with you for quite some time.

Rationality and natural virtue, friendships, reshaping expectations, and avoiding comparisons can be hugely complementary to prayer and can transform a potentially negative experience of suffering into an opportunity for growth in identity, virtue, love, and salvation. If this is to occur, we will have to do something more than mitigate anxiety. We will have to open ourselves to the truth of God's love and his promise of our resurrection, confront the falsity of darkness, and seek the consolation that God desires to offer us. We will then be free to know the opportunities awaiting us. Before we do this, we will want to look more deeply into the nature of love, particularly Jesus' self-sacrificial love for the world, which is the subject of the next chapter.

PHASE THREE

Benefitting from Suffering in the Long-Term

Foundations 6–9

Chapter Six

Love One Another as I Have Loved You

Sixth Foundation: The Unity of Suffering and Love in Self-Sacrifice

Introduction

Suffering is not antithetical to love; rather, it is ingredient to love's highest expression: self-sacrifice. Perhaps the best way of showing this is to explore the nature of love through the paradigm given in Volume I of this Quartet: the four levels of happiness. The four levels of happiness give rise to four levels of love, and as we shall see, suffering has virtually *no* value for those living for Level One and Level Two love; however, suffering has *immense* value for those living for Level Three love, and *ultimate* value for those living for Level Four love. We will also be discussing four *kinds* of love: *storgē* (affection), *philia* (friendship), *eros* (romantic love leading to exclusive commitment), and *agapē* (love directed toward the other alone that is forgiving, compassionate, and self-sacrificial). As we will show, *agapē* is the primary *opportunity* of suffering. The more we understand Level Four love and *agapē*, the better we will understand the opportunities of suffering and the positive momentum that can come from it.[1]

This chapter will shed light on the deepest manifestations of love and why love is our reason for being, our highest dignity, and our eternal destiny. When we understand "love" in this way, we will also see the goodness and power of suffering to help us actualize this

[1] See Chapter 7 (the opportunities of suffering) and Chapter 8 (the mystical opportunity of suffering).

highest love in our lives, and in view of this, we will no longer be able to view suffering as a mere negative, but as one of the most powerful agents of positive change in our lives. As such, suffering cannot be meaningless—for it leads us to our *ultimate* purpose: eternal and unconditional love with God and the blessed throughout eternity.

Our dominant view of happiness will influence (and probably determine) the way we view love. Furthermore, the way we view happiness and love will affect the way we view suffering. Hence we will structure this chapter as follows:

  I.   Brief Review of the Four Levels of Happiness
 II.   Four Levels of Love
III.   Four *Kinds* of Love
 IV.   Exceptional Love and the Lives of Some Saints

I. Brief Review of the Four Levels of Happiness

Volume I of the Quartet was dedicated to finding true happiness, and specifically the four levels of happiness. We have revisited those four levels in various chapters of this volume. However, a brief review of them might help in understanding the four levels of love. Recall that the lower levels are immediately gratifying, surface apparent, and intensive, while the higher levels are pervasive, enduring, and deep—but not vice versa. Level One arises out of the satisfaction of physical-material desires, such as a good bowl of linguini, nice clothes, a good car, and a fine bottle of wine. Level Two arises out of ego-comparative advantage, coming to us from increases or comparative advantage in status, popularity, power, control, giftedness, intelligence, athleticism, beauty, and of course winning. Level Three comes from making a positive difference to someone or something beyond ourselves, making the world optimally better off for our having lived, such as making a contribution to family, friends, community, church, Kingdom of God, society, or culture. Level Four comes from satisfaction of our transcendental desires—the desire to be in relationship with God through religious community, prayer, worship, and sacred time and symbols. It is incited not only by our interior experience of God (the numinous experience), but also our conscience and our desire for perfect and unconditional truth, love, goodness, beauty, and home.

In Volume I (Chapter 3), we looked at three fundamental problems with remaining on Levels One and Two—namely, underliving our lives (not making the contributions or legacy we could have), existential emptiness, and the negative emotions of the "comparison game" (jealousy, fear of loss of esteem, inferiority, superiority and contempt, loneliness, resentment, self-pity, ego rage, ego sensitivities, etc.). We saw that these difficulties could lead to a profoundly unhappy, unmeaningful, and empty life if we do not move to Levels Three and Four. Moreover, we saw that Level Three is not capable of satisfying our restless hearts; for without Level Four, we feel a sense of cosmic emptiness, loneliness, alienation, and guilt coming from the absence of a relationship with the Divine and an absence of ultimate purpose, dignity, and destiny.

We concluded from this that true happiness includes transcendent happiness, which brings Level Three contributive happiness to its fulfillment and allows Level Three happiness, in turn, to bring Levels One and Two happiness to their proper fulfillment. When the four levels are present, we do not have to worry about living for physical gratifications alone—they can bring us happiness in their own proper way without bearing the burden of having to bring us ultimate, pervasive, enduring, and deep happiness, which they cannot do. Similarly, when we allow Levels Three and Four happiness to have a higher place, we don't have to make intelligence, athleticism, beauty, status, power, etc., ends in themselves. We can enjoy the gifts we have—not because they make us better than others, but because we can use them to make an optimal positive difference to family, friends, community, church, the Kingdom of God, and so forth. Finally, we don't have to make contributions in this world an end in themselves. When we allow Level Four to have the highest place, we can make contributions for the sake of the eternal salvation of others, the Kingdom of God, and the will of the Lord, who calls us ultimately to Himself. All four levels of happiness are good, but only the fourth level of happiness can bring the others to their proper fulfillment. If we make lower levels of happiness ends in themselves, they will ultimately leave us dissatisfied, empty, and alienated—opening the way to disappointment, calamity, and even despair.

II. Four Levels of Love

As noted above, as our view of happiness goes, so also goes our view of love; so inasmuch as there are four levels of happiness, there will also be four levels of love. We will discuss each level in turn.

A. Levels One and Two Love

If we have a dominant Level One view of happiness, we are likely to think of love as the fulfillment of libidinal or sexual desires. If external pleasure is most important to our happiness (and quality of life), then it is unlikely that we will be able to look beyond physical gratification in our search for love. Even though the other desires for happiness (and love) are present in us, they will be overshadowed by our dominant view of happiness and will truncate the search for the other three levels of love.

If we have a dominant Level Two view of happiness, then we are likely to view love as the quest to *be loved* by other people. We will generally associate with people who might be able to advance our status, position, wealth, and power, or who might be able to satisfy our needs for affection, romance, and sexual gratification. Recall that all of us have Level Two desires that are good and necessary for our lives, but when Level Two becomes dominant, it tends to restrict our view of "love" to what Aristotle might have called "friendships of utility" or what Maslow called "the need for esteem and the need *to be* loved". Thus, a dominant Level Two view of love is not *truly* generative. It might appear to be generative, but such actions generally expect some "return on investment" (a quid pro quo). Thus, a generous gesture or an offer of help very probably anticipates a return of generosity or help of equal or greater worth. Romance is also viewed in this way—the offer of romantic "gifts and services" anticipates comparable or greater romantic "gifts or services".

In Chapter 7, we will discuss in detail how suffering can help us move from Levels One and Two love to Levels Three and Four love. As we shall see, suffering cannot do this by itself; it provides only the *impetus* to move toward Levels Three and Four. If we actually are to *make* the move, we will have to see Levels Three and Four as not only "an end to the pain of the comparison game", but also the key to our highest fulfillment, dignity, and destiny. If we recognize this, we can transform suffering from sheer meaninglessness into a powerful lever to achieve the fulfillment and self-identity for which we were created. If we *sustain* this move to Levels Three and Four, the highest levels of love will be within our purview, and we will be well on the way to the eternal salvation promised us by Jesus Christ and His unconditionally loving Father.

B. Level Three Love

If we have a dominant Level Three view of happiness, then we are likely to have a truly generative view of love. Thus, we will be interested in *other people's* happiness—alongside our own. Likewise, we will be interested in their welfare, security, and advancement—alongside our own. Though Level Three does not entail the loss of desire for our own happiness, welfare, security, etc., it allows the other's happiness, welfare, and security to be important *in its own right*, meaning that the other's welfare need not be subordinated to *our* welfare or a "return on investment".

For example, I might have a Level Three friendship with someone with whom I expect mutual or reciprocal attentiveness to my needs, welfare, etc. However, if I see that the other's needs are greater or more urgent than my own (in a particular situation), then I am free to attend to those needs without asking myself, "Am I giving more than he is giving?" "Am I getting my fair share out of this friendship?" The freedom that Level Three incites enables me to mitigate my concern for "equality", "just compensation", and the resentments that can arise out of these viewpoints. Level Three enables me to serve others in their needs when they truly need it, without having to keep a strict accounting of the debt owed.

Recall that Level Three happiness is interested in making a positive difference to someone or something beyond myself for no other reason than "making the world a better place". In Level Three, the primary interest is in the betterment of others, the community, and the culture. People who give anonymously to others or who are dedicated to serving others, the community, or the Kingdom of God generally do so because they really want those other people, the community, or the Kingdom of God to be advanced by their efforts and contribution. If they receive recognition, it's a "nice thing", but it is not the reason for the generosity or service.

Viktor Frankl learned this lesson in a concentration camp, and it was reinforced so powerfully throughout his life that he made it the centerpiece of his psychotherapeutic school (logotherapy):

> Being human always points, and is directed, to something or someone, other than oneself—be it a meaning to fulfill or another human being to encounter. The more one forgets himself—by giving himself to a cause to serve or another person to love—the more human he is and the more he actualizes himself. What is called self-actualization is not an attainable aim at all, for the simple reason that the more one would strive for it, the more he would miss it. In other words, self-actualization is possible only as a side-effect of self-transcendence.[2]

If we have a dominant Level Three view of love, it does not mean that we will be detached from our egos. As we saw in Volume I (Chapter 4), it is all too easy to slip into a dominant Level Two viewpoint—sometimes for a few minutes, or a few hours, or a few days, or even longer. However, if we are moderately vigilant about putting Level Three ahead of Level Two, we can keep our view of love relatively generative and detached from surges or spikes of egocentricity. If we look to the good of the other, even when we are seeking our own fulfillment, we will be less inclined to use or diminish the other for egocentric ends. This helps us to free ourselves from objectifying ("thing-a-fying") others, using others, and controlling others. If we can see the other's good as equal to or more important than our good, we become *free* to be generous with our time and self-gift—which makes us free for commitment to the other.

There are three primary powers within us that help us to move to this Level Three perspective: empathy, conscience, and prayer-grace (Level Four). Let's begin with empathy. Recall from Volume I (Chapter 1) that empathy is a strong power of connection or unity

---

[2] Viktor Frankl, *Man's Search for Meaning: An Introduction to Logotherapy* (New York: Beacon Press, 1984), p. 101.

with another person that breaks down our barriers of autonomy and egocentricity, so that doing the good for the other is just as easy, if not easier, than doing the good for ourselves. Recall also from Volume I (Chapter 4) that empathy must get its start from "looking for the good news in the other"—looking for kindness, strength, virtue, delightfulness, and transcendent mystery in the other. This ability to "look for the good news in the other", in its turn, depends on having at least a dominant Level Three view of happiness—to live for making an optimal positive difference to the people and world around us. But what does this mean?

If we are going to use our remarkable capacity for empathy to strengthen the bond between ourselves and others, we will have to commit ourselves to looking for the good news in the other, which entails a dominant desire to make an optimal positive difference to the world with our lives. Thus, the move to dominant Level Three is critical to unleashing the power of empathy. Once empathy has been unleashed, then "caring about" and "caring for" others becomes almost effortless. Battling our egocentricity is manageable through the power of empathy, but without it—at least in my case—it would be unmanageable. Empathy and care for others moves us to restrict our egocentricity without relying on strength of the will. The strength of our care *automatically* diminishes the strength of our Level Two desires, making them less compelling. The dominant Level Three viewpoint needed for this freedom is within the range of our *natural* ability to choose. As we shall see, our natural ability can be assisted and supported by prayer and grace (Level Four).

Let us proceed now to the second interior capacity that helps us move to a dominant Level Three view of love: *conscience*. Recall from Volume I (Chapter 1) that conscience is one of the most important human faculties. It is generally viewed as an inner attraction to and love of goodness and justice and an inner shunning and fear of evil and injustice. Our love of the good leads to feelings of nobility and fulfillment when we do the good, while our shunning and fear of evil leads to feelings of guilt and alienation when we do evil. Thus this two-sided inner sense causes not only feelings, but a sense of our inner self before and after we do good or evil. Recall also that Immanuel Kant and John Henry Newman attempted to show that conscience has a *divine* origin, and that Lewis and Tolkien recognized its role in our sense of a cosmic struggle between good and evil.[3]

This powerful attraction to the good and fear-revulsion toward evil helps us in our relationships with others. If we are attentive to our conscience, we will not want to hurt, harm, or use others. If we do, then we will probably feel alienated for treating them basely and unjustly (which they do not deserve). We will also sense our cooperation with evil, which moves us away from the perfectly good source of our conscience. Even the anticipation of hurting, harming, or using others causes feelings of self-alienation and guilt. When we take cognizance of our conscience, then we are imbued with the Silver Rule in our hearts and our whole being: "do not do unto others what you would not have them do unto you."

Recall also that there is another dimension to conscience—namely, the attraction to the good, and the feelings of nobility and "home with self" that arise when we follow that attraction and do the good. This dimension of the power of conscience is one of the primary forces behind our desire for Level Three. Recall that Level Three is not only a *choice*, but also a *desire*. Inasmuch as our desire to make an optimal positive difference to others and the world comes from the attraction to the good and the noble (from conscience), then we could say that the desire for Level Three is inspired by conscience. So, conscience inspires the desire for Level Three, and when we *choose* to follow that desire, it becomes stronger within us, and the stronger the desire becomes, the easier it is to follow. After a while, the desire can become so strong that it subordinates the desires for Level One and Level Two to itself—and becomes a habit of mind and heart, what the ancients called "a virtue". Thus, continually choosing the desires of conscience creates the condition necessary for making Level Three happiness and Level Three love not only a dominant *desire*, but also a dominant part of our identity—*who* we are. As with empathy, this process induced by conscience (and choosing to follow conscience) is within the range of our *natural* capacity, but it can be greatly enhanced by prayer-grace (Level Four), which is our next topic.

[3] For an extended treatment of these subjects, see Volume II, Chapter 2, and the sequel to the Quartet, *Called out of Darkness: Contending with Evil through Virtue and Prayer* (San Francisco: Ignatius Press, forthcoming).

C. How Prayer and Grace Enhance Level Three Love

We may now proceed to prayer and grace, which arises out of Level Four desire and choice. As we shall see in Chapters 7 and 8, the power of empathy and conscience can be greatly enhanced by prayer and grace. With respect to empathy, our relationship with the loving God—particularly through contemplative prayer and the Examen Prayer[4]—frees our emotions and desires from egocentric dominance. The more we know the heart of God from our interior life and Christian revelation, the more God's love becomes co-natural with us— God's heart of unconditional love speaks more and more clearly to our hearts.[5] As this occurs, our love becomes more like His, and we are gradually purified from our egocentric desires and perspectives. As God's heart speaks more easily to our hearts, it becomes easier to look for and see the good news in the other, and as a result, easier to empathize with the other, and care about and for the other.

It should be noted that this transformation of our hearts through identification with the heart of God does not arise out of a stoic act of will. For example, I don't repeatedly insist to myself that "I'm going to have the heart of Jesus Christ; I'm going to have the heart of Jesus Christ—I really, really am . . ." This will not do anything except frustrate us because we cannot "power" ourselves out of egocentricity. Exerting our "will to power" serves only to turn us in on ourselves instead of toward the One whose love we want to imitate.

A far better strategy is to involve our *hearts* and the Lord of love. How? By contemplating on Him, praying to Him, and expressing our desire to become more like Him in His love. As we contemplate on the unconditional love of God, we become more and more aware of how much He has loved us and continues to love us. This incites trust, gratitude, and love, which in turn incites the desire to be more like Him—to be His companion in the salvation of the world. This process allows the Lord's heart to speak to our hearts, which produces a gentle yet persistent transformation through loving identification with the Lord.

---

[4] See Volume I, Chapters 7 and 9.

[5] See Fulton J. Sheen, *Cor ad Cor Loquitor: Heart Speaks to Heart* (Bethesda, Md.: Ministr-o-Media, 1979).

Evidently, transformation through contemplation and prayer is radically different from a stoic act of will in which we attempt to beat ourselves into submission to the will of a stoic god. Even if we succeed in doing this, we do not arrive at greater empathy and the third level of love—but rather at a kind of hard-hearted self-righteousness. Jesus' Parable of the Tax Collector and the Pharisee praying in the Temple is most instructive here. The Pharisee has been very successful at fulfilling the prescriptions of the law, and Jesus says that the "Pharisee stood and prayed thus with *himself*, 'God, I thank you that I am not like other men, extortioners, unjust, adulterers, or even like this tax collector'" (Lk 18:11; emphasis mine).

In sum, prayer, particularly contemplation and the Examen, allows *God* to touch our hearts (grace), which frees us from our egocentricity so that we might empathize and care for others with ever-greater compassion, humility, and authenticity—in imitation of Jesus. In this way, Level Four supports and enhances Level Three desires, which in turn enhance Level Three love.

Prayer-grace also supports and enhances the natural power of *conscience*. An important series of studies shows that religious people may not necessarily *know* more about ethics than nonreligious people; however, they are less willing to be unethical—particularly at the moment of decision. For example, an empirical study by K. Praveen Parboteeah[6] used the religious typology of Marie Cornwall[7] to confirm the findings of previous studies,[8] showing that religious belief is negatively related to individuals' willingness to justify unethical behaviors. In other words, religiously affiliated people are less willing

[6]See K. Praveen Parboteeah, Martin Hoegl, and John B. Cullen, "Ethics and Religion: An Empirical Test of a Multidimensional Model", *Journal of Business Ethics* 80, no. 2 (June 1, 2008): 387–98.

[7]See Marie Cornwall et al., "The Dimensions of Religiosity: A Conceptual Model with an Empirical Test", *Review of Religious Research* 27, no. 3 (March 1986): 226–44.

[8]See Charles R. Tittle and Michael R. Welch, "Religiosity and Deviance: Toward a Contingency Theory of Constraining Effects", *Social Forces* 61, no. 3 (March 1983): 653–82; Gary R. Weaver and Bradley R. Agle, "Religiosity and Ethical Behavior in Organizations: A Symbolic Interactionist Perspective", *Academy of Management Review* 27, no. 1 (January 2002): 77–97; Jonathan H. Turner, *The Institutional Order* (New York: Addison-Wesley Educational Publishers, 1997); and Thomas J. Fararo and John Skvoretz, "Action and Institution, Network and Function: The Cybernetic Concept of Social Structure", *Sociological Forum* 1, no. 2 (March 1, 1986): 219–50.

to engage in unethical conduct at the moment of decision.[9] If religion helps us to follow the dictates of our conscience, then it will also support and enhance our capacity for Level Three love.

Prayer-grace supports Level Three love beyond the enhancement of empathy and conscience, because it puts us in touch with and partially fulfills our transcendental nature. Recall the study of Kanita Dervic in the *American Journal of Psychiatry*, which showed that religiously unaffiliated subjects had higher rates of suicide, impulse aggressivity, meaninglessness, familial tension, and past substance abuse (see the Introduction in this volume).[10] All of these characteristics negatively influence our capacity to love others and ourselves. Put the other way around—prayer and grace enhance the factors that lead to love of neighbor and self. Psychiatric studies seem to verify what Jesus said long ago—that love of God would lead to love of neighbor and self.[11]

D. Level Four Love

Is there any other way in which prayer and grace support and enhance love? The above three ways (the enhancement of empathy, conscience, and our transcendent nature) show how Level Four enhances *Level Three* love, but as you may suspect, it also enhances specifically *Level Four* love. Level Three love is oriented toward specific individuals with whom we have empathy. It does not necessarily extend to the transcendental nature and salvation of those individuals, but only to contributive and ethical treatment of them. However, Level Four love recognizes the transcendental nature, dignity, and destiny of every individual, and so seeks the ultimate

[9] See Paraboteeah, Hoegl, and Cullen, "Ethics and Religion", p. 393.

[10] "Religiously unaffiliated subjects had *significantly* more lifetime suicide attempts and more first-degree relatives who committed suicide than subjects who endorsed a religious affiliation.... Furthermore, subjects with no religious affiliation perceived fewer reasons for living, particularly fewer moral objections to suicide. In terms of clinical characteristics, religiously unaffiliated subjects had more lifetime impulsivity, aggression, and past substance use disorder. No differences in the level of subjective and objective depression, hopelessness, or stressful life events were found." Kanita Dervic et al., "Religious Affiliation and Suicide Attempt", *American Journal of Psychiatry* 161, no. 12 (December 1, 2004): 2303–8, http://ajp.psychiatryonline.org/article.aspx?articleid=177228.

[11] This point is fully explicated in Volume I, Chapters 7–10.

salvific good of those individuals. For dominant Level Four individuals, being empathetic, contributive, and ethically responsible is not enough because Level Four seeks the ultimate transcendental and eternal fulfillment of others. For Christians, this means we will want to help others discover and move toward the unconditional love of God revealed by Jesus.

Dominant Level Four individuals view Level Three love as incomplete—for it only takes into consideration a *small* part of the nature, dignity, and destiny of each person. Level Three love can even lead to the frustration of the much larger part of our nature by overemphasizing the fulfillment of the smaller part. Even though we cannot force or "hound" people into recognizing their transcendental nature and destiny, we can present reasonable and responsible evidence of our transcendence to those who are willing to listen (see Volume II of this Quartet). To those who are willing to look further, we can also give reasonable and responsible evidence for the historicity, Resurrection, and divinity of Jesus (presented in Volume III of this Quartet). At the very least, we can all be witnesses to the increased empathy, conscience, and transcendental happiness coming from our faith, which may provoke some to wonder how they might be able to move toward the joy we seem to "naturally", or perhaps better, "supernaturally", exemplify.

Furthermore, Level Four love extends beyond Level Three love by acknowledging the transcendental significance of good and evil. In Level Three, good and evil are considered to be opposite qualities and effects of our actions and intentions *in this world*. Even though conscience reveals supernatural qualities in goodness (from God) and evil (from a malevolent force), a Level Three perspective does not explicitize these qualities. They remain hidden in the background until we take an interest in our transcendental nature (Level Four), in which case the supernatural dimension of good and evil become explicitized. Similarly, the archetypal myth of our involvement in the cosmic struggle between good and evil will remain solely in the world of our dreams until we become interested in our transcendental nature and destiny (see Volume II, Chapter 2). Sometimes our interest in the cosmic struggle between good and evil can be aroused by reading the Tolkien trilogy (*The Lord of the Rings*) or going to a *Star Wars* movie, but if we have no sense of our transcendental nature, our engagement in it will remain solely on the level of "mere interest" or entertainment. However, if we do have a sense of our transcendental nature and destiny, then these myths have the significance intended by Tolkien for them, who remarked that myths "are not lies". Tolkien argued, according to Joseph Pearce, that

> far from being lies they are the best way—sometimes the only way—of conveying truths that would otherwise remain inexpressible. We have come from God and inevitably the myths woven by us, though they contain error, reflect a splintered fragment of the true light, the eternal truth that is with God.[12]

When we acknowledge transcendence and our transcendent destiny, the archetypal myth within us takes on supernatural significance and we no longer see "good and evil" as the qualities and effects of our actions and intentions *in this world alone*, but rather in the totality of reality that includes both absolute love and absolute egocentricity, absolute light and absolute darkness, and absolute good and absolute evil. Once we recognize this dimension of reality, our love for others cannot stop at fair conduct and ethical propriety; we will want to protect people from the power of darkness by helping them to see the power of absolute light and love. We will desire this not only for individuals, but also for our culture, and even the whole community. In Level Four, love naturally extends itself to promoting supernatural good and absolute love, and defeating supernatural evil and absolute darkness, for the whole community.

III. Four *Kinds* of Love

We are now in a position to correlate the four *levels* of love with the four *kinds* of love presented in Volume III (Chapter 1). In brief, C. S. Lewis presents the four *kinds* of love from classical and Christian writings as follows:[13]

---

[12]Joseph Pearce, "J.R.R. Tolkien: Truth and Myth", *Lay Witness*, September 2001, http://www.catholiceducation.org/en/culture/literature/j-r-r-tolkien-truth-and-myth.html.

[13]See C.S. Lewis, *The Four Loves* (New York: Harcourt, 1960).

- *Storgē*—a *feeling* of affection
- *Philia*—friendship that entails *mutual* gift of self, loyalty, support, and commitment
- *Eros*—sexual-*romantic* love, which is brought to fulfillment through "highest friendship" in a "highest, exclusive relationship"
- *Agapē*—love that seeks only the good of the *other* arising out of the recognition of the unique intrinsic goodness and lovability of that other, leading toward forgiveness, care, compassion, and self-sacrifice for the other

Now let us correlate these four *kinds* of love with the four *levels* of love mentioned above.

A. Storgē—*Affection*

Storgē can be present in all four levels of love. Since it is only a *feeling* of delight or affection, it needs nothing other than an object of affection or delight to be engendered, such as a child or a pet. People who are pursuing physical gratification (Level One); the need to be esteemed or loved (Level Two); empathetic, contributive, and generative love (Level Three); and transcendental love (Level Four) can all experience objects of affection and delight, and the feelings associated with them. *Storgē* is the only kind of love for which the four levels are not significant.

B. Philia—*Friendship*

Philia (friendship) is an entirely different matter. In Level One love, friendship is virtually illusory. Since the other person is viewed mostly as an "object" of gratification—some *thing* to gratify *another*—there is virtually no recognition of another *person* deserving of loyalty, support, contribution, and commitment.[14] We do not think of mere

---

[14] The "objectification" or "thingafication" of another person is explained by Martin Buber as an "I-it relationship". See Martin Buber, *I and Thou* (Eastford, Conn.: Martino Publications, 2010), pp. 10–13.

objects (things) as being worthy or deserving of these subjective qualities. Therefore, *mutual or reciprocal* loyalty, support, contribution, and commitment are virtually nonexistent.

In Level Two love, friendship is not illusory, but it is reduced to what Aristotle called "friendships of utility".[15] A "friend" is someone who can do something for me, can open a door for me, or provide a needed service for me—but is certainly not a *person* with whom I would be in a relationship of mutual concern, care, and commitment. Notice that the person is still objectified (thingafied) in this view of friendship. In Martin Buber's words, we are still on the level of "I-it" instead of "I-thou".[16] What is friendship without the awareness of personhood—that is, without the elements of concern, care, loyalty, support, and commitment? Not much! It barely brings to fruition the potentiality of mutual care and commitment, and is the faintest glimmer of what Jesus called "friendship with His disciples".[17]

As people make the transition from Level Two to Level Three, they may notice fluctuations in their view of others, from "I-it" to "I-thou" back to "I-it", and so forth. It is human nature to return to attitudes and feelings that we have habitually appropriated and used for many years. However, if we make a concerted attempt to live for contribution before ego-comparative advantage and physical gratification, we will eventually see our "grip on old habits" begin to loosen. As will be explained below, prayer-grace (Level Four) can be exceedingly helpful in this process.

As we begin to transition into a Level Three view of the individual person—that is, as a "thou" instead of an "it"—it becomes easier to look for the good news in the other. Why? Because we can see the "good news" beyond characteristics that will bring us ego-comparative advantage. The "good news" is no longer limited to utility, outward beauty, or status enhancement; it extends to the kindness, virtue, friendliness, delightfulness, mystery, transcendence,

[15]See Aristotle, *Aristotle on Friendship: Being an Expanded Translation of the Nicomachean Ethics Books VIII and IX*, trans. and ed. Geoffrey Percival (Cambridge: Cambridge University Press, 2015), pp. 11–19.

[16]See Buber, *I and Thou*, pp. 10–13.

[17]See John 15:15: "No longer do I call you servants, for the servant does not know what his master is doing; but I have called you friends, for all that I have heard from my Father I have made known to you."

and lovability of others. This is the good news from which empathy, concern, and care are fashioned.

In short, if we want to actualize true *philia*, we will want to move to Level Three love, because it entails a Level Three view of happiness (contribution and empathy) and a Level Three view of person— that is, "thou". Level Three individuals can be friends with people having any level of happiness, though the ensuing friendship cannot have the same qualities from level to level because Level Two and Level One people cannot reciprocate in a Level Three way. Since it is difficult for dominant Level One and Level Two people to experience genuine empathy, concern, and care for others (making it difficult to contribute and commit to them freely), we cannot expect reciprocity of friendship in the way that it is given, if we are Level Three or Level Four. This means that a dominant Level Three person will "not grow" very much in friendship with dominant Level One and Level Two people, because the latter do not love others in the same deeply personal way. However, Level Three people can extend themselves to Level One and Level Two people in generosity, genuine care, joy, and commitment without expecting the same level of reciprocity or a deep personal friendship.

If Level Three people are looking for deep personal friendships (or a potential spouse), it is best to seek out Level Three or Level Four friends; otherwise, they can expect a life filled with frustration and disappointed expectations. Some Level Three people believe that they can "make" or "change" dominant Level One-Two people into Level Three-Four people by befriending or marrying them. This strategy rarely works unless the people in question are already in the process of moving toward Level Three and Level Four *on their own*.

Level Three friendships have the potential to grow in depth, contribution, and commitment for decades; true friends can take greater joy in one another, find greater peace through one another, find themselves at home (less alienated) through the other, as well as experiencing the mutuality of care and "being cared for", of supporting and being supported, of committing and "being committed to"— almost indefinitely. As the Book of Sirach says:

> A faithful friend is a sturdy shelter:
> he that has found one has found a treasure.
> There is nothing so precious as a faithful friend,

and no scales can measure his excellence.
A faithful friend is an elixir of life;
and those who fear the Lord will find him.
Whoever fears the Lord directs his friendship aright,
for as he is, so is his neighbor also. (6:14–17)

This passage leads us to Level Four. As we saw above, Level Four (prayer and grace) can be very important in attaining and maintaining Level Three love, and therefore Level Three friendship. Christians' commitment to the teachings of Jesus will incite them to look for the "good news" in others in a Level Three way. They will not only know what to look for, but they will want to look at the other person as Jesus does; and even though it may be difficult to stay focused on these qualities, they will feel moved by their love of the Lord and the grace of the Holy Spirit to hold on to this perspective. It is easier to do something difficult with a friend who is supportive than to do it by ourselves. Speaking personally, I cannot imagine trying to keep my focus on "the good news in the other", amid the bad news, without my faith in Jesus and grace from His Spirit. I do not have enough natural virtue to do this without my commitment to the Lord and His inspiration and love in my life. Frankly, I am not very successful at keeping my focus on Level Three love, even with faith, prayer, and grace, but without it, I would have very few successes and would have long ago succumbed to the bad news and the superficial good news in others (utility, surface beauty, status enhancement, etc.). I am aware of other people who have more natural virtue than myself, and so I would say that if you are *anything* like me, then faith, prayer, and grace are absolutely essential to Level Three happiness, love, and friendship.

Level Four prayer and grace does not stop at helping us to attain and maintain *Level Three* love and friendship. As noted earlier, it helps us to see the transcendent, eternal, and sacred dimension of others; and for Christians, it enables us to see them as brothers and sisters of Jesus, and even as the image of Jesus Himself: "[A]s you did it to one of the least of these my brethren, you did it to me" (Mt 25:40). This brings friendship into a whole new domain. It sees the eternal and transcendent mystery in the other, the presence of Christ in the other, and the dignity that comes from this, and so it seeks to treat others in a fashion commensurate with their eternal, sacred, and divine identity, seeking to bring it to fruition in the eternal Kingdom of unconditional love with Jesus Christ. This perspective changes everything, because love can no longer be focused on the other person *alone*—it must also be focused on the person as a "child of" the loving God. However, when the transition is made, a new kind of love that allows God to possess the other, and the other to belong to God, comes into being. This love recognizes that even a very best friend cannot belong only to *us*, and we cannot belong only to *them*. We must open the relationship to the loving God who alone can fulfill the *eternal and transcendental* nature of the sacred mystery who we call our "friend" or "beloved".

In his insightful autobiography about love and suffering,[18] Sheldon Vanauken describes a change in his relationship with his wife, Davy, when they return to America after a profound conversion to Christianity during their studies with C. S. Lewis at Oxford. Davy takes her conversion to Christianity very seriously and begins to pray and read the Bible daily, poring over it for her Sunday school classes and opening herself to being transformed in the image of Jesus.

Prior to their conversion, they grew in an ever-deepening *Level Three* commitment and love, perhaps as deep as Level Three *philia* (or in their case, *eros*) could go. They describe the exclusivity of their love as a "Shining Barrier", indicating the *sufficiency* of each one for the *completion* and *fulfillment* of the other. When Davy began to take her faith seriously, and to fall more deeply in love with Jesus and His teaching, she discovered that their profound Level Three love was not capable of completing or fulfilling their transcendental nature and their need for redemption by Jesus. She knew that she could not redeem and fulfill Sheldon in this most important respect, and that he could not do the same for her.

Sheldon, on the other hand, was far more reluctant to break the "Shining Barrier" because it was so filled with love, joy, and fulfillment in both the present and his memory of the past. To even think about "breaking the Barrier" brought a sense of deep grief. So as Davy deepened in her loving relationship with Christ, Sheldon became disturbed and resentful toward her journey through the

---

[18] Sheldon Vanauken, *A Severe Mercy: A Story of Faith, Tragedy, and Triumph* (New York: HarperCollins, 1980).

"Shining Barrier". *Intellectually* he knew that she was progressing in love, but *emotionally* he was unable and unwilling to accept it, particularly his insufficiency to complete and fulfill his part in it. At one point he thinks to himself:

> I wanted—what did I want? I wanted the fine keen bow of a schooner cutting the waves with Davy and me—just Davy and me and Flurry— happy and loving and comradely on her decks. Well, there was nothing unChristian about that, as long as God was there, too, and as long as we were neglecting no service of love. But, I wanted Him approving from a considerable distance. I didn't want to be thinking of Him. I wanted to be free—like Gypsy. I wanted life itself, the colour and fire and loveliness of life. And Christ now and then, like a loved poem I could read when I wanted to. I didn't want us to be swallowed up in God. I wanted holidays from the school of Christ. We should, somehow, be able to have the Shining Barrier intact *and* follow the King of Glory. I didn't want to be a saint. Almost none of this did I consciously know—just longings.[19]

As Davy grew in love of Jesus, her love for Sheldon was also transformed. She no longer saw herself as being the completion and fulfillment of her beloved, because she knew that Jesus and His Father alone could do this. So she decided to love Sheldon the best way she could, in her new realization of what love means. He describes it as follows:

> It was the year when Davy, a month or so before its end, offered up her life in holy exchange and utter love for me. Tonight, after Bourges and the "Requiem Mass," she told me, to my horror and dread.[20]

In her Level Four perspective, through the heart of her Christian conversion, Davy felt that the highest possible love for Sheldon would be his salvation in Christ with her, and so she offered up her very life in loving exchange for him and his salvation. Sheldon, still clinging to the Shining Barrier of Level Three, was horrified. Davy's progression in love, and her willingness to sacrifice herself in imitation of Jesus, was now at odds with Sheldon's view of love and life.

[19] Ibid., p. 136.
[20] Ibid., p. 149.

Shortly thereafter Davy contracted a virus that relentlessly attacked her liver. Medical treatment at the time was unable to stop its progress. She was expected to die within a few months. During this period Sheldon knew he would have to evolve in his view of love in order to reach her so that their love could again be truly reciprocal. So he began to allow God, whom he formerly thought would swallow them up, to play a greater role in *his* part of the relationship. He found that by so doing, his love of Davy increased profoundly. As he grew in humility, he was happy to let Jesus fulfill Davy where he could not, and was happy to let go of Davy in order for Jesus to fulfill her. He knew that he had to do this so that Davy could be truly happy and fulfilled, and he trusted that Jesus would not take her away from him, but would give her back to him when she was truly fulfilled. Later, He would give Sheldon back to Davy when he was likewise fulfilled. Davy's offering of herself was successful, because Sheldon, in his *freedom*, chose to respond in faith.

Level Four love is categorically different from Level Three love because it entails an abandonment to divine providence, or in Sheldon's and Davy's case an abandonment to Jesus. This abandonment leads to a personal transformation that places our destiny in the hands of the unconditionally loving God, a transformation that allows us to give our lives freely in loving exchange for the salvation of others, in imitation of Jesus who gave His life for the salvation of the world.

C. Eros—*Romantic and Exclusive Love*

Though *eros* is identified with romantic or sexual love, it is quite complex, reaching to the highest levels of personal generativity, freedom, and commitment. It combines sexual drive, beauty, gender complementarity, and romance with intimacy, generativity, the highest levels of *philia*, commitment of our future, and the promise of exclusivity.[21] A brief survey of these characteristics reveals that some can be shared by all four levels of love—namely, sexual drive, beauty, gender complementarity, and romance—while others are more proper to Levels Three and Four: intimacy, generativity, the

---

[21] See Lewis, *Four Loves*, pp. 91–115.

highest levels of *philia*, commitment of our future, and the promise of exclusivity. This means that *eros* within a Level One or Two person will not be able to reach its proper fulfillment, because that fulfillment requires generativity and higher levels of commitment, which are proper to Levels Three and Four. The four levels of *eros* are explained in Volume III (Chapter 1), and we might summarize them as follows.

The first two levels of *eros* are quite superficial and do not reach the depth of personhood, goodness, lovability, and transcendental value in the "beloved" that can be reached in Levels Three and Four. As a result, Levels One and Two romantic relationships do not reach the same degree and scope of common cause, commitment, familial interest, and generativity reached in Level Three and Four relationships. In Levels One and Two, the focus is directed at physical appeal, status appeal, and utility appeal. However, as one moves into Levels Three and Four, the nature of *eros* changes dramatically. It is less focused on physical gratification and being admired and loved, and more focused on forming a "first priority" friendship, which can lead to mutual support, common cause, and ultimately, commitment and family. Sexuality and romance are still present, but they are reconfigured. Sexuality is no longer an end in itself, but serves the union and commitment of the beloveds. The same holds true for being loved and admired; it is not an end in itself but serves a generative end beyond itself. This means that "romance" has a much more enhanced meaning in Levels Three and Four than in Levels One and Two. In Levels Three and Four, romance includes mutual support, care, intimacy, appreciation, common cause, respect, and commitment, which means that it is laden with the attributes of love that Paul speaks of: patience, kindness, not boasting, not growing angry, etc. (see 1 Cor 13:4–7).

Level Three *eros* may be likened to what Sheldon and Davy enjoyed in their years before their conversion at Oxford. They had a very heightened view of romance, including intimacy, mutual contribution and support, common cause, and self-sacrifice, which led to and sustained their "highest priority commitment" that they alone could experience. At first they interpreted this heightened romance in terms of a "Shining Barrier" that indicated their sufficiency to fulfill one another completely. However, their encounter with C. S.

Lewis and subsequent conversion to Christianity showed Davy that there was much more to Sheldon's life than her, and much more to her life than Sheldon—namely, salvation in the unconditional love of Jesus Christ. Davy could not help herself; she proceeded to Level Four *eros* and breached the Shining Barrier.

At this juncture, Davy loved Sheldon in a much deeper and broader way than Sheldon was capable of loving her. Her love (*eros*) was so great that she offered her life to Christ in loving exchange for Sheldon's salvation, for which there is no greater love. This horrified Sheldon, who later understood what she had done for him. This caused him to offer himself completely for her. This absolute concern for the transcendent eternal salvation of the other is the height of *eros* (Level Four *eros*), which Level Three, though remarkable, cannot reach because of its limited (nontranscendent) vision of the individual person.

Unfortunately, our culture is becoming progressively more disconnected not only from the Level Four perspective of Davy and Sheldon after their conversion, but also their Level Three perspective before their conversion. Inasmuch as parts of our culture are moving to a dominant Level One and Two viewpoint, it is losing a Level Three and Four view of sexuality, intimacy, and romance. As a result, we are becoming progressively more shallow in our relationships, and even substituting "fashioned images of ourselves" in social media for the "real us". This has led to a devaluation of marriage and marital relationships, an undermining of marital commitment, and an increase in the rate of divorce. Some young people claim that they do not know the difference between cohabitating and being married, as if public commitment were completely unintelligible. If we are to reverse this trend, we will first have to help people move toward dominant Level Three and Four happiness, then to Level Three and Four friendships, and then to a reexamination of the positive characteristics of commitment, marriage, and family.

We will also have to reexamine how technology is affecting our ability to relate to others in a Level Three-Four way. The rapid progress made in communication, technology, Internet, and social media seem to be intensifying the decline in Level Three-Four friendship and *eros*. In many respects, we are relating just as much to machines and computers as to real people. Though computers can deliver real-time communication with others, they tend to be faceless and terse. Social media encourages people to make "images of themselves" instead of conveying their real selves. E-mails can be harsh and arrogant because we are not attending to the feelings and reactions of a real person. Though business, creative work, and scholarship are considerably enhanced by these tools, *personal* relationships are not. If our "computer associations" are complemented by real interpersonal relationships, then they will cause little harm. However, if "computer associations" begin to replace personal relationships, the harm to Level Three-Four friendships and *eros* can be significant.

D. Agapē—*Selfless Love*

We may now proceed to the fourth kind of love: *agapē*, which is sometimes translated as "charity" (*caritas*) and was advanced and developed by Jesus and the Christian Church.[22] Though it may include giving alms to the poor (which is promoted by most religions), it is much more, including an interior disposition and a vision of the other coming from Jesus' teaching on "compassion" and "neighbor", particularly in the Parable of the Good Samaritan (see Volume III, Chapter 1, and Lk 10:25–37).

Agapē is the kind of love arising out of our recognition of the unique goodness, lovability, and transcendentality of the other. It seeks no reward other than that of protecting, promoting, and fostering the good of an intrinsically valuable individual. Hence, this kind of love is not interested in who is being loved, whether it be a potential friend, a real friend, or a total stranger. Furthermore, it needs no reason to justify its occurrence other than the fact that all persons deserve to be loved (cared about, cared for, and contributed to) simply because they are intrinsically valuable transcendent mysteries.

---

[22]See ibid., pp. 115–25. Though Lewis does not use the term *agapē*, he considers the immense contribution of Jesus' teaching to the propagation of this kind of love. John McKenzie notes that the term *agapē* was chosen by the Christian Church to refer to Jesus' unique kind of love, exemplified, for example, in the Parable of the Good Samaritan. This kind of love goes far beyond the three *natural* loves, and so the Christian Church needed another term to refer to it, hence, the selection of *agapē*. See John McKenzie, *Dictionary of the Bible* (New York: Macmillan Publishing, 1965), p. 521.

Unlike friendship and *eros*, *agapē* does not seek mutuality or reciprocity, and it is indifferent to emotional rewards such as gratitude or romance. Hence, *agapē* can fuel a love of strangers, the marginalized, criminals, enemies, the destitute, and others who are incapable of reciprocating. Furthermore, *agapē* can be self-sacrificial, even to the point of death. It is the kind of love promoted by Jesus and the kind of love most intimately tied to virtue and suffering. When people practice this kind of love as a matter of habit, they are probably in the highest attainable state of personal virtue, bringing their human nature to its highest level of freedom, dignity, and fulfillment.

By now it will be evident that a dominant Level One-Two viewpoint is virtually incapable of giving rise to or sustaining *agapē*. Indeed, the whole idea of *agapē*—with its forgetfulness of self, and its inclination toward nonreciprocal, nonrewarded self-sacrifice—is antithetical to a dominant Level One-Two viewpoint. Level One and Level Two are not self-forgetful, and their orientation is toward reciprocity and reward. For this reason, dominant Level One-Two people have a very difficult time responding to and aspiring to be like Jesus. Thus, if we are to engage in *agapē*, we will have to be at least at Level Three.

Level Three is sufficient for *agapē*, but Level Four can support *agapē* by supporting Level Three. We noted above that prayer and grace (arising out of Level Four) could support Level Three love. We cited several studies that showed how religion supports familial relationships, adherence to conscience, and meaning in life, and decreases lifetime impulsivity and aggression, substance abuse, and suicide rates.[23] All of these qualities enhance empathy, responsibility to others, and awareness of others' transcendental and eternal significance. Level Four love also views our completeness and fulfillment through a divine Being who is perfect truth, love, goodness, beauty, and home. It shows that we are incapable of bringing ourselves to complete happiness and shows us a path of love that is humble and responsible to a divine power (as well as to ourselves). Since all of these attributes are essential to *agapē*, we may conclude that faith

---

[23] See Dervic et al., "Religious Affiliation and Suicide Attempt"; Parboteeah, Hoegl, and Cullen, "Ethics and Religion"; Weaver and Agle, "Religiosity and Ethical Behavior"; Cornwall et al., "Dimensions of Religiosity"; Tittle and Welch, "Religiosity and Deviance"; and Turner, *Institutional Order*.

and religion (prayer and grace) support the initiation, sustenance, and growth of *agapē*.[24] This is particularly true for the Christian religion where Christ preaches *agapē* as the epitome of joy, purpose, fulfillment, and God's Kingdom.[25]

E. Agapē *and Christianity*

In Volume III (Chapter 1), we gave an extended description of *agapē*, showing that Jesus explains its dynamic character through the Parable of the Good Samaritan (see Lk 10:25–37). Recall that Samaritans and Jews were enemies—so that the Jew who was beaten and left for dead by the side of the road was not only a stranger, but an enemy to the Samaritan. Nevertheless, the sight of the man who was beaten and robbed moved the Samaritan to a deep compassion. Luke translates Jesus' Aramaic by the Greek word *splagchnizomai*, which refers to a deep interior sympathy and sorrow that physically affects the "pit of one's stomach".[26] Though this deeply felt interior state can be achieved in Level Three, it is found most profoundly in people of faith and deep prayer.[27] Though this kind of Level Four love is by no means limited to Christianity (e.g., Gandhi), it is frequently and profoundly manifest in Christianity because it lies at the heart of the teaching and example of Jesus. Jesus not only teaches this kind of love in the Parables of the Good Samaritan and the Prodigal Son, as well as the attributes of *agapē* (love of strangers, enemies, the unjust, the poor, the sick, the oppressed, and prisoners); He also manifests it in His actions, particularly in His self-sacrificial love for the redemption of the world.

When Christians take their faith seriously, they not only go to Mass, but also try to enter into the heart and spirit of Jesus, both in attitude and action. Frequently, they will get involved in church activities—perhaps teaching, helping the needy, helping to

[24] See Lewis, *Four Loves*, pp. 119ff.

[25] See, for example, John 15:11–15; Galatians 5:22–23; 1 Corinthians 13:1; and Philippians 2:2–3.

[26] See James Strong, *The New Strong's Exhaustive Concordance of the Bible* (New York: Thomas Nelson, 2003), no. 4697, "splagchnizomai".

[27] See Lewis, *Four Loves*, pp. 119ff.

administrate the parish, etc. This deep interest in faith is shared with their family members, who in turn create a "familial community of faith and prayer". This rises to a high level of priority within the family and the personal lives of most of its members. This kind of faith is filled with Level Four love—interest in the *salvation* of family members, church members, people served by the church, people who are taught in classes or Bible studies, and frequently going beyond "the call of duty" to help friends and strangers who are in need to "get back on their feet". The Lord is pleased with this love and does not *require* more. However, He often *inspires* us to engage in extraordinary acts of charity or heroism when urgent needs arise—and so many of us are able to look back on our lives and see our call to what might be called heroic or saintly Level Four love. Perhaps we defended the faith against someone who was attacking it, stood up to somebody who was undermining decency or virtue in the culture, defended a victim who could not defend himself, or volunteered to serve in a place of extreme poverty or destitution. Despite the legitimate excuses that could have been made to avoid such sacrifices, we responded to them anyway—perhaps because others asked us to do so, we felt that the Lord wanted us to do so, or we felt a deep compassion for those who are suffering. Whatever the motive, we responded to a "call" we felt within our hearts—a call to *sacrifice ourselves*, entering into the realm of extraordinary Level Four love.

IV. Exceptional Love and the Lives of Some Saints

When we enter the domain of Level Four love, the inspiration of the Holy Spirit becomes incredibly powerful. The Spirit does not violate our freedom, but inspires us in proportion to our willingness to be inspired to greater and greater acts of *agapē* and self-sacrifice for the good of those in need, for the culture, the Mystical Body of Christ (the Church), and the Kingdom of God. There is no small number of such individuals, many of whom are acknowledged by the current culture, but a particularly impressive list may be found among the canonized saints of the Catholic Church. Though all of these saints had their personal shortcomings and cultural limitations, because they were human beings still *not perfected* in love, they were inspired by the love and self-sacrifice of Jesus and sought to imitate Him by serving the needy, the culture, and the Kingdom.

Most of these individuals began their lives like most of us, learning about and growing in their faith—some rich and some poor, some well-educated and relatively uneducated. Some of them, such as Saint Thomas Aquinas, Saint Aloysius Gonzaga, Saint Catherine Drexel, and Saint Elizabeth Ann Seton, took a *direct* route to sainthood, generally in three stages:

1. They experienced a remarkable growth in faith and love in childhood and adolescence.
2. They developed a strong personal relationship with Jesus in prayer.
3. They had a profound contemplative experience of the self-sacrifice and Passion of Jesus, producing such deep love of Him that they too wanted to imitate Him completely—especially in self-sacrificial love.

Some saints took an indirect—and even a *very* indirect—route toward their sainthood, such as Saint Augustine, Saint Francis of Assisi, and Saint Ignatius Loyola. For example, Saint Augustine left the Church and Christianity to lead a rather "excessive life", including seducing his friends to get addicted to the bloodlust of the coliseum; Saint Francis of Assisi wanted to lead the life of a rich heir and heroic soldier; and Saint Ignatius Loyola was a vainglorious dueler, ladies' man, and a military commander. These individuals seemed to have gone through five stages in their path to exceptional Level Four love:

1. They were disinterested in faith and love while growing up—aspiring to "honors, riches, power, and glory".
2. They experienced a period in their adult lives where they in fact pursued "honors, riches, power, and glory".
3. They had two or three major experiences that turned their lives around—that is, conversion experiences.
4. They had a resultant, almost insatiable appetite, to learn everything about Jesus Christ and His teaching.

5. They had a deep contemplative experience of the self-sacrifice and Passion of Jesus, producing such a profound love for Him that they wanted to imitate Him in self-sacrificial love.

There are huge variations within these two general scenarios, and some saints fall outside of both scenarios, but the vast majority of them have one thing in common—they were inspired by the love of Jesus, particularly manifest in His suffering and death on the Cross for the world. As they contemplated on the crucified Jesus, they did not focus on the hatred and ugliness underlying His tortured death, because they were inspired by His unconditional love, which they perceived as emanating from His crucified body. For them, the crucifix was a living symbol of perfect love for the world. They experienced the profundity of Jesus' self-sacrifice with such great empathy and gratitude that they abandoned themselves completely to His providence and the service of the needy, the culture, and the Kingdom.

Notice that all these individuals—even those who started out as vainglorious—sought *humility* in imitation of the Lord they loved. Thus even though their love was truly exceptional, they would have never considered themselves to be heroic, because it would have implied that their love was *self*-motivated instead of being inspired by the love and self-sacrifice of their living Lord. The saints who took the "indirect route" had to struggle against pride and passion— precisely because they were passionate and strong-willed. Most of them would have stated outright that they were not perfect in controlling their pride and passions, but because they made the virtue of humility and compassionate love so central to their spiritual lives, they learned how to mitigate pride's negative influence. Once again we see that the quest for humility and self-restraint is not primarily *self*-motivated, but rather is inspired by the humility and self-restraint of Jesus—particularly in His Passion and death.

It is difficult to give a detailed discussion of only a *few* saints because there are so many. Virtually all canonized saints in the Catholic Church manifest extraordinary love, which is inspired by the unconditional love of Jesus—particularly on the Cross. Nevertheless, I selected Saint Francis of Assisi and Saint Ignatius Loyola as representatives of the indirect route, and Saint Peter Claver and Saint Teresa of Calcutta as representatives of the direct route to attain extraordinary Level Four love.

A. Saint Francis of Assisi[28]

Throughout much of his youth, Saint Francis focused on a life of riches and military glory. As a young man he worked as a merchant for his father selling cloth and velvet. He wore bright clothes, befriended the rich, and enjoyed worldly pleasures. On one occasion God called him through a beggar who asked him for some help. Francis was so moved that he took all of the day's receipts and gave them to the beggar, provoking his father's anger and disdain. Nevertheless, Francis continued his worldly life and went on campaign against Perugia, where he was captured and spent one year in prison. During this time, he seems to have had a deeper spiritual conversion. Once again, he returned to the life of a soldier and had his father commission armor (laden with gold) for him to go out on another military campaign. After one day, God called him in a dream, telling him that his life of riches and military glory was leading Francis away from Him, and that he should return home and turn his life around. He did this to the great disdain of his father and to the ridicule of all his former friends and neighbors—moving, as it were, from vainglory to humiliations for the sake of Christ in one day. Following this, Francis began to give himself progressively more to prayer, in which he felt great contrition for his sin, as well as great consolation from Jesus. All the while, he grew in trust and knowledge of the love of Jesus and grew in love of "Lady Poverty".

On another occasion, Francis entered the little church of San Damiano outside of Assisi. Accustomed to praying before the crucifix, he entered the church and prayed before the icon of Jesus crucified, at which point he had a mystical experience in which Jesus said to him, "Francis, Francis, go and repair My house which, as

---

[28] The following events are recounted by Saint Francis' official biographer, Thomas of Celano, a Franciscan monk and a contemporary of Saint Francis. See Thomas of Celano, *The First Life of St. Francis of Assisi*, trans. Christopher Stace (London: Society for Promoting Christian Knowledge, 2000).

you can see, is falling into ruins."[29] He took this to mean the ruined church of San Damiano, but later discovered that Jesus meant the "universal church", which incited him to rebuild the spirituality of the Church, based on prayer and poverty.

His experience in prayer was tested one day when he was riding in a forest and was confronted by a leper whose appearance and smell revolted him. Nevertheless, the love of Christ dwelling in him (from his lengthy period of prayer) incited him to get off his horse and kiss the leper—who, in turn, kissed him. When he rode off and looked back, the leper had disappeared. He concluded from this that he had "passed the test" from the Lord. At this juncture, his conversion was complete, and he set himself about the mission given to him in the church at San Damiano. He was about to enshrine a life of *self-sacrificial love* in his own person and in the religious order he was about to found.

Francis began to preach and work with the poor throughout the towns of the province of Umbria. His exhortations were so impassioned—and more importantly, his work with the poor was so edifying—that he inspired eleven men to follow him. At this juncture, he needed a "primitive rule" to start a religious order devoted specifically to poverty and work with the poor. Though Pope Innocent III did not officially approve the order, he did permit Francis to continue in it until he had additional growth. Francis' complete dedication to the crucified Jesus and His self-sacrificial love for the world was so extraordinary that it edified dozens upon dozens of men to join him in his life of poverty. Many of these new followers were wealthy and educated, and gave up everything to be near him. Though his new order grew at an unprecedented rate (by comparison with other orders at the time), Francis did not attribute it to himself, but rather to the loving God moving his new followers as He moved Francis himself. After this period of growth, Francis returned to Rome, where his new order was approved by Pope Innocent III.

Francis and his friars then proceeded to preach all over Italy, beyond the province of Umbria. Again additional friars began to

[29]Recounted by Thomas of Celano, a Franciscan monk and a contemporary of Saint Francis. See Thomas of Celano, *Saint Francis of Assisi: First and Second Life of St. Francis with Selections from the Treatise on the Miracles of Blessed Francis*, trans. Placid Hermann (Chicago: Franciscan Herald Press, 1988), p. 182.

join the order, and Francis started houses throughout Italy. During this period Francis was preaching in the church of San Rufino. A noblewoman—Clare of Assisi—was moved by his preaching and clandestinely left her palace and family to join Francis in a life of poverty, self-sacrifice, and charity. She later started the women's correlate of the Franciscans, which she named the "Poor Ladies", which was later renamed as the "Poor Clares".

Francis then began to travel beyond Italy, establishing his most important missions in the Holy Land, which at that time was occupied by the Saracens. Before going to the Holy Land, Francis attempted to convert the sultan of Egypt (the nephew of the great Saladin). The sultan listened to the preaching of Francis, but it had no effect at that time. Later, however, some hagiographers reported that the sultan secretly converted to Christianity on his deathbed. Whether this actually occurred or not, the sultan gave Francis and his companions permission to enter the Holy Land and to establish houses and missions at various holy places. This truly extraordinary gesture shows the effects that Francis' preaching and presence had on the sultan.

When he returned to San Damiano in Italy, he worked on administrative tasks to solidify the internal organization of the Franciscan order (which he called the "lesser brothers—the fratres minores"). He was later given the stigmata,[30] the wounds of Christ, to fulfill his spirituality of complete abandonment to the crucified Christ. Sensing that the end was near, he dictated some of his personal memoirs to his biographer, Thomas of Celano.[31] He died shortly thereafter, fully aware that he was going to his Lord of unconditional love.

Saint Francis' life is a testimony to how profoundly the Holy Spirit can work through the sufferings of Jesus and through extraordinary self-sacrificial love. After Saint Francis' vision of the crucified Christ in the little chapel of San Damiano, he was moved to identify with the humble, poor, and crucified Christ completely. His conversion to extraordinary love (in imitation of his Lord) made his

[30] Some saints, like Saint Francis of Assisi and Saint Pio, had the wounds of Christ appear in their hands, feet, and sides, and Saint Pio (who lived in the twentieth century) had his wounds examined by several physicians, some of whom concluded that they did not appear to be self-inflicted.

[31] See Thomas of Celano, The First Life of St. Francis of Assisi, trans. by Christopher Stace (London: Society for Promoting Christian Knowledge, 2000).

example and preaching almost addictive to those who were open to it. No other religious order had grown so rapidly prior to the time of Saint Francis—and despite the fact that Francis tried to make it "the lesser brothers", it became a major influence both inside and outside the Christian Church. Francis never took the credit for this but gave it all to the Lord, who loved him and gave Himself for him. As Francis showed, the Holy Spirit can work through suffering, self-sacrifice, and extraordinary love (i.e., Level Four love), to bring immense and lasting good for the needy, the culture, and the Kingdom of God.

B. Saint Ignatius Loyola[32]

Saint Ignatius Loyola provides yet another example of the same pattern: (1) the call of Christ through suffering, (2) devotion to the crucified Christ and His self-sacrificial love for the world, and (3) dedication of his life to following Christ in self-sacrificial love.

Ignatius was born in Loyola, Spain, in 1491 of parents of minor nobility, and like Saint Francis, he focused on a life of honors and military glory. Saint Ignatius enjoyed the military life because it gave him many opportunities for glory, honor, and vanity. He was known to be a "ladies' man" and a dueler. On one occasion, when a Moor denied the divinity of Christ, he challenged him to a duel and ran him through. He apparently engaged in many such duels.

He took up arms with the duke of Nájera (viceroy of Navarre) and went on campaign with him, proving himself as a valiant soldier and good leader. On one occasion, completely outnumbered by a French army in Pamplona, Ignatius was trying to rally his small band of Spanish soldiers to continue fighting. A French cannonball hit him squarely in the leg, causing a severe fracture. The French soldiers were impressed by his bravery and returned him to his home in Loyola to recover.

---

[32] The original account of most of the events discussed below in Saint Ignatius' early life is given in his autobiography. See Saint Ignatius Loyola, *A Pilgrim's Journey: The Autobiography of St. Ignatius of Loyola* (San Francisco: Ignatius Press, 2001). For an excellent biography of Saint Ignatius that delves deeply into his spiritual formation, see James Brodrick, *St. Ignatius Loyola: The Pilgrim Years* (San Francisco: Ignatius Press, 1998).

During this time of recovery, Ignatius asked for books of romance and military glory, but none were available. Instead, he was given an illustrated life of Christ and biographies of Saint Francis and Saint Dominic. The *Life of Christ*, written by Ludolph of Saxony, was remarkably detailed and theologically insightful, which greatly edified Ignatius. Moreover, it recommended a technique of simple contemplation—to place oneself within the scene of Jesus' life—which captivated Ignatius, who had an active imagination. This volume, as well as some lives of the saints, became the foundation for his conversion—as well as his *Spiritual Exercises*, which he wrote during and after his experience at Manresa (see below).

During this time, he would daydream prolifically—sometimes about chivalry and military exploits, and sometimes about doing deeds of love for his Lord. Both kinds of daydreams produced considerable excitement and delight, but he noticed that the former kind left him sad and empty, while the latter left him continuously consoled and hopeful. He came to realize that the affective and spiritual states following his daydreams were ways in which the Lord was communicating with him—the feelings of sadness and emptiness indicated a path away from the Lord of consolation, while the feelings of consolation and hope indicated a path leading toward the Lord. This became the basis for his rules for the discernment of spirits (in the *Spiritual Exercises*).

He was then moved to go to Jerusalem to convert the Muslim world and regain the sacred city for Christ, his Lord. On his journey, he went to the well-known Benedictine Abbey of Montserrat to visit the shrine of our Lady, and there before her statue he gave away his sword and dagger and pledged himself completely to the service of Christ. He was then moved to go to the nearby town of Manresa, where he procured lodgings near a hospital (in which he served) for ten months. During that time, he spent every free moment going to a nearby cave to pray, experiencing a wide range of spiritual states and feelings—consolations, desolations, genuine sorrow for sins, visions, scruples, inspiration, and discouragement, which bordered on despair. As he reflected on these affective and spiritual states, he began to learn how the Holy Spirit can use both consolation and desolation, and how the Evil One could use both desolation and false consolation, and even masquerade as an "angel of light" (2 Cor 11:14).[33] He not only recognized God's call to him, but also how God was guiding him in his service. Like Saint Francis, Ignatius' communion with the heart and love of Jesus moved him to a life of Level Four love (*agapē*), which included a complete self-offering in imitation of the crucified Jesus. He placed the Anima Christi prayer[34] at the beginning of the *Spiritual Exercises* to signify this:

> Soul of Christ, sanctify me; Body of Christ, save me; Blood of Christ, inebriate me; Water from Christ's side, wash me; Passion of Christ, strengthen me; O good Jesus, hear me; Within Thy wounds hide me; Suffer me not to be separated from Thee; From the malicious enemy defend me; In the hour of my death call me; And bid me come unto Thee; That I may praise Thee with Thy saints and with Thy angels; Forever and ever; Amen.

In his ardent desire to serve the Lord, he proceeded toward Jerusalem, but after a few weeks, he was told by the church there that he was quite counterproductive and needed to return to Europe. Though he was downcast, he used his knowledge of discernment to follow the Lord's guiding hand to his new mission—to share the *Spiritual Exercises*, work with the poor and homeless, catechize children, and follow the Lord's call to poverty, chastity, and service. After the completion of his elementary studies, he proceeded to the University of Paris, where he spent seven years obtaining a master's degree in theology. During that time, he gave the *Spiritual Exercises* to several fellow students who were so moved by him and the experience of the exercises that they became his first companions—Francis Xavier, Alfonso Salmeron, Diego Laynez, and Nicholas Bobadilla (Spaniards); Peter Faber, a Frenchman; and Simão Rodrigues of Portugal. He was later joined by Saint Francis Borgia, a member of the House of Borgia who was the main aide of Emperor Charles V, and other nobles.

On August 15, 1534, Saint Ignatius and his companions proceeded to the church of Saint Denis (now San Piere) on Montmartre (a hill

---

[33] For a full explanation of discernment of spirits and God's providential guidance, see Volume I (Chapter 8). A summary of this is also given in Chapter 9 of this volume.

[34] A medieval prayer composed by Jean-Baptiste Lully. It was a favorite of Saint Ignatius Loyola since the time of his conversion.

in northern Paris) to take their first vows in their new order "the Company of Jesus"—also called the Society of Jesus or the Jesuits. Saint Ignatius' dedication to extraordinary love—manifest not only in the *Spiritual Exercises*, but also in his spiritual *practice* to the poor, orphans, and prostitutes—moved these students of the University of Paris to pledge themselves to a life of evangelization, poverty, chastity, and service to the poor and needy.

In 1537, Ignatius and his companions proceeded to Rome to put themselves at the service of the Pope. On the way there, he had a very palpable and moving vision of God the Father placing him with His Son, after which he determined to dedicate the Spirit of his new order to following Christ crucified. Saint Ignatius was brought to tears not only by his vision of the crucified Jesus, but in his subsequent meditations on Him. This moved him with ever-greater ardor to imitate the Lord, who had loved him so, by accepting and even pursuing the cross that would empower his continued self-transformation and effectiveness in mission.

That same year, the companions received permission from Pope Paul III to be formally recognized as a religious order. He gave them temporary approval and allowed them to be ordained, which occurred at the church of Saint Denis in Paris. In 1540 the Company of Jesus was formally approved by Pope Paul III.

Since the time of its formal approval, the Jesuits experienced meteoric expansion. They started classically based schools across Europe, became involved in the reform and strengthening of seminaries, and initiated missions in countries as far away as Paraguay, Bolivia, Columbia, China, Japan, India, Ontario, and Ethiopia. They were also responsible for the Counter-Reformation in Germany, Poland, and Eastern Europe. Saint Francis Xavier alone was so successful that he initiated missions in India, Japan, and Borneo, converting approximately thirty thousand people before he died on an island outside China, hoping to gain entrance there to establish a mission.

Like Saint Francis of Assisi, Ignatius' charisma was grounded not only in his preaching and spiritual direction, but in his authentic love for Christ, the poor, and the deprived. His example was so great that the little Jesuit order initiated on the Hill of Montmartre in 1534 grew to over one thousand priests worldwide by the time of his death in 1556. Again we see the riveting, if not addictive, quality of Level

Four love. People found Saint Ignatius and Saint Francis Xavier not only to be interesting, but almost irresistibly authentic and truthful. Their poverty, humility, self-sacrifice, and compassion gave credibility to their words of faith, which allowed them to have enormous impact for the needy, the culture, and the Church. Was this addictive quality and enormous impact attributable to the charisma of Saint Ignatius and Saint Francis Xavier alone? Was it attributable to their heroism and natural talent alone? *They* certainly did not think so— they gave credit, all the credit, to the Lord of love working through their humble love and zeal to bring His word of hope to the world. In so doing they testified by word and action that love's self-sacrificial and compassionate "power" is beyond pride and *worldly* power.

C. Saint Peter Claver[35]

Peter Claver was born in 1581 in Verdu, Catalonia (Spain). His parents were prosperous farmers and devout Catholics, and Peter took an early and deep interest in their faith. He was noted for his intelligence and piety, which enabled him to gain entrance to the Society of Jesus at the age of twenty.

Prior to entering the Society, Claver studied at the University of Barcelona, where he advanced not only in his education, but in his faith. He felt compelled to follow Jesus in his call to be a servant/slave[36] of all (see Mt 20:26–27), and he wrote in his journal, "I must dedicate myself to the service of God until death, on the understanding that I am like a slave." As it turned out, this was an incredibly prescient remark.

After Claver completed his novitiate, he proceeded to his philosophical and theological studies at Majorca. There, he met a very pious brother, Saint Alphonsus Rodriguez, who was a humble porter at the door. Saint Alphonsus was no ordinary porter; he was the spiritual director of many of the seminarians (as well as townspeople), and was noted for his prophetic gift. When he saw Peter Claver, he

[35] For a spiritual biography of Saint Peter Claver, see John Slattery, *St. Peter Claver: Apostle to the Negroes* (Philadelphia: H. L. Kilner, 2015).

[36] The Greek word *doulos* used in the New Testament can be translated as either "servant" or "slave", because servants were almost universally slaves in ancient culture.

felt that the Lord was calling him quite strongly to minister to the slaves in the New World. Saint Alphonsus believed this so strongly, that he mentioned it on several occasions to Claver, who eventually decided to follow this lead as a way of fulfilling his call by Jesus to be at the service of all "like a slave". In 1610, he volunteered to work in New Granada and arrived at the port city of Cartagena in Colombia. There he witnessed the exceedingly harsh treatment of the black slaves, which deeply disturbed him. The call of Jesus to be a slave, even of the slaves (a servant of the servants), became solidified in his heart. Claver had to delay this call for six years so that he could complete his theological studies and be ordained a priest. After that, he pursued his heart's desire.

Cartagena was a large slave-trading post. Ships filled with black slaves regularly came from Africa and docked at the port there. Slave owners would come to a large auction area to bid on the slaves who survived the transit. Approximately one-third of the slaves died in transit, and the lower decks (where the slaves were "stored") were so crowded and foul that even Claver was overcome by the experience. Two popes (Paul III and Urban VIII) had already vehemently condemned the slave trade, and Pope Pius IX later called it "the supreme villainy". Nevertheless, the need for black slaves to work in the mines (rather than the weaker Indian natives) and the huge profits associated with the slave trade (who were sold for fifty times their cost in Africa) motivated most of the traders to ignore the papal pronouncements. This provoked Claver to become a "street preacher", reminding the slave owners incessantly of their responsibility to the slaves before Christ and the Church. Though much of his preaching went unheeded, he did convince many to treat their slaves more humanely.

Claver felt deeply for the slaves, whom he believed were his equals in every way. He became associated with Father Alonso de Sandoval, another Jesuit who ministered to the slaves in the places they worked. He studied the slaves' customs and languages (most of whom came from Ethiopia, Angola, and Congo) and later wrote a book about them. Claver learned these customs and used translators to speak with the different slave groups, for purposes of ministry and catechesis.

Where Sandoval ministered to the slaves in the workplace, Claver chose to do so on the ship at their point of entry. When a ship would come in, he would rush onto it and go immediately to the slave decks, enduring the incredible stench and horrible sight, to minister to the slaves. He would bring food, drink, medicine, and other provisions to help them in their next stage of transit. When possible, he would try to educate the slaves in the faith, and if they wanted, baptize them. According to virtually all reports, he cared for, catechized, and baptized at least three hundred thousand slaves before his death. After their Baptism, Claver reminded the slave traders that they must treat the slaves as "fellow Christians" who had the same status as they did according to Jesus. After the slaves were sold, he followed up with the slave owners to make sure that the slaves were accorded their proper Christian and civil rights. In doing this work, he did not stay with the slave traders, but rather in the slave quarters, where Jesus his Lord would have been content to stay.

Claver became seriously ill in 1650. His Jesuit Superior hired a former slave to care for him, but when placed in charge of him, the former slave physically abused and starved him in his last years. Claver never judged this former slave negatively for his harsh treatment; he saw it as a path to greater humility in imitation of the Lord of love. He died four years later in 1654 and, ironically, was given a large state funeral, precisely the opposite of the way he lived and would have wanted, representing the final humiliation.

What motivated Peter Claver? Prior to entering the Jesuits, Claver's great devotion to Jesus led him to what he believed to be the highest form of imitation: to be like a slave for everyone in the service of his Lord, who was the servant of all and gave His life as a ransom for all. This early commitment (at the University of Barcelona) led him to the Jesuits, where in the novitiate he would have discovered Saint Ignatius' meditation on the "Two Standards" and the "Three Degrees of Humility" (in the *Spiritual Exercises*). In those meditations, Saint Ignatius exhorts the retreatant to be poor with Christ's poor, and to be humble with Christ's humble; these two virtues help to resist the temptations of the Evil One, who exhorts us instead to riches, honors, and glory, which will ultimately undermine our capacity for love and our desire for the Kingdom.

No doubt, Claver responded to these meditations in the spirit of the third week of the exercises, which focuses solely on the Passion and death of Jesus. He loved his Lord, particularly in his perfect self-sacrifice and love for everyone. This opened him to the imitation of Christ and the appropriation of a spirit of poverty and humility for the sake of love and service. The Lord had set the stage for his meeting with Saint Alphonsus Rodriguez, and when the latter suggested being "the slave of the slaves", Claver could not resist. He was impelled by desire, grace, and love to follow his Lord to the fullest expression of service and self-sacrifice: the fullness of love.

D. Saint Teresa of Calcutta (Mother Teresa)

Saint Teresa of Calcutta is an extraordinary example of Level Four love inspired by the love of Jesus. Born in 1910 of humble parents in an obscure town of Macedonia (Skopje), Anjezë (Agnes) Gonxhe Bojaxhiu fell in love with the Person of Christ and a life of service at the age of twelve. From that time on she experienced remarkable development leading to the spirituality that would underlie and nourish her extraordinary apostolic zeal. Her apostolic life was devoted to seeing the face of her beloved Jesus in the poorest of the poor and imitating Him in His love for them in her every action.

Her devotion was so strong and her love so pure, that she drew disciples to herself in precisely the same way as Saint Francis of Assisi and Saint Ignatius Loyola. In 1950 with only thirteen sisters, Mother Teresa started the Missionaries of Charity, a Catholic religious order devoted to loving and serving the poorest of the poor. The order grew quite rapidly, and by the time of her death (1997), it had grown to more than 4,000 sisters and 450 brothers in 120 countries worldwide. Her charism was so powerful that her order continued to grow by another 1,000 sisters a decade after her death.

How did this "little" woman from such humble beginnings soar to such heights of love and service? In a phrase, it was the Lord's powerful inspiration, call, and guidance. It seems that the Lord called Agnes to a life of service at a very early age. She was so intrigued with the service of missionaries in Bengal that she would spend hours reading their biographies, all the while intensely desiring (a sign of the inspiration of the Holy Spirit) to serve the poor in mission countries. At the age of twelve, she resolved to become a religious sister and serve in the missions.[37] At the age of eighteen, while praying before the

[37] See Joan Clucas, *Mother Teresa* (New York: Chelsea House Publications, 1988), p. 24.

shrine of the Black Madonna of Letnice, she became certain of God's call to her, and resolved to join the Sisters of Loreto as a missionary.[38] Though the details of these experiences are not known, it must have been significant enough to move her to a remarkable lifelong commitment to the poor. She was well on the way to Level Four love at the age of eighteen.

Agnes joined the Sisters of Loreto, took the name "Teresa" (after Thérèse of Lisieux), and took final vows in 1937 (at the age of twenty-seven). During her years of formation, she became deeply interested in the spirituality of Thérèse, who emphasized self-sacrifice in imitation of Jesus for the salvation of souls (see Chapter 8, Section III). Saint Thérèse transformed her sufferings (from tuberculosis) into acts of loving self-sacrifice for the salvation of those in need. Teresa was struck by this and placed self-sacrifice at the center of her spirituality. She would experience heightened suffering in a "dark night of the soul" (in imitation of Saint Thérèse) throughout the last thirty years of her life (explained below in this section).

Teresa spent twenty years teaching in the mission school associated with the convent in Calcutta and eventually became headmistress of the school. Though she was a skilled teacher and administrator and loved the students, she sympathized deeply with the poor in Calcutta, particularly during two extended periods of famine. This led to her "call" to start the Missionaries of Charity, dedicated to serving the poorest of the poor.

After spending twenty years at the convent school, she experienced what she called "a call within a call" on a train ride from Calcutta to Darjeeling in 1946 (at the age of 36). The experience was so powerful and convincing that she considered it to be "an order from the Lord". Teresa found herself following in the footsteps of Saint Thérèse's mystical experience of Jesus on the Cross, who declared to her: "I thirst" (see Jn 19:28). Like Thérèse, Teresa interpreted Jesus' cry to be an unquenchable thirst to bring as many as possible to the heights of love and the salvation of their souls. She desired to love Christ in the poorest of the poor and to offer her sacrifices for their needs and salvation. At this point she had given herself over to Level

[38] See Meg Green, *Mother Teresa: A Biography* (Westport, Conn.: Greenwood Press, 2004), p. 11.

Four love—complete self-sacrifice for the good of the Kingdom. Her "call within a call" (interpreted through the mystical love of Saint Thérèse) led to the mission statement of her new religious order: "to quench the infinite *thirst* of Jesus on the cross for love and souls ... [by] labouring for the salvation and sanctification of the poorest of the poor".

After taking a brief course in medical training in Patna, Teresa moved into the slums of Calcutta and began to serve the poorest of the poor as a poor person. She saw the image of Christ in those she served—particularly the dying, diseased, and destitute, and found a spiritual joy in her service and love of Jesus in the poor. Teresa's love was heroic yet humble and self-effacing and her joy palpable and mystical—even amid the sickening smells and disturbing sights of Calcutta's slums. This love and joy led to an explosion of vocations in her newly found order, which in turn led to an explosion of hospitals, charity centers, houses for the dying, mobile medical units, food pantries, and soup kitchens. Her spirituality of humble-heroic love (complemented by spiritual joy) fascinated many; and when some joined her religious order, they found it to be "tough but addictive", certainly not for the faint of heart, but filled with an expressed love for Jesus.

At this juncture, the Lord asked Mother Teresa for the ultimate sacrifice, similar to that experienced by Saint Thérèse of Lisieux: the dark night of the soul. We must pause here for a moment to address this important spiritual phenomenon, which is generally restricted to those with a well-developed spiritual life immersed in humble and heroic Level Four love, such as Saint John of the Cross (who wrote extensively about it[39]), Saint Teresa of Avila, Saint Thérèse of Lisieux (the main inspiration of Mother Teresa), and Saint Paul of the Cross. Saint John of the Cross explains the Lord's rationale for introducing such darkness into the lives of his devoted beloveds, as follows:

> The soul not only suffers the void and suspension of these natural supports and apprehensions, which is a terrible anguish (like hanging in

---

[39] See Saint John of the Cross, *Dark Night of the Soul*, in *The Collected Works of St. John of the Cross*, ed. Kieran Kavanaugh (Washington, D.C.: Institute of Carmelite Studies Press, 1979), pp. 293–389.

midair, unable to breathe), but it is also purged by this contemplation. As fire consumes the tarnish and rust of metal, this contemplation annihilates, empties, and consumes all the affections and imperfect habits the soul contracted throughout its life.[40]

As Saint John of the Cross indicates, the "dark night" is yet another form of suffering, experienced by only a few truly holy and loving people, and given by the Lord as a stage of *final purgation* to help purify Level Four love of any remaining imperfections—residual attachments, aberrant affections, and spiritual pride. It may seem bewildering that the Lord would (lovingly) cause the most loving people to experience emptiness, darkness, and profound loneliness in order to complete their purification in love. To be sure, He does not do this with the vast majority of people, even those who are very advanced in holiness and love; yet, He does do this for a select few whom *He knows* can endure it and benefit from it. Several Catholic *contemplatives and mystics* experience this kind of purgation, but it is less frequent in active contemplatives such as Saint Teresa of Calcutta. Nevertheless, the Lord knew that she, having chosen Thérèse of Lisieux as her primary inspiration, would be able to endure the pain of final purgation, like her spiritual mother who declared:

> When I want to rest my heart, wearied by the darkness which surrounds it, by the memory of the luminous country to which I aspire, my torment redoubles; it seems to me that the darkness, borrowing the voice of sinners, says mockingly to me: "You are dreaming about the light, about a country fragrant with the sweetest perfumes; you are dreaming about the *eternal* possession of the Creator of all these things; you believe that one day you will walk out of this fog which surrounds you! Dream on, dream on; rejoice in death which will give you not what you hope for, but even deeper night, the night of nothingness!"[41]

In spite of this trial, which robs me of all comfort, I still can say: "Thou hast given me, O Lord, delight in all Thou dost." For what

---

[40] Ibid., p. 364.

[41] Saint Thérèse of Lisieux, *The Story of a Soul: The Autobiography of St. Thérèse of Lisieux*, trans. John Clarke, O.C.D. (Washington, D.C.: ICS Publications, 1996), p. 213.

joy can be greater than to suffer for Thy Love? The more the suffering
is and the less it appears before men, the more is it to Thy Honour
and Glory.[42]

It is crucial to note that the Lord is not causing "the voice of sinners" to make suggestions about the fictitiousness of eternal life and
His love. Rather, the Lord simply removes his normal consolation
and supports from the saint's consciousness, leaving him open to his
own dark unconscious suggestions as well as those of an evil spirit.[43]
These other voices (not belonging to the Lord) are part of the
purification process. Their suggestions about ultimate darkness are
temptations against hope that must be confronted and defeated,
including their suggestions about the Lord's infidelity and uncaring
nature (temptations against faith and trust). Most importantly, their
suggestions to "cut and run", "to give it all up", and to proclaim the
falsity of unconditional love cynically are temptations against love—
the ultimate temptation of pride and egocentricity. They too must be
confronted and defeated, and when the trial is over—and it will
be over—there will be the perfect joy of completely purified love
with the Lord.
    This is precisely what happened to Mother Teresa in her final
weeks on this Earth. According to Benedict Groeschel, who documented the accounts of Saint Teresa's sisters and witnessed it himself, Mother Teresa suddenly emerged from her serious and somber
demeanor and became filled with a joy and hope that was both giddy
and intensely ecstatic. Groeschel writes:

> Fr. Brian [Kolódiejchuk—postulator general of her cause] records the
> sisters' observation when Mother Teresa returned to Calcutta shortly
> before her death: "After her return from Rome [and New York] ...
> Mother had been extremely happy, joyful, optimistic, and talkative.
> Her face was always radiant, full of fun. The Lord must have revealed
> to her the impending end of her life." ...

---

[42] Saint Thérèse of Lisieux, *The Story of a Soul: The Autobiography of St. Thérèse of Lisieux
with Additional Writings and Sayings of St. Thérèse* (1912), pp. 93–94, http://www.catholic
bible101.com/St.%20Therese%20Story%20of%20a%20soul.pdf.
[43] For an explanation of "normal consolation and supports", see Volume I, Chapter 8,
Section II. For an explanation of the reality of evil and the deceptions of the Evil One, see
Spitzer, *Called out of Darkness.*

I personally observed this joyfulness the day before Mother returned to Calcutta. I was asked by her sisters to offer Mass for her. She was so weak that she could not stand, but attended Mass lying on a cot. My confrere Fr. Andrew Apostoli and I were utterly astonished after Mass when she was "bubbly." She laughed and told us with great joy the number of sisters and convents they had throughout the world. Mother never spoke about this before, and she was not doing so in any boastful way. Rather, she was rejoicing "with triumphant exultation" at the great blessings God had been able to grant through the Missionaries of Charity.[44]

Saint Teresa was longsuffering, but following Jesus (her beloved) and Saint Thérèse (her inspiration), she knew well the power of offering her suffering (especially her spiritual suffering) as a loving, self-sacrificial offering for the strength of the Church and the salvation of souls (see Chapter 8, Section II). She also knew that her suffering would purify her in the manner described above, and so she knew that even though darkness pervaded her interior life, she could present the joy of Christ to others through her exterior love and life. Hence, even in her darkest days, she was able to begin with her adaptation of a prayer by John Henry Cardinal Newman:

> Dear Jesus, help us to spread your fragrance everywhere
>   we go.
> Flood our souls with your spirit and life.
> Penetrate and possess our whole being so utterly,
> that our lives may only be a radiance of yours.
> Shine through us, and be so in us,
> [so] that every person we should come in contact with
> may we feel your presence in our soul.
> ——
> Let them look up and see no longer us, but only Jesus.
> Stay with us, and then we shall begin to shine as you
>   shine;
> so to shine as to be a light to others;
> the light, Jesus, will be all from you.
> None of it will be ours.

[44]Benedict Groeschel, "Mother Teresa Remembered", *First Things*, September 11, 2007, http://www.firstthings.com/web-exclusives/2007/09/mother-teresa-remembered.

Let us thus praise you in the way you love best,
by shining on those around us.
Let us preach you without preaching:
not by words, but by our example,
by the catching force,
the sympathetic influence of what we do,
the evident fullness of the love our hearts bear for you.
Amen.[45]

As Saint Teresa experienced a void within, she continued to see Jesus in the faces and figures of the people she served, and in serving them, continued to love the One whom she desired more than anyone else. It gave her *genuine* joy to lift up those who had no joy. This seeming bifurcation of interior and exterior life was brought back to complete integration in her final days when the joy she found serving Christ through the poor penetrated her very soul, revealing her ultimate home with Jesus and His heavenly Father. Patient endurance of her suffering led her to the heights of love, and she knew well that in the "twinkling of an eye" there would be no suffering, only unconditional love with her beloved forever.

V. Conclusion

At the height of the fourth level of love, suffering and love are unified, but only for a while—that is, for the remainder of our earthly lives. Suffering calls forth loving self-sacrifice for others and the Kingdom of God. It purifies us in love, by bestowing gifts of humility, empathy for the weak, and trust in God. It enables us to offer ourselves in sacrifice to the Lord for salvation of the world in imitation of Jesus' act of unconditional love (see Volume III, Chapter 3, Section IV).

When suffering has done its purifying work—and when it has been freely embraced as an act of love—it is no longer necessary. At that point, our free choices toward the higher levels of love, inspired

[45] WorldPrayers.org, accessed June 16, 2016, http://www.worldprayers.org/archive/prayers/invocations/dear_jesus_help_us_to.html.

by the grace of God, will have shaped our eternal identity. Like Saint Francis, Saint Ignatius, Saint Peter Claver, and Saint Teresa, it remains only for the Lord to call us into the Kingdom of His perfectly loving joy.

The above biographies shed light on how the Lord inspires us to the heights of love through suffering. The misery and emptiness caused by the negative emotions of the comparison game lead us toward Level Three and Level Four. The suffering coming from cosmic emptiness, loneliness, and alienation opens the way to a deeper relationship with the Lord, who alone can satisfy our restless hearts. This movement toward the Lord reveals His love, a love recognized by virtually all the world's religions, but brought to fruition in the revelation of Jesus Christ, who showed us in word and action His unconditional love and that of His Father—a love of perfect humility, empathy, and compassion demonstrated in His free and complete self-sacrifice on the Cross.

Meditating on the Passion and death of Jesus has led scores of Christians toward the heights of humble-heroic Level Four love— not only Saint Francis, Saint Ignatius, Saint Peter Claver, Saint Teresa, and virtually every known saint, but also the unheralded self-sacrificial love of tens of thousands of "Davys"[46] who give themselves completely for others and the Kingdom. The powerful example of Jesus is a conduit for inspiration to move toward ever-greater acceptance of suffering (i.e., ever-greater heights of love) for the sake of the One who loved us in the same way. Once inspired, we leave a legacy of incomparable good, and after our hearts have been purified, we inherit the Kingdom prepared for us from the beginning of time.

We are now in a position to examine the opportunities of suffering (Chapters 7 and 8)—for as now might be clear, the primary opportunity of suffering is love, a legacy of love, purification of love, and the inheritance of unconditional love. Bearing these opportunities in mind, we will be able to learn how to follow the Holy Spirit during times of suffering (Chapter 9) and why the unconditionally loving God would allow suffering in the world (Chapter 10).

---

[46]That is, Vanauken's wife, Davy, as discussed above in his reference to his *Severe Mercy*.

Chapter Seven

Finding Light in the Darkness

Seventh Foundation: Interior and Exterior Opportunities of Suffering

Introduction

The nineteenth-century American artist Thomas Cole portrayed the voyage of life in a series of four paintings: childhood, youth, manhood, and old age.[1] Each painting was set in a river with varying landscapes and a guardian angel overlooking the scene. In childhood, the waters are serene, the landscape fresh, and the angel is in the boat with the child. In youth, the angel has positioned itself onshore, the waters are moving faster, and the young man has the boat's tiller in his hand; the angel is waving to him from the shore, letting him control the boat as it goes onto an ever-wider path. The young man is looking at a castle in the sky, representing his dreams and ideals. In manhood, the scene changes completely. The angel has positioned itself overhead, and the man cannot see it, so he must take it on faith that the angel is there. The waters have turned quite turbulent; they are filled with surging and challenging currents and rapids. The landscape is no longer fresh, but filled with rocks and leafless trees that have been worn down by storms. The man no longer has the tiller and has to follow the current of the river by trying to maintain the boat's stability— and praying. Evil spirits are looking down from the stormy heavens, yet there is a faint glimmer of light in the background toward the right in the painting (toward the direction of the currents). In old age, the waters have become still again, and the old man is looking in

---

[1] Enlarged images of all four paintings in "The Voyage of Life" may be viewed on the following website: http://www.explorethomascole.org/tour/items/73.

the direction indicated by his guardian angel, toward some angels at the far end of the painting.

I always imagined that Cole did not see manhood as a predominantly negative period of life, but rather as an exceedingly challenging time that has benefits and opportunities leading toward salvation. Though the guardian angel is present and watching, the man cannot see him; further, he has lost the tiller (some of his youthful autonomy), so he is reliant on faith and prayer to keep the boat steady amid the churning of the current. This detachment from self-possession and self-control, and this need for faith and prayer, indicates some of the opportunities that suffering and challenge offer us on the road to salvation. By the time the old man has emerged on the other side of the rapids, he is detached from egocentricity and autonomy, and he is allowing the angel who is hovering nearby to lead him to the radiant beauty on the horizon.

So, what is the opportunity of suffering according to Cole? In a phrase, detachment from self, reliance on God, and bravely following Him through the challenges and sufferings of life. We can extend Cole's view of suffering by adding several Christian opportunities to it—namely, compassion, humility, forgiveness, contributing to the common good, and building the Kingdom of God. As Cole suggests, God never leaves us, even during the most turbulent and dangerous times in our lives; He is present to us, helping us to mold and shape our identities and characters, particularly when the tiller of control has disappeared and the rapids seem ready to envelop us. If we bravely put our trust in Him, and we take advantage of the opportunities in challenge and suffering, we will emerge on the other side of the rapids, heading toward the salvation prepared for us by Jesus Christ and His Father.

The forthcoming explanation of the opportunities in suffering will be divided into two parts:

1. Interior Opportunities of Suffering (Section I)
2. External Opportunities of Suffering (Section II)

The forthcoming explanation of the opportunities in suffering will help to give an answer to the question of why an all-loving God allows suffering, which will be explored in Chapter 10. We might offer a preliminary answer to this question to frame the more detailed discussion given in this chapter and Chapter 10: God allows suffering in order to create a context of interdependence, mutual need, common cause, and esprit de corps that will bring us to our individual and collective best in courage, faith, and love—a context that will help us use our freedom of choice to shape our identities toward the eternal salvation of unconditional love He has prepared for us. When suffering is seen within this context, its interior and exterior opportunities come to light.

I. Interior Opportunities of Suffering

By "interior" I mean pertaining to the self—to principles, ideals, character, purpose, and identity that shape *who* we are and *who* we will become. Philosophers throughout the ages have followed the lead of Plato and Aristotle in suggesting that our personal identity is governed by the *end* or objective we habitually or continuously pursue as our main reason for living, as well as the means we habitually use to pursue that end or objective. The idea of habit is very important here, because the more habituated we become to particular ends and means, the more they become engrained in our character and identity. Habits become "second *nature*" to us, and after a while, they become almost permanent, by constituting our identity.

There are both good habits and bad habits. Good habits are those that pursue the highest and most noble ends and means within our reach; they make the best use of our powers of intellect, creativity, emotions, and will. Bad habits are precisely the opposite; they orient us in a direction that will either underutilize our powers or focus them on negative and destructive ends. Virtues are good habits, and they are indispensable not only for living our present lives, but for constituting our eternal identity. We are taught that there are three theological virtues (faith, hope, and love) and four cardinal virtues (prudence, justice, temperance, and fortitude). As we saw in Volume I (Chapter 1), the virtue of love (*agapē*) is vast in its implications and reach. It includes humility, gentleness, forgiveness, and compassion, as well as the ability to accept compassion, the desire to serve the common good, and the desire to serve the eternal Kingdom of God.

Since the time of Jesus, Christians have advocated that *suffering* is an indispensable path to virtue and, therefore, an indispensable means for solidifying and establishing our eternal character and identity.[2] Christians have not made this suggestion cavalierly or stoically, and they certainly do not advocate expressions such as, "Shut up and take it; it will make you tougher and more self-reliant!" Rather, Christians have spent themselves trying to *alleviate* suffering, and encouraging trust and hope in God, by helping those who "find life burdensome" to seize the opportunity within it—opportunities for faith, hope, prudence, justice, temperance, fortitude, humility, forgiveness, and compassion, as well as acceptance of compassion and the desire to build the common good and the Kingdom of God.

The question now arises, why does suffering present such a remarkable opportunity for solidifying and establishing our eternal character and identity, and how do we take advantage of those opportunities so that suffering will lead to optimal growth in virtue, character, identity, and ultimately to salvation? In this section devoted to *interior* opportunities in suffering, I will examine how suffering helps us choose and develop

- prudence, the first natural virtue (Section I.A);
- the natural virtues of fortitude and temperance (Section I.B); and
- *agapē*—compassionate, forgiving, self-sacrificial love for the good of the *other*, including specific treatment of empathy, vulnerability, humility, forgiveness, compassion, and the acceptance of compassion (Section I.C).

A. First Interior Opportunity: Prudence and Identity Transformation

In Chapter 5, we noted that the natural virtue of prudence is first and foremost the awareness of what is truly important and meaningful in life. Thus, prudence is grounded in the awareness of

---

[2] See Volume III, Chapter 3, Section I.

knowing our most proper *end* or objective in life—that is, what will bring greatest meaning, dignity, fulfillment, and destiny. However, prudence does not stop there. It includes awareness of the essential *means* to get to those ends—the principles and virtues (good habits) that will support achievement of this ultimate end. In so doing, it also considers the vices and behaviors that undermine this end. Finally, prudence goes beyond being *aware* of these good ends, principles, and virtues; it appreciates their beauty and "lovability", both in themselves and as a source of the good life. As such, prudence *desires* them, and in this desire, it moves us naturally toward them, which ultimately habituates them. This is why prudence is the first of the natural virtues, and why it must be our first consideration in the opportunities of suffering.

We dedicated the whole of Volume I of this Quartet (*Finding True Happiness*) to the subject of prudence—that is, to knowing our highest and most noble end. We considered it under the rubric of "Four Levels of Happiness". Recall that we have four kinds of desire based on nine powers or capacities within us:

1. Bodily desires—connected with bodily powers
2. Ego-comparative desires—connected with the power of self-consciousness
3. Contributive and loving desires—connected with the powers of empathy and conscience
4. Transcendental desires—connected with our desires for perfect and unconditional truth, love, justice/goodness, beauty, and home

We then noted that "happiness" comes from the fulfillment of a desire and that, conversely, "unhappiness" comes from the nonfulfillment of a desire. Inasmuch as there are four kinds of desire, then there must also be four kinds of happiness.

We then showed—along with Plato and Aristotle, as well as with many contemporary philosophers, psychologists, and theologians— that these four kinds of happiness could be ranked according to how pervasive, enduring, and deep they are. "Pervasive" indicates the extent to which their effects go beyond the self; "endurance" refers to how long these effects are likely to last; and "depth" refers to the *quality* of effect. With respect to depth, do they come from the highest use of our powers—that is, intelligence, creativity, love, moral reasoning, spiritual awareness, intuition, and will? Using these three criteria, it is clear that the first kind of happiness (physical-material happiness) is the least pervasive, enduring, and deep. The second kind of happiness (ego-comparative) is more pervasive, enduring, and deep, but not optimally so. The third kind of happiness (contributive and loving happiness) is more pervasive, enduring, and deep, but still not optimally so. Finally, the fourth kind of happiness (transcendental happiness) is the most pervasive, enduring, and deep because it promises perfect, unconditional, universal, and eternal truth, love, justice/ goodness, beauty, and home in a loving Being who can support and ground these perfections: God.

At this point we began to see clearly where prudence was pointing: toward the highest levels of happiness. We noted that all levels of happiness are good and fulfill important aspects of life's purpose and dignity, but that the higher ones have to direct the lower ones—lest the lower ones undermine the higher ones. We might say then that the wise or prudent person will seek first the transcendental desires, then the contributive and loving desires in light of them, the ego-comparative desires in light of the higher two kinds, and finally the bodily desires in light of the higher three kinds. The prudent person will also see the beauty and lovability of this ordering—that is, desire it and move naturally toward it, which will eventually make it habitual.

In the process of explaining this, we noted that one of these levels of desire or happiness will have to be dominant; it will have to be our first priority (either implicitly or explicitly), because we cannot have two first priorities if a conflict of desires should arise. We noted also that the above ordering was not intuitively obvious, because children tend to stress Level One, and adolescents (who have a modicum of opportunity) stress Level Two. There is no guarantee that adults will move to Levels Three or Four. They can habituate themselves to Levels One and Two, even if these lower levels are destroying them. Why?

The lower levels of happiness/identity are more surface apparent, immediately gratifying, and intense. They tend to easily attract us and hold our attention more (instead of requiring discipline and effort), so we more easily gravitate toward them. If we do not educate ourselves, search for something more, and discipline ourselves to attain the higher levels, we could easily drift into a hedonistic inertia. This would mean living for what is most surface apparent and immediately gratifying, while neglecting what is most pervasive, enduring, and deep—which expresses our highest, most noble, eternal, and unconditional purpose, dignity, and fulfillment. If we want to move toward what is most pervasive, enduring, and deep, we will have to allow Levels One and Two to become recessive; we will have to let go of them (enticing as they are), and this is where suffering frequently comes in.

It cannot be said that we *require* suffering in order to move from the more superficial levels of happiness/identity to the higher (more pervasive, enduring, and deep) ones, for we can see the intrinsic goodness and beauty of making an optimal positive difference to family, friends, community, organization, culture, and even the Kingdom of God. They can be attracted to this noble, beautiful, and even transcendent identity as a fulfillment of their higher selves, or even their transcendent eternal selves. However, this more positive impetus to move toward the more pervasive, enduring, and deep identity can be greatly *assisted* by emptiness, weakness, and vulnerability, as well as by the negative emotions of the comparison game (see Volume I, Chapter 3). It is precisely these negative conditions which can break the spell of the lower levels of happiness/identity.

Physical pleasures (Level One) can be so riveting that they can produce addiction. The same holds true for status, esteem, control, and power. In my life, I have seen how powerful (and even addictive) these lower levels of identity can be. Yet, I truly desired (and saw the beauty and nobility of) the higher levels of happiness/identity. Though this vision was quite powerful in me, I found myself transfixed by the lower levels and almost unable to move myself beyond them. This is where the "power" of suffering (emptiness, weakness, and vulnerability) came into my life. Experiences of my limitations (including progressive blindness) broke the spell of pursuing ego, status, and power. I had a genuine Pauline experience of having to look at life anew—to look for more pervasive purpose in the face of a loss of power, to reexamine what I was living for in light of a loss of control. I had to become more dependent on God, to trust in His ways, and to trust more radically in His logic of love. Thank God for suffering; thank God for the imperfect natural order that gave rise to weaknesses and limitations. Without them, I would have been locked into the spell of ego, status, and power, even though I saw the beauty and nobility of optimal contribution and love. My appreciation of the noble was not strong enough to break the spell of superficiality. Without suffering, I would have been trapped in its powerful inertia. Ironically, weakness and suffering gave me the freedom to overcome the far greater suffering of living beneath myself, of shunning noble purpose, and of consciously wasting my life. Physical and psychological weakness helped me overcome the underliving of my life, the underestimation of my dignity, and the emptiness intrinsic to them.

There are probably some who do not need suffering to make a move from Level Two to Levels Three and Four. I was not one of them. Suffering was my liberation, my vehicle, my pathway to what was most worthy of my life, and what was most noble and perduring in me. I suspect that there are others like me (and Saint Paul) who need suffering, weakness, and vulnerability to call them to their most noble, perduring, and true selves. For these individuals, the imperfect world is indispensable.

Speaking for myself, if I had been born in a *perfect* world, I would not have been called out of Levels One and Two meanings in life— and very likely would never have discovered contribution, humility, compassion, love, and faith, as well as service to the common good and service to the Kingdom. I would likely have been content to simply enjoy life, instead of struggling to define my character and make a difference to the world and the Kingdom of God. Life might have been more enjoyable, but not nearly as meaningful, dignified, fulfilling, or noble.

This liberating power of suffering is not restricted to physical or psychological weakness. It applies most poignantly to the anticipation of death. I once had a student ask, "Why do we need to die? If God is perfect and He intended to give us eternal life, why does He make us die in order to get there? Why not just allow us to continue living without all the mystery about the beyond?" I initially responded that eternal life is not merely a continuation of this current earthly life; it is a *transition* from this life to a completely new kind of life. She responded, "Well, why isn't the 'new' life a continuation of this one? Why wouldn't God create us immediately in the 'new' life?" I indicated to her that the goodness, joy, and beauty of the "new" life consists in perfect love that will exist between God and us, and between all of us in God. I further indicated that this "love" would consist in a perfect act of empathy with another, whereby doing the good for the other would be just as easy, if not easier, than doing the good for oneself, where empathy would take over the desire for ego-satisfaction and bring us to our completion through others and God.

The student almost intuitively agreed that this would be perfect joy, which led her to reask the question: "Well, why didn't God just create us in a situation of perfect love?" At this point, the reader will probably recognize my answer to her question from the foregoing chapters—that love is our *free* choice. God cannot create us into a "world of perfect love"; we have to create the condition of love for ourselves and others by our free decisions. As noted immediately above, our decision to love (to live for a contributive identity) can be assisted considerably by weakness and vulnerability; but even more importantly, it can be assisted by the anticipation of death.

As many philosophers have noted—those coming from both a transcendental perspective, such as Karl Rahner[3] and Edith Stein,[4] and a purely naturalist perspective, such as Martin Heidegger[5] and Jean-Paul Sartre[6]—death produces a psychological finality that compels us to make a decision about what truly matters to us and what truly defines our lives, sooner rather than later. It really does not matter whether we have a strong belief in an afterlife or not; the finality of death incites us to make a statement about the "predeath" meaning of our lives. Most of us view an ongoing deferral of fundamental options (such as to live for love or not, to live for integrity or not, to live for truth or not, etc.) to be unacceptable because death calls us to give authentic definition to our lives; the finality of death says to

[3] See Karl Rahner, *On the Theology of Death* (New York: Herder and Herder, 1961).

[4] See Edith Stein, *Finite and Eternal Being: An Attempt at an Ascent to the Meaning of Being* (Washington, D.C.: ICS Publications, Institute of Carmelite Studies, 2002).

[5] See his extensive treatment of "Being toward Death", in Martin Heidegger, *Being and Time* (New York: Harper Perennial Classics, 2008), pp. 237–99.

[6] See the role of death in Jean-Paul Sartre, *Being and Nothingness*, trans. Hazel Barnes (New York: Washington Square Press, 1993), pp. 65–66, 76, 165–66.

our innermost being that we must express our true selves prior to the termination of the life we know.

Death may well be one of the best gifts we have been given because it calls us to our deepest life definition and self-definition, and in the words of Jean-Paul Sartre, to the creation of our essence.[7] If we believe in an afterlife, we take this authentic self-definition (say, love) with us into our eternity. But even if we do not believe in an afterlife, death still constitutes an indispensable gift of life, for it prevents us from interminably delaying the creation of our essence. It calls us to proclaim who we truly are and what we really stand for—sooner rather than later. We cannot interminably waste our lives in indecision.

In light of death, the choice of one's fundamental essence (say, love) becomes transformative and "life-giving". Death gives life, an authentic, reflective, and free life through a more pervasive, enduring, and deep purpose.

Ironic as it may seem, our need to move *freely* to higher levels of happiness, purpose, dignity, fulfillment, and destiny makes emptiness, weakness, vulnerability, and death, as well as the negative emotions of the comparison game, indispensable. Without them, most of us would be left in the inertia of superficiality, underrated dignity, and underestimated destiny. Left in unhindered hedonism and ego-comparative identity, many of us, if not most of us, would fail to choose, develop, and make habitual the prudence, virtue, and love leading to our eternal transcendental fulfillment.

B. Second Interior Opportunity: Growth in Natural Virtues

Weakness and vulnerability are the conditions necessary for two of the cardinal virtues: courage and self-discipline. Notice that these virtues define our character precisely because they are chosen in the midst of adversity. They define our ability to "pay a price" for our principles and ideals. This "price" gives existential weight to our principles and ideals, for we cannot hold them cheaply.

This is particularly evident with respect to courage. The principles of love, truth, and justice are good in themselves, and they are

[7]See ibid., pp. 15, 60, 129, 724.

honorable in action, but when we have to choose them in the midst of the possibility of injury, embarrassment, mortification, or death, we not only admire them for their intrinsic goodness; we claim them as our own. The greater the price we must pay to live the principles and ideals we admire and honor, the more they become part of us— the more they define our identity. If we admire an honorable ideal because it is honorable, it speaks only partially to who we are; but if we choose an honorable ideal not only because we honor it, but because we want to live it even at the cost of injury, sacrifice, embarrassment, or death, then it truly defines us. Ironically, an imperfect natural order (which gives rise to the real possibility of injury or death) not only gives rise to the possibility of courage, but also to that courage, lending existential weight (and therefore dignity) to our choice of the honorable ideal.

Is it worth it? Is it worth sacrifice, injury, and death to choose the noble thing in the midst of adversity? Only the reader can answer for himself. Would you rather have a very safe world where you can only be a bystander, or would you rather have an unsafe world where you can enter into the fray and see who you truly are (how you truly embrace the honorable), even at the cost of injury or death? What would you want for your children: a safe world without the dignity and self-definition of challenge and self-sacrifice, or an unsafe world, holding out the possibility and actuality of that ultimate dignity? The answer to these questions may depend on whether we believe in eternal life—though not necessarily. If we do believe in eternal life, then the answer will very probably be, "I would rather have challenge, the possibility of courage, and the possibility of self-sacrifice for a noble cause—for then I will know who I truly am, and I will have defined myself in the face of adversity for all eternity." If we do not believe in eternal life, the answer is more ambiguous, though some naturalistic and atheistic thinkers, such as Heidegger[8] and Sartre,[9] acknowledge even a temporary benefit of knowing and defining our true selves.

I am presuming that most readers are open to at least the possibility of eternal life with an unconditionally loving God; otherwise, you would not have made it this far in the Quartet and would not be considering why an unconditionally loving God would allow suffering

---

[8] See Heidegger, "Being toward Death", pp. 272–74.
[9] See Sartre, *Being and Nothingness*, pp. 140–43, 177, 465–67.

and evil. If I am correct, then the suffering you endure for the sake of the noble, love, and the Kingdom of God will define your being— not just in this life, but throughout eternity, where suffering, according to Jesus, is replaced completely by the joy of unconditional love. We will not need to suffer for an eternity to give ourselves eternal self-definition; the suffering we endure in this short life will be sufficient to leave an indelible mark on who we are forever.

Now use the lens of eternal love to ask yourself the above questions once again: Would you rather have a very safe world where you can only be a bystander, or would you rather have an unsafe world where you can enter into the fray and see who you truly are and will be throughout eternity? What would you want for your children: a safe world without the possibility of challenge or self-sacrifice, or an unsafe world, holding out the possibility of establishing a meaningful identity throughout eternity? If you chose the "unsafe world" for the sake of eternally meaningful self-definition, then the rest of this chapter will be beneficial; however, if you chose the "safe world", then this chapter may prove quite challenging.

We now move to the second natural virtue: self-control or self-discipline. While courage is the pursuit of virtue over against the possibility of pain, self-control is the pursuit of virtue through the avoidance of destructive indulgence in pleasure and passion. Many philosophers have recognized that an unmitigated pursuit of pleasure can interfere with, or even undermine, the pursuit of what is most noble, most pervasive, and most enduring. It can even lead to the destruction of ourselves and others. Yet these pleasures are not intrinsically evil. Food is obviously good for us, but an unmitigated pursuit of food (to the point of gluttony) will likely undermine (or at least slow down) the pursuit of the noble. A glass of wine may be good during a convivial meal, but excessive indulgence in it could lead to alcoholism and the undermining of family, job, and friends. Sexuality is a powerful binding force within marriage and family, but excessive indulgence in it can lead to broken relationships, a sense of betrayal, breakdown in commitments, and crimes of passion.

Similarly, ego-satisfactions can also play a beneficial part in life. Success in a speech might encourage one to do more speaking. Achievement in studies might encourage one to pursue a Ph.D. Praise from others could build up self-esteem, but an unmitigated pursuit of success, achievement, and praise (as ends in themselves) will produce egocentricity, narcissism, and the negative emotions of the comparison game: jealousy, fear of failure, ego-sensitivity, blame, rage, contempt, inferiority, superiority, self-pity, and emptiness (see Volume I, Chapter 3).

Both sensorial and ego pleasures are a mixed blessing; in their proper place they can bring happiness, conviviality, and encouragement toward certain forms of achievement; but pursued uncontrollably as ends in themselves, they will very likely interfere with, and even undermine, the pursuit of what is noble, pervasive, and enduring—what is most meaningful and purposeful in life.

This gives rise to the question of why God didn't create a more perfect person in a more perfect world. Why didn't God just give us an "internal regulator" that would *not allow* us to eat too much, drink too much, or desire too much? Why didn't God put us in a world with just enough resources to satisfy our sensorial and ego appetites just enough for health but not enough to undermine our deepest purpose in life? We return to the same words we have seen time and time again: "choice" and "freedom".

Choosing to limit pleasure can be just as difficult as enduring pain for the sake of the good or noble. Thus the limiting of pleasure can be just as self-definitional as enduring pain. There is a real sacrifice involved in limiting pleasure; sometimes it entails saying no amid an irresistible urge; sometimes it means dealing with an addiction; sometimes it causes a profound restriction to freedom because we deny ourselves what we could have otherwise pursued; and sometimes it can make us look prudish in the midst of friends who do not share our view of happiness/identity.

So, why didn't God just create us with a behavioral governor inside our brains? Why didn't God create a better individual in a better world without the possibility of unmitigated desire for pleasure and ego satisfaction? Because God wants *us* to define ourselves in terms of ordinary, nonheroic choices, by choosing noble aspirations above the world of material pleasures. In the day-to-day, ordinary, nonheroic choices we make, an essence (self-definition) begins to form, etched in our character beyond mere thought and aspiration, through the constant pursuit of the little things that enable nobility to emerge from our souls.

We might fail in this pursuit countless times, but our perseverance in the midst of struggles and failures can be extraordinarily effective in etching self-definition into our eternal souls. In God's logic of unconditional love (which includes unconditional forgiveness and healing), our struggles to control pleasure and passion, our hope in forgiveness, our perseverance amid failures, and our humble endurance of criticism are all "part of the cost" of virtue, which makes that virtue more than a mere thought or aspiration—it etches that virtue into our eternal souls.

For this reason, God has created us with the freedom to pursue the Seven Deadly Sins—gluttony, lust, sloth, greed, anger, envy, and pride—and a capacity to desire more than we need even to the point of undermining a good and noble life. God has done this to give us the privilege and freedom to choose the noble over against the possibility of the ignoble so that our virtue—or at least our struggle in pursuit of the virtuous—might be our own; so that it might be chosen and etched into our eternal souls; so that it might be part of our self-definition for all eternity.

Up to this point, we have discussed why God would create us in an imperfect world giving rise to pain, weakness, vulnerability, death, and grief—so that we might *freely* choose the higher levels of purpose and identity as well as the virtues of courage and self-discipline for the sake of the noble. If this is part of the reason why an all-loving God allows suffering, then we would waste our suffering if we fail to seek these opportunities in it. As we have discussed in previous chapters, particularly Chapter 5, it is very difficult to concentrate on seeking opportunities in suffering when we are besieged by fear, anxiety, loneliness, anger, bitterness, and grief. This is precisely why I did not present the opportunities of suffering until this late point in the book. The first step in dealing with suffering is to bring fear, anxiety, and other negative emotions into perspective with prayer, rationality, prudence, and friends. Once we have a modicum of peace and stability—workable backup plans, a sense of God's presence and help, and support from our friends—then we can begin to mine our suffering for the riches of higher purpose and identity, courage, and self-discipline, not to mention the forthcoming virtues of *agapē*, contribution, faith, and building the Kingdom of God.

How do we begin the process of mining our suffering for these virtues? *Ask questions* directed at these virtues. In the case of the above virtues, we might ask, "How can I use my suffering to pursue a higher level of meaning and identity? Can I use my suffering to enter more deeply into Level Three contributive purpose and identity? Can I use my suffering to enter more deeply into Level Four transcendent identity? Can I use my suffering to enhance my faith and my relationship with the loving God? Can I use my suffering to be more deliberate about pursuing the noble, even at the cost of self-sacrifice? Can I use my suffering to be more temperate and disciplined for the sake of the noble?" These questions are not meant to be answered immediately. They are meant to stimulate both conscious and unconscious reflection, and when we repeat them in the midst of our suffering, they direct our conscious and subconscious mind to *look for* answers within ourselves, our dreams, our conversations, and every other aspect of our lives. We become like Archimedes—that is, with open-ended anticipation of an answer to our questions—and eventually when we see the water rising in the baths of Syracuse, we get the clue and shout, "Eureka, I have found it!"

I think it would be just like an unconditionally loving God not only to give us the free choice to appropriate higher levels of purpose and identity as well as the virtues of courage and self-discipline, but also to give us the opportunity and creativity to discover, pursue, and develop our own particular way to do this. Though suffering is painful and negative, it provides this opportunity for growth, creativity, and self-definition.

C. Third Interior Opportunity: Growth in Agapē

We now move from the natural virtues of Plato, Aristotle, and other philosophers to the religious virtue of *agapē*. Though most religions acknowledge the importance of love, philosophers have not given it its due, by leaving it on the periphery of philosophical reflection.[10] Among religions, Christianity alone has made love central, taking great care to define it in detail.[11] The reason for this is obvious. Jesus

[10] The notable exceptions to this are Christian philosophers such as Saint Augustine, Saint Thomas Aquinas, and Saint Bonaventure, and contemporary Christian philosophers such as Bernard Lonergan, Karl Rahner, and Gabriel Marcel.
[11] See Volume II, Chapter 1, Section V.

made love the highest commandment, defined love (*agapē*) through His preaching and parables, asserted the unconditional love of His Father, and demonstrated His unconditional love through His relationship with sinners and His self-sacrificial actions.[12] I will again make the assumption that most readers are at least open to Christianity; otherwise, you probably would not be asking why an *all-loving* God (distinctive and central to Christianity) would allow suffering. If this is the case, this section will be of paramount importance; for inasmuch as love is the highest virtue for Jesus (which all other natural virtues must be consistent with and serve), it must be at the heart of Jesus' explanation for why His Father would allow suffering.

Volume III (Chapter 1) was dedicated to defining Jesus' distinctive view of love, for which early Christians used the term *agapē*. This will be briefly summarized in Section I.C.1, after which six specific characteristics of *agapē* will be considered in their relationship to suffering: empathy (Section I.C.2), love's vulnerability (Section I.C.3), humility (Section I.C.4), forgiveness (Section I.C.5), compassion (Section I.C.6), and acceptance of compassion (Section I.C.7).

1. Definition of Agapē

As we saw in the previous chapter, *agapē* is a gift of self, which is frequently expressed in self-sacrifice. It is grounded in empathy with the other, which makes apparent the unique and *intrinsic* goodness, worthiness, and lovability of that other; this creates a unity with that other whereby doing the good for the other is just as easy, if not easier, than doing the good for oneself. As such, *agapē* arises out of a desire to give life to the intrinsically valuable and lovable other, who could be a stranger or a friend.

We must pause for a moment here to address the idea of *intrinsic* goodness or dignity. This idea must be distinguished from *extrinsic* goodness or dignity, which is grounded in personal and social utility, the ability to make a productive or economically valuable contribution to others and society. Intrinsic goodness or dignity belongs to individuals independently of their usefulness. It comes from their souls—their unique capacity for friendship and love as

---

[12]See Volume III, Chapters 1–3.

well as their capacity to pursue perfect truth, love, goodness, beauty, and home, and to relate to the transcendent interpersonal Being who has given us these transcendental capacities. In the moment of empathy, we recognize a unique interpersonal person who manifests these empathetic and transcendental capacities—the unique and irreplaceable *person* who emanates empathy, goodness, and transcendental mystery. We behold and appreciate the uniquely good and loving transcendental mystery before us, encountering this mystery through a benevolent glance, an amiable voice, a "feeling of unity" with someone of ultimate significance and preciousness. In this act of empathy, the *intrinsic* mysterious lovable good and transcendental dignity of a unique individual is beheld, which is quite distinct from capturing and objectifying the usefulness of that being. Viktor Frankl states it this way:

> But today's society is characterized by achievement orientation, and consequently it adores people who are successful and happy and, in particular, it adores the young. It virtually ignores the value of all those who are otherwise, and in so doing blurs the decisive difference between being valuable in the sense of dignity and being valuable in the sense of usefulness. If one is not cognizant of this difference and holds that an individual's value stems only from his present usefulness, then, believe me, one owes it only to personal inconsistency not to plead for euthanasia along the lines of Hitler's program, that is to say, "mercy" killing of all those who have lost their social usefulness, be it because of old age, incurable illness, mental deterioration, or whatever handicap they may suffer. Confounding the dignity of man with mere usefulness arises from conceptual confusion that in turn may be traced back to the contemporary nihilism transmitted on many an academic campus and many an analytical couch.[13]

Furthermore, *agapē* seeks no reward—neither the reward of romantic feelings intrinsic to *eros* (romantic love) nor the reward of reciprocal commitment and care intrinsic to *philia* (friendship), nor even the feelings of love and delight intrinsic to *storgē* (affection). *Agapē* seeks only the goodness and lovability of others *in themselves*.

---

[13] Viktor Frankl, *Man's Search for Meaning: An Introduction to Logotherapy* (New York: Beacon Press, 1984), p. 138.

The well-being of the intrinsically good, lovable, and transcendental other is a sufficient reward for the commitment of one's time, future, psychic energy, physical energy, resources, and even self-sacrifice. It is its own reward.

2. Empathy[14]

Agapē begins with empathy—a feeling for another, or perhaps better, a feeling *with* another, which produces "unity with", "caring about", and "caring for" the other. This unity with the other breaks down interpersonal barriers (rising out of self-interest) so that doing the good for the other is just as easy if not easier than doing the good for oneself. Most would agree that this "feeling for and with another" is quite natural. We can meet others for a few moments and get a sense of their goodness and lovability. When we see others in need and intuit their worthiness from our empathetic connection with them, we will likely respond with sympathy, assistance, or words of consolation. Mere presence, mere tone of voice, mere glance, and mere feeling of connectedness can engender a recognition of unique and intrinsic goodness and lovability, which causes us to care about the other, to protect the other, to attend to the other's needs, to spend time with the other, and even to sacrifice oneself for the other—even a total stranger. It is as if we have a receptor, like a radio antenna, that is attuned to the frequency of the other's unique and intrinsic goodness and lovability, and when the signal comes, whether it be from a smile, an utterance, or a look of need, we connect in a single feeling that engenders a gift of self.

Though most would agree that empathy is natural to us, we must hasten to add that our own desires for autonomy and ego-fulfillment can block our receptivity to the other's "signal". We can become so self-absorbed or self-involved that we forget to turn on the receiver, and even if we have turned on the receiver, we have the volume turned down so low that it cannot produce adequate output in our hearts. It is at this juncture that suffering, particularly the suffering of weakness and vulnerability, proves to be most helpful.

---

[14]Perhaps the most nuanced treatment of empathy available today is Edith Stein's phenomenological *On the Problem of Empathy* (Washington, D.C.: ICS Publications, 1989). The first chapter on the "Essence of the Act of Empathy" is particularly valuable (see pp. 6–17).

This point may be illustrated by a story my father told me when I was an adolescent. I think he meant it more as a parable about how some attitudes can lead some people to become believers and other people to become unbelievers and even malcontents. But it became for me a first glimpse into the interrelationship between suffering and compassion, love and lovability, trust and trustworthiness, co-responsibility and dignity, and the nature of God.

Once upon a time, God created a world at a banquet table.[15] He had everyone sit down, and served up a sumptuous feast. Unfortunately, He did not provide any of the people at the table with wrists or elbows. As a consequence, they could not feed themselves. All they could do was feel acute hunger while gazing at the feast.

This provoked a variety of responses. At one end of the table, a group began to conjecture that God could not possibly be all-powerful, for if He were, He would have been all-knowing and would have realized that it would have been far more perfect to create persons with wrists and elbows, so that they could eat sumptuous feasts placed before them. The following refrain was frequently heard: "Any fool can see that some pivot point on the arm would be preferable to the impoverished straight ones with which we have been provided!"

A second group retorted, "If there really is a God, it would seem that He would *have* to be all-powerful and all-knowing, in which case, He would not make elementary mistakes. If God is God, He could have made a better creature (e.g., one with elbows). If God exists, and in His omniscience has created us without elbows or wrists, He must have a cruel streak, perhaps even a sadistic streak. At the very minimum, He certainly cannot be all-loving."

A third group responded by noting that the attributes of "all-powerful" and "all-loving" would seem to belong to God by nature, for love is positive, and God is purely positive; therefore, God—not being devoid of any positivity—would have to be pure love. They then concluded that God did not exist, for it was clear that the people

[15] This parable is attributed to Rabbi Haim of Romshishok, who used it as an allegory to illustrate the difference between Hell and Heaven. In Hell, everyone tries to feed himself, but gets nothing, while in Heaven people reach across the table and are fed. Apparently my father made a very creative adaptation of this parable.

at the table were set into a condition that was certainly less than perfect (which *seemed* to betoken an imperfectly loving God). They conjectured, "We should not ask where the banquet came from, let alone where we came from, but just accept the fact that life is inexplicable and absurd. After all, we have been created to suffer, but an all-loving God would not have done this. Our only recourse is to face, with authenticity and courage, the absence of God in the world, and to embrace the despair and absurdity of life."[16]

A fourth group was listening to the responses of the first three, but did not seem to be engaged by the heavily theoretical discourse. A few of them began to look across the table, and in an act of empathy and compassion, noticed that even though they could not feed themselves, they could feed the person across the table. In an act of freely choosing to feed the other first, of letting go of the resentment about not being able to do it by themselves, they began to feed one another. At once, *agapē* was discovered in freedom, while their very real need to eat was also satisfied.

This parable reveals a key insight into suffering—namely, that "empathy has reasons that negative theorizing knows not of". The first three groups had all assumed that weakness and vulnerability were essentially negative, and because of this, they assumed that either God had made a mistake or He was defective in love. Their preoccupation with the negativity of weakness distracted them from discovering, in that same weakness, the positive, empathetic, and compassionate responsiveness to the need of the other that grounds the unity and generativity of love. This lesson holds the key not only to the meaning of suffering but also to the life and joy of *agapē*. If we are to be drawn by suffering into the richness of empathy and compassion, we will have to let go of the stoic presumption that weakness and vulnerability are essentially negative, and invest ourselves in Jesus' revelation of the positivity of suffering—its invitation to eternal love and joy.

The experience of the fourth group at the table reveals why God would allow us to suffer—because the imperfection of the human condition leads to weakness and vulnerability, which in turn provide

---

[16]Albert Camus explicitly states this absurdist philosophy in *The Myth of Sisyphus and Other Essays* (New York: Vintage Books, 1991).

invaluable assistance in directing us toward empathy and compassion, and even to receiving the empathy and compassion of others.

Weakness and vulnerability are not *required* for empathy and compassion, because many people find empathy and compassion to be their own reward. They will see the positivity of empathy and compassion as good for both others and themselves. This was certainly not the case for me. Though I saw the intrinsic goodness and worthiness of empathy and compassion (for both myself and others), my egocentricity and desire for autonomy created such powerful blocks that I could not move myself to what I thought was intrinsically valuable and meaningful. I needed help to break through my self-imposed barrier to others—and be released from the spell of autonomy and egocentricity; I needed a "thorn ... in the flesh ... an angel of Satan, to beat me, to keep me from getting proud" (2 Cor 12:7, NAB). As noted earlier, I was given this gift through various weaknesses, particularly the deterioration of my eyesight.

Like the fourth group in the parable, my imperfect condition gave me a moment to reconsider the entire meaning of life, what really made life worth living, and it was here that I discovered empathy, love, and compassion. The process was gradual, but the "thorn in the flesh" gave me the very real assistance I needed to open myself to love as the meaning of life.

The first step to unleashing the power of empathy is recognizing the impossibility of being self-sufficient. Looking back on it I was never self-sufficient; I was content to live under the *illusion* of it. Nevertheless, the dispelling of the illusion made me confront the reality that we are interdependent, and therefore, we need one another; we need each other's friendship, support, companionship, complementarity, inspiration, and compassion.

The second step requires *accepting* help and compassion from others. In my twenties and thirties I had a great deal of difficulty doing this because it made me feel inferior to the people who were only trying to help me. Though I recognized their good intent intellectually, I could not help myself; I felt horribly demeaned. Nevertheless, I needed their help, and I disliked my resentful feelings toward them. At this juncture an important philosophical distinction came to the rescue: Viktor Frankl's distinction (mentioned above) between "value in the sense of dignity" and "value in the sense of usefulness".[17] I have characterized these qualities elsewhere as "intrinsic dignity" and "extrinsic value", respectively. At the very moment I felt inferiority and resentment for not being able to be self-sufficient, I became more detached from a merely extrinsic self-valuation. If I had not done this, I would have been reduced to a continual state of torment. As I became detached from mere extrinsic valuation, I discovered my *intrinsic* dignity. At first I counted this kind of self-valuation as "sub-par", secretly yearning for the old extrinsic valuation to be restored. But it wasn't, and so gradually I began to accept my intrinsic dignity as *truly* valuable—my presence to others, my friendship, empathy, and capacity to help and care for others. Eventually I began to see this kind of self-valuation as more important than extrinsic valuation. This led in turn to my ability to value *others* more for their intrinsic dignity than their extrinsic value, which gave me the freedom to love them for who they are—instead of esteeming them for what they do. Suffering broke down the barrier of errant self-valuation, which eventually gave me the freedom to love. Upon reflection, I had been like a character in my father's parable of the banquet table. Thank God for suffering!

I did not make this transition by myself—I was greatly helped by others who recognized some intrinsic goodness and lovability in *me*, and were trying to help me for no other reason than to respond to my need. They recognized something in me that I did not recognize in myself, because I had long since replaced my "lovable self" with a merely "esteemable self" (a "thingafied self"), and I had to recapture the lovable self through the love that others gratuitously offered to me.

Thus, my weakness and vulnerability *freed* me to empathize with others. If I had not had weaknesses and vulnerability, I probably would not have discovered the beauty of empathy and the lovability of both others and myself. In retrospect, I can say with Saint Paul that I thank God for my weakness and suffering, because they broke the spell of Level Two identity and the myth of autonomy, virtually compelling me to recognize my own and others' intrinsic dignity. Weakness gave me the *opportunity* to appreciate others' gratuitous love, their lovability in that love, and my lovability as a reflection of that love. Without suffering, my life would be categorically different; it would be caught up in superficiality and filled with the darkness,

---

[17] Frankl, *Man's Search for Meaning*, p. 138.

emptiness, and loneliness that merely extrinsic self-valuation inevitably brings.

3. Love's Vulnerability

Love has vulnerability built into it. There is a softness to love—it opens itself to being completed by the other; it reveals weakness (the need for complementarity by the other); it is forgiving of the other in times of failure; it anticipates forgiveness by the other in one's own failings; its empathy can elicit tears.

Some of us are able to accept and even live in this vulnerability through a simple vision of its intrinsic beauty and goodness. Others like myself (as illustrated above) need some extrinsic prodding to help break the spell of self-sufficiency and ego-centricity, which is built on the illusion that complementarity, weakness, and gentleness are negative. Some of us need to experience vulnerability in order to see its goodness in relationship to love. Some of us need the assistance of weakness to accept the love of others. Some of us need to be reduced to tears in order to experience the tears of sympathy. Some of us need to experience weakness and vulnerability in order to sympathize with others' weaknesses and vulnerabilities.

There is a silent, if not overt, suspicion of and aversion to weakness and vulnerability in our culture. The reason for this lies in a false view of courage and self-discipline. As noted above and in Chapter 5, God wants us to possess the natural virtues of rational reflection, prudence, courage, and temperance. He does not want us to be the archetypal "needy person"—helpless and overly dependent on others for everything. Instead, He wants us to be strong and self-reliant in every way that is feasible. *However*, He does not want us to be self-reliant, rational, prudent, courageous, and self-disciplined to the *exclusion* of real interdependency and need for others. God does not want us to lie to ourselves, or others, and create a façade of being *purely* self-reliant, rational, courageous, and self-disciplined. He wants our rationality, courage, self-discipline, and self-reliance to be based on reality and truth—and therefore he wants us to acknowledge our interdependency with others as well as the areas in which we truly need their help and support.

The façade of being *purely* self-sufficient is not only dangerous to self and others; it reveals an arrogance that reduces us to complete inauthenticity. To perpetuate this arrogance, we have to make ourselves believe the most fundamental lie of all: complete autonomy; and if we can be that false to ourselves, then it must follow (as the night, the day) that we will be false to every other person.

So how do we acquire love's vulnerability, which leads to gentleness and humbleness of heart, without abandoning the natural virtues of rationality, prudence, courage, and temperance? We must be truthful to ourselves, discerning where we have genuine needs and how we can respond to others' genuine needs, *then* cultivate the natural virtues around this truth.

Here is where the opportunity and efficacy of suffering comes into play. Our personal weakness and our inability to fulfill perfectly the needs of others compels all but the most stubborn to confront the myth of perfect autonomy, which in turn points to the truth about ourselves—our interdependency, including our ability to complement and be complemented by another, and our ability to serve and to be served by others.

4. Humility

As Jesus and virtually every saint recognized, humility is the condition necessary for the possibility of *agapē*. Most of us recognize the necessity of humility in attaining empathy and "gift of self". Self-absorption does not permit the "signal" of the other to be received. Moreover, it makes us so obsessed with fulfilling our egos that we barely notice the goodness and mystery of the other, and feel compelled to use the other as a mere instrument of self-satisfaction. These conditions undermine the very possibility of love.

Some people are able to see the goodness and beauty of humility and to move almost effortlessly toward it, but judging from the history of philosophy, most of us do not belong to this group. We have all heard the following phrase from the Book of Proverbs: "Pride goes before destruction, and a haughty spirit before a fall" (16:18); we have also heard Jesus' proclamation that the "greatest among you shall be your servant; whoever exalts himself will be humbled, and whoever humbles himself will be exalted" (Mt 23:11–12). Jesus illustrates this further in the Gospel of Luke when He notices guests trying to pick the places of honor at table at a Pharisee's house:

FINDING LIGHT IN THE DARKNESS

When you are invited by any one to a marriage feast, do not sit down in a place of honor, lest a more eminent man than you be invited by him; and he who invited you both will come and say to you, "Give place to this man," and then you will begin with shame to take the lowest place. But when you are invited, go and sit in the lowest place, so that when your host comes he may say to you, "Friend, go up higher"; then you will be honored in the presence of all who sit at table with you. For every one who exalts himself will be humbled, and he who humbles himself will be exalted. (14:7–11)

It is no accident that Jesus places humble-heartedness (the poor in spirit) as the first Beatitude, which affects and conditions not only the rest of the Beatitudes, but the entire Sermon on the Mount; so we should not be surprised that Jesus, in one of the few references to His personal characteristics, states, "For I am meek and *humble* of heart" (Mt 11:29, NAB; emphasis mine).

Though Socrates recognized the need for humility in the process of inquiry and the acquisition of wisdom,[18] he did not link it specifically to love. As noted above, most non-Christian philosophers do not spend considerable time or energy on the definition or virtue of love, and so they do not recognize the importance of humility in achieving *agapē* as the highest virtue. Christian philosophers are a notable exception to this. Saint Augustine said that "it was pride that changed angels into devils; it is humility that makes men as angels."[19] Christian philosophical tradition has followed this prioritization of humble love until the present day.[20] For Jesus and the Christian tradition, humility

---

[18] See Plato, *Apology* 20e–23c.

[19] This is attributed to Saint Augustine in a popular medieval Latin handbook used for sermons called *Manipulus Florum* (*A Handful of Flowers*), edited by Thomas Hibernicus (Thomas of Ireland) in about 1306. He was an anthologist who collected over six thousand patristic sayings from the libraries at the Sorbonne. He bequeathed it to the Sorbonne, and it was printed in 1483 as a patristic handbook for sermons and writings.

[20] Though the contemporary Thomistic tradition acknowledges the importance of humility, Christian existentialism (beginning with Søren Kierkegaard) makes it *central*. Robert Roberts shows that humility and gratitude underlie the whole of Kierkegaard's writings on virtue, and is integral to the whole of Christian moral psychology. See Robert Roberts, *Emotions: An Essay in Aid of Moral Psychology* (Cambridge: Cambridge University Press, 2003). The centrality of humility is followed by other Christian existentialists and phenomenologists, most notably Gabriel Marcel, Carl Jaspers, Max Scheler, and Dietrich von Hildebrand. See especially Dietrich von Hildebrand, *Humility: Wellspring of Virtue* (Manchester, N.H.: Sophia Institute Press, 1976).

is the entryway to *agapē* and *agapē* the entryway to true joy. As Jesus says in the Gospel of John:

> If you keep my commandments [to love], you will abide in my love, just as I have kept my Father's commandments [to love] and abide in his love. These things I have spoken to you, that my joy may be in you, and that your joy may be full. This is my commandment, that you love one another as I have loved you. (15:10–12)

The Christian philosophical tradition acknowledges that the wisdom and goodness of humility is not easy to see, appreciate, and appropriate, because it is contrary to our propensity to pursue ego-gratification, comparative advantage, status, and power. I have elsewhere described this propensity as the outcome of a dominant Level Two view of happiness (see Volume I, Chapter 3).

I, for one, never belonged to the group that found the wisdom and goodness of humility to be self-evident. It was difficult for me to understand, even more difficult to appreciate, and still more difficult to appropriate. I was about twenty years old when I first got an inkling about the "possible value" of humility. At that time, I was still equating my lovability with my esteemability and respectability. Yes, I was a friend to others; I could have a great time with my friends—but I wanted these friendships to be on my terms and to be based on my friends' *esteem* for me. Though I had a sense that my friends loved me for *who* I was, and that they appreciated my presence and personality, I really wanted them to respect my accomplishments first. Esteemability trumped lovability. I needed extrinsic prodding from deprivation and difficulty to reexamine what I considered to be friendship.

At that time, I saw intelligence, courage, achievement, and my newly burgeoning faith to be valuable. But to be honest, I didn't even notice humility, empathy, and the vulnerability intrinsic to *agapē*, so I was in no position to consider them valuable. Once again, suffering came to the rescue—and this time, it was complemented by faith and grace.

In my novitiate (the beginning of Jesuit formation), I had a two-fold experience leading toward humility: an experience of weakness combined with an experience of the beauty of humility in the heart of Christ. The experience of weakness came as a virtual inevitability in the area of athletics (which was never my strong suit). In college, I had always oriented my athletic endeavors around activities I could do fairly well, thus avoiding any potential embarrassments. However, in the novitiate, we had mandated sports activities, such as volleyball and basketball. On one occasion while playing volleyball, we were at "game point", and the serve went to a man on the opposite team who was six feet six and had a powerful serve. I thought to myself, "He is going to pound that ball right at me," the weak link in the chain—and sure enough, he did! I tried to get my hands perfectly positioned under the ball to knock it high in the air so another teammate could pound it back over the net. I was off by about an inch, and the ball went flying sideways, and we lost the game. I was humiliated—humiliated by the fact that everyone knew *before the shot* that I was the weak link in the chain, and further humiliated by living up to their low expectations. As I was walking off the court with my head hanging low, one of my fellow novices (with whom I am still a good friend) said to me, "Spitzer, what does this have to do with the whole order of salvation?" I thought to myself, "Not much!" At first I applied his advice only to being the efficient cause of our team losing the game, but later it occurred to me that being weak and humiliated in athletics might have a potential value in helping me to embrace the teachings of Jesus, and this synergized well with the next experience: the love and humility of Jesus.

In my thirty-day silent retreat, I experienced the *heart* of Christ. This experience, combined with my experience of athletic weakness, led to a reexamination of life's meaning, dignity, and fulfillment. Curiously, I came to an awareness of Level Three through my faith (Level Four). When I experienced the profound love of Jesus and His Father for me and began to see how important love (*agapē*) is for meaning, dignity, fulfillment, and destiny, I knew that I would have to take Jesus' teachings on love very seriously. This led to a slow and reluctant, but nevertheless effective, appreciation of the Parable of the Good Samaritan and the Beatitudes. I began to look at these passages in light of the crucified Jesus, noting carefully what He tried to show us and give us through His suffering. I perceived a faint glimmer of the value of humility and self-sacrifice, sufficient to extricate myself from the darkness of pride and egocentricity.

I thought back to the volleyball game and reflected on the humiliation and weakness I felt in that moment, and how these painful and
seemingly negative experiences led me—or should I say "compelled
me"—to look for life's meaning *beyond* esteemability and egocentric
satisfaction. On the horizon, I could see other meanings central to
Jesus' heart, such as contribution, love, and faith, and recognized
how they could be far more meaningful and fulfilling than mere
comparative and egocentric satisfactions. Once I had this insight, I
was not about to let it go. The example of Jesus enabled me to see
the positive value of weakness and humility in the pursuit of love,
which, in turn, began to free me to accept them—though at the time,
I could not embrace them.

A meditation in the *Spiritual Exercises* called "The Three Degrees
of Humility" was central to my thirty-day retreat. When I encountered it, it produced great fear and anxiety because the greater degrees
of humility seemed to be beyond my reach. Saint Ignatius counseled
that we should not pursue this as a stoic enterprise but rather should
imitate the love and goodness of Jesus, who loves us unconditionally.
Even with this understanding, I found myself resisting Ignatius' direction quite strenuously. Fortunately, he anticipated people like myself,
and counseled that if we cannot desire such humility, then we should
begin by trying to *desire the desire* for humility (*whewwwww*—that got
me through the meditation).

I made recourse to this story because it speaks to a truth of the
heart—namely, that weakness and humiliation, seen within the context of the love and suffering of the Son of God, opened my otherwise
tightly closed heart to both humility and the efficacy of suffering. It
started a journey, which lasts to this very day and will not be completed until after I leave this world. In a word, suffering in light of
the love and suffering of Christ is the pathway to humble love, patient
love, compassionate love, gentle love, and self-sacrificial love—what
the early Christians called *agapē*, which is the pathway to ultimate
authenticity, meaning, dignity, destiny, and above all, joy.

In sum, weakness and humiliation were essential in my life to
loosen the grip of Level Two dominance, the comparison game, and
the esteemable self. As such, they were integral to my freedom to
love and the rediscovery of my "lovable self". This path to humility
involved three components:

1. The encounter with weakness and vulnerability in my life, first in the novitiate and early formation, and later and much more profoundly in my progressive blindness
2. My discovery of the heart of Jesus and His Father (particularly in the *Spiritual Exercises*), whose love I desired—and desired to imitate
3. The interpretation of my weakness, vulnerability, and suffering through the words and actions of Jesus and Saint Paul, who not only showed me the efficacy of suffering, but also the light and exaltation of humility

5. Forgiveness

For Jesus, forgiveness is the most important facet of *agapē*; it is mentioned more often than any other prescript in the New Testament. Forgiveness enables us to start again without having to live under the burden of our past offenses. If we cannot forgive from the heart, love (*agapē*) has little chance of getting off the ground.

Forgiveness requires both humility and empathy because it entails letting go of a *just* grievance against another. If someone has unintentionally hurt us, it can be *excused*; but if someone *intentionally* insults or hurts us, forgiveness is required because we have to give up our *just* claim to retribution. Difficult as this might be, it is necessary to restore the possibility of love. The fact is, retribution begets retribution, vengeance begets vengeance, and violence begets violence. If we are to interrupt this ever-expanding cycle of vengeance and violence, if we are to allow the parties in the cycle to begin the long process of healing, and if we are to restore equanimity to a shattered peace, we will have to *let go* of our *just* claims against the other.

How is this possible? We must see the intrinsic value and need of the unjust perpetrator, like Bishop Myriel in *Les Miserables*, who sees the goodness and need of Jean Valjean, despite the fact that Jean stole his silver after the bishop allowed him to stay at his house. He is so convinced of Jean's potential goodness that he gives him two additional silver pieces to protect him from being arrested, and then tells him to do some good with the money he obtains. Jean lives up to the bishop's expectations more than the latter could have expected.

If we are to forgive, we must not only see the intrinsic goodness and redeemability of unjust perpetrators, but also see the goodness of interrupting the cycle of vengeance begetting vengeance and violence begetting violence; and we must want the good of our enemy (even though we may have to protect ourselves against him in the future). But how can we do this, particularly when we are still stinging from the injustice of a seemingly callous attack? Here is where empathy and humility become relevant. It might best be explained by extending the personal story given above.

My gradual appropriation of empathy and humility in the novitiate made me more aware of the unique goodness and lovability of the many people I encountered in college, some of whom I had judged and treated quite basely. I reflected on times when I intimated that people were not as quick or knowledgeable as I might have expected. I also let people know the privilege of my family background without regard to the hardships they may have had to endure. At the time, I was almost oblivious to the pain I was causing to others, but the enhancement of empathy and humility in the novitiate allowed me to feel the pain they must have felt at my disrespect and indifference. I not only wanted to be forgiven for my offense; I wanted the Lord to heal the injuries that I had caused. I literally begged the Lord to "make good come out of whatever harm I might have caused" (see Chapter 4, Section IX), and trusted that He would work miracles in the hearts of the people I had grieved.

What did this have to do with my forgiving others? It occurred to me that if I so desperately needed to be forgiven and healed by God, others who had offended me would need the same forgiveness from me—and God. Once again, empathy and humility had given me new freedom. Empathy enabled me to feel the need others had for forgiveness by association with *my* need for it, and humility enabled me to see that the need of others to be freed from past burdens was just as great if not greater than my own. In retrospect, all this happened because weakness, vulnerability, and embarrassment, combined with the love of Jesus, opened me to empathy, humility, and love. Once opened, it was quite easy for the Spirit to lead me to my own need for forgiveness, and by association, to the need of others to be forgiven by me.

Weakness and suffering enabled me to see the goodness and lovability of others *and* what I could have done to befriend them.

Though this filled me with another kind of suffering—the guilt and regret for my indifference, callousness, and arrogance—it led me to realize that I had been forgiven much and loved much by both God and neighbor; this led me to the freedom to forgive others who had unjustly offended me. I could now ask the Lord for the grace to imitate Him in His forgiveness, and pray for my persecutors by putting injustices in the hands of the perfectly just and merciful judge. This *freedom* which came through a combination of suffering and the love of God has enabled me, albeit imperfectly, to forgive from the heart.

I have a long way to go in the pursuit of humility, empathy, respect, and forgiveness, so I expect that I will need additional assistance to further purify my love. Though I know some of this assistance will entail additional experiences of weakness and vulnerability, I have come to trust that God can transform these initial negative experiences into deeper empathy, humility, and forgiveness. I have also come to realize that these dimensions of love will ultimately lead to true happiness—eternal joy with the unconditionally loving God.

6. Compassion

Compassion is yet another gift that suffering helps to appropriate. Jesus taught that compassion for strangers and enemies was the highest form of love, and best manifests His Father's perfect love (Mt 5:43–48). The word means literally "to suffer with", and in the Parable of the Good Samaritan, Jesus describes it as a feeling of profound identification with the suffering of another person that moves one to merciful action.[21]

When we *are* compassionate (not merely *showing* compassion, which feels like pity to the receiving party) we become like the Good Samaritan. We feel miserable because someone of unique intrinsic goodness and lovability *is* miserable, and this sense of "sympathetic sadness" moves us to do as much as we can to comfort the one who is suffering. Comfort sometimes takes the form of *doing* something beneficial (e.g., giving medical treatment or providing housing). But

---

[21] In Latin, *passio* means suffering; and *cum* means with. Hence, *cum passio* (compassion) means suffering with. It signifies being deeply moved by the suffering of another. See also Jesus' reaction to the widow of Nain who has lost her only son (Lk 7:11–17).

frequently enough, we cannot *do* anything but give our time, presence, and attention; we can only *be with* the other—we are capable only of using our presence, our friendship, and our love to give comfort. Yet this imparts dignity. Spending time with another proves to the other that he is valuable, because most everyone intuitively recognizes the preciousness of time.

No matter how compassion is manifested (doing something for someone, or simply being with someone), it always has the capacity to impart dignity. There is something about an act of loving sympathy with another's misery that elicits comfort and proves to another that he not only has esteemability or status, but genuine lovability (belovedness). This "loving sympathy giving rise to comfort" is the deepest and most positive gift that can be given, because the awareness of genuine belovedness is also a recognition of our profound *intrinsic* dignity.

There is only one hitch: we have to be suffering in order to receive compassion. This is one of the most paradoxical aspects of the human condition; if we are to receive the deep affirmation of our belovedness, which leads to our deepest moments of dignity, freedom, self-affirmation, and joy, we must be in a state of weakness, pain, or need.

Most children experience this when they are sick and stay home from school. Instead of their mothers, or caretakers, being revolted by their illness, or angry at the inconvenience of their illness, they probably receive loving sympathy, comfort, and a genuine affirmation of their belovedness. This gift of compassion leaves an indelible mark on children. If it recurs again and again, an intuitive belief begins to form that they are intrinsically lovable. They are beloved just in themselves, without all the accomplishments and comparative advantage that can make them *exteriorly* esteemable. This will eventually enable them to love themselves and to accept love from another, which will make all the difference between a life of love and a life of trying to win the love that they believe they do not deserve.

Suffering not only provides the condition necessary for recognizing our intrinsic dignity and our "lovable selves"; it also helps us be compassionate to others. We have already seen how suffering helps us break the spell of Level Two identity, giving us the freedom for empathy, humility, and forgiveness; so it should come as no surprise that it can also help us become compassionate, helping others in their suffering by profoundly identifying with them in their pain. It is almost a cliché to say that our suffering helps us sympathize with others in their suffering. If we know from firsthand experience what suffering is like, we will have a better idea of what others must be feeling in their suffering, which opens us to sympathetic identification with them. This reveals yet another paradox: inasmuch as compassion is one of the highest and most positive activities of the human spirit, which according to Jesus reflects His Father's perfect love,[22] then suffering supports and leads to this highest of human activities. Though suffering can be profoundly negative, it can also be profoundly positive, in different respects at the same time.

As I noted earlier, this has truly been the case in my life—in broken relationships, athletic ineptness, and progressive blindness. Always, suffering has led to an increased awareness of other people's pain, and therefore to an increased desire to help them through it. In addition to this, my suffering has led to an increased awareness of the sufferings of Jesus—the price He paid to sacrifice Himself completely to create an unconditional act of love for the world.[23] The more I have endured suffering and weakness, the less abstract His unconditional act of love has become, and conversely, the more I have been able to *feel* the sacrifice intrinsic to His unconditional act of love. This has helped me to grow not only in faith and love of Jesus, but also to offer my suffering as an act of self-sacrifice for the redemption of the world (see Chapter 8).

I might sum up by reiterating the conclusion drawn at the end of the previous chapter that suffering, faith, and love (*agapē*) are complementary and integral to one. When seen through the eyes of Christian faith, suffering can greatly enhance love, empathy, humility, forgiveness, and compassion. This leads to my last point in this section.

---

[22] Luke explicitizes Jesus' phrase in Matthew "be perfect, as your heavenly Father is perfect" (Mt 5:48) as "[b]e compassionate (*oiktirmones*) as your Father is compassionate" (Lk 6:36; my translation), showing that compassion is the highest expression of the Father's perfect love. "Luke 6:36: 'Be compassionate (oiktirmones | οἰκτίρμονες | nom pl masc), just as your Father is compassionate (oiktirmōn | οἰκτίρμων | nom sg masc)'", https://www.billmounce.com/greek-dictionary/oiktirmon. See *Strong's Concordance*, number 3629, Greek number 3881 "merciful, compassionate".

[23] See Volume III, Chapter 3, Section IV. See also Chapter 8 of this volume.

Christian faith is indispensable for transforming suffering into the highest levels of love. Jesus gives ultimate meaning to suffering through His promise of eternal salvation, His Holy Spirit (who inspires, guides, consoles, and protects us), His presence and love (to alleviate fear and bring consolation), and the example of His suffering, which shows us how to use our suffering as a self-offering for the salvation of the world. All of these graces help lift suffering into the heights of love, leading us to our eternal salvation with the unconditionally loving God.

7. Acceptance of Compassion

Most of us who have reached our midtwenties no longer have the attitude of children who are capable of accepting the compassion of parents, friends, and teachers. We have learned that we are supposed to be capable of taking care of ourselves, carrying our own weight, and that our respectability depends on this. We have also learned that we should never take another person's time for our personal needs. Even though we could not possibly live this way, we try to believe the myth so that we can content ourselves with our autonomy and self-sufficiency. If we believe the myth, we tell ourselves that we are not needy, and as a consequence, we would never admit to being needy, but we do find ways, "acceptable ways", of getting our needs met.

How do people find the freedom to accept another's compassion? As implied above, some people do this naturally. Others remember the acts of compassion they received as children and carry them over into adulthood. And still others, like myself, *need suffering* in order to do this.

As I noted, my gradual blindness caused me to lose my driver's license when I was thirty-one. Now if there is one thing in this culture that proves we are self-sufficient, it is the fact that we can get into our cars and go wherever we want whenever we want. But I found myself, at a young age, unable to do so. As a result, I became dependent on others for rides.

At first I could not ask anyone for a ride because of embarrassment. I felt that the mere admission of bad eyesight and the inability to drive *myself* (not carrying my own weight) would not only trouble a prospective driver, but also cause shock and disdain. People never really reacted like this, but I *thought* that people felt this way. After two years of having my secretaries ask for rides for me, I still did not believe that people respected me as much as they would have if I had not been losing my eyesight. I thought they were disguising it incredibly well. So, as I took the rides from compassionate people, I would sit there believing that they were annoyed at the inconvenience, troubled by my inferiority, and pitying me for it. I really hated getting into those cars.

One day, when I was going from Seattle University to my parish (Saint Philomena's), a lady mentioned to me that she was really grateful that she was able to get on the list of people who wanted to give me a ride. I said, "A list? Why would there be a list?" And she said that this was something that many people thought they could do, that it was relatively easy, and it would give them some time with me. I was truly surprised. They were not annoyed at my weakness. They found it a rather pleasing and interesting idiosyncrasy in a person who seemed, at times, distant because of his use of complex sentences and concepts. They said that my eye problem made me human, and that they were able to empathize with a person that they had otherwise found to be somewhat intimidating. In fact, this lady said that it made me "*un*intimidating".

After some reflection on this incident, I discovered that people liked me, just for myself, not for my intellect or my gifts of speaking. They wanted to get to know *me*; they wanted me to be unintimidating. They enjoyed being around me, not despite my weakness, but because of it. They really enjoyed being of service, and giving a ride was something they could do (which I obviously could not do). I had the peculiar role of *allowing* these wonderful people an opportunity to practice *agapē* through selfless service. In their attempt to make my life easier—in their loving sympathy with my weakness and self-sacrifice to care for me—I too was able to impart dignity back to them by merely *accepting* their compassion as compassion, by *accepting* their love as genuine love. It occurred to me that their smiles were not an act, but genuine joy arising out of an authentic act of empathy, graciously accepted by someone in need.

I discovered that people were better than I had expected. The fault was my own; *I* was not up to their level. *I* was not capable of that kind of compassion. Formerly, I believed that their compassion and joy were contrived (they were doing it because the pastor had put pressure on them, and they were making the best out of a bad situation), but I came to learn that people really *are* that good; they *are* much better than I expected, and so I felt called to be more compassionate in imitation of *them*. The more I responded to this call, the more I was able to accept the compassion of others.

Showing and accepting compassion are complementary and give rise to an expanding cycle—accepting compassion can incite awareness of the genuine goodness of people, and this in turn calls us to imitate that goodness in them, inspiring us to greater compassion. Suffering provided the impetus for this cycle, and all I had to do was notice the genuine goodness of others, accept their compassion, and allow myself to be edified by their goodness—and imitate them.

My faith in Jesus truly helped in this expanding cycle. If I had to rely on myself alone, without the example of Jesus and the inspiration of the Holy Spirit, there is a very good chance I would have let the above opportunity simply pass me by. I can see myself letting the preoccupation with my weakness and embarrassment block my awareness of the beauty, goodness, and love of others who were trying to help me; and I consider myself incredibly fortunate to have been in a relationship with my Lord, who allowed His feet to be washed with a woman's tears, allowed Himself to be fed by tax collectors and sinners, and allowed Himself to be defended by a thief on a cross. He broke through my defenses, reminding me of John Donne's Holy Sonnet 14:

> Batter my heart, three-person'd God, for you
> As yet but knock, breathe, shine, and seek to mend;
> That I may rise and stand, o'erthrow me, and bend
> Your force to break, blow, burn, and make me new.
> I, like an usurp'd town to another due,
> Labor to admit you, but oh, to no end:
> Reason, your viceroy in me, me should defend,
> But is captiv'd, and proves weak or untrue.
> Yet dearly I love you, and would be lov'd fain,
> But am betroth'd unto your enemy;
> Divorce me, untie or break that knot again,

Take me to you, imprison me, for I,
Except you enthrall me, never shall be free,
Nor ever chaste, except you ravish me.[24]

Though God has allowed me to suffer—bending, breaking, blowing, burning me—He has filled me with His grace and love. Despite my attempts to return to former darkness, He ravished me and made me new.

There was another hidden benefit underlying my increased ability for compassion and the acceptance of it: the further breaking of the spell of Level Two purpose and identity. I am not sure how my attachment to Level Two grew so strong, because my parents never emphasized Level Two characteristics, but rather Levels Three and Four. I suppose it happened throughout my academic studies because I was in competition with other students in three master's programs and a doctoral program—and I wanted to win the esteem of my professors as much as my religious superiors, perhaps more (I hate to admit it). This emphasis on intelligence, research, writing, and lecturing did not undermine my faith, but it did undermine my capacity for love (*agapē*).

During my studies, I was willing to help people with their final and comprehensive exams, but they would hint that "I did not suffer fools gladly" or "Wow, you were a little rough with that guy" or "Intellectual precision is not the most important thing, you know." I would always ask, "You really think I was that overbearing?" Most people would just say, "Figure it out for yourself."

My eye disease changed all that; it laid bare how much I truly valued the benefits of Level Two, to the virtual exclusion of *agapē*. As I began to accept the genuine acts of compassion from others, and to see how truly good people are, I began the long process of going back to what my parents had taught me through their loving actions. Thinking back on it, if I had not been blessed with this gift of progressive blindness (and my faith), I might have become quite heartless—and if that had occurred, I might have wandered into profound darkness. Faith showed me that I did not have to find my way

[24]John Donne, "Holy Sonnets: Batter My Heart, Three-Person'd God", Poetry Foundation, accessed June 17, 2016, www.poetryfoundation.org/poem/173362.

out of the darkness by myself: "Who will deliver me from this mortal body? Thanks be to God through Jesus Christ our Lord" (Rom 7:24–25, NAB). Supported by God's love and salvific intention, I was free to allow suffering to move and shape me toward the love of Christ, which would ultimately lead to eternal joy.

I have been going through this for more than thirty years now, and I have received a lot of rides—I mean *a lot* of rides. I have seen the benefits of accepting and giving compassion again and again, and I feel that God called me to be a magnet of compassion, with a concomitant deepening of my own compassion. All this happened because of my need for help, which was met by my accepting the compassion of others. If I lived for the acceptance and gift of compassion alone, skipping the accomplishments, it would have been more than enough.

D. Conclusion to Section I

Is suffering really *necessary* for *agapē* (empathy, the acceptance of love's vulnerability, humility, forgiveness, compassion, and the acceptance of compassion)? For God, it is not, for He can—in a timeless, completely transparent act, through His perfect power and love—achieve perfect empathy, perfect acceptance of love's vulnerability, perfect humility, perfect forgiveness, and perfect compassion. As I have indicated many times above, I believe there are some people who can more easily move to this position without much assistance from suffering. However, for people like me, suffering is absolutely indispensable for removing the blocks to *agapē*, arising out of my egocentric and autonomous desires (e.g., my belief in the cultural myth of self-sufficiency, my underestimation of the goodness and love of other people, and all the other limitations to my heart and head).

I have to believe that God allowed an imperfect physical nature and an imperfect world for people like me not only to actualize *agapē* freely, but also, and perhaps more importantly, to notice it. I really believe that God asks us to bear patiently with suffering and trials so that we can arrive at an insight about ourselves that will be advanced by empathy, humility, forgiveness, and compassion.

God works through this suffering. He doesn't waste any of it. For those who are open to seeing the horizon of love embedded in it, there is a future, nay, an eternity for each of us to manifest our own unique brand of unconditional love within the symphony of love that is God's Kingdom. Without suffering, I do not think I could have even begun to move freely toward that horizon which is my eternal destiny and joy.

II. External Opportunities of Suffering

By "external opportunities of suffering", I mean ways in which suffering can open new avenues to make a positive difference to the world around us (Section II.A) as well as the Kingdom of God (Section II.B). We have already discussed both kinds of opportunities in Volume I—opportunity in the world around us (Chapter 4), and opportunities for the Kingdom of God (Chapter 8). Though we can expand considerably on the previous discussion of opportunities for the Kingdom of God, we cannot do as much for the rather complete exposition of opportunities for the world around us given in Volume I.

A. First External Opportunity of Suffering: Making the World a Better Place

As noted in Section I.A above, suffering provides a significant opportunity for identity transformation. When Level One and Level Two happiness and purpose give rise to deep feelings of emptiness and the negative emotions of the comparison game, we are moved to ask, "Is there any more to life than what I am doing, and is there anyway of stopping the relentless emotions of inferiority, superiority, jealousy, fear of loss of esteem, narcissism, loneliness, ego-sensitivity, ego-rage and blame, and emptiness?" With some help from a wise friend or mentor, we may find ourselves looking seriously at either Level Three or Level Four happiness. Some people turn first to Level Three, while others, like myself, turn first to Level Four and subsequently discover Level Three contributive identity through their faith.

When we feel motivated to investigate either level, we will not simply want to think about it, but also *choose* it and then *move it into action*. If we do not convert our thoughts into actions, they will not become a real part of our purpose and identity, but if we do put them into action, they etch themselves into the character and identity we take with us into God's eternity. Hence, we must be prepared to seek opportunities for action when we are impelled toward identity transformation.

Opportunities to contribute can be focused on the world around us as well as the Kingdom of God. As Jesus makes clear, *both* are important. Though Jesus said, "[S]eek first the kingdom [of God] ... and all these things will be given you besides" (Mt 6:33, NAB), He did not mean seek exclusively opportunities to build the Kingdom. He showed many times in both His actions and words that it is essential to alleviate the sufferings of others, which means not only sharing our faith, but giving our time, energy, creativity, and resources to concretely alleviating suffering, where we can.

This can take many forms—simply listening to someone who needs support (a gift of time and presence), giving consolation through friendship and support (a gift of compassion), or contributing resources (such as funds, clothes, food, drink, or shelter), as well as providing a gift of work (such as serving on a food line, making care packages, and visiting shut-ins, children, the sick, and prisoners) or a gift of education (tutoring children, teaching immigrants, and teaching courses in practical skills,). This is by no means an exhaustive list.

We will want to choose the kind of service that best fits the skills, education, and talents we have, because we cannot do everything. Indeed, we all have a limited amount of psychic energy and time, and most of us have spouses and families who must be our first responsibility. So, we should follow the advice of Saint Paul, who says:

> [T]here are varieties of gifts, but the same Spirit; and there are varieties of service, but the same Lord; and there are varieties of working, but it is the same God who inspires them all in every one. To each is given the manifestation of the Spirit for the common good.... All these are inspired by one and the same Spirit, who apportions to each one individually as he wills. (1 Cor 12:4–7, 11)

Though Saint Paul here is speaking about spiritual gifts, the same can be applied to charitable gifts. Some of us are more equipped for education or for visiting the sick; some for working with young

people, for working in homeless shelters, for working in a food distri-
bution center, for working with the underprivileged, or for working
with the physically or mentally challenged; and some for distributing
food to shut-ins. We can apply the same logic to these ministries
as Paul did to spiritual ministries: "[T]here are varieties of service,
but the same Lord; and there are varieties of working, but it is the
same God who inspires them all in every one." Wherever we serve
the needy in love (*agapē*), Jesus is also present. As He proclaims in
the Gospel of Mathew, "[A]s you did it to one of the least of these
my brethren, you did it to me" (25:40).

Though these pursuits are important, according to Jesus and our
commitment to Him we must remember that our first priority is to
our families. Thus, we do not want to volunteer to the extent that
we neglect our spouses or children, jeopardize their livelihood, or
create a sense of competition between them and our contributive
work. This will lead to a breakdown of the family and a resentment
of our charitable work, which may also lead to a resentment of Jesus
and the Church. Thus, we will want to choose charitable work that is
supported by our families, and if possible, work in which our families
can participate.

Sometimes the most important contribution we can make is to listen to our children who may be having difficulties in school or with
friends, or sometimes merely listening to our spouses who are trying
to connect with us and establish common cause with us. Other times
we might listen to our friends who are in need of support or are having difficulties; might actively try to do good for those friends who
are in need of help; might fulfill a request to teach the seventh-grade
catechism class that no one else wants to teach; or might want to help
neighborhood kids with their math homework. And sometimes we
may want to contribute by working in a food line, homeless shelter,
hospital, etc. We only have a limited amount of time and psychic
energy, and we cannot do everything. Since we have committed
ourselves to family and friends, we owe them the first priority, within
reason, and when these commitments have been fulfilled, we can
move to more acute needs of the poor and suffering around us.

People with financial resources who are limited in time because of
families and leadership positions will want to "give alms", particularly
to the poor and destitute. It is best to involve family members when

giving to the needy. Religious people will likely seek out religious charitable organizations; many will prefer to support *local* charitable organizations, such as food banks, homeless shelters, shut-in services, etc. Some people reserve a part of their monthly income to give to charitable organizations who serve the very poor, destitute, and suffering. Those who have time will want to give some of it; those who have physical abilities will want to give that gift; those with an ability to help children, that gift, and so forth.

Now let us return to suffering. When suffering strikes, causing vulnerability, weakness, or loss, we do not want to miss its opportunity. If we have faith, we will want to pray that God will use this vulnerability, weakness, or loss to cause a transformation in us, or perhaps a deeper transformation into a Level Three and Four purpose and identity. As we move more deeply into this identity, we will want to pray for the enhanced *desire* to contribute to the needy and the building of the Kingdom of God. We will also want to pray for the *enhanced desire* to empathize more deeply with the vulnerable, weak, and suffering among our family members, friends, colleagues, and associates, and those who are less fortunate than we. When the Holy Spirit grants this increased desire (though it may come slowly because He will respect our freedom)—we will want to act on it according to our natural priorities—contribution to and empathy for, first, family members; second, friends, associates, and those in desperate need of help.

As we do this, we will notice a transformation of our hearts. The more time, energy, and resources we give to alleviating suffering of the people around us, the more gentle-hearted ("meek") we become, and this in its turn leads to greater humble-heartedness ("poverty of spirit"), and even greater mercy and compassion. Thinking and imagining are the beginning of transformation; choice is its next necessary step, and action is its consummation. When we combine this with faith and prayer, we inch progressively closer to the heart of the loving God.

B. Second External Opportunity of Suffering: Building the Kingdom of God

As noted above, suffering can be of invaluable assistance in leading us to our eternal and loving reward. In Section I we saw how suffering could be truly helpful to moving from a merely materialistic identity (Level One) and an egocentric identity (Level Two), to a contributive, loving identity (Level Three) and a transcendently good and loving identity (Level Four). The movement toward a Level Three/Level Four identity is not for this world alone, for love is eternal by nature, and faith is oriented toward a loving eternity. Hence, any progress toward Level Three and Level Four is also progress toward the eternal Kingdom of God. If suffering helps us to progress toward Levels Three and Four, it must also help us to progress toward the Kingdom of God.

The same holds true for the points made in Section I.C. We saw there how suffering could be helpful in embracing deeper empathy, humility, compassion, and *agapē*, and in Section I.B, we saw how suffering could be helpful in appropriating deeper courage and self-discipline, which are intrinsic to the pursuit of authentic love. Inasmuch as suffering is helpful in developing the elements and conditions of authentic love, and unconditional love is intrinsic to the eternal Kingdom of God, suffering must again be helpful in moving toward the Kingdom of God.

Furthermore, if Jesus was correct in asserting the unconditional love of His Father, then His intention is to redeem every dimension of suffering. Thus, whenever we suffer, God is already working through it to bring about optimal empathy, humility, authenticity, compassion, courage, and self-discipline, and through these, to bring about the optimal path toward eternal salvation in His love. We may not clearly apprehend the direction, timeline, and nuances of this plan, but we may be sure that an unconditionally loving God will do everything to optimize our salvation (without violating our and others' freedom).

There are four other ways in which suffering is involved in the road to salvation: (1) room to participate in building the Kingdom, (2) deeper appropriation of faith, (3) serving and building the Kingdom of God, and (4) offering up our suffering as an act of love for the salvation of the world. We will discuss the first three opportunities in this chapter, and defer the fourth—which is a more spiritual or mystical opportunity—until the next.

1. Room to Participate in Building the Kingdom

The more we cooperate with God's plan to bring love and salvation out of suffering, the more we can become instruments of God's hope, love, and salvation to others, which allows us, in turn, to be genuine participants in building the Kingdom of God.

God does not expect our *perfect* cooperation with His loving plan in order to bestow salvation upon us, because He knows our limitations and redeems us through *His* unconditional love. This is a very happy truth, because the vast majority of us (or perhaps I should speak only for myself) are incapable of even approaching *perfect* cooperation with God's loving plan. Yet God has left enough room for us to participate in His work of salvation (albeit imperfectly), and so, the more we consciously cooperate with His plan, the more good we will be able to do for ourselves and others in the work of eternal salvation.

The above thought provokes a question: Why try to cooperate with God's loving plan if God will save repentant people anyway, even amid their imperfections? Because cooperating with God's loving plan will

1. make suffering less painful and depressing for us and others,
2. deepen *our* conversion toward authentic unconditional love more quickly (which brings us closer to true joy), and
3. help *us* to play an important role in actualizing eternal salvation.

The first two points may by now be evident from the explanation of suffering given above, but the third point merits closer consideration.

As noted in the previous section, God did not do everything for us. He created us in an imperfect world so that we might be able to make a significant contribution in bringing about both love in the world *and* unconditional love in His eternal Kingdom.

Consider the following: God did not create a *perfectly* loving Kingdom on Earth. This is obvious not only in the imperfect natural world in which we live, but also in the millions of unloving human actions awaiting redemption in His future eternal Kingdom. In God's Kingdom there will be no acts of unlove because God's grace will eventually purify our freedom so that our actions truly reflect a pure desire to love authentically and unconditionally. Inasmuch as our freedom is not yet completely purified, the Kingdom of God is not and cannot be perfectly manifest on Earth.

So how do we move from imperfect freedom to perfectly purified freedom? Christians believe this occurs through the redemptive act

of Christ, our desire for His redemption, and the Holy Spirit working in our hearts and minds. We believe that Jesus' unconditionally
loving death and Resurrection and the action of the Holy Spirit will
redeem every person of goodwill who seeks this redemption.[25] Yet,
Christ did not redeem the world in a way that would preclude us
from participating in His work of salvation. Quite the contrary. Just
as the Creator gives us room to make a better world, so also Jesus
gives us room to participate in the work of salvation. As noted in
Chapter 1, Paul acknowledges this in a passage from the Letter to
the Colossians:

> Now I rejoice in my sufferings for your sake, and in my flesh I *com-
> plete* what is *lacking* in Christ's afflictions for the sake of his body, that
> is, the Church, of which I became a minister according to the divine
> office which was given to me for you, to make the word of God fully
> known. (1:24–25; emphasis mine)

As noted earlier, Paul does not think there is anything *intrinsically*
lacking in the sufferings of Christ. This would be both heretical and
self-refuting, for if something were lacking in Christ's redemptive act
(necessary for salvation), then we would not be definitively saved!
Paul clearly does not intend this for both doctrinal and logical reasons. Moreover, he argues the precise opposite many other times
throughout his corpus.

One may also get the impression that Paul is being arrogant when
he claims that *he* completes what is lacking in the sufferings of Christ.
Once again, this must be a misinterpretation, because it conflicts with
his desire for humility and love, and his awareness that humility and
love are the essence of Jesus and His Father.

So, what *does* he mean? He means that there is nothing necessary
for salvation lacking in the sufferings of Christ, *but* that Christ has
left enough room *for us* to participate in His redemptive work. Jesus'
redemptive act (His Incarnation and Passion) constitutes an unconditional gift of self (an unconditional act of love) indelibly actualized

---

[25] See the explanation of this doctrine in the Dogmatic Constitution on the Catholic
Church (*Lumen Gentium*) and the Pastoral Constitution on the Catholic Church (*Gaudium et
Spes*) in Chapter 1, Section IV, of this volume.

and concretized in the world. This is sufficient to redeem every person who freely accepts it or tries to follow God according to the dictates of his conscience.[26] Yet He does not complete every aspect of the *propagation* of this salvific love. Rather, He leaves this open for the Church and us to help accomplish. He gives us the Holy Spirit to *assist* with this ministry, not to take it over. He lets us be His instruments and participate in the greatest of all possible earthly actions— namely, the propagation of His *eternal* love and joy. He allows us to play an integral part in giving His greatest gift to mankind. What could be a greater dignity, privilege, and purpose in life? What could be a greater joy?

Yet, as Paul makes clear, this great joy is punctuated by suffering ("Now I rejoice in *my sufferings* for your sake, and in my flesh I complete what is lacking in Christ's afflictions"). Though Paul is speaking of *his* sufferings here, he is also implicitly referring to all our sufferings in spreading the gospel and building the Kingdom. It seems that the noble project of giving away the eternal and unconditional love of Christ can involve misunderstanding, misinterpretation, and even heresy. It can engender resentment, infighting, and jealousy, as well as inauthenticity and hypocrisy and having to face false allegations for the sake of Christ, having to be courageous to stay true to His word, and having to make sacrifices of a thousand other kinds. This is why Jesus concludes the Beatitudes with the promise that every kind of persecution for the faith will be redeemed in the Kingdom of God:

> Blessed are those who are persecuted for righteousness' sake, for theirs is the kingdom of heaven. Blessed are you when men revile you and persecute you and utter all kinds of evil against you falsely on my account. Rejoice and be glad, for your reward is great in heaven, for so men persecuted the prophets who were before you. (Mt 5:10–12)

It seems that the privilege, purpose, and joy we have been given in preaching the unconditional love of God entails many pitfalls and sufferings, but there is no greater dignity or purpose we can have than

---

[26] See the previous note. Please note that this occurs through the influence of God's grace.

this salvific project, because its effects are *eternal*. If we help someone to find faith and stay on the road to salvation, that has an *eternal*
effect; if we help to prevent a person from discouragement, despair,
or unbelief, that too has an eternal effect; and if we inhibit a destructive momentum—which might cause the loss of transcendence or
virtue, within the culture—that too has an eternal effect. So if we
are ridiculed, harassed, or even persecuted for doing these things, it is
worth it, for it is a temporal sacrifice for an eternal effect. Moreover,
the trusting and courageous endurance of such sufferings can be an
act of *self-sacrificial love* in imitation of Jesus, who turned hatred and
persecution into self-sacrificial love for the world (see Chapter 8). In
the Second Letter to the Corinthians, Saint Paul exhorts us to perse-
vere in this mission of absolute and eternal significance in the midst
of suffering:

> But we have this treasure in earthen vessels, to show that the tran-
> scendent power belongs to God and not to us. We are afflicted in
> every way, but not crushed; perplexed, but not driven to despair;
> persecuted, but not forsaken; struck down, but not destroyed; always
> carrying in the body the death of Jesus, so that the life of Jesus may
> also be manifested in our bodies. For while we live we are always
> being given up to death for Jesus' sake, so that the life of Jesus may
> be manifested in our mortal flesh. So death is at work in us, but life
> in you. (4:7–12)

This faith enables Saint Paul to say, "Now I *rejoice* in my sufferings
for your sake" (Col 1:24; emphasis mine). He knows that suffering
is anything but meaningless because it is filled with eternal salvific
significance. Paul rejoices because the eternal and unconditional dignity of the ministry he has been given far outweighs the sufferings
he must endure to carry it out. This does not reduce the hardship of
spreading the gospel, but it does infuse that hardship with a profound
meaning of eternal and unconditional love.

Furthermore, this hardship is a manifestation of *our* love, a purification of our freedom, and an act of love for the One who redeemed
us by His blood—a gift of self to complement Christ's total gift of
self on the Cross. Thus, the suffering intrinsic to spreading the gospel

is not only filled with meaning (i.e., eternal meaning), but also with self-transformation and love destined to last throughout eternity.

2. Deeper Appropriation of Faith

Suffering can also lead us to a relationship with God and membership in a church community. This is clearly evidenced in tens of thousands of adult conversions and reconversions. As noted above, suffering can compel us to look for more profound meaning in life, to seek purpose in places we had never anticipated, and to find meaning and consolation in those new places. The most significant potential source of such meaning, dignity, destiny, and consolation is a relationship with God, particularly, an unconditionally loving God. When suffering breaks down our superficiality and opens the way to our true purpose, fulfillment, and destiny, the leap to faith lies before us. If we take the leap, we will discover that this loving God is not simply a *potential* source of meaning and fulfillment; He is the source of all *reality*.

If we believe that our potential can be met by the fulfillment of Level One-Two desires, we might settle for mediocrity and superficiality in life's purpose. Fortunately, for most of us, suffering finds its way into our lives and compels us to look for higher meaning, not just contributive meaning, but ultimate and eternal meaning, leading us to the heart of the loving God. This can occur for people who were raised in a religious tradition as well as those who were not.

I grew up in a strong Catholic household, and so when suffering and the feeling of powerlessness entered into my life, I reflexively turned toward God to hold the center when I could not hold it myself. I have known other people who did not grow up with faith and whose turning toward God had to be learned over the course of months or years—through dialogue with friends, little or great "miracles" occurring in their lives, reading religious books or journals, watching religious television, listening to religious radio, participating in a twelve-step program, listening to a chaplain in a hospital, or a myriad of other ways. As noted in Chapter 5 (Section IV), when we reach out to the Lord in our suffering, we will likely find that our sense of powerlessness is replaced with consolation—if we choose it. When we realize that we are powerless, we have a perfect opportunity to strengthen our reliance on the Lord as well as our relationship with Him. All we need do is remove the blocks, admit our need, and choose the consolation and guidance He wants to bring. Remember, it is generally unwise to propose a plan and timetable for how God "should" alleviate our suffering; we need to be open to *His* plan to actualize His six objectives.

The radical admission of need *allows* the God of love to move into our center. Recall that He would not do this unless we, in our freedom, invite Him. As noted earlier, God's love is so great, He would not impose Himself on us, but rather will wait until *we* allow Him to help. This help may not be a *direct* solution to our problems, or the help that *we* expect; but it *will* open us to His unconditional love, protect our freedom, and lead to our and others' salvation, while *ultimately* alleviating our suffering. Much of the time, this process can be greatly facilitated by a church community.

The above process of redemption through suffering can be initiated in a variety of ways, some of them quite tacit. Sometimes it can start with expressions or actions of faith and love from others; sometimes it can literally leap off a page of the New Testament; sometimes it can come from spiritual beauty—the beauty of people serving God, the beauty of faith and love exemplified by the saints, and the beauty of Jesus' teachings on love, as well as the beauty of the Eucharist, the sacraments, the liturgy, the liturgical year, living tradition, and the beauty of spiritual music, art, and architecture. Whether suffering "calls" us to faith, love, and redemption through words, actions, church community, revelation, or spiritual beauty, we find ourselves entering an ethos of love, goodness, beauty, and truth that leads evermore deeply into the mystery of God's presence and majesty.

This mysterious presence calls us to itself. It enchants us, fascinates us, enriches us, and fills us quietly but deeply. We become very interested in things theological, almost addicted to asking questions about God, Heaven, Scripture, and Tradition—everything having to do with this mysterious, beautiful love. God might not solve our problems or resolve our sufferings immediately, but He will make us aware of His presence through our *admission of need*, and He will invite us more deeply into His mystery, enchant and enrich us with it, and then lead us by *His* own path to a new meaning of life in humility, service, and love. To be sure, this path may not be easy, but in the long run, it will lead us out of superficiality into a life filled with transcendent truth, love, goodness, beauty, and home—to a life betokening our eternal destiny of love with Him.

That's not all. When we have been "rescued" from a life of superficiality, meaninglessness, or hopelessness, we develop a *natural* inclination to *share* this blessing with others. At this point, the Lord of love again inspires us—enflaming us with wisdom and energy, with knowledge and compassion, and with a love and faith beyond our temporal understanding—to go out and share the good news that there is ultimate and eternal meaning, fulfillment, goodness, love, beauty, and joy. The source of this ultimate meaning is perfect love itself: Emmanuel, who has come to be with us, to show us the way to our eternal dignity and destiny. We can trust Him completely, especially during times of suffering.

This desire to share the Word of hope with others—to share the Word that gives more than superficial life, the Word that reaches into mystery, perfection, and eternity—builds on itself. When we see the depth and breadth, the hope and love, the richness and joy that comes from our ministry and service, we cannot resist the inspiration to do more—increasingly more. We want to serve the Lord of love who has made this possible for us. As we do this, we not only find an increased meaning, depth, love, and joy in our lives; we grow in certitude that we are being led. God then becomes for us more than an intelligent Creator; He becomes the God of providential love concerned not just for me but for us, concerned to lead us toward greater freedom and love—caring enough to invite us into His very divine life of love. After living a life of service and ministry, we can scarcely doubt the love and presence of God. Certitude has worked its way into our life experience through the acceptance of God's invitation given to us in suffering.

The unfolding of these "loving tactics of God" has certainly been the story of my life, but I have seen it manifest even more profoundly in the lives of those with greater challenges than my own. Sometimes the people with the greatest challenges in life, whether physical, familial, or mental, give some of the strongest and most articulate testimonies to the love of God. Their faith, peace, confidence, awareness of God, capacity for compassion, and, above all, their joy and "being at home with God" are incredibly profound. I frequently find this to be a sign of God's presence because I cannot fathom how they could have all these qualities without some direct inspiration from the God of love.

This holds true even for children, particularly those who face illness and physical deprivation. Many of the children I have met in hospitals who are facing severe illnesses and even death have a profound faith, peace, and confidence, which allows them to console their parents when their parents are incapable of consoling them. When I first heard children say, "Don't worry, Mom; everything is going to be all right," I thought, "Well, that is the naïve optimism of a child." But then I came to realize that most of these children didn't think their life *in this world* was going to be all right; they thought their life with God would make everything all right. I asked some of these parents whether they had brought up their children in a religious household. Many of them had, but interestingly enough, many of the children who had not been brought up in a religious household expressed just as profound a peace and confidence in the life to come as the ones who had been raised with that expectation. One might still insist that this seemingly profound perspective is mixed with the naïve optimism of a child, but I don't think so, because the prospect of death (powerful as this finality is) did not seem to shake the peace which these children felt.

There is one major point that is shared by both children and adults who experience this peace, "which passes all understanding" (Phil 4:7)—namely, they both have acknowledged their need for God and have invited Him into their center. Children seem to do this naturally, not just with God, but also with their parents and with everyone else. This is the distinctive advantage of children. But adults can do this too; they can acquire the heart of a child, but they generally need to do this through suffering, which causes them to invite God into their center, which in turn allows God to invite them more deeply into His mysterious loving presence. This inspires many to serve God by sharing with others the life and meaning of eternal and perfect love, which leads to peace beyond all understanding. Adults frequently need suffering to reach the state of authentic openness to God, but children seem to possess it in their very being. Far from naïveté, they exemplify a confidence, peace, and love originating in God Himself.

3. Serving and Building the Kingdom of God

When suffering shocks us out of superficiality—when it leads us to humility and to the search for God, and our need for Him—and when it has worked its "miracle" of opening us to the world of eternal significance and eternal effects, we will want to *do* something about it. This "doing" frequently consists first in getting involved in a church community, and then learning more about our faith. This leads invariably to the desire to share with others the eternal significance and salvation we have received. We need to act on this natural inclination when we feel it most strongly—at the time we have drawn closer to God and eternity. Unfortunately, our desire to share the eternal gift we have been given with others tends to diminish if we do not follow through on it—that is, if we do not put it into action. However, if we do put it into action, the sense of our eternal significance and destiny grows stronger and stronger, creating the impetus to share it with more people as often as we can.

Jesus' parables of the Kingdom frequently reflect this theme. He compares this gift of eternal significance and destiny to a mustard seed that when planted in the ground (shared with others) turns into the largest of trees where the birds of the sky come and make their nest (see Mt 13:31–32; Mk 4:30–32; Lk 13:18–19). He also speaks of it as leaven that a woman kneaded into a small batch of flour until the entire dough began to rise (see Mt 13:33; Lk 13:20–21). Though He speaks most often about the *growth* of our faith through building "the Kingdom" (by sharing the gift of eternal significance and destiny with others), He also speaks of the opposite effect.

The Parable of the Talents speaks of both growth and diminishment (see Mt 25:14–30; Lk 19:11–27). Two of the servants invest (build up) the master's money (ultimate and eternal meaning and fulfillment), and they predictably make much more. One servant decides not to do this, burying his talents in the ground. The master then takes the "money" from that servant and gives it to the others who have more, and concludes by saying, "[T]o every one who has will more be given, and he will have abundance; but from him who has not, even what he has will be taken away" (Mt 25:29). The meaning of the parable is clear: if we do not share the gift of eternal significance and destiny with others, it will simply grow weaker and weaker in us until we no longer recognize it or care about it. However, if we do share it with others, it will grow into abundance, not only for others but for ourselves, because sharing this gift enables us to produce eternal effects in the world, and this cannot help but deepen the eternal significance of our lives and being.

Therefore, when we have been given the gift of faith whether we received it directly without the need for suffering, or indirectly because suffering shocked us out of our superficiality, then we will want to act on our natural inclination to share it with others, and this means finding some way to be "the salt of the earth" and "the light of the world" (Mt 5:13–14). As noted above, there can be no greater dignity than this because the effects of our efforts are eternal and universal.

When considering how we might share our faith, it is advisable to begin with those closest to us, and then, if we are in a position to reach further, to do so in proportion to our time, energy, and talent. Thus, we will want to start with *personal evangelization*—our personal witness to family, to friends, and then to colleagues and associates at work or in the community. Personal witness does not have to be deep and complex. We need only testify to how faith has helped us in our lives—how it has helped us in life's trials, in our relationships, to give direction to our lives, and to elevate our sense of meaning, fulfillment, dignity, and destiny. This testimony does not have to be as interesting as a novel, but only a light for people to reorient their lives.

This personal witness is especially important in times of *suffering*. Sometimes we feel reticent to talk about our faith out of respect for our friends and colleagues, because it seems like it might be "laying a trip" on them. However, I have found in the vast majority of instances, when I felt such reticence to do this (because I suspected it might not be greeted well), my friends and colleagues have responded with gratitude and appreciation. I truly think it is worth the risk to take the opportunity during a friend's or colleague's suffering to introduce him to the Lord, and to the whole new transcendent meaning, dignity, and destiny He presents.

We can move beyond the domain of personal evangelization by getting involved in our church or in our diocese. This can take dozens of forms, because there are so many ways of making contributions—serving on one of the church committees, being a lector or extraordinary minister of Holy Communion, working with the poor of the parish or diocese, taking Communion to the sick, teaching catechism or Confirmation classes to young people, and so forth. If you are unsure of how or where to make a contribution, ask the pastor for a list of committees on which you might serve, or ask about other ministerial opportunities. Getting involved in a church or diocese is an excellent way of building the Kingdom of God (see the rules for discernment and following the Holy Spirit in Chapter 9, Section II).

When we move beyond our families, friends, colleagues, churches, and dioceses, we enter into a less personal realm in which it is more difficult to make a direct contribution to the Kingdom of God, but there is still a need, particularly the need for evangelization. Since we cannot rely on personal connections and personal witness, we will have to become more familiar with the rationale and arguments that address peoples' questions and difficulties with faith. There are many websites that have a large number of apologetical, catechetical, psychological, and spiritual resources to help seekers move beyond their doubts and difficulties.[27] We do not have to be experts in all of these areas to help those who are seeking to deepen their faith. Most of the time, it is sufficient to give them access to videos, articles, and books that will give a direct answer to their questions. If they want to proceed further, and you are not able to help them, refer them to the relevant websites. They are likely to answer the questions of those seriously pursuing faith. If you are interested in mastering some of the information on these websites, all the better, because you can help seekers in a more personal and detailed way.

In sum, the opportunities for building the Kingdom of God are immense, and we need not go beyond the areas with which we are acquainted and comfortable. If we do what we can, we will create

[27]For apologetical resources in the areas of science, reason, and faith; happiness and suffering; virtue and freedom; and the reality of Jesus, I would recommend the Magis Center website (www.magiscenter.com). There are dozens of free resources on this site that answer many, if not most, of the fundamental questions seekers have about God, the soul, Jesus, and virtue.

gifts of unconditional and eternal truth, love, goodness, beauty, and home, by introducing seekers to the One who has been calling them to Himself. This is a very good use of our time and talent because the effects of our efforts will endure throughout an eternity of love.

III. Conclusion

As Louis Pasteur once said, "Chance favors the prepared mind." We might extend this by noting "and so does Divine Providence". If we are aware of the opportunities that suffering can unleash, even suffering that happens by pure chance (e.g., by the blind forces of nature), then we are much more likely to *seize* them and *benefit from* them. As we have noted repeatedly above, suffering does not *automatically* lead to the above interior and exterior opportunities. We need to be *prepared* with the following:

- *Faith* in a perfectly loving God who desires to give us eternal life with Him
- *Prayers* to help us ask for His protection, inspiration, redemption, and guidance during times of suffering
- *Natural virtues*, particularly the virtue of prudence that helps us to know the levels of happiness, purpose, dignity, fulfillment, and destiny, and how to maintain Levels Three and Four
- *Knowing what opportunities await us*; explained in this chapter

The following list gives a helpful summary of the opportunities embedded in suffering. Readers may want to photocopy it as a guide to where the Holy Spirit may be leading or to what He wants us to consider. If chance and providence favor the prepared mind, then it might be wise to reflect on the list given below *before* unexpected suffering occurs. It will make the negativity of suffering ultimately and eternally worthwhile, not only for us, but also for the people we touch. There are other opportunities of suffering associated with imitating Jesus' self-sacrificial action on the Cross. These more spiritual or mystical opportunities will be taken up in the next chapter.

OPPORTUNITIES OF SUFFERING

I. Interior Opportunities of Suffering

　1. Prudence: Appropriation of Higher Levels of Purpose and Identity
- Appropriation—Level Three *contributive* identity (see Volume I, Chapters 3 and 4)
- Appropriation—Level Four *faith* identity (see Volume I, Chapters 5 through 10)

　2. Other Natural Virtues
- Rationality (see this volume, Chapters 5 through 6)
- Fortitude and courage (see this volume, Chapters 5, 6, and 12)
- Temperance/self-discipline (see this volume, Chapters 5, 6, and 12)

　3. *Agapē*—Other-Centered Love
- Empathy (see above in this chapter, and Volume I, Chapter 4)
- Acceptance of love's vulnerability (see above in this chapter)
- Humility (see above in this chapter and Volume III, Chapter 1)
- Forgiveness (see above in this chapter and Volume III, Chapters 1 through 3)
- Compassion (see above in this chapter and Volume III, Chapters 1 through 3)
- Acceptance of compassion (see above in this chapter and Volume I, Chapter 4)

II. External Opportunities of Suffering

　1. Good for the World
- Good for the family
- Good for organization/institution
- Good for the community
- Good for culture or society

　2. Building the Kingdom of God
- Personal evangelization—to family, friends, and colleagues
- Contributing to a local church or diocese
- Contributing to the larger Church mission (national or international)
- Evangelizing within the community (apologetical, catechetical, or moral)
- Evangelizing the culture (apologetical, catechetical, or moral)

Chapter Eight

Mystical Self-Offering

Eighth Foundation: Offering Suffering as a Loving Self-Sacrifice

Introduction

Up to this point, we have been addressing opportunities and benefits of suffering that can be *noticed* in our lives. Though the *interior* benefits of suffering may not be perceptible right away, if we are open to them and pursue them, we will assuredly notice them in the short- to long-term. So, for example, if we use our suffering as a lever to move to higher levels of identity, we will eventually see ourselves becoming more and more transformed in Levels Three and Four regarding purpose in life. Similarly, if we use our suffering as a lever to pursue the natural virtues of prudence, fortitude, and temperance, and the supreme virtue of *agapē* (with its seven important dimensions discussed in the previous chapter), we will also see progress in our desire and capacity for these virtues.

The same holds true for the exterior opportunities of suffering. If we use our suffering as a lever to pursue a better world and the Kingdom of God, we will see our lives taking a distinctively new turn toward optimizing the good for family, friends, community, and organizations, as well as the Church, the faith of others, and the Kingdom of God. The effects may at first be gradual and even imperceptible, but eventually they will manifest themselves quite powerfully as we lever our sufferings for these purposes.

As noted in the previous chapter, all these transformations help *us*, as well as others, to create the eternal identity with which we will enter into the Kingdom of God; hence, they pave the way for us to enter into eternal salvation and joy. Of course, we will not be perfect at the time of our death—and I certainly do not imagine myself as even approaching such perfection—but the direction we have set for ourselves will allow the Lord at the time of our death, and even after it, to complete the process of preparation, through our freedom, to love perfectly and unconditionally in His Kingdom. Jesus and Saint Paul make provision for both pardon and purification after death, and the Catholic Church has called this postmortem purification "Purgatory".[1]

Suffering is quite helpful for this preparation or purification unto perfect love, whether it takes place in this life or the next. We can encourage one another to use suffering for this preparation for perfect love during this lifetime, and we can pray that the deceased will be able to reach final purification as quickly as possible and with the least possible suffering. If this were the total purpose for suffering, it would be more than enough—indeed, it would be an infinite and eternal benefit for us and others. Yet there is more.

As noted in Chapter 1, Jesus teaches us to make our suffering a loving self-sacrifice to the Father for the salvation of all people. Saint Paul indicates that this self-offering will benefit the *whole* body of Christ, including those who are alive and those who have passed to the next life. By implication then, we can make our suffering a loving self-sacrifice for the deceased who are undergoing purification unto perfect love (i.e., the souls in Purgatory). Thus, the grace coming from making our suffering a loving self-sacrifice for others is not limited to those still alive in this world; it can benefit the deceased as well. Jesus intended this in His own self-sacrificial death, as implied

---

[1] The Catholic Church has decreed the doctrine of Purgatory to explain this process of purification *after death*. According to the *Catechism of the Catholic Church*, "All who die in God's grace and friendship, but still imperfectly purified, are indeed assured of their eternal salvation; but after death they undergo purification, so as to achieve the holiness necessary to enter the joy of heaven. The Church gives the name *Purgatory* to this final purification of the elect, which is entirely different from the punishment of the damned." *Catechism of the Catholic Church*, 2nd ed. (Washington, D.C.: Libreria Editrice Vaticana—United States Conference of Catholic Bishops, 2000), nos. 1030–31.

Jesus makes provision for purification after death when He declares that blasphemy "against the Holy Spirit will not be forgiven, either in *this age or in the age to come*" (Mt 12:32; emphasis mine). Therefore, by implication, Jesus believed that there is pardon and purification in the coming age. Saint Paul apparently adheres to Jesus' view as well as the Old Testament tradition of prayer for the dead (2 Mac 12:38–45), by praying for his deceased friend Onesiphorus (2 Tim 1:16–18).

in His dying words during His recitation of Psalm 22 (see below, Section I).

Jesus bestowed three permanent gifts on us through His Incarnation, ministry, death, and Resurrection, which all play an essential role in our conversion, salvation, and capacity to serve the Kingdom:

1. The gift of His *word* (enshrined in the New Testament, His Eucharistic words, His designation of Peter as "head", and the living memory of His presence and intention)
2. The gift of His *unconditional love*, a perfect gift of self that could outshine any finite evil or darkness within us or perpetrated by us (given through His Passion and death)
3. The gift of His *Holy Spirit*, not only as the fleeting "voice" of the prophets, but as a *permanent* gift to dwell within us individually and within the Church collectively

We have already addressed the word of Jesus in Volume III. This chapter will be devoted to the second gift, His gift of unconditional love for the redemption of the world. The next chapter will be concerned with His gift of the Holy Spirit.

Jesus' gift of unconditional love for the salvation of the world not only creates the unconditional love underlying our forgiveness and salvation; it also provides the way to transform *our* suffering into the same redemptive love. In order to understand this, we must look into Jesus' mindset and intention—and in grasping it (at least in part), imitate Him in this work of love and salvation.

When the Son of God became incarnate as Jesus of Nazareth, His intention was not only to show us the meaning of love, the purpose of suffering, and the way to salvation, but also to *give himself* to us *completely*. He intended to do this in three stages—first, by His Incarnation, in which He subjected Himself to the finitude of space, time, natural forces, and the vagaries of power and evil; second, by His sacrificial actions during His ministry, from enduring the temptations of the Evil One, the ridicule and chastisement of the religious authorities, and His continuous ministering to those in need "from town to town and village to village"; and finally, by sacrificing Himself on the Cross unto death, to bring His gift of self (i.e., His unconditional love) to perfect and unconditional completion. In doing this, Jesus wanted not only to love us perfectly, unconditionally, and infinitely, but also to give us an *example* of how we too could love others through our suffering and self-sacrifice:

> When [Jesus] had washed their feet, and taken his garments, and resumed his place, he said to them, "Do you know what I have done to you? You call me Teacher and Lord; and you are right, for so I am. If I then, your Lord and Teacher, have washed your feet, you also ought to wash one another's feet. For I have given you an *example*, that you also should do as I have done to you. Truly, truly, I say to you, a servant is not greater than his master; nor is he who is sent greater than he who sent him. If you know these things, blessed are you if you do them. (Jn 13:12–17; emphasis mine)

He left us this example not as an obediential command—"you better do this, or else!"—but rather to show us how to transform self-sacrifice into redemptive love. This may be perplexing to the contemporary mind, which may not be able to understand directly Jesus' teaching and its efficacy, so we will first study how Jesus intended to use self-sacrifice as redemptive love (Section I), and then discuss how we might imitate Him in our own ministry of self-sacrificial suffering (Section II).

I. Jesus' Use of Suffering as Self-Sacrificial Redemptive Love

In Volume III (Chapter 3) of the Quartet, *God So Loved the World*, we discussed three passages of Scripture that are integral to understanding Jesus' own mission to create an unrestricted, unconditional, and perfect act of love that could redeem *all* human evil and darkness throughout the history of the world—from the creation of the first person to the end of the human race:

1. Isaiah 52:13—53:12 (the Fourth Suffering Servant Song)
2. Jesus' Eucharistic words recounted in Mark 14:22–25 and Matthew 26:26–29, especially the words "poured out for many" (Mk 14:24; Mt 26:28)

3. Jesus' dying words on the Cross, especially His recitation of the first line of Psalm 22, recounted in the Gospel of Mark (15:34): "My God, my God, why have you forsaken me?"

We noted in Volume III that it would be difficult for the contemporary mind to understand Jesus' intention because He had a significantly different view of sacred time, real presence, and the efficacy of self-sacrifice than we do today. Our dominant view of reality is empirical and scientific—that is, conditioned by physical theories of space, time, and nature—while Jesus' view was what Mircea Eliade called "sacred, transtemporal, and transpatial". Recall that Eliade's view was based on a comprehensive study of world religions, both past and present, through which he discovered a remarkable similarity: sacred history was seen as superseding profane history (physical history), and through ritual and myth, prophets and priests could return to the sacred time of history as if profane time were not relevant.[2] Though this view of time and history is significantly different from our view, it is not incompatible with it—if we have faith.

Even if we hold to the truth of the physical-scientific view of space, time, and nature—as I do—we can still believe that there is an entire realm of transtemporal, transpatial, and transphysical reality that is—for lack of a better term—superimposed on the physical world. This "supernatural superstructure" of sacred reality is not opposed to physical reality—it is consistent with physical reality, supersedes it, and can bring about transtemporal, transpatial, and transphysical effects within physical reality. How is this possible? God's mentative activity is the cause of this sacred, supernatural superstructure which is superimposed on physical reality. He is perfectly free to "think" His efficacious grace from one physical moment to another physical moment in the past or the future, without regard to the physical barrier that constrains us as physical beings. Thus, God can make Jesus' view of sacred history occur within physical history whenever the Eucharistic ritual—or other rituals—are relived by priests or prophets.

[2] See Mircea Eliade, The Sacred and the Profane: The Nature of Religion (New York: Harcourt Brace Jovanovich, 1987), pp. 93–97; and Mircea Eliade, The Myth of the Eternal Return, or Cosmos and History (Princeton, N.J.: Princeton University Press, 1971). See also Volume II, Chapter 2, and Volume III, Chapter 3, of this Quartet.

The same holds true for Jesus' view of "real presence" that is related to His view of sacred history. Joachim Jeremias describes it succinctly:

> God's remembrance is, namely (this is an important fact to which O. Michel called attention), never a simple remembering of something, but always and without exception "an *effecting and creating* event." When Luke 1.72 says that God remembers his covenant, this means that he is *now fulfilling* the eschatological covenant promise.[3]

In other words, Jesus' view of "being present" or "making present" is different from a merely physical viewpoint. All that is required for Jesus' historical presence on the Cross to be present in the here-and-now moment is for God to simply remember it—for when God remembers it, He "remembers it *into* our present". The effecting of God's remembrance occurs through the prophetic or priestly remembrance of the salvific event according to the ritual designated by Jesus or a prophet like Moses (who gives a similar instruction to remember and relive the Passover sacrifice).[4] Thus, in order for Jesus and His unconditionally loving self-sacrificial act to be present here and now, a priest need only follow the prescribed ritual that concludes, "Do this in *remembrance* of me" (Lk 22:19; 1 Cor 11:24). God's remembrance of His Son's salvific action in the past, commemorated by a priest, makes Jesus and His loving action present in the here and now. As noted above, there is no opposition between our physical view of "the present" and Jesus' supernaturally sacred view of "making present". God's action supersedes that of the natural world and can "make present" a past person and his love in the present moment without regard to the physical separation that constrains us as physical beings.

What does all this have to do with Jesus' view of the efficacy of suffering, and further, what does it have to do with the efficacy of *our*

---

[3] Joachim Jeremias, *The Eucharistic Words of Jesus* (London: SCM Press, 1966), p. 348; emphasis mine.

[4] After Moses has given the instructions from God on celebrating the first Passover (Ex 12:1–13), he continues: "This day shall be for you a *memorial* [a remembrance] day, and you shall keep it as a feast to the LORD; throughout your generations you shall observe it as an ordinance forever" (Ex 12:14; emphasis mine). The Hebrew word "זִכָּרֹ֑ון" may be translated as memorial or remembrance, and it has the precise meaning of *anamnesis* (in New Testament Greek), as Joachim Jeremias and O. Michel have described it.

suffering? In order to comprehend this, we need to understand one more piece of the puzzle—Jesus' view of the equivalence of self-sacrifice with redemptive grace and love. To do this we must first understand the Old Testament view of "grace" and "sacrifice", in which Jesus is immersed.

The Old Testament view of grace (hen) centers on the idea of favor. When applied to God, it has two parts. When God "finds favor" (hen) with the actions of people, He responds by "showing favor" (hanan) to those people. He does not respond automatically to certain actions, but interprets the motives of those performing the action.[5] If He deems both the actions and the motives to be good, He will find favor with them. There are many kinds of actions with which God finds favor (when our motives are good)—helping the needy, observing the law, and (germane to our case) making a sacrifice. Again, it is important that the person making a sacrifice have good motives—that is why God *found* favor with Abel's sacrifice but not with the sacrifice of Cain, his brother. As a result, God *showed* favor to Abel but not to Cain, provoking Cain's jealousy.[6]

So when God shows favor, how is it manifest? As McKenzie notes: "One shows favor by sparing from punishment, by rendering assistance, by gifts. When the word ['favor'] is used of *Yahweh*, the *same* benevolence is seen in Him."[7] Thus, a *sacrifice* (like that of Abel's) can find favor with God, and when it does, God responds by showing favor—such as relenting punishment, rendering assistance, or providing gifts. This is Jesus' viewpoint when He decides to make *Himself* a sacrifice for the world, particularly for the forgiveness of sins (sparing punishment), giving eternal life (the highest of gifts), and freeing us from the slavery and darkness of evil (rendering the highest assistance).

We now proceed to the idea of sacrifice, which like the sacred view of time (mentioned above) is present in virtually *every* religion in the ancient world, including in the time of Jesus. As with the sacred

---

[5] John L. McKenzie, *Dictionary of the Bible* (New York: Macmillan Publishing, 1965), p. 324.

[6] Notice the phrasing of Genesis 4:4: "[T]he LORD had regard for Abel and his offering, but for Cain and his offering he had no regard."

[7] McKenzie, *Dictionary of the Bible*, p. 324; emphasis mine.

view of time (and the ability of ritual to bring the efficacy of past grace into the present), the practice and belief in the efficacy of sacrifice is *not* the result of "mutual borrowing" among religions[8]—it seems to be intrinsic to *each* culture, irrespective of influences from other cultures. Hence, it seems to be universally present in human consciousness or, if Jung and Eliade are correct, the unconscious psyche.[9] In either case, it seems to be an "in-built" awareness and desire within *all* people.[10] There's one other element that also seems to be built into personal awareness and desire: the fivefold *meaning* of sacrifice, also present in *every* world religion without mutual borrowing. According to McKenzie, this fivefold meaning is as follows:

> (1) The gift of man to the deity; (2) the homage of the subject to the lord; (3) the expiation of offenses; (4) communion with the deity in the sacrificial banquet; (5) life released from the victim, transmitted to the deity, and conferred upon the worshipers.[11]

Inasmuch as the Old Testament view is no different from the universal one (given above), and inasmuch as Jesus is immersed in the Old Testament view, we can be confident that He believed that His Father would *show* three kinds of favor from His well-intended sacrifice: (1) *expiation* of offenses, (2) *communion* with His Father, and (3) the gift of (eternal) *life*. We are now in a position to understand Jesus' view of offering up his suffering as self-sacrifice. To do this, we will briefly review the three central passages that Jesus used to interpret His suffering (as self-sacrifice) and why He believed that it would *show* the above three favors on a new transcendent and eternal scale to everyone throughout the whole of human history. If we can understand this, we can also understand why Jesus and Saint Paul exhort us to do the same—and to expect the same redemptive and salvific results.

---

[8] Ibid., p. 754.

[9] See Volume II, Chapter 2 of this Quartet.

[10] Eliade believes that modern nonreligious man has lost this intrinsic awareness and desire to be close to the sacred through ritual and sacrifice. However, contemporary religious people can awaken these intrinsic desires when they practice religious rituals without allowing the merely scientific-physical viewpoint to "trump" them. This is discussed in detail in Volume II (Chapters 1 and 2) of this Quartet.

[11] McKenzie, *Dictionary of the Bible*, p. 754.

In Volume III (Chapter 3) we investigated all three of Jesus' inter-
pretive passages: Isaiah 52:13—53:12; His Eucharistic words "poured
out for many" in Mark 14:24 and Matthew 26:28; and Psalm 22,
recounted in His dying words. The first passage, Isaiah 52:13—53:12
(the Fourth Suffering Servant Song), apparently inspired Jesus to
apply the idea of "sacrifice" to Himself, and to see that such self-
sacrifice would be an expiation of the sins of many—indeed, *everyone*.
The passage runs as follows:

> Behold, my servant shall prosper,
> he shall be exalted and lifted up,
> and shall be very high.
> As many were astonished at him—
> his appearance was so marred, beyond
> human semblance,
> and his form beyond that of the sons of
> men—
> so shall he startle *many nations*;
> kings shall shut their mouths because of
> him;
> for that which has not been told them they
> shall see,
> and that which they have not heard they
>
> shall understand.
> Who has believed what we have heard?
> And to whom has the arm of the LORD
>
> been revealed?
> For he grew up before him like a young plant,
> and like a root out of dry ground;
> he had no form or comeliness that we should
> look at him,
> and no beauty that we should desire him.
> He was despised and rejected by men;
> a man of sorrows, and acquainted with
> grief;
> and as one from whom men hide their faces

he was despised, and we esteemed him not.
Surely he has borne *our* griefs
and carried *our* sorrows;
yet we esteemed him stricken,
struck down by God, and afflicted.
But he was wounded for *our* transgressions,
he was bruised for *our* iniquities;
upon him was the chastisement that made *us*
whole,
and with his stripes *we* are healed.
All we like sheep have gone astray;
we have turned every one to his own way;
and the LORD has laid on him

the iniquity of *us all*.
He was oppressed, and he was afflicted,
yet he opened not his mouth;
like a lamb that is led to the slaughter,
and like a sheep that before its shearers is
silent,
so he opened not his mouth.
By oppression and judgment he was taken
away;
and as for his generation, who considered
that he was cut off out of the land of the
living,
stricken for the transgression of my
people?
And they made his grave with the wicked
and with a rich man in his death,
although he had done *no* violence,
and there was no deceit in his mouth.
Yet it was the will of the LORD to bruise him;
he has put him to grief;
when he makes himself an offering for sin,
he shall see his offspring, he shall prolong
his days;
the will of the LORD shall prosper in his hand;

he shall see the fruit of the travail of his
soul and be satisfied;
by his knowledge shall the *righteous one*, my
servant,
make many to be accounted righteous;
and he shall bear their iniquities.
Therefore I will divide him a portion with the
great,
and he shall divide the spoil with the
strong;
because he *poured out his soul to death,*
and was numbered with the transgressors;
yet he bore the sin of *many*,
and made intercession for the transgressors.
(Is 52:13—53:12; emphasis mine)[12]

We must assume that Jesus was quite familiar with this song, because
he used the expressions "poured out for the many for the forgiveness
of sins" in his Eucharistic words (Mt 26:28; Mk 14:24; my translation).[13] As can be seen throughout this song, Isaiah continuously links

[12] Lucien Cerfaux first made the strong case not only for the parallelism between the Fourth
Suffering Servant Song of Isaiah and the Christological Hymn in Paul's Letter to the Philip-
pians (Phil 2:6–11), but also the likelihood of this Fourth Song of Isaiah being in the mind of
Jesus Himself. Jesus' Eucharistic words "poured out for the many" repeat the end of that song,
showing that He had it in mind prior to his Passion and perhaps in His ministry. See Lucien
Cerfaux, "L hymne au Christ-Serviteur de Dieu (Phil., II, 6-11 - Is., LII, 13,-LIII, 12)", in
*Miscellanea historica in honorem Alberti de Meyer Universitatis Catholicae in oppido Lovaniensi iam
annos XXV professoris* (Louvain: Bibliothèque de l'Université, 1946), 1:117–30.

[13] Recall the Semitism "the many" is a literal translation of the Hebrew *rabbim* with the
definite article which means "all". See the detailed explanation of this—and the probable
reason why "many" should be interpreted as "all"—in Volume III, Chapter 3, of the Quartet.
See also Jeremias' detailed justification for resolving the "many or all" problem in favor of
"*all*". He notes in this regard, "While 'many' in Greek (as in English) stands in opposition to
'all,' and therefore has the exclusive sense ('*many, but not all*'), Hebrew *rabbim* can have the
inclusive sense ('*the whole, comprising many individuals*'). This inclusive use is connected with
the fact that Hebrew and Aramaic possess no word for 'all'." Jeremias, *Eucharistic Words of
Jesus*, p. 179. This is why the highly unusual phrase *to pollōn* (*the* many) reveals a Greek transla-
tor's attempt to translate a Semitism—Jesus' use of *rabbim* with a definite article. Since Hebrew
has no word for "all", it uses *rabbim* with the definite article to refer to it. Hence Jesus' Eucharistic words in Mark and Matthew show that He very probably meant "poured out *for all*".

the *self*-sacrifice of the *innocent* Servant to the salvation of "the many" (see the italicized words in the above passage).

Recall from Volume III (Chapter 3) that there is no distinctive Hebrew word for "all". The same word *rabbim* is used to signify both "all" and "many". The two words are distinguished by the definite article ("the"). When *rabbim* is accompanied by the definite article, it means "all", but without the definite article, it means "many". Therefore, every time "*the* many" is used in the above passage, it translates *rabbim* with a definite article, meaning that it likely refers to "*all*".

Now let us return to the passage. Jesus' use of Isaiah's Suffering Servant Song in His Eucharistic words ("poured out for the many") indicates His acceptance of Isaiah's meaning—the *self*-sacrifice of an *innocent* victim is a perfect sacrifice which must have benefit beyond the innocent victim making it, because the innocent victim has no need for it since he is innocent. Both Jesus and Isaiah believe that this perfect sacrifice not only goes to "many" throughout the world, but to *all* throughout the world (as the use of the definite article with *rabbim* suggests). Thus, when Jesus set His face resolutely toward Jerusalem, knowing that He will there be persecuted and killed, He planned to make Himself the perfect sacrifice for the expiation of the sins of everyone.

This intention is clearly manifest in both His Eucharistic words and in Psalm 22 (His dying words). A brief review of each of these texts will clarify this point.[14] We will begin with Jesus' Eucharistic words (relying on Joachim Jeremias' analysis of Jesus' original words).

Also recall from Chapter 3 of Volume III that when Jesus celebrated the Passover meal with His disciples, He waited until after He received one of the four Passover cups to institute the new ritual of His body and blood. He then initiated the ritual of the bread, identifying it with His body: "Jesus took bread, and blessed, and broke it, and gave it to the disciples and said, 'Take, eat; this is my body'" (Mt 26:26; see Mk 14:22; Lk 22:19; 1 Cor 11:23–24). Then, after the completion of the Passover meal, Jesus initiated the ritual of the wine that He identifies with the covenant in His blood. He took a cup of

---

[14]For a detailed review of both texts, see Volume III (Chapter 3, Section IV) of this Quartet.

red wine, gave thanks, and gave it to His disciples, saying, "[T]his [cup] is my blood of the covenant,[15] which is poured out for [the] many[16] [all]."[17] The reason Jesus separates the rite of the bread/body from the rite of the red wine/blood is to indicate that He is making a *sin* offering, in which it is common to remove the blood from the flesh of a sacrificial animal, and then to offer the bloodless flesh first and *then* the blood as an oblation for sin.

There is one important difference between Jesus' rite and traditional sin offerings: Jesus does not use a sacrificial animal for the sacrifice, but instead refers directly to Himself, *His* body and then *His* blood. This unmistakably refers back to the Fourth Suffering Servant Song of Isaiah, in which the *self*-sacrifice of the *innocent* victim is said to lead to the expiation of the sins of *all* throughout the world. The parallel between Jesus' Eucharistic words and Isaiah's Fourth Suffering Servant Song is solidified when Jesus uses the expression of the last line of the song, "poured out [His life unto death] for [*the*] many [all]". The parallels are so close that it is difficult to imagine that Jesus did not have Isaiah's Fourth Suffering Servant Song in mind when he instituted the rite of His body and blood. If this is the case, then Jesus fully expected that His self-sacrifice would lead to the expiation of the sins of *all* throughout the world.

---

[15] Though Jesus identifies the red wine with His "blood of the covenant", it is clear from the red wine, the parallelism with the bread, and the use of "this cup" that Jesus is identifying the red wine with *both* His *blood* and the covenant in His blood. Jeremias notes that the color of the wine is significant here: "The *tertium comparationis* in the case of the bread is the fact that it was broken, and in the case of the wine the red colour. We have already seen ... that it was customary to drink red wine at the Passover.... The comparison between *red wine* and blood was common in the Old Testament (Gen. 49.11; Deut. 32.14; Isa. 63.3,6), further Eccl 39.26; 50.15; I Macc. 6.34; Rev. 14.20; Sanh. 70a, etc." Jeremias, *Eucharistic Words of Jesus*, pp. 223–24.

[16] Mark and Matthew report "poured out for many", but Luke reports "poured out for *you*"; emphasis mine. Jeremias holds that "for the many" is the more original on the basis of linguistic grounds; namely, "for the many" is a Semitism while "you" is not. Jeremias attributes the replacement of "the many" by "you" as having a liturgical purpose where each worshipper feels him to be individually addressed (by "you"), which would not happen with the indefinite "the many". See ibid., p. 172.

[17] As noted above, the Greek expression *to pollōn* means "*the* many". Since this expression makes no sense in Greek, it is very likely a Greek translation of a Hebrew or Aramaic expression (a Semitism). It very probably refers to *rabbim* accompanied by the definite article, which means "*all*".

Is there additional evidence that Jesus believed His suffering would lead to the expiation of sins and the salvation of all throughout the world? The answer is contained in His dying words. Recall from Volume III (Chapter 3, Section IV.B) that Mark's version of Jesus' dying words is very probably historical, because it does not refer to the Hebrew (official) version of Psalm 22, but rather to a northern Galilean Aramaic version of the Psalm, which Jesus probably learned as a child from His Mother: *"Elōi, Elōi, lama sabachthani"* ("My God, my God, why have you forsaken me?" [Mk 15:34]).[18] Recall also that Jesus' use of the first line of the Psalm refers to the *whole* Psalm, not to just the first line. Edward Mally explains this succinctly:

> As a quotation of an Old Testament Psalm [Jesus' dying words] can hardly be taken literally as an expression of real despair or dereliction. Rather, Jesus applies to himself an Old Testament passage that sums up the *suffering of the upright individual* who turns to his God in the stress of hostile opposition and its ensuing depression. In using the Psalm, Jesus does not express the feeling that his life's work has failed and that God has therefore abandoned him; he identifies himself with a biblical precedent, *the persecuted upright man* who has trusted in Yahweh, and found in him *the source of his consolation and ultimate triumph.*[19]

So why did Jesus select this particular Psalm for His dying words? As Mally indicates, Jesus' dying words "can hardly be taken literally as an expression of real despair or dereliction"; rather, He selects Psalm 22 for three major reasons:

1. It manifests His true trust in His Father, and His belief in the redemption that will come through His suffering (vv. 19–24).
2. It has an uncanny resemblance to His own Crucifixion one thousand years later (vv. 7–8, 11–18).

[18] See Brown's linguistic analysis of the likely dialect of Jesus' dying words (in Mark) in Raymond Brown, *The Death of the Messiah: From Gethsemane to the Grave; A Commentary on the Passion Narratives in the Four Gospels* (New York: Doubleday, 1994), pp. 1051–52. Notice that Matthew, who was writing for a sophisticated Jewish audience, believes he has to correct Mark's unsophisticated Aramaic version, and so he changes it to the correct Hebrew; he changed Mark's Aramaic *Elōi* to the Hebrew *'Ēlî:* "*'Ēlî, 'Ēlî, lema sabachthani*" (Mt 27:46).

[19] Edward Mally, "The Gospel according to Mark", in *The Jerome Biblical Commentary*, ed. Raymond Brown, Joseph A. Fitzmyer, and Roland E. Murphy (Englewood Cliffs, N.J.: Prentice-Hall, 1968), 2:58; emphasis mine.

3. Most importantly, it points to the universal salvation that His sacrifice will bring—not just to Israel, but to all nations; not just to the present age, but to the whole of the past and the future (vv. 25–31).

We will here restrict ourselves to Jesus' third rationale for using Psalm 22. In order to understand it, we must see the theme of "the persecuted upright man" (as quoted above by Mally) in light of Isaiah's Fourth Suffering Servant Song, of which Jesus is conscious when reciting the Psalm. In light of Isaiah's song, we now know what the triumph is: the expiation and redemption of the world through the perfect self-sacrifice of the innocent victim. Psalm 22 extends this one step further by revealing the whole scope of Jesus' redemptive action. It is not limited only to *His* time and place, but extends to the whole past, the whole future, and to all places. This is clear from the last stanzas of the Psalm:

> For he has not despised or abhorred
> the affliction of the afflicted;
> and he has not hidden his face from him,
> but has heard, when he cried to him.
> From you comes my praise in the great
> congregation;
> my vows I will pay before those who fear
> him.
> The afflicted shall eat and be satisfied;
> those who seek him shall praise the LORD!
> May your hearts live for ever!
> *All* the ends of the earth shall remember
> and turn to the LORD;
> and *all* the families of the nations
> shall worship before him.
> For dominion belongs to the LORD,
> and he rules over the nations.
> Yes, to him shall *all* the proud of the earth
> bow down;
> before him shall bow *all* who go down to the
> dust,
> and he who *cannot* keep himself alive.

Posterity shall serve him;
men shall tell of the Lord to the *coming*
generation,
and proclaim his deliverance to a *people yet*
unborn,
that he has wrought it. (Ps 22:24–31; emphasis mine)

The magnitude of the triumph of the innocent victim is *completely* universal. The Psalmist says that Yahweh has heard his plea, and responds with unexpected magnanimity. The benefit of the victim's suffering will lead not just to the benefit of Israel, but to "all the ends of the earth" and "all the families of the nations", who will "turn to the LORD" (v. 27). By turning to the Lord the Psalmist probably means "giving praise to *Yahweh*". However, Jesus probably has a much fuller interpretation of this phrase in light of His mission to bring salvation and eternal life to the world. He may well have viewed this phrase as indicating expiation, justification, redemption, and salvation. The reference to "all the ends of the earth" and "all the families of nations" refers to everybody—Jew and Gentile alike.

What is most interesting is that the Psalmist also includes in this redemption and salvation *all* who are *dead*—"all who go down to the dust" (v. 29)—that is, Sheol, the domain of the dead, those who cannot keep themselves alive. This is a difficult passage to interpret, because Sheol does not seem to have been thought of as a place of the living—let alone a place of worship (implying righteousness)—but rather a place where souls of the dead lay in darkness, both the righteous and the unrighteous. Though it is difficult to say what the Psalmist was thinking—writing about 1,000 B.C.[20]—it is likely that Jesus, in light of His mission to save the world and bestow eternal life, used this phrase to apply His self-sacrificial action to those who have gone into the realm of the dead so that they too (or at least some of them) might receive expiation, justification, and eternal life.

Finally, the Psalmist proclaims that the Lord's work will be known by *future* generations: "Posterity shall serve him; men shall tell future

---

[20] According to Craig Davis, Psalm 22 should be viewed as a preexilic Psalm dating to about 1,000 B.C. because "*Bashan* in v12 points to a united monarchy time frame, since *Bashan* was lost to Judah upon the division of the kingdom. The older '*anoki*' in v6 (Heb v7) helps rule out a late date." Craig Davis, *Dating the Old Testament* (New York: RJ Communications, 2007), p. 317.

generations about the Lord and proclaim his deliverance to a people yet unborn" (vv. 30–31; my translation). Again, Jesus probably had a fuller interpretation of this phrase in light of His mission to bring salvation and eternal life to the world. He was probably applying His self-sacrificial action to the expiation, justification, and salvation of future generations who desire and try to follow Him.

We can draw two conclusions from Jesus' Eucharistic words and His reference to the Fourth Suffering Servant Song and Psalm 22:

1. He saw suffering, particularly the suffering of an innocent, as an opportunity for perfect self-sacrifice that could be offered to the Father to help in the redemption of all people.
2. He considered His suffering to be this *perfect* self-sacrifice which would lead to *perfect* expiation, justification, and redemption for the whole world.[21]

Recall that the Old Testament view of sacrifice (which Jesus accepted) follows the universal meaning of sacrifice, which according to McKenzie has three major *effects*:

1. The expiation of offenses
2. Communion with the deity in the sacrificial banquet
3. Life released from the victim, transmitted to the deity, and conferred upon the worshippers[22]

Recall also that Jesus extends this view of sacrifice through His use of Isaiah's Fourth Suffering Servant Song. By doing this, He intended His perfect *self*-sacrifice (the sacrifice of the Innocent One) to lead to expiation, communion, and life for all people. As we shall see,

---

[21] For Jesus, expiation of sins was not only an act of forgiveness (i.e., a restoration to favor with His Father) but also a release from the bondage of evil—specifically, from the bondage of Satan. According to Wright, Jesus viewed His self-sacrificial death as a final victory over Satan, the complete self-sacrifice that would conquer not just darkness, but the dark power himself. This conquest of Satan would make Jesus the new universal temple for all nations. See N. T. Wright, *Jesus and the Victory of God* (Minneapolis: Fortress Press 1996), pp. 463–67. Saint Paul interprets Jesus becoming the new temple as "His body"; it is the substance unifying the members of the Christian Church (see 1 Cor 12 and Rom 12:5). The topic of Jesus' conquest of Satan will be taken up in detail in a sequel to this Quartet, *Called out of Darkness: Contending with Evil through Virtue and Prayer* (San Francisco: Ignatius Press, forthcoming).

[22] McKenzie, *Dictionary of the Bible*, p. 754.

the early Church did not think that Jesus restricted efficacious self-offering to *His* suffering and death alone. It held that all of us could turn *our* suffering into efficacious expiation of sins, communion with God, and grace to help in the work of salvation. Evidently, none of us can be a *perfectly* innocent victim, and so our self-sacrifice will be different from that of Jesus'. Nevertheless, Saint Paul makes clear that we too can enter into this mystical meaning of suffering through the graciousness of God (see Col 1:24 and the detailed explanation below in Section II).

Before explaining our participation in this mystical meaning of suffering, sacrifice, and redemption, it will be helpful to see how the Gospel of John interprets it in light of love (*agapē*), Jesus' highest virtue. In John 15:13 we can detect Jesus' implicit definition of love, indeed, perfect love: "Greater love has no man than this, that a man lay down his life for his friends." According to this passage, love is self-sacrifice (gift of self) and perfect love is complete self-sacrifice (complete gift of self). Though this interpretation is explicitized best in John's Gospel, it is consistent with Jesus' intention of establishing love as the highest commandment and associating love with sacrifice, which is clearly manifest in the Synoptic Gospels.

In view of this, we can now see Jesus' perfect self-sacrifice through a new lens, the lens of the highest virtue that characterizes His and the Father's heart—unconditional love. The reason that Jesus' perfect self-sacrifice is capable of universal expiation, justification, and redemption is not only found in the dynamics of "sacrifice to God", but also in the dynamics of love, which naturally goes beyond the self. Thus, when Jesus gave Himself for us on the Cross, He did so linking His perfect self-sacrifice to His unconditional love for us. And we, according to Saint Paul in Colossians 1:24, can also offer our self-sacrifice (given in love) to strengthen the Church and assist in the work of redemption.

II. Imitating Jesus in the Mystical Purpose of Suffering

Jesus not only atoned for our sins through His self-sacrificial suffering; He left the way open to *us* to participate in this mystery as well—to use our suffering to strengthen the Church in the work of redemption by offering it up to the Father as an act of loving self-sacrifice. This may be the *most* noble purpose and use of our suffering. This may seem difficult to imagine because there are so many important opportunities in suffering that lead to the salvation and good of ourselves and others (see Chapter 7). Yet for Jesus, the mystical purpose of suffering seems to be the highest, both in His life and, by implication, for us as well. Jesus did many things to bring the Kingdom of God to us—by performing healings and miracles as well as by preaching the word of love, raising the dead, defeating evil through His ministry of exorcism, proclaiming the good news to sinners and the poor, and bestowing on us the gifts of the resurrection and the Holy Spirit. Yet none of these extraordinary gifts seems to be more central to His mission of redemption and salvation than His unconditional gift of self, in letting Himself be unjustly accused, ridiculed, crucified, and put to death.

Jesus' priority here points to the intrinsic value of suffering for *our* redemption and the redemption of others. Of course, we need faith in Jesus, and recognition of love as our highest calling, to understand this supreme value of suffering. If we do have this faith, we too can offer our suffering to the Father as self-sacrifice to help in the work of redemption. Saint Paul makes this clear in the Letter to the Colossians:

> Now I rejoice in my sufferings for your sake, and in my flesh I complete what is lacking in Christ's afflictions for the sake of his body, that is, the Church. (1:24)

Recall from the detailed explanation of this passage given in Volume III (Chapter 3) that Saint Paul is not suggesting that there is anything lacking in the sufferings of Jesus for the redemption of the world, but rather that Jesus has provided a place for Him to use His suffering to help the Church—that is, to help in the *work* of salvation. Paul is fully aware that Jesus has provided the unconditionally loving sacrifice—the infinite love necessary for the redemption of *everyone*, which, according to Church teaching, includes

> those who, through no fault of their own, do not know the Gospel of Christ or his Church, but who nevertheless seek God with a sincere

heart, and, moved by grace, try in their actions to do his will as they
know it through the dictates of their conscience.[23]

So if nothing is lacking in Jesus' redemptive act, how did He leave
room for us to participate in the work of salvation?

Saint Paul views his loving self-sacrifice for the Colossians as having a *strengthening effect* not only in the Church of Colossae, but also
for the *whole* Church. When we imitate Jesus in an act of loving self-
sacrifice (by offering our suffering to God for the Church), the grace
(favor) given by God for our and others' salvation[24] moves into the
Church through the unifying and grace-filled spiritual body of Jesus
and strengthens her. Paul teaches that God's generosity is so great
that He allows *our* suffering, offered as loving self-sacrifice, to have
a similar effect to that of His Son, though not to the same degree,
for ours is not perfect and universal. When we make our sufferings
a self-offering to God, God shows favor not only to the Church as a
whole but to all individuals in His Mystical Body, which includes
those who have not heard of Christ, but try to seek God according
to the dictates of their conscience.

In the First Letter to the Corinthians, Paul speaks about Christ's
spiritual body as the unifying bond of all of us—its members.[25] He
then notes that "[i]f one member suffers, all suffer together; if one
member is honored, all rejoice together" (12:26). The implication is
clear: each individual member affects the whole body, and therefore,
every member of it; so if one member suffers, the whole body suffers,
and if one is honored, the whole body is honored. Yet these are not
the only qualities that affect the body of Christ. We can infer from
Paul's analysis that if members are strong in their love, it will positively affect the whole body, and conversely if members are weak in
their love, it will weaken the whole body. As noted above, offering
our suffering as self-sacrifice for the good of the body of Christ is an

[23] Dogmatic Constitution on the Church, *Lumen Gentium*, November 21, 1964, no. 16, in
Vatican Council II, Vol. 1: The Conciliar and Postconciliar Documents, ed. Austin Flannery (Northport, N.Y.: Costello Publishing, 1975), p. 376.

[24] Recall from Section I above that "grace" (in Hebrew *hanan*) means the favor showed by
God *when* He finds favor with us. In contrast, Jesus offers salvation (unconditional favor) to *all*
mankind through His loving self-sacrifice, irrespective of whether He finds favor with us. His
loving self-sacrifice gives salvation to contrite sinners as well as saints.

[25] Saint John uses the image of "the vine and the branches" to convey the same message
(see Jn 15:1–7).

act of *love* for the Church—so when we offer our sufferings to the Lord as self-sacrifice, we strengthen the whole body, and therefore, every member of it.

Paul reinforces the importance and dignity of offering our whole selves to the Lord in the Letter to the Romans:

> I appeal to you therefore, brethren, by the mercies of God, to present your bodies [*somata*] as a living sacrifice, holy and acceptable to God, which is your spiritual worship [*latreian*]. (12:1)

The word for "bodies" here is "*somata*", which can mean the physical body, but can also have a more abstract meaning referring to the *whole self*. It can also refer figuratively to the Mystical Body of Christ, which unifies many individual people. Thus, we could interpret this passage to mean that we should offer our whole selves as a living sacrifice to God, for which there can be no greater or more proper service to Him.

Paul later implies that all our gifts, presumably including the offering of ourselves, build up the body, and so we do not belong to ourselves alone, but rather belong to one another in the one body:

> For as in one body we have many members, and all the members do not have the same function, so we, though many, are one body in Christ, and individually members one of another. (Rom 12:4)

Inasmuch as we have the remarkable capacity to build up the body of Christ through the offering of ourselves, particularly our suffering, to the Father in imitation of Jesus, we cannot afford to waste our suffering as members of the body of Christ. When we suffer, we need to *remember* to make it a self-sacrificial offering so that we can unify our sufferings to that of Jesus for the good of the body. As implied by Paul, there is no more noble service to the Church and the Kingdom of Christ than this.

There are several prayers we can use to offer our sufferings to the Lord for the good of the Church and the work of redemption, not the least of which is the traditional Catholic morning offering.[26] I

---

[26] "O Jesus, through the Immaculate Heart of Mary, I offer you my prayers, works, joys, and sufferings of this day for all the intentions of your Sacred Heart, in union with the Holy Sacrifice of the Mass throughout the world, for the salvation of souls, the reparation of sins, the reunion of all Christians, and in particular for the intentions of the Holy Father. Amen."

add to this a spontaneous prayer that I can use when events come up during the day: "Lord Jesus, I want to unite my suffering with Your sufferings as a self-sacrifice for the Church and the work of redemption." Readers should make their own spontaneous prayer (try to make it easy to remember and repeat). All the essential elements have been described above:

1. Uniting our sufferings with those of Jesus, so that we are with Him in the common ministry of redemption through the offering of suffering
2. Making our suffering into self-sacrificial love by offering it to the Father in imitation of Jesus
3. Asking the Lord to use this offering of love to help the Church (the body of Christ) and His work of redemption

There is also a tradition of asking the Lord to apply the grace and love of our self-sacrifice to *specific* people and *specific* intentions. It is difficult to imagine that the Lord would not look favorably on this, so long as our petitions will help the salvation of that person according to God's six objectives—the promotion of our own and others' salvation, the protection of our own and others' freedom, and then the alleviation of our own and others' suffering. Parents will frequently do this for their children, spouses for one another, and friends for friends. We can also offer our sufferings for a local church, a specific cause (to further the work of redemption), or a specific organization (furthering the cause of redemption or the alleviation of suffering).

People who are quite sick or debilitated will want to make a spirituality and ministry out of offering their sufferings to the Lord. This can be done by integrating prayers to "offer our suffering" into other prayers throughout the day, perhaps after each decade of a Rosary, after *Lectio Divina*,[27] or simply after saying the Our Father. Some may want to focus their prayer on Jesus' Passion, either by meditating on the Gospel narratives, the Sorrowful Mysteries of the Rosary, or a reflection on Jesus' suffering. As they contemplate, they may want to consider specifically Jesus' intention to bestow His love on the world through His self-sacrificial suffering, and ask for the freedom to offer themselves in love as He did through their sufferings. This has a double effect:

[27] *Lectio Divina* (Latin for "Divine Reading") is a contemplative reading of the Scriptures.

1. It strengthens the Church and advances the work of redemption (as described above).

2. It transforms those making the prayer, for the more we can accept suffering in faith as our highest calling and dignity (in imitation of Jesus), the more we place ourselves in His hands, trusting in His loving will.

The greater our freedom to *imitate* Jesus in offering our suffering, the more we enter into *spiritual union* with Him, bringing us closer to His loving heart, which in turn helps us become more like Him in love (*agapē*).

When events conspire to make suffering a large part of our lives, we have an opportunity to imitate the greatest of saints. We can use our suffering as a foundation for a "contemplative vocation", which puts "self-sacrificial offering" at its center. Though most people who have this opportunity have not entered a monastery or subjected themselves to a rule, they can order their lives, much like a contemplative brother or sister, toward meditating on Jesus' Passion and recognizing His love in that Passion, as well as uniting their suffering to His. As they ask for the grace to *imitate* Him in the freedom to use suffering as a source of love and grace for redemption, they will notice all the fruits of a real contemplative vocation, for they will receive the grace they ask for and will draw closer to Him and His loving heart, so as to be like Him in love. These individuals may not be in a monastery, but they are bringing the monastery and its rule into their hearts by uniting their self-offering with the sufferings of Jesus as they meditate on His loving actions. Though the paradigm for this is Saint Thérèse of Lisieux (see below), who was a contemplative Carmelite, she would have been the first to advocate that nonmonastic individuals join the ranks of her "little way" through this kind of contemplation and self-offering.

III. Saint Thérèse of Lisieux as Exemplar of the Mystical Purpose of Suffering

Saint Thérèse of Lisieux (born 1873) was raised in a devout Catholic family in France. As a young adolescent she felt called to religious life, but was overcome with anxiety at the loss of her mother when

Thérèse was only four years old. However, a turning point occurred in her life on Christmas Eve 1886 (at the age of thirteen), when she overheard her father saying to her sisters, "Fortunately this will be the last year," referring to the last year to keep up the childhood story of the Child Jesus dropping gifts into the shoes of children at the hearth. Although she was greatly distressed by this seeming rejection of her and her childhood by her father, she immediately received the grace from the Lord not only to forgive the perceived insult but also to forget herself. She suddenly felt relief from the anxiety over her mother's death—and felt herself freed from her childhood and self-centeredness. Two months later, Thérèse was sitting before the image of the crucified Christ, contemplating the bleeding from His hands, when she was overwhelmed by a sense of the presence of Christ saying to her, "I thirst." She described the experience as follows:

> One Sunday, looking at a picture of Our Lord on the Cross, I was struck by the blood flowing from one of the divine hands.... I was resolved to remain in spirit at the foot of the Cross and to receive the divine dew. I understood I was then to pour it out upon souls. The cry of Jesus on the Cross sounded continually in my heart: "I thirst!" These words ignited within me an unknown and very living fire. I wanted to give my beloved to drink and I felt myself consumed with a thirst for souls.[28]

This experience moved Thérèse to offer her whole self, particularly her sufferings, for the redemption of the world—especially for those who were in the grip of spiritual darkness. A few years later, at the age of fifteen, she entered the Carmelite convent, where she joined her two sisters and wrote about her "little way", a simple spirituality based on her confidence in the unconditional love of Jesus. During this time, Thérèse was found to have an advanced case of tuberculosis, which caused her to suffer immensely. She joined her sufferings to those of Jesus—offering them to the Father for the redemption of the world. Though Thérèse did not engage in active ministries, she nonetheless exemplified the highest form of love for the Lord, and the highest form of passion for the salvation of souls. She formulated

---

[28] Thérèse of Lisieux, *Story of a Soul: The Autobiography of St. Thérèse of Lisieux*, 3rd ed., ed. and trans. John Clarke (Washington, D.C.: Institute of Carmelite Studies, 1996), p. 99.

a profound spirituality of suffering by responding to the Lord's call to endure great pain, both physically and psychologically, throughout her life. Her "little way" consisted in patiently welcoming the sufferings given her, humbly enduring them, and trusting in the Lord by joining her sufferings to His as a perfect prayer of self-offering and love. Her spirituality and autobiography were so influential that Saint Pius XI called her "the greatest saint of modern times".

Since the time of her "little miracle" ("freedom from childhood and self") on Christmas Eve 1886, Thérèse had in mind that she wanted to be a *victim* for the sake of love. After entering the Carmelite convent, she grew more fervent in her desire to be a perfect "little victim" so that she could be a perfect gift of love to Jesus, her beloved. She knew that the trials of this world were temporary and that her sufferings would have three effects:

1. They would purify her love and give her ever-greater freedom to lose herself in the desire to be with and serve her Lord.
2. They could be offered up to the Lord as a holocaust (self-sacrifice), as reparation and grace for those immersed in darkness.
3. They were the vehicle through which she could become ever-more progressively a perfect gift of love to the one who loved her—Jesus crucified and risen.

As her tuberculosis progressed and the pain consumed her, she became more convinced of the efficacy of the three graces intrinsic to being a "little victim". In 1897, she wrote:

> In order that my life may be one act of *perfect* love, I offer myself as a *victim* of holocaust to Thy merciful love, imploring Thee to *consume me* unceasingly, and to allow the floods of infinite tenderness gathered up in Thee to overflow into my soul, that so I may become a very *martyr of Thy love*, Oh my God! May this martyrdom, after having prepared me to appear in Thy presence, *free me* from this life at the last, and may my soul take its flight without delay into the eternal embrace of Thy merciful love![29]

---

[29] Thérèse of Lisieux, *Soeur Thérèse of Lisieux, the Little Flower of Jesus: A New and Complete Translation of L Histoire d'une Ame, with an Account of Some Favours Attributed to the Intercession of Soeur Thérèse*, ed. T. N. Taylor (London: Burns and Oates, 1912), p. 312, https://archive.org/stream/saintthaeraeseofoothaeuoft/saintthaeraeseofoothaeuoft_djvu.txt.

In a particularly illuminating conversation with Mother Agnes (Thérèse's sister Pauline), Thérèse explained the twofold source of her inner strength:

1. The trials God sends are *good*.
2. Since the trials are sent by the One she loves, then she accepts them in *trust and love*, knowing it will be good for her purification in love and for the body of Christ (especially those immersed in darkness).

She knew that the more she endured difficulty for the sake of the One she loved, the more perfect her love for Him would be—she would present herself as a purer gift of self. The dialogue begins with Mother Agnes:

> You have had many trials today? Yes, but I love them.... I love all the good God sends me! Your sufferings are terrible! No they are not terrible: can a little victim of love find anything terrible that is sent by her spouse? Each moment He sends me what I am able to bear, and nothing more, and if He increases the pain, my strength is increased as well. But I could never ask for greater sufferings, I am too little a soul. They would then be of my own choice.[30]

The assurance with which Thérèse tells Mother Agnes that God continuously gives her the strength to endure pain must have been genuine, because her face was transformed in "unearthly joy", even when she was racked in pain.[31]

Thérèse did not consider her endurance of pain as *heroic*, for that would call attention to *her* strength and virtue. She was so deeply aware of the need for *humility*, selflessness, and truth in her love that she did not dare attribute her patient endurance of pain to her own strength; the strength, as she said, is the Lord's alone. In order to avoid the possibility of attributing heroic virtue to herself, she even

---

[30] Ibid., p. 214.

[31] "A certain Sister entertained doubts concerning the patience of Thérèse. One day, during a visit, she remarked that the invalid's face wore an expression of unearthly joy, and she sought to know the reason. It is because the pain is so acute just now. Thérèse replied, I have always forced myself to love suffering and to give it a glad welcome." Ibid.

refused to ask for *more* pain, because that would imply she could do more than the Lord had given her in conjunction with *His* strength. In order to make herself a perfect gift of love to the Lord she loves, she knew that she would have to be attentive to *welcoming* the pain, enduring it *patiently* and *humbly* while putting herself in the hands of her loving Lord.

In Chapter 6, we discussed the higher stages of the fourth level of love. There we saw that at the highest stages of Level Four love, genuinely holy people (imitating Jesus in His suffering) see *no contradiction* between love and suffering, not even between love and ever-increasing intense suffering. Suffering is at once purification in love and transformation of self into a perfectly loving gift for the Lord. This was the grace of Saint Thérèse of the Little Flower of Jesus, and her perfect appropriation of it led to her very quick canonization twenty-eight years after her death.

Thérèse reiterated her spirituality of suffering and love in her dying words to Mother Agnes, which she recorded in an entry to her auto-biography as follows:

> At last dawned the eternal day. It was Thursday, September 30, 1897. In the morning, the sweet victim, her eyes fixed on Our Lady's statue, spoke thus of her last night on earth: "Oh! With what fervor I have prayed to her! And yet it has been pure agony, without a ray of con-solation.... Earth's air is failing me: when shall I breathe the air of Heaven?" For weeks she had been unable to raise herself in bed, but at half-past two in the afternoon, she sat up and exclaimed: "Dear Mother, the chalice is full to overflowing! I could never have believed that it was possible to suffer so intensely.... I can only explain it by my extreme desire to save souls ... :" and a little while later: "Yes, all that I have written about my thirst for suffering is really true! I do not regret having surrendered myself to love." She repeated these last words several times.[32]

By making herself "a little victim for the sake of love", she graced the world with her love and allowed the Lord to transform her into a perfect gift of love, which was her true desire and joy.

[32] Ibid., p. 220.

Some readers are probably thinking, "God forbid that I should be reduced to such hardship and suffering in my life! I can't even begin to see this as an opportunity for anything, let alone an opportunity for a contemplative vocation to grow closer to Christ in love! I don't care how great Saint Thérèse of Lisieux was (or how doable her 'little way'); I don't want to imagine myself ever being in this kind of situation where I would be 'condemned' to this kind of life." If this is going through your mind, consider that God will not call you to this kind of life unless He gives you the specific grace to live it. The vast majority of us are not called to this kind of life, but we can still learn from the little way of Saint Thérèse how to use our more manageable sufferings to give strength to the Church and be transformed in love.

I take away four lessons from her "little profound way":

1. When suffering strikes—not only debilitating suffering, but any suffering—offer it up to the Lord as a self-sacrifice for the good of the Church and those in need of help toward redemption.
2. Unite the offering of yourself with the sufferings of Christ, so that both of you can be on mission together.
3. If possible, reflect on the Passion of Christ as you make your offering with Him to the Father.
4. Ask Him for the healing you desire, so long as it is commensurate with His will, by using Jesus' prayer in the Garden of Gethsemane: "Abba, Father, *all* things are possible to you. *Take* this cup away from me, but not what I will but what you will" (Mk 14:36, NAB; emphasis mine).

If you have a significant negative reaction to the "little way" of Saint Thérèse, do *not* force yourself to affirm what she is saying or doing—nothing good will come from this (see Volume I, Chapter 9, Section I). Instead, simply ask the Lord for the *"desire for the desire"* to offer your suffering freely as self-sacrifice for the strength of the Church and the redemption of souls. Don't play mind games with yourself, forcing yourself into a position of Saint Thérèse which the Lord at this time has not given you the grace to bear. As Thérèse herself said, "Each moment He sends me what I am able to bear, and nothing more, and if He increases the pain, my strength is increased as well."[33] It is best to imitate her humility and to allow the Lord to help us "His way", trusting that He will bring optimal fruit out of our suffering—for ourselves, the people we touch, and the Church. If we ask the Father to do this, while offering our suffering to Him as self-sacrifice in imitation of Jesus, He will bring unimagined goodness and salvation out of our offering, which He will reveal to us when we inherit eternal joy with Him.

---

[33] Thérèse of Lisieux, *The Story of a Soul*, trans Rev. Thomas N. Taylor (New York: Cosimo Classics, 2004), p. 183.

Chapter Nine

The Spirit of Truth Will Guide You

Ninth Foundation: Following the Inspiration and Guidance of the Holy Spirit

Introduction

The objective of this chapter is to give *practical* advice on following the Holy Spirit during times of suffering. There are many good books that address the role of the Holy Spirit in the time of Saint Paul and the apostles,[1] as well as the role of the Holy Spirit in our lives.[2] These books give additional explanation for the contents of this chapter.

In the Letter to the Romans, Saint Paul summarizes the deep interior and external role of the Holy Spirit in inspiring and guiding us, particularly in times of suffering:

> [T]he Spirit helps us in our weakness; for we do not know how to pray as we ought, but the Spirit himself intercedes for us with sighs too deep for words. And he who searches our hearts knows what is the mind of the Spirit, because the Spirit intercedes for the saints according to the will of God. (8:26–27; my translation)

---

[1] See, for example, James Dunn, *Jesus and the Spirit: A Study of the Religious and Charismatic Experience of Jesus and the First Christians as Reflected in the New Testament* (Philadelphia: Westminster Press, 1975). For an extended analysis of the Holy Spirit throughout the ages, see Alan Schreck, *The Gift: Discovering the Holy Spirit in Catholic Tradition* (Orleans, Mass.: Paraclete Press, 2013).

[2] See Alan Schreck, *Your Life in the Holy Spirit: What Every Catholic Needs to Know and Experience* (Frederick, Md.: Word Among Us Press, 2007). There are other books dedicated to the discernment of spirits that show how the Holy Spirit inspires and leads us in our lives. See, for example, Timothy Gallagher, *The Discernment of Spirits: An Ignatian Guide for Everyday Living* (New York: Crossroad Publishing, 2005).

How can we know the content and direction of the Holy Spirit's intercessions on our behalf? How can we make the "wordless groans" of the Holy Spirit intelligible so that we can follow them? Many Christian saints have written extensively about this, but perhaps none more clearly and completely than Saint Ignatius Loyola in his "Rules for the Discernment of Spirits" in *The Spiritual Exercises*. I have discussed these rules extensively in Volume I, Chapter 8, Section II, and will summarize them with respect to following the Spirit in times of suffering in this chapter (Sections II.C–II.E).

My intention in this chapter is to give a "how to" approach for following the Spirit in times of suffering. This consists in a preliminary observation about our "mindset" when attempting to follow the Spirit (Section I), and then a five-step process for recognizing the guidance of the Spirit in our minds, hearts, and lives (Section II). As might be expected, it will incorporate all the elements from the previous chapters of this volume, so that we will be able to see the predominately subtle signs of the Spirit amid the blur of suffering.

I. Our Mindset When Following the Holy Spirit

So what kind of mindset must we have to follow the Holy Spirit? Four qualities are necessary:

1. Awareness of God's objectives in alleviating suffering (Section I.A)
2. Humility in light of our inability to understand God's providential plan (also Section I.A)
3. Trust in the face of doubts and suspicion (Section I.B)
4. The patience to wait for the unfolding of God's plans (Section I.C)

A. God's Six Objectives and the Need for Humility

We have discussed God's six objectives and the need for humility in Chapter 3, but a brief review here will be helpful in using the forthcoming five-step process for following the Holy Spirit (Section II).

With respect to the Lord's six objectives in alleviating suffering, recall that He is first and foremost interested in *eternal salvation* for both us and others. For God, this life—and the good of this life—is but a mere blip within the vast domain of eternity. It is a critically import-ant "blip" because He gives us the opportunity to *choose* the identity with which we will proceed into eternity, and therefore the kind of eternity we will experience—loving or egocentric, caring or domi-neering, worship of God or worship of ourselves. God's whole pur-pose is to help us choose an eternity of love, care, and a relationship with Him that will make our joy complete. The words of Saint Paul truly reflect the Holy Spirit's perspective (God's perspective) about suffering and eternal love:

> For all who are led by the Spirit of God are sons of God. For you did not receive the spirit of slavery to fall back into fear, but you have received the spirit of sonship. When we cry, "Abba! Father!" it is the Spirit himself bearing witness with our spirit that we are children of God, and if children, then heirs, heirs of God and fellow heirs with Christ, provided we suffer with him in order that we may also be glo-rified with him. I consider that the *sufferings* of this present time *are not* worth comparing with the glory that is to be revealed to us. For the creation waits with eager longing for the revealing of the sons of God; for the creation was subjected to futility, not of its own will but by the will of him who subjected it in hope; because the creation itself will be set free from its bondage to decay and obtain the glorious liberty of the children of God. (Rom 8:14–21; emphasis mine)

Recall also that God's other objective is the protection of our own and others' freedom. If we are not free to choose the identity we want throughout eternity, then we are not free to choose the kind of eternity we wish to enter; and if we are not free to choose this, the purpose of this life is reduced to nothing—in God's perspective. Recall that this life, though but a mere blip amid eternity, is criti-cally important for *choosing* who we are and who we will become and, therefore, *choosing* the kind of eternity in which we will best fit. As noted repeatedly above, very few of us, if any, will make these choices perfectly. We will likely fail thousands of times and will hopefully repent and return to the Lord. As we continue on our somewhat "rocky" journey, we will begin to form an identity toward love, albeit imperfectly, that will enable God to bring us to perfection in love, either in this life or the next,[3] so that we can enter into eternal salvation with Him and the blessed.

Some might wonder, "Why would God give us such an awesome power of freedom that would allow us to choose an eternity without Him, the blessed, and love?" As we have repeatedly said throughout the Quartet, love is not our own unless it is freely chosen. If we do not have the capacity to choose "unlove" and "antilove", then our love is not our own; it does not originate within us—it is only an instinctive program installed in our brains by the "divine programmer". So God has to allow us to choose "unlove" and "antilove" so that we might be able to *choose* love as the identity we want to actualize throughout eternity. Unfortunately, if God allows us to choose "unlove" and "antilove", we can begin to fall "in love" with them—falsely. And if we give our hearts over to them, we will not be able to enter the Kingdom of God because we will be opposed to everything in it—a destructive and dark force within the Kingdom of light and love.

If we understand God's priority to bring us and others to salvation and to protect our own and others' freedom *before* He alleviates suffering *in this life,* then we will be able to understand the need for the second quality of our mindset: *humility.* We cannot possibly understand the immense complexity of God's providential plan for us and the world, because we do not even remotely have the capacity to understand the path to our salvation, let alone the path to others' salvation; we do not even remotely have the capacity to understand the protection of *our* freedom, let alone others' freedom; and we do not even remotely have the capacity to understand how God can best alleviate *our* suffering in light of these priorities, let alone understand how He would do so for others. At the very best, we have

---

[3] God can bring us to this perfection in love *after* we have passed from this world—in Purgatory. Those who are in this state of purification are *assured* of salvation after this purification is complete. See *Catechism of the Catholic Church*, 2nd ed. (Washington, D.C.: Libreria Editrice Vaticana—United States Conference of Catholic Bishops, 2000), nos. 1030–31. Recall that Jesus made provision for this in Matthew 12:32, when He teaches that blasphemy "against the Holy Spirit will not be forgiven, either in this age or *in the age to come*" (emphasis mine), implying that pardon and purification can take place after death. Saint Paul also makes provision for this by advocating prayer for the dead in 2 Timothy 1:16–18.

but a glimmer of insight into the vast conspiracy of providence; and so as Elihu advises Job, we should be humble about our capacity to understand suffering and its alleviation, refrain from attributing any negative motive to God, and resist giving God ultimatums, timelines, and specified plans for the alleviation of our suffering (Job 36–37).

If we do not admit in all humility our intrinsic incapacity to understand even a little part of the vast divine plan for us and others, then we are likely to make the error of attributing false motives to God that will lead to discouragement, anger, resentment, and possibly despair, as well as lead to loss of faith and loss of all the above-mentioned opportunities (see Chapter 3, Section II of this volume).

B. Trust and Doubts

We now come to the third quality of the mindset needed to follow the Holy Spirit: *trust*. Unfortunately, trust can be quite difficult when suffering strikes. There is a truism that applies here: when things are going well, we are naturally inclined toward optimism, but when things are going poorly, we are naturally inclined to pessimism. This natural pessimism during times of suffering directly interferes with following the Holy Spirit because it creates *doubts*.

Frequently, when I have suggested to people who are suffering that they place their trust in the loving God, they respond to me, "Father, I've been going to church all my life, and I've never had more doubts about God than I do right now; how can I put my trust in a Being whose very existence I'm questioning?" Doubts are particularly powerful and pernicious during times of suffering, because they undermine trust in God at the very moment we need it most. It almost seems like a vicious plot—suffering causes doubt, and doubt undermines the trust we need during times of suffering! When these doubts arise, it is very difficult to simply muster a "*subjective* act of the will" to overcome them, because our interior attitudes are extremely distorted. That is why Saint Ignatius Loyola recommended that we never make an important decision or discernment in times of desolation. So what *can* we do to overcome this problem? *Be objective.*

The reader may have wondered why we dedicated Volumes II and III of the Quartet to explaining the *objective* evidence for God, a transcendent soul, and Jesus. Aside from the fact that this evidence is helpful in securing our "little leap of faith", and important for dialoguing with an increasingly materialistic and secular culture, it is indispensable during times of suffering. When our subjective disposition, intentions, and will are distorted by suffering, objective evidence can be of immense assistance, because it stands on its own, requiring a minimal act of the will.

Why does objective evidence require *any* act of the will? Because no objective evidence is completely persuasive, even if its denial leads to an intrinsic contradiction or a contradiction of fact. Assent to God requires a movement of the heart, a *desire* to open ourselves to a supreme Being beyond ourselves, a Being that has a moral dimension leading us to a life of unconditional goodness and love. If we do not want to believe in such a Being—that is, if we are not open to and accepting of it—then no objective evidence will ever convince us; we will resign ourselves to total skepticism before assenting to it. Thus, the disposition of our hearts influences our desires, intentions, and choices; it is intrinsic to our *free will*. If the reality of a supreme Being irritates or repulses us, or we are closed to a supreme moral authority beyond ourselves, then we will never believe even if "someone were to rise from the dead" and present himself unmistakably to us. We would think later, "Wow, that was a powerful illusion."

The necessity of a movement of the heart—an act of the will, a little leap of faith or belief—is by *God's* own design. Recall the words of Fyodor Dostoyevsky's *Brothers Karamazov* that God would not "enslave man with a miracle" (Volume I, Chapter 5);[4] He would not create objective evidence so persuasive that it would overrule our hearts and free choice, so persuasive that we would not be able to resist it even if we wanted to. Though this life is a mere blip amid the vastness of eternity, it has one major purpose for God: to have us choose the fundamental identity that will follow us into eternity and determine the kind of eternity we will experience. Will our eternity be self-centered or other-centered, dominating or caring? Will we worship ourselves or worship a supreme Being beyond ourselves? Will we respect others or disdain them? Will we be like

---

[4]Fyodor Dostoyevsky, "The Grand Inquisitor", in *The Brothers Karamazov*, trans. David McDuff (New York: Penguin, 2003), p. 334.

the Good Samaritan or like the greedy Gordon Gekko (from the film *Wall Street*)? The whole meaning of our lives depends on these *choices*. If God were to create irresistibly persuasive evidence that could over-rule our hearts and free will, He would undermine the very reason for creating us in this mortal stage of our eternal lives.

Though objective evidence can never be irresistibly persuasive (without undermining God's purpose), it can go a long way to securing our *belief* (which includes our free choice) in God, a transcendent soul, and Jesus, particularly during times of suffering. This was the rationale for writing Volumes II and III of this Quartet.

What's the point? When suffering strikes and our subjective disposition becomes distorted—making trust in God quite difficult, when doubt is stronger than certainty—we will first want to ground our belief in the *objective* evidence of God. Though it will not be irresistibly persuasive, it can be strongly probative, particularly when we *combine* different kinds of evidence, such as the *verifiable* evidence of a transcendent soul from near-death experiences, the proof of a unique uncaused reality, the numinous experience (and other experiences of the transcendent), the evidence of our transcendental desires, and the scientific evidence of intelligent creation.

This evidence from experience and reason can lay the foundation for a *little* leap of faith, avoiding the need for a perfect act of the will to get us over an infinite chasm between us and God (see Volume I, Chapter 6, Section I). God gives us *objective* evidence of our tran-scendence and His existence so that our choices, our leap of faith, can reach reasonable and responsible *belief* without a *perfect* act of will, which we are unlikely to have in times of suffering. God has created a balance between our minds and hearts, leaving our wills free to choose—not overruling our wills with objective evidence, but pro-viding enough of it to make a reasonable choice to believe in both His existence and benevolence, even in times of suffering. Thus, God intends that we familiarize ourselves with some of this evidence, and use it in combination with our openness to and acceptance of Him, in our acts of trust.

Before discussing trust in God and the five-step process for fol-lowing the Holy Spirit, I recommend reviewing the material from Volumes II and III that speak most powerfully to *you*. With respect to Volume II, you might want to look at the following:

1. If you are empirically oriented, you may want to review the evidence of near-death experiences that not only reveal veridical evidence of surviving bodily death, but also a heavenly domain in which there is a loving deity amid deceased relatives and friends (Chapter 5).

2. If you are logically inclined, you may want to review the two proofs of God: the Lonerganian proof (Chapter 3, Sections III–IV) and the Thomistic proof (Appendix 2).

3. If you are scientifically inclined, you may want to review the evidence for an intelligent Creator from contemporary physics (Appendix 1).

4. If you are inclined toward interior evidence, you might want to review Rudolf Otto's numinous experience, Mircea Eliade's intuition of the sacred, John Henry Newman's proof of God from conscience, and Carl Jung's and J. R. R. Tolkien's view of the universal awareness of a cosmic struggle between good and evil (Chapters 1 and 2).

5. If you are philosophically inclined, you may want to review the evidence of God's presence to you in your awareness of and desire for perfect truth, love, justice-goodness, and beauty (Chapter 4), as well as the evidence for transphysical consciousness from heuristic notions (Chapter 3), Gödel's proof (Chapters 3 and 6), and self-consciousness—that is, the hard problem of consciousness (Chapter 6).

6. Though this was not discussed in Volume II, if you are empirically inclined, you may want to investigate well-documented miracles from the International Medical Committee of Lourdes[5] and from the work of Craig Keener.[6] Since these miracles are associated with Jesus, they are explained in more detail in the list of objective evidence from Volume III (see below).

God has left us with multiple clues to His existence and our transcendence because we are all different, and some forms of evidence

---

[5] See the website of the International Medical Committee of Lourdes at http://en.lourdes-france.org/deepen/cures-and-miracles/the-international-medical-committee.

[6] See Craig Keener, *Miracles: The Credibility of the New Testament Accounts*, 2 vols. (Grand Rapids, Mich.: Baker Academic Publishing, 2011).

will speak to us more strongly than others. I have had students who recognize the necessity of at least one uncaused reality and intuitively saw that such a reality would have to contain within itself the complete set of correct answers to the complete set of questions—if it could explain its own existence. Upon seeing this, they knew that the reality in question would have to be a unique unrestricted act of thinking.

I have also had students who after reading about the major medical studies of near-death experiences—examining the veridical evidence of patients who reported highly unusual events completely accurately and the evidence of blind people seeing during clinical death—come to a recognition that there is probably something beyond the material world. Their conviction was based on not only the thousands of cases studied, but the failure of current physicalist hypotheses to explain this phenomenon.

I have known still other students who went through the philosophical arguments for the five transcendental desires and proclaimed, "That's me." They recognized that they had a desire for *perfect* truth, love, goodness, and beauty, and also had a capacity to recognize seemingly every imperfection in these qualities in everything around them. They then realized that they could not have done this without having at least a tacit awareness of *perfect* truth, love, goodness, and beauty. From where, or what, could they have derived this awareness? Certainly not the imperfect world around them, or from the imperfect physical processes constituting their brains, and so they concluded that the cause of their tacit awareness of perfect truth, love, goodness, and beauty had to be commensurate with its effects. The cause had to be perfect truth, love, goodness, and beauty itself: God.

I've also had students who had an intrinsic suspicion about the physical universe's capacity to explain itself—students who were well apprised of current physics with its hypotheses about multiverses, bouncing universes, and higher dimensional string universes—and concluded that temporal limits were probably unavoidable (implying a creation), and that a *transphysical* explanation of universal conditions and constants was more reasonable than the alternative: a multiverse that itself has to be *fine-tuned*.

Finally, I have had students who read Otto's *Idea of the Holy*[7] or Newman's "proof of God from conscience"[8] or Jung's[9] and Tolkien's[10] universal awareness of the cosmic struggle between good and evil, and said, "That applies to me; I have sensed the mysterious, fascinating, immense, inviting 'wholly Other' within me."

As we saw above, the probative force of each kind of evidence, and the even greater probative force of their combination (as Newman implied in his "informal inference"[11]), will only get us to the *probability* of God and the transcendent soul, because assent to God entails a movement of the *heart*. If we are *not* open to a supreme transcendent reality, and if we do not want to accept it, we will try to explain away all the above evidence by

- claiming that a universe filled with only caused realities (which are *nothing* before being caused) can *exist* without an uncaused reality, even though this is an evident intrinsic contradiction (Volume II, Appendix 2, Section I);
- claiming that the evidence of near-death experiences can be explained by a *physical* cause within the brain, even though such causes such as hallucination, anoxia, temporal lobe stimulation, and narcotics cannot explain accurate accounts of verifiable data during clinical death and 80 percent of blind people seeing, most for the first time (Volume II, Chapter 5, Section III);
- claiming that it is possible to recognize virtually *every* imperfection in trust, love, goodness, and beauty, without having even a

[7] Rudolf Otto, *The Idea of the Holy: An Inquiry into the Non-Rational Factor in the Idea of the Divine and Its Relation to the Rational* (New York: Oxford University Press, 1958).

[8] John Henry Newman, "Proof of Theism" (unpublished manuscript), in *The Argument from Conscience to the Existence of God*, eds. Adrian Boekraad and Henry Tristram (London: Mill Hill, 1961).

[9] Carl Jung, *The Archetypes and The Collective Unconscious*, in *Collected Words of C. G. Jung*, vol. 9, part 1, trans. R. F. C. Hull (Princeton, N.J.: Princeton University Press, 1981).

[10] J. R. R. Tolkien, *The Lord of the Rings*, 3 vols. (New York: HarperCollins, 1954).

[11] According to Newman, an "informal inference" is derived from multiple antecedently and independently probable sources of data that corroborate and complement one another. This allows for modifications of data in one or more sources, without affecting the probative force of the combined data in their mutual corroboration. See John Henry Newman, *An Essay in Aid of a Grammar of Assent* (Worcester, Mass.: Assumption Press, 2013), pp. 189–215.

tacit awareness of what perfect truth, love, goodness, and beauty would be like—a seeming contradiction (Volume II, Chapter 4, Section I);

- claiming that something can come out of nothing, or that nothing is really gravitational equation (e.g., Stephen Hawking[12]) to escape the high likelihood of temporal limits of the physical universe shown in the Borde-Vilenkin-Guth proof (Volume II, Appendix 1, Section III) and universal entropy (Volume II, Appendix 1, Section IV); and

- claiming that the experience of the numinous, the authority of conscience, and the universal awareness of the cosmic struggle between good and evil are mere figments of the imagination (when all of them are filled with a distinctive subjective presence more powerful and authoritative than ourselves) (Volume II, Chapter 2).

As inadequate and frequently contradictory as these counterpositions can be, they provide a possibility for people to avoid belief if they wish. As noted above, this is by God's own design, for God does not want us to be persuaded by mere evidence of the mind alone; He wants us to be open to Him and accepting of His "way to life". The clues and evidence He leaves us are ways of lending objective credibility to the conviction of our hearts; they are not a replacement for our hearts. With this in mind, keep the above list of objective evidence from experience and reason handy for the day you may need it—when suffering comes.

It is not only imperative to have *objective* evidence for the existence of God in our transcendent souls; we will also want to have objective evidence for the unconditional *love* of God and the revelation of His *way* to eternal life. In Volume III, we discussed why Jesus would be the most likely source of this revelation. The following list outlines the evidence presented in that volume:

1. If you are empirically and scientifically inclined, you may want to review the scientific study of the Shroud of Turin, particularly the four kinds of dating tests that show its origin to be

---

[12] Stephen Hawking, *The Grand Design* (New York: Random House, 2010), p. 8.

THE SPIRIT OF TRUTH WILL GUIDE YOU

around A.D. 50, and the evidence for a transphysical resurrection in the five anomalies of its image formation (Appendix 1).

2. If you are empirically inclined, you may want to investigate the charismatic manifestation of the Holy Spirit today, particularly in healing miracles (Chapter 5, Section II[13]). There are other very well-documented healing miracles associated with Jesus, such as those occurring through Marian apparitions approved by the Catholic Church. Of particular importance are those documented by the Lourdes International Medical Committee.[14]

3. If you are inclined toward historical investigation, particularly the application of historical criteria, you will want to investigate the evidence for the historicity of the Resurrection from N. T. Wright and others (Chapter 4). You may also want to investigate the historical evidence of Jesus' miracles from John P. Meier, Raymond Brown, and others (Chapter 5).

4. If you are philosophically inclined, you may want to investigate the six steps leading from an intelligent Creator to Jesus, "the unconditional love of God with us" (Chapter 2, Section I.A).

5. If you are inclined toward evidence of the *heart* of God, you may want to investigate the evidence for Jesus' revelation of the unconditional love of His Father, and the demonstration of *His* unconditional love in His love of sinners, the poor, and the sick, as well as His complete self-sacrifice on the Cross (Chapters 2 and 3).

As we saw above, this objective evidence can only support the *likelihood* that Jesus is "the unconditional love of God with us", and the *likelihood* that His revelation of His Father's unconditional love is true. Once again, we have to be open to His revelation that love is the highest commandment, and that it entails humility, gentleness,

---

[13] Also, see Keener, *Miracles.*

[14] The International Medical Committee of Lourdes is very selective in the miracles it approves and documents. The selection criteria are so rigorous that of the thousands of miracles that have occurred at Lourdes, it has only definitively approved of sixty-nine (as of 2015). However, those sixty-nine miracles are very well-documented and deserve the readers' scrutiny. See their website at http://en.lourdes-france.org/deepen/cures-and-miracles. Of particular note is the validation of a miraculous healing of tuberculosis by the Nobel Prize winner Alexis Carrel, documented in his own book: Alexis Carrell, *The Voyage to Lourdes* (New York: Harper and Brothers, 1950).

forgiveness, compassion, and self-sacrifice. If we find this revelation to be distasteful or even repulsive in our *hearts*, then all the evidence in the world will not convince us that Jesus is Emmanuel, "the unconditionally loving God with us". Without acceptance of Jesus and His message in our hearts, we will try to "explain it away"— finding some "reason" to negate all the scientific evidence from the Shroud of Turin, the miracles at Lourdes and other contemporary miracles, the historical evidence of Jesus' Resurrection and miracles, and the philosophical evidence for why a creator would be unconditionally loving. However, if we are open to Jesus and His message of unconditional love, the above evidence will probably be sufficiently probative.

As noted above, objective evidence may be sufficient to allay doubts, but it cannot by itself produce an act of trust during times of suffering, because it only influences the *mind*. An act of trust also requires our *heart and will*.

In Chapter 5 we addressed several *emotional* blocks to faith in times of suffering, particularly those arising out of the resentment, fear, skepticism, and cynicism borne naturally out darkness. We recommended that we address these emotional blocks and *choose* consolation so that our hearts would not impede the objective deliberation of our minds. This requires a decision—an act of the *will*—to remove oneself from the power of negative emotion. This cannot be done by simply telling oneself, "I'm going to stop being angry now," or "I won't let myself slip into the depth of despair," and so forth. These uses of negative energy to stop negative energy only serve to feed it. Rather, we must make a decision to let our *minds* have some "space" and "time" in our consciousness. We must make a decision to push our negative emotions aside (*a little*) so that our mental deliberation can have a small place to initiate its appropriate activities. Once we seriously begin to engage the evidence, negative emotions *will* subside.

Rational deliberation can be so engaging that we can overdo *it* too—and therefore, we must be on the lookout for the temptation to achieve "unachievable *perfect* certitude". If we find ourselves caught up in this search, we will have to make a second decision—another act of the will—to move beyond our acts of thinking, conceiving, ruminating, and deliberating. We must allow the probative force of the evidence we *do* have to ground reasonable and responsible belief. At this point, we must decide that God *is* worthy of trust—and stop asking the questions of *whether* He exists, cares, and *can* be trusted. In Chapter 5 (Section IV) we recommended two ways of allowing *God* to help us do this:

1. Entering into the domain of the sacred (through a church, an icon, or religious objects like a Bible or a rosary)
2. Acknowledging God's presence and offering simple prayers such as "Lord, I know you are here and I know that you love me"

The combination of our mental certitude and our awareness of the sacred (i.e., of God's presence) can help us make an act of trust. This act of trust does not have to be extravagant; we need only a decisive declaration: "Okay, Lord, I place my trust in You," or "Okay, Lord, I trust that You are leading me, and I'm going to stop my mental machinations; please lead me." Notice that doing this requires yet another decision—another act of the will. In addition to choosing the cessation of my mental machinations, I must also get about the business of action and life. Once we have decided to trust the Lord, we must *act* on that trust. If we do this, we will not be disappointed. Believe me, God is quite real, and so is the action of the Holy Spirit in our lives. If we give ourselves over to Him in trust, He will act on our behalf *immediately*—though we might not recognize it immediately.

Recall what was said above about our inability to know *how* He will work in our lives. Even though we are aware of His objectives in redeeming suffering—the promotion of our own and others' salvation, the protection of our own and others' freedom, and the alleviation of our own and others' suffering—we cannot hope to know *how* those objectives will be worked out in reality. As noted above, we don't even know what is good for *our* salvation and freedom, let alone that of everyone else we might touch; we don't even know *our* future, let alone the future of others; and so we are completely incapable of understanding the immense complexity of how we fit into the Lord's loving providential plan. Thus, we must *decide* to let God do it His way. This entails refraining from giving Him a plan, a timetable, and of course, an ultimatum, tempting as all of this might be. When we make an act of trust, we also decide that we will *wait* for Him to carry out *His* providential plan.

C. Waiting on the Lord

The theme of waiting for the Lord or "waiting on the Lord" is central to the Psalms[15] and the prophets,[16] as well as to the Gospels and the New Testament Epistles.[17] It is certainly one of the most important spiritual "disciplines", because it will almost inevitably be used when we are involved in serious suffering. It not only requires keeping our expectations in check, but also believing that the Lord *is* working when we cannot perceive it. Therefore, we will want to wait expectantly through the inspiration of the Psalmist:

> I waited patiently for the LORD; he inclined to me and heard my cry. He drew me up from the desolate pit, out of the miry bog, and set my feet upon a rock, making my steps secure. He put a new song in my mouth, a song of praise to our God. Many will see and fear, and put their trust in the LORD. (Ps 40:1–3)

We must distinguish between waiting on the Lord and doing nothing. Waiting on the Lord does not mean passively sitting back and waiting for the Lord to do *everything*. He has created us with free will, intellect, desire, aspiration, energy, conscience, moral judgment, empathy, and love, as well as transcendental and spiritual awareness—to allow us *to choose and act*. God wants us to be involved not only in choosing our values, ideals, dignity, and destiny—that is, to choose among the four levels of happiness and love; He wants us to choose how and when we are going to put those values and ideals into *practice* and action, so that they will become habits, second nature to us. He wants us to choose and act so that we might engage in the process of forming our eternal identity. Therefore, it is incumbent upon us to engage in all the activities mentioned in Chapter 5—being rational; making backup plans; strategizing how to limit the damage; considering who can help us; asking our friends for support, wisdom, and help; and putting our plans into *action*.

[15] See Ps 25:4–5; 27:1–14; 33:20–22; 37:3, 7, 9, 34; 40:1–17; 62:1, 5; 119:48; 123:1–2; 130:5–6.
[16] See Is 1:1–31; 4:1–6; 30:18; 40:31; Amos 1:1–15; Mic 7:7; Hab 2:1–3; Zeph 3:8; Mal 3:11.
[17] See Mt 6:33, 34; 25:1–13; Jn 3:16–17; 5:6; Rom 5:3–4; 8:18; 12:1–7; 2 Cor 1:22; Col 1:11; Jas 5:7–8; 2 Pet 3:9; 1 Jn 4:4.

God works through our *choices* and *actions*. Have you ever noticed that when you are developing a backup plan or a "damage control" strategy *after praying*, that your thoughts become quite lucid, extending far beyond anything you might have originally conceived? Have you noticed that when you put those plans into action, new almost inexplicable opportunities emerge in front of you? We might think that our extended insight is attributable to the brilliance of our subconscious and that our new opportunities are simply coincidence; however, I prefer to think of them realistically as the work of the Holy Spirit, because I have learned that my subconscious mind is not that smart or prescient.

The new insights and opportunities coming from rational reflection *and prayer* may not lead to what we might have wanted or expected, but they will undoubtedly lead to our salvation and the salvation of others, helping us actualize greater empathy, humility, other-centeredness, compassion, virtue, faith, and the service of God's Kingdom.

Though we must refrain from imposing a request plan or timetable on the Lord, we must still be rational and proactive while being attentive to the new insights and opportunities leading to our own and others' salvation. We must then be *patient* while we await the unfolding of His plan. I have never been naturally patient, and so as I wait for the Lord's plan to unfold, I pray some of the Psalms mentioned above. It is not necessary to use the Psalms; a simple spontaneous prayer will suffice, such as, "Lord, help me to be patient; I know that if I am, You will lead me steadily to Your Kingdom."

We have mentioned several spontaneous prayers throughout this section—some to make an act of trust, some to stop our mental machinations, and some to help us be patient as the Lord unfolds His providential plan. One prayer can be substituted for all these prayers: "Thy loving will be done" (which was discussed in detail in Chapter 4, Section X). This is a perfect way of making an act of trust, because it acknowledges that God will optimize love, salvation, and goodness in us and through us—when we place our trust in Him. As I noted in Chapter 4, this prayer can be used many times per day, during times of fear, impatience, anger, temptation, and virtually every other occasion.

The reader may by now be wondering, "How can we patiently wait for the Lord's plan to unfold if God expects us to be thinking, creating, choosing, and acting to contend with our suffering? Isn't this a contradiction?" It could be a contradiction if we did not put these two seemingly opposed pieces together properly. Fortunately, Saint Ignatius Loyola provided rules for the discernment of spirits that would enable a person on Levels Three and Four to make rational choices and perform efficacious actions to alleviate suffering *while* waiting on the Lord and attending to the inspiration and guidance of His Spirit. A five-step process for doing this will be suggested in Section II, but before proceeding there, we might want to pause for a moment and review the four dimensions of the mindset for following the Holy Spirit, because these will be necessary to implement Saint Ignatius Loyola's rules for discernment:

1. God's six objectives for alleviating suffering
2. Humility in view of our inability to understand God's providential plan
3. Trust and objectivity in the face of suspicion and doubts
4. The patience to wait for God's plan to manifest itself

II. Five-Step Process for Following the Holy Spirit in Times of Suffering

The Holy Spirit works within the parameters of our freedom. Therefore, He will not "enslave us to a miracle" by manifesting Himself in a coercive way—for example, by saying, "Bob, I want you to do X, Y, and Z according to the following timetable." Instead, He will use a set of much more subtle tools: consolations, desolations, fascination, energy, and desirability, as well as the words and actions of others and new external opportunities. These tools are designed to assure both guidance and our freedom of choice. Subtle as they may be, they are noticeable, if we are open to the Spirit's guidance. If we choose to pursue the opportunities to which they lead, they will direct us to our salvation and the facilitation of others' salvation.

There is one exception to the "subtlety rule". In certain cases where the Lord is intent on calling a person to an important mission, and He sees that that person's freedom will not be jeopardized, He can manifest Himself in a very *explicit* way. This was certainly the case with Saint Paul. Before his conversion, the Lord gave Paul an explicit revelation of Himself because He intended to call him to be the apostle to the Gentiles. He knew Paul's heart and knew that, if explicitly asked, Paul would *freely* change from a persecutor to an apostle, since his faith was so strong. When He asked Paul the question, "Saul, Saul, why do you persecute me?" (Acts 9:4), He did not tell Paul everything "upfront", but instead gradually revealed His plan, allowing Paul the opportunity to choose his new mission over the course of three years in the desert. When Paul completed his discernment, he freely became the Lord's apostle to the Gentiles. Though such incidents occur throughout the history of salvation, they are an exception to the Lord's general plan—to use subtlety and signs (instead of overt direction) to protect our freedom.

The five-step program suggested below combines elements of Saint Ignatius' rules for the discernment of spirits (given in Volume I, Chapter 8) and the opportunities for the long-term benefits of suffering (given in Chapters 7 and 8 of this volume):

1. Spontaneous prayer, mitigating fear, and choosing consolation
2. Offering our suffering to the Lord as loving self-sacrifice for the good of souls and the Church
3. Opening ourselves to the opportunities of suffering
4. Making an initial discernment
5. Making a second and final discernment leading toward action

The first two steps in the process have been discussed in previous chapters, the third step was partially discussed, and the final two steps are new.

A. First Step: Spontaneous Prayer, Mitigating Fear, and Choosing Consolation

In Chapter 4 we explained ten spontaneous prayers that could be used in times of suffering. These prayers are not only conduits for God's grace, but vehicles for keeping us oriented toward "God's bigger picture" while avoiding theological and spiritual mistakes. When serious suffering comes, I would highly recommend reviewing the entire chapter, to refamiliarize yourself with the many forms of God's grace and the ways to pray for it. As noted earlier, these prayers can be repeated many times per day throughout times of suffering.

In Chapter 5 (Sections II and III), we discussed various methods for mitigating fear and anxiety, including prayer as well as using prudence and reason; developing courage, fortitude, and temperance; connecting with our friends for both emotional support and practical help; controlling our expectations; and avoiding comparisons. Again, a brief review of these practical points will be helpful in following the Holy Spirit to the Lord's bigger picture for our lives and salvation.

In Chapter 5 (Section IV), we discussed the three dimensions of choosing God's consolation and summarized them in this chapter (Section I.B). This is particularly important for opening ourselves to God's affective consolation, and to the guidance and inspiration of the Holy Spirit that frequently comes through it.

B. Second Step: Offering Our Suffering to the Lord for the Strength of the Church and the Salvation of Souls

In the previous chapter, we addressed the efficacy of offering our sufferings as self-sacrifice to the Lord in imitation of Jesus. Jesus showed us through His Passion and death that this is one of the most positive and efficacious opportunities in suffering. If we do not imitate Him in our lives, we let much of suffering's benefit and opportunity go to waste. To obtain this remarkable effect, we need only pray the following: "Lord, I offer You my sufferings of this day for the salvation of souls and the Church throughout the world; I unite my sufferings to those of Your Son, whose perfect sacrifice leads to my salvation." This prayer, or a similar one, can be repeated throughout the day, particularly when pain, loss, or grief are acute.

C. Third Step: Opening Ourselves to the Opportunities of Suffering

When fear and anxiety are managed and we have made our offering to the Lord, we can turn our attention to the opportunities of suffering. The list given at the end of Chapter 7 will prove quite helpful, and so we have provided it here.

If you can't remember what the terms on the chart mean, go back to the corresponding sections in Chapter 7. As you review each of the opportunities, see if anything stands out more than the other opportunities: Does this "stand-out opportunity" intrigue you—that is, are you drawn toward it? Does it seem fascinating or even inviting? If so, it may be a sign from the Holy Spirit to look for this opportunity during your time of suffering.

Be attentive also to "little coincidences" between the words on the list of opportunities and those of your family members and friends, as well as those in books, journals, television programs, or other forms of media. Frequently, the Holy Spirit can inspire your family members and friends to say something that strikes a coincidental chord with words or concepts on the list of opportunities. The Spirit can also lead you with words on the printed page or on a television program. Whatever the case, if this little coincidence occurs multiple times, it may again be a sign from the Holy Spirit about a potential opportunity in your suffering.

The Lord works with subtle increases in tone and volume, subtle coincidences and gentle proddings. For example, after using the breviary for many years, I am *very* familiar with the Psalms in it. Though this has the unfortunate effect of making these roll too easily off of my tongue, it has the reverse effect of making a "subtle increase in tone or volume" stand out. Thus, when I am reading a Psalm, with which I am very familiar, and suddenly a verse or two in it (that I have read a thousand times) "flies off the page", I become aware of where the Spirit is leading me. Generally, I stay with that passage a bit longer and bear it in mind throughout the day, because it helps me to spot potential opportunities. This leads to an important point: looking for opportunities.

If after reviewing the above list of opportunities, one or more stands out as intriguing, and they begin to appear in conversations, books, and other media, it may mean that the Holy Spirit is prompting (or, perhaps better, coaxing) us to look for this opportunity in our lives. The Holy Spirit gives us the "clue" of what to look for, but *we* must be attentive to how that opportunity might be actualized in our lives. This is generally not immediately evident; we must be

OPPORTUNITIES OF SUFFERING

I. Interior Opportunities of Suffering

  1. Prudence: Appropriation of Higher Levels of Purpose and Identity
     * Appropriation—Level Three *contributive* identity (see Volume I, Chapters 3 and 4)
     * Appropriation—Level Four *faith* identity (see Volume I, Chapters 5 through 10)

  2. Other Natural Virtues
     * Rationality (see this volume, Chapters 5 through 6)
     * Fortitude and courage (see this volume, Chapters 5, 6, and 12)
     * Temperance/self-discipline (see this volume, Chapters 5, 6, and 12)

  3. *Agapē*—Other-Centered Love
     * Empathy (see above in this chapter, and Volume I, Chapter 4)
     * Acceptance of love's vulnerability (see above in this chapter)
     * Humility (see above in this chapter and Volume III, Chapter 1)
     * Forgiveness (see above in this chapter and Volume III, Chapters 1 through 3)
     * Compassion (see above in this chapter and Volume III, Chapters 1 through 3)
     * Acceptance of compassion (see above in this chapter and Volume I, Chapter 4)

II. External Opportunities of Suffering

  1. Good for the World
     * Good for the family
     * Good for organization/institution
     * Good for the community
     * Good for culture or society

  2. Building the Kingdom of God
     * Personal evangelization—to family, friends, and colleagues
     * Contributing to a local church or diocese
     * Contributing to the larger Church mission (national or international)
     * Evangelizing within the community (apologetical, catechetical, or moral)
     * Evangelizing the culture (apologetical, catechetical, or moral)

like Archimedes, who opened himself to opportunities and clues that could come by analogy, from life's circumstances.

Recall that Archimedes was given a task by the king of Syracuse to find out whether a crown he had been given was truly made of gold. Archimedes knew the weight of gold per cubic unit of space, but because of the crown's irregularity, he did not know what the volume of the crown was. He couldn't melt it into a Pythagorean sphere or a Pythagorean cube to make the measurement, so he was baffled. Nevertheless, he carried this question around in his mind, and one day as he went to the baths of Syracuse, he noticed how the water rose uniformly (and therefore measurably) in the tub when his irregularly shaped body was submerged in the water. He realized that by knowing the volume of water in a container, he could simply put the crown into it and measure the displacement of the uniformly rising water. Upon seeing the solution, he cried out, "Eureka, I have found it!" and raced down the streets of Syracuse to his home—naked.

Though this happened to Archimedes in a naturalistic way, the Holy Spirit can also use the same "technique" to provide us with analogical clues from inspiration, the words of others, new opportunities, and so forth. When we obtain a clue from the Holy Spirit about a particular opportunity that stands off the page, we need to keep it in the back of our minds, like Archimedes. At some point a datum, like the rising water in the bathtub, will likely manifest itself. We may not recognize it immediately like Archimedes, but maybe after a day or two. How does this happen? When the datum manifests itself, we may not notice it consciously, but if we are searching for it, we could notice it *unconsciously*. If that datum matters enough to us, it will work its way to our conscious minds, and when it does, we have *insight*. All we need do now is make a discernment, and if that discernment goes well, put it into *practice*, which are our next two steps.

Before proceeding to the "practice and discernment" process in the fourth and fifth steps, the distinction between *interior* and *external* opportunities of suffering, return to the chart on the opportunities of suffering given earlier in this section. Notice that the *interior* opportunities of suffering (e.g., growth in empathy, humility, forgiveness, compassion, and acceptance of compassion) can be actualized *without* having to select a *particular path*. However, the *external* opportunities of suffering (e.g., contributions to family, friends, community, and culture, as well as personal evangelization and contributions to church and cultural evangelization) *do* require a particular path, a specific way of pursuing the opportunity in our lives. In view of this, with one notable exception the pursuit of *interior* opportunities of suffering does *not* require the discernment process in the fourth and fifth steps: avoiding the problem of the Evil One, appearing "as an angel of light" (2 Cor 11:14), which is explained below in the fifth step (Section II.E). However, the pursuit of *external* opportunities of suffering *does* require the discernment process in the fourth and fifth steps, because it entails a *particular path* of actualization in our lives.

D. Fourth Step: Making an Initial Discernment

As noted above, this section pertains to *external* opportunities of suffering. When we achieve insight into a potential path to actualize an external opportunity of suffering (e.g., to volunteer at a food bank or join the finance committee of a parish), it is best not to act immediately, but to make what might be called an initial discernment. This consists in putting the potential particular opportunity before the Lord, to see if it is His will. The Lord will not respond immediately by saying, "Bob, it is my will," because that could undermine our freedom. Instead, He will generally give us a sense of *peace* as we continue to put it before Him over the course of several days. If *peace persists* and lasts, it is a positive sign from the Holy Spirit that this particular external opportunity is worthy of pursuit.

However, if *discord* and *anxiousness* occur, it could be a sign that the Spirit is moving us away from this particular external opportunity. Generally, if we find a particular opportunity to be attractive, interesting, intriguing, and even desirable in the *abstract* (e.g., making a contribution to the Kingdom of God), but then find ourselves repeatedly feeling discord and anxiety when considering a *particular path* to actualizing that opportunity (e.g., serving on the church finance committee or engaging more deliberately in evangelization among friends and colleagues), it is not a good sign; and if the discord and anxiety persist, we will not want to pursue that particular path to actualizing the opportunity. We will then want to consider other paths to actualizing the same opportunity (e.g., serving on another church committee, or teaching catechism).

There is an important rule in Saint Ignatius' "Rules for the Discernment of Spirits" that is relevant here: "Never make an important decision in time of desolation." Such decisions can lead in precisely the opposite direction from that of the Holy Spirit, because it may well be urged by an evil spirit. Recall from Volume I (Chapter 8) that there are two kinds of desolation: affective desolation and spiritual desolation. Affective desolation refers to my affective or emotional state—that is, *feeling* dark, depressed, empty, arid, desolate, or even despairing. Spiritual desolation refers to the state of my *soul*—that is, moving in a direction of *decreased* faith, hope, and love (explained below). For Saint Ignatius, feelings of darkness, depression, emptiness, and despondency, and a state of soul marked by a decrease in faith, hope, and love, can be signs of the presence or involvement of an evil spirit. Such a spirit will twist an opportunity for the good into a spiritual decline.

If you are in a state of affective desolation (feeling dark, depressed, and empty) or spiritual desolation (declining faith, hope, and love), do *not* proceed any further with a particular path to actualize an external opportunity. These kinds of desolation could indicate a problem with a *particular* path you have chosen—*or* a more fundamental problem such as unresolved fear or anxiety (discussed in Chapter 5), a false notion of God (discussed in Chapter 2), a false notion of God's intention in allowing suffering (discussed in Chapter 3), or a false notion of God's objectives in alleviating suffering (also discussed in Chapter 3). If changing your path to actualizing a particular external opportunity does *not* resolve your desolation, you will want to review the chapters concerned with the aforementioned problems.

Doubts may also accompany states of affective and spiritual desolation. If such doubts increase or become acute, use the objective evidence presented in Volumes II and III (and summarized above) to mitigate them.

If you are still in a state of affective or spiritual desolation after using the above material to alleviate it, you may want to consult a priest, pastor, or spiritual director to determine whether there might be another spiritual problem or a deeper *psychological* problem. In any case, if desolation persists, it is advisable to delay selecting a particular path to actualizing an external opportunity until the desolation is effectively neutralized.

E. Fifth Step: Action and the Second Discernment

If you persistently and repeatedly feel *peace* when considering a *particular path* to actualizing an external opportunity, put it into action— *temporarily and experimentally*. Once again we see the need for fiat, putting an end to the process of thinking, considering, and ruminating, by making an act of the will: "Let it be done!" It is best to pursue a new opportunity with some degree of caution, to make sure that we are listening to the Holy Spirit—and not to some other spirit. Saint Paul teaches us how to do this with remarkable balance:

> Do not quench the Spirit, do not despise prophesying, but test everything; hold fast what is good, abstain from every form of evil. (1 Thess 5:19–22)

Though Saint Paul is speaking about prophecies in this passage, it applies to every guiding action of the Holy Spirit. He counsels that we should have faith in the Spirit's guidance. This is particularly true when we are seeking opportunities (in our suffering) to contribute to others, the common good, and the Kingdom of God. If we "quench the Spirit", if we do not look for the Spirit's guidance, we waste a tremendous spiritual gift that can lead to our well-being and salvation. However, Paul continues, we should not rush to an affirmative judgment, because there are two kinds of spirits, good and evil, and evil spirits will try to deceive us. He counsels us, therefore, to test the spirits, and to hold on to what is good, and reject what is evil.

So how do we implement the advice of Saint Paul? We have to *choose and act upon* a particular path of actualizing an external opportunity that passes the test of our initial discernment (discussed in the fourth step). After pursuing this opportunity for at least *three weeks*, we will want to engage in a *second* discernment beyond the initial discernment in the fourth step. How do we do this? By implementing two important rules given by Saint Ignatius Loyola for the discernment of spirits:

1. Test to see whether a particular decision or action leads to an increase or decrease in faith, hope, and love.
2. Beware of the Evil One, who can appear like "an angel of light" (2 Cor 11:14).

An extended explanation of these two rules was given in Volume I (Chapter 8), but I will review them here because they are of paramount importance for following the Holy Spirit.

We have already encountered the first rule in the fourth step with respect to spiritual desolation—a decline in faith, hope, and love. Recall that this could mean the presence or involvement of an evil spirit in the decision we have made or the external opportunity we have chosen to pursue. Recall also that a decrease in faith refers to a decline in our trust in God, a decrease in hope refers to a tendency toward despair (losing hope in our salvation), and a decrease in love refers to a decrease in the characteristics elucidated by Saint Paul in First Corinthians 13 (patience, kindness, etc.).

Therefore, if after at least three weeks of pursuing a particular external opportunity, we find ourselves feeling a decreased trust in God, decreased hope in our salvation, and a decreased ability to actualize love (as defined in 1 Cor 13), we will then want to seriously question the opportunity we have pursued, because an evil spirit may well be present or involved in our pursuit of that external opportunity. This means that we should at least modify *the way* in which we are pursuing that opportunity. If such modifications do not redress the decrease in faith, hope, and love, then we should abandon the pursuit of that particular way of actualizing opportunity all together. Unfortunately this will mean returning to the third and fourth steps to find another path of external opportunity. It should be mentioned that this does not happen frequently, but when it does, it could exacerbate the "fallout" from suffering, and so it must be wisely and speedily addressed.

There is a second sign that a particular path to a new external opportunity will need to be modified. If our pursuit of that particular path is leading to neglect of our families or work performance, we will want to *taper back* on the amount of time, psychic energy, and physical energy we are devoting to it. Such neglect is manifest when family members begin to complain that we are never around, and we really aren't. Or our manager is beginning to complain that our work performance is sliding, and it really is. We need to take these complaints seriously because our first priority is to our families, and our work performance is integral to the way in which we can take care of our families.

Most of the time, the external opportunity we have chosen to pursue *is not* the problem, but only the *amount of time* we have dedicated to it. Sometimes when we are pursuing a new opportunity inspired by the Holy Spirit, particularly external opportunities that come from suffering, we can become quite enthusiastic—and in that enthusiasm, we begin to set aside some of our very high priorities. The fact that we are inspired and enthusiastic is a very good sign that the Holy Spirit is present, particularly if we are experiencing an increase in trust in God, hope in our salvation, and love. So we certainly do not want to abandon our pursuit of that particular opportunity. Instead, we need to exercise the virtues of *prudence* and *temperance*, and modulate the time, psychic energy, and physical energy we are devoting to it. Later, when the children move out of the house, or our jobs allow it, we can devote more time to this opportunity, and allow it to define our legacy as well as our eternal identity.

We now arrive at the final rule in the discernment process that is embodied in the words of Saint Paul: "Satan disguises himself as an angel of light" (2 Cor 11:14). This rule applies to *both interior* and *external* opportunities of suffering. What does Saint Paul mean here? When we are developing spiritually and contributing to the world and the Kingdom (through our suffering), we are warned that the Evil One will attempt to impede us. Yet this will be difficult to do, because we are in an inspired state of mind. His usual tactic, according to Saint Paul and Saint Ignatius, is to masquerade as "an angel of light", which means that he will try to present us with suggestions that *appear* good (and consistent with our spiritual pursuits), but in *reality* contain *exaggerations* that are designed to discourage us and cause us to withdraw from the opportunities we are pursuing. Dale Ahlquist, summarizing the thought of G. K. Chesterton, gives us a critical insight into this tactic: "Heresy is at best a half-truth, but usually even less than that. A heresy is a fragment of the truth that is exaggerated at the expense of the rest of the truth."[18]

---

[18] Dale Ahlquist, "Lecture 8: Heretics", American Chesterton Society, 2014, http://www.chesterton.org/lecture-8/.

The important word here is "exaggeration". When we are pursuing a new interior or external opportunity, and are inspired by the Holy Spirit, the Evil One will suggest to us that "doing *more* would be *better*" and "doing it *faster*" would be better and "the *harder* it is, the better."

For example, we might be attempting to be more humble (an *interior* opportunity of suffering), and we may have achieved some success in this with the inspiration and help of the Holy Spirit. Since we are experiencing spiritual fervor, enthusiasm, and success, the Evil One will find it difficult to dissuade us from the pursuit of this interior opportunity altogether; so, he tries a different tactic. Instead of saying, "Abandon the pursuit of humility," he suggests, "You could be a lot more humble than you currently are; you have so many layers of pride, arrogance, and inauthenticity, that if you don't 'step up the pace', you'll be in a state of overweening pride forever. You have been successful thus far; you can do it. You can have the humility of Jesus; it's right around the corner—go for it!"

An objective observer who is not in a state of spiritual fervor and enthusiasm might be able to see what is likely to happen here. The victim of the Evil One, appearing as an angel of light, will try to pursue greater depths of humility at a pace far beyond his capability, and eventually, will find himself failing at every turn. Finally, he will grow discouraged and *give up*. At this juncture, an evil spirit suggests that it was *God* who wanted him to become perfectly humble overnight, and therefore that God "wants the impossible; He is never satisfied." At this point the victim is quite close to spiritual desolation, and he will have to take some steps to reverse the destructive momentum on which he is being carried. This can be done quickly by first identifying the presence of an evil spirit, and then modifying his course of action by tapering his pursuit of humility to a realistic pace and level.

The same holds true for *external* opportunities. Let us suppose that our suffering has helped us to transition from Levels One and Two to Levels Three and Four, and as a result we decide to become involved in personal evangelization of friends and colleagues as well as volunteering at church. Again, since we are in a state of spiritual fervor and enthusiasm, an evil spirit has little chance of dissuading us from this opportunity altogether. So he uses the same tactic: "You could do more to awaken your family's faith, and you are practically indolent in evangelizing your colleagues at work. Step up the pace; say more and do more. You could become a small version of Billy Graham; you can do it."

A potential victim of the Evil One, posing as an angel of light, could easily take the bait, and he might find himself pushing hard to get deeper conversion and commitment out of family, friends, and colleagues. After a while, he will likely find himself alienating most of them—with the possible exception of his mother. Instead of trying to help them patiently, humbly, respectfully, and lovingly understand his perspective by using personal examples of how it has helped him (in imitation of Jesus), he pushes it by saying, "You should . . . ," or "You ought to do . . ." Obviously, he is not in a position to be imposing divine admonitions, because he does not know the situation of the people with whom he is speaking, and he has probably not asked *God* what *He* wants for them. Unfortunately, this may not only lead to alienation from family, friends, and colleagues; it may also alienate family, friends, and colleagues from faith in God. Moreover, he pursues his personal crusade at the expense of his family and job, doubling the damage. As people begin to abandon him, he justifies his actions by saying that they are unworthy of God, because if they were worthy, they would have known that *he* holds the key to God's truth, and they would have followed his admonitions assiduously; after all, he is speaking for God. This, of course, is the final straw; he has now made himself the "mouthpiece" of God and is in a state of real spiritual pride (the antithesis of love defined in the Beatitudes and 1 Corinthians 13).

The Evil One now has the upper hand—if the victim's spiritual pride does not destroy him, the discouragement from all the damage he has done certainly will. What can be done? First, the victim must recover Jesus' teaching on the father of the prodigal son, who patiently, humbly, respectfully, and lovingly awaits the return of his son; secondly, he must recover the tactics of Jesus, who called tax collectors and sinners humbly, patiently, respectfully, caringly, and lovingly. In other words, the victim needs to pursue some of the *interior* opportunities of suffering (e.g., empathy, humility, forgiveness, and compassion) along with his pursuit of the external opportunities of suffering (e.g., personal evangelization and volunteering in church). When Jesus' way of evangelizing has been recaptured, the victim will want to adjust his method of personal evangelization to conform to it, and to apologize to those who may have been alienated by his messianic presumptions.

Notice how the Evil One uses exaggeration to move fervent and enthusiastic people to discouragement or spiritual pride—or both. Without adjustments to our interior attitudes and our level of pursuing new opportunities, a victim can find himself in a very dark state of spiritual desolation.

So let's review how the Evil One appears as an angel of light. At first he plays on our enthusiasm and egos to incite us to the above *exaggerations*, but eventually he gets around to suggesting that this is what *God* wants and prefers. Since there is no limit to the "more, faster, harder, and better", he can bring us to the point of exhaustion or spiritual pride—or both. At this point he uses divergent tactics, depending on whether he is trying to move us to discouragement or spiritual pride. If the Evil One is trying to move us to *discouragement*, he suggests that since *God* wants this, we can't possibly please Him—no matter how much we do, how fast we go, and how hard we work. He hopes to change our view of God from the Father of the Prodigal Son to a harsh task master who will never be pleased with anything we do—and then push us into the darkness of discouragement and despair. If he is trying to move us to spiritual pride, he suggests that God wants us to push harder and harder on family, friends, and colleagues, and that we could not possibly be wrong, because we must be doing God's will—after all, we are His "mouthpiece". It is truly a brilliant tactic, and it is particularly effective with those who are new in the spiritual life, because they are experiencing the inspiration of "first fervor" and are not yet acquainted with how an evil spirit can sneakily use their enthusiasm and egos.

So how do we prevent ourselves from being deceived by Satan himself masquerading "as an angel of light"? (2 Cor 11:14). Go back to the first *rule* discussed above in this step; if in the midst of enthusiastically pursuing a new spiritual opportunity you find yourself *decreasing* in trust, hope, and love—if you find yourself discouraged and thinking, "God is a harsh task master who can never be pleased," or thinking, "God has made me His new messiah, and I can do no wrong in promoting His cause even if I am uncaring, disrespectful, arrogant, and impatient"—then you can be reasonably sure that the Evil One has worked his tactic well.

When you discover this, look for the following words, which you may have been thinking while pursuing your new spiritual opportunity: "more, faster, better, and harder". If you become caught up in this deception, first, go back to who God is: the Father of the Prodigal Son. Second, think back to the time when you were still enthusiastic about pursuing your new spiritual opportunity—before the discouragement and the decrease in trust, hope, and love—or the time when you valued the humility, patience, care, and love of Jesus as much as the importance of your new ministry. How much were you doing at that point? How fast were you doing it? How hard was it? How hard were you trying? How important were humility and care?

After detecting this, go back to *that level* of pursuit—*no more*. Don't let the Evil One use your enthusiasm or ego to talk you back into the increase—"more must be better, and harder is a proof of my faith". If you get into that mentality, you will reexperience discouragement and spiritual pride, resulting in spiritual desolation. Be prudent and temperate; stop at the level where your spiritual life is growing and being fostered. This is the will of the *Holy* Spirit—"more, faster, harder, and better" are usually the tactics of the Evil One.

F. Making the Five-Step Process Habitual

The reader may be thinking that this five-step process is somewhat complicated, but it really isn't—once we get used to it. We can make it a habit after successfully implementing it one or two times. It is definitely worth the effort, because the inspiration and guidance of the Holy Spirit is *invaluable*. Much of the time, the new opportunities we pursue *because of suffering* become the most important features of our lives. If we avail ourselves of the Holy Spirit's power, and are alert to the deceptions of the Evil One, we will find ourselves attaining levels of virtue and "kingdom building" of which we had never dreamt. By doing this, we open ourselves to the Holy Spirit, who will lead us through our suffering to a life far beyond the life we could have made for ourselves.

Now try to begin the task of making the above five-step process habitual. We can become habituated to the first two steps by practicing spontaneous prayers and rational techniques for managing suffering, as well as choosing consolation and offering our suffering to the Lord in our everyday lives. The third, fourth, and fifth steps may present more of a challenge because they are focused more on times of suffering than on our everyday lives. Nevertheless, studying the "lists of opportunities in suffering" (given above in Section II.C) and the techniques for the first and second discernment (given in Section II.D and II.E) can make these more focused steps familiar enough to become habitual. For ease of learning, the steps of the first and second discernment are given in the chart below.

III. Conclusion

We have now completed eight of the nine foundations for suffering well. A brief review of those foundations may prove helpful, because this one (following the Holy Spirit) presumes the others and brings them to completion:

1. Conviction about eternal life and the resurrection (Chapter 1)
2. Who God is and is not—according to Jesus (Chapter 2)
3. God's presence in our suffering (Chapter 3)
4. Spontaneous prayers in times of suffering (Chapter 4)
5. Mitigating fear and choosing consolation (Chapter 5)
6. Awareness of the opportunities of suffering (Chapter 7)
7. Offering up our suffering as self-sacrifice in imitation of Jesus (Chapter 8)
8. Following the inspiration and guidance of the Holy Spirit (Chapter 9)

It is not necessary to have a detailed memory of all these chapters—I doubt that I could do this myself! However, it is important to remember the names of the above eight foundations, so that when suffering strikes we can situate ourselves in the larger context of faith, avoid pitfalls and mistakes that could exacerbate suffering, and avail ourselves of the teaching of Jesus and the inspiration and guidance of the Holy Spirit. This larger context for suffering will not only enable us to mitigate the negative effects of suffering, but also to seize the

RULES FOR THE FIRST AND SECOND DISCERNMENT

Rules for the First Discernment

- Never make an important decision in times of affective or spiritual desolation. If you are in desolation, return to the first step and stay with spontaneous prayers and the management of fear and anxiety. If this does not lead eventually away from desolation, review Chapter 2 on who God is and is not as well as rational evidence for God and Jesus (in Volumes II and III).
- Review the list of opportunities, and note whether something "stands out" as interesting, intriguing, or desirable. Notice if this opportunity is coincident with other things in your life—words of family and friends, books or media, etc. If it is, then move forward.
- Once you have selected an area of opportunity from the list (in abstract), open yourself, like Archimedes, to a particular path to actualize that opportunity. Normally, the opportunity comes to you—someone asking a favor, reading a church bulletin, listening to some friends, etc.
- If a particular path to actualizing an opportunity stands out, place it before the Lord to see whether it is His will. After one or two weeks of doing this, ask yourself, "Do I feel a sense of peace and hopefulness, or a sense of discord and dejection?" If there is a *persistent* sense of peace, then pursue it. If there is persistent discord, abandon it and start the third step again.

Rules for the Second Discernment

- After pursuing a particular path to actualizing an opportunity, ask yourself whether you are experiencing an increase or a decrease in trust in God, hope in your salvation, and love (1 Cor 13). If you experience a decrease, either modify or abandon that particular path. If you experience an increase, continue your pursuit of that opportunity.
- After pursuing the opportunity, ask yourself if it is creating tensions with your family or workplace. If so, and you are still experiencing an increase in trust, hope, and love, then *modify* the amount of time, psychic energy, and physical energy you are committing to the pursuit of that opportunity.
- If after pursuing an opportunity for two or more months, you feel a sense of discouragement followed by a decrease in trust, hope, and love (after you had previously been inspired and enthusiastic—increasing in trust, hope, and love), it probably means that you succumbed to an evil spirit masquerading as a "angel of light" (2 Cor 11:14). If in your enthusiasm you felt that "more, faster, and harder is better", and got carried away with it, try to identify the point in your past when you were still enthusiastic and growing in trust, hope, and love, and then modify your pursuit of that opportunity to the level at *that* time.

opportunities in it to move toward a much richer life—and ultimately the Kingdom of God.

We are now in a position to answer the question of why an all-
loving God would allow suffering, which will conclude our treatment of suffering.

A Vexing Question and a Synopsis
of the Relationship among
Suffering, Freedom, Love, and God

Chapter Ten

Why the All-Loving God Allows Suffering

We know that in everything God works for good with those who love him, who are called according to his purpose.

—Romans 8:28

Introduction

In view of what has been said about the unconditional love of God and His redemption of suffering, one might ask the question, why would God have allowed suffering to occur in the first place? We might rephrase the question as follows: If God intends to redeem every aspect of suffering in His unconditional love, why didn't He simply eliminate the possibility of suffering altogether so that we could avoid pain and He wouldn't have to redeem it?

As we have implied in the foregoing chapters, there are several reasons why God allows suffering to occur in the world, but all of them, according to the Christian view, are linked to the advancement and free appropriation of love. As Saint Paul implies in the above quotation, God allows suffering to make *all* things work for the *good* of those who love Him. Thus, when God allows us to cause suffering to one another, He does so for reasons of advancing the free appropriation of love. Similarly, the reason God creates us in a world with natural laws that *indirectly* cause suffering is to advance the same purpose.[1]

---

[1] Some Judeo-Christian believers may be wondering how this contention squares with the enmity between nature and man caused by the sin of Adam: "[T]o Adam [God] said, 'Because you listened to the voice of your wife, and have eaten of the tree of which I commanded you, "You shall not eat of it," cursed is the ground because of you; in toil you shall eat of it all the days of your life'" (Gen 3:17). This is explained in the context of other Old Testament and New Testament passages in Chapter 3 (Section II.D).

There are three major sources of suffering, none of them directly caused by God:[2]

1. Suffering caused by our decisions about happiness, purpose, and identity
2. Suffering caused by other people or groups (e.g., Joe causes suffering to Mary, or a political regime persecuting minorities)
3. Suffering caused by natural forces (e.g., tsunamis, earthquakes, drought, disease, old age, etc.)

We gave an extended discussion of the first kind of suffering (caused by our decisions about happiness, purpose, and identity) in Volume I (Chapters 1–5, which are concerned with the four levels of happiness) and gave a summary of it in this volume (Chapter 6, Section I). We explained there the unhappiness (the suffering) that can come from dominant Level Two happiness—emptiness and the comparison game. We also explained the unhappiness that can come from rejecting transcendent happiness (Level Four)—cosmic emptiness, loneliness, alienation, and guilt. Throughout these discussions, we showed that this pain could be quite positive because it could lead us, like Saint Augustine, to our highest fulfillment, dignity, and destiny—transcendent happiness with the unconditionally loving God. If we open ourselves to a "little leap of faith", we will find a path out of the pain caused by lower-level identity decisions and discover a new kind of spirit, purpose, and happiness leading toward eternal love and joy. Since this cause of suffering has been thoroughly discussed, we will limit ourselves in this chapter to the other two causes of suffering—suffering caused by others and suffering caused by natural forces.

Recall the fundamental revelation of Jesus, that God does not *passively* look upon our suffering. Like the father of the prodigal son, He

---

[2] In Chapter 3 (Section III.E), we give an explanation of why God does not *directly* cause suffering arising out of the forces of nature. The reason lies in the concept of secondary causation, which stands at the forefront of the scientific revolution. According to this view, which arose out of Christian theology in the Middle Ages, God creates laws of nature at the very creation of the universe itself and then allows these natural causes to give rise to human beings who interact with them. Thus, He does not *directly* cause suffering through nature; He only *indirectly allows* suffering to occur through these natural laws in their independent interaction with man. God can miraculously intervene in this system of secondary natural causes, but He does not do this with great frequency, because it would interfere with freedom of choice (see also Chapter 3, Section III.A).

empathizes with our pain, involves Himself in our interior and exterior lives (if we allow Him to), and guides us through that pain to His Kingdom of unconditional love. God may be compared to unconditionally loving parents who would rather rush out in front of their children to "take the hit" for them instead of allowing them to take the hit themselves. There is only one problem with this strategy for both God and parents—if they don't allow their children to "take the hit" they will never allow them the opportunity to react to and learn from pain, deprivation, and grief—to develop courage, self-discipline, humility, empathy, compassion, contribution to the world, and contribution to the Kingdom. Parents who try to prevent their children from suffering leave them on the shallowest of levels—in a sort of "womb", a sort of "pleasure bubble"—that leaves them at Level One identity, thereby leaving them undeveloped in efficacy, virtue, contribution and love. The result of being an overprotective parent is at best the creation of a perpetually superficial child, and at worst the creation of a noncontributory, unvirtuous, unloving monster—and most parents know it. They know that wisdom requires them to step back, allowing their children to experience the hard world that will develop them in virtue, contribution, and love. The best they can do is help them, guide them, and love them as they move through the difficult stages on life's way.

According to Jesus, God intimately understands us in our suffering, and He intends to redeem all suffering in His providence for all eternity.[3] Indeed, God the Father sent His only-begotten Son into the world to suffer with us and for us, so that He could be a companion with us in our suffering and bring us to our eternal salvation. God *allows* suffering to occur in the world (for the reasons mentioned below), but His intention is to transform it into love. If He does not do this now, He could do it later in this world, and if He does not do that, He will do it in the eternal world to come. The key idea to remember is that God has an eternal perspective and that He will transform all suffering in this world into love for all eternity—if we let Him.

Thus, there can be only one kind of suffering that is *completely* tragic—the suffering occurring in the self-exclusion from God and

---

[3] See the passages from Jesus in the Gospels promising God's complete redemption of suffering discussed in the Introduction to this book (Section II): Mt 5:4; 11:28; Jn 5:24; 8:12; 16:20. See also the same promise interpreted by Saint Paul (in Chapter 1, Sections IV–VI): Rom 5:3–5; 8:17–18, 26–28; Phil 3:8–14; 12:7–10; and Col 1:24.

the blessed, the pain arising out of the rejection of love for the sake of egocentricity, domination, and self-worship—that is, the pain of Hell.

Outside of this one possibility, which ironically comes from free choice and preference, tragedy is only temporary and limited. It may exist for a while, but in the hands of God, it will eventually be turned into love, and that love will last for all eternity. Even incredible tragedies, like the death of a child, are not *ultimately and completely* tragic; they are only *partially and temporarily* so, because the temporary loss and grief that parents feel in such circumstances is already compensated in the *life of the child* by God bestowing unconditional love upon him in His heavenly Kingdom. God intimately understands the grief of the loving parents, who miss their beloved, and He will do so for as long as the parents experience it; but God simultaneously bestows unconditional and eternal love and fulfillment on the child whose loss is the cause of that grief.

Therefore, in the Christian view, suffering is complex. It includes the genuine experience of deep grief, loss, and pain, as well as the experience, arising out of faith, of God redeeming that suffering completely and eternally. It also includes an experience of peace and consolation, if we choose it; a myriad of opportunities to grow in faith, love, and service, if we focus on them; and the inspiration, protection, and guidance of the Holy Spirit, if we are attentive to Him.

This complexity of thoughts and emotions can be quite confusing and trying, even for a person of faith, but at the end of the day, that same faith allows us to give the upper hand to the eternity that awaits us, the opportunities available to us, and the inspiration, protection, and guidance of the Holy Spirit, who is present to us. If we do this, we will *never* give up, and love will be victorious over darkness and despair. Thus, Christians are capable of experiencing grief and profound loss as well as hope in unconditional love and hope in eternal reuniting and "peace beyond all understanding" at the same time, until unconditional love can make sense of it all. This can be incredibly difficult, but our faith will lead inevitably to the transformation of suffering into love, and through this to the eternal Kingdom of joy.

In a remarkable passage from the Letter to the Romans, Saint Paul expresses this hope in the redemption of suffering, not only for us, but also for the whole of creation:

I consider that the sufferings of this present time are not worth comparing with the glory that is to be revealed to us. For the creation waits with eager longing for the revealing of the sons of God; for the creation was subjected to futility, not of its own will but by the will of him who subjected it in hope; because the creation itself will be set free from its bondage to decay and obtain the glorious liberty of the children of God. We know that the whole creation has been groaning with labor pains together until now; and not only the creation, but we ourselves, who have the first fruits of the Spirit, groan inwardly as we wait for adoption as children, the redemption of our bodies. For in this hope we were saved. Now hope that is seen is not hope. For who hopes for what he sees? But if we hope for what we do not see, we wait for it with patience. Likewise the Spirit helps us in our weakness; for we do not know how to pray as we ought, but the Spirit himself intercedes for us with sighs too deep for words. And he who searches the hearts of men knows what is the mind of the Spirit, because the Spirit intercedes for the saints according to the will of God. (8:18–27)

I present the above overriding principle because I am concerned that the reader might think that the forthcoming presentation about why God allows suffering is a bit too philosophical, too cold, and too detached from the real emotion and sadness of suffering. I do not intend this at all. I do not want to distract the reader from the pathos intrinsic to suffering or present a detached philosophical view of it. I only want to give a sense of the rationale for why God would allow suffering caused by human agents and an imperfect world. I beg the reader's indulgence to grant me the above overriding principle as I do so.

With this in mind, we may now proceed to the two major extrinsic causes of suffering and why God would allow them to occur:

1. Why God allows us to cause suffering (Section I)
2. Why God allows nature to cause suffering (Section II)

I. Why Does God Allow Us to Cause Suffering?

Why would an unconditionally loving God allow us to cause suffering to one another? Because love requires the *freedom* to be *unloving*, and "unlove" frequently causes suffering. In other words, without the capacity to cause suffering (through choices of unlove), we would not be able to choose love, and if we could not choose love, our love would not originate from within us—it would not be our own. If we do not have the freedom to choose *unloving* behaviors, then our *loving* behaviors are not really chosen; they are merely programmed (like impulses, desires, or instincts). Beings that have no real alternatives are not the true *initiators* of their actions; they are merely responding to stimuli in the *only* way they can. Thus, without the possibility to cause suffering intentionally by choices of unlove, we are reduced to mere robots or programmed machines, falling far short of "beings created in the image and likeness of God" (see Gen 1:26).

This insight may be deepened by examining what would happen if God made us incapable of unloving behaviors. Let us suppose that I did not have the capacity to choose unloving behaviors. It would seem that the world would be a better place. After all, I would not have to worry about acting on a greedy impulse that could cause harm to another person; I would not have to worry about insulting my friend out of a sense of fear or pride; I wouldn't even have to worry about any of the Ten Commandments or the Seven Deadly Sins. I would be *incapable* of lying, stealing, coveting, egocentricity, arrogance, anger, jealousy, contempt, and all of the other attitudes or dispositions that could cause me to do harm to another person.

Yet there is one little problem with this seemingly perfect scenario. If we do not have the choice to do something contrary to love, then we also do not have the choice to do something commensurate with love. The unfortunate part about choice is that we must have both options—to do or not to do, to love or not to love; choice is not choice if we can *only* do one of two possible options. Thus, if we do not have the possibility to cause suffering to others through unloving choices, we do not have the capacity to initiate an act of love—we are mere robots.

Now we can see that the Creator is caught in a fundamental dilemma: either He can create beings without the capacity to do harm (which would mean creating them with a program to perform or emulate prescribed loving behaviors, but without the capacity to initiate love), or He can create beings with the capacity to initiate love (which would mean creating them with the choice to love or *not* to love, allowing them the possibility to do harm). He cannot do both in the same being.

One might think that such a dilemma reveals a limitation to God's power, but in fact it does not. God has the power to create *both* kinds of beings, but He cannot create their opposed qualities in the same being at the same time; He cannot create a contradiction, a being that can and cannot initiate love in the same respect at the same time.

Contradictions arise out of finitude or restrictions. For example, a spatial restriction, like a square, cannot also have the restriction of a circle or a trapezoid in the same respect at the same place and time. Thus, once God creates finitude or restriction, He also creates the possibility of contradictory states, and in so doing He allows one restriction to exclude the possibility of another restriction in the same place and time. By creating finitude, God creates exclusions intrinsic to that finitude, which he cannot overcome; they are built into the nature of *finitude* itself. Hence, when God creates the restrictions of a square, He creates the impossibility of a square-circle of the same area at the same place and time; He creates a condition that He cannot overcome because it is "built" into His creation.

If I am six feet tall, I cannot be six feet one or six feet two at the same time. If I weigh 200 pounds, I cannot weigh 201 or 202 pounds at the same time; and God cannot make this happen—not because He lacks power, but because He creates me with an intrinsic restriction that disallows other incompatible restrictions at the same time. Incidentally, since God has no restrictions, He is compatible with everything. As we saw in Volume II, there can only be one unrestricted reality; therefore, there can only be one purely inclusive reality. All of us are subject to the exclusions caused by our restrictions.

Now let us return to the question of God's dilemma: Should he create a perfectly loving programmed being (incapable of initiating love), or an imperfectly loving being capable of choosing and initiating love (as well as choosing and initiating "unlove")? Since the first condition *excludes* the second condition (and vice versa), God can only choose one of them—because He is limited by the exclusive nature of the conditions He Himself freely created. Evidently, God was not interested in creating a perfectly loving robot, marionette, or stimulus-response machine, and so He chose to create beings capable of choosing and initiating love, beings that could love one another and receive and appreciate love from one another, as well as love Him and receive and appreciate love from Him. God wanted to create beings in His own image and likeness, beings who could be in a freely loving relationship with Him and others throughout eternity.

In order for God to create beings capable of initiating love, He had to give them the capacity for free choice, which requires giving them self-consciousness (to be aware of themselves over against others) and the power of empathy (to connect naturally with others). He also had to create beings that are intelligent, beings capable of analysis, symbolic representation, language, and narrative (as explained in Volume II, Chapter 6). He also had to create them with the power of conscience to feel and understand the distinction between good and evil. Finally, to create beings capable of entering into relationship with Him, He had to create them with transcendental awareness, a tacit awareness of perfect truth, love, goodness, beauty, and home, and above all, the tacit awareness of Him—His personal intersubjective self-consciousness. This is why Karl Rahner insisted:

> God wishes to communicate himself, to pour forth the love which he himself is. This is the first and the last of his real plans and hence of his real world too. Everything else exists so that this one thing might be: the eternal miracle of infinite Love. And so God makes a creature whom he can love: he creates man. He creates him in such a way that he *can* receive this Love which is God himself, and that he can and must at the same time accept it for what it is: the ever astounding wonder, the unexpected, unexacted gift.[4]

Beautiful and loving as God's objective is, it presents an incredible risk, for He has given us immense power in our self-consciousness, intelligence, free will, and transcendental awareness to do tremendous evil. He has given us not only the power for egocentric, narcissistic, domineering, and destructive attitudes and actions, but also the power to "call ourselves God", and even to make ourselves a false god before others. Hence, His creation of self-conscious, intelligent, and transcendental beings can go "both ways"—toward empathy,

[4] Karl Rahner, *Foundations of Christian Faith: An Introduction to the Idea of Christianity*, trans. William V. Dych (New York: Crossroad Publishing, 1982), pp. 123–24; emphasis mine.

conscience, and relationship with Him, or toward egocentricity (away from empathy and love), evil (away from the good), and radical separation from Him. He has to give us both of these options if He wants our love and goodness to originate from within us.

Thus, the precious gift of free will (entailing self-consciousness, intelligence, empathy, conscience, and transcendental awareness) can give rise to Saint Francis of Assisi or Adolf Hitler, to Mother Teresa or Joseph Stalin. God must not only create us with the capacity to use our freedom justly and lovingly; He must also create us with the freedom to use it unjustly and unlovingly. He cannot selectively lobotomize people who are going to misuse their freedom, such as Hitler or Stalin, because doing so would violate their freedom. He really can't make exceptions to this rule and eliminate the freedom of *only* those who will do *considerable* harm. Besides, if He did this, none of us would know who would be next—or where the dividing line is between those who will be lobotomized or struck down by God versus those who won't. God has to maintain the freedom of everyone in order to be certain that everyone is free to choose love and goodness without external compulsion.

When God decided to create restricted yet transcendental human beings—distinct from Him, yet made in His own image—He took a risk, knowing that only some of us, with the help of His redeeming love and grace, would ultimately produce more good than evil, and more love than unlove. Though He intended to forgive even the most grievous of sinners (if they asked Him), He could not prevent the damage that these sins would produce to others, culture, and society. Though He intended to redeem the suffering brought about by human evil, He could not prevent it without destroying the freedom necessary for love. This is why Jesus tells the Parable of Weeds among the Wheat:

> The kingdom of heaven may be compared to a man who sowed good seed in his field; but while men were sleeping, his enemy came and sowed weeds among the wheat, and went away. So when the plants came up and bore grain, then the weeds appeared also. And the servants of the householder came and said to him, "Sir, did you not sow good seed in your field? How then has it weeds?" He said to them, "An enemy has done this." The servants said to him, "Then do you

want us to go and gather them?" But he said, "No; lest in gathering the weeds you root up the wheat along with them. Let both grow together until the harvest." (Mt 13:24–30)

Note that God does not create the *actuality* of suffering in the world, but only the *possibility* of suffering, by creating agents who have the real choice, the real power to act contrary to love. As noted above, God *must* create this possibility; otherwise, He could not create a free agent and therefore could not create a loving being, a beloved with the freedom to love others with self-initiated love. God's purpose in creating "little beloveds who are loving" would be frustrated.

In sum, if God is to create a being *incapable* of unlove, He would also have to create a being *incapable* of love. Thus, if He does not create beings capable of jealousy, egocentricity, or hatred, He cannot create beings that are capable of the opposite. To create a being incapable of jealousy is to create a being incapable of magnanimity; to create a being incapable of egocentricity is to create a being incapable of altruism; and to create a being incapable of hatred is to create a being incapable of forgiveness and compassion. Since God wanted to create beings in His own image and likeness, He had to create them capable of unloving choices and behaviors—with self-consciousness and free will, as well as with creative thought and imagination. Since He wanted to create beings in His own image and likeness, He had to create them with a power for evil, meaning that He had to create the *possibility*, but not the actuality, of evil. The possibility of unlove is the price of creating the possibility of self-initiated love—and God paid the price, not only in creating personal freedom, but also in the redemption He would actualize through the Incarnation, death, and Resurrection of His beloved Son.

II. Why Does God Allow Nature to Cause Suffering?

It is somewhat easier to understand why God would allow suffering to occur through human agents than through nature. After all, it would seem that if God creates the natural order, He could have created it perfectly, so perfectly that there would be no possibility of human suffering.[5] Why couldn't He have created each person in a perfectly self-sufficient way so we would have no need? Need entails weakness, effort, inconvenience, and pain, that is, the possibility of suffering, but it seems that God could have eliminated the possibility of such suffering at the outset by creating completely self-sufficient beings in a world of perfectly abundant resources. So why did God create an imperfect natural order? Why did He create a natural order that would allow for scarcity, a natural order that would give rise to earthquakes, volcanoes, and tsunamis, a natural order that would permit vulnerabilities within the human genome causing blindness, deafness, or muscular degeneration, a natural order that would permit debilitating diseases?

The brief answer lies in the fact that a perfect natural order would leave no room for need, weakness, and vulnerability; yet these kinds of suffering (coming from seeming defects of nature) frequently open the way to many positive human characteristics, perhaps the most important characteristics, such as (1) identity transformation, (2) natural virtues, (3) compassionate love (*agapē*), (4) interdependence and human community, (5) the possibility of contributing to others and the common good, and (6) the possibility of contributing to the Kingdom of God. We discussed each of these characteristics in detail in Chapter 7 of this volume. Recall that these characteristics represent the most noble of human qualities and endeavors that strive for greater justice, love, civility, culture, and civilization; it also gives glimpses of a Perfection that is unconditional and eternal by its very nature. Though need, weakness, and vulnerability cause suffering, and in many cases seem to undermine human potential, they very frequently detach us from what is base and superficial so that we might freely see and move toward what is truly worthy of

---

[5] The question about enmity between us and nature coming through the sin of Adam and Eve is discussed in Chapter 3 (Section II.D). As explained there, the story of Adam and Eve is only a *partial* answer to the question of why God created an imperfect world. It does not explain why God allows just people (like Job) to be affected by such a world—or why the enmity between us and nature was not immediately remediated by the perfect self-sacrificial act of His Son. To answer these questions we must probe more deeply into Christian revelation as well as the opportunities for love and redemption that come through suffering, the purpose of this chapter and Chapter 7.

ourselves, what has truly lasting effects, and what leads us to our true destiny: eternal and unconditional love.

Let us turn again to Saint Paul's insight in Second Corinthians:

> [A] thorn was given me in the flesh, a messenger of Satan, to harass me, to keep me from being too elated. Three times I begged the Lord about this, that it should leave me; but he said to me, "My grace is sufficient for you, for my power is made perfect in weakness." I will all the more gladly boast of my weaknesses, that the power of Christ may rest upon me. For the sake of Christ, then, I am content with weaknesses, insults, hardships, persecutions, and calamities; for when I am weak, then I am strong. (12:7–10)

As noted earlier, Paul probably had a physical malady (possibly progressive blindness), which caused him to experience a loss of natural power and autonomy, yet he felt that his power had increased. The power about which he is speaking here is love, a love that moved him to make significant changes in his life and identity, and that drew him toward greater virtue and compassion toward others, and above all, the loving God manifest in Jesus Christ. His most noble power was truly perfected by weakness, a decline in natural power. His experience provides a significant clue as to why God would create a natural order with intrinsic imperfections that could cause genuine suffering.

So what is the problem with a perfect world? It seems quite attractive, and perhaps the solution to all our problems. As Paul implies, the perfect world might leave us content with pure autonomy and superficiality, which would deprive us of the help we might need to deepen our virtue, relationships, community, compassion, and noble striving for the common good and the Kingdom of God. The "perfect world" might deprive us of the impetus toward *real* perfection— the perfection of love, the perfection that is destined to last forever.

Some readers might object that the above observations may well be true for Christianity—particularly its view of eternal life, the unconditionally loving triune God, God's desire to bring us to perfect joy with Him and one another, and the immensity of our freedom. Yet does suffering caused by nature help people of other religions and cultural perspectives? Do imperfections in our own abilities and characteristics help *non*-Christians; does an imperfect world with earthquakes and disease help people who have no real acquaintance with Jesus? Was the imperfect world and human condition helpful for the pre-Christian world? Did God intend suffering to help everybody? I believe that this was His plan from all eternity—a plan that began with the creation of the first person with self-consciousness, abstract intelligence, free will, empathy, conscience, and transcendental awareness. We will discuss this plan in the next section (II.A)—three *universal* messages and choices intrinsic to an imperfect world—and then discuss (in Section II.B) God's more nuanced plan according to the Christian view.

A. Three Universal Messages Intrinsic to an Imperfect World

There are many universal messages and choices presented by an imperfect world. I will focus on three that are pertinent to the formation of our character, purpose, and identity. As noted in previous chapters, the formation of our identity is the main purpose of life—for it will determine the kind of person we will become and the kind of eternity we will pursue. We form our character, purpose, and identity with and through others—our families, friends, colleagues, communities, societies, and churches—yet at the end of the day the most important factor is our *free choice*. I would contend that God placed *every* person, belonging to every religion and culture, within an imperfect world to present three messages necessary for shaping our identity and eternity:

1. We are not God—or gods (Section II.A.1).
2. We must develop our natural abilities and virtues (Section II.A.2).
3. We are a small part of a larger interdependent community (Section II.A.3).

Irrespective of our religion or culture, the above three messages of an imperfect world will set the *parameters* for choosing our identity and eternity. An imperfect world—with its vulnerabilities, weaknesses, and needs—will also elicit choices on how we will relate to those who are relatively weaker or stronger. Whatever our religion or culture, the choices we make will begin to define who we are and the kind of eternity we would prefer.

Some readers may be thinking that it is presumptuous to assume that people of all times, cultures, and religions define their identities for eternity, because some religions do not subscribe to the Christian view of eternal unconditional love as the true fulfillment of our transcendental nature. Though there are religions that do not subscribe to this view, I would contend that if God is unconditionally loving (as Jesus has proclaimed), then He would want to bestow His eternal unconditional love to all people who pursue Him and act according to their consciences. As noted earlier, the Catholic Church, summarizing Jesus' revelation of the universal salvific intention of His unconditionally loving Father, gave this doctrinal pronouncement:

> Those who, through no fault of their own, do not know the Gospel of Christ or his Church, but who nevertheless seek God with a sincere heart, and, moved by grace, try in their actions to do his will as they know it through the dictates of their conscience—those too may achieve eternal salvation.[6]

If this is God's plan, then He would have to create all people in a world that provides the messages and fundamental options needed to shape our identity and eternity toward justice or injustice, service or exploitation, compassion or heartlessness, respect or disdain, collaboration or domination, and worship or self-idolatry. We will now briefly discuss each of these messages and choices of an imperfect world.

1. We Are Not God (or Gods)

Our imperfect human condition and world makes one thing perfectly clear in virtually every religion—we are not gods. Virtually every religion makes a distinction between us—who are mortal, and comparatively weak—and God (or the gods), who is eternal

---

[6]Dogmatic Constitution on the Church, *Lumen Gentium*, November 21, 1964, no. 16, in *Vatican Council II, Vol. 1: The Conciliar and Postconciliar Documents*, ed. Austin Flannery (Northport, N.Y.: Costello Publishing, 1975), p. 376.

and comparatively stronger. Though the ancient Greeks believed that the gods could mate with human beings (producing a demigod like Hercules), such demigods were still not considered "gods". Their humanity has pulled them from a purely divine status to a partial one—and their human mortality and weakness continues to affect them. Thus, our imperfect world gives us an essential clue to who we are—something less than divine.

Most religions hold that we have a spark of the divine within us, that God (or the gods) has shared *something*, but not all, of His (their) nature with us; and many ancient and contemporary religions believe that we have a transphysical nature that will survive bodily death— *eternally*. In so doing, these religions are careful to teach that we are not *fully* divine.

The comprehensive historian and philosopher of religion Mircea Eliade held that in virtually every religion, the imperfect world, as imperfect, is seen as profane—that is, distinct from the sacred. The Divine (the Sacred) breaks into the world to make it sacred.[7] Recall from Volume II (Chapters 1 and 2), that prior to the nineteenth century, virtually every person (and culture) was religious, and even today 84 percent are religious.[8] Eliade believes that this is attributable to the universal interior experience of the numinous,[9] and a fundamental religious intuition about the Sacred breaking into the profane, imperfect, physical world.[10] The vast majority of people throughout ancient and modern culture combine their experience of the numinous and the sacred with their experience of the imperfect physical world and conclude that we are immersed in a profane environment that needs to be sacralized—that is, made holy by the Divine. They also conclude that the Divine does break through into the profane world, makes it sacred, and creates a sacred time and place to which we can draw close to share in its holiness.[11] In Eliade's words:

[7] Mircea Eliade, *The Sacred and the Profane: The Nature of Religion* (New York: Harcourt Brace Jovanovich, 1987), pp. 11, 45, 58, 64–67.

[8] See Pew Research Center, "The Global Religious Landscape", December 18, 2012, http://www.pewforum.org/2012/12/18/global-religious-landscape-exec.

[9] See Rudolf Otto, *The Idea of the Holy: An Inquiry into the Non-Rational Factor in the Idea of the Divine and Its Relation to the Rational* (New York: Oxford University Press, 1958).

[10] See Eliade, *Sacred and the Profane*, pp. 64–67, 202–6.

[11] Ibid.

Religious man assumes a particular and characteristic mode of existence in the world and, despite the great number of historico-religious forms, this characteristic mode is always recognizable. Whatever the historical context in which he is placed, *homo religiosus* always believes that there is an absolute reality, *the sacred*, which transcends this world but manifests itself in this world, thereby sanctifying it and making it real. He further believes that life has a sacred origin and that human existence realizes all of its potentialities in proportion as it is religious—that is, participates in reality. The gods created man and the world, the culture heroes completed Creation, and the history of all these divine and semidivine works is preserved in the myths. By reactualizing sacred history, by imitating the divine behavior, man puts and keeps himself close to the gods—that is, in the real and significant.[12]

Thus, the imperfect world presents us with a key parameter about who we are and how we relate to the Divine—we are not the Divine, but we need to draw close to the Divine to share in Its holiness and to fulfill our transcendent nature. When combined with the numinous experience and religious intuition, the imperfect world (and the imperfect human condition) instills in us a fundamental *humility*—what Otto calls *"creature consciousness"* before the sacred and mysterious wholly Other.[13] Though we recognize the spark of divinity within us, we also recognize our creatureliness, humility, and our desire and need for the Divine. Our religious practice fascinates and fulfills us in ways that no profane reality can, and it inspires us to seek the wisdom and goodness of the Divine—which is beyond the profane, imperfect, physical world.[14] If for this reason alone, God created us in an imperfect world (and in an imperfect human condition), it would have been completely justifiable—for we learn at once that we are not fully divine (God or gods), that we need the Divine, and that the Divine holds out wisdom and goodness that the profane world cannot give.

Eliade also indicated that some modern people mistakenly believe that scientific and social-scientific method can give a *complete* explanation of human nature and in so doing have unjustifiably excluded

---

[12] Ibid., p. 202.
[13] Otto, *Idea of the Holy*, pp. 6–26.
[14] See Eliade, *Sacred and the Profane*, pp. 64–67, and ibid., pp. 6–16.

from reality everything that these two methods cannot explain. Beyond the intellectual problem of committing a glaring unjustifiable error of omission, this viewpoint has alienated its subscribers from their transcendental and religious nature[15] and in so doing has proscribed the highest fulfillment of their nature from themselves—giving themselves, as it were, an unnecessary transcendental lobotomy. The result of this decline in religion is becoming ever more apparent—increased suicide rates, substance abuse, feelings of meaningless and despondency, impulse aggressivity, and familial tension.[16]

There is another consequence of the eclipsing of our transcendental and religious nature. To the extent that we do not recognize our religious nature, we will also be unable to understand suffering, and the imperfect physical world causing suffering. Religious people do not see the imperfect physical world as "all there is", but rather as a profane place into which the Sacred has entered to call us toward Itself—and in most cases to a reality beyond this life and the physical world. Thus, for religious people, the imperfect physical world is not a stumbling block producing *unintelligible* suffering, but rather a starting point, stepping stone, and testing ground, for life and reality with the Divine—beyond the profane world.

In contrast, modern *nonreligious* people do not view the imperfect physical world within the context of the divine horizon—yet many persist in asking the question, why would an all-loving God create an imperfect world producing suffering? They will likely find this question vexing because they do not subscribe to a transcendent reality. Therefore, the term "God" in their question is merely hypothetical. It is not infused with the prospect of eternal life, perfect truth, love, goodness, and beauty, and an interpersonal relationship with a loving God. Since "God" is merely hypothetical, they are not aware of His intention to bestow on us an eternal life of unconditional goodness or love—and consequently are unaware of the conditions necessary to freely choose this eternal life of love. As a result, they do not see the value of detaching themselves from egocentricity, domination, and

---

[15] Eliade, *Sacred and the Profane*, pp. 202–6.

[16] See, for example, Kanita Dervic et al., "Religious Affiliation and Suicide Attempt", *American Journal of Psychiatry* 161, no. 12 (December 2004), pp. 2303–8, http://ajp.psychiatryonline.org/article.aspx?articleid=177228.

self-idolatry (i.e., the profane) and replacing it with the sacred (i.e., reverence, humility, justice, and love).[17] As such, they see a radical dichotomy between suffering and love, concluding that an unconditionally loving God would not allow suffering—when in fact the opposite is true. Ironically, the only way we can see the opportunities suffering provides to the pursuit of love is to *embark* on a journey toward the Sacred (i.e., God) and to find our ultimate fulfillment through Him.

In my case, faith was an essential step for embarking on the journey toward love, because I would not have discovered the truth, goodness, joy, and fulfillment of love (understood as *agapē*) without the teaching, example, and grace of Jesus. In view of this, I would ask anyone who has not yet embarked on the journey toward love (*agapē*) not to ask the question of why an all-loving God would allow suffering before trying to enter into religious belief. By doing the latter before the former, we will better understand God's intention to bring us to eternal love, which will in turn clarify the meaning of "love" ("*agapē*") and the relationship between suffering, love, and eternal life with the Divine. This will help to answer coherently the question of why an unconditionally loving God would allow suffering.

We may now return to the significance of an imperfect world (and the suffering it produces) in the shaping of our eternal identity and destiny. For both Christian and non-Christian religious believers, the imperfect human condition and world alerts people to the falsity of self-idolatry while encouraging both humility and piety (respect for the sacred mysterious wholly Other). As we shall see below (Section II.A.3), this humility and piety lie not only at the foundation of justice, but also social authority, the law, and civil society—for they encourage adherence to the law and integration within society.

---

[17] According to Friedrich Heiler, the vast majority of world religions have seven beliefs/values in common: (1) the transcendent, the holy, the divine Other is real; (2) the transcendent reality is immanent in human awareness; (3) this transcendent reality is the highest truth, highest good, and highest beauty; (4) this transcendent reality is loving and compassionate and seeks to reveal its love to human beings; (5) the way to God requires prayer, ethical self-discipline, purgation of self-centeredness, asceticism, and redressing of offenses; (6) the way to God also includes service and responsibility to others; and (7) the highest way to eternal bliss in the transcendent reality is through love. See Friedrich Heiler, "The History of Religions as a Preparation for the Cooperation of Religions", in *The History of Religions*, ed. Mircea Eliade and J. Kitagawa (Chicago: Chicago University Press, 1959), pp. 142–53.

Without an imperfect human condition and world, individual egos would likely go unchecked, with each person vying for the highest level of self-deification—an anarchy of Neitzschean superegos, the opposite of a just and ordered community to which we are called by the sacred and mysterious Divine Reality.

The imperfect world is even more significant in the Christian viewpoint, because it reveals who we truly are (called to eternal unconditional love by God), which gives us the opportunity to choose our identity for eternity. Therefore, the imperfections of this world are opportunities to call us out of superficiality, egocentricity, and domination, providing a conduit to humility, empathy, compassion, contribution, and faith (see Chapter 7). Hence, suffering—and the imperfect world producing it—has immense value, for it helps to release us from the bondage of superficiality, egocentricity, injustice, domination, and self-idolatry, and to usher us into an identity and eternity of unconditional love.

Whatever our religion—Christian or non-Christian—the imperfect world, and the suffering coming from it, is an essential help to moving us to our true, good, and loving transcendental nature.

2. The Call to Develop Our Natural Abilities and Virtues

The imperfect human condition and world provides a second essential message to people of all cultures and religion—it tells us that life is not going to be easy, and that we, and the human spirit, will have to rise to the occasion and deal with the challenges confronting us with strength, hard work, resilience, courage, and prudence (the natural virtues). Without an imperfect human condition and world, there would be no challenges and hardships to be overcome—and therefore no need for the human spirit to move itself from passivity to self-possession, self-expression, self-communication, engagement in the world, transformation of the world, and engagement with others for the common good. Without the hardships and challenges of the world around us, we would likely have an indolent spirit content to absorb and enjoy the pleasures of the moment. We would be left in a childlike state without *self-efficacy*—actualizing a mere fraction of our potential, without self-possession, self-expression, self-communication, engagement in the world, etc. This presents us with yet another irony—we need hardship, suffering, and challenge to actualize the full potential of our human spirit. We need a partially "unfriendly" world to be *over against us* so that we will make recourse to *interior* resources to meet these hardships and challenges. Our imperfect condition and world incite us to find *from within ourselves* the spirit and energy to meet, fight, and overcome challenges— to *exert* ourselves and even to put ourselves at risk so that we will not be overcome by them.

Of course we cannot live in a *purely* unfriendly or hostile world, for we would find no joy in life and would ultimately be overcome by hardship. The ideal kind of world for the human spirit to discover and actualize itself is a *partially* unfriendly world, a world that is essentially benevolent and beautiful, but not perfectly so, so that the human spirit can come alive, find its inner resilience in the midst of challenges, and actualize itself in overcoming them. Additionally, the partially unfriendly world need only be *temporary*, because once the human spirit has discovered and actualized its resilience and efficacy, it can continue in this vein without having to interminably rediscover and reactualize it. Once the human spirit has been lifted out of dormancy into the light of self-possession, self-expression, etc., it will not lose these qualities—even throughout eternity.

Why is it that some people seem to have more than their fair share of hardships and challenges and some less? The answer seems to lie in *natural* causes and forces, such as climate conditions, geological conditions, environmental conditions, and genetic conditions, and to some extent *human* causes, such as family conditions, migration patterns, human effects on climate, and human failure to respond to crises (disease, famine, natural disasters, etc.). In God's eternal plan, such inequities in the imperfect world are only temporary conditions of darkness within an infinitely extending perfect light. As will be discussed below (Section II.B.4), those who receive proportionately more challenge and suffering during this life are not necessarily worse off in the progression toward eternal joy than those who have received less. Indeed, most of the time, those who have received proportionately more challenges and suffering have greater opportunities to detach themselves from superficial and destructive purpose and identity, and grow in humility, empathy, and compassion, leading toward eternal unconditional love and joy.

In the Christian view, there is an additional purpose for the imperfect world, particularly the inequities of imperfection within it—namely, the call to loving service. When we see that one person has more than their fair share of burdens, hardships, and challenges, it is incumbent upon us to help alleviate them to the extent that we can, by giving of our time, advice, resources, love, and prayers, or to find other avenues of relief where possible. At the very least, if we cannot substantially alleviate these burdens, we can, like Saint Mother Teresa of Calcutta, provide love and hope to those who are suffering and even dying. Our mode of service should be commensurate with our gifts—teachers might tutor or educate, carpenters might provide shelter, business people might provide organization and resources, people of faith might share it, and so forth (see Chapter 7, Section II). The more we individually and collectively respond in love to "the cry of the poor" (see Ps 34), the more the inequities of the imperfect world can be redressed. For Christians, all such inequities of burdens and challenges will be *ultimately* and *completely* redressed in the Kingdom of God in accordance with Jesus' proclamation, "Blessed are those who mourn, for they shall be comforted" (Mt 5:4).

The imperfect world not only calls us to discover and actualize the above components of our human spirit (self-possession, self-expression, etc.); it also calls forth four essential *natural* virtues in all religions and cultures—diligent work, fortitude, courage, and prudence. It does not take much imagination to see that the virtue of diligence (diligent work) will help to overcome the hardships and challenges of an imperfect world, and that it will foster and enhance the above qualities of the human spirit—self-possession and self-expression, as well as slothfulness and indolence, at least in more basic societies, are almost immediately penalized by the very hardships and challenges diligence would have overcome. Moreover, slothfulness leaves much of the human spirit undiscovered and unactualized—leading to only *partial* self-possession, self-expression, self-communication, engagement in the world, etc. In more advanced societies, additional wealth may often prevent the immediate penalization of slothfulness with hardship, but it cannot alleviate the merely partial discovery and actualization of the human spirit, which lies wasted and fallow.

The imperfect human condition and world also calls forth the virtue of fortitude—that is, "stick-to-it-ness", the inner resolve to keep going and pushing in the midst of obstacles and resistance, the refusal to give up or abandon a worthy or noble pursuit—to resolve to be undaunted by opposing circumstances, forces, and people. We see here again how this virtue enhances and develops the human spirit, giving us the inner resources to overcome persistent, long-term hardships and challenges. Without persistent obstacles and challenges, this virtue would likely not come to the fore (because it would be unnecessary), and so without the imperfect world, our human spirit would only be *partially* discovered and actualized.

The same holds true for courage, the ability to face fear in a detached and rational fashion. As with the other virtues, courage would be unnecessary without fear, and fear would not occur without the possibility of threats to our life, health, well-being, and the life, health, and well-being of our family and friends. Though such threats can come from others, they frequently come from an imperfect world. We have to learn how to resist panic to summon rationality and to act decisively in our own defense—and when we do, we discover and actualize our human spirit in deeper and greater ways. When we display courage and overcome very dangerous and desperate situations, we often look back on it as one of the most significant and self-defining moments in our lives. We see in these situations something about ourselves that shows our most honorable character that would never have emerged without human enemies and an imperfect world. Strange as it may sound, some of our most profound and noble moments are the most traumatic ones.

The imperfect world also calls forth prudence—practical knowhow arising out of training, education, and ingenuity. We have all heard the expression that necessity is the mother of invention, and such necessity frequently arises out of the challenges of an imperfect world. This is true not only for individuals who apply their learning and ingenuity to overcome personal hardships and challenges, but also for groups, communities, and societies who apply collective learning and ingenuity to overcome the problems of disease, food shortages, natural disasters, and every other form of natural challenge. When we look at the history of technology and the incredible progress we have made in agriculture, medicine, engineering (electrical, mechanical, civil, and environmental), running water, electrical transmission, communication, prediction and response to natural disasters, and literally hundreds of other areas of technological progress, we frequently see the imperfect human condition and world as their major impetus. Once again we see that some of the achievements of the collective human spirit come from the hardships, challenges, and even cruelties of an imperfect world.

It must be asked whether it is fair for some people to suffer in order for others to ingeniously, courageously, and undauntingly overcome the causes of that suffering. The answer would be no if there was no life beyond this world. However, if an unconditionally loving God truly exists and is calling us into eternal life with Him, then these inequitable sufferings will not ultimately be unfair—for He intends to transform them into unconditional life, love, and joy, if we "seek God with a sincere heart ... and try in [our] actions to do his will as [we] know it through the dictates of [our] conscience."[18] Moreover, inequities in challenge and suffering can lead more quickly and profoundly to eternal life, love, and joy with God (see below Section II.B.4). Ultimately, such inequitable suffering will simply melt away—as proclaimed in the Book of Revelation:

> [A] great voice from the throne [said], "Behold, the dwelling of God is with men. He will dwell with them, and they shall be his people, and God himself will be with them; he will wipe away every tear from their eyes, and death shall be no more, neither shall there be mourning nor crying nor pain any more, for the former things have passed away." And he who sat upon the throne said, "Behold, I make all things new." (Rev 21:3–5)

There is one major problem with discovering and actualizing the human spirit—and appropriating the natural virtues that enhance it (diligent work, fortitude, courage, and prudence). If we make the enhancement of the *human* spirit, and the *natural* virtues, the sole meaning of our lives and the sole measure of our success, they can undermine and destroy us, the people around us, and even the fabric of society. History is replete with examples of exceedingly hardworking, committed, courageous, and ingenious tyrants—people who have used their discovery and actualization of the human spirit to

---

[18] See *Lumen Gentium*, no. 16.

exploit and dominate others willfully, particularly the less gifted and vulnerable. Unfortunately, the above four natural virtues are not self-regulating—they only help to release interior *strength*, but they do not show us how best to use that strength exteriorly, in our relationships with others and the Divine. Thus, if they are not complemented by other virtues, such as piety, justice, and love (i.e., humility, empathy, and compassion), they can actually encourage extreme egocentricity and even ruthlessness. Little wonder, then, that some of history's most callous persecutions were carried out by individuals who attained the highest levels of the above four virtues—causing them to believe in their intrinsic superiority and "divine status".[19]

The radically incomplete nature of the above four virtues (diligent work, fortitude, courage, and ingenuity) reveal the need to balance them with the other two messages of the imperfect world—"we are not God or gods" (see above Section II.A.1) and "we are a small part of an interdependent community" (see below Section II.A.3). The former message *tempers* the actualized human spirit with the reality that it is immersed within a cosmos that it does not control—a cosmos that can effortlessly crush it. Moreover, the awareness of this more powerful cosmos is accompanied by the numinous experience and religious intuition that suggest there is a creative force of the cosmos that is even more powerful and mysterious—a force that is intelligent and in some ways benevolent, as the order and beauty of nature suggest. For this reason, the Psalmist declares universally that only "[t]he fool says in his heart, 'There is no God'" (Ps 14:1).

This tacit awareness of a powerful, intelligent, creative force—which pervades every culture and the vast majority of individuals—confronts the actualized human spirit and declares the need for humility, respect, and reverence, echoing the refrain that "you are not me, the master of the cosmos, but a mere part of the cosmos created by me."

---

[19] For example, Adolf Hitler was very diligent, hard-working, courageous, persistent, and ingenious, but he lacked any real sense of justice, humility, and love. The natural virtues alone (without justice, humility, and love) gave him the ability to initiate and maintain the world's worst persecutions, and convinced him of his own divine status. See William L. Shirer and Ron Rosenbaum, *The Rise and Fall of the Third Reich: A History of Nazi Germany* (New York: Simon and Schuster, 2011), pp. xxii–xxiv.

One can of course revolt against this interior awareness and declare in an overriding will to power, as Nietzsche did, that "you, God, are dead—and I am supreme." But this generally results in tragedy, for Nietzsche became insane according to his own self-prophecy:

> All superior men who were irresistibly drawn to throw off the yoke of any kind of morality and to frame new laws had, if they were not actually mad, no alternative but to make themselves or pretend to be mad.[20]

Madness frequently besets self-proclaimed "superior men" in their dreams, delusions, and pretentions, because they have falsely claimed themselves to be masters of a reality they cannot control—a truth that comes back to haunt them with the prospect of their delusions being fully exposed.

The actualization of the human spirit must also be tempered by the third message of an imperfect world—that we are parts of an interdependent community. As will be discussed below, this message arises out of the fact that we need one another. No matter how blessed we might be in intelligence, strength, self-actualization, skills, dexterity, beauty, etc., we are not complete—*we* remain *imperfect*. The imperfection of our condition requires us to seek community with others—not simply to obtain sustenance, shelter, and protection, but also to obtain knowledge, wisdom, companionship, and friendship. From the moment we are born, our imperfect human condition and imperfect world necessitate dependence on others who take care of the needs that are beyond us. We are inescapably part of an interdependent network, which never fully disappears—no matter how self-sufficient and independent we try to become.

When we are true to ourselves, and recognize that we are not completely autonomous and independent, we acknowledge that we are beholding to this greater social reality—we *owe* something to it. This gives rise to a sense of being responsible to the larger community. We cannot undermine it and must in some way contribute to it and help it to flourish. As will be seen below, this helps to reinforce our belief

---

[20] Frederick Nietzsche, *Daybreak: Thoughts on the Prejudices of Morality*, Cambridge Texts in the History of Philosophy, ed. Maudemarie Clark and Brian Leiter (Cambridge: Cambridge University Press, 1997), p. 14.

444   RELATIONSHIP AMONG SUFFERING, FREEDOM, LOVE, AND GOD

in the law and social order. This belief, in turn, tempers the actualized human spirit by suggesting that its activities must stay within the confines of the law and the good of the community. Betrayal and destruction of the law and the community for selfish benefit and self-aggrandizement creates a sense of alienation—not only from the community but from the truth of ourselves.

Of course we can always revolt against these interior beliefs, feelings, and truths, and assert our superiority over the law and the community's good. We may even get away with this for a while, but after we have undermined the social network that gave and gives us life, it too will reassert its superiority over *us* by either ostracizing or punishing us. If we get too "big for our britches", we will, as the Chinese proverb says, put ourselves in the position of a nail standing above the rest, which will likely be first to be pounded down. This attitude of complete disregard for the law and the community is quite distinct from the attitude of individuals who fight against *unjust* laws and government. These individuals are not putting themselves above the law and community, but only attempting to correct *unjust* laws for the sake of the community and the law itself.

In sum, the three messages of an imperfect world balance one another within our psyche—the discovery and actualization of the human spirit, culminating in self-possession, self-expression, self-communication, engagement in the world, and transformation of the world, are tempered by our awareness of a divine mystery that we cannot control and an interdependent community to which we are obliged. If we assert ourselves over these greater realities, if we forget the truths of the imperfect world about our partiality and incompleteness, the greater realities will likely reassert themselves *over us*, producing our undoing.

3. We Are a Small Part of an Interdependent Community

As noted above, the imperfect world conveys a third imperative message—that we are not an island, but part of a social reality that precedes us, goes beyond us, and succeeds us. The imperfection and incompleteness of our human condition dictate our dependence on and need for the larger community. As John Donne so eloquently explained:

No man is an island,
Entire of itself,
Every man is a piece of the continent,
A part of the main.
If a clod be washed away by the sea,
Europe is the less.
As well as if a promontory were.
As well as if a manor of thy friend's
Or of thine own were:
Any man's death diminishes me,
Because I am involved in mankind,
And therefore never send to know for whom the bell tolls;
It tolls for thee.[21]

This dependence and need betokens a reciprocal obligation to protect and assist the community that protects and assists us. Most individuals within ancient cultures had a strong sense of this reciprocity, which manifests itself in what anthropologist Mary Douglas calls "high group cultures".[22] In such cultures, individuals tend to subordinate their identity to that of the group, deriving their purpose and place in society from it. This produces a strong sense of loyalty to both the group and authority figures in it.

This allegiance and obligation to the community (the "group") is further enhanced by the first message of an imperfect world—namely, that we are not God or gods, and that we should be humble, respectful, and reverent toward the Sacred and Divine. Why? Inasmuch as the Divine Reality controls the cosmos, and the community is part of that cosmos, most societal groups concluded that the community springs forth from the Divine Reality, and as noted above, the Divine Reality comes to it to make it sacred and to draw it to Itself. The Sacred Reality is thus thought to be not only the wellspring of the community, but also the source of the epics, customs, and laws that animate it.

---

[21] John Donne, "Meditation 17, 'For Whom the Bell Tolls' ", in The Best of John Donne, Classic Poet (Seattle: CreateSpace Independent Publishing Platform, 2012), p. 45.

[22] See Mary Douglas, Natural Symbols: Explorations in Cosmology, 3rd ed. (New York: Routledge, 2003), pp. 57–71.

Recall from above that the vast majority of religions teach that the Sacred Reality has broken into the profane world and has partially sacralized it. The closer people draw to the place of the Sacred Reality's entrance ("the sacred place"), the more they participate in the sacralization brought by It.[23] Furthermore, the sacred time can be reinstated by recounting the sacred myths of the Divine Reality's entrance into the world.[24] Inasmuch as a community or village is proximate to the sacred place and recounts the myths of the sacred time, it too is made sacred—and its leaders and religious figures participate in its sacredness.[25] In this way, the customs, rules, and rituals of the community are endowed with sacredness and deserve the respect—and even reverence—of community members. This reinforces the natural sense of allegiance, obligation, and subordination of individuals to the community felt within "high group" communities or societies.

Customs and rules are of two kinds—those which are specifically religious (such as making sacrifices or ritual washings, i.e., ablutions[26]) and those which are a blend of religious and legal prescriptions/proscriptions (such as defending the community, social place within the community, obedience to chiefs and other leaders within the community, etc.). This means that there are two kinds of divine mandate that individuals are expected to choose (obligate themselves to): ritualistic prescriptions/proscriptions (the obligations of piety) and legal prescriptions/proscriptions (the obligations to the sacred community and its leaders). Every ancient legal code (e.g., the Levitical code of the Bible or the Code of Hamarabi) springs from both kinds of proscriptions/prescriptions.

[23] Eliade, *Sacred and the Profane*, p. 88.

[24] Ibid., p. 95.

[25] Ibid., pp. 88–97.

[26] Recall McKenzie's observations about these religious rituals such as sacrifice—namely, that they occur in virtually *every* culture and community without evidence of mutual borrowing. They seem to be *intrinsic* to all individuals and the various communities they constitute. It is also remarkable how similar the view of sacrifice and ritual ablution are among vastly different and separated cultures. For example, McKenzie asserts that the same fivefold meaning of sacrifice pervades virtually all cultures: "(1) The gift of man to the deity; (2) the homage of the subject to the lord; (3) the expiation of offenses; (4) communion with the deity in the sacrificial banquet; (5) life released from the victim, transmitted to the deity, and conferred upon the worshipers". John L. McKenzie, *Dictionary of the Bible* (New York: Macmillan, 1965), p. 754. This strongly supports Rudolf Otto's universal numinous experience (within individuals) and Mircea Eliade's religious intuition (giving rise to religious community and ritual expression).

Though there is tremendous pressure for individuals to obey these prescriptions and proscriptions, they can also be evaded without being detected. Some community members may avoid doing appropriate sacrifice or ritual ablution, some may deceitfully acquire others' property or animals, still others may pursue another's spouse, etc. As will be seen below (Section II.B), these pietistic-legal obligations require a decision on the part of every community member—"Will they adhere to the rules of piety or not—and will they be law abiding or not?" The decisions that they habitually make will eventually form their identity—the way they seek God in their hearts and try to follow Him through the dictates of their conscience.[27]

4. Conclusion: The Need for an Imperfect Human Condition and World

What do the above observations have to say about God creating an imperfect human condition and world that can cause suffering? As we have noted above, the imperfect world is an essential part of the formation of both pietistic and legal obligations—and without an imperfect world, it is quite doubtful that either set of obligations would have arisen. Pietistic obligations come not only from the numinous experience and sacred intuition within all individuals, but also from the acute awareness that we are not God or gods, which our *imperfections*—and the *imperfections* of the world—plainly reveal. Our and the worlds' imperfections are so manifest that the Sacred Reality must break into it to sacralize it. Without an imperfect human condition and world, we would probably view ourselves as divine without need for sacrifice and ritual to help us commune with the Divine Reality. In combination with the numinous experience and sacred intuition, the imperfect world reveals the need for various religious and legal obligations.

Furthermore, our imperfect human condition and world reveal that we are not self-sufficient, but rather must be part of a larger group that can provide protection, familial support, and efficient division of labor. In order to deal with our own weaknesses and the larger kinds of calamity that may confront us, we must integrate ourselves into community or societal units for mutual protection and

[27] See *Lumen Gentium*, no. 25.

benefit. This places another obligation on us—whether to adhere to the sacred customs, rules, and laws of the community or not.

What's the point? Our reactions and choices to honor or not to honor religious and social obligations will shape who we are—the kind of person we will be—and whether or not we will seek God with a sincere heart and try to follow Him through the dictates of our conscience. The decisions we make will determine the kind of eternity we desire—one that honors God and the larger community or one that dishonors them. These obligations, identity choices, and "eternity choices" are present even in the most ancient of cultures and religions—existing thousands of years before Christ. If the divine plan of the unconditionally loving God is to bring us to an eternal life with Him *through our free choices*, then He will have to create a world in which these choices can be made—and in order to do this, He must create us with an imperfect human nature in an imperfect world. It is not enough to reveal His presence to us (through the numinous experience); He must also provide an impetus to *choose* piety, honor, respect, and reciprocal obligation, or their contraries. If the all-loving God had not subjected us to imperfections in ourselves and in the world, He would have deprived us of most of the profound opportunities to choose and appropriate the character that would define us throughout eternity.

The above analysis reveals why God would create an imperfect world for *all* people of *all* times and cultures—to help us *choose* our identity and eternity with Him. We now turn to the revelation of Jesus that gives us a much richer explanation of the opportunities and benefits of our imperfect human condition and world—and the suffering coming from it.

B. The Opportunities and Benefits of an
Imperfect World according to Jesus

In Volume III of this Quartet, we explained the likelihood that God is unconditionally loving (Chapter 2), and Jesus' confirmation of it—in His preaching, healing ministry, love of the poor and sinners, and the Eucharist, as well as His self-sacrificial Passion, Resurrection, and gift of the Holy Spirit (Chapters 3–7). Jesus provides an incredibly deep and substantial revelation of what self-sacrificial love is—and then confirms by word and action that He and the Father are the perfect manifestation of that love. This revelation of the nature of love and its perfect manifestation in God shines a clear light not only on God's *willingness* to give us eternal life, but also the *kind* of eternal life to which He is calling us (perfect joy through perfect *agapē* with Him and the blessed). This revelation in turn presents us with a much deeper and broader array of suffering's opportunities and benefits. We discussed these opportunities and benefits extensively in Chapters 7 and 8 of this volume, but it might be helpful here to review them in light of our imperfect human condition and world—for they will show in a much more extensive way why an all-loving God would create us in a condition that would inevitably give rise to suffering.

There is one major underlying similarity between the pre-Christian and Christian rationale for an imperfect world—the vulnerability and weakness that opens us to our need for God and others, presenting us with four fundamental options:

- Will we respect God or only ourselves?
- Will we exploit others' needs or assist them in their needs?
- Will we exploit the community or contribute to the community?
- Will we be law abiding, or will we attempt to shirk the law?

Our choices in these matters will indicate the kind of identity we are forming and the eternity we are pursuing. Yet there is so much more to the way suffering can open opportunities and benefits to us if we affirm the teaching of Jesus and recognize the eternal joy and love to which we are being called, particularly what we have called the fourth level of love (see Chapter 6). So what are these additional opportunities and benefits of suffering arising out of Jesus' revelation? In Chapter 7 we elucidated several of them, but we will summarize them under five points in the sections below:

1. An Imperfect World Can Shock Us Out of Superficial Purpose in Life (Section II.B.2).
2. An Imperfect World Can Deepen Our Faith and Transcendent Purpose (Section II.B.3).

3. An Imperfect World Provides the Conditions for Contributing to Others (Section II.B.4).
4. An Imperfect World Provides the Impetus for Deeper Love (Empathy, Humility, and Compassion) (Section II.B.5).
5. An Imperfect World Provides the Condition for Offering Our Sufferings to God in Imitation of Jesus (Section II.B.6).

Before elucidating these additional opportunities and benefits from the teaching of Jesus, we will review three aspects of the Christian view of an imperfect world and suffering (Section II.B.1).

1. Three Aspects of the Christian View of an Imperfect World

In Chapter 3 of this volume, we gave an extensive discussion of Jesus' view of God's involvement in our suffering, and how the Christian Church interpreted it to accommodate the idea of "secondary causation". We might summarize this teaching under three points:

1. The physical world is essentially good, though there are imperfections in it that can give rise to suffering.
2. God does not directly cause suffering to punish the unjust, but allows suffering to occur in the lives of both the just and the unjust.
3. God does not directly cause every instance of suffering in the physical world, but creates a network of secondary causes that can do so without His direct causal act.

With respect to the first point, Jesus accepts the teaching of Genesis that God created the world as essentially *good* (see Gen 1:4, 10, 12, 18, 21, 25, 31). Nevertheless, Jesus implies (and Saint Paul states) that God allows nature to be partially inhospitable to us in order to help us freely move from an inclination toward self-centeredness toward love and faith (see 2 Cor 12:7–10). Though this partial inhospitable condition may sometimes be acute (e.g., earthquakes, floods, diseases, etc.), it is not the general state of nature, which is hospitable to life, particularly human life. When we encounter suffering in the forces of nature, we become inclined to look for higher purpose in life and to seek the help and comfort of God. Both inclinations help to open us to Level Four (transcendent) happiness and purpose in life, and in the Christian vision, to eternal salvation with the unconditionally loving God (see below, II.B.2–4).

With respect to the second point, Jesus supersedes the Old Testament notion that suffering is the punishment of God for sinfulness (Ex 34:6–7; Deut 5:8–10; Lev 26:39), and replaces it with the view that "[H]e makes his sun rise on the evil and on the good, and sends rain on the just and on the unjust" (Mt 5:45). In this passage, Jesus explains this new doctrine as a dimension of God's love of enemies, while other New Testament passages indicate additional reasons for it—suffering helps us to grow in faith (see II.B.2–3), to grow in love (see II.B.4–5), and to offer ourselves for the salvation of souls in imitation of Jesus (see II.B.6). Thus, for Jesus, suffering has a *positive* value in combination with faith to lead us to salvation and enable us to help others toward their salvation. When we bring faith to bear on our suffering, we unleash a powerful momentum for growth in trust, hope, and love (*agapē*), which opens upon our salvation and helps us to encourage others toward their salvation. Recall that God's highest purpose for creating us *in this world* is to enable us to *choose freely* a self-identity and eternity of unconditional love with Him. Every other objective, including the alleviation of our own and other's suffering, is secondary to this. Hence, when we are suffering, we will want to interpret it and utilize it *through our Christian faith*, which will in turn strengthen our trust, hope, and love toward our own and other's salvation.

We now proceed to the third point, the Christian Church's teaching on "secondary causation". At first glance, Jesus' teaching that God *causes* His sun to shine and His rain to fall on both the just and unjust may seem to contradict physical laws and scientific explanation, because it suggests that God is *directly* causing suffering in the world. As noted in Chapter 3 (Section III.E), Saint Thomas Aquinas introduced the formal notion of "secondary causality" to explain and defend natural causation (as previously elucidated by Aristotle), human freedom, and chance occurrences.[28] According to this view, the physical world is endowed with its own intrinsic potentiality and is empowered to evolve according to natural laws. This insight

[28] See *Summa Theologica* I, q. 22, art. 2–4.

enabled later thinkers to develop the idea of scientific explanation and natural physical laws. Contemporary views of natural physical laws (which include the indeterminacy of quantum mechanics) hold that natural laws are not completely deterministic, allowing for random occurrences and human free will.

If we accept this view of physical causes,[29] then God does *not directly* cause the suffering brought by natural physical events, such as earthquakes, floods, diseases, or genetic disorders. Rather, He *allows* natural physical causes to bring about such suffering while achieving their own ends. God could suspend a particular physical cause (a miracle), but will only do this rarely. If miracles were common occurrences, we would never be able to predict our future with any accuracy, making freely chosen actions virtually impossible (see Chapter 3, Section III.E), and so God allows the order of physical causation to be mostly fixed, to enable us to reasonably predict the future and freely accommodate our behavior to it.

In light of this, it would be inaccurate to blame God for causing an earthquake, which arises out of natural physical causes and laws. It would also be inaccurate to fault Him for not performing a miracle to prevent the earthquake (because He cannot suspend natural laws continuously without removing the possibility of reasonable prediction and free choice). So the real question is, why did God create the physical universe with laws and causal structures that would allow earthquakes, diseases, genetic defects, etc? This is precisely the question we are attempting to answer in this chapter. Section II.A gave a response from a *universal* religious perspective, and this section will respond from a Christian viewpoint. In both cases, the intention of God is the same—to use the imperfections of the physical world (and the sufferings coming from it) to help us freely seek Him with a sincere heart (by following the dictates of our conscience), so that He can bring us into the fullness of joy and love with Him forever. The Christian view advances the universal one by showing how we can use our faith in times of suffering to deepen our relationship with God and our appropriation of love

---

[29] "This Christian view holds that secondary causes, such as natural physical laws, are responsible for their own proper ends, but the primary cause must maintain all secondary causes in existence.

WHY THE ALL-LOVING GOD ALLOWS SUFFERING   453

(especially empathy, humility, and compassion), and through this, help others to their salvation.

Viktor Frankl implicitly grasped God's purpose in allowing suffering by pointing to the importance of our *decisions* during *negative circumstances* to form the basis of our character—which in the Christian view becomes, after purification, our *eternal identity*:

> A human being is not one thing among others; things determine each other, but man is ultimately self-determining. What he becomes—within the limits of endowment and environment—he has made out of himself. In the concentration camps, for example, in this living laboratory and on this testing ground, we watched and witnessed some of our comrades behave like swine while others behaved like saints. Man has both potentialities within himself; which one is actualized depends on *decisions* but not on conditions.[30]

2. An Imperfect World Can Shock Us Out of Superficial Purpose in Life

Let us begin with a brief review of the four levels of happiness—which are also four levels of purpose in life. Recall from Chapter 6 that Level One (physical-material happiness) and Level Two (ego-comparative happiness) are like a "default drive" for children and adolescents. Yet we can get stuck in this default drive, as if it were addictive, if we are not *called* out of it. Sometimes that call consists in suffering, particularly, the negative emotions of the comparison game and/or existential emptiness. This occurs when we are not fulfilling our Level Three desires (contribution and love arising out of empathy and conscience) and our Level Four desires (our transcendental desires for perfect truth, love, goodness, beauty, and home—as well as our desire for a relationship with a perfect personal transcendental Being who invites us to this fulfillment). Though the pain of the comparison game and existential emptiness can be quite acute, some may choose to endure it by striving for ever-greater Level One and Two satisfaction—and this is where the imperfect human condition and world come to our rescue.

---

[30] Viktor Frankl, *Man's Search for Meaning: An Introduction to Logotherapy* (New York: Beacon Press, 1984), p. 121; emphasis mine.

In our quest for ever-greater creature comforts and ego satisfaction, we will get older, our abilities will decrease, our health will be more challenged, and we will have to confront our mortality. When these challenges of our imperfect human condition and world combine with the negative emotions of the comparison game and existential emptiness, they virtually compel us, unless we are utterly obstinate, to look for meaning beyond what we have been pursuing for decades. We could, of course, remain obstinate and become resentful and bitter toward God and others—or we could look outward and ask if perhaps our lives would be more meaningful if we gave some of the fruits of our knowledge and success to an imperfect world in desperate need. Mortality and death may also be of considerable assistance to us. We could view them as a terrible and absurd end to life, generating bitterness and anger, or we might ask ourselves a serious question of whether there is life beyond the grave— whether there really is something to the religions we have been ignoring throughout our lives. If we take these questions seriously and we seek answers to them, we will likely find ourselves pursuing Levels Three and Four in ways that will change our purpose in life, self-identity, and our eternal destiny. All of this positive transformation, leading to eternal love and joy, could well be missed were it not for the impetus provided by an imperfect world and an imperfect human condition. Without weakness, old age, health problems, and death, many of us might consign ourselves to the most egocentric and superficial lives—but our imperfect human condition and world can provide invaluable assistance to moving beyond this partial and incomplete life.

At this point, the revelation of Jesus becomes important, for as He repeats throughout His preaching and parables, all are welcome into the Kingdom—no matter when the act of repentance (regret for the past and choice toward a future of faith and love) occurs. Workers who are hired at the end of the day will ultimately be given the same wage as those who were hired in the morning (see Mt 20:1–16). If we allow suffering to call us out of superficiality into a new pervasive, enduring, and deep meaning in life—no matter when we heed the call—it will most likely lead us not only to greater meaning, love, and faith, but also to our true and eternal fulfillment in the unconditionally loving God.

3. An Imperfect World Can Deepen Our Faith and Transcendent Purpose

An imperfect world can lead not only to a *basic* pursuit of Level Four (transcendent) happiness, but also to a deep interior conversion to Christian faith, hope, and love. Recall that God's first priority in helping us through suffering is *our own and others' salvation*. Above, we saw that sickness, weakness, old age, debilitation, loss, and death can be essential for refocusing our purpose in life toward what is transcendent and eternal—and can incite us to turn to the Lord for help. These dimensions of our imperfect world can go much further; they can open us to the search for knowledge of God beyond the domain of science, logic, and reason (which can reasonably affirm a transcendent, intelligent Creator),[31] to the search for God's own self-revelation. When the imperfect world incites us to seek God's help, we become interested in the Helper. At this point, God steps in and inspires us to know Him with ever-greater depth—to move from the domain of His transcendence, intelligence, and creativity (science and logic) to His *heart* (which can only be known through His self-revelation).This may cause us to find theology and spirituality fascinating and important in ways we had never previously conceived. This thirst for knowledge will likely lead to a deeper interest in the love and heart of God, which will require a form of revelation that speaks to these essential characteristics. We will not have to search long to discover that this is the center of Jesus' revelation of His Father and Himself. He not only defines love as empathy, humility, forgiveness, compassion, and self-sacrifice; He shows unequivocally that He and His Father are *unconditional* love.[32]

[31] Recall from Volume II that metaphysics can support reasonable and responsible affirmation of a unique, unrestricted, uncaused reality that is an unrestricted act of thinking and the Creator of everything else (see Volume II, Chapter 3 and Appendix 2). Recall also that contemporary science can support reasonable and responsible affirmation of a transcendent, intelligent Creator from the Borde-Vilenkin-Guth proof, the evidence of entropy, and the exceedingly high improbability of necessary anthropic conditions (see Volume II, Appendix 1). These contentions are supported by the verifiable evidence of near-death experiences from peer-reviewed medical studies (see Volume II, Chapter 5).

[32] Recall from Volume III that Jesus teaches his disciples to use "Abba" to address His Father, that He defines love as the highest commandment, and that He reveals the heart of His Father through the Parable of the Prodigal Son (see Volume III, Chapter 2). Recall also

At this juncture, the imperfect world serves an even greater purpose, for in following Jesus, we become interested in serving others and alleviating *their* suffering. This leads to a desire to make a positive contribution to others, the common good, and the Kingdom of God (see below Section II.B.4), a desire to be more like Jesus in empathy, humility, compassion, and self-sacrifice (see below Section II.B.5), and a desire to offer our sufferings to the Father for the salvation of souls in imitation of Jesus (see below Section II.B.6). Thus, suffering can open us to Level Three purpose in life, which in turn can move us to deeper love and contribution. Though suffering can lead *without faith* to external expressions of love (contributions to family, friends, organizations, community, Church, Kingdom of God, and culture), and to the interior purification of love (empathy, humility, compassion, and self-sacrifice), its effects are greatly enhanced *with* faith, particularly Christian faith.

Why? Because the revelation of Jesus teaches us how to express and purify love (*agapē*), and a relationship with Him opens us to the inspiration and grace of the Holy Spirit, who moves us deeply toward the imitation of His heart and loving actions. This teaching and inspiration inflame our hearts; we want to imitate Jesus, who has loved us, and want to become more like Him in our hearts, words, and actions. Though the sufferings of this world can initiate our move to Level Three (contributive) identity, its effects are compounded tremendously when we move to Level Four (transcendent) identity and embrace Jesus as the revelation of how to live a life of love. Since this section concerns the *Christian* viewpoint on the imperfect world, the following three subsections (II.B.4, II.B.5, and II.B.6) will be concerned with levering the sufferings of this world toward the more enhanced actualization of love, made possible by the teaching and grace of Jesus.

4. An Imperfect World Provides the Conditions for Contributing to Others

The need, weakness, and suffering brought on by our imperfect human condition and world provide the occasion to make a significant

---

that Jesus demonstrates *His* unconditional love in His love for sinners, the poor and suffering, and especially His disciples. More importantly, He shows His *unconditional* love for the world in His self-sacrificial death (see Volume III, Chapter 3).

contribution to those within our purview. If God had created the human condition and the world perfectly, there would be absolutely nothing for us to do—no positivity to offset negativity; no assistance to alleviate poverty, sickness, and suffering; no social contribution to offset deprivation; no faith to offset existential emptiness, loneliness, and alienation; and no hope to offset despair. If God had created us in a perfect world, we could not make sacrifices for something noble or loving, and we could leave no legacy worthy of our existence.

Imagine a life where there is no contribution to make, no sacrifice to offer for the good of others or humanity, no way in which you could positively affect the lives and salvation of others. Such a life would not allow us to *define our identity* by our loving actions (or our egocentric ones), our courageous actions (or our cowardly ones), our self-sacrificial actions (or our refusal to sacrifice), our sharing of faith (or our rejection of it). This scenario would effectively undermine the central purpose of our short mortal life, which has as its end eternal self-definition through the decisions we make in the face of need, vulnerability, weakness, and suffering in ourselves and others.

The reader may again be thinking: "Why would a loving God allow some people to suffer in order to give other people an opportunity to help them?" This is not an accurately phrased question, because the imperfect world will invariably cause *all of us* to suffer—physically, psychologically, and existentially. Just as no one will get out of this life alive, no one will get out of it without suffering. Furthermore, it is not accurate to say that only some of us are called to help people during their time of suffering—*all of us* are called to do this. So the proper way of asking the question is, why would an all-loving God allow *everyone* to suffer so that *everyone* will be called to help and serve one another?

This question is best answered, and perhaps can only be answered, within the context of Jesus' revelation and grace, because they provide three essential elements for actualizing God's purpose for suffering:

1. We are not created for this worldly life alone, but for eternal life in unconditional love with Jesus, who revealed this not only in word, but through His Resurrection.
2. Jesus gives us indispensable gifts to help us in times of suffering—guidance, inspiration, and grace of the Holy Spirit—as well as

the sacraments, community, and Word of God given through the Church.

3. Jesus provides an example and call through His Passion and death to synthesize our suffering and our faith by imitating Him in the pursuit of the highest level of self-sacrifice and love.

When we embrace God's purpose for suffering, along with the gifts provided from Jesus, we can no longer view suffering as ultimately tragic, or ultimately negative. In recognizing that neither this life nor the sufferings in it are ultimate, we infer that this life is only a "staging area" for us to choose and solidify our identity, which will then characterize us throughout eternity. This life, with its sufferings and joys, is but a temporary moment in which to make fundamental choices—to respond to the needs of others or to ignore them, to make a contribution to others or to exploit them, to elevate people's dignity and destiny or to tear them down, to listen to and heal others or to ignore them, to bring hope or despair, etc. Without an imperfect world—without the needs and vulnerabilities that allow us to make a positive difference to the world, and without the possibility of sacrificing ourselves for a noble cause—we would not be able to choose freely who we are and who we will be throughout eternity.

The all-loving God would not allow us to remain in the inertia of indecision and indeterminateness—and so He created us in a condition and world where we would be called to make a contribution, a sacrifice, and a legacy that will define and shape us throughout eternity. If we go on the path of love, even if imperfectly, He will bring us to the fullness of eternal love, for which we were created. In order to fulfill us completely and eternally, God allows us the opportunity to *choose* love through contribution, sacrifice, sympathy, and service; and this requires an imperfect human condition and world—for a brief time. Once again we see the synergistic combination of suffering and faith providing not only the call to contribution and compassion, but also the inspiration and grace to pursue it. The aims of love, which are the aims of God, are ironically fulfilled through the synthesis of negative and positive, deprivation and transcendence, suffering and faith.

Some readers may still be thinking, "Well, that's all very well and good, but why do some people have to suffer proportionately more than others in order to achieve the above result? Couldn't God have created the imperfect world so that it would lead to more equal suffering for all of us?" Though this questioning is understandable, it betrays an unfounded and generally specious assumption—namely, that proportionately more suffering is *bad* for us. There can be no doubt that "proportionately more suffering" initially produces more stress, strain, and pain in our lives, but recall that Jesus' view of "good" and "bad" is not so much concerned with the *initial* stress, strain, and pain of suffering, as with our *salvation* at the end of this life. For Jesus, proportionately more suffering is likely to lead to deeper faith—and deeper faith to deeper love (empathy, humility and compassion), *if* we are open to faith and love. The poor, sick, and grieving may well have more strain, stress, and pain in this life, but if they are open to faith and love, they will likely have an easier and more efficacious path to salvation. Jesus promises this in the Sermon on the Plain:

> Blessed are you poor, for yours is the kingdom of God.
> Blessed are you that hunger now, for you shall be satisfied.
> Blessed are you that weep now, for you shall laugh.
> Blessed are you when men hate you, and when they exclude you and revile you, and cast out your name as evil, on account of the Son of man! Rejoice in that day, and leap for joy, for behold, your reward is great in heaven. (Lk 6:20–23)

Conversely, proportionately less suffering may give rise to less stress, pain, and strain, but this is not necessarily good for our salvation. As Jesus suggests, such benefits of this life may lead *away* from greater faith and love—to egocentricity, arrogance, domination, exploitation, and self-worship. Evidently, this scenario could present greater challenges to choosing an eternal identity grounded in love. Jesus was concerned that "the rich" could easily invest more of themselves in their wealth, status, power, and comparative advantage than in care and compassion for others, the common good, trust in God, and building His Kingdom. This need not happen if the rich are conscientious about faith and love in their lives, but the "default attraction" to Level One and Level Two satisfaction, and the self-importance coming from it, could present a strong distraction, and even a hindrance to the deeper appropriation of faith and love. That is why he says to his disciples:

Truly, I say to you, it will be hard for a rich man to enter the kingdom of heaven. Again I tell you, it is easier for a camel to go through the eye of a needle than for a rich man to enter the kingdom of God. (Mt 19:23–24)

"Rich" (*plousious*) is derived from the root *ploutos* and refers not only to material wealth, but "*abundance*" both literally and metaphorically.[33] Thus, "rich" here can signify abundance of material goods, power, status, popularity, talents, intellectual gifts, rhetorical gifts, beauty, athletic prowess, and other possessions and characteristics— that is, those who have proportionately *less* suffering.

At first glance this passage seems to suggest that those who have "comparatively less suffering" (an abundance of possessions, abilities, power, and status) have almost no chance of entering the Kingdom of God. However, this conclusion is mitigated by two important considerations. First, this figure of speech (a camel passing through the eye of a needle) is a colorful *exaggerated* image used to capture the attention and imagination of Jesus' listeners. Such exaggerated metaphors are quite common in Semitic culture, and Jesus' audience would have been aware of the intent of His exaggeration. Second, Jesus' audience knew that every image must be set within the context of the *whole* passage. The end of this passage is critically important for its interpretation: "With men this is impossible, but with God all things are possible" (Mt 19:26).

So in the above context, what does the passage mean? In brief, hope is not lost for those who have proportionately more gifts and proportionately less suffering in their lives. They must be saved in the same way as everyone else: through the grace and mercy of the unconditionally loving God. If they turn to God in faith for His mercy, and try to remain faithful, they will be saved. However, it will be harder for the rich to do this than it will be for the poor (those who have proportionately more suffering) because the rich can easily become attached to, distracted by, and reliant upon the abundance they have in this world. Oftentimes, suffering comes into the lives of the fortunate, and this shocks them out of their attachment to and reliance upon Level One and Level Two "riches", which helps them to focus on God, salvation, contribution, and love.

[33] James Strong, *The New Strong's Exhaustive Concordance of the Bible* (New York: Thomas Nelson, 2003), no. 4145, "plousious", http://lexiconcordance.com/greek/4145.html.

Thus, for Jesus, those who have proportionately more suffering in this life may well be more fortunate than those who have proportionately less suffering—for those who suffer will have far fewer impediments to Level Three (contributive) and Level Four (transcendent) purpose in life. We may conclude from this that the combination of suffering and faith provides a powerful and almost irresistible impetus toward deeper levels of love and eternal salvation.

As noted in previous chapters, I am very thankful for my progressive blindness, which some view as "proportionately more suffering than the average person". Though this disability has given rise to more *initial* stress, strain, and pain than might occur in the lives of those with normal eyesight, I, like Saint Paul (with his "thorn in the flesh"), count myself very fortunate to have it, because it has lessened my focus on self-aggrandizement and helped me to focus on empathy, humility, care, compassion, trust in God, and building the Kingdom. It has even helped me be comfortable with obvious weakness and comparative disadvantage, which I used to disdain and fear. The effects of this disability are so powerful and positive that they really have changed my identity and purpose in life, which has opened me to the Lord's invitation to His Kingdom of Love. I am absolutely certain that when I get to the Kingdom of Heaven, I will look back on my life and say, "Whew! Thank you so very, very much, Lord, for my progressive blindness. It was what I really needed to help me out of intransigent self-aggrandizement and comparative advantage into a life commensurate with the love that leads to true joy—the humble and compassionate love of Your Son. I am sorry I fought You so many times, and I am thankful You did not listen to my folly, but allowed Your wisdom to prevail so that I would choose You, Your love, and the love of neighbors, instead of the darkness of self-obsession. I can see how hard it would have been to choose life without progressive blindness. It was the perfect cross for me. Thank You for the suffering."

5. An Imperfect World Provides the Impetus for Deeper Love (Empathy, Humility, and Compassion)

Some people are naturally empathetic—they see the vulnerability and needs of others and respond to it without hesitation, even from the time they were children (like Saint Teresa of Calcutta—see

Chapter 6, Section IV.D). However, I suspect that most of us are like me—like Saint Francis of Assisi or Saint Ignatius Loyola. We need motivation to draw us out of our concern for self toward concern for others. Though empathy and conscience provide us with a desire to connect with and respect others, concern for ourselves can be so strong that we ignore their call. Breaking through the barrier of self-concern frequently requires an *external* cause, which then will allow empathy and conscience to enter our consciousness. Most of the time, this external cause is provided by our own pain, weakness, and vulnerability—like the cannonball hitting the leg of Saint Ignatius Loyola.

As I explained in Chapter 7, I was resistant to the call of empathy and compassion for others and was happy to live amid good intelligent friends and the security of my family's love and wealth—with an intellectual life embracing philosophy, science, literature, and history. It was a terrific little "bubble", but unfortunately it permitted me to ignore the needs of people around me. The Lord used my intellectual interests to first fascinate me with ultimate causation and meaning through metaphysics, physics, and ultimately philosophical theology. As I began to see His presence at the inception and culmination not only of the universe, but of reality itself, I turned toward Him and to the Church in which I had discovered Him. Though I had found God and was discovering Jesus, I had not yet let Jesus' teaching on love affect me. This was a gradual process, which gained considerable momentum during my novitiate, and then again during my theological studies in Rome.

As noted above, in my final year of study in Rome, when I was most acutely aware of the teaching of Jesus and most desirous to follow His example, I was given another grace—progressive blindness. This challenge shook me out of my pride, self-sufficiency, and impatience, introducing me wholesale to my need for God and others. This showed me love (*agapē*) in a way I had never known before. Even though it was painful to accept humility and compassion, I discovered their beauty, and I wanted to imitate their lead—not only because they were beautiful and helped the people around me, but also because the Lord whom I loved and wanted to imitate possessed them. It has been a long and difficult road of conversion, but my imperfect human condition in the imperfect world has been indispensable for directing me toward the road to humility and compassion.

At this juncture we might pause to consider the reflections of Viktor Frankl about his experience in the darkness of a Nazi concentration camp. Through all the deprivation, pain, hatred, cruelty, and death, he discovered with great clarity the central meaning of life, which he never forgot, making it the foundation of his marriage, psychotherapeutic school, and future service to humanity:

> For the first time in my life I saw the truth as it is set into song by so many poets, proclaimed as the final wisdom by so many thinkers. The truth—that Love is the ultimate and highest goal to which man can aspire. Then I grasped the meaning of the greatest secret that human poetry and human thought and belief have to impart: The salvation of man is through love and in love.[34]

This corresponds with the experience of Saint Paul. Recall from Chapter 7 that he had a physical malady, probably gradual blindness, which he saw as "a thorn in the flesh" and "a messenger of Satan, to harass [him]" (2 Cor 12:7). As he testified, he was grateful for it because it had given him two essential gifts necessary for his salvation and service to the Church: humility (his physical malady prevented him from being proud), and a reliance on Christ's strength rather than his own (see 2 Cor 12:7–10). Saint Paul's experience corresponds to that of many other saints. Recall from Chapter 6 (Section IV) how the synergy between suffering and faith led to other saints' attainment of the highest levels of agapē, particularly Saint Francis of Assisi, Saint Ignatius Loyola, Saint Teresa of Calcutta, and Saint Thérèse of Lisieux.

There are literally millions of unheralded "saints" whose lives demonstrate how the combination of suffering and faith lead to the deepest levels of love—and ultimately to salvation. Recall the poignant case study (given in Chapter 6) from Sheldon Vanauken's *A Severe Mercy*, showing how sickness and death, combined with faith, led to the highest levels of compassion and self-sacrifice. In this autobiographical work, he tells of how he and his wife, Davy, were transformed in love by their experiences at Oxford. When they arrived there, they had already created a "Shining Barrier" around themselves, separating them from others. The barrier signified the *complete* sufficiency of each for the fulfillment of the other. This idyllic "little bubble" was first penetrated when they met C. S. Lewis and discovered that they could not satisfy one another's desire for perfect truth, love, goodness, beauty, and home, and so they would have to make room for a Being that could do this, a God who would come to be with us—Jesus. Though Davy began to take seriously a life of self-sacrifice and service to God and others, Sheldon remained somewhat resentful of the penetration and breakdown of the "Shining Barrier". Davy worried about this and made a complete offering of herself for the sake of Sheldon. When she revealed this to him, he was shocked: "It was the year when Davy, a month or so before its end, offered up her life in holy exchange and utter love for me. Tonight, after Bourges and the 'Requiem Mass,' she told me, to my horror and dread."[35]

Davy soon contracted an irreversible deadly illness brought on by a rare virus, which led to her death, but this seemingly tragic result of the blind forces of an imperfect world had a remarkable effect on him. Instead of withdrawing in bitterness and anger, he rose to the heights to which Davy had called him—and found himself embracing the complete self-sacrificial love she had given to him, and that Jesus had given to the world. Once again, the imperfect world had shown itself to be indispensable in providing the opportunity for greater conversion to love as Jesus revealed it.

A recurrent paradoxical truth in the Christian view of an imperfect world has manifested itself once again—that suffering plus faith leads to Level Four love. This love not only leads to our eternal salvation with Jesus, but allows us to serve His people and Kingdom in remarkable ways. The greater our faith, the more suffering will lead to higher forms of Level Four love. At these levels of love, our service and prayers for others and the Kingdom are highly effective, and we can become like Davy, or even Saint Francis or Saint Ignatius.

6. An Imperfect World Provides the Condition for Offering Our Suffering to God in Imitation of Jesus

There is yet another way in which "suffering plus faith leads to the highest levels of love", the offering of our suffering to God as

---

[35] Sheldon Vanauken, *A Severe Mercy: A Story of Faith, Tragedy, and Triumph* (New York: HarperCollins, 1980), p. 149.

self-sacrificial love in imitation of Jesus. In the previous subsection, we saw how this formula works to transform our hearts and lives *visibly*, leading to the *visible* service of others and the Kingdom. Yet this effect is not limited to the visible domain; it also occurs in the *invisible* domain of our hearts, the lives of others, the Church (the Mystical Body of Christ), and the Kingdom. As we noted in Chapter 8, one of Jesus' main reasons for coming to be with us was to reveal the efficacy of offering our sufferings to His Father as self-sacrificial love. Though He fully revealed and clarified this kind of Level Four love in His words and actions, He showed how His Father revealed it initially to the Psalmists (Psalm 22) and to Isaiah (in the Fourth Suffering Servant Song). Beginning with His Eucharistic words and actions, and concluding with His self-sacrificial death on the Cross, He revealed that this invisible form of Level Four love was just as efficacious, if not more so, than the *visible* forms of Level Four love. Saint Paul had a profound recognition of this and declared:

> Now I rejoice in my sufferings for your sake, and in my flesh I complete what is lacking in Christ's afflictions for the sake of his body, that is, the Church. (Col 1:24)

Throughout history, this *invisible* form of Level Four love has been central in the lives of many saints—from the sufferings of the martyrs, who frequently offered their lives for the salvation of their persecutors as well as the Church, to the lives of Saint Francis of Assisi and Saint Thérèse of Lisieux, who offered their sufferings as self-sacrificial love for the salvation of those in most need of God's mercy.

Evidently, this kind of self-sacrifice is not limited to suffering from the imperfect world (e.g., Davy and Saint Thérèse of Lisieux), but can also come from the unjustified acts of man (e.g., Jesus and the martyrs). In both cases, we will want to follow the example of Jesus. Instead of resenting the seeming unfairness of our misfortune or the injustice of others, we can, like Jesus, offer it to the Father as self-sacrificial love. This does not mean we have to be passive in our response to suffering. If we have a disease, we will want to find doctors and other means of alleviating it. If we are lonely and depressed, we will want to seek out friends who can help us. If we are fearful, we will want to follow the advice in Chapter 5, using prayer, rationality, and natural virtue to mitigate damage and formulate backup plans.

Above all, we will want to follow Jesus in praying the prayer of Gethsemane: "Abba, Father, *all* things are possible to you; remove this chalice from me; yet not what I will, but what you will" (Mk 14:36). If suffering persists after we have taken the above steps, then we must believe, as Jesus did, that there are *invisible* opportunities of "self-sacrificial offering" in that suffering—beyond the visible opportunities (addressed in Chapter 7). The best way to make this prayer is with the same kind of trust Jesus exemplified toward His Father on the Cross as He recited Psalm 22 (see Chapter 8, Section I).

As we make our self-sacrificial offering of suffering for the salvation of the world, it may be helpful to recall the example of Saint Thérèse of Lisieux, who united her sufferings with those of her beloved Jesus, knowing that He would assure its efficacy for the salvation of souls, especially those who are alienated from Him. We will not know the true effects of our loving offering until we understand it through the eyes and heart of God in His Kingdom. Yet if we trust in Him, we will be confident that each little bit of suffering will, like the mustard seed, be turned into an abundance of grace available to those who need it most, grace that will strengthen the Church and, through her, the culture. For those with faith, this may be the most important and efficacious benefit of suffering.

We now turn to another dimension of the Christian view of the efficacy of suffering—extending beyond the personal domain, to that of culture, society, and world history.

III. The Imperfect World, the Human Spirit, and the Lord of Culture and History

We now move from an individual and personal perspective on suffering to a social and cultural one. We saw in Section II.B how God uses an imperfect world, and the challenge and suffering it can cause, to call and lead *individuals* to eternal salvation by providing an impetus toward personal transformation, deepening of faith, contribution to the world and the Kingdom of God, growth in natural virtue and love, and loving self-sacrifice. The value of suffering from others and an imperfect world goes even further. God can also use suffering to advance the *collective* human spirit, particularly in culture and society.

WHY THE ALL-LOVING GOD ALLOWS SUFFERING

As noted in Section II.A above, suffering helps us to recognize our need for others, and to form interdependent associations in communities and societies. These associations, communities, and societies take on a life of their own. They not only support and sustain the individuals within them, but also take on a distinctive identity, ethos, culture, and historical momentum. Some definitions of these terms will clarify how suffering can benefit community, culture, society, and historical momentum.

A society is a cohesive group with a generic common culture and ethos. Larger societies may have multiple subcultures (with distinctive ethoses) within the common culture. The "ethos" of a society is its common virtues, vices, principles, and ideals that give meaning, value, and identity to individuals and the group. The "culture" is imbued with the common habits and patterns of life that enable the ethos to be actualized. Religious, educational, legal, and cultural leaders attempt to convey and influence the ethos and culture of society, and so they create a dynamic momentum, which allows the culture to move forward and prosper or to decay and dissolve. This dynamic momentum is called either a "cultural momentum" or "historical momentum". If a society has an essentially positive and edifying cultural and historical momentum, it will attract other individuals and communities to it, and will grow in numbers, cohesiveness, and strength. If the momentum is negative, it will discourage individuals, leading to the weakening of the society and to its eventual dissolution and absorption into a stronger society. Moral and cultural decadence are just as responsible for the dissolution of societies as outright military conquests, and frequently, the former leads to the latter.

Just as suffering can shock *individuals* out of superficial meaning, values, and identity, it can do the same for communities and societies. Hence, an economic depression, civil strife, or even a war could lead a Level One–Level Two society to embrace Level Three–Level Four meaning, values, and identity, which in turn could cause it to grow in numbers, cohesiveness, and strength.[36] Conversely, an *absence* of collective adversity, challenge, or suffering can undermine the ideals, principles, aspirations, and hopes of a society, letting it slip into a state

---

[36] See the analysis of this phenomenon below, and the example from Tom Brokaw, *The Greatest Generation* (New York: Random House, 2001).

of dogmatic slumber satisfied with Level One pleasure and entertainment, and Level Two ego-gratification.[37] This gradual decay can weaken the culture's cohesiveness, resolve, collective drive for excellence, and vision of the future.

Collective adversity and suffering alone are not sufficient to create positive cultural and historical momentum; positive thought leaders—religious, educational, literary, scientific, and legal—are also required. A "*positive*" thought leader is capable of charismatically communicating Level Three-Four (contributive, empathetic, conscientious, responsible, and transcendent) values and purpose in life. Just as Levels Three and Four values and purpose can rescue *individuals* from existential emptiness and the negative conditions of the comparison game, so also they can do this for communities and societies. Level Three–Level Four meaning and purpose can animate both the heart of individuals and the collective heart of societies (the collective embrace of its cultural ethos).

When collective suffering is accompanied by positive thought leaders, it almost inevitably leads to a positive cultural and historical momentum. If collective suffering is not accompanied by these positive thought leaders, or is accompanied by *negative* thought leaders, then it can accelerate the decline of a society, leading to a breakdown in the family, to negative cultural influences, and to a decline in the individuals reliant on them. As a society's cultural ethos declines (from Levels Three and Four to Levels One and Two), it will lead not only to a breakdown in the family and neighborhoods, but also to a marked increase in existential emptiness, the negative emotions of the comparison game, and individual and collective malaise, which in turn leads to increased substance abuse, depression, unethical behavior, suicide attempts, impulse aggressivity, and antisocial and criminal behavior.[38]

---

[37] For example, "the roaring twenties". See the analysis of this phenomenon below in this section.

[38] This trend has been manifesting itself increasingly in the last twenty years. Two recent Pew Research Center surveys indicate a sharp decline of religion in America, especially among *millennials*. See Pew Research Center, "America's Changing Religious Landscape: Christians Decline Sharply as Share of Population; Unaffiliated and Other Faiths Continue to Grow", May 12, 2015, http://www.pewforum.org/2015/05/12/americas-changing-religious-landscape/; Pew Research Center, "Religion among the Millennials", February 17, 2010, http://www.pewforum.org/2010/02/17/religion-among-the-millennials/.

As noted above, recent research reported by the American Psychiatric Association shows that a decrease in religious affiliation leads to an increase in meaninglessness, despondency,

Culture and family reinforce one another. Thus, a decline in culture will lead to a breakdown in the family, which will in turn lead to a further decline in culture. The family is a special social unit that imparts values, principles, ideals, and self-transcendence in a loving and nurturing context, allowing children to assimilate goodness, transcendence, principles, and love. As the family breaks down, we can expect to find a corresponding breakdown in Level Three and Level Four values, principles, ideals, and worldview, which will manifest itself in the above-mentioned increase in depression, malaise, and substance abuse; unethical, antisocial, criminal behaviors; and suicides, as well as an increase in existential emptiness and the negative emotions of the comparison game.[39]

---

substance abuse, familial tensions, impulse aggressivity, and suicide rates. See Dervic et al., "Religious Affiliation and Suicide Attempt".

The Journal of the American Academy of Child and Adolescent Psychiatry reports increases and earlier onset in both major depressive disorder (MDD) and dysthymic disorder (DD). See Boris Birmaher, "Childhood and Adolescent Depression: A Review of the Past 10 Years. Part I", Journal of the American Academy of Child and Adolescent Psychiatry 35, no. 11 (November 1996): 1427–39, http://www.sciencedirect.com/science/article/pii/S0890856709664030. A report in Scientific American reveals a decline in empathy among young people, which affects the degree to which we adhere to conscience. See Jamil Zaki, "What, Me Care? Young Are Less Empathetic: A Recent Study Finds a Decline in Empathy among Young People in the U.S.", Scientific American, January 1, 2011, http://www.scientificamerican.com/article/what-me-care/?page=1. Darcia Narvaez, a psychologist at the University of Notre Dame, sees the same decline in conscience from the vantage point of the diminishment of moral valuation within culture. See Darcia Narvaez, "The Decline of Children and the Moral Sense: Problems That Used to Be Rare Are Becoming Mainstream", Psychology Today, August 15, 2010, https://www.psychologytoday.com/blog/moral-landscapes/201008/the-decline-children-and-the-moral-sense. As noted in Chapter 6, a recent comprehensive study using the methods of Cornwall and others shows that religious affiliation increases individuals' unwillingness to be unethical. See K. Praveen Parboteeah, Martin Hoegl, John B. Cullen, "Ethics and Religion: An Empirical Test of a Multidimensional Model", Journal of Business Ethics 80, no. 2 (June 1, 2008): 387–98.

The Josephson Institute's "2012 Report Card on the Ethics of American Youth" shows a steady decline in ethics of American youth over the last two decades. See Josephson Institute: Center for Youth Ethics, "The Ethics of American Youth: 2012, Installment 1: Honesty and Integrity", news release, November 20, 2012, https://charactercounts.org/national-report-card/2012-report-card/.

[39] According to a Pew Research Center survey on the decline of marriage, the institution of marriage is experiencing a sharp decline in the United States; the number of couples getting married in their twenties has moved from 68 percent to 26 percent since 1960. This rapid decline has taken place along class lines. Those with a college education have not declined much, but those without a college education have experienced huge declines. Four out of ten respondents believed that marriage was an outdated institution. See Pew Research Center, "The Decline of Marriage and Rise of New Families", November 18, 2010, http://www.pewsocialtrends.org/files/2010/11/pew-social-trends-2010-families.pdf. Inasmuch as

We might conclude from this that societies that lack either collective adversity or positive thought leaders are likely to experience heightened rates of depression, family breakdown, substance abuse, and collective malaise; as a result, the society loses cohesiveness, unity, resilience, idealism, and vision, as well as collective hope and aspirations. Such societies will experience a decline in marriages and birthrates, creating a need for youthfulness and labor from other societies to support and prop up its aging population.[40] The immigration of needed youth and labor will come from societies having "family friendly" cultures and values (Level Three and Level Four), which will mitigate the depression, malaise, substance abuse, and dissolution of the social fabric. Eventually, these new "family friendly" participants in the culture will replace the participants of the old culture who will naturally "die out" both in population and cultural influence.[41]

We may now make one additional conclusion about collective adversity. Societies that face collective adversity *and* who embrace positive thought leaders are likely to *benefit* from that adversity. When this occurs, their participants can be expected to increase in happiness, fulfillment, purpose, resilience, hope, and vision for the future. These societies will likely experience an increase in cohesiveness regarding family strength and the community, as well as an increase in collective ethics, mutual respect, idealism, and hope in the future. Ironically, collective adversity strengthens culture and society, so long as the society is open to Level Three and Level Four values and principles, which will enable them to embrace Level Three and Level

---

marriage provides a solid foundation to convey religious affiliation, ethical beliefs, familial bonding, and children's psychological security and stability, we might expect that the decline in marriage will lead to the above-mentioned problems connected with decreased religious affiliation, ethical beliefs, empathy, and psychological security and stability.

[40] With respect to the United States, see ibid.; with respect to Europe, see Arthur C. Brooks, "An Aging Europe in Decline", *New York Times*, op-ed, January 6, 2015. See also Russell Shorto, "No Babies? Declining Population in Europe", *New York Times*, June 29, 2008.

[41] This is occurring quite rapidly in Europe in direct proportion to the decline in traditional European populations. See the following Berlin Institute's comprehensive study: Steffen Krohnert, Iris Hobmann, and Reiner Klingholz, *Europe's Demographic Future: Growing Regional Imbalances* (Berlin: Berlin Institute for Population and Development, 2008). For the effects of changing demographics in the United States, see Teaching Tolerance, a Project of the Southern Poverty Law Center, "Changing Demographics, Changing Identity, Changing Attitudes", 2016, http://www.tolerance.org/lesson/changing-demographics -changing-identity-changing-attitudes.

Four thought leaders.[42] If the above social-cultural analysis is correct, it shows yet another way in which suffering can be positive, leading to strong positive cultures through collective Level Three and Level Four transformation.

The opportunity to contribute to culture and society entails a commitment to advance the culture's ethos—to transform its ideas, ideals, values, and habits from Level One and Level Two purpose to Level Three and Level Four purpose. This commitment to the culture's ethos may seem more intangible than helping an organization or institution by volunteering or contributing funds. Though this may be the case, transforming a culture's ethos can be far more significant and influential in the long-term than more tangible or concrete contributions.

How do we engage in this kind of contribution or service? It generally takes two forms:

1. Fighting a negative trend toward greater Level One and Level Two dominance within the culture
2. Promoting a positive trend toward Level Three and Level Four values within the culture

Both kinds of contribution require alertness and courage, but not necessarily high degrees of education, wealth, or influence. The one key condition for making these essential contributions is a common-sense grasp of the destructiveness of *purely* Level One and Level Two values and ideals and the necessity of Level Three and Level Four values and ideals within individual lives and the culture. Armed with this central insight, we can seek opportunities to introduce this perspective in conversations with family and friends as well as in discussions with team members and colleagues, in community centers, service organizations, and yes, even churches; and when the opportunity arises,

[42] See Brokaw, *Greatest Generation*. Brokaw holds that America's greatness arose out of the adversity of the Second World War. This occurred because of America's strong religious affiliation and its ethical principles and ideals, which were used by thought leaders across America's entire demographic spectrum. He further showed that the very positive American ethos (which we have called "Level Three and Level Four") prepared the generation of the Great Depression and the Second World War to interpret the nation's collective suffering in terms of righteous self-sacrifice; it was "the right thing to do".

we must summon the courage to actually say something—prudently, humbly, and diplomatically, but to say something.

We do not have to look far to see an accelerating trend toward Level One and Level Two values and ideals within our culture, even amid an increased interest in service, the delivery of social goods, and philanthropy. Unfortunately, these positive trends are rather small subtrends within a much larger general trend toward increased materialism (Level One) and ego-comparative (Level Two) purpose and identity within the culture. This is revealed not only by increased anxiety in young people arising out of existential emptiness, the negative emotions of the comparison game, and a generalized loss of meaning or purpose beyond ego-comparative satisfaction, but also by a marked decrease in empathy, conscience, objective principles, faith, and religious affiliation, producing the attendant problems of increased depression, malaise, substance abuse, familial tensions, and suicide attempts within the culture.[43]

This negative trend is probably attributable to the two above-mentioned causes—a decrease in collective adversity and suffering within our increasingly prosperous and privileged society, as well as a diminishment of spokesmen for Level Three and Level Four values and ideals within the culture. There seems to be fewer charismatic Level Three and Level Four thought leaders, as well as fewer popular spokesmen, among families, friends, community centers, schools, and political organizations—and it is hurting our culture. It is too easy to "let somebody else do it" or to justify remaining silent in the face of opportunity by thinking that we have done enough, that we don't want to impose ourselves on others, or that we don't want to be arrogant by taking the moral high ground. We have to resist the forces of cultural inertia and summon the courage to say something humbly, compassionately, and diplomatically to get people thinking—or to change their minds.

When the temptation arises to say nothing amid cultural decline, we will want to keep in mind the prophetic statement of Edmund

---

[43] See the following studies: Dervic et al., "Religious Affiliation and Suicide Attempt"; Birmaher, "Childhood and Adolescent Depression"; Zaki, "What, Me Care?"; Narvaez, "Decline of Children and the Moral Sense"; Parboteeah, Hoegl, and Cullen, "Ethics and Religion"; and Josephson Institute, "Ethics of American Youth: 2012".

Burke: "The only thing necessary for the triumph of evil is for good men to do nothing."

We may now return to the question with which we started: Did God intend that the imperfect world (and the challenge, adversity, and suffering coming from it) would lead ultimately to not only *individual* salvation, faith, and love, but also to *societal* and *cultural* growth and development? It is difficult to believe that He did not, because so many destructive natural and human disasters have been accompanied by history's most positive thought leaders, which in turn has led to a host of remarkable cultural and societal developments—in everything from justice theory to rights theory, as well as to the development of science and medicine, public health, public education and social welfare, the abolition of slavery, the decline of social classes, development of economic systems, international cooperation, and global social and economic concern. Virtually all of these developments have sprung from collective challenge and ingenious positive thought leaders. Necessity and hardship were the mothers of invention and collective beneficence, which has created not only resolution to societal crises, but remarkable advancements in ethos and culture through those necessities and hardships. Before examining some of these historical developments, it may prove helpful to take account of how collective adversity and suffering have not only helped us to form associations for mutual benefit, but also to develop our "collective spirit"—esprit de corps.

When collective adversity strikes, whether it be from the imperfect world or human strife, it is quite typical for us to "close ranks", tighten our bonds, join a team, and devote ourselves to it so that we can collectively face and resolve this adversity. When we devote ourselves to this collective effort, we strengthen the collective human spirit, standing above our individual human spirit, which creates a unifying force intensifying and magnifying our individual efforts. This "collective spirit" goes beyond a sense of "belonging"; it unifies us, energizes us, enhances our efforts, and ennobles us, making the creative, moral, and sacrificial spirit of individuals into a dynamic whole in which the spirit of each individual courses through our collective veins. When *we* fight the good fight together, we enhance and ennoble one another, which makes our efforts all the more effective and ennobling. Though great sacrifices are made for the group, we are individually and collectively enhanced by one another through them—and these moments are frequently considered to be our most memorable and noble collective peak experiences.

It would have been noble indeed, and a fulfillment of both individual and collective purpose, to have played a small part in the history of irrigation; the synthesis of metals; the building of roads; the discovery of herbs and medicines; the development of elementary technologies and of initial legal codes; the initial formulation of the great ideas (such as justice and love); the discoveries of modern chemistry, modern biology, modern medicine, modern particle and quantum physics, contemporary astronomy and astrophysics; the development of justice theory, inalienable rights theory, political rights theory, economic rights theory; the development of contemporary structures of governments as well as the development of psychology, sociology, literature, history—indeed, all the humanities, arts, and social sciences, to have played a small part in the great engineering and technological feats that have enabled us to meet our resource needs amid a growing population, to be part of the communication and transportation revolutions that have brought our world so much closer together; to have been a small part of the commerce that not only ennobled human work, but also generated the resources necessary to build a better world; and to have been a small part in these monumental creative efforts meeting tremendous collective challenges and needs in the course of human history. Yet, none of these achievements (and the individual and collective purpose and fulfillment coming from them) would have been possible without an imperfect world. If God had done everything for us, life would have been much less interesting (to say the least) and would have been devoid of the great purpose and achievement of the collective human spirit.

Did God create an imperfect world, and the adversity and challenge coming from it, to incite us toward the discovery of our collective human spirit, common cause, the common good, and collective noble endeavor and purpose? It is hard to escape the thought that He did—that He did not want to create us for a merely comfortable existence, but a difficult, challenging, ennobling, and edifying one. It is difficult to resist the thought that He created us to rise to the challenge of collective adversity and to discover our collective human spirit, and through it to make the world progressively more unified, just, humane, compassionate, and technologically developed. For if we sacrifice ourselves for this collective endeavor, it could lead to a deepening of love opening upon eternal salvation with Him.

There is another opportunity arising out of collective adversity and suffering. It frequently enables us to build culture—the animating ethos arising out of our collective heart that impels us not only toward a deeper and broader vision of individuals, but also of groups, communities, societies, and the world. This broader and deeper vision includes a deeper appreciation of individual and collective potential, and therefore a deeper respect for the individual and collective human spirit. Thus, we have the capacity not only to build a legal *system*, but also to infuse it with an *ideal* of justice and rights, a scrupulous concern for accuracy and evidence, and a presumption of innocence and care for the individual. We have the ability not only to make tremendous scientific discoveries, but also to use them for the common good rather than the good of just a privileged class. We have the ability not only to build great structures, but also to use our architecture to reflect the beauty and goodness of the human spirit. We have the capacity not only to do great research, but also to impart the knowledge and wisdom gained by it in a humane and altruistic educational system. And the list goes on.

One of the greatest ironies of human history is the progression of remarkable cultural achievements from the most extreme moments of human suffering and tragedy (whether these be caused by natural calamities like disease, shortages of food, or floods, or out of humanly induced tragedies such as slavery, persecution of groups, world wars, and genocide). The cruelty of Rome, particularly its harsh form of slavery and the bloodthirsty entertainment of the coliseum, led many to seek humane solace in the Christian Church[44]—particularly its care for the sick, the needy, and the uneducated. Eventually this trend led to the humanization of the empire—thanks to Constantine.

---

[44] See, for example, Helmut Koester et al., "The Great Appeal: What Did Christianity Offer Its Believers That Made It Worth Social Estrangement, Hostility from Neighbors, and Possible Persecution?" Frontline, PBS.org, April 1998, pbs.org/wgbh/pages/frontline/shows /religion/why/appeal.html. See also James M. Robinson and Helmut Koester, *Trajectories through Early Christianity* (Philadelphia: Fortress Press, 1971; repr., Eugene, Ore.: Wipf and Stock, 2006).

The horrific abuses of slavery in Africa and the New World eventually led to the abolitionist movement and the proclamation of the universality of individual rights—intimated first by the Dominican friar Bartolomé de las Casas in his defense of the Indians against the slavery of the Spanish and Portuguese conquistadores.[45] This led to the first formalization of the universal and inalienable rights to life, liberty, property, and the pursuit of happiness by the Jesuit priest and philosopher Francisco Suarez in his tractate *De Legibus* in 1612.[46] The famous Calvinist philosopher and father of international law, Hugo Grotius, read the works of Suarez quite carefully and used his doctrine of universal natural rights to develop the basis for international law.[47] John Locke soon discovered the doctrine of inalienable rights in the works of Grotius, and used it as the foundation for his *Second Treatise on Government*.[48] Thomas Jefferson and other European Democrats used these foundations to establish the inalienable rights doctrine standing at the heart of every modern democracy.[49] This doctrine also stands at the foundation of international human rights as enshrined in the United Nations' "Universal Declaration of Human Rights":

[45] See Bartolomé de las Casas, *In Defense of the Indians: The Defense of the Most Reverend Lord, Don Fray Bartolomé de las Casas, of the Order of Preachers, Late Bishop of Chiapa, against the Persecutors and Slanderers of the Peoples of the New World Discovered across the Seas*, trans. and ed. Stafford Poole (DeKalb: Northern Illinois University Press, 1992).

[46] See Francisco Suarez, *De Legibus* (Madrid: Consejo Superior de Investigaciones Cientificas, Instituto Francisco de Vitoria, 1971). See also John Finnis, *Natural Law and Natural Rights* (New York: Oxford University Press, 1980), p. 207.

[47] Grotius' major work on jurisprudence *On the Laws of War and Peace* was written in 1625, thirteen years after the publication of Francisco Suarez' *DeLegibus* (1612). Grotius studied Suarez' work and borrowed extensively from it (as well as from Aquinas' *Summa Theologica*). According to Terence Irwin, Grotius borrowed so much from Suarez and Aquinas that he cannot be considered a pioneer of natural rights. See Terence Irwin, *The Development of Ethics*, vol. 2 (Oxford: Oxford University Press, 2008), pp. 98ff.

[48] See John Locke, *Second Treatise on Government*, ed. C.B. Macpherson (Indianapolis: Hackett Publishing, 1980), p. 48.

[49] "We hold these truths to be self-evident, that all men are created equal, that they are endowed by their Creator with certain unalienable Rights, that among these are Life, Liberty and the pursuit of Happiness—That to secure these rights, Governments are instituted among Men, deriving their just powers from the consent of the governed—That whenever any Form of Government becomes destructive of these ends, it is the Right of the People to alter or to abolish it, and to institute new Government, laying its foundation on such principles and organizing its powers in such form, as to them shall seem most likely to effect their Safety and Happiness." Thomas Jefferson, *Declaration of Independence*, Preamble.

Whereas recognition of the inherent dignity and of the equal and inalienable rights of all members of the human family is the foundation of freedom, justice and peace in the world,

Whereas disregard and contempt for human rights have resulted in barbarous acts which have outraged the conscience of mankind, and the advent of a world in which human beings shall enjoy freedom of speech and belief and freedom from fear and want has been proclaimed as the highest aspiration of the common people,

Whereas it is essential, if man is not to be compelled to have recourse, as a last resort, to rebellion against tyranny and oppression, that human rights should be protected by the rule of law ...[50]

This progression of the formulation and institutionalization of natural rights—as the principal guarantor of just laws and just governments as well as the key protector of individuals within states—would never have happened without social abuse, suffering, and struggle that motivated Level Three and Level Four thought leaders to ignite and animate the collective human spirit to declare "never again".

Though slavery, unjust laws, and social inequities provided a strong impetus for the development of natural rights, they did not lead inevitably to this doctrine. Every one of the above philosophers and statesmen were not only Level Three but also Level Four thought leaders. They were Christians who not only took their faith seriously,[51] but also took from their faith the central idea of the intrinsic dignity of *every* person and the inviolability of their life and freedom to advance themselves and pursue happiness (on all four levels). Standing at the base of their conviction was Jesus' teaching: "[A]s you did it to one of the least of these my brethren, you did it me" (Mt 25:40).

The outbreak of plagues led eventually to advances in medicine and public health, as well as a deeper appreciation of *individual* life and personhood; large-scale economic marginalization and injustice

[50] United Nations, "The Universal Declaration of Human Rights", December 10, 1948, Preamble, www.un.org/en/documents/udhr/index.shtml.

[51] Bartolomé de las Casas was a Dominican friar in the Catholic Church, Francisco Suarez was a Jesuit priest in the Catholic Church, Hugo Grotius was a Calvinist philosopher and a noted Christian apologist, and John Locke was a Calvinist—who modified his Christological position throughout his life—and was a significant philosophical Christian apologist, writing *The Reasonableness of Christianity as Delivered in the Scriptures* (1695).

during the industrial revolution led eventually to economic rights theory (and to systems of economic rights); and world wars led eventually to institutions of world justice and peace. There seems to be something in collective tragedy and suffering that awakens the human spirit—awakens a prophet or a visionary, such as Saint Francis of Assisi, William Wilberforce, Mahatma Gandhi, or Martin Luther King, Jr.—which then awakens a collective movement of the human heart (such as the abolitionist movement). These movements have to endure suffering and hardship in order to accomplish social change, but when they do, it brings us to a greater awareness of what is humane. Through the leadership of Level Three and Level Four prophetic figures like these, the ashes of collective tragedy inspire the advancement of social good and human culture; and more than this, a collective resolve, a determination of the collective human spirit to perpetuate the values, principles, ideals, and ideas that will advance justice, love, intrinsic dignity, and the common good for everyone— and even more than this, to construct political-legal systems to shepherd this collective resolve into the future.

As may now be evident, the greatest collective human achievements in science, law, government, philosophy, politics, and human ideals seem to have at their base not just an imperfect world, not just individual suffering, not just collective suffering, but epic and even monumental collective suffering. Was an imperfect world necessary for these greatest human achievements? It would seem so; otherwise, there would have been no room to grow, no challenges to overcome, no deficits to inspire and animate visionary leaders, no common cause to rally around, no noble endeavor to elicit self-sacrifice, and no ideals to be formulated to perpetuate the goodness of collective human striving. Without an imperfect world and the struggle to overcome human evil, there would be little inspiration and output from the collective human spirit; at best, it would be infantile.

Nothing could be worse for a child's development than overprotective parents who think they are doing the child a favor by doing his homework for him, constructing his project, and thinking for him. To remove all imperfections from a child's living conditions; to take away all challenges and opportunities to meet adversity, all opportunities to rise above imperfect conditions; to take away all opportunities to create and invent a better future; and to remove the opportunity to exemplify courage and love amid these challenges and opportunities would be tantamount to a decapitation. God would not decapitate the individual or collective human spirit any more than loving parents would decapitate the spirit of their child; and so, God not only *allowed* an imperfect world filled with challenge and adversity, but He *created* it.

Once again we encounter the question of why God allows so much suffering to come from the imperfect world and human evil. Did humanity really have to suffer the horrors of World War II in order to move to the current system of international political and economic rights, international courts, and the propensity toward democracy? No, but the outrages of World War II were not caused by an imperfect world; they were the result of human evil raised to a state of madness. Unlike natural laws, which blindly follow pattern sequences of cause and effect, human evil has embedded in it injustice, egocentrism, hatred, and cruelty, which are *freely* chosen. Nevertheless, even in the midst of the unnecessary and gratuitous suffering arising out of moral evil, the collective human spirit (galvanized by the Holy Spirit according to Christian faith) rises above this suffering and seems eventually to produce advancements in culture and the common good in proportion to the degree of suffering.

As noted above in Section I, God could not have eliminated the possibility of human evil by eradicating its perpetrators because He would have undermined personal freedom, the necessary condition for our love to be our own. In order for God to make us in His own image, He had to allow us to choose our purpose and identity—and this allowance entails the possibility of our choosing evil. Though God allows us to cause evil to one another, He can also inspire us to overcome it. So He inspires those who have chosen Level Three and Level Four identity, and who are willing to courageously sacrifice themselves for the common good and His Kingdom, to animate the collective human spirit to fight against tyranny and injustice, and to create institutions that will shield against them into the future.

The reader may be thinking, "The above rationale pertains only to suffering caused by *human* evil; what about appalling suffering coming from the imperfect world alone? Why did God allow the imperfect world to bring about the bubonic plague and the Black Death? Why did He allow one hundred million people to die in the Middle

East and Europe from this disease? Couldn't He have prevented *that* much devastation?"

At this juncture, we will want to recall that God's intention, according to Jesus, is to bring us into eternal love and joy. As noted above, God intends to redeem all our suffering and to transform it into the symphony of eternal love, which is His Kingdom. At the time of the plague (1330–1360), religious faith was central to the lives of most people in medieval Europe. Though the horror and suffering of the Black Death cannot be underestimated, it was generally seen through this religious lens which anticipated the resurrection and eternal life. As a result, millions of people focused on their spiritual preparation for the life to come, which partially mitigated the daily horror and loss from Europe's greatest natural disaster. Though the plague induced great fear and grief, it was not viewed as ultimately tragic, because the prospect of eternal life remained strong, though confidence in the Church was weakened.[52]

The plague also incited one of the most significant social and economic reforms in history. The sudden decrease in the population created shortages of labor, which meant that merchants had to pay wages to those who were serfs, and higher wages to those who were in the lower economic strata. This brought an end to feudalism and created the foundation for a waged working class.[53] The rise of this economic class led to greater freedom and autonomy among Europe's population, which led in its turn to a greater sense of the intrinsic dignity of mankind. This opened the door to Christian humanism and the Renaissance, which led to a new sense of equality and individual political rights. Ironically, the horror of the plague gave rise to the

[52] See Kenneth Pennington, "The Black Death and Religious Impact", Catholic University of America, CUA.edu, accessed June 27, 2016, http://faculty.cua.edu/pennington /churchhistory220/LectureTen/BlackDeath/Religious%20Impact%20page.htm.

[53] For example, David Routt at the University of Richmond notes, "The rural worker indeed demanded and received higher payments in cash (nominal wages) in the plague's aftermath. Wages in England rose from twelve to twenty-eight percent from the 1340s to the 1350s and twenty to forty percent from the 1340s to the 1360s." David Routt, "The Economic Impact of the Black Death", Economic History Association, *EH.net Encyclopedia*, ed. Robert Whaples, July 20, 2008, https://eh.net/encyclopedia/the-economic-impact-of -the-black-death. See also Samuel Cohn, "After the Black Death: Labour Legislation and Attitudes towards Labour in Late-Medieval Western Europe", *Economic History Review* 60, no. 3 (August 2007): 457–85. See also David Herlihy, *The Black Death and the Transformation of the West* (Cambridge, Mass.: Harvard University Press, 1997).

social and economic foundations of what might be called "the modern world".

Was this radical transition of the social economic and political order worth the price of the plague? This question can only be answered from the perspective of God, and therefore, we must approach it with the humility and trust of Elihu, who imparted this wisdom to Job (see Chapter 3). Bearing this in mind, one might argue that the sacrifice of the "plague generation" gave rise to generations upon generations of people who emerged from veritable serfdom and political obscurity into the light of the universal natural, political, religious, and economic rights enshrined in modern culture by Francisco Suarez, Hugo Grotius, John Locke, Thomas Jefferson, and their successors. Given the centrality of faith in the resurrection within the vast majority of Europe's population, it could be argued that if any generation had to make the sacrifice, this would be the one. The timing of this radical socioeconomic revolution could not have been better, for the world was prepared not only for the advent of natural rights, but also the expansion of universities, the rise of natural science, and the advent of modern economics.

With our limited knowledge and perspective, we will not be able to answer the question, why did God allow the imperfect world to have its way with so many victims? But we can be fairly certain that the centrality of faith in the culture of that time, God's promise of the resurrection, the need for social and economic reform, and the road to political rights were all involved in God's outlook. Yet this cannot be the ultimate answer to the question of suffering, because the victims of the plague, as well as the martyrs of human depravity such as those in Nazi concentration camps, did not suffer for the progress of this world alone, as if they were pawns in the movement of some Hegelian world spirit. As we have noted above, the ultimate answer to the question of suffering lies in God's intention to use and redeem it for the *eternal salvation* of all people who seek Him with a sincere heart according to the dictates of their conscience.

According to Jesus, all suffering will be used by the unconditionally loving God to bring optimal salvation and consolation to us and the people we touch. At the moment of what seems to be senseless suffering and death, God takes its victims into the fullness of His love, light, and life while initiating a momentum toward a greater common good within the course of human history. People of faith must continually bring to mind God's objectives in resolving individual and collective human suffering—the promotion of our own and others' salvation, the protection of our own and others' freedom, and the alleviation of our own and others' suffering. We must look intently for the action of His Spirit, not only to move individuals to salvation, but also to catalyze and inspire the collective human spirit to rise from the ashes of indignity and callousness to whole new levels of justice and love in world history.

As noted above, there is no guarantee that humanity will continue to progress in justice and love in the future, because this progress depends on the emergence and success of Level Three and Level Four thought leaders to inspire this progress in the public, and a public who is willing to be inspired by Level Three and Level Four ideals and principles. If these conditions are not met, then the direction of human history will turn decidedly downward, and the ensuing decadence could cause its destruction and even its ultimate demise.

In conclusion, the annals of human history are replete with examples of tragic periods of collective human suffering that provide the essential impetus to unify the collective human spirit and move it to rise above negation and darkness by creating higher levels of science, medicine, engineering, principles, ideals, laws, art, literature, architecture, systems, organizations, and institutions—all leading to a better life in a better world. Of course, much of this progress in the areas of principles, ideals, laws, and societal organization can be lost if a society's cultural ethos becomes more materialistic and self-interested (Levels One and Two) to the detriment of contribution, justice, the common good, and transcendence (Levels Three and Four). This regressive move in a society's culture frequently occurs in the absence of suffering, during times of prosperity (like the "roaring twenties").[54]

[54] This point was explained in some detail above in this section where the following was concluded: "As a society's cultural ethos declines (from Levels Three and Four to Levels One and Two), it will lead not only to a breakdown in the family and neighborhoods, but also a marked increase in existential emptiness, the negative emotions of the comparison game, and individual and collective malaise, which in turn leads to increased substance abuse, depression, unethical behavior, suicide attempts, impulse aggressivity, and antisocial and criminal behavior." Eventually these conditions will lead to a further breakdown in marriage, leading to markedly decreasing birthrates. These declines in birthrates will usher in a radical demographic change with new "family friendly" participants reintroducing

As noted above, suffering alone is not sufficient to bring about this phoenixlike phenomenon; it also requires Level Three and Four charismatic leaders possessed of courage, commitment, and enduring fortitude as well as Level Three and Four individuals who are inspired by these leaders to sacrifice themselves to make a better world out of the ashes of human suffering. If one has faith, one will likely attribute this "phoenix-like" phenomenon to the Holy Spirit working within the collective human spirit. If one does not have faith, one will simply have to marvel at the incredible goodness of the collective human spirit. Perhaps the human spirit is capable of such goodness, but in light of the evils that it has also produced, the seemingly continuous victory of good over evil should make us wonder. Are we really that good in ourselves, or is an unconditionally good God orchestrating our goodness to His ultimately good end?

Whatever our answer to this question, it seems evident that our imperfect world has provided an impetus for us to build a social and cultural reality with historically ascending levels of efficacy and goodness in the areas of justice, rights, legal systems, governance systems, medicine, biology, chemistry, physics, psychology, sociology, and every other discipline that has as its noble end the advancement of the common good. Without an imperfect world, without some suffering in the world, it seems highly unlikely that any of this would have arisen out of the collective human spirit in the course of history. Though these ascending levels of efficacy and goodness have been punctuated by negative and even tragic declines, the collective human spirit seems to reemerge on an ever-greater level, defying common sense by its counterentropic trend. Once again we must ask, is the collective human spirit *solely* responsible, or is there a higher guiding spirit that is inspiring and guiding the reemergence of the phoenix?

---

religious affiliation, family unity, ethical principles and ideals (from religious affiliation), and a renewed sense of resilience, hope, and vision for the future. See the following studies: Dervic et al., "Religious Affiliation and Suicide Attempt"; Pew Research Center, "Global Religious Landscape"; Pew Research Center, "America's Changing Religious Landscape"; Pew Research Center, "Religion among the Millennials"; Pew Research Center, "Decline of Marriage and Rise of New Families"; Josephson Institute, "Ethics of American Youth: 2012"; Birmaher, "Childhood and Adolescent Depression"; Zaki, "What, Me Care?"; and Parboteeah, Hoegl, and Cullen, "Ethics and Religion".

At the very least, we might conclude that the pain, hardship, and challenge of suffering throughout world history has been partially off-set by the gains made in culture and society, as well as gains in the individual spirit and the collective human spirit. What about the pain, hardship, and challenge that is *not* offset by these gains? Is it only an unjust tragic waste? What about the victims who were never able to experience or benefit from these gains? Are they simply unwilling martyrs? Not for Jesus. One of the reasons Jesus came to be with us *and to suffer for us* was to reveal His Father's desire to transform all suffering into eternal love and joy, and to use suffering as an impetus to free us from egocentricity and dominance into the empathy, humility, contribution, and compassion of the "children of God". Yet, Jesus' intention goes beyond *our* eternal resurrection in love; it extends to the whole created imperfect world, which remains frustrated and in bondage to decay until the final times. As Saint Paul teaches:

> For the creation waits with eager longing for the revealing of the sons of God; for the creation was subjected to futility, not of its own will but by the will of him who subjected it in hope; because the creation itself will be set free from its bondage to decay and obtain the glorious liberty of the children of God. We know that the whole creation has been groaning with labor pains together until now; and not only the creation, but we ourselves, who have the first fruits of the Spirit, groan inwardly as we wait for adoption as sons, the redemption of our bodies. (Rom 8:19–23)

In the perspective of Christian faith, no pain, suffering, or challenge need be wasted or ultimately tragic. *If we have faith*, we can lever these sufferings toward freedom from egocentricity and dominance—toward love and contribution to others in the Kingdom of God—and offer them up for the salvation of souls, especially those in most need of God's help. For Christians, all pain, suffering, and challenges are intended by God to lead to eternally loving and joyful salvation for all people—if we "seek God with a sincere heart, and moved by grace, try in our actions to do His will as we know it through the dictates of our conscience".[55]

---

[55] *Lumen Gentium*, no. 16. This universal promise of salvation is evident in the New Testament and is part of the dogmatic constitution of the Catholic Church—*Lumen Gentium*.

I do not mean to trivialize the history of human suffering or the lives of individuals who have suffered the indignity of systematic injustice and an imperfect natural order. Yet we should not fail to find some hope in light emerging from darkness, and goodness emerging from evil. Inasmuch as God is all-powerful and all-loving, He can seize upon this goodness and light to reinforce its historical momentum, and more importantly to transform it into an unconditionally loving eternity. If this is correct, then an imperfect world shaped by an imperfect, yet transcendently good, human spirit brought to fulfillment by an unconditionally loving God will equate to an eternal symphony of love.

IV. Conclusion

So why does the all-loving God allow suffering? The answer may be found in the interrelationship among four ideas—freedom, love, eternal salvation, and personal identity. In Section I, we considered God's dilemma in creating beings truly capable of love, noting that God had to create us with the potential to cause suffering, for if He did not, we would not have the capacity to choose evil, injustice, and unloving behaviors, in which case we would have had *no choice* but to do good, just, and loving behaviors. If we had no choice, then we would have been *compelled* or programmed to do these positive behaviors. They would not have originated from within us, but from a preset program, and hence we would not be loving creatures, but only robots programmed to perform loving behaviors. If God wanted to create genuinely loving beings, He had to create the potential for evil and suffering caused by those beings.

In Section II, we considered why God would have created us in an imperfect world, so that the blind forces of nature could cause famine, disease, genetic defects, floods, and other natural disasters, producing all manner of pain, suffering, and deprivation. It was here that the idea of "personal identity" became important—for when we are confronted by the forces of the imperfect world, we have to make *choices* that will determine not only who we are, but the kind of eternity that we would prefer. The impending reality of death in the imperfect world incites us to *choose* the way in which we are going to live in the short time we have in the physical world: Are we going to accumulate things for *ourselves*, aggrandize *ourselves*, gain ego-comparative advantage for *ourselves*, dominate others for the sake of *our* personal benefit, and worship *ourselves*, or will we use our gifts and resources to help *others*, edify *others*, contribute to *others*, respect *others*, show compassion to *others*, and worship the true God? Without death, these fundamental choices and identity decisions could be interminably delayed, allowing us to avoid the critical decisions constituting our personal and eternal identity.

In Section II.A, we noted how the imperfect world provides the impetus for natural virtue, particularly prudence, courage, and self-discipline. Without an imperfect world, we would have no practical need to use our rational faculties, because everything would be perfectly obvious and accessible. Furthermore, there would be no need for courage to face our fears, because the perfect world would present no fear; there would be no need to sacrifice ourselves to make the world a better place, because the world would already be a perfect place; there would be no need to exert effort and restrain the pursuit of pleasure, because everything would be effortless and there would be no worthier pursuit than the mere pursuit of pleasure. Without an imperfect world, life would be pleasant, painless, and simple, but we would have no opportunity to make a contribution, a positive difference, to anybody or anything. There would be no impetus from the natural world to sacrifice ourselves, use our wits, face our fears, exert effort, and restrain ourselves. We would remain at the level of little children, completely unfamiliar with the challenges, self-efficacy, self-knowledge, virtue, self-sacrifice, self-transcendence, and *choices* of the adult world. Though life would be more pleasant, we would not be able to reach most of our potential—and therefore, most of our personal identity.

In Section II.B, we saw other important benefits from the imperfect world brought to light by the revelation of Jesus. We saw how personal and bodily weakness and limitations can lead to humility, empathy, and compassion, and how the needs of others can call us to make contributions, show compassion, and build systems, structures, and cultures for the common good. We also saw how the imperfect world can shock us out of superficial Level One and Level Two purpose in life, calling us to look for something more—something contributive, loving, and transcendent—and we also saw how the imperfect world tells us that we are *not* God and helps us to acknowledge our need *for* God. Additionally, we saw how the sufferings of the imperfect world provide the conditions for making a self-sacrificial offering to God for the salvation of souls. All these dimensions of suffering lead to a deepening of love within our consciousness and personal identity, thereby opening the way to eternal salvation with the unconditionally loving God.

In Section III, we saw that suffering also provides the impetus to build cultures of justice, compassion, and unity, cultures that will inspire creativity, service, intrinsic dignity, mutual respect, individual and economic rights, hope, vision, and transcendence. We indicated that such cultures could inspire individuals to work with others, in spirit and common cause, to overcome suffering and to lead individuals to their highest personal and interpersonal identity, and through this to lives of great fulfillment and even to eternal salvation. We noted that cultural decline (from Levels Three and Four to Levels One and Two) could have the opposite effect—giving rise to decreased empathy, contribution, ethics, and sense of transcendence, resulting in increased depression, malaise, meaninglessness, despondency, substance abuse, familial tensions, antisocial and criminal behavior, and suicides.

Great cultures can produce the phoenix phenomenon, transforming collective adversity and suffering into the highest levels of achievement in the areas of science, law, ethics, engineering, medicine, humanities, art, and architecture. However, base cultures can have the opposite effect—exacerbating the negative effects of suffering, undermining the family and social structures, and lowering the levels of intrinsic dignity, mutual respect, and peaceful coexistence. We concluded from this that suffering provides an impetus to all of us to be alert to opportunities to promote and defend Level Three and Level Four values, principles, and ideals, and to summon the courage to say something when those opportunities present themselves. Though this may be difficult, and earn us the disdain of others and may require great self-sacrifice, it usually results in some of the greatest contributions of our lives—contributions to society, the common good, and the Kingdom of God. When we speak the truth about Level Three and Level Four values, principles, and ideals, amid palpable resistance, we can produce tremendous good to galvanize the "silent majority", and to interrupt a momentum of decline.

As we examine the lives of history's greatest cultural heroes—whether they be religious, philosophical, literary, historical, and legal, and especially ordinary men and women who rise to the occasion—we see a common thread: the desire to make the imperfect world a better place, to improve the lot of humanity, and to inspire our collective spirit to rise above the din toward a future even better than the one undermined by calamity and collective adversity. Suffering not only contains the call for us to respond to *individual* needs, but also to *collective* needs, not just collective *material* needs, but to collective *cultural* needs—to dare to lift up the spirit of humanity. The imperfect world, and human evil, can and do incite us to the highest levels of individual spirit, collective spirit, and human endeavor, and this can make an important contribution not only to our salvation, but also to the salvation of others—sometimes dozens and hundreds of others.

We may close with a consideration of the role of suffering in the highest levels of love. Let us return to the formula we have seen throughout this book—*suffering plus faith equals extraordinary love*. In the context of Christian faith, we saw how personal suffering could lead to freedom from self-centeredness, and how the sufferings of others could call us to sacrifice ourselves for them. Suffering can call us to greater trust in God, and when He responds, to a greater awareness of His love for us. The more we are aware of His love, the more we love Him in return—desiring to serve Him in the needy, the suffering, the physically deprived, the spiritually deprived, the Church, and the culture.

In Christianity, this process can reach particularly great heights because of the example and sacrifice of Jesus, and the grace provided us by the inspiration of the Holy Spirit. Saint Francis of Assisi, Saint Ignatius Loyola, Saint Peter Claver, and Saint Teresa of Calcutta entered into the purifying process of suffering as most of us do—by turning to God for help during times of adversity, pain, deprivation, and challenge. Like most of us, these individuals became more aware of how God works through our suffering to call us to salvation, and to help us call others to their salvation. These saints connected deeply with the teaching, life, and self-sacrificial death of Jesus; and the love they initially felt for Him intensified so greatly that they wanted to serve not only the poor, but *Him* in the poor. They not only wanted to imitate His humility, empathy, and compassion, but also to emulate His complete self-sacrifice for the salvation of souls. For these extraordinary individuals, the formula of "suffering plus faith equals love" came to its highest synergistic actualization through their faith in *Jesus*.

As these saints considered the life of Jesus, they became increasingly aware of the sacrifices He made for them (and the world) to love and redeem them. Moved with great gratitude, they responded spontaneously with love for Him. They were so moved with love that they wanted to imitate the One who had loved them and had provided the path to their eternal salvation. As they considered the needs of the world—bodily needs, spiritual needs, and cultural needs—they wanted to do as much as they could to help, in the way that Jesus taught, with empathy, humility, respect, and compassion; and so they gave their whole heart to Him, to His way of love, and to those in need.

As we examine the prayers that each wrote, they contain the four terms that lie at the heart of suffering's opportunities and benefits— freedom, love, eternal salvation, and personal identity. These prayers reflect the highest levels of spiritual *freedom*, the highest levels of compassion and self-sacrificial love, and the highest levels of trust in God and hope in eternal salvation. As Saint Ignatius Loyola expressed it:

> Take Lord receive all my liberty,
> my memory, understanding, and my entire will.
> Whatsoever I have or hold, you have given to me.
> I give it all back to you—dispose of it entirely according
>   to your will.
> Give me only your love and your grace—that's enough
>   for me, and I ask for nothing more.

(Suscipe, Spiritual Exercises, no. 234)

CONCLUSION

There is light in the darkness—the light of salvation, love, freedom, transcendence, and personal actualization. The darkness, through faith, makes this light all the more profound and precious, refining our freedom and love to an ever-greater, authentic, purified, and unconditional state. We cannot hope to recapture the depth of philosophy, psychology, theology, and spirituality used to examine this remarkable light throughout this book, so we might best conclude by providing an outline of some of the practical steps to help us contend with suffering and benefit from it.

When suffering finds its way into our lives, we can review this outline to get the "big picture" of how to use our faith to turn suffering into love and salvation. Our review will be divided into the three phases used throughout this book:

1. Theological Preparation for Suffering
2. Contending with Suffering in the Short-Term
3. Benefitting from Suffering in the Long-Term

These review documents are meant to stimulate memory and imagination. If some of the points do not look familiar, you may want to go back to the appropriate chapter and section to refresh them. The outline for the first phase may be studied at any time; it need not be confined to times of suffering. The outline for the second phase will be most useful if reviewed when suffering strikes. The outline for the third phase will prove most useful when the initial debilitating effects of suffering have subsided, and consolation is beginning to recur. This will open the way to the lasting benefits your faith can bring to suffering.

PHASE ONE—Theological Preparation for Suffering
Foundations 1–3

Foundation No. 1—Conviction about the Resurrection

1. Affirming faith in the resurrection

   - Reasons of the heart—God is unconditional love who desires to give resurrection
   - Historicity of Jesus' Resurrection—testimony of Saint Paul, as well as historical criteria of N. T. Wright and others
   - Shroud of Turin—four dating tests and other evidence of early first-century Jerusalem; evidence of the Resurrection; excimer lasers
   - Near-death experiences—medical studies with veridical evidence; visual perception of the blind; witnessing of deceased relatives
   - Miracles done in the name of Jesus or the intercession of His Mother—Craig Keener's documentation of Jesus' miracles; International Medical Committee of Lourdes' documentation of miracles attributed to the Blessed Mother

2. Hope in the resurrection

   - The hope of Saint Paul—"He who did not spare his own Son but gave him up for us all, will he not also give us all things with him?" (Rom 8:32).
   - The confidence in the Letter to the Ephesians—God "is able to do far more abundantly than all that we ask or think" (3:20).
   - What Jesus makes clear—we can fail as miserably as the prodigal son, and his Father will accept us back to the Kingdom if we are sincerely contrite (Lk 15:11–32).
   - Dogmatic Constitution on the Church (*Lumen Gentium*)—all those who "seek God with a sincere heart" and try "to do his will ... through the dictates of their conscience" may achieve the fullness of salvation (no. 16)

3. The nature of the resurrection

   - The transformation of our bodies in spirit, power, and glory

- The messianic banquet—unconditionally loving appreciation and self-communication with Jesus and all others in the Kingdom
- The creation itself—set free from its bondage to obtain the glorious freedom of the children of God
- Linda Stewart's NDE: "I knew I was in the arms of a being who cherished me with perfect love and carried me from the dark void into a new reality.... I beheld a radiant, Spirit being, so magnificent and full of love that I knew I would never again feel the sense of loss.... I knew the Spirit was Christ" (Kevin Williams, "Linda Stewart's Near-Death Experience", Near-Death Experiences and the Afterlife, 2014, http://www.near-death.com/experiences/notable/linda-stewart.html).

4. Six Christian insights about suffering and resurrection

- Suffering is completely redeemed in the Resurrection.
- The purpose of suffering is to help us toward our salvation and help us bring others to their salvation—purification of freedom, virtue, and love.
- Suffering can be offered as loving self-sacrifice to God for the salvation of souls and the strength of the Mystical Body; suffering becomes grace.
- God is compassionately present to us in our times of suffering, and through it guides and inspires us toward our own and others' salvation.
- God can transform our suffering into Level Four holiness and love—if we are open.
- God can use suffering to transform the culture—if there are leaders who will take up the challenge.

Foundation No. 2—Affirming the Unconditional Love of God

- God is Abba, the Father of the Prodigal Son.
- God is *not* "the angry god".
- God is *not* "the payback god".
- God is *not* "the domineering god".
- God is *not* "the terrifying god".
- God is *not* "the stoic god".
- God is *not* "the disgusted god".

Foundation No. 3—Recognizing God's Presence in Our Suffering

- God does not use suffering to punish us or our children; He forgives His enemies.
- God must manage six issues during our suffering: our salvation, others' salvation, the protection of our freedom, the protection of others' freedom, the alleviation of our suffering, and the alleviation of others' suffering. The alleviation of suffering is secondary to our and others' salvation and freedom.
- God does not directly cause natural events; He creates a universe with secondary causes.
- We need humility and trust, to give God the benefit of the doubt.

PHASE TWO—Contending with Suffering in the Short-Term

Foundations 4–5

Foundation No. 4—Spontaneous Prayers in Times of Suffering

- "Lord, help me."
- "Abba, Father, all things are possible to you; remove this chalice from me; yet not what I will, but what you will" (Mk 14:36).
- "Hail Mary, full of grace" (Lk 1:28).
- "Lord, do not let any of this suffering go to waste; make optimal good come out it for me, others, and Your Kingdom."
- "Lord, snatch victory from the jaws of defeat."
- "I give up—You take care of it."
- "Lord, push back this darkness and foreboding."
- "Lord, You are the just, wise, and merciful Judge—You take care of it."
- "Thank You."
- "God, be merciful to me a sinner!" (Lk 18:13).
- "Lord, save me" (Mt 14:30).
- "Lord, I accept Your forgiveness."
- "Lord, I will try with all my heart to walk in Your light and love."

- "Lord, make good come out of whatever harm I might have caused."
- "Thy loving will be done."
- "Lord, I offer up my sufferings to You."

Foundation No. 5—Mitigating Fear and Choosing Consolation

1. Mitigating fear and anxiety through natural virtues

   - Use reason and prudence to create backup plan, damage control, and team response.
   - Seek the help of supportive and practical friends.
   - Reshape expectations by stopping the refrain, "I can't be happy without ..." and replacing it with, "I can be happy in a new way ..."
   - Avoid comparisons to the way you were in the past, and avoid comparisons to people who do not have your challenges.

2. Choosing consolation

   - Confronting emotional blocks and negative frames of mind with the truth about the Resurrection, Jesus Christ, and positive opportunities of suffering.
   - Find a sacred domain—go into a church; position yourself next to a sacred image or icon; use a sacred object, such as a Bible or rosary.
   - Acknowledge God's presence and love: "Lord, I know You love me, and I know You are here."
   - Say simple prayers to the Father, Son, and Holy Spirit.
   - The Lord will eventually bring peace and consolation.

Foundation No. 6—The Unity of Suffering and Love in Self-Sacrifice

1. Bringing love to perfection brings suffering to perfection:

   - Level One and Level Two "love" is not really love (focused on the other) and therefore cannot bring suffering to perfection.
   - Level Three love (focused on neighbor) brings love to *partial* perfection—and therefore brings suffering to *partial* perfection.

- Level Four love (love of neighbor in the context of love and surrender to God) brings love to full perfection (self-sacrifice for the immanent and transcendent good of the other with the help and grace of God), which in turn brings suffering to its full perfection.

2. *Philia* (friendship), *eros* (exclusive and highest love relationship with a human being), and *agapē* (self-sacrificial love for the good of the other) are open to being perfected on Levels Three and Four.

   - If we focus on perfecting all three of these kinds of love, not only will it improve our friendships, marriages, and self-sacrificial love, but it will also perfect suffering.
   - In Level Three and Level Four love, suffering can call and help us toward deeper empathy, compassion, humility, and generativity in our friendships and marriages.
   - Level Four love can bring suffering and love (*agapē*) into union with one another—in self-sacrifice, gift of self to neighbor, and gift of self to God.

3. The grace, teaching, support, and example of the *Christian Church* can bring about the union of *agapē* and suffering through self-sacrifice.

   - The grace of the sacraments and Christian prayer
   - Self-sacrificial offering of suffering to the Lord in imitation of Jesus for the good of souls and the Church
   - The example of Saint Paul and Saint Thérèse of Lisieux in self-sacrificial self-offering
   - The union of *agapē* and suffering in the lives and ministries of Saint Francis of Assisi, Saint Ignatius Loyola, Saint Peter Claver, and Saint Teresa of Calcutta

PHASE THREE—Benefitting from Suffering in the Long-Term

Foundations 7–9

Foundation No. 7—Interior and Exterior Opportunities of Suffering

OPPORTUNITIES OF SUFFERING

I. Interior Opportunities of Suffering

1. Prudence: Appropriation of Higher Levels of Purpose and Identity

   - Appropriation—Level Three *contributive* identity (see Volume I, Chapters 3 and 4)
   - Appropriation—Level Four *faith* identity (see Volume I, Chapters 5 through 10)

2. Other Natural Virtues

   - Rationality (see this volume, Chapters 5 through 6)
   - Fortitude and courage (see this volume, Chapters 5, 6, and 12)
   - Temperance/self-discipline (see this volume, Chapters 5, 6, and 12)

3. *Agapē*—Other-Centered Love

   - Empathy (see above in this chapter, and Volume I, Chapter 4)
   - Acceptance of love's vulnerability (see above in this chapter)
   - Humility (see above in this chapter and Volume III, Chapter 1)
   - Forgiveness (see above in this chapter and Volume III, Chapters 1 through 3)
   - Compassion (see above in this chapter and Volume III, Chapters 1 through 3)
   - Acceptance of compassion (see above in this chapter and Volume I, Chapter 4)

II. External Opportunities of Suffering

1. Good for the World

- Good for the family
- Good for organization/institution
- Good for the community
- Good for culture or society

2. Building the Kingdom of God

- Personal evangelization—to family, friends, and colleagues
- Contributing to a local church or diocese
- Contributing to the larger Church mission (national or international)
- Evangelizing within the community (apologetical, catechetical, or moral)
- Evangelizing the culture (apologetical, catechetical, or moral)

Foundation No. 8—Offering Suffering to God as a Loving Self-Sacrifice

1. For Jesus, the primary purpose of suffering is to make a self-sacrificial offering of it to the Father.

   - This offering is effectively an act of love (gift of self) for reparation of sins and salvation for all who are in need of it.
   - See Jesus' Eucharistic words and His interpretation of the Fourth Suffering Servant Song of Isaiah (52:13–53:12) and Psalm 22 (His dying words).

2. Saint Paul rejoices in his sufferings because he can join them to the sufferings of Christ for the good of the Church and the redemption of the world (see Col 1:24–25).

   - By implication, Saint Paul encourages us to do likewise.

3. Saint Thérèse of Lisieux went beyond this and made the offering of her suffering into her life's vocation.

   - Since her suffering prevented her from doing more active work, she felt privileged to turn her whole life—her whole religious vocation—into becoming a self-sacrificial, loving oblation to God for the salvation of the world.

4. Saint Thérèse's prayer to make her whole life and self a loving, sacrificial offering to the Lord:

"In order that my life may be one Act of *perfect* love, I offer myself as a *Victim* of holocaust to Thy merciful love, imploring Thee to *consume me* unceasingly, and to allow the floods of infinite tenderness gathered up in Thee to overflow into my soul, that so I may become a very *martyr of Thy love*, Oh my God!"[1]

5. The morning offering of the apostleship of prayer:

"O Jesus, through the Immaculate Heart of Mary, I offer you my prayers, works, joys, and sufferings of this day for all the intentions of your Sacred Heart, in union with the Holy Sacrifice of the Mass throughout the world, for the salvation of souls, the reparation of sins, the reunion of all Christians, and in particular for the intentions of the Holy Father. Amen."

Foundation No. 9—Following the Inspiration and Guidance of the Holy Spirit

RULES FOR THE FIRST AND SECOND DISCERNMENT

Rules for the First Discernment

- Never make an important decision in times of affective or spiritual desolation. If you are in desolation, return to the first step and stay with spontaneous prayers and the management of fear and anxiety. If this does not lead eventually away from desolation, review Chapter 2 on who God is and is not as well as rational evidence for God and Jesus (in Volumes II and III).
- Review the list of opportunities, and note whether something "stands out" as interesting, intriguing, or desirable. Notice if this opportunity is coincident with other things in your life—words

---

[1] Thérèse of Lisieux, *The Story of the Soul*, trans. Rev. Thomas N. Taylor (New York: Cosimo Classics, 2007), 278; emphasis mine.

of family and friends, books or media, etc. If is is, then move
forward.

- Once you have selected an area of opportunity from the list (in abstract), open yourself, like Archimedes, to a particular path to
actualize that opportunity. Normally, the opportunity comes to
you—someone asking a favor, reading a church bulletin, listening to some friends, etc.
- If a particular path to actualizing an opportunity stands out,
place it before the Lord to see whether it is His will. After one
or two weeks of doing this, ask yourself, "Do I feel a sense of
peace and hopefulness, or a sense of discord and dejection?"
If there is a persistent sense of peace, then pursue it. If there is
persistent discord, abandon it and start the third step again.

Rules for the Second Discernment

- After pursuing a particular path to actualizing an opportunity,
ask yourself whether you are experiencing an increase or a
decrease in trust in God, hope in your salvation, and love (1
Cor 13). If you experience a decrease, either modify or abandon that particular path. If you experience an increase, continue
your pursuit of that opportunity.
- After pursuing the opportunity, ask yourself if it is creating tensions with your family or workplace. If so, and you are still
experiencing an increase in trust, hope, and love, then *modify*
the amount of time, psychic energy, and physical energy you
are committing to the pursuit of that opportunity.
- If after pursuing an opportunity for two or more months, you
feel a sense of discouragement followed by a decrease in trust,
hope, and love (after you had previously been inspired and
enthusiastic—increasing in trust, hope, and love), it probably
means that you succumbed to an evil spirit masquerading as
a "angel of light" (2 Cor 11:14). If in your enthusiasm you
felt that "more, faster, and harder is better", and got carried
away with it, try to identify the point in your past when you
were still enthusiastic and growing in sturs, hope, and love,
and then modify your pursuit of that opportunity to the level
at *that* time.

In the Introduction to Volume I of the Quartet, I mentioned that this fourth volume would have two parts:

1. Contending with suffering through faith
2. Contending with evil through virtue and faith

As can be seen, I was only able to take the first of these two topics in this volume, and I am therefore constrained to write yet another volume on the topic of evil, virtue, and faith. It will be a sequel to the Quartet entitled *Called out of Darkness: Contending with Evil through Virtue and Prayer* (San Francisco: Ignatius Press, forthcoming). When that volume is completed, I will give a brief synopsis of all the volumes and the vision for transcendent happiness with which they are concerned.

BIBLIOGRAPHY

Ahlquist, Dale. "Lecture 8: Heretics". American Chesterton Society, 2013. http://www.chesterton.org/lecture-8/.

Anonymous. *The Cloud of Unknowing*. Edited by James Walsh. New York: Paulist Press, 1981.

Aquinas, Thomas. *Commentary on Aristotle's Physics*. Books I–II. Translated by Richard J. Blackwell, Richard Spath, and W. Edmund Thirlkel. New Haven, Conn.: Yale University Press, 1963. http://www.dhspriory.org/thomas/Physics.htm.

―――. *Summa Theologica*. Vol. 2. Translated by Fathers of the English Dominican Provence. Grand Rapids, Mich.: Christian Classics, 1981.

―――. *The Summa Theologica of St. Thomas Aquinas*. Vol. 1. Translated by Fathers of the English Dominican Province. New York: Benzinger Brothers, 1947.

Aristotle. *Aristotle on Friendship: Being an Expanded Translation of the Nicomachean Ethics Books VIII and IX*. Translated and edited by Geoffrey Percival. Cambridge: Cambridge University Press, 2015.

Augustine. *Confessions*. Translated by F.J. Sheed. Edited by Michael P. Foley. Indianapolis: Hackett Publishing, 2006.

Austin Institute. "Are Religious People Happier?" January 23, 2015. http://www.austin-institute.org/research/media/are-religious-people-happier/.

Basford, T.K. *Near-Death Experiences: An Annotated Bibliography*. New York: Garland, 1990.

Birmaher, Boris. "Childhood and Adolescent Depression: A Review of the Past 10 Years. Part I". *Journal of the American Academy of Child and Adolescent Psychiatry* 35, no. 11 (November 1996): 1427–39. http://www.sciencedirect.com/science/article/pii/S0890856709664030.

Brodrick, James. *St. Ignatius Loyola: The Pilgrim Years*. San Francisco: Ignatius Press, 1998.

Brokaw, Tom. *The Greatest Generation*. New York: Random House, 2001.

Brooks, Arthur C. "An Aging Europe in Decline". *New York Times*, op-ed, January 6, 2015.

Brown, Raymond. *The Death of the Messiah: From Gethsemane to the Grave; A Commentary on the Passion Narratives in the Four Gospels*. New York: Doubleday, 1994.

Brunschwig, Jacques, and Pierre Pellegrin. *Greek Thought: A Guide to Classical Knowledge*. Cambridge, Mass.: Harvard University Press, 2000.

Buber, Martin. *I and Thou*. Eastford, Conn.: Martino Publications, 2010.

Camus, Albert. *The Myth of Sisyphus and Other Essays*. New York: Vintage Books, 1991.

Carrell, Alexis. *The Voyage to Lourdes*. New York: Harper and Brothers, 1950.

Catechism of the Catholic Church. 2nd ed. Washington, D.C.: Libreria Editrice Vaticana—United States Conference of Catholic Bishops, 2000.

Cerfaux, Lucien. "L hymne au Christ-Serviteur de Dieu (Phil., II, 6–11 -Is., LII, 13, -LIII, 12)". In *Miscellanea historica in honorem Alberti de Meyer Universitatis Catholicae in oppido Lovaniensi iam annos XXV professoris*, 1:117–30. Louvain: Bibliothèque de l'Université, 1946.

Clucas, Joan. *Mother Teresa*. New York: Chelsea House Publications, 1988.

Cohn, Samuel. "After the Black Death: Labour Legislation and Attitudes towards Labour in Late-Medieval Western Europe". *Economic History Review* 60, no. 3 (August 2007): 457–85.

Cook, E. W., B. Greyson, and I. Stevenson. "Do Any Near-Death Experiences Provide Evidence for the Survival of Human Personality After Death? Relevant Features and Illustrative Case Reports". *Journal of Scientific Exploration* 12 (1998): 377–406.

Cornwall, Marie, Stan L. Albrecht, Perry H. Cunningham, and Brian L. Pitcher. "The Dimensions of Religiosity: A Conceptual Model with an Empirical Test". *Review of Religious Research* 27, no. 3 (March 1986): 226–44.

Davis, Craig. *Dating the Old Testament*. New York: RJ Communications, 2007.

De La Croix, Paul Marie. *Carmelite Spirituality in the Teresian Tradition.* Washington, D.C.: Institute of Carmelite Studies, 1994.

————. "St. Therese's Life in the Carmel of Lisieux and the Influence of Her 'Little Way'". Taken from *Carmelite Spirituality.* EWTN. Accessed June 8, 2016. http://www.ewtn.com/therese /carmel.htm.

Dervic, Kanita, Maria Oquendo, Michael Grunebaum, Steve Ellis, Ainsley Burke, and J. John Mann. "Religious Affiliation and Suicide Attempt". *American Journal of Psychiatry* 161, no. 12 (December 1, 2004): 2303–8. http://ajp.psychiatryonline.org/article.aspx ?articleid=177228.

Di Lazzaro, Paolo, Daniele Murra, Antonino Santoni, Giulio Fanti, Enrico Nichelatti, and Giuseppe Baldacchini. "Deep Ultraviolet Radiation Simulates the Turin Shroud Image". *Journal of Imaging Science and Technology* 54, no. 4 (July–August 2010): 40302-1–40302-6.

Donne, John. "Holy Sonnets: Batter My Heart, Three-Person'd God". *Poetry Foundation.* Accessed June 17, 2016. www.poetry foundation.org/poem/173362.

————. "Meditation 17, 'For Whom the Bell Tolls'". In *The Best of John Donne,* p. 45. Seattle: CreateSpace Independent Publishing Platform, 2012.

Dostoyevsky, Fyodor. "The Grand Inquisitor". In *The Brothers Karamazov,* translated by David McDuff, pp. 322–44. New York: Penguin, 2003.

Douglas, Mary. *Natural Symbols: Explorations in Cosmology.* 3rd ed. New York: Routledge, 2003.

Dunn, James. *Jesus and the Spirit: A Study of the Religious and Charismatic Experience of Jesus and the First Christians as Reflected in the New Testament.* Philadelphia: Westminster Press, 1975.

Edwards, Jonathan. "Sinners in the Hands of an Angry God". Sermon delivered in Enfield, Connecticut, July 8, 1741. Christian Classics Ethereal Library. Accessed January 31, 2016. http://www .ccel.org/ccel/edwards/sermons.sinners.html.

Einstein, Albert. *Ideas and Opinions.* Translated by Sonja Bargmann. New York: Crown Publishers, 1954.

Eliade, Mircea. *The Myth of the Eternal Return, or Cosmos and History.* Princeton, N.J.: Princeton University Press, 1971.

————. *The Sacred and the Profane: The Nature of Religion*. New York: Harcourt Brace Jovanovich, 1987.

Evans, Christopher. *Saint Luke*. London: SCM Press, 1990.

Fararo, Thomas J., and John Skvoretz. "Action and Institution, Network and Function: The Cybernetic Concept of Social Structure". *Sociological Forum* 1, no. 2 (March 1, 1986): 219–50.

Fenwick, P., and E. Fenwick. *The Truth in the Light: An Investigation of Over 300 Near-Death Experiences*. New York: Berkeley Books, 1995.

Finnis, John. *Natural Law and Natural Rights*. New York: Oxford University Press, 1980.

Flannery, Austin, ed. *Vatican Council II, Vol. 1: The Conciliar and Post-conciliar Documents*. Northport, N.Y.: Costello Publishing, 1975.

Frankl, Viktor. *Man's Search for Meaning: An Introduction to Logotherapy*. New York: Beacon Press, 1984.

Gallagher, Timothy. *The Discernment of Spirits: An Ignatian Guide for Everyday Living*. New York: Crossroad Publishing, 2005.

Green, Meg. *Mother Teresa: A Biography*. Westport, Conn.: Greenwood Press, 2004.

Greyson, Bruce. "Seeing Dead People Not Known to Have Died: 'Peak in Darien' Experiences". American Anthropological Association, November 21, 2010. http://onlinelibrary.wiley.com/doi/10.1111/j.1548-1409.2010.01064.x/abstract.

Greyson, Bruce, and C.P. Flynn, eds. *The Near-Death Experience: Problems, Prospects, Perspectives*. Springfield, Ill.: Charles C. Thomas, 1984.

Groeschel, Benedict. "Mother Teresa Remembered". *First Things*, September 11, 2007. http://www.firstthings.com/web-exclusives/2007/09/mother-teresa-remembered.

————. *Spiritual Passages: The Psychology of Spiritual Development*. New York: Crossroads, 1984.

Heidegger, Martin. *Being and Time*. New York: Harper Perennial Classics, 2008.

Heiler, Friedrich. "The History of Religions as a Preparation for the Cooperation of Religions". In *The History of Religions*, edited by Mircea Eliade and J. Kitagawa, pp. 142–53. Chicago: Chicago University Press, 1959.

Herlihy, David. *The Black Death and the Transformation of the West*. Cambridge, Mass.: Harvard University Press, 1997.

Holden, Janice. *Handbook of Near Death Experiences: Thirty Years of Investigation*. Westport, Conn.: Praeger Press, 2009.

Ignatius Loyola. *A Pilgrim's Journey: The Autobiography of St. Ignatius of Loyola*. San Francisco: Ignatius Press, 2001.

International Association for Near Death Studies. "Children's Near-Death Experiences". Last updated February 22, 2016. http://iands.org/childrens-near-death-experiences.html.

International Medical Committee of Lourdes. http://en.lourdes-france.org/deepen/cures-and-miracles/the-international-medical-committee.

Irwin, Terence. *The Development of Ethics*. Vol. 2. Oxford: Oxford University Press, 2008.

Jaki, Stanley L. *The Origin of Science and the Science of Its Origin*. Edinburgh: Scottish Academic Press, 1978.

Jeremias, Joachim. *The Eucharistic Words of Jesus*. London: SCM Press, 1966.

————. *New Testament Theology*. Vol. 1. New York: Charles Scribner and Sons, 1971.

————. *The Parables of Jesus*. London: SCM Press, 1972.

John of the Cross. *Dark Night of the Soul*. In *The Collected Works of St. John of the Cross*, edited by Kieran Kavanaugh, pp. 295–392. Washington, D.C.: Institute of Carmelite Studies, 1979.

————. "The Living Flame of Love". In *The Collected Works of St. John of the Cross*, translated by Kieran Kavanaugh and Otilio Rodriguez, pp. 569–649. Washington, D.C.: ICS Publications, 1979.

John Paul II. "Homily on Mother Teresa on the Occasion of her Beatification". October 19, 2003. https://w2.vatican.va/content/john-paul-ii/en/homilies/2003/documents/hf_jp-ii_hom_20031019_mother-theresa.html.

Josephson Institute: Center for Youth Ethics. "The Ethics of American Youth: 2012, Installment 1: Honesty and Integrity", news release, November 20, 2012. https://charactercounts.org/national-report-card/2012-report-card/.

Jung, Carl. *The Archetypes and the Collective Unconscious*. In *Collected Works of C. G. Jung*. Vol. 9, pt. 1, translated by R. F. C. Hull. Princeton, N.J.: Princeton University Press, 1981.

Keener, Craig. *Miracles: The Credibility of the New Testament Accounts*. 2 vols. Grand Rapids, Mich.: Baker Academic Publishing, 2011.

Kelly, Emily, B. Greyson, and I. Stevenson. "Can Experiences Near Death Furnish Evidence of Life After Death?" *Omega: Journal of Death and Dying* 40 (2000): 39–45.

Koester, Helmut, L. Michael White, Wayne A. Meeks, Elizabeth Clark, Paula Fredriksen, and Elaine H. Pagels. "The Great Appeal: What Did Christianity Offer Its Believers That Made It Worth Social Estrangement, Hostility from Neighbors, and Possible Persecution?" Frontline, PBS.org, April 1998. pbs.org/wgbh/pages /frontline/shows/religion/why/appeal.html.

Krohnert, Steffen, Iris Hobmann, and Reiner Klingholz. *Europe's Demographic Future: Growing Regional Imbalances*. Berlin: Berlin Institute for Population and Development, 2008.

Kübler-Ross, Elisabeth. *On Death and Dying: What the Dying Have to Teach Doctors, Nurses, Clergy and Their Own Families*. New York: Scribner, 2003.

Las Casas, Bartolomé de. *In Defense of the Indians: The Defense of the Most Reverend Lord, Don Fray Bartolomé de las Casas, of the Order of Preachers, Late Bishop of Chiapa, against the Persecutors and Slanderers of the Peoples of the New World Discovered across the Seas*. Translated and edited by Stafford Poole. DeKalb: Northern Illinois University Press, 1992.

Lewis, C. S. *The Four Loves*. New York: Harcourt, 1960.

————. *Surprised by Joy: The Shape of My Early Life*. New York: Harcourt, Brace, Jovanovich, 1966.

Locke, John. *Second Treatise on Government*. Edited by C. B. Macpherson. Indianapolis: Hackett Publishing, 1980.

Lonergan, Bernard. *Insight: A Study of Human Understanding*. In *Collected Works of Bernard Lonergan* 3, edited by Frederick E. Crowe and Robert M. Doran. Toronto: University of Toronto Press, 1992.

MacKenzie, R. A. F., and Roland E. Murphy. "Job". In *The New Jerome Biblical Commentary*, edited by Raymond E. Brown, Joseph A. Fitzmyer, and Roland E. Murphy, pp. 466–88. Englewood Cliffs, N.J.: Prentice Hall, 1990.

Mally, Edward J. "The Gospel according to Mark". In *The Jerome Biblical Commentary*, edited by Raymond Brown, Joseph A. Fitzmyer, and Roland E. Murphy, 2:21–61. Englewood Cliffs, N.J.: Prentice-Hall, 1968.

McKenzie, John L. *Dictionary of the Bible*. New York: Macmillan Publishing, 1965.

———. "The Gospel according to Matthew". In *The Jerome Biblical Commentary*, edited by Raymond E. Brown, Joseph A. Fitzmyer, and Roland E. Murphy, pp. 62–114. Englewood Cliffs, N.J.: Prentice Hall, 1968.

Meier, John P. *A Marginal Jew: Rethinking the Historical Jesus*. Vol. 2, *Mentor, Message, and Miracles*. New York: Doubleday, 1994.

Merrill, Eugene. "Fear". In *Baker's Evangelical Dictionary of Biblical Theology*, edited by Walter Elwell. Grand Rapids, Mich.: Baker Books, 1996. http://www.biblestudytools.com/dictionaries/bakers-evangelical-dictionary/fear.html.

Moody, Raymond A. *Life after Life*. New York: HarperCollins, 1975.

———. *The Light Beyond*. New York: Bantam Books, 1988.

———. *Reunions: Visionary Encounters with Departed Loved Ones*. New York: Random House, 1993.

Narvaez, Darcia. "The Decline of Children and the Moral Sense: Problems That Used to Be Rare Are Becoming Mainstream". *Psychology Today*, August 15, 2010. https://www.psychologytoday.com/blog/moral-landscapes/201008/the-decline-children-and-the-moral-sense.

Nietzsche, Friedrich. *Daybreak: Thoughts on the Prejudices of Morality*. Cambridge Texts in the History of Philosophy. Edited by Maudemarie Clark and Brian Leiter. Cambridge: Cambridge University Press, 1997.

Newman, John Henry. *An Essay in Aid of a Grammar of Assent*. Worcester, Mass.: Assumption Press, 2013.

———. "Proof of Theism". In *The Argument from Conscience to the Existence of God*, edited by Adrian Boekraad and Henry Tristram. London: Mill Hill, 1961.

Otto, Rudolf. *The Idea of the Holy: An Inquiry into the Non-Rational Factor in the Idea of the Divine and Its Relation to the Rational*. New York: Oxford University Press, 1958.

Parboteeah, K. Praveen, Martin Hoegl, and John B. Cullen. "Ethics and Religion: An Empirical Test of a Multidimensional Model". *Journal of Business Ethics* 80, no. 2 (June 1, 2008): 387–98.

Parnia, Sam, et al. "AWARE—AWAreness during REsuscitation; A Prospective Study". *Journal of Resuscitation*, October 6, 2014, pp. 1799–805. http://www.resuscitationjournal.com/article/S0300 -9572(14)00739-4/abstract.

Pearce, Joseph. "J.R.R. Tolkien: Truth and Myth". *Lay Witness* (September 2001). http://www.catholiceducation.org/en/culture /literature/j-r-r-tolkien-truth-and-myth.html.

Pelikan, Jaroslav. *Mary through the Centuries*. New Haven, Conn.: Yale University Press, 1998.

Pennington, Kenneth. "The Black Death and Religious Impact". Catholic University of America, CUA.edu. Accessed June 27, 2016. http://faculty.cua.edu/pennington/churchhistory220/Lecture Ten/BlackDeath/Religious%20Impact%20page.htm.

Perrin, Nicholas. *Jesus the Temple*. Ada, Mich.: Baker Academic, 2010.

Pew Research Center. "America's Changing Religious Landscape: Christians Decline Sharply as Share of Population; Unaffiliated and Other Faiths Continue to Grow". May 12, 2015. http://www .pewforum.org/2015/05/12/americas-changing-religious-land scape/.

———. "The Decline of Marriage and Rise of New Families". November 18, 2010. http://www.pewsocialtrends.org/files/2010/11 /pew-social-trends-2010-families.pdf.

———. "Global Religious Landscape". December 18, 2012. http:// www.pewforum.org/2012/12/18/global-religious-landscape -exec.

———. "Religion among the Millennials". February 17, 2010. http://www.pewforum.org/2010/02/17/religion-among-the -millennials/.

Plato. *The Collected Dialogues of Plato*. Edited by Edith Hamilton and Huntington Cairns. Princeton, N.J.: Princeton University Press, 1973.

Rahner, Karl. *Foundations of Christian Faith: An Introduction to the Idea of Christianity*. Translated by William V. Dych. New York: Cross-road Publishing, 1982.

———. *On the Theology of Death*. New York: Herder and Herder, 1961.

Ring, Kenneth. *Life at Death: A Scientific Investigation of the Near-Death Experience*. New York: Coward, McCann and Geoghegan, 1980.

Ring, Kenneth, and Madelaine Lawrence. "Further Evidence for Veridical Perception during Near-Death Experiences". *Journal of Near-Death Studies* 11, no. 4 (Summer 1993): 223–29.

Ring, Kenneth, Sharon Cooper, and Charles Tart. *Mindsight: Near-Death and Out-of-Body Experiences in the Blind*. Palo Alto, Calif.: William James Center for Consciousness Studies at the Institute of Transpersonal Psychology, 1999.

Ring, Kenneth, and Evelyn Elsaesser Valarino. *Lessons from the Light: What We Can Learn from the Near-Death Experience*. New York: Insight Books, 2006.

Roberts, G., and J. Owen. "The Near-Death Experience". *British Journal of Psychiatry* 153 (1988): 607–17.

Roberts, Robert. *Emotions: An Essay in Aid of Moral Psychology*. Cambridge: Cambridge University Press, 2003.

Robinson, James M., and Helmut Koester. *Trajectories through Early Christianity*. Philadelphia: Fortress, 1971; repr., Eugene, Ore.: Wipf and Stock, 2006.

Rogers, Raymond N. "Studies on the Radiocarbon Sample from the Shroud of Turin". *Thermochimica Acta* 425, nos. 1–2 (January 20, 2005): 189–94.

Routt, David. 2012. "The Economic Impact of the Black Death". Economic History Association, *EH.net Encyclopedia*. Edited by Robert Whaples, July 20, 2008. https://eh.net/encyclopedia/the-economic-impact-of-the-black-death.

Sabom, M.B. *Recollections of Death: A Medical Investigation*. New York: Harper and Row, 1982.

Sartre, Jean-Paul. *Being and Nothingness*. Translated by Hazel Barnes. New York: Washington Square Press, 1993.

Scheler, Max. *Ressentiment*. Edited by Lewis B. Coser. Milwaukee, Wis.: Marquette University Studies in Philosophy, 1994.

Schnackenburg, Rudolph. *The Moral Teaching of the New Testament*. New York: Herder and Herder, 1965.

Schreck, Alan. *The Gift: Discovering the Holy Spirit in Catholic Tradition*. Orleans, Mass.: Paraclete Press, 2013.

—————. *Your Life in the Holy Spirit: What Every Catholic Needs to Know and Experience*. Frederick, Md.: Word Among Us Press, 2007.

Seligman, Martin. *Learned Optimism: How to Change Your Mind and Your Life*. New York: Simon and Schuster, 1998.

Seneca, Lucius. *De Clementia.* In *World Essays.* Translated by John W. Basore. Vol. I, 2.6–7. Loeb Classical Library. London: W. Heinemann, 1928.

Sheen, Fulton J. *Cor ad Cor Loquitor: Heart Speaks to Heart.* Bethesda, Md.: Ministr-o-Media, 1979.

Shirer, William L., and Ron Rosenbaum. *The Rise and Fall of the Third Reich: A History of Nazi Germany.* New York: Simon and Schuster, 2011.

Shorto, Russell. "No Babies? Declining Population in Europe". *New York Times,* June 29, 2008.

Slattery, John. *St. Peter Claver: Apostle to the Negroes.* Philadelphia: H. L. Kilner, 2015.

Spitzer, Robert. *Called out of Darkness: Contending with Evil through Virtue and Prayer.* San Francisco: Ignatius Press, forthcoming.

———. *Finding True Happiness: Satisfying Our Restless Hearts.* San Francisco: Ignatius Press, 2015.

———. *God So Loved the World: Clues to Our Transcendent Destiny from the Revelation of Jesus.* San Francisco: Ignatius Press, 2016.

———. *New Proofs for the Existence of God: Contributions of Contemporary Physics and Philosophy.* Grand Rapids: Mich.: Eerdmans, 2010.

———. *The Soul's Upward Yearning: Clues to Our Transcendent Nature from Experience and Reason.* San Francisco: Ignatius Press, 2015.

Stein, Edith. *Finite and Eternal Being: An Attempt at an Ascent to the Meaning of Being.* Washington, D.C.: ICS Publications, Institute of Carmelite Studies, 2002.

———. *On the Problem of Empathy.* Washington, D.C.: ICS Publications, 1989.

Strong, James. *The New Strong's Exhaustive Concordance of the Bible.* New York: Thomas Nelson, 2003.

Suarez, Francisco. *De Legibus.* Madrid: Consejo Superior de Investigaciones Cientificas, Instituto Francisco de Vitoria, 1971.

Sutherland, Cherie. "Near Death Experiences of Children". In *Making Sense of Near-Death Experiences: A Handbook for Clinicians,* edited by Karuppiah Jagadheesan, Anthony Peake, and Mahendra Perera, pp. 63–79. London: Jessica Kingsley Publishers, 2012.

Teaching Tolerance, a Project of the Southern Poverty Law Center. "Changing Demographics, Changing Identity, Changing Attitudes", 2016. http://www.tolerance.org/lesson/changing-demographics-changing-identity-changing-attitudes.

Teresa of Avila. "The Book of Her Life". In *The Collected Works of St. Teresa of Avila*, translated by Kieran Kavanaugh and Otilio Rodriguez. Washington, D.C.: ICS Publications, 1976.

Thayer, Joseph. *Thayer's Greek-English Lexicon of the New Testament: Coded with Strong's Concordance Numbers*. Peabody, Mass.: Hendrickson Publishers, 1995. www.biblehub.com/greek/3986.htm.

Thérèse of Lisieux. *Soeur Thérèse of Lisieux, the Little Flower of Jesus: A New and Complete Translation of L'Histoire d'une Ame, with an Account of Some Favours Attributed to the Intercession of Soeur Thérèse*. Edited by T. N. Taylor. London: Burns and Oates, 1912. https://archive.org/stream/saintthaeraeseofoothaeuoft/saintthaeraeseofoothaeuoft_djvu.txt.

———. *Story of a Soul: The Autobiography of St. Thérèse of Lisieux*. 3rd ed. Edited and translated by John Clarke. Washington, D.C.: Institute of Carmelite Studies, 1996.

———. *The Story of a Soul: The Autobiography of St. Thérèse of Lisieux with Additional Writings and Sayings of St. Thérèse*. 1912. http://www.catholicbible101.com/St.%20Therese%20Story%20of%20a%20soul.pdf.

Thomas of Celano. *The First Life of St. Francis of Assisi*. Translated by Christopher Stace. London: Society for Promoting Christian Knowledge, 2000.

———. *Saint Francis of Assisi: First and Second Life of St. Francis with Selections from the Treatise on the Miracles of Blessed Francis*. Translated by Placid Hermann. Chicago: Franciscan Herald Press, 1988.

Tittle, Charles R., and Michael R. Welch. "Religiosity and Deviance: Toward a Contingency Theory of Constraining Effects". *Social Forces* 61, no. 3 (March 1983): 653–82.

Turner, Jonathan H. *The Institutional Order*. New York: Addison-Wesley Educational Publishers, 1997.

Underhill, Evelyn. *Mysticism: A Study in the Nature and Development of Man's Spiritual Consciousness*. London: Methuen, 1930.

United Nations. "The Universal Declaration of Human Rights", Preamble, December 10, 1948. www.un.org/en/documents/udhr/index.shtml.

Van Lommel, Pim. *Consciousness beyond Life*. New York: HarperOne, 2010.

Van Lommel, Pim, Ruud van Wees, Vincent Meyers, and Ingrid Elfferich. "Near-Death Experience in Survivors of Cardiac Arrest:

A Prospective Study in the Netherlands". *The Lancet* 358, no. 9298 (2001): 2039–45.

Vanauken, Sheldon. *A Severe Mercy: A Story of Faith, Tragedy, and Triumph*. New York: HarperCollins, 1980.

Vawter, Bruce. "The Gospel according to John". In *The Jerome Biblical Commentary*, edited by Raymond E. Brown, Joseph A. Fitzmyer, and Roland E. Murphy, pp. 414–66. Inglewood Cliffs, N.J.: Prentice Hall, 1968.

———. "Introduction to Prophetic Literature". In *The New Jerome Biblical Commentary*, edited by Raymond E. Brown, Joseph A. Fitzmyer, and Roland E. Murphy, pp. 186–97. Englewood Cliffs, N.J.: Prentice Hall, 1968.

Viviano, Benedict. "The Gospel according to Matthew". In *The New Jerome Biblical Commentary*, edited by Raymond E. Brown, Joseph A. Fitzmyer, and Roland E. Murphy, pp. 630–74. Englewood Cliffs, N.J.: Prentice Hall, 1990.

Viviano, Frank. "Why Shroud of Turin's Secrets Continue to Elude Science". *National Geographic* (April 17, 2015). http://news.nationalgeographic.com/2015/04/150417-shroud-turin-relics-jesus-catholic-church-religion-science/.

Von Hildebrand, Dietrich. *Humility: Wellspring of Virtue*. Manchester, N.H.: Sophia Institute Press, 1976.

Weaver, Gary R., and Bradley R. Agle. "Religiosity and Ethical Behavior in Organizations: A Symbolic Interactionist Perspective". *Academy of Management Review* 27, no. 1 (January 2002): 77–97.

Williams, Kevin. *Nothing Better than Death*. Bloomington, Ind.: Xlibris Corp., 2002.

Wright, N. T. *Jesus and the Victory of God*. Minneapolis: Fortress Press, 1996.

———. *The Resurrection of the Son of God*. Minneapolis: Fortress Press, 2003.

Zaki, Jamil. "What, Me Care? Young Are Less Empathetic: A Recent Study Finds a Decline in Empathy among Young People in the U.S." *Scientific American* (January 1, 2011). http://www.scientificamerican.com/article/what-me-care/?page=1.

Zaleski, C. *Otherworld Journeys: Accounts of Near-Death Experience in Medieval and Modern Times*. Oxford: Oxford University Press, 1987.

The Happiness, Suffering, and
Transcendence Quartet:

NAME INDEX

Abel (biblical figure), 359
Abram/Abraham (biblical figure), 39n1,
    104, 166
Adam (biblical figure), 141–43, 146,
    419n1, 429n5
Mother Agnes (Pauline of Lisieux), 378,
    379
Ahlquist, Dale, 408
Albright, W.F., 113
Apostoli, Andrew, 294
Aquinas. See Saint Thomas Aquinas
Archimedes, 311, 403, 414, 500
Aristotle, 76, 83, 119, 149, 254, 265,
    299, 301, 311, 451
Augustine, Saint, 17, 134, 137, 153, 277,
    311n10, 321, 420

Bartimaeus (biblical figure), 167
Blessed Mother. See Mary
Bobadilla, Nicholas, 284
Bonaventure, Saint, 311n10
Borde, Arvind, 20, 392, 455n31
Borgia, Saint Francis, 284
Brokaw, Tom, 467n36, 471n42
Brown, Raymond, 52, 366n18, 393
Buber, Martin, 264n14, 265
Burke, Edmund, 472–73

Cain (biblical figure), 359
Camus, Albert, 316n16
Carrel, Alexis, 393n14
Cerfaux, Lucien, 363n12
Chalmers, David, 20
Charles V (Holy Roman Emperor), 284
Chesterton, G.K., 408
Clare of Assisi, Saint, 281
Claver, Saint Peter, 33, 78, 278–79,
    286–89, 296, 488, 496
Cole, Thomas, 297–98

Constantine I the Great (Roman
    emperor), 475
Cooper, Sharon, 50
Cornwall, Marie, 260, 469n38

Davis, Craig, 368n20
Dervic, Kanita, 261
the Devil. See Satan
Di Lazzaro, Paolo, 47
Dominic, Saint, 283
Donne, John, 332–33, 444–45
Dostoyevsky, Fyodor, 25, 387
Douglas, Mary, 445
Drexel, Saint Catherine, 277

Eccles, Sir John, 21
Edwards, Jonathan, 90–91n9, 115, 125
Einstein, Albert, 83
Eliade, Mircea, 19, 245, 357, 360, 389,
    433–35, 446n26
Elihu (in Book of Job), 130, 131, 138,
    139, 157–60, 386, 481
Eliphaz (in Book of Job), 109
Elizabeth (cousin of Mary), 181
Epictetus, 120
Eve (biblical figure), 141, 429n5
Evil One. See Satan
Ezekiel (biblical figure), 190

Faber, Peter, 284
Fanti, Giulio, 45
Francis of Assisi, Saint
    freedom in life of, 78, 427
    grace in suffering received by, 137
    Ignatius Loyola and, 282, 283, 284,
        285
    indirect route to sainthood, 277, 278
    love and suffering in life of, 279–82,
        463, 464, 465, 488, 496

SUBJECT INDEX